D1603783

Computers
and
Thought

COMPUTERS
and THOUGHT

edited by

EDWARD A. FEIGENBAUM
& JULIAN FELDMAN

AAAI Press / The MIT Press

MENLO PARK • CAMBRIDGE • LONDON

First AAAI Press Edition, 1995
Copyright © 1995, American Association for Artificial Intelligence
445 Burgess Drive
Menlo Park, CA 94025

Copublished and distributed by The MIT Press, Massachusetts Institute of Technology, Cambridge, Massachusetts and London, England.

ISBN 0-262-56092-5

First published in 1963 by McGraw-Hill Book Company

Preface to the AAAI Edition

Julian Feldman and I wrote the preface to the first edition of *Computers and Thought* in 1962. At that time the now omnipresent computer science departments had not yet been invented by universities. Julian and I were young assistant professors at the University of California, Berkeley, School of Business Administration. Artificial Intelligence was a tiny field of a few hardy pioneers, their graduate students, little funding, almost no published books, and no textbook.

Julian and I introduced a course in computer modeling of thought (at the Business School!) but had no book to teach from. Eureka! A niche, in which two young professors could help the field, as well as easing their own teaching. The easiest way to do that was to assemble the papers of the time that we thought were seminal or particularly noteworthy; knit them together with interstitial material explaining their importance; and publish an extensive bibliography of papers of the growing field. Thus was born *Computers and Thought*.

One of the founders of AI, one of AI's major contributors throughout its history, and its only Nobel laureate, Herbert Simon, was a consulting editor for Prentice Hall at the time. He recommended against publishing *Computers and Thought* because of its potentially small sale. That was probably one of Herb's worst judgement calls. McGraw Hill was willing to gamble. *Computers and Thought* was published in 1963 and indeed was a big seller for a decade. In an odd way, *Computers and Thought* had an impact upon publishing in the embryonic field of Computer Science. Publishers were wary of venturing their money on books in this new field. They would call Julian and me, seeking information on sales of *Computers and Thought,* the thought being that if books were selling in the arcane sibling AI field, then maybe Computer Science was not such a gamble.

Computers and Thought was translated in several foreign editions. The Russians removed the article by Armer that discussed Soviet AI work, and substituted another of their choice, all without permission. They promised to pay royalties, but in the end never did. An edition in Japanese helped to launch AI in Japan. Other editions were Polish and Spanish.

Eventually McGraw-Hill decided to take the book out of print, and sold the reprint rights to a publisher specializing in otherwise-out-of-print books. Another version was thus available for about a decade. Then, a few years ago the second publisher took it out of print, seemingly with finality.

But by that time, the book had become a "classic" and there was continuing demand for it. McGraw-Hill returned the rights to Julian and me, and we donated them to the American Association of Artificial Intelligence for the publication of this historical edition.

Computers and Thought is indeed a treasure. Some of the papers are as important today for their fundamental ideas as they were in the late 1950s and early 1960s when they were written. Others are interesting as early milestones of fields that have expanded and changed dramatically. A few are interesting in that they represent work that simply did not go anywhere. Some of the papers describe key work that is not typically taught any more, but is "buried" deeply in the conceptual structure of AI—a heritage that needs to be honored and preserved.

The papers of *Computers and Thought* had all been published somewhere else. Equity demanded that the royalties be divided equally among the authors of papers. But the royalties were expected to be small, and one-*nth* of the royalties would make no noticeable dent in anyone's style of living. So Julian and I got the permission of all to donate the royalties in the service of a good AI cause. Allen Newell was asked to chair the committee that determined what that good cause was to be. He accepted on the condition that the committee be a committee of one. Eventually, the good cause emerged: a prize for excellence of contribution to AI by a young researcher. This prize is called the Computers and Thought Award, and is administered by the International Joint Conference on Artificial Intelligence (IJCAI). It has matured into one of the most prestigious awards offered in the AI field.

From the hardy band of pioneers grew a professional scientific field that is very large and vigorous. Tens of thousands of its researchers and practitioners belong to the AAAI, the IEEE, ACM's SIGART, the Association for Computational Linguistics, similar societies in Europe, Japan, and indeed all over the world. As the field grew and matured, it spun off professional groups in neural networks, fuzzy systems, expert systems, pattern recognition, and host of other subspecialties. AI is not one enterprise but a whole family of related enterprises. There are tens of thousands of practicing software engineers who are doing applied AI work. Recently I attended a planning meeting in which the US Army was defining an official professional career path called "AI Specialist" for the staffing of their two hundred AI projects!

Today's young AI researcher can not easily imagine the excitement of the early years of AI, from which the papers of this volume are drawn. Nor can they imagine the computer resources that were used to do the early work. The Macintosh with which I write this preface has by far more processing power, more RAM, and more disk memory than the sum of all the computers that were being used by all the AI researchers of the period 1956-62. I wrote the earliest version of the EPAM program described in this book in 2000 words of rotating drum memory of the IBM 650 (by count that was 20K bytes, but they couldn't be used very efficiently as bytes). It was seen as a tremendous leap upward that later I could do EPAM II (my thesis program) on the 32K words of an IBM 709 and 7090. Newell, Shaw and Simon did their landmark work on the Logic Theorist on an early machine called Johnniac (after John Von Neumann) with a memory of 4K words. There were no word processors, not even time-sharing, and the only interaction came if someone let you take over the multi-million dollar machine. You sat at the console, and interacted through the console lights and switches. The amount of computer power that each of us has routinely available was (I think) not dreamed of by the researchers whose work is in this book.

Let me tell you something else about the papers in this book. With two exceptions (one being the famous survey paper of early AI by Minsky), a critical selection criterion was that the paper had to describe the experimental results from a running computer program. The view was that if a cognitive theory on which you were basing your approach to AI was worthy of the time and attention of others, it had to have been stated in a language of a computer; and it had to have run on a set of appropriate cognitive tasks to demonstrate at least the sufficiency of the theory. The theory might be wrong, but at least it generated detailed predictions (results of running the program) that were testable.

Newell once called the running-program criterion "the coin of the realm" in our field. All else was talk, philosophy not science. Some researchers of the early days did not use the methodology of the running program, nor even believe in it. Their work did not make it into *Computers and Thought*. Today, there are many more who theorize but do not write programs. For decades, around the world of AI programs there has been a world of AI "talk," but little has come out of the "talk." The quest for the intelligent machine has not been a fruitful field for the philosopher or the formalist.

Working in AI has been a privilege and a great gift. The gift was given to Julian and me by Herb Simon during the magic period following the invention of the Logic Theory program. We both carried it with us, to Berkeley, and then to the University of California, Irvine (Julian) and to Stanford University (me). At Stanford I had a double gift of colleagues: John McCarthy, one of AI's great scientists; and Joshua Lederberg, the Genetics Nobel laureate who helped me and Bruce Buchanan in the creation of the DENDRAL program and expert systems. Always, the science and technology in AI gave me the challenge and exhilaration of working at the cutting edge of something truly grand. And throughout, we all had the gift of a brilliant and generous role model and friend, the late Allen Newell.

The AI field gave me the privilege of serving as a President of the AAAI. And my work in AI led in 1994 to the thrill of sharing the ACM Turing Award with my colleague and friend of thirty years, Raj Reddy of Stanford and Carnegie Mellon Universities. It is from my Turing Award speech that I would like to close this preface.

"The vision of computational models of intelligence, to which we regularly apply (and then unapply) transient and trendy labels, is one of the great goals that science has envisioned.

It is a truly grand challenge for Computer Science.

Edward Feigenbaum
Stanford University,
& Chief Scientist
United States Air Force

With help from
Julian Feldman
University of California
Irvine

MAY 1, 1995

Preface

These research reports and discussions are concerned with the information processing activity that underlies intelligent behavior in human beings and computers. We were motivated to prepare such an anthology for three reasons.

First, since the topic is of general interest, controversial, and of potentially great scientific and social significance, we wished to make available to a wide audience a collection of the significant research papers. Most have been available only in relatively inaccessible technical journals, and most are reprinted here just as they originally appeared.

Second, we felt it important to make these particular readings easily available for use in graduate-level and undergraduate courses being offered (or planned) at many colleges and universities.

Third, we wished to provide a convenient reference volume for researchers working in or entering the fields of artificial intelligence and simulation of thought processes. An invaluable component of such a reference volume is a good bibliography. We believe that Minsky's descriptor-indexed bibliography will be a particularly useful tool for the researcher.

The lot of the anthology editor is not a happy one. He may be damned not only for presumed sins of commission but also for sins of omission. When the anthology is the first in an area as ductile as the one we are labeling Computers and Thought, the problems of selection are compounded.

In the introduction to Part 1 on artificial intelligence, we present our understanding and interpretation of the goal of this research. We have selected reports of research efforts which we feel outdistance all others in advancement toward this goal. Such a criterion, as we see it, gives high priority to a particular brand of research, loosely labeled "cognitive models." An opposing school of thought, sometimes called "neural cybernetics" or "self-organizing systems," has intrinsic fascination and has produced a considerable number of particular projects. Neural cybernetics approaches the problem of designing intelligent machines by postulating a large number of very simple information processing elements, arranged in a random or organized network, and certain processes for facilitating or inhibiting their activity. Cognitive model builders take a much more macroscopic approach, using highly complex information processing mechanisms as the basis of their designs. They believe that intelligent performance by a machine is an end difficult enough to achieve without "starting from scratch," and so they build into their systems as much complexity of information processing as they are able to understand and communicate to a computer (using their programming techniques).

The cognitive models approach has led to tangible progress (displacement toward the ultimate goal) in the field of artificial intelligence, while the progress to date in the neural cybernetics approach is barely discernible. On this basis, we feel that there is reason for our bias in favor of cognitive models, though of course there are other dimensions along which to evaluate the research.

We have tried to focus on papers that report *results*. In this collection, the papers that deal with specific projects describe actual working computer programs that produced interesting and significant behavior. Because of the limited space available, we chose to avoid the more speculative, albeit stimulating and thought-provoking, pieces that have been written on intelligent machines. It is for this reason that the writings of some of the well-known theorists in the area are not included.

Related research areas, such as machine translation of languages, automatic information retrieval, and automata theory, were not treated, since they constitute separate subdisciplines of the computer sciences and deserve full treatment in their own right.

Many papers in psychology and the life sciences are relevant to an understanding of information processing in human thought, but we did not include these, because we wished to keep a sharp focus on computer processes and techniques.

For reasons of sharp focus also, we have not included a paper on an important topic, the social implications of intelligent machines.

We have used the papers here collected for a graduate-level course in artificial intelligence and computer simulation of cognitive processes, in which we have had students from business administration, psychology, linguistics, philosophy, biology, physics and biophysics, and electrical engineering. The course has no mathematics prerequisite, but some knowledge of mathematics is helpful (e.g., in understanding Slagle's work on integration). An introductory course in psychology would also be helpful to the student, but it is not required. We have required some elementary knowledge of computers and an ability to program a computer, preferably in one of the list processing languages, e.g., Information Processing Language V (IPL-V), FORTRAN List Processing Language (FLPL), COMIT, or LISP. For students who have not had this preparation, we have provided extra instruction in IPL-V.

As a road map to the collection we offer the following guidelines:

For the general reader: The major introductions to Part 1 on artificial intelligence and Part 2 on simulation of cognitive processes, the introductory article by Turing, followed by the other articles in a sequence dictated by the tastes of the reader and his competence in the subject matter discussed, and finally the summary and review articles by Armer and Minsky. The Minsky critical review might also usefully be the midpoint in a reading of this collection.

For the computer scientist and the management scientist: The major introductions, followed by Minsky's critical review. Perhaps of highlighted interest, Samuel's treatment of learning programs, Tonge's management science application, and the research on theorem-proving programs (Newell, Shaw, and Simon, and Gelernter).

For the psychologist and the philosopher: The introduction to Part 2 on simulation of cognitive processes, the articles on problem-solving, verbal learning, two-choice behavior, concept formation, social behavior, and decision-making, in a sequence dictated by the interests of the reader, and finally the papers on artificial intelligence research.

We should like to express our gratitude to the authors who graciously allowed us to reprint their articles; to those who advised us on the selection problems; to Robert Lindsay, Leonard Uhr and Charles Vossler, John and Jeanne Gullahorn, and Geoffrey Clarkson, who prepared articles or revisions specifically for this collection; to Arthur Samuel for service beyond the call of duty in arranging and running the 7090-Nealey checker game; and especially to Marvin Minsky for the time and energy he spent in preparing a revision of his earlier bibliography. We owe a special debt to A. Newell and H. A. Simon for their guidance and research collaboration over the years. Our final expression of appreciation is to Mrs. Pamela Tellefsen, who offered this manuscript her toil, patience, and care over many months, and to Rita R. Feldman, who compiled the Index.

Edward Feigenbaum
Julian Feldman

Acknowledgments

A. M. Turing, Computing machinery and intelligence, by permission from the editors of *Mind,* October, 1950, **59**:433–460.

A. Newell, J. C. Shaw, and H. Simon, Chess playing programs and the problem of complexity, by permission from the *IBM Journal of Research and Development,* October, 1958, **2**:320–335.

A. L. Samuel, Some studies in machine learning using the game of checkers, by permission from the *IBM Journal of Research and Development,* July, 1959, **3**:211–229. The author acknowledges:

> *Many different people have contributed to these studies through stimulating discussions of the basic problems. From time to time the writer was assisted by several different programmers, although most of the detailed work was his own. The forbearance of the machine room operators and their willingness to play the machine at all hours of the day and night are also greatly appreciated.*

A. Newell, J. C. Shaw, and H. Simon, Empirical explorations with the Logic Theory Machine, by permission of the authors from the *Proceedings of the Western Joint Computer Conference,* 1957, **15**:218–239. This research was part of a project conducted jointly by Newell and Shaw of the RAND Corporation, Santa Monica, and H. Simon of the Carnegie Institute of Technology.

H. Gelernter, Realization of a geometry-theorem proving machine, by permission from the *Proceedings of an International Conference on Information Processing,* Paris: UNESCO House, 1959, pp. 273–282. The author acknowledges:

> *The technical and programming assistance of J. R. Hansen and D. W. Loveland has been indispensable to the success of this project. N. Rochester and J. McCarthy contributed much to the early development of ideas, and Rochester supplied the necessary administrative support as well. Other members of the Information Research Department of IBM, and W. G. Bouricius, P. C. Gilmore, J. P. Lazarus, and P. D. Welch, in particular, contributed to the author's understanding of the problem in his conversations with them.*
>
> *The research project itself is a consequence of the Dartmouth Summer Research Project on Artificial Intelligence held in 1956, during which M. L. Minsky pointed out the potential utility of the diagram to a geometry theorem-proving machine.*

H. Gelernter, J. R. Hansen, and D. W. Loveland, Empirical explorations of the geometry-theorem proving machine, by permission of the authors. It first appeared in *Proceedings of the Western Joint Computer Conference,* 1960, **17:**143–147.

J. Slagle, A heuristic program that solves symbolic integration problems in freshman calculus, by permission of the author and Lincoln Laboratory of Massachusetts Institute of Technology. Some of the many persons who helped the author with the project and manuscript are D. Edwards, E. Freed, A. Greene, J. McCarthy, M. Minsky, H. Rogers, Jr., S. Russell, O. Selfridge, C. Shannon, and G. Shapiro.

F. M. Tonge, Summary of a heuristic line balancing procedure, by permission from *Management Science,* 1960, **7:**21–42. This is based on a doctoral dissertation submitted to the Graduate School of Industrial Administration, Carnegie Institute of Technology. The research has been supported in varying degrees by the Graduate School, an IBM fellowship, the RAND Corporation, and the Westinghouse Electric Corporation. While many persons have contributed to developing this topic, the author particularly acknowledges the stimulation and encouragement of A. Newell, J. C. Shaw, and H. Kanter of the RAND Corporation.

B. F. Green, A. K. Wolf, C. Chomsky, and K. Laughery, Baseball: An automatic question answerer, by permission of the authors. It first appeared in the *Proceedings of the Western Joint Computer Conference,* 1961, **19:**219–224. The authors gratefully acknowledge the guidance of F. Frick, O. Selfridge, and G. P. Dineen.

O. Selfridge and U. Neisser, Pattern recognition by machine, by permission from *Scientific American,* August, 1960, **203:**60–68.

L. Uhr and C. Vossler, A pattern-recognition program that generates, evaluates, and adjusts its own operators, by permission of the authors. The bulk of this report first appeared under the same title in the *Proceedings of the Western Joint Computer Conference,* 1961, **19:**555–570, and important additions came from the authors' chapter "The Search to Recognize," in the *Symposium on Optical Character Recognition,* 1962, Washington, D.C.: Spartan Books, by permission.

A. Newell and H. Simon, "GPS, a program that simulates human thought," by permission from *Lernende Automaten,* Munich: R. Oldenbourg KG, 1961. The authors acknowledge:

> *We would like to express our indebtedness to J. C. Shaw, who has been our colleague in most of our research into complex information processes, including the GPS program which forms the basis of this paper.*

E. A. Feigenbaum, The simulation of verbal learning behavior, first appeared in the *Proceedings of the Western Joint Computer Conference,* 1961, **19:**121–132. The author acknowledges:

I am deeply indebted to H. Simon for his past and present collaboration in this research. This research has been supported by the Computer Sciences Department, the RAND Corporation, and the Ford Foundation. I wish to express appreciation for the help and critical comments of J. Feldman, A. Newell, J. C. Shaw, and F. Tonge.

E. B. Hunt and C. I. Hovland, Programming a model of human concept formulation, by permission of the authors. It first appeared in the *Proceedings of the Western Joint Computer Conference*, 1961, **19**:145–155. The authors acknowledge:

> *The work reported in this paper was supported by a grant for the study of concept learning from the Ford Foundation to C. I. Hovland. The computational work involved was supported, for the most part, by the Computation Center, Massachusetts Institute of Technology. B. F. Green, Jr., and A. Wolf, of Lincoln Laboratory, M.I.T., made available the 709 version of the IPL-V interpreter and instructed Hunt in its use. The aid received is gratefully acknowledged.*

G. P. E. Clarkson, A model of the trust investment process, by permission from *A Simulation of Trust Investment*, Englewood Cliffs, N.J.: Prentice-Hall, 1961.

J. Feldman, Simulation of behavior in the binary choice experiment, first appeared in the *Proceedings of the Western Joint Computer Conference*, 1961, **19**:133–144. The author is indebted to A. Newell for advice and suggestions made during the course of the research summarized in this report.

J. Gullahorn and J. Gullahorn, A computer model of elementary social behavior. The authors wish to acknowledge the helpful suggestions of H. Simon, E. Feigenbaum, J. Feldman, F. Marzocco, and C. Baker. The authors also acknowledge:

> *Thanks are also due the Committee on Simulation of Cognitive Processes of the Social Science Research Council for support during the early phases of this research at the School of Business Administration, University of California at Berkeley, and to the System Development Corporation, Santa Monica, for continued sponsorship of the project.*

P. Armer, Attitudes toward intelligent machines, by permission from the *Symposium on Bionics*, 1960, Wadd Technical Report 60 600, pp. 13–19. The author acknowledges:

> *I would like to express my gratitude for many long discussions of this topic with W. H. Ware, M. E. Maron, F. J. Gruenberger, E. A. Feigenbaum, A. Newell, J. C. Shaw, and H. A. Simon, and the influence of the research efforts of the latter four on my thinking. In*

this paper I have quoted many people. In so doing I have strived to avoid quoting out of context. However, one runs this risk when only a portion of a man's statement is repeated. If I have misrepresented the intended meaning of anyone in this paper, it has been accidental.

M. Minsky, Steps toward artificial intelligence, by permission from the *Proceedings of the Institute of Radio Engineers,* January, 1961, **49:**8–30.

M. Minsky, A selected descriptor-indexed bibliography to the literature on artificial intelligence, by permission from the *IRE Transactions on Human Factors in Electronics,* March, 1961, **HFE-2:**39–55.

Contents

part 1
Artificial Intelligence

The purpose of this volume is to inform the nonspecialist about current research on intelligent behavior by computer—not by exhortation or reinterpretation, but by the collection of key scientific research reports which collectively represent the state of progress in this field. Each is an important paper for an informed understanding of research in artificial intelligence. In this introduction we hope to provide the reader with a set of guidelines to a thoughtful reading of the collected papers.

What Is a Computer? Is It Just a "Number Factory"?

In the popular conception, a computer is a high-speed number calculator. This view is only partly correct. A digital computer is, in fact, a general symbol-processing device, capable of performing any well-defined process for the manipulation and transformation of information.

All general-purpose digital computers are basically alike. They have:

1. One or more "input" devices for transforming symbolic information external to the machine into internally usable form. These internal forms are the *symbols* which the machine manipulates. A punched-card reader is an example of an input device.

2. One or more "output" devices for transforming the internal symbols back into external form. The computer's printer is an example of an output device.

3. One or more "memory" devices capable of storing symbols before, during, and after processing.

4. An "arithmetic unit." One of the possible interpretations that can be given to a computer's symbols is the interpretation as *numbers*. The arithmetic unit is a piece of electronic gear which will operate upon these numbers to produce (under the numerical interpretation) sums, differences, products, etc. Most of the computation described in this volume is nonnumeric. For example, the chess pieces manipulated by the Newell-Shaw-Simon Chess Player are represented and handled as symbols, not numbers.

5. A "control unit." The control unit is the executive of the computer organization. It is wired to understand and obey a repertory of *instructions* (or commands), calling the other units into action when necessary. The instructions are generally elementary processes, *e.g.*, fetch a symbol from a specified place in memory, return a symbol to some place in memory, shift a symbol a certain number of places to the left or right in "working storage."

A very important instruction, "compare and transfer control," enables the computer to make a simple two-choice decision—to take one of two specified courses of action depending on the information found in some cell of the memory. By cascading these simple decisions, highly complex decisions can be fashioned.

Information processes more complicated than those "wired into" the computer can be carried out by means of a sequence of the elementary instructions, called a *program*. The program is the precise statement of the information process that the user desires the machine to carry out. A computer's program is stored in the memory along with all the other problem information and data. One part of a program can call in another part of the program from the memory to the working storage and alter it. The general-purpose digital computer can do any information processing task for which a program can be written. The same computer which one moment is computing a company's payroll may in the next moment be computing aircraft designs or insurance premiums. Any program for a general-purpose computer effectively converts this general-purpose machine into a special-purpose machine for doing that task intended by the user who wrote the program.

Is It Possible for Computing Machines to Think?

No—if one defines thinking as an activity peculiarly and exclusively *human*. Any such behavior in machines, therefore, would have to be called thinking-like behavior.

No—if one postulates that there is something in the essence of thinking which is *inscrutable, mysterious, mystical.*

Yes—if one admits that the question is to be answered by *experiment and observation,* comparing the behavior of the computer with that behavior of human beings to which the term "thinking" is generally applied.

We regard the two negative views as unscientifically dogmatic. The positive, or empirical, view is explored with cogency by Turing in an article reprinted in this volume. Armer, in another reprinted article, qualifies the positive view by pointing out that there exists a continuum of intelligent behavior, that the question of how far we can push machines out along that continuum is to be answered by research, not dogma. We might add one further qualification: to assert that thinking machines are possible is not necessarily to assert that thinking machines with human capabilities already exist (or that they will exist in the near future). The reader of this volume is invited to form a judgment on the matter. The reports reprinted here constitute, we think, the best evidence available on the subject at present.

What, then, is the goal of artificial intelligence research? As we interpret the field, it is this: *to construct computer programs which exhibit behavior that we call "intelligent behavior" when we observe it in human beings.*

Because this research area is still in the formative stage of its development, many different research paths are being explored. Our goal definition may be too ambitious for some researchers, not ambitious enough for others (chiefly because it is tied to human behavior).

Many of the research projects reported in Part 1 achieve this goal within their special problem areas. Shall we call this computer behavior "thinking," or shall we not? Perhaps this is an individual's choice. In our opinion, it is neither an important nor a fruitful topic for debate.

But Doesn't a Computer Do Exactly What It Is Told To Do and No More?

Commenting on this familiar question, a well-known researcher in the field had this to say:

This statement—that computers can do only what they are programmed to do—is intuitively obvious, indubitably true, and supports none of the implications that are commonly drawn from it.

A human being can think, learn, and create because the program his biological endowment gives him, together with the changes in that program produced by interaction with his environment after birth, enables him to think, learn, and create. If a computer thinks, learns, and creates, it will be by virtue of a program that endows it with these capacities. Clearly this will not be a program—any more than the human's is—that calls for highly stereotyped and repetitive behavior independent of the stimuli coming from the environment and the task to be completed. It will be a program that makes the system's behavior highly conditional on the task environment—on the task goals and on the clues extracted from the environment that indicate whether progress is being made toward those goals. It will be a program that analyzes, by some means, its own performance, diagnoses its failures, and makes changes that enhance its future effectiveness (Simon, 1960, p. 25).

Similarly, it is wrong to conclude that a computer can exhibit behavior no more intelligent than its human programmer and that this astute gentleman can accurately predict the behavior of his program. These conclusions ignore the enormous complexity of information processing possible in problem-solving and learning machines. They presume that, because the programmer can write down (as programs) general prescriptions for adaptive behavior in such mechanisms, he can comprehend the remote consequences of these mechanisms after the execution of millions of information processing operations and the interaction of these mechanisms with a task environment. And, more importantly, they presume that he can perform the same complex information processing operations equally well with the device within his skull.

Is It True That a Computer Will Be a Chess Champion Because the Computer Is So Fast That It Can Examine All Possible Moves and Their Consequences?

This view of the problem-solving potential of computers rests on the assumption that, because computers are so fast, they can "think of everything." This kind of computing might be called *brute-force* computing. Brute-force programs generally have a simple structure, employing exhaustive enumeration of possibilities and exhaustive search. Is brute-force computing a general method for handling problems that are usually thought of as having some "intellectual content"?

To answer this question, we must look first at what *a problem* is. A problem exists for a problem-solver when he is faced with the task of choosing one of a set of alternatives placed before him by the problem environment. The problem-solver has no problem if the environment presents him with only one alternative; he must take that alternative. What is troublesome about alternatives is not so much their number as their consequences. Alternatives usually have elaborate consequences, which need to be evaluated before one alternative is chosen. The formal expression of this notion leads us to the so-called *maze model of a problem.* Let us look at this in an example.

Consider the problem of choosing a move at some point in a game of chess. If the position allows the player only one alternative, there is no problem—the move is *forced.* If, however, there is a genuine problem, the decision can be made by examining the immediate and remote consequences of selecting particular alternatives—the moves opened up to the opponent, the possible replies to these moves, etc. This "tree of possibilities" is pictured in Fig. 1.

In principle, this tree can be completely elaborated; the end points can be identified as wins, losses, or draws; and a strategy can be employed to determine the best alternative available at the top of the tree.

Since this procedure can in principle be programmed on modern, high-speed computers, why is chess still an interesting game? Why are computers not unbeatable champions at chess?

The answer is simple: the size of the chess maze is enormous. It has been estimated that there are about 10^{120} different paths through a complete chess maze (give or take, perhaps, many powers of ten). Even under the most generous assumptions about the power of modern computing machinery, now or in the future, it is beyond the limits of plausibility that a computer will ever be able to play "optimum" chess by the exhaustive strategy mentioned above.

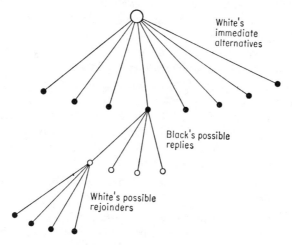

Figure 1.

Brute-force computing through problem mazes (for any but the most trivial problems) just won't do. Problem-solving by this method is beyond the realm of practical possibility.

How, then, are we to construct an intelligent problem-solver?

It appears that the clue to intelligent behavior, whether of men or machines, is *highly selective search,* the drastic pruning of the tree of possibilities explored. *For a computer program to behave intelligently, it must search problem mazes in a highly selective way, exploring paths relatively fertile with solutions and ignoring paths relatively sterile.*

What Is a Heuristic Program?

A *heuristic* (*heuristic rule, heuristic method*) is a rule of thumb, strategy, trick, simplification, or any other kind of device which drastically limits search for solutions in large problem spaces. Heuristics do not guarantee optimal solutions; in fact, they do not guarantee any solution at all; *all that can be said for a useful heuristic is that it offers solutions which are good enough most of the time.* A *heuristic program* is a program that employs heuristics in solving complex problems.

Heuristic methods have sometimes been contrasted with *algorithmic methods* for finding problem solutions, and a certain amount of intellectual blood has been shed unnecessarily on this battlefield. Without getting into the subtleties of the disagreement, we observe that the term "algorithm" is used with considerable ambiguity in mathematics and logic. Under one commonly held definition, algorithms are decision procedures which are *guaranteed* to produce the solution being sought, given enough time. The brute-force program described above for playing chess is such an algorithm. But algorithms (under this concept) are known, or practical, for only a very small subset of all interesting problems one would like to have computers solve. Over the spectrum of the broader class, heuristic methods seem to offer more general applicability.

The payoff in using heuristics is greatly reduced search and, therefore, practicality. Often, but not always, a price is paid: by drastic search limitations, sometimes the best solution (indeed, *any or all* solutions) may be overlooked.

Heuristics come in at least two varieties: special-purpose and general-purpose. Let us examine these by example:

1. The chess duffer might typically use this rule of thumb: Stop exploring any sequence that puts the queen in immediate danger of being captured. This is a special-purpose chess heuristic. It is useful

to the duffer because it keeps him out of one kind of trouble. By using this especially crude search-limiting device, the duffer will never discover those exciting queen-sacrifice combinations which get "!!" annotations in books on chess.

2. In proving theorems, a mathematician usually works backward from the theorem he is trying to prove to known theorems or axioms, instead of working forward from known expressions, using the rules of inference, until he stumbles on the theorem he has to prove. Under certain conditions, "working backward" is a powerful general heuristic for utilizing information in the problem to guide search for the solution.

3. A useful rule of thumb used by human beings in most of their problem-solving is this: Attack a new problem by methods that have solved similar problems in the past. The criteria for "similarity" may themselves be heuristic. If the environment is in a kind of steady state with respect to problem types, this heuristic may be very useful. In environments demanding a high degree of innovative problem-solving, this heuristic will hinder rather than facilitate problem-solving.

4. Two general-purpose heuristic problem-solving methods commonly employed in human reasoning are *means-ends analysis* and *planning*. In means-ends analysis, an initial problem state is transformed into a target state by selecting and applying operations which, step by step, reduce the difference between the states. In the planning method, a simplified statement of the original problem is constructed, and means-ends analysis is applied to this new, simpler problem. The result is a set of plans (guesses at possible operator sequences), hopefully one of which will work, *i.e.*, solve the original problem. Means-ends analysis is discussed in detail in the reprinted article on the General Problem Solver (GPS).

What Are Some Unsolved Problems of Artificial Intelligence Research?

In an area so new and exploratory, most of the problems remain unsolved, indeed unattacked. At this stage, it is not easy even to identify and state the problems, except in a very general way. We offer some examples of problems we think are ripe for attack:

1. The learning of heuristics. A puzzling, fascinating, and extremely important question is this: How can computers (and how do people) learn new heuristic methods and rules, both special-purpose and general-purpose? At the moment, our knowledge of learning mechanisms for problem-solving programs is rudimentary. Any significant breakthrough in this area would offer the promise of enabling

us to "bootstrap" our way into very much more powerful problem-solving programs.

2. Inductive inference. Artificial intelligence currently is strong on deductive inference, weak on inductive inference. Yet, in the melting pot of everyday intelligence, induction is certainly the more significant ingredient. One way of looking at the problem is that we need programs which will in some sense induce internally stored "models" of external environments—models from which the programs can make valid and useful predictions of future environmental states. Looked at in another way, this is the problem of hypothesis formation by machine. It is the general pattern recognition problem. Today we know very little about this crucial problem.

3. Understanding natural language. A problem of great theoretical and practical interest is that of constructing a program to understand communication in natural language (the word "understand" is here used with its full human connotation). To put it simply, one would like to be able to engage in a dialog with a computer—a dialog in which the computer will hold up its end of the conversation adaptively, intelligently, with understanding. Research on question-answering programs (*e.g.*, the BASEBALL program reprinted in this volume) is a good start. There is much that can be transferred from research on mechanical translation, on information retrieval, on models of human associative memory, and other areas of information science. The problem is ripe for intensive, interdisciplinary study.

What Are the Limits of Artificial Intelligence Research?

No one can answer this question today.

Perhaps the question has more fascination than importance. In terms of the continuum of intelligence suggested by Armer, the computer programs we have been able to construct are still at the low end. What is important is that we continue to strike out in the direction of the milestone that represents the capabilities of human intelligence. Is there any reason to suppose that we shall never get there? None whatever. Not a single piece of evidence, no logical argument, no proof or theorem has ever been advanced which demonstrates an insurmountable hurdle along the continuum.

Today, despite our ignorance, we can point to that biological milestone, the thinking brain, in the same spirit as the scientists many hundreds of years ago pointed to the bird as a demonstration in nature that mechanisms heavier than air could fly.

section 1

Can a Machine Think?

One of the unfortunate circumstances of the early post-World War II history of computer technology was that the high-speed electronic digital computer became styled as a "giant brain." The widespread use of this term by science popularizers, science-fiction writers, and their advertising-agency counterparts caused a vigorous and widespread reaction among the members of the rapidly expanding computer profession. The experience of the time was that it was difficult to program computers to do even the simplest data processing and computational jobs (*e.g.*, computerizing a payroll procedure).

To the theorists, however, the question of thinking by machine still held considerable interest. They were interested in defining the question more clearly and in discerning the existence or nonexistence of various kinds of theoretical upper bounds on the intelligence of computing devices. One of the best-known papers to emerge from these deliberations was by the famous English mathematician and logician, A. M. Turing, reprinted in this section. Turing's paper appeared five years before concrete developments in intelligent behavior by machine began to occur. Yet it remains today one of the most cogent and thorough discussions in the literature on the general question "Can a machine think?"

Turing takes a behavioristic posture relative to the question. The question is to be decided by an unprejudiced comparison of the alleged "thinking behavior" of the machine with normal "thinking behavior" in human beings. He proposes an experiment—commonly called "Turing's test"—in which the unprejudiced comparison could be made. Though the test has flaws, it is the best that has been proposed to date.

A. M. Turing died suddenly in 1954 after a short but brilliant career. Shortly before his death, while at the National Physical Laboratory in England, he completed the design of one of the world's first modern high-speed digital computers.

COMPUTING MACHINERY
AND INTELLIGENCE

by A. M. Turing

1. The Imitation Game

I propose to consider the question, "Can machines think?" This should begin with definitions of the meaning of the terms "machine" and "think." The definitions might be framed so as to reflect so far as possible the normal use of the words, but this attitude is dangerous. If the meaning of the words "machine" and "think" are to be found by examining how they are commonly used it is difficult to escape the conclusion that the meaning and the answer to the question, "Can machines think?" is to be sought in a statistical survey such as a Gallup poll. But this is absurd. Instead of attempting such a definition I shall replace the question by another, which is closely related to it and is expressed in relatively unambiguous words.

The new form of the problem can be described in terms of a game which we call the "imitation game." It is played with three people, a man (A), a woman (B), and an interrogator (C) who may be of either sex. The interrogator stays in a room apart from the other two. The object of the game for the interrogator is to determine which of the other two is the man and which is the woman. He knows them by labels X and Y, and at the end of the game he says either "X is A and Y is B" or "X is B and Y is A." The interrogator is allowed to put questions to A and B thus:

C: Will X please tell me the length of his or her hair?

Now suppose X is actually A, then A must answer. It is A's object in the game to try and cause C to make the wrong identification. His answer might therefore be:

"My hair is shingled, and the longest strands are about nine inches long."

11

In order that tones of voice may not help the interrogator the answers should be written, or better still, typewritten. The ideal arrangement is to have a teleprinter communicating between the two rooms. Alternatively the question and answers can be repeated by an intermediary. The object of the game for the third player (B) is to help the interrogator. The best strategy for her is probably to give truthful answers. She can add such things as "I am the woman, don't listen to him!" to her answers, but it will avail nothing as the man can make similar remarks.

We now ask the question, "What will happen when a machine takes the part of A in this game?" Will the interrogator decide wrongly as often when the game is played like this as he does when the game is played between a man and a woman? These questions replace our original, "Can machines think?"

2. Critique of the New Problem

As well as asking, "What is the answer to this new form of the question," one may ask, "Is this new question a worthy one to investigate?" This latter question we investigate without further ado, thereby cutting short an infinite regress.

The new problem has the advantage of drawing a fairly sharp line between the physical and the intellectual capacities of a man. No engineer or chemist claims to be able to produce a material which is indistinguishable from the human skin. It is possible that at some time this might be done, but even supposing this invention available we should feel there was little point in trying to make a "thinking machine" more human by dressing it up in such artificial flesh. The form in which we have set the problem reflects this fact in the condition which prevents the interrogator from seeing or touching the other competitors, or hearing their voices. Some other advantages of the proposed criterion may be shown up by specimen questions and answers. Thus:

Q: Please write me a sonnet on the subject of the Forth Bridge.
A: Count me out on this one. I never could write poetry.
Q: Add 34957 to 70764.
A: (Pause about 30 seconds and then give as answer) 105621.
Q: Do you play chess?
A: Yes.
Q: I have K at my K1, and no other pieces. You have only K at K6 and R at R1. It is your move. What do you play?
A: (After a pause of 15 seconds) R-R8 mate.

The question and answer method seems to be suitable for introducing almost any one of the fields of human endeavour that we wish to include.

We do not wish to penalise the machine for its inability to shine in beauty competitions, nor to penalise a man for losing in a race against an aeroplane. The conditions of our game make these disabilities irrelevant. The "witnesses" can brag, if they consider it advisable, as much as they please about their charms, strength or heroism, but the interrogator cannot demand practical demonstrations.

The game may perhaps be criticised on the ground that the odds are weighted too heavily against the machine. If the man were to try and pretend to be the machine he would clearly make a very poor showing. He would be given away at once by slowness and inaccuracy in arithmetic. May not machines carry out something which ought to be described as thinking but which is very different from what a man does? This objection is a very strong one, but at least we can say that if, nevertheless, a machine can be constructed to play the imitation game satisfactorily, we need not be troubled by this objection.

It might be urged that when playing the "imitation game" the best strategy for the machine may possibly be something other than imitation of the behaviour of a man. This may be, but I think it is unlikely that there is any great effect of this kind. In any case there is no intention to investigate here the theory of the game, and it will be assumed that the best strategy is to try to provide answers that would naturally be given by a man.

3. The Machines Concerned in the Game

The question which we put in §1 will not be quite definite until we have specified what we mean by the word "machine." It is natural that we should wish to permit every kind of engineering technique to be used in our machines. We also wish to allow the possibility than an engineer or team of engineers may construct a machine which works, but whose manner of operation cannot be satisfactorily described by its constructors because they have applied a method which is largely experimental. Finally, we wish to exclude from the machines men born in the usual manner. It is difficult to frame the definitions so as to satisfy these three conditions. One might for instance insist that the team of engineers should be all of one sex, but this would not really be satisfactory, for it is probably possible to rear a complete individual from a single cell of the skin (say) of a man. To do so would be a feat of biological technique deserving of the very highest praise, but we would not be inclined to regard it as a case of "constructing a thinking machine." This prompts us to abandon the requirement that every kind of technique should be permitted. We are the more ready to do so in view of the fact that the present interest in "thinking machines" has been aroused by a particular kind of machine, usually called an "electronic computer" or "digital computer." Following this suggestion we only permit digital computers to take part in our game.

This restriction appears at first sight to be a very drastic one. I shall attempt to show that it is not so in reality. To do this necessitates a short account of the nature and properties of these computers.

It may also be said that this identification of machines with digital computers, like our criterion for "thinking," will only be unsatisfactory if (contrary to my belief), it turns out that digital computers are unable to give a good showing in the game.

There are already a number of digital computers in working order, and it may be asked, "Why not try the experiment straight away? It would be easy to satisfy the conditions of the game. A number of interrogators could be used, and statistics compiled to show how often the right identification was given." The short answer is that we are not asking whether all digital computers would do well in the game nor whether the computers at present available would do well, but whether there are imaginable computers which would do well. But this is only the short answer. We shall see this question in a different light later.

4. Digital Computers

The idea behind digital computers may be explained by saying that these machines are intended to carry out any operations which could be done by a human computer. The human computer is supposed to be following fixed rules; he has no authority to deviate from them in any detail. We may suppose that these rules are supplied in a book, which is altered whenever he is put on to a new job. He has also an unlimited supply of paper on which he does his calculations. He may also do his multiplications and additions on a "desk machine," but this is not important.

If we use the above explanation as a definition we shall be in danger of circularity of argument. We avoid this by giving an outline of the means by which the desired effect is achieved. A digital computer can usually be regarded as consisting of three parts:

    (i) Store.
    (ii) Executive unit.
    (iii) Control.

The store is a store of information, and corresponds to the human computer's paper, whether this is the paper on which he does his calculations or that on which his book of rules is printed. In so far as the human computer does calculations in his head a part of the store will correspond to his memory.

The executive unit is the part which carries out the various individual operations involved in a calculation. What these individual operations are will vary from machine to machine. Usually fairly lengthy operations can be done such as "Multiply 3540675445 by 7076345687" but in some machines only very simple ones such as "Write down 0" are possible.

We have mentioned that the "book of rules" supplied to the computer is replaced in the machine by a part of the store. It is then called the "table of instructions." It is the duty of the control to see that these instructions are obeyed correctly and in the right order. The control is so constructed that this necessarily happens.

The information in the store is usually broken up into packets of moderately small size. In one machine, for instance, a packet might consist of ten decimal digits. Numbers are assigned to the parts of the store in which the various packets of information are stored, in some systematic manner. A typical instruction might say—

"Add the number stored in position 6809 to that in 4302 and put the result back into the latter storage position."

Needless to say it would not occur in the machine expressed in English. It would more likely be coded in a form such as 6809430217. Here 17 says which of various possible operations is to be performed on the two numbers. In this case the operation is that described above, *viz.*, "Add the number. . . ." It will be noticed that the instruction takes up 10 digits and so forms one packet of information, very conveniently. The control will normally take the instructions to be obeyed in the order of the positions in which they are stored, but occasionally an instruction such as

"Now obey the instruction stored in position 5606, and continue from there"

may be encountered, or again

"If position 4505 contains 0 obey next the instruction stored in 6707, otherwise continue straight on."

Instructions of these latter types are very important because they make it possible for a sequence of operations to be replaced over and over again until some condition is fulfilled, but in doing so to obey, not fresh instructions on each repetition, but the same ones over and over again. To take a domestic analogy. Suppose Mother wants Tommy to call at the cobbler's every morning on his way to school to see if her shoes are done, she can ask him afresh every morning. Alternatively she can stick up a notice once and for all in the hall which he will see when he leaves for school and which tells him to call for the shoes, and also to destroy the notice when he comes back if he has the shoes with him.

The reader must accept it as a fact that digital computers can be constructed, and indeed have been constructed, according to the principles we have described, and that they can in fact mimic the actions of a human computer very closely.

The book of rules which we have described our human computer as using is of course a convenient fiction. Actual human computers really remember what they have got to do. If one wants to make a machine mimic the behaviour of the human computer in some complex operation one has to ask him how it is done, and then translate the answer into the form of an instruction table. Constructing instruction tables is usually described as "programming." To "programme a machine to carry out the operation A" means to put the appropriate instruction table into the machine so that it will do A.

An interesting variant on the idea of a digital computer is a "digital computer with a random element." These have instructions involving the throwing of a die or some equivalent electronic process; one such instruction might for instance be, "Throw the die and put the resulting number into store 1000." Sometimes such a machine is described as having free will (though I would not use this phrase myself). It is not normally possible to determine from observing a machine whether it has a random element, for a similar effect can be produced by such devices as making the choices depend on the digits of the decimal for π.

Most actual digital computers have only a finite store. There is no theoretical difficulty in the idea of a computer with an unlimited store. Of course only a finite part can have been used at any one time. Likewise only a finite amount can have been constructed, but we can imagine more and more being added as required. Such computers have special theoretical interest and will be called infinitive capacity computers.

The idea of a digital computer is an old one. Charles Babbage, Lucasian Professor of Mathematics at Cambridge from 1828 to 1839, planned such a machine, called the Analytical Engine, but it was never completed. Although Babbage had all the essential ideas, his machine was not at that time such a very attractive prospect. The speed which would have been available would be definitely faster than a human computer but something like 100 times slower than the Manchester machine, itself one of the slower of the modern machines. The storage was to be purely mechanical, using wheels and cards.

The fact that Babbage's Analytical Engine was to be entirely mechanical will help us to rid ourselves of a superstition. Importance is often attached to the fact that modern digital computers are electrical, and that the nervous system also is electrical. Since Babbage's machine was not electrical, and since all digital computers are in a sense equivalent, we see that this use of electricity cannot be of theoretical importance. Of course electricity usually comes in where fast signalling is concerned, so that it is not surprising that we find it in both these connections. In the nervous system chemical phenomena are at least as important as electrical. In certain computers the storage system is mainly acoustic. The feature of using electricity is thus seen to be only a very superficial similarity. If we wish to find such similarities we should look rather for mathematical analogies of function.

5. Universality of Digital Computers

The digital computers considered in the last section may be classified amongst the "discrete-state machines." These are the machines which move by sudden jumps or clicks from one quite definite state to another. These states are sufficiently different for the possibility of confusion between them to be ignored. Strictly speaking there are no such machines. Everything really moves continuously. But there are many kinds of machine which can profitably be *thought of* as being discrete-state machines. For instance in considering the switches for a lighting system it is a convenient fiction that each switch must be definitely on or definitely off. There must be inter-mediate positions, but for most purposes we can forget about them. As an example of a discrete-state machine we might consider a wheel which clicks round through 120° once a second, but may be stopped by a lever which can be operated from outside; in addition a lamp is to light in one of the positions of the wheel. This machine could be described abstractly as follows. The internal state of the machine (which is described by the position of the wheel) may be q_1, q_2 or q_3. There is an input signal i_0 or i_1 (position of lever). The internal state at any moment is determined by the last state and input signal according to the table

		Last State		
		q_1	q_2	q_3
Input	i_0	q_2	q_3	q_1
	i_1	q_1	q_2	q_3

The output signals, the only externally visible indication of the internal state (the light) are described by the table

State	q_1	q_2	q_3
Output	o_0	o_0	o_1

This example is typical of discrete-state machines. They can be described by such tables provided they have only a finite number of possible states.

It will seem that given the initial state of the machine and the input signals it is always possible to predict all future states. This is reminiscent of Laplace's view that from the complete state of the universe at one moment of time, as described by the positions and velocities of all particles, it should be possible to predict all future states. The prediction which we are considering is, however, rather nearer to practicability than that considered by Laplace. The system of the "universe as a whole" is such that quite small errors in the initial conditions can have an overwhelming effect at a later time. The displacement of a single electron by a billionth of a centimetre at one moment might make the difference between a man being killed by an avalanche a year later, or escaping. It is an essential property of the mechanical systems which we have called "discrete-state machines" that this phenomenon does not occur. Even when we consider the actual physical machines instead of the idealised machines, reasonably accurate knowledge of the state at one moment yields reasonably accurate knowledge any number of steps later.

As we have mentioned, digital computers fall within the class of discrete-state machines. But the number of states of which such a machine is capable is usually enormously large. For instance, the number for the machine now working at Manchester is about $2^{165,000}$, *i.e.*, about $10^{50,000}$. Compare this with our example of the clicking wheel described above, which had three states. It is not difficult to see why the number of states should be so immense. The computer includes a store corresponding to the paper used by a human computer. It must be possible to write into the store any one of the combinations of symbols which might have been written on the paper. For simplicity suppose that only digits from 0 to 9 are used as symbols. Variations in handwriting are ignored. Suppose the computer is allowed 100 sheets of paper each containing 50 lines each with room for 30 digits. Then the number of states is $10^{100 \times 50 \times 30}$, *i.e.*, $10^{150,000}$. This is about the number of states of three Manchester machines put together. The logarithm to the base two of the number of states is usually called the "storage capacity" of the machine. Thus the Manchester machine has a storage capacity of about 165,000 and the wheel machine of our example about 1.6. If two machines are put together their capacities must be added to obtain the capacity of the resultant machine. This leads to the possibility of statements such as "The Manchester machine contains 64 magnetic tracks each with a capacity of 2560, eight electronic tubes with a capacity of 1280. Miscellaneous storage amounts to about 300 making a total of 174,380."

Given the table corresponding to a discrete-state machine it is possible to predict what it will do. There is no reason why this calculation should not be carried out by means of a digital computer. Provided it could be carried out sufficiently quickly the digital computer could mimic the behavior of any discrete-state machine. The imitation game could then be played with the machine in question (as B) and the mimicking digital computer (as A) and the interrogator would be unable to distinguish them. Of course the digital computer must have an adequate storage capacity as well as working sufficiently fast. Moreover, it must be programmed afresh for each new machine which it is desired to mimic.

This special property of digital computers, that they can mimic any discrete-state machine, is described by saying that they are *universal* machines. The existence of machines with this property has the important consequence that, considerations of speed apart, it is unnecessary to design various new machines to do various computing processes. They can all be done with one digital computer, suitably programmed for each case. It will be seen that as a consequence of this all digital computers are in a sense equivalent.

We may now consider again the point raised at the end of §3. It was suggested tentatively that the question, "Can machines think?" should be replaced by "Are there imaginable digital computers which would do well in the imitation game?" If we wish we can make this superficially more general and ask "Are there discrete-state machines which would do well?" But in view of the universality property we see that either of these questions is equivalent to this, "Let us fix our attention on one particular digital computer C. Is it true that by modifying this computer to have an adequate storage, suitably increasing its speed of action, and providing it with an appropriate programme, C can be made to play satisfactorily the part of A in the imitation game, the part of B being taken by a man?"

6. Contrary Views on the Main Question

We may now consider the ground to have been cleared and we are ready to proceed to the debate on our question, "Can machines think?" and the variant of it quoted at the end of the last section. We cannot altogether abandon the original form of the problem, for opinions will differ as to the appropriateness of the substitution and we must at least listen to what has to be said in this connexion.

It will simplify matters for the reader if I explain first my own beliefs in the matter. Consider first the more accurate form of the question. I believe that in about fifty years' time it will be possible to programme computers, with a storage capacity of about 10^9, to make them play the imitation game so well that an average interrogator will not have more than 70 per cent chance of making the right identification after five minutes of questioning. The original question, "Can machines think?" I believe to be too meaningless to deserve discussion. Nevertheless I believe that at the end of the century the use of words and general educated opinion will have altered so much that one will be able to speak of machines thinking without expecting to be contradicted. I believe further that no useful purpose is served by concealing these beliefs. The popular view that scientists proceed inexorably from well-established fact to well-established fact, never being influenced by any improved conjecture, is quite mistaken. Provided it is made clear which are proved facts and which are conjectures, no harm can result. Conjectures are of great importance since they suggest useful lines of research.

I now proceed to consider opinions opposed to my own.

(1) The Theological Objection

Thinking is a function of man's immortal soul. God has given an immortal soul to every man and woman, but not to any other animal or to machines. Hence no animal or machine can think.[1]

I am unable to accept any part of this, but will attempt to reply in theological terms. I should find the argument more convincing if animals were classed with men, for there is a greater difference, to my mind, between the typical animate and the inanimate than there is between man and the other animals. The arbitrary character of the orthodox view becomes clearer if we consider how it might appear to a member of some other religious community. How do Christians regard the Moslem view that women have no souls? But let us leave this point aside and return to the main argument. It appears to me that the argument quoted above implies a serious restriction of the omnipotence of the Almighty. It is admitted that there are certain things that He cannot do such as making one equal to two, but should we not believe that He has freedom to confer a soul on an elephant if He sees fit? We might expect that He would only exercise this power in conjunction with a mutation which provided the elephant with an appropriately improved brain to minister to the needs of this soul. An argument of exactly similar form may be made for the case of machines. It may seem different because it is more difficult to "swallow." But this really only means that we think it would be less likely that He would consider the circumstances suitable for conferring a soul. The circumstances in question are discussed in the rest of this paper. In attempting to construct such machines we should not be irreverently usurping His power of creating souls, any more than we are in the procreation of children: rather we are, in either case, instruments of His will providing mansions for the souls that He creates.

However, this is mere speculation. I am not very impressed with theological arguments whatever they may be used to support. Such arguments have often been found unsatisfactory in the past. In the time of Galileo it was argued that the texts, "And the sun stood still . . . and hasted not to go down about a whole day" (Joshua x. 13) and "He laid the foundations of the earth, that it should not move at any time" (Psalm cv. 5) were an adequate refutation of the Copernican theory. With our present knowledge such an argument appears futile. When that knowledge was not available it made a quite different impression.

[1] Possibly this view is heretical. St. Thomas Aquinas [*Summa Theologica,* quoted by Bertrand Russell (1945, p. 458)] states that God cannot make a man to have no soul. But this may not be a real restriction on His powers, but only a result of the fact that men's souls are immortal, and therefore indestructible.

(2) The "Heads in the Sand" Objection

"The consequences of machines thinking would be too dreadful. Let us hope and believe that they cannot do so."

This argument is seldom expressed quite so openly as in the form above. But it affects most of us who think about it at all. We like to believe that Man is in some subtle way superior to the rest of creation. It is best if he can be shown to be *necessarily* superior, for then there is no danger of him losing his commanding position. The popularity of the theological argument is clearly connected with this feeling. It is likely to be quite strong in intellectual people, since they value the power of thinking more highly than others, and are more inclined to base their belief in the superiority of Man on this power.

I do not think that this argument is sufficiently substantial to require refutation. Consolation would be more appropriate: perhaps this should be sought in the transmigration of souls.

(3) The Mathematical Objection

There are a number of results of mathematical logic which can be used to show that there are limitations to the powers of discrete-state machines. The best known of these results is known as Gödel's theorem (1931) and shows that in any sufficiently powerful logical system statements can be formulated which can neither be proved nor disproved within the system, unless possibly the system itself is inconsistent. There are other, in some respects similar, results due to Church (1936), Kleene (1935), Rosser, and Turing (1937). The latter result is the most convenient to consider, since it refers directly to machines, whereas the others can only be used in a comparatively indirect argument: for instance if Gödel's theorem is to be used we need in addition to have some means of describing logical systems in terms of machines, and machines in terms of logical systems. The result in question refers to a type of machine which is essentially a digital computer with an infinite capacity. It states that there are certain things that such a machine cannot do. If it is rigged up to give answers to questions as in the imitation game, there will be some questions to which it will either give a wrong answer, or fail to give an answer at all however much time is allowed for a reply. There may, of course, be many such questions, and questions which cannot be answered by one machine may be satisfactorily answered by another. We are of course supposing for the present that the questions are of the kind to which an answer "Yes" or "No" is appropriate, rather than questions such as "What do you think of Picasso?" The questions that we know the machines must fail on are of this type, "Consider the machine specified as follows. . . . Will this machine ever answer 'Yes' to any question?" The dots are to be replaced by a description of some machine in a standard form, which could be something like that used in §5. When the machine described bears a certain comparatively simple relation to the machine which is under interrogation, it can be shown that the answer is either wrong or not forthcoming. This is the mathematical result: it is argued that it proves a disability of machines to which the human intellect is not subject.

The short answer to this argument is that although it is established that there are limitations to the powers of any particular machine, it has only been stated, without any sort of proof, that no such limitations apply to the human intellect. But I do not think this view can be dismissed quite so lightly. Whenever one of these machines is asked the appropriate critical question, and gives a definite answer, we know that this answer must be wrong, and this gives us a certain feeling of superiority. Is this feeling illusory? It is no doubt quite genuine, but I do not think too much importance should be attached to it. We too often give wrong answers to questions ourselves to be justified in being very pleased at such evidence of fallibility on the part of the machines. Further, our superiority can only be felt on such an occasion in relation to the one machine over which we have scored our petty triumph. There would be no question of triumphing simultaneously over *all* machines. In short, then, there might be men cleverer than any given machine, but then again there might be other machines cleverer again, and so on.

Those who hold to the mathematical argument would, I think, mostly be willing to accept the imitation game as a basis for discussion. Those who believe in the two previous objections would probably not be interested in any criteria.

(4) The Argument from Consciousness

This argument is very well expressed in Professor Jefferson's Lister Oration for 1949, from which I quote. "Not until a machine can write a sonnet or compose a concerto because of thoughts and emotions felt, and not by the chance fall of symbols, could we agree that machine equals brain—that is, not only write it but know that it had written it. No mechanism could feel (and not merely artificially signal, an easy contrivance) pleasure at its successes, grief when its valves fuse, be warmed by flattery, be made miserable by its mistakes, be charmed by sex, be angry or depressed when it cannot get what it wants."

This argument appears to be a denial of the validity of our test. According to the most extreme form of this view the only way by which one could be sure that a machine thinks is to *be* the machine and to feel oneself thinking. One could then describe these feelings to the world, but of course no one would be justified in taking any notice. Likewise according to this view the only way to know that a *man* thinks is to be that particular man. It is in fact the solipsist point of view. It may be the most logical view to hold but it makes communication of ideas difficult. A is liable to believe "A thinks but B does not" whilst B believes "B thinks but A does not." Instead of arguing continually over this point it is usual to have the polite convention that everyone thinks.

I am sure that Professor Jefferson does not wish to adopt the extreme and solipsist point of view. Probably he would be quite willing to accept the imitation game as a test. The game (with the player B omitted) is frequently used in practice under the name of *viva voce* to discover whether some one really understands something or has "learnt it parrot fashion." Let us listen in to a part of such a *viva voce:*

Interrogator: In the first line of your sonnet which reads "Shall I compare thee to a summer's day," would not "a spring day" do as well or better?
Witness: It wouldn't scan.
Interrogator: How about "a winter's day." That would scan all right.
Witness: Yes, but nobody wants to be compared to a winter's day.
Interrogator: Would you say Mr. Pickwick reminded you of Christmas?
Witness: In a way.
Interrogator: Yet Chrismas is a winter's day, and I do not think Mr. Pickwick would mind the comparison.
Witness: I don't think you're serious. By a winter's day one means a typical winter's day, rather than a special one like Christmas.

And so on. What would Professor Jefferson say if the sonnet-writing machine was able to answer like this in the *viva voce?* I do not know whether he would regard the machine as "merely artificially signalling" these answers, but if the answers were as satisfactory and sustained as in the above passage I do not think he would describe it as "an easy contrivance." This phrase is, I think, intended to cover such devices as the inclusion in the machine of a record of someone reading a sonnet, with appropriate switching to turn it on from time to time.

In short then, I think that most of those who support the argument from consciousness could be persuaded to abandon it rather than be forced into the solipsist position. They will then probably be willing to accept our test.

I do not wish to give the impression that I think there is no mystery about consciousness. There is, for instance, something of a paradox connected with any attempt to localise it. But I do not think these mysteries necessarily need to be solved before we can answer the question with which we are concerned in this paper.

(5) Arguments from Various Disabilities

These arguments take the form, "I grant you that you can make machines do all the things you have mentioned but you will never be able to make one to do X." Numerous features X are suggested in this connexion. I offer a selection:

Be kind, resourceful, beautiful, friendly, have initiative, have a sense of humour, tell right from wrong, make mistakes, fall in love, enjoy strawberries and cream, make some one fall in love with it, learn from experience, use words properly, be the subject of its own thought, have as much diversity of behaviour as a man, do something really new.

No support is usually offered for these statements. I believe they are mostly founded on the principle of scientific induction. A man has seen thousands of machines in his lifetime. From what he sees of them he draws a number of general conclusions. They are ugly, each is designed for a very limited purpose, when required for a minutely different purpose they are useless, the variety of behaviour of any one of them is very small, etc., etc. Naturally he concludes that these are necessary properties of machines in general. Many of these limitations are associated with the very small storage capacity of most machines. (I am assuming that the idea of storage capacity is extended in some way to cover machines other than discrete-state machines. The exact definition does not matter as no mathematical accuracy is claimed in the present discussion.) A few years ago, when very little had been heard of digital computers, it was possible to elicit much incredulity concerning them, if one mentioned their properties without describing their construction. That was presumably due to a similar application of the principle of scientific induction. These applications of the principle are of course largely unconscious. When a burnt child fears the fire and shows that he fears it by avoiding it, I should say that he was applying scientific induction. (I could of course also describe his behaviour in many other ways.) The works and customs of mankind do not seem to be very suitable material to which to apply scientific induction. A very large part of space-time must be investigated, if reliable results are to be obtained. Otherwise we may (as most English children do) decide that everybody speaks English, and that it is silly to learn French.

There are, however, special remarks to be made about many of the disabilities that have been mentioned. The inability to enjoy strawberries and cream may have struck the reader as frivolous. Possibly a machine might be made to enjoy this delicious dish, but any attempt to make one do so would be idiotic. What is important about this disability is that it contributes to some of the other disabilities, *e.g.,* to the difficulty of the same kind of friendliness occurring between man and machine as between white man and white man, or between black man and black man.

The claim that "machines cannot make mistakes" seems a curious one. One is tempted to retort, "Are they any the worse for that?" But let us adopt a more sympathetic attitude, and try to see what is really meant. I think this criticism can be explained in terms of the imitation game. It is claimed that the interrogator could distinguish the machine from the man simply by setting them a number of problems in arithmetic. The machine would be unmasked because of its deadly accuracy. The reply to this is simple. The machine (programmed for playing the game) would not attempt to give the *right* answers to the arithmetic problems. It would deliberately introduce mistakes in a manner calculated to confuse the interrogator. A mechanical fault would probably show itself through an unsuitable decision as to what sort of a mistake to make in the arithmetic. Even this interpretation of the criticism is not sufficiently sympathetic. But we cannot afford the space to go into it much further. It seems to me that this criticism depends on a confusion between two kinds of mistake. We may call them "errors of functioning" and "errors of conclusion." Errors of functioning are due to some mechanical or electrical fault which causes the machine to behave otherwise than it was designed to do. In philosophical discussions one likes to ignore the possibility of such errors; one is therefore discussing "abstract machines." These abstract machines are mathematical fictions rather than physical objects. By definition they are incapable of errors of functioning. In this sense we can truly say that "machines can never make mistakes." Errors of conclusion can only arise when some meaning is attached to the output signals from the machine. The machine might, for instance, type out mathematical equations, or sentences in English. When a false proposition is typed we say that the machine has committed an error of conclusion. There is clearly no reason at all for saying that a machine cannot make this kind of mistake. It might do nothing but type out repeatedly "0 = 1." To take a less perverse example, it might have some method for drawing conclusions by scientific induction. We must expect such a method to lead occasionally to erroneous results.

The claim that a machine cannot be the subject of its own thought can of course only be answered if it can be shown that the machine has *some* thought with *some* subject matter. Nevertheless, "the subject matter of a machine's operations" does seem to mean something, at least to the people who deal with it. If, for instance, the machine was trying to find a solution of the equation $x^2 - 40x - 11 = 0$ one would be tempted to describe this equation as part of the machine's subject matter at that moment. In this sort of sense a machine undoubtedly can be its own subject matter. It may be used to help in making up its own programmes, or to predict the effect of alterations in its own structure. By observing the results of its own behaviour it can modify its own programmes so as to achieve some purpose more effectively. These are possibilities of the near future, rather than Utopian dreams.

The criticism that a machine cannot have much diversity of behaviour is just a way of saying that it cannot have much storage capacity. Until fairly recently a storage capacity of even a thousand digits was very rare.

The criticisms that we are considering here are often disguised forms of the argument from consciousness. Usually if one maintains that a machine *can* do one of these things, and describes the kind of method that the machine could use, one will not make much of an impression. It is thought that the method (whatever it may be, for it must be mechanical) is really rather base. Compare the parentheses in Jefferson's statement quoted on page 22.

(6) Lady Lovelace's Objection

Our most detailed information of Babbage's Analytical Engine comes from a memoir by Lady Lovelace (1842). In it she states, "The Analytical Engine has no pretensions to *originate* anything. It can do *whatever we know how to order it* to perform" (her italics). This statement is quoted by Hartree (1949) who adds: "This does not imply that it may not be possible to construct electronic equipment which will 'think for itself,' or in which, in biological terms, one could set up a conditioned reflex, which would serve as a basis for 'learning.' Whether this is possible in principle or not is a stimulating and exciting question, suggested by some of these recent developments. But it did not seem that the machines constructed or projected at the time had this property."

I am in thorough agreement with Hartree over this. It will be noticed that he does not assert that the machines in question had not got the property, but rather that the evidence available to Lady Lovelace did not encourage her to believe that they had it. It is quite possible that the machines in question had in a sense got this property. For suppose that some discrete-state machine has the property. The Analytical Engine was a universal digital computer, so that, if its storage capacity and speed were adequate, it could by suitable programming be made to mimic the machine in question. Probably this argument did not occur to the Countess or to Babbage. In any case there was no obligation on them to claim all that could be claimed.

This whole question will be considered again under the heading of learning machines.

A variant of Lady Lovelace's objection states that a machine can "never do anything really new." This may be parried for a moment with the saw, "There is nothing new under the sun." Who can be certain that "original work" that he has done was not simply the growth of the seed planted in him by teaching, or the effect of following well-known general principles. A better variant of the objection says that a machine can never "take us by surprise." This statement is a more direct challenge and can be met directly. Machines take me by surprise with great frequency. This is largely because I do not do sufficient calculation to decide what to expect them to do, or rather because, although I do a calculation, I do it in a hurried, slipshod fashion, taking risks. Perhaps I say to myself, "I suppose the voltage here ought to be the same as there: anyway let's assume it is." Naturally I am often wrong, and the result is a surprise for me for by the time the experiment is done these assumptions have been forgotten. These admissions lay me open to lectures on the subject of my vicious ways, but do not throw any doubt on my credibility when I testify to the surprises I experience.

I do not expect this reply to silence my critic. He will probably say that such surprises are due to some creative mental act on my part, and reflect no credit on the machine. This leads us back to the argument from consciousness, and far from the idea of surprise. It is a line of argument we must consider closed, but it is perhaps worth remarking that the appreciation of something as surprising requires as much of a "creative mental act" whether the surprising event originates from a man, a book, a machine or anything else.

The view that machines cannot give rise to surprises is due, I believe, to a fallacy to which philosophers and mathematicians are particularly subject. This is the assumption that as soon as a fact is presented to a mind all consequences of that fact spring into the mind simultaneously with it. It is a very useful assumption under many circumstances, but one too easily forgets that it is false. A natural consequence of doing so is that one then assumes that there is no virtue in the mere working out of consequences from data and general principles.

(7) Argument from Continuity in the Nervous System

The nervous system is certainly not a discrete-state machine. A small error in the information about the size of a nervous impulse impinging on a neuron, may make a large difference to the size of the outgoing impulse. It may be argued that, this being so, one cannot expect to be able to mimic the behaviour of the nervous system with a discrete-state system.

It is true that a discrete-state machine must be different from a continuous machine. But if we adhere to the conditions of the imitation game, the interrogator will not be able to take any advantage of this difference. The situation can be made clearer if we consider some other simpler continuous machine. A differential analyser will do very well. (A differential analyser is a certain kind of machine not of the discrete-state type used for some kinds of calculation.) Some of these provide their answers in a typed form, and so are suitable for taking part in the game. It would not be possible for a digital computer to predict exactly what answers the differential analyser would give to a problem, but it would be quite capable of giving the right sort of answer. For instance, if asked to give the value of π (actually about 3.1416) it would be reasonable to choose at random between the values 3.12, 3.13, 3.14, 3.15, 3.16 with the probabilities of 0.05, 0.15, 0.55, 0.19, 0.06 (say). Under these circumstances it would be very difficult for the interrogator to distinguish the differential analyser from the digital computer.

(8) The Argument from Informality of Behaviour

It is not possible to produce a set of rules purporting to describe what a man should do in every conceivable set of circumstances. One might for instance have a rule that one is to stop when one sees a red traffic light, and to go if one sees a green one, but what if by some fault both appear together? One may perhaps decide that it is safest to stop. But some further difficulty may well arise from this decision later. To attempt to provide rules of conduct to cover every eventuality, even those arising from traffic lights, appears to be impossible. With all this I agree.

From this it is argued that we cannot be machines. I shall try to reproduce the argument, but I fear I shall hardly do it justice. It seems to run something like this. "If each man had a definite set of rules of conduct by which he regulated his life he would be no better than a machine. But there are no such rules, so men cannot be machines." The undistributed middle is glaring. I do not think the argument is ever put quite like this, but I believe this is the argument used nevertheless. There may however be a certain confusion between "rules of conduct" and "laws of behaviour" to cloud the issue. By "rules of conduct" I mean precepts such as "Stop if you see red lights," on which one can act, and of which one can be conscious. By "laws of behaviour" I mean laws of nature as applied to a man's body such as "if you pinch him he will squeak." If we substitute "laws of behaviour which regulate his life" for "laws of conduct by which he regulates his life" in the argument quoted the undistributed middle is no longer insuperable. For we believe that it is not only true that being regulated by laws of behaviour implies being some sort of machine (though not necessarily a discrete-state machine), but that conversely being such a machine implies being regulated by such laws. However, we cannot so easily convince ourselves of the absence of complete laws of behaviour as of complete rules of conduct. The only way we know of for finding such laws is scientific observation, and we certainly know of no circumstances under which we could say, "We have searched enough. There are no such laws."

We can demonstrate more forcibly that any such statement would be unjustified. For suppose we could be sure of finding such laws if they existed. Then given a discrete-state machine it should certainly be possible to discover by observation sufficient about it to predict its future behaviour, and this within a reasonable time, say a thousand years. But this does not seem to be the case. I have set up on the Manchester computer a small programme using only 1,000 units of storage, whereby the machine supplied with one sixteen-figure number replies with another within two seconds. I would defy anyone to learn from these replies sufficient about the programme to be able to predict any replies to untried values.

(9) The Argument from Extrasensory Perception

I assume that the reader is familiar with the idea of extrasensory perception, and the meaning of the four items of it, *viz.,* telepathy, clairvoyance, precognition and psychokinesis. These disturbing phenomena seem to deny all our usual scientific ideas. How we should like to discredit them! Unfortunately the statistical evidence, at least for telepathy, is overwhelming. It is very difficult to rearrange one's ideas so as to fit these new facts in. Once one has accepted them it does not seem a very big step to believe in ghosts and bogies. The idea that our bodies move simply according to the known laws of physics, together with some others not yet discovered but somewhat similar, would be one of the first to go.

This argument is to my mind quite a strong one. One can say in reply that many scientific theories seem to remain workable in practice, in spite of clashing with ESP; that in fact one can get along very nicely if one forgets about it. This is rather cold comfort, and one fears that thinking is just the kind of phenomenon where ESP may be especially relevant.

A more specific argument based on ESP might run as follows: "Let us play the imitation game, using as witnesses a man who is good as a telepathic receiver, and a digital computer. The interrogator can ask such questions as 'What suit does the card in my right hand belong to?' The man by telepathy or clairvoyance gives the right answer 130 times out of 400 cards. The machine can only guess at random, and perhaps gets 104 right, so the interrogator makes the right identification." There is an interesting possibility which opens here. Suppose the digital computer contains a random number generator. Then it will be natural to use this to decide what answer to give. But then the random number generator will be subject to the psychokinetic powers of the interrogator. Perhaps this psychokinesis might cause the machine to guess right more often than would be expected on a probability calculation, so that the interrogator might still be unable to make the right identification. On the other hand, he might be able to guess right without any questioning, by clairvoyance. With ESP anything may happen.

If telepathy is admitted it will be necessary to tighten our test up. The situation could be regarded as analogous to that which would occur if the interrogator were talking to himself and one of the competitors was listening with his ear to the wall. To put the competitors into a "telepathy-proof room" would satisfy all requirements.

7. Learning Machines

The reader will have anticipated that I have no very convincing arguments of a positive nature to support my views. If I had I should not have taken such pains to point out the fallacies in contrary views. Such evidence as I have I shall now give.

Let us return for a moment to Lady Lovelace's objection, which stated that the machine can only do what we tell it to do. One could say that a man can "inject" an idea into the machine, and that it will respond to a certain extent and 'then drop into quiescence, like a piano string struck by a hammer. Another simile would be an atomic pile of less than critical size: an injected idea is to correspond to a neutron entering the pile from without. Each such neutron will cause a certain disturbance which eventually dies away. If, however, the size of the pile is sufficiently increased, the disturbance caused by such an incoming neutron will very likely go on and on increasing until the whole pile is destroyed. Is there a corresponding phenomenon for minds, and is there one for machines? There does seem to be one for the human mind. The majority of them seem to be "subcritical," i.e., to correspond in this analogy to piles of subcritical size. An idea presented to such a mind will on average give rise to less than one idea in reply. A smallish proportion are supercritical. An idea presented to such a mind that may give rise to a whole "theory" consisting of secondary, tertiary and more remote ideas. Animals minds seem to be very definitely subcritical. Adhering to this analogy we ask, "Can a machine be made to be supercritical?"

The "skin-of-an-onion" analogy is also helpful. In considering the functions of the mind or the brain we find certain operations which we can explain in purely mechanical terms. This we say does not correspond to the real mind: it is a sort of skin which we must strip off if we are to find the real mind. But then in what remains we find a further skin to be stripped off, and so on. Proceeding in this way do we ever come to the "real" mind, or do we eventually come to the skin which has nothing in it? In the latter case the whole mind is mechanical. (It would not be a discrete-state machine however. We have discussed this.)

These last two paragraphs do not claim to be convincing arguments. They should rather be described as "recitations tending to produce belief."

The only really satisfactory support that can be given for the view expressed at the beginning of §6, will be that provided by waiting for the end of the century and then doing the experiment described. But what can we say in the meantime? What steps should be taken now if the experiment is to be successful?

As I have explained, the problem is mainly one of programming. Advances in engineering will have to be made too, but it seems unlikely that these will not be adequate for the requirements. Estimates of the storage capacity of the brain vary from 10^{10} to 10^{15} binary digits. I incline to the lower values and believe that only a very small fraction is used for the higher types of thinking. Most of it is probably used for the retention of visual impressions. I should be surprised if more than 10^9 was required for satisfactory playing of the imitation game, at any rate against a blind man. (*Note:* The capacity of the *Encyclopaedia Britannica,* 11th edition, is 2×10^9.) A storage capacity of 10^7 would be a very practicable possibility even by present techniques. It is probably not necessary to increase the speed of operations of the machines at all. Parts of modern machines which can be regarded as analogs of nerve cells work about a thousand times faster than the latter. This should provide a "margin of safety" which could cover losses of speed arising in many ways. Our problem then is to find out how to programme these machines to play the game. At my present rate of working I produce about a thousand digits of programme a day, so that about sixty workers, working steadily through the fifty years might accomplish the job, if nothing went into the wastepaper basket. Some more expeditious method seems desirable.

In the process of trying to imitate an adult human mind we are bound to think a good deal about the process which has brought it to the state that it is in. We may notice three components.

(*a*) The initial state of the mind, say at birth,
(*b*) The education to which it has been subjected,
(*c*) Other experience, not to be described as education, to which it has been subjected.

Instead of trying to produce a programme to simulate the adult mind, why not rather try to produce one which simulates the child's? If this were then subjected to an appropriate course of education one would obtain the adult brain. Presumably the child brain is something like a notebook as one buys it from the stationer's. Rather little mechanism, and lots of blank sheets. (Mechanism and writing are from our point of view almost synonymous.) Our hope is that there is so little mechanism in the child brain that something like it can be easily programmed. The amount of work in the education we can assume, as a first approximation, to be much the same as for the human child.

We have thus divided our problem into two parts. The child programme and the education process. These two remain very closely connected. We cannot expect to find a good child machine at the first attempt. One must experiment with teaching one such machine and see how well it learns. One can then try another and see if it is better or worse. There is an obvious connection between this process and evolution, by the identifications

Structure of the child machine = hereditary material
Changes of the child machine = mutations
Natural selection = judgment of the experimenter

One may hope, however, that this process will be more expeditious than evolution. The survival of the fittest is a slow method for measuring advantages. The experimenter, by the exercise of intelligence, should be able to speed it up. Equally important is the fact that he is not restricted to random mutations. If he can trace a cause for some weakness he can probably think of the kind of mutation which will improve it.

It will not be possible to apply exactly the same teaching process to the machine as to a normal child. It will not, for instance, be provided with legs, so that it could not be asked to go out and fill the coal scuttle. Possibly it might not have eyes. But however well these deficiencies might be overcome by clever engineering, one could not send the creature to school without the other children making excessive fun of it. It must be given some tuition. We need not be too concerned about the legs, eyes, etc. The example of Miss Helen Keller shows that education can take place provided that communication in both directions between teacher and pupil can take place by some means or other.

We normally associate punishments and rewards with the teaching process. Some simple child machines can be constructed or programmed on this sort of principle. The machine has to be so constructed that events which shortly preceded the occurrence of a punishment signal are unlikely to be repeated, whereas a reward signal increased the probability of repetition of the events which led up to it. These definitions do not presuppose any feelings on the part of the machine. I have done some experiments with one such child machine, and succeeded in teaching it a few things, but the teaching method was too unorthodox for the experiment to be considered really successful.

The use of punishments and rewards can at best be a part of the teaching process. Roughly speaking, if the teacher has no other means of communicating to the pupil, the amount of information which can reach him does not exceed the total number of rewards and punishments applied. By the time a child has learnt to repeat "Casabianca" he would probably feel very sore indeed, if the text could only be discovered by a "Twenty Questions" technique, every "NO" taking the form of a blow. It is necessary therefore to have some other "unemotional" channels of communication. If these are available it is possible to teach a machine by punishments and rewards to obey orders given in some language, *e.g.,* a symbolic language. These orders are to be transmitted through the "unemotional" channels. The use of this language will diminish greatly the number of punishments and rewards required.

Opinions may vary as to the complexity which is suitable in the child machine. One might try to make it as simple as possible consistently with the general principles. Alternatively one might have a complete system of logical inference "built in."[2] In the latter case the store would be largely occupied with definitions and propositions. The propositions would have various kinds of status, *e.g.,* well-established facts, conjectures, mathematically proved theorems, statements given by an authority, expressions having the logical form of proposition but not belief-value. Certain propositions may be described as "imperatives." The machine should be so constructed that as soon as an imperative is classed as "well established" the appropriate action automatically takes place. To illustrate this, suppose the teacher says to the machine, "Do your homework now." This may cause "Teacher says 'Do your homework now'" to be included amongst the well-established facts. Another such fact might be, "Everything that teacher says is true." Combining these may eventually lead to the imperative, "Do your homework now," being included amongst the well-established facts, and this, by the construction of the machine, will mean that the homework actually gets started, but the effect is very satisfactory. The processes of inference used by the machine need not be such as would satisfy the most exacting logicians. There might for instance be no hierarchy of types. But this need not mean that type fallacies will occur, any more than we are bound to fall over unfenced cliffs. Suitable imperatives (expressed *within* the systems, not forming part of the rules *of* the system) such as "Do not use a class unless it is a subclass of one which has been mentioned by teacher" can have a similar effect to "Do not go too near the edge."

The imperatives that can be obeyed by a machine that has no limbs are bound to be of a rather intellectual character, as in the example (doing homework) given above. Important amongst such imperatives will be ones which regulate the order in which the rules of the logical system concerned are to be applied. For at each stage when one is using a logical system, there is a very large number of alternative steps, any of which one is permitted to apply, so far as obedience to the rules of the logical system is concerned. These choices make the difference between a brilliant and a footling reasoner, not the difference between a sound and a fallacious one. Propositions leading to imperatives of this kind might be "When Socrates is mentioned, use the syllogism in Barbara" or "If one method has been proved to be quicker than another, do not use the slower method." Some

[2] Or rather "programmed in" for our child machine will be programmed in a digital computer. But the logical system will not have to be learnt.

of these may be "given by authority," but others may be produced by the machine itself, *e.g.* by scientific induction.

The idea of a learning machine may appear paradoxical to some readers. How can the rules of operation of the machine change? They should describe completely how the machine will react whatever its history might be, whatever changes it might undergo. The rules are thus quite time-invariant. This is quite true. The explanation of the paradox is that the rules which get changed in the learning process are of a rather less pretentious kind, claiming only an ephemeral validity. The reader may draw a parallel with the Constitution of the United States.

An important feature of a learning machine is that its teacher will often be very largely ignorant of quite what is going on inside, although he may still be able to some extent to predict his pupil's behavior. This should apply most strongly to the later education of a machine arising from a child machine of well-tried design (or programme). This is in clear contrast with normal procedure when using a machine to do computations: one's object is then to have a clear mental picture of the state of the machine at each moment in the computation. This object can only be achieved with a struggle. The view that "the machine can only do what we know how to order it to do,"[3] appears strange in face of this. Most of the programmes which we can put into the machine will result in its doing something that we cannot make sense of at all, or which we regard as completely random behaviour. Intelligent behaviour presumably consists in a departure from the completely disciplined behaviour involved in computation, but a rather slight one, which does not give rise to random behaviour, or to pointless repetitive loops. Another important result of preparing our machine for its part in the imitation game by a process of teaching and learning is that "human fallibility" is likely to be omitted in a rather natural way, *i.e.,* without special "coaching." (The reader should reconcile this with the point of view on pages 23 and 24.) Processes that are learnt do not produce a hundred per cent certainty of result; if they did they could not be unlearnt.

It is probably wise to include a random element in a learning machine. A random element is rather useful when we are searching for a solution of some problem. Suppose for instance we wanted to find a number between 50 and 200 which was equal to the square of the sum of its digits, we might start at 51 then try 52 and go on until we got a number that worked. Alternatively we might choose numbers at random until we got a good one. This method has the advantage that it is unnecessary to keep track of the values that have been tried, but the disadvantage that one may try the same one twice, but this is not very important if there are several solutions. The systematic method has the disadvantage that there may be

---

[3] Compare Lady Lovelace's statement which does not contain the word "only."

an enormous block without any solutions in the region which has to be investigated first. Now the learning process may be regarded as a search for a form of behaviour which will satisfy the teacher (or some other criterion). Since there is probably a very large number of satisfactory solutions the random method seems to be better than the systematic. It should be noticed that it is used in the analogous process of evolution. But there the systematic method is not possible. How could one keep track of the different genetical combinations that had been tried, so as to avoid trying them again?

We may hope that machines will eventually compete with men in all purely intellectual fields. But which are the best ones to start with? Even this is a difficult decision. Many people think that a very abstract activity, like the playing of chess, would be best. It can also be maintained that it is best to provide the machine with the best sense organs that money can buy, and then teach it to understand and speak English. This process could follow the normal teaching of a child. Things would be pointed out and named, etc. Again I do not know what the right answer is, but I think both approaches should be tried.

We can only see a short distance ahead, but we can see plenty there that needs to be done.

section 2

Machines That Play Games

A favorite area of research in artificial intelligence, past and present, is in computer programs that play games. Why should one be interested in game playing, a mere human pastime? Or, as a Soviet acquaintance once put the question to one of the editors of this volume, "Who allows you to do it?"

Game playing has many fascinating aspects to the researcher. Affectively, it provides a direct contest between man's wit and machine's wit. On a more serious level, game situations provide problem environments which are relatively highly regular and well defined, but which afford sufficient complexity in solution generation so that intelligence and symbolic reasoning skills play a crucial role. In short, game environments are very useful task environments for studying the nature and structure of complex problem-solving processes.

The game of chess is one of man's valued intellectual diversions, and a number of chess-playing programs have been constructed. A history and critique of these efforts are given by Newell, Shaw, and Simon in the paper reprinted in this section. The greater part of their paper is devoted to a detailed explanation of the working of their own chess-playing program (NSS Chess Player). Following this theoretical explanation is a game played by the NSS Chess Player. It is annotated by a number of chess experts, including a partial annotation by chess master Edward Lasker.

The NSS Chess Player is one of those research efforts which lie in the shadowy area between artificial intelligence and simulation of human problem-solving. In the strict sense, it is not intended to be a model of human problem-solving in the chess environment. But the authors, in conceiving their program, were convinced that humanlike problem-solving methods, involving highly adaptive and highly selective search techniques, would be more effective in chess problem-solving than other computational schemes that had been proposed and tried. The behavior of their chess-playing program tends to support their conviction.

The focus on human problem-solving methods which is characteristic of the research of Newell, Shaw, and Simon predates the existence of their research team. In this connection, it is instructive to read the essays in Simon's *Models of Man* entitled "A Behavioral Theory of Rational Choice" and "Rational Choice and the Structure of the Environment." These essays, written more than a decade ago, contain a large part of the basic conceptual scheme of the decision-making mechanisms embodied in the Chess Player and the Logic Theorist, as well as in the portfolio selection program of Clarkson (reprinted in Part 2 of this volume).

Samuel's checker-playing program, on the other hand, sits squarely in the artificial intelligence camp. In its basic mechanism, especially in its position-evaluation scheme, it does not employ humanlike problem-solving mechanisms. Samuel believes that the effective path to progress in artificial intelligence is probably not that of imitating and adapting human processes. The rather high level of skill attained by Samuel's program is reassuring as to this point of view.

In terms of actual proficiency as exhibited in behavior, Samuel's program is one of the landmarks of artificial intelligence research to date. A recent game played by the program, in which it defeated a checkers champion, follows the Samuel article.

Of special interest in the checker-playing program are the learning routines, which improve the performance of the program as it gains experience with actual games. This learning scheme is important because it represents the only really successful attempt at machine learning in problem-solving situations.

A. Newell is Institute Professor of Systems and Communication Sciences at Carnegie Institute of Technology. H. A. Simon is Professor of Administration and Psychology in the Graduate School of Industrial Administration at the same institution. J. C. Shaw is a member of the research staff of the RAND Corporation. A. Samuel is Director of Research Communications at the IBM Research Center.

CHESS-PLAYING PROGRAMS
AND THE PROBLEM
OF COMPLEXITY

by Allen Newell, J. C. Shaw, & H. A. Simon

Man can solve problems without knowing how he solves them. This simple fact sets the conditions for all attempts to rationalize and understand human decision-making and problem-solving. Let us simply assume that it is good to know how to do mechanically what man can do naturally—both to add to man's knowledge of man, and to add to his kit of tools for controlling and manipulating his environment. We shall try to assess recent progress in understanding and mechanizing man's intellectual attainments by considering a single line of attack—the attempts to construct digital computer programs that play chess.

Chess is the intellectual game *par excellence*. Without a chance device to obscure the contest, it pits two intellects against each other in a situation so complex that neither can hope to understand it completely, but sufficiently amenable to analysis that each can hope to outthink his opponent. The game is sufficiently deep and subtle in its implications to have supported the rise of professional players, and to have allowed a deepening analysis through 200 years of intensive study and play without becoming exhausted or barren. Such characteristics mark chess as a natural arena for attempts at mechanization. If one could devise a successful chess machine, one would seem to have penetrated to the core of human intellectual endeavor.

The history of chess programs is an example of the attempt to conceive and cope with complex mechanisms. Now there might have been a trick—one might have discovered something that was as the wheel to the human leg: a device quite different from humans in its methods, but supremely effective in its way, and perhaps very simple. Such a device might play

39

excellent chess, but would fail to further our understanding of human intellectual processes. Such a prize, of course, would be worthy of discovery in its own right, but there appears to be nothing of this sort in sight.

We return to the original orientation: Humans play chess, and when they do they engage in behavior that seems extremely complex, intricate, and successful. Consider, for example, a scrap of a player's (White's) running comment as he analyzes the position in Fig. 1:

> *Are there any other threats? Black also has a threat of Knight to Bishop 5 threatening the Queen, and also putting more pressure on the King's side because his Queen's Bishop can come over after he moves his Knight at Queen 2; however, that is not the immediate threat. Otherwise, his Pawn at King 4 is threatening my Pawn. . . .*

Notice that his analysis is qualitative and functional. He wanders from one feature to another, accumulating various bits of information that will be available from time to time throughout the rest of the analysis. He makes evaluations in terms of pressures and immediacies of threat, and gradually creates order out of the situation.

How can we construct mechanisms that will show comparable complexity in their behavior? They need not play in exactly the same way; close simulation of the human is not the immediate issue. But we do assert that complexity of behavior is essential to an intelligent performance—that the complexity of a successful chess program will approach the complexity

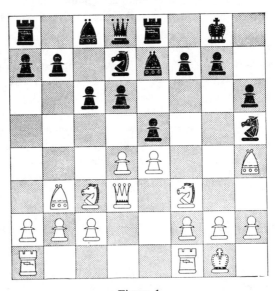

Figure 1.

of the thought processes of a successful human chess player. Complexity of response is dictated by the task, not by idiosyncrasies of the human response mechanism.

There is a close and reciprocal relation between complexity and communication. On the one hand, the complexity of the systems we can specify depends on the language in which we must specify them. Being human, we have only limited capacities for processing information. Given a more powerful language, we can specify greater complexity with limited processing powers.

Let us illustrate this side of the relation between complexity and communication. No one considers building chess machines in the literal sense —fashioning pieces of electronic gear into automatons that will play chess. We think instead of chess programs; specifications written in a language, called machine code, that will instruct a digital computer of standard design how to play chess. There is a reason for choosing this latter course—in addition to any aversion we may have to constructing a large piece of special-purpose machinery. Machine code is a more powerful language than the block diagrams ·of the electronics engineer. Each symbol in machine code specifies a larger unit of processing than a symbol in the block diagram. Even a moderately complicated program becomes hopelessly complex if thought of in terms of gates and pulses.

But there is another side to the relation between communication and complexity. We cannot use any old language we please. We must be understood by the person or machine to whom we are communicating. English will not do to specify chess programs because there are no English-understanding computers. A specification in English is a specification to another human who then has the task of creating the machine. Machine code is an advance precisely because there are machines that understand it—because a chess program in machine code is operationally equivalent to a machine that plays chess.

If the machine could understand even more powerful languages, we could use these to write chess programs—and thus get more complex and intelligent programs from our limited human processing capacity. But communication is limited by the intelligence of the least participant, and at present a computer has only passive capability. The language it understands is one of simple commands—it must be told very much about what to do.

Thus it seems that the rise of effective communication between man and computer will coincide with the rise in the intelligence of the computer—so that the human can say more while thinking less. But at this point in history, the only way we can obtain more intelligent machines is to design them—we cannot yet grow them, or breed them, or train them by the blind proccdures that work with humans. We are caught at the wrong equilibrium of a bistable system: we could design more intelligent machines if we could communicate to them better; we could communicate to them better if they were more intelligent. Limited both in our capabilities for design and communication, every advance in either separately requires a momentous effort. Each success, however, allows a corresponding effort on the other side to reach a little further. At some point the reaction will "go," and we will find ourselves at the favorable equilibrium point of the system, possessing mechanisms that are both highly intelligent and communicative.

With this view of the task and its setting, we can turn to the substance of the report: the development of chess programs. We will proceed historically, since this arrangement of the material will show most clearly what progress is being made in obtaining systems of increasing complexity and intelligence.

Shannon's Proposal

The relevant history begins with a paper by Claude Shannon in 1949. He did not present a particular chess program, but discussed many of the basic problems involved. The framework he introduced has guided most of the subsequent analysis of the problem.

As Shannon observed, chess is a finite game. There is only a finite number of positions, each of which admits a finite number of alternative moves. The rules of chess assure that any play will terminate: that eventually a position will be reached that is a win, loss, or draw. Thus chess can be completely described as a branching tree (as in Fig. 2), the nodes corresponding to positions and the branches corresponding to the alternative moves from each position. It is intuitively clear, and easily proved, that for a player who can view the entire tree and see all the ultimate consequences of each alternative, chess becomes a simple game. Starting with the terminal positions, which have determinate payoffs, he can work backwards, determining at each node which branch is best for him or his opponent as the case may be, until he arrives at the alternative for his next move.

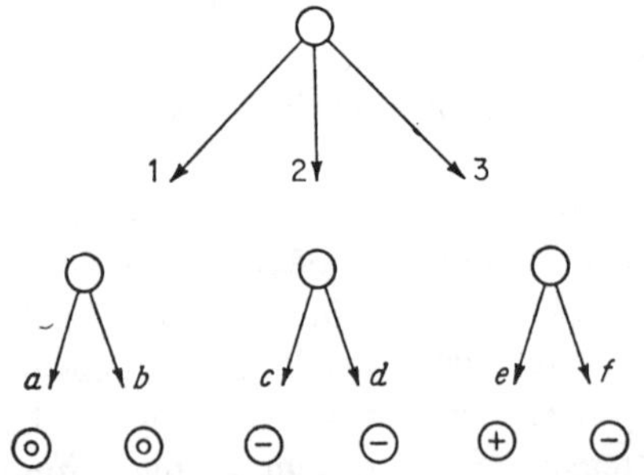

This inferential procedure—called *minimaxing* in the theory of games—is basic to all the attempts so far to program computers for chess. Let us be sure we understand it. Figure 2 shows a situation where White is to move and has three choices, (1), (2), and (3). White's move will be followed by Black's: (*a*) or (*b*) in

Figure 2. The game tree and minimaxing.

case move (1) is made; (c) or (d) if move (2) is made; and (e) or (f) if move (3) is made. To keep the example simple, we have assumed that all of Black's moves lead to positions with known payoffs: (+) meaning a win for White, (0) meaning a draw, and (−) meaning a loss for White. How should White decide what to do—what inference procedure allows him to determine which of the three moves is to be preferred? Clearly, no matter what Black does, move (1) leads to a draw. Similarly, no matter what Black does, move (2) leads to a loss for White. White should clearly prefer move (1) to move (2). But what about move (3)? It offers the possibility of a win, but also contains the possibility of a loss; and furthermore, the outcome is in Black's control. If White is willing to impute any analytic ability to his opponent, he must conclude that move (3) will end as a loss for White, and hence that move (1) is the preferred move. The win from move (3) is completely insubstantial, since it can never be realized. Thus White can impute a value to a position—in this case draw—by reasoning backward from known values.

To repeat: If the entire tree can be scanned, the best move can be determined simply by the minimaxing procedure. Now minimaxing might have been the "wheel" of chess—with the adventure ended almost before it had started—if the tree were not so large that even current computers can discover only the minutest fraction of it in years of computing. Shannon's estimate, for instance, is that there are something like 10^{120} continuations to be explored, with less than 10^{16} microseconds available in a century to explore them.

Shannon then suggested the following framework. Playing chess consists of considering the alternative moves, obtaining some effective evaluation of them by means of analysis, and choosing the preferred alternative on the basis of the evaluation. The analysis—which is the hard part—could be factored into three parts. First, one would explore the continuations to a certain depth. Second, since it is clear that the explorations cannot be deep enough to reach terminal positions, one would evaluate the positions reached at the end of each exploration in terms of the pattern of men on the chessboard. These static evaluations would then be combined by means of the minimaxing procedure to form the effective value of the alternative. One would then choose the move with the highest effective value. The rationale behind this factorization was the reasonableness that, for a given evaluation function, the greater the depth of analysis, the better the chess that would be played. In the limit, of course, such a process would play perfect chess by finding terminal positions for all continuations. Thus a metric was provided that measured all programs along the single dimension of their depth of analysis.

To complete the scheme, a procedure was needed to evaluate positions statically—that is, without making further moves. Shannon proposed a numerical measure formed by summing, with weights, a number of factors or scores that could be computed for any position. These scores would correspond to the various features that chess experts assert are important. This approach gains plausibility from the existence of a few natural quantities in chess, such as the values of pieces, and the mobility of men. It also gains plausibility, of course, from the general use in science and engineering of linearizing assumptions as first approximations.

To summarize: the basic framework introduced by Shannon for thinking about chess programs consists of a series of questions:

1. Alternatives
   Which alternative moves are to be considered?
2. Analysis
   a. Which continuations are to be explored and to what depth?
   b. How are positions to be evaluated statically—in terms of their patterns?
   c. How are the static evaluations to be integrated into a single value for an alternative?
3. Final choice procedure
   What procedure is to be used to select the final preferred move?

We would hazard that Shannon's paper is chiefly remembered for the specific answers he proposed to these questions: consider all alternatives; search all continuations to fixed depth, n; evaluate with a numerical sum; minimax to get the effective value for an alternative; and then pick the best one. His article goes beyond these specifics, however, and discusses the possibility of selecting only a small number of alternatives and continuations. It also discusses the possibility of analysis in terms of the functions that chessmen perform—blocking, attacking, defending. At this stage, however, it was possible to think of chess programs only in terms of extremely systematic procedures. Shannon's specific proposals have gradually been realized in actual programs, whereas the rest of his discussion has been largely ignored. And when proposals for more complex computations enter the research picture again, it is through a different route.

Turing's Program

Shannon did not present a particular program. His specifications still require large amounts of computing for even such modest depths of analysis as two or three moves. It remained for A. M. Turing (1950) to describe a program along these lines that was sufficiently simple to be simulated by hand, without the aid of a digital computer.

In Table 1 we have characterized Turing's program in terms of the framework just defined. There are some additional categories which will become clear as we proceed. The table also provides similar information for each of the other three programs we will consider.

TABLE 1 Comparison of Current Chess Programs

	Turing	Kister, Stein, Ulam, Walden, Wells (Los Alamos)	Bernstein, Roberts, Arbuckle, Belsky (Bernstein)	Newell, Shaw, Simon (NSS)
Vital statistics				
Date	1951	1956	1957	1958
Board	8 × 8	6 × 6	8 × 8	8 × 8
Computer	Hand simulation	MANIAC-I 11,000 ops./sec	IBM 704 42,000 ops./sec	RAND JOHNNIAC 20,000 ops./sec
Chess program				
Alternatives	All moves	All moves	7 plausible moves Sequence of move generators	Variable Sequence of move generators
Depth of analysis	Until dead (exchanges only)	All moves 2 moves deep	7 plausible moves 2 moves deep	Until dead Each goal generates moves
Static evaluation	Numerical Many factors	Numerical Material, mobility	Numerical Material, mobility Area control King defense	Nonnumerical Vector of values Acceptance by goals
Integration of values	Minimax	Minimax (modified)	Minimax	Minimax
Final choice	Material dominates Otherwise, best value	Best value	Best value	1. First acceptable 2. Double function
Programming				
Language		Machine code	Machine code	IPL-IV, interpretive
Data scheme		Single board No records	Single board Centralized tables Recompute	Single board Decentralized List structure Recompute
Time	Minutes	12 min/move	8 min/move	1–10 hr/move (est.)
Space		600 words	7000 words	Now 6000 words, est. 16,000
Results				
Experience	1 game	3 games (no longer exists)	2 games	0 games
Description	Loses to weak player Aimless Subtleties of evaluation lost	Beats weak player Equivalent to human with 20 games experience	Passable amateur Blind spots Positional	Some hand simulation Good in spots (opening) No aggressive goals yet

Turing's program considered all alternatives—that is, all legal moves. In order to limit computation, however, he was very circumspect about the continuations the program considered. Turing introduced the notion of a "dead" position: one that in some sense was stable, hence could be evaluated. For example, there is no sense in counting material on the board in the middle of an exchange of Queens: one should explore the continuations until the exchange has been carried through—to the point where the material is not going to change with the next move. So Turing's program evaluated material at dead positions only. He made the value of material dominant in his static evaluation, so that a decision problem remained only if minimaxing revealed several alternatives that were equal in material. In these cases, he applied a supplementary additive evaluation to the positions reached by making the alternative moves. This evaluation included a large number of factors—mobility, backward pawns, defense of men, and so on—points being assigned for each.

Thus Turing's program is a good instance of a chess-playing system as envisaged by Shannon, although a small-scale one in terms of computational requirements. Only one published game, as far as we know, was played with the program. It proved to be rather weak, for it lost against a weak human player (who did not know the program, by the way), although it was not entirely a pushover. In general its play was rather aimless, and it was capable of gross blunders, one of which cost it the game. As one might have expected, the subtleties of the evaluation function were lost upon it. Most of the numerous factors included in the function rarely had any influence on the move chosen. In summary: Turing's program was not a very good chess player, but it reached the bottom rung of the human ladder.

There is no *a priori* objection to hand simulation of a program, although experience has shown that it is almost always inexact for programs of this complexity. For example, there is an error in Turing's play of his program, because he—the human simulator—was unwilling to consider all the alternatives. He failed to explore the ones he "knew" would be eliminated anyway, and was wrong once. The main objection to hand simulation is the amount of effort required to do it. The computer is really the enabling condition for exploring the behavior of a complex program. One cannot even realize the potentialities of the Shannon scheme without programming it for a computer.

The Los Alamos Program

In 1956 a group at Los Alamos programmed MANIAC I to play chess (Kister et al., 1957).[1] The Los Alamos program is an almost perfect

[1] There are two other explorations between 1951 and 1956 of which we are aware

example of the type of system specified by Shannon. As shown in the table, all alternatives were considered; all continuations were explored to a depth of two moves (*i.e.,* two moves for Black and two for White); the static evaluation function consisted of a sum of material and mobility measures; the values were integrated by a minimax procedure,[2] and the best alternative in terms of the effective value was chosen for the move.

In order to carry out the computation within reasonable time limits, a major concession was required. Instead of the normal chessboard of eight squares by eight squares, they used a reduced board, six squares by six squares. They eliminated the Bishops and all special chess moves: castling, two-square Pawn moves in the opening, and *en passant* captures.

The result? Again the program is a weak player, but now one that is capable of beating a weak human player, as the machine demonstrated in one of its three games. It is capable of serious blunders, a common characteristic, also, of weak human play.

Since this is our first example of actual play on a computer, it is worth looking a bit at the programming and machine problems. In a normal 8×8 game of chess there are about 30 legal alternatives at each move, on the average, thus looking two moves ahead brings 30^4 continuations, about 800,000, into consideration. In the reduced 6×6 game, the designers estimate the average number of alternatives at about 20, giving a total of about 160,000 continuations per move. Even with this reduction of five to one, there are still a lot of positions to be looked at. By comparison, the best evidence suggests that a human player considers considerably less than 100 positions in the analysis of a move (De Groot, 1946). The Los Alamos program was able to make a move in about 12 minutes on the average. To do this the code had to be very simple and straightforward. This can be seen by the size of the program—only 600 words. In a sense, the machine barely glanced at each position it evaluated. The two measures in the evaluation function are obtained directly from the process of looking at continuations: changes in material are noticed if the moves are captures, and the mobility score for a position is equal to the number of new positions to which it leads—hence is computed almost without effort when exploring all continuations.

The Los Alamos program tests the limits of simplification in the direction of minimizing the amount of information required for each position evaluated, just as Turing's program tests the limits in the direction of minimizing the amount of exploration of continuations. These programs, espe-

---

—a hand simulation by F. Mosteller and a Russian program for BESM. Unfortunately, not enough information is available on either to talk about them, so we must leave a gap in the history between 1951 and 1956.

[2] The minimax procedure was a slight modification of the one described earlier, in that the mobility score for each of the intermediate positions was added in.

cially the Los Alamos one, provide real anchor points. They show that, with very little in the way of complexity, we have at least entered the arena of human play—we can beat a beginner.

Bernstein's Program

Over the last two years Alex Bernstein, a chess player and programmer at IBM, has constructed a chess-playing program for the IBM 704 (for the full 8×8 board) (Bernstein and Roberts, 1958b; Bernstein et al., 1958a). This program has been in partial operation for the last six months, and has now played one full game plus a number of shorter sequences. It, too, is in the Shannon tradition, but it takes an extremely important step in the direction of greater sophistication: only a fraction of the legal alternatives and continuations are considered. There is a series of subroutines, which we can call plausible move generators, that propose the moves to be considered. Each of these generators is related to some feature of the game: King safety, development, defending own men, attacking opponent's men, and so on. The program considers at most seven alternatives, which are obtained by operating the generators in priority order, the most important first, until the seven are accumulated.

The program explores continuations two moves ahead, just as the Los Alamos program did. However, it uses the plausible move generators at each stage, so that, at most, 7 direct continuations are considered from any given position. For its evaluation function it uses the ratio of two sums, one for White and one for Black. Each sum consists of four weighted factors: material, King defense, area control, and mobility. The program minimaxes and chooses the alternative with the greatest effective value.

The program's play is uneven. Blind spots occur that are very striking; on the other hand it sometimes plays very well for a series of moves. It has never beaten anyone, as far as we know; in the one full game it played it was beaten by a good player, (Bernstein and Roberts, 1958b), and it has never been pitted against weak players to establish how good it is.

Bernstein's program gives us our first information about radical selectivity, in move generation and analysis. At 7 moves per position, it examines only 2,500 final positions two moves deep, out of about 800,000 legal continuations. That it still plays at all tolerably with a reduction in search by a factor of 300 implies that the selection mechanism is fairly effective. Of course, the selections follow the common and tested lore of the chess world; so that the significance of the reduction lies in showing that this lore is being successfully captured in mechanism. On the other hand, such radical selection should give the program a strong proclivity to overlook moves and consequences. The selective mechanisms in Bernstein's program have none of the checks and balances that exist in human selection on the chessboard. And this is what we find. For example, in one situation a Bishop was successively attacked by three Pawns, each time retreating one square to a post where the next Pawn could attack it. The program remained oblivious to this possibility since the successive Pawn pushes that attacked the Bishop were never proposed as plausible moves by the generators. But this is nothing to be unhappy about. Any particular difficulty is removable: in the case of the Bishop, by adding another move generator responsive to another feature of the board. This kind of error correction is precisely how the body of practical knowledge about chess programs and chess play will accumulate, gradually teaching us the right kinds of selectivity.

Every increase in sophistication of performance is paid for by an increase in the complexity of the program. The move generators and the components of the static evaluation require varied and diverse information about each position. This implies both more program and more computing time per position than with the Los Alamos program. From Table 1, we observe that Bernstein's program takes 7000 words, the Los Alamos program only 600 words: a factor of about 10. As for time per position, both programs take about the same time to produce a move—8 and 12 minutes respectively. Since the increase in problem size of the 8×8 board over the 6×6 board (about 5 to 1) is approximately canceled by the increase in speed of the IBM 704 over the MANIAC (also about 5 to 1, counting the increased power of the 704 order code), we can say they would both produce moves in the same 8×8 game in the same time. Hence the increase in amount of processing per move in Bernstein's program approximately cancels the gain of 300 to 1 in selectivity that this more complex processing achieves. This is so, even though Bernstein's program is coded to attain maximum speed by the use of fixed tables, direct machine coding, and so on.

We have introduced the comparison in order to focus on computing speed versus selectivity as sources of improvement in complex programs. It is not possible, unfortunately, to compare the two programs in performance level except very crudely. We should compare an 8×8 version of the Los Alamos program with the Bernstein program, and we also need more games with each to provide reliable estimates of performance. Since the 8×8 version of the Los Alamos program will be better than the 6×6, compared to human play, let us assume for purposes of argument that the Los Alamos and Bernstein programs are roughly comparable in performance. To a rough approximation, then, we have two programs that achieve the same quality of performance with the same total effort by two different routes: the Los Alamos program by using no selectivity and being very fast, and the Bernstein program by using a large amount of selectivity and taking much more effort per position examined in order to make the selection.

The point we wish to make is that this equality is an accident: that selectivity is a very powerful device and speed a very weak device for improving the performance of complex programs. For instance, suppose both the Los Alamos and the Bernstein programs were to explore three moves deep instead of two as they now do. Then the Los Alamos program would take about 1000 times (30^2) as long as now to make a move, whereas Bernstein's program would take about 50 times as long (7^2), the latter gaining a factor of 20 in the total computing effort required per move. The significant feature of chess is the exponential growth of positions to be considered with depth of analysis. As analysis deepens, greater computing effort per position soon pays for itself, since it slows the growth in number of positions to be considered. The comparison of the two programs at a greater depth is relevant since the natural mode of improvement of the Los Alamos program is to increase the speed enough to allow explorations three moves deep. Furthermore, attempts to introduce selectivity in the Los Alamos program will be extremely costly relative to the cost of additional selectivity in the Bernstein program.

One more calculation might be useful to emphasize the value of heuristics that eliminate branches to be explored. Suppose we had a branching tree in which our program was exploring n moves deep, and let this tree have four branches at each node. If we could double the speed of the program—that is, consider twice as many positions for the same total effort—then this improvement would let us look half a move deeper ($n + \frac{1}{2}$). If, on the other hand, we could double the selectivity—that is, only consider two of the four branches at each node, then we could look twice as deep ($2n$). It is clear that we could afford to pay an apparently high computing cost per position to achieve this selectivity.

To summarize, Bernstein's program introduces both sophistication and complication to the chess program. Although in some respects—*e.g.,* depth of analysis—it still uses simple uniform rules, in selecting moves to be considered it introduces a set of powerful heuristics which are taken from successful chess practice, and drastically reduce the number of moves considered at each position.

Newell, Shaw, and Simon Program

Although our own work on chess started in 1955, it took a prolonged vacation during a period in which we were developing programs that discover proofs for theorems in symbolic logic (Newell, Shaw, and Simon, 1957; Newell and Simon, 1956). In a fundamental sense, proving theorems and playing chess involve the same problem: reasoning with heuristics that select fruitful paths of exploration in a space of possibilities that grows exponentially. The same dilemmas of speed versus selection and uniformity versus sophistication exist in both problem domains. Likewise, the programming costs attendant upon complexity seem similar for both. So we have recently returned to the chess programming problem equipped with ideas derived from the work on logic.

The historical antecedents of our own work are somewhat different from those of the other investigators we have mentioned. We have been primarily concerned with describing and understanding human thinking and decision processes (Newell, Shaw, and Simon, 1958a, 1958c). However, both for chess players and for chess programmers, the structure of the task dictates in considerable part the approach taken, and our current program can be described in the same terms we have used for the others. Most of the positive features of the earlier programs are clearly discernible: The basic factorization introduced by Shannon; Turing's concept of a dead position; and the move generators, associated with features of the chess situation, used by Bernstein. Perhaps the only common characteristic of the other programs that is strikingly absent from ours—and from human thinking also, we believe—is the use of numerical additive evaluation functions to compare alternatives.

Basic Organization

Figure 3 shows the two-way classification in terms of which the program is organized. There is a set of goals, each of which corresponds to some feature of the chess situation—King safety, material balance, center control, and so on. Each goal has associated with it a collection of processes, corresponding to the categories outlined by Shannon: a move generator, a static evaluation routine, and a move generator for analysis. The routine for integrating the static evaluations into an effective value for a proposed move, and the final choice procedure are both common routines for the whole program, and therefore are not present in each separate component.

Goals

The goals form a basic set of modules out of which the program is constructed. The goals are independent: any of them can be added to the

		Goal specification	Move generator	Static evaluation	Analysis generator
Goals	King safety				
	Material balance				
	Center control				
	Development				
	King-side attack				
	Promotion				

Figure 3. Basic organization of the NSS chess program.

program or removed without affecting the feasibility of the remaining goals. At the beginning of each move a preliminary analysis establishes that a given chess situation (a "state") obtains, and this chess situation evokes a set of goals appropriate to it. The goal specification routines shown for each goal in Fig. 3 provide information that is used in this initial selection of goals. The goals are put on a list with the most crucial ones first. This goal list then controls the remainder of the processing: the selection of alternatives, the continuations to be explored, the static evaluation, and the final choice procedure.

What kind of game the program will play clearly depends on what goals are available to it and chosen by it for any particular move. One purpose of this modular construction is to provide flexibility over the course of the game in the kinds of considerations the program spends its effort upon. For example, the goal of denying stalemate to the opponent is relevant only in certain end-game situations where the opponent is on the defensive and the King is in a constrained position. Another purpose of the modular construction is to give us a flexible tool for investigating chess programs— so that entirely new considerations can be added to an already complex but operational program.

Move Generation

The move generator associated with each goal proposes alternative moves relevant to that goal. These move generators carry the burden of finding positive reasons for doing things. Thus, only the center-control generator will propose P-Q4 as a good move in the opening; only the material-balance generator will propose moving out of danger a piece that is *en prise*. These move generators correspond to the move generators in Bernstein's program, except that here they are used exclusively to generate alternative moves and are not used to generate the continuations that are explored in the course of analyzing a move. In Bernstein's program—and *a fortiori* in the Los Alamos program—identical generators are used both to find a set of alternative moves from which the final choice of next move is made, and also to find the continuations that must be explored to assess the consequences of reaching a given position. In our program the latter function is performed by a separate set of analysis generators.

Evaluation

Each move proposed by a move generator is assigned a value by an analysis procedure. We said above that the move generators have the responsibility for finding positive reasons for making moves. Correspondingly, the analysis procedure is concerned only with the acceptability of a move once it has been generated. A generator proposes; the analysis procedure disposes.

The value assigned to a move is obtained from a series of evaluations, one for each goal. The value is a vector, if you like to think of it that way, except that it does not necessarily have the same components throughout the chess game, since the components derive from the basic list of goals that is constructed from the position at the beginning of each move. Each component expresses acceptability or unacceptability of a position from the viewpoint of the goal corresponding to that component. Thus, the material-balance goal would assess only the loss or gain of material; the development goal, the relative gain or loss of *tempi;* the Pawn structure goal, the doubling and isolation of Pawns; and so on. The value for a component is in some cases a number—*e.g.,* in the material-balance goal where we use conventional piece values: 9 for a Queen, 5 for a Rook, and so on. In other cases the component value is dichotomous, simply designating the presence or absence of some property, like the blocking of a move or the doubling of a Pawn.

As in the other chess programs, our analysis procedure consists of three parts: exploring continuations to some depth, forming static evaluations, and integrating these to establish an effective value for the move. By a process that we will describe later, the analysis move generators associated with the goals determine what branches will be explored from each position reached. At the final position of each continuation, a value is assigned using the static evaluation routines of each goal to provide the component values. The effective value for a proposed move is obtained by minimaxing on these final static values. Minimaxing seems especially appropriate for an analysis procedure that is inherently conservative, such as an acceptance test.

To be able to minimax, it must be possible to compare any two values and decide which is preferable, or whether they are equal in value. For values of the kind we are using, there must be a complete ordering on the vectors that determine them. Further, this ordering must allow variation in the size and composition of the goal list. We use a lexicographic ordering: Each component value is completely ordered within itself; and higher priority values completely dominate lower priority values, as determined by the order of goals on the goal list. To compare two values, then, the first components are compared. If one of these is preferable to the other, this determines the preference for the entire value. If the two components are equal, then the second pair of components is compared. If these are unequal in value, they determine the preference for the entire value; otherwise the next components are compared, and so on.

Final Choice

It is still necessary to select the move to be played from the alternative moves, given the values assigned to them by the analysis procedure. In the other programs the final choice procedure was simply an extension of the minimax: choose the one with highest value. Its obviousness rests on the assumption that the set of alternatives to be considered is a fixed set. If this assumption is relaxed, by generating alternatives sequentially, then other procedures are possible. The simplest, and the one we are currently using, is to set an acceptance level as final criterion and simply take the first acceptable move. The executive routine proceeds down the goal list, activating the move generators of the goals in order of priority, so that important moves are considered first. The executive saves the best move that has been found up to any given moment, and if no moves reach the specified level of acceptability, it makes the best move that was found.

Another possible final choice procedure is to search for an acceptable move that has a double function—that is, a move that is proposed by more than one generator as having a positive effect. With this plan, the executive proceeds down the list of goals in order of priority. After finding an acceptable move, it activates the rest of the generators to see if the move will be proposed a second time. If not, it works from the list of unevaluated moves just obtained to see if any move proposed twice is acceptable. If not, it takes the first acceptable move or the best if none has proved acceptable. This type of executive has considerable plausibility, since the concept of multiple function plays an important role in the chess literature.

Yet a third variation in the final choice procedure is to divide the goals into two lists. The first list contains all the features that should normally be attended to; the second list contains features that are rare in occurrence but either very good or very bad if they do occur. On this second list would be goals that relate to sacrificial combinations, hidden forks or pins that are two moves away, and so on. The executive finds an acceptable move with the first, normal list. Then the rest of the available time is spent looking for various rare consequences derived from the second list.

Analysis

In describing the basic organization of the program we skipped over the detailed mechanism for exploring continuations, simply assuming that certain continuations were explored, the static values computed, and the effective value obtained by minimaxing. But it is clear that the exact mechanisms are very important. The analysis move generators are the main agents of selectivity in the program: They determine for each position arrived at in the analysis just which further branches must be explored, hence the average number of branches in the exploration tree and its average depth. The move generators for the alternatives and the final choice procedure also affect the amount of exploration by determining what moves are considered. But their selection operates only once per move, whereas the selectivity of the analysis generators operates at each step (half move) of the exploration. Hence the selectivity of the analysis generators varies geometrically with the average depth of analysis.

The exploration of continuations is based on a generalization of Turing's concept of a dead position. Recall that Turing applied this notion to exchanges, arguing that it made no sense to count material on the board until all exchanges that were to take place had been carried out. We apply the same notion to each feature of the board: The static evaluation of a goal is meaningful only if the position being evaluated is "dead" with respect to the feature associated with that goal—that is, only if no moves are likely to be made that could radically alter that component static value. The analysis move generators for each goal determine for any position they are applied to whether the position is dead with respect to their goal; if not, they generate the moves that are both plausible and might seriously affect the static value of the goal. Thus the selection of continuations to be explored is dictated by the search for a position that is dead with respect to all the goals, so that, finally, a static evaluation can be made. Both the number of branches from each position and the depth of the exploration are controlled in this way. Placid situations will produce search trees containing only a handful of positions; complicated middle game situations will produce much larger ones.

To make the mechanics of the analysis clearer, Fig. 4 gives a schematic example of a situation. P_0 is the initial position from which White, the machine, must make a move. The arrow, α, leading to P_1 represents an alternative proposed by some move generator. The move is made internally (*i.e.*, "considered"), yielding position P_1, and the analysis procedure must then obtain the value of P_1, which will become the value imputed to the proposed alternative, α. Taking each goal from the goal list in turn, an attempt is made to produce a static evaluation. For P_1 this attempt is successful for the first and second components, yielding values of 5 and 3 respectively. (Numbers are used for values throughout this example to keep the picture simple; in reality, various sets of ordered symbols are used, their exact structure depending on the nature of the computation.) However, the third component does not find the position dead, and generates two moves, β and γ. The first, β, is considered, leading to P_2, and an attempt is made to produce a static evaluation of it. This proceeds just as with P_1, except that this time all components find the

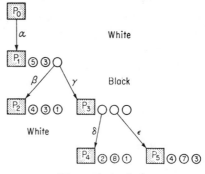

Figure 4. Analysis

position dead and the static value $(4,3,1)$ is obtained. Then the second move, γ, from P_1 is considered, leading to P_3. The attempt to produce a static value for P_3 runs into difficulties with the first component, which generates one move, δ, to resolve the instability of P_3 with respect to its feature. This move leads to P_4 which is evaluable, having the value $(2,8,1)$. However, the second component also finds P_3 not dead and generates a single move, ϵ, leading to P_5. This is also evaluable, having the value $(4,7,3)$. The third component finds P_3 dead and therefore contributes no additional moves. Thus the exploration comes to an end with all terminal positions yielding complete static values. Since it is White's move at P_3, White will choose the move with the highest value. This is ϵ, the move to P_5, with a value of $(4,7,3)$ (the first component dominates). The value of this move is the effective value assigned to P_3. Black now has a choice between the move, β, to P_2, yielding $(4,3,1)$ and the move, γ, to P_3, yielding $(4,7,3)$. Since Black is minimizing, he will choose β. This yields $(4,3,1)$ as the effective value of the alternative, α, that leads to P_1, and the end of the analysis.

The minimaxing operation is conducted concurrently with the generation of branches. Thus if P_5, which has a value of $(4,7,3)$, had been generated prior to P_4 no further moves would have been generated from P_3, since it is already apparent that Black will prefer P_2 to P_3. The value of P_3 is at least as great as the value of P_5, since it is White's move and he will maximize.

This analysis procedure is not a simple one, either conceptually or technically. There are a number of possible ways to terminate search and reach an effective evaluation. There is no built-in rule that guarantees that the search will converge; the success depends heavily on the ability to evaluate statically. The more numerous the situations that can be recognized as having a certain value without having to generate continuations, the more rapidly the search will terminate. The number of plausible moves that affect the value is also of consequence, as we discussed in connection with Bernstein's program, but there are limits beyond which this cannot be reduced. For example, suppose that a position is not dead with respect to Material Balance and that one of the machine's pieces is attacked. Then it can try to (a) take the attacker, (b) add a defender, (c) move the attacked piece, (d) pin the defender, (e) interpose a man between the attacker and the attacked, or (f) launch a counterattack. Alternatives of each of these types must be sought and tried—they are all plausible and may radically affect the material balance.

As an example of the heuristics involved in achieving a static evaluation, imagine that the above situation occurred after several moves of an exploration, and that the machine was already a Pawn down from the early part of the continuation. Then, being on the defensive implies a very remote chance of recovering the Pawn. Consequently, a negative value of at least a Pawn can be assigned to the position statically. This is usually enough in connection with concurrent minimaxing to eliminate the continuation from further consideration.

Summary

Let us summarize our entire program. It is organized in terms of a set of goals: these are conceptual units of chess—King safety, passed Pawns, and so on. Each goal has several routines associated with it:

1. A routine that specifies the goal in terms of the given position;
2. A move generator that finds moves positively related to carrying out the goal;
3. A procedure for making a static evaluation of any position with respect to the goal, which essentially measures acceptability;
4. An analysis move generator that finds the continuations required to resolve a situation into dead positions.

The alternative moves come from the move generators, considered in the order of priority of their respective goals. Each move, when it is generated, is subjected to an analysis. This analysis generates an exploration of the continuations following from the move until dead positions are reached and static evaluations computed for them. The static evaluations are compared, using minimax as an inference procedure, so that an effective value is eventually produced for each alternative. The final choice procedure can rest on any of several criteria: for instance, choosing the first move generated that has an effective value greater than a given norm.

Examples of Goals

In this section we will give two examples of goals and their various components to illustrate the type of program we are constructing. The first example is the center-control goal:

CENTER CONTROL

Specification. Goal is always operative unless there are no more center Pawns to be moved to the fourth rank.

Move Generator

1. Move P-Q4, P-K4 (primary moves).
2. Prevent the opponent from making his primary moves.
3. Prepare your own primary moves:
   a. Add a defender to Q4 or K4 square.
   b. Eliminate a block to moving QP or KP.

Static Evaluation. Count the number of blocks to making the primary moves.

Analysis Move Generators. None; static evaluation is always possible.

To interpret this a little: Goals are proposed in terms of the general situation—*e.g.,* for the opening game. The list of goals is made up for a position by applying, in turn, the specification of each of the potential goals. Whether any particular goal is declared relevant or irrelevant to the position depends on whether or not the position meets its specification. For Center Control, no special information need be gathered, but the goal is declared irrelevant if the center Pawns have already been moved to the fourth rank or beyond.

The most important part of the center-control program is its move generator. The generator is concerned with two primary moves: P-Q4 and P-K4. It will propose these moves, if they are legal, and it is the responsibility of the analysis procedures (for all the goals) to reject the moves if there is anything wrong with them—*e.g.,* if the Pawns will be taken when moved. So, after 1. P-Q4, P-Q4, the center-control move generator will propose 2. P-K4, but (as we shall see) the evaluation routine of the material balance goal will reject this move because of the loss of material that would result from 2. . . . , P × P. The center-control generator will have nothing to do with tracing out these consequences.

If the primary moves cannot be made, the center-control move generator has two choices: to prepare them, or to prevent the opponent from making his primary moves. The program's style of play will depend very much on whether prevention has priority over preparation (as it does in our description of the generator above), or vice versa. The ordering we have proposed, which puts prevention first, probably produces more aggressive and slightly better opening play than the reverse ordering. Similarly, the style of play depends on whether the Queen's Pawn or the King's Pawn is considered first.

The move generator approaches the subgoal of preventing the opponent's primary moves (whenever this subgoal is evoked) in the following way. It first determines whether the opponent can make one of these moves by trying the move and then obtaining an evaluation of it from the opponent's viewpoint. If one or both of the primary moves are not rejected, preventive moves will serve some purpose. Under these conditions, the center-control move generator will generate them by finding moves that bring another attacker to bear on the opponent's K4 and Q4 squares or that pin a defender of one of these squares. Among the moves this generator will normally propose are N-B3 and BP-B4.

The move generator approaches the subgoal of preparing its own primary moves by first determining why the moves cannot be made without preparation—that is, whether the Pawn is blocked from moving by a friendly piece, or whether the fourth-rank square is unsafe for the Pawn. In the former case, the generator proposes moves for the blocking piece; in the latter case, it finds moves that will add defenders to the fourth-rank square, drive away or pin attackers, and so on.

So much for the center-control move generators. The task of the evaluation routine for the center-control goal is essentially negative—to assure that moves, proposed by some other goal, will not be made that jeopardize control of the center. The possibility is simply ignored that a move generator for some other goal will inadvertently provide a move that contributes to center control. Hence, the static evaluation for Center Control is only concerned that moves not be made that interfere with P-K4 and P-Q4. A typical example of a move that the center-control evaluation routine is prepared to reject is B-Q3 or B-K3 before the respective center Pawns have been moved.

The second example of a goal is Material Balance. This is a much more extensive and complicated goal than Center Control, and handles all questions about gain and loss of material in the immediate situation. It does not consider threats like pins and forks, where the actual exchange is still a move away; other goals must take care of these. Both the negative and positive aspects of material must be included in a single goal, since they compensate directly for each other, and material must often be spent to gain material.

MATERIAL BALANCE

Specification. A list of exchanges on squares occupied by own men, and a list of exchanges on squares occupied by opponent's men. For each exchange square there is listed the target man, the list of attackers, and the list of defenders (including, *e.g.,* both Rooks if they are doubled on the appropriate rank or file). For each exchange square a static exchange value is computed by playing out the exchange with all the attackers and defenders assuming no indirect consequences like pins, discovered attacks, etc. Exchange squares are listed in order of static exchange value, largest negative value first. Squares with positive values for the defender are dropped from the list. At the same time a list of all pinned men is generated.

Move Generator. Starting with the exchange squares at the top of the list, appropriate moves are generated. If the most important exchange square is occupied by the opponent, captures by attacking pieces are proposed, the least valuable attacker being tried first. If the move is rejected because the attacker is pinned, the next attacker is tried. If the move is rejected for another reason, the possibility of exchange on this square is abandoned, and the next exchange square examined.

If the exchange square under examination is occupied by the program's own piece, a whole series of possible moves is generated:

   a. Try "no move" to see if attack is damaging.

   b. Capture the attacker.

   c. Add a defender not employed in another defense.

   d. Move the attacked piece.

   e. Interpose a man between the attacker and the target; but not a man employed elsewhere, and not if the interposer will be captured.

   f. Pin the attacker with a man not employed elsewhere and not capturable by the attacker.

Static Evaluation. For each exchange square, add the values of own men and subtract the values of opponent's men. Use conventional values: Q-9, R-5, B-N-3, P-1.

Move Generators toward Dead Positions. A position is dead for this goal only if there are no exchanges—that is, if the specification list defined above is empty. Then a static evaluation can be made. Otherwise, the various kinds of moves defined under the move generator are made to resolve the exchanges. However, various additional qualifications are introduced to reduce the number of continuations examined. For example, if in a particular exchange material has already been lost and a man is still under attack, the position is treated as dead, since it is unlikely that the loss will be recovered. When a dead position is reached, the static evaluation is used to find a value for the position.

It is impossible to provide here more than a sketchy picture of the heuristics contained in this one goal. It should be obvious from this brief description that there are a lot of them, and that they incorporate a number of implicit assumptions about what is important, and what isn't, on the chessboard.

Performance of the Program

We cannot say very much about the behavior of the program. It was coded this spring and is not yet fully debugged. Only two goals have been coded: Material Balance and Center Control. Development is fully defined as well as a Pawn structure goal sufficient for the opening, where its role is primarily to prevent undesirable structures like doubled Pawns. These four goals—Material Balance, Center Control, Development, and Pawn Structure—in this order seem an appropriate set for the first phase of the opening game. Several others—King Safety, Serious Threats, and Gambits—need to be added for full opening play. The serious threats goal could be limited initially to forks and pins.

We have done considerable hand simulation with the program in typical positions. Two examples will show how the goals interact. In Fig. 5 the

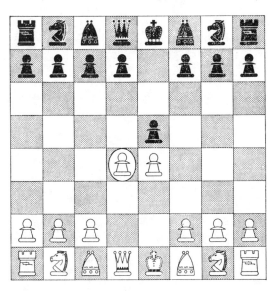

Figure 5.

machine is White and the play has been 1. P-K4, P-K4. Assuming the goal list mentioned above, the material-balance move generator will not propose any moves since there are no exchanges on the board. The center-control generator will propose P-Q4, which is the circled move in the figure. (In the illustration, we assume the center-control move generator has the order of the primary moves reversed from the order described earlier.) This move is rejected—as it should be—and it is instructive to see why. The move is proposed for analysis. Material Balance does not find the position dead, since there is an exchange, and generates Black's move, 2. . . . , P × P. The resulting position is still not dead, and 3. Q × P, is generated. The position is now dead for Material Balance, with no gain or loss in material. The first component of the static evaluation is "even." There are obviously no blocks to Pawn moves, so that the center control static value is acceptable. However, the third component, Development, finds the position not dead because there is now an exposed piece, the Queen. It generates replies that both attack the piece and develop—*i.e.*, add a tempo. The move 3. . . . , N-QB3 is generated. This forces a Queen move, resulting in loss of a tempo for White. Hence Development rejects the move, 2. P-Q4. (The move 3. . . . , B-B4 would not have sufficed for rejection by Development, since the Bishop could be taken.)

The second example, shown in Fig. 6, is from a famous game of Morphy against Duke Karl of Brunswick and Count Isouard. Play had proceeded 1. P-K4, P-K4; 2. N-KB3, P-Q3; 3. P-Q4. Suppose the machine is Black

Figure 6.

in this position. The move 3. . . . , B-N5 is proposed by Material Balance to deal with the exchange that threatens Black with the loss of a Pawn. This is the move made by the Duke and Count. The analysis proceeds by 4. P × P, P × P. This opens up a new exchange possibility with the Queens, which is tried: 5. Q × Q, K × Q; 6. N × P. Thus the Pawn is lost in this continuation. Hence, alternative moves are considered at Black's nearest option, which is move 4, since there are no alternative ways of recapturing the Queen at move 5. The capture of White's Knight is possible, so we get: 4'. . . . , B × N; 5'. P × B, P × P; 6'. Q × Q, K × Q. This position is rejected by Development since the forced King move loses Black his castling privilege, and this loss affects the tempo count. This is a sufficient reason to reject the move 3. . . . , B-N5, without even examining the stronger continuation, 5''. Q × B, that Morphy as White chose. In our program, 5. P × B is generated before 5. Q × B. Either reply shows that 3. . . . , B-N5 is unsound.

One purpose of these examples is to illustrate a heuristic for constructing chess programs that we incline to rather strongly. We wish not only to have the program make good moves, but to do so for the right reasons. The chess commentary above is not untypical of human analysis. It also represents rather closely the analysis made by the program. We think this is sound design philosophy in constructing complex programs. To take another example: the four-goal opening program will not make sacrifices, and conversely, will always accept gambits. The existing program is unable to balance material against positional advantage. The way to make the program take account of sacrifices is to introduce an additional goal having to do with them explicitly. The corresponding heuristic for a human chess player is: don't make sacrifices until you understand what a sacrifice is. Stated in still another way, part of the success of human play depends on the emergence of appropriate concepts. One major theme in chess history, for example, is the emergence of the concept of the center and the notion of what it means to control the center. One should not expect the equivalent of such a concept simply to emerge from computation based on quite different features of the position.

Programming

The program we have been describing is extremely complicated. Almost all elements of the original framework put forward by Shannon, which were handled initially by simply uniform rules, have been made variable, and dependent on rather complicated considerations. Many special and highly particular heuristics are used to select moves and decide on evaluations. The program can be expected to be much larger, more intricate, and to require much more processing per position considered than even the Bernstein program.

In the introduction to this paper we remarked on the close connection between complexity and communication. Processes as complex as the Los Alamos program are unthinkable without languages like current machine codes in which to specify them. The Bernstein program is already a very complicated program in machine code; it involved a great deal of coding effort and parts of it required very sophisticated coding techniques. Our own program is already beyond the reach of direct machine coding: it requires a more powerful language.

In connection with the work on theorem-proving programs we have been developing a series of languages, called information processing languages (IPL's) (Newell, 1961e). The current chess program is coded in one of them, IPL-IV. An information processing language is an interpretive pseudocode—that is, there exists a program in JOHNNIAC machine code that is capable of intepreting a program in IPL and executing it. When operating, JOHNNIAC contains both the machine code and the IPL code.

It is not possible to give in this report a description of IPL-IV or of the programming techniques involved in constructing the chess program. Basically IPL is designed to manipulate lists, and to allow extremely complicated structures of lists to be built up during the execution of a program without incurring intolerable problems of memory assignment and program planning. It allows unlimited hierarchies of subroutines to be easily defined, and permits recursive definition of routines. As it stands —that is, prior to coding a particular problem—it is independent of subject matter (although biased toward list manipulation in the same sense that algebraic compilers are biased toward numerical evaluation of algebraic expressions). To code chess, a complete "chess vocabulary" is built up from definitions in IPL. This vocabulary consists of a set of processes for expressing basic concepts in chess: tests of whether a man bears on another man, or whether two men are on the same diagonal; processes for finding the direction between two men, or the first man in a given direction from another; and processes that express iterations over all men of a given type, or over all squares of a given rank. There are about 100 terms in this basic process vocabulary. The final chess program, as we have been describing it in this paper, is largely coded in terms of the chess vocabulary. Thus there are four language "levels" in the chess program: JOHNNIAC machine code, general IPL, basic chess vocabulary, and finally the chess program itself.

We can now make a rough assessment of the size and complexity of this program in comparison with the other programs. The table indicates that the program now consists of 6000 words and will probably increase to 16,000. The upper bound is dictated by the size of the JOHNNIAC drum and the fact that JOHNNIAC has no tapes. In terms of the pyramiding structure described above, this program is already much larger than Bernstein's, although it is difficult to estimate the "expansion" factor involved in converting IPL to machine code. (For one thing, it is not clear how an "equivalent" machine-coded program would be organized.) However, only about 1000 words of our program are in machine code, and 3000 words are IPL programs, some of which are as many as ten definitional steps removed from machine code. Further, all 12,000 words on the drum will be IPL program: no additional data or machine code are planned.

The estimated time per move, as shown in Table 1, is from one to ten hours, although moves in very placid situations like the opening will take only a few minutes. Even taking into account the difference in speed between the 704 and JOHNNIAC, our program still appears to be at least ten times slower than Bernstein's. This gap reflects partly the mismatch between current computers and computers constructed to do efficiently the kind of information processing required in chess (Shaw et al., 1958). To use an interpretive code, such as IPL, is in essence to simulate an "IPL computer" with a current computer. A large price has to be paid in computing effort for this simulation over and above the computing effort for the chess program itself. However, this gap also reflects the difficulty of specifying complex processes; we have not been able to write these programs and attend closely to the efficiency issue at the same time.

On both counts we have felt it important to explore the kind of languages and programming techniques appropriate to the task of specifying complex programs, and to ignore for the time being the costs we were incurring.

Conclusion

We have now completed our survey of attempts to program computers to play chess. There is clearly evident in this succession of efforts a steady development toward the use of more and more complex programs and more and more selective heuristics; and toward the use of principles of play similar to those used by human players. Partly, this trend represents—at least in our case—a deliberate attempt to simulate human thought processes. In even larger part, however, it reflects the constraints that the task itself imposes upon any information processing system that undertakes to perform it. We believe that any information processing system—a human, a computer, or any other—that plays chess successfully will use heuristics generically similar to those used by humans.

We are not unmindful of the radical differences between men and machines at the level of componentry. Rather, we are arguing that for tasks that could not be performed at all without very great selectivity—and chess is certainly one of these—the main goal of the program must be to achieve this selection. The higher-level programs involved in accomplishing this will look very much the same whatever processes are going on at more microscopic levels. Nor are we saying that programs will not be adapted to the powerful features of the computing systems that are used—e.g., the high speed and precision of current digital computers, which seems to favor exploring substantial numbers of continuations. However, none of the differences known to us—in speed, memory, and so on—affect the essential nature of the task: search in a space of exponentially growing possibilities. Hence the adaptations to the idiosyncrasies of particular computers will all be secondary in importance, although they will certainly exist and may be worthwhile.

The complexity of heuristic programs requires a more powerful language for communicating with the computer than the language of elementary machine instructions. We have seen that this necessity has already mothered the creation of new information processing languages. But even with these powerful interpretive languages, communication with the machine is difficult and cumbersome. The next step that must be taken is to write programs that will give computers a problem-solving ability in understanding and interpreting instructions that is commensurable with their problem-solving ability in playing chess and proving theorems.

The interpreter that will transform the machine into an adequate student for a human instructor will not be a passive, algorithmic translator—as even the most advanced interpreters and compilers are today—but an active, complex, heuristic problem-solving program. As our explorations of heuristic programs for chess playing and other tasks teach us how to build such an interpreter, they will at last enable us to make the transition from the low-level equilibrium at which man-machine communication now rests to the high-level equilibrium that is certainly attainable.

Appendix: Game Played by H. A. Simon and the NSS Chess Program

The following chess game was played by the NSS chess program, CP-I. Its opponent was Prof. H. A. Simon, playing black. CP-I played white. The program was run on JOHNNIAC, and the moves each took 2 to 50 min of processing. The program has three goals: material balance, center control, and development. The lack of goals corresponding to king safety, serious threats, or pawn promotion seriously unbalances the play and makes the program insensitive to certain aspects of the play. Games by machines evoke commentary even more abundantly than do regular chess games. The italicized comments are those of Edward Lasker, a well-known chess master who has been much interested in chess machines; the other notes are by G. W. Baylor and S. M. Strassen.

	CP-I	*H. A. Simon*
1	P-Q4	N-KB3
2	N-QB3	

White prepares to occupy the center with P-K4, but the text move has the disadvantage of blocking the Queen's Bishop's Pawn, which when advanced to Queen Bishop Four, controls Queen Five with a pawn.

	2 . . .	P-Q4
3	Q-Q3?	

This move does prepare P-K4; however, (1) minor pieces should generally be developed before the Queen, (2) the Queen is now subject to early attack by Black's minor pieces, and (3) the text move decreases the mobility of the King's Bishop.

In your game 3. Q-Q3 shows that you need an order that minor pieces should be developed ahead of the queen unless other orders in the program lead to the decision that a queen move is preferable.

	3 . . .	P-QN3

3 . . . , P-QN3 is difficult to evaluate. Probably best was (*a*) 3 . . . , P-B4; if then 4. P-K4, P × KP; 5. N × P, P × P; 6. N × Nch, NP × N with a fine pawn plus. Also, considerable was (*b*) 3 . . . , P-KN3 so as to develop the Queen's Bishop on King Bishop Four, thus exploiting the misplacement of the White Queen.

4	P-K4

Thematic!

4 . . .	B-N2
5 P×P	

Best I think. If, for example, (a) 5. P-K5, N-K5 gives Black strong control of Queen Four and King Five with a devastating P-QB4 to follow shortly; while (b) 5. P-B3 leaves White no good squares on which to develop his King side pieces.

P × P shows that your definition or "development" must probably be amplified to give a higher rating to moves which do not increase the mobility of one of the opponent's pieces.

5 . . .	N × P
6 N-B3	

White can effectively gain control of the center (especially Queen Five) with 6. N × N, Q × N (6 . . . , B × N is no better); 7. P-QB4!, Q-Q2; 8. N-KB3, P-K3; 9. B-K3 preventing Black's P-QB4 for a while. If, of course, 8 . . . , P-QB4; 9. P-Q5, P-K3 will be met simply by 10. P × P, in any case, with a good position for White.

6 . . .	P-K3

For now if 7. N × N, P × N is best because then the effect of 8. P-B4 is negated simply by 8 . . . , P × P which frees the Bishop and isolates the White Queen Pawn.

7 B-K2

"A developing move and hence cannot be bad."

7 . . .	B-K2
8 B-K3	

Not bad: 8 . . . , N × B; 9. P × N is certainly not to be feared for when White gets P-K4 in, he will have the superior game. 8. B-K3 also has the added advantage of restraining Black's Queen Bishop Pawn. A more constructive placement of the pieces, however, might be accomplished by 8. N × N, 9. O-O, 10. B-KB4, and 11. R-K1 with strong control of King Five. And if . . . , P-QB4, then White can play P-QB3 effectively.

8 . . .	O-O
9 O-O	N-Q2
10 KR-K1	

The two Rook moves are not really good. White does not yet (and never will!) have a constructive plan: he is simply developing pieces on the center files where they are not necessarily optimally placed. Generally first rank Rook moves consolidate concrete plans. Thus White should attempt either to continue with (a) 10. N × N and 11. P-QB4 after which his Rooks will probably best be placed on Queen One and Queen Bishop One, or (b) 10. N-K5, N × N; 11. P × N after which the Queen file requires foremost attention. 10. N-K5 also enhances the mobility of the White King's Bishop which has been sadly restricted due to the misplacement of the White Queen (*i.e.*, B-KB3 will then be in order).

<table>
<tr><td></td><td>10 . . .</td><td>P-QB4</td></tr>
</table>

Finally!

<table>
<tr><td>11 QR-Q1</td><td>Q-B2</td></tr>
</table>

Although this move does prevent 12. N-K5, it is not good. For instance on 12. N-QN5, Q-N1 (to be consistent); 13. P-B4!, N-N5; 14. Q-N1 threatening 15. P-QR3 and 16. P-Q5 is good for White so that 14 . . . , P × P; 15. N/5 × QP is probably in order for Black but still gives White the edge. Therefore Black should have continued pressure on the Queen Bishop file with 11 . . . , R-B1 and not have allowed the opportunity to White of playing 12. N-QN5 and 13. P-B4. Even after 11 . . . , R-B1, however, White could continue well with 12. N-K5.

<table>
<tr><td>12 N × N</td><td></td></tr>
</table>

Missing the sharpest continuation, but the text is not bad; *e.g.,* 12 . . . , P × N; 13. P-B4, P × QP; 14. B × P, P × P; 15. Q × BP with at least equality for White.

<table>
<tr><td>12 . . .</td><td>B × N?</td></tr>
</table>

This allows the now strong continuation 13. P-B4 after which 13 . . . , B-N2; 14. P-Q5, P × P; 15. P × P yields a strong passed pawn (an immediate threat of 16. P-Q6) as well as control of the board.

<table>
<tr><td>13 P-QR4?</td><td></td></tr>
</table>

A terrible move: just defends the Queen Rook Pawn whereas the multifunctional 13. P-B4 defends the Queen Rook Pawn and also attacks the center.

I am wondering why your "center control" orders did not suggest 13. P-QB4 rather than P-QR4. It would really have given the machine a very good game. 13. P-QR4 shows that an order—or a series of orders—is missing which would lead to the preparation of protection of pawns located in a file the opponent has opened for a Rook.

<table>
<tr><td>13 . . .</td><td>QR-B1</td></tr>
<tr><td>14 Q-B3</td><td></td></tr>
</table>

After 14 . . . , P × P; 15. Q × Q, R × Q; 16. N × P, White can solidify his position with P-QB3, but even so 14. Q-B3 doesn't really contribute anything to the position. 14. P-B4 is still best.

14 . . .	B-KB3!

Capitalizing on White's shortsightedness! 14 . . . , N-KB3 is also good (heading for King Five).

15 B-QN5	

Clever: Black was threatening to win a pawn with 15 . . . , P × P; 16. Q × Q, R × Q; 17. N × P, B × N; 18. B × B and 18 . . . , R × P. After the text move, however, the Queen Knight must be defended. The alternative (other than a Rook move) 15. B-Q3 does not actually defend the Queen Bishop Pawn because of 15 . . . , B × N; 16. P × B, P × P; 17. B × P (17. Q × Q, R × Q and White cannot recapture the pawn), Q-N1!; 18. Q-N4, P-QR4; 19. Q-N5, B × B; 20. Q × N, KR-Q1 with a strong attack for Black.

15 . . .	B × N

Good. If 15 . . . , KR-Q1 first, then 16. B × N, R × B; 17. N-K5, P × P; 18. B × P holding on admirably well.

16 P × B	KR-Q1
17 B × N?	

White loses his last opportunity to defend his Queen Bishop Pawn. Some Queen move, for instance 17, Q-Q2, holds the pawn: 17. Q-Q2, P × P; 18. B × P, B × B; 19. Q × B, Q × BP; 20. B × N winning (20 . . . , R-B2; 21. Q-KB4!, P-KR3; 22. R-Q2!).

17 . . .	Q × B
18 P-N3	

As good as many and better than some: White must lose a pawn anyhow.

18 . . .	P × P
19 Q-Q2!	

Very good. White finds the only way (other than Q-Q3) to avoid losing a piece by capitalizing on the immobility of the Black Queen Pawn.

19 . . .	Q-B3!
20 B-B4	Q × QBP
21 Q × Q	R × Q
22 R-QB1	

White is lost but relatively best was 22. R-Q3 blockading the passed Queen Pawn.

22. R-QB1 indicates that an order is missing to avoid exchanges after losing material, unless such exchanges deserve a high rating for specific reasons covered by other orders.

22 . . .	KR-QB1
23 QR-Q1	

White is just floundering in a lost position.

23 . . .	KR-B6
24 P-N4	

"There are no good moves in bad positions!"

24 . . .	KR × P
25 B-N3	

Best; White at least stops the mating attack.

25 . . .	P-Q6
26 R-QB1	B-N4

26. R-QB1 indicates that an order is missing that would make the machine avoid getting forked.
Better was 26 . . . , P-Q7 winning instantly (26 . . . , P-Q7; 27. R × R, P × R = Qch; 28. K-N2, Q-Q8!, 29. R-B8ch, B-Q1).

27 R × R	P × R
28 B-K5	P-B8 = Q
29 R × Q	B × R
30 Resigns	

Best, but I'm sure the programmers were just getting tired!
Such test games give indeed excellent indications as to the type of general principles the program should include in addition to material balance, development, and center control, to eliminate antipositional moves as much as possible.

SOME STUDIES IN
MACHINE LEARNING USING
THE GAME OF CHECKERS

by A. L. Samuel

Introduction

The studies reported here have been concerned with the programming of a digital computer to behave in a way which, if done by human beings or animals, would be described as involving the process of learning. While this is not the place to dwell on the importance of machine-learning procedures, or to discourse on the philosophical aspects,[1] there is obviously a very large amount of work, now done by people, which is quite trivial in its demands on the intellect but does, nevertheless, involve some learning. We have at our command computers with adequate data-handling ability and with sufficient computational speed to make use of machine-learning techniques, but our knowledge of the basic principles of these techniques is still rudimentary. Lacking such knowledge, it is necessary to specify methods of problem solution in minute and exact detail, a time-consuming and costly procedure. Programming computers to learn from experience should eventually eliminate the need for much of this detailed programming effort.

General Methods of Approach

At the outset it might be well to distinguish sharply between two general approaches to the problem of machine learning. One method, which might be called the *Neural-Net Approach,* deals with the possibility of inducing learned behavior into a randomly connected switching net (or its simula-

---

[1] Some of these are quite profound and have a bearing on the questions raised by Nelson Goodman in *Fact, Fiction and Forecast,* Cambridge, Mass.: Harvard, 1954.

tion on a digital computer) as a result of a reward-and-punishment routine. A second, and much more efficient approach, is to produce the equivalent of a highly organized network which has been designed to learn only certain specific things. The first method should lead to the development of general-purpose learning machines. A comparison between the size of the switching nets that can be reasonably constructed or simulated at the present time and the size of the neural nets used by animals, suggests that we have a long way to go before we obtain practical devices.[2] The second procedure requires reprogramming for each new application, but it is capable of realization at the present time. The experiments to be described here were based on this second approach.

Choice of Problem

For some years the writer has devoted his spare time to the subject of machine learning and has concentrated on the development of learning procedures as applied to games.[3] A game provides a convenient vehicle for such study as contrasted with a problem taken from life, since many of the complications of detail are removed. Checkers, rather than chess (Shannon, 1950; Bernstein and Roberts, 1958b; Kister et al., 1957; Newell, Shaw, and Simon, 1958b), was chosen because the simplicity of its rules permits greater emphasis to be placed on learning techniques. Regardless of the relative merits of the two games as intellectual pastimes, it is fair to state that checkers contains all of the basic characteristics of an intellectual activity in which heuristic procedures and learning processes can play a major role and in which these processes can be evaluated.

Some of these characteristics might well be enumerated. They are:

(1) The activity must not be deterministic in the practical sense. There exists no known algorithm which will guarantee a win or a draw in checkers, and the complete explorations of every possible path through a checker game would involve perhaps 10^{40} choices of moves which, at 3 choices per millimicrosecond, would still take 10^{21} centuries to consider.

(2) A definite goal must exist—the winning of the game—and at least one criterion or intermediate goal must exist which has a bearing on the achievement of the final goal and for which the sign should be known. In checkers the goal is to deprive the opponent of the possibility of moving,

[2] Warren S. McCulloch (1949) has compared the digital computer to the nervous system of a flatworm. To extend this comparison to the situation under discussion would be unfair to the worm, since its nervous system is actually quite highly organized as compared with the random-net studies by Farley and Clark (1954), Rochester, Holland, Haibt, and Duda (1956), and by Rosenblatt (1958).

[3] The first operating checker program for the IBM 701 was written in 1952. This was recoded for the IBM 704 in 1954. The first program with learning was completed in 1955 and demonstrated on television on February 24, 1956.

and the dominant criterion is the number of pieces of each color on the board. The importance of having a known criterion will be discussed later.

(3) The rules of the activity must be definite and they should be known. Games satisfy this requirement. Unfortunately, many problems of economic importance do not. While in principle the determination of the rules can be a part of the learning process, this is a complication which might well be left until later.

(4) There should be a background of knowledge concerning the activity against which the learning progress can be tested.

(5) The activity should be one that is familiar to a substantial body of people so that the behavior of the program can be made understandable to them. The ability to have the program play against human opponents (or antagonists) adds spice to the study and, incidentally, provides a convincing demonstration for those who do not believe that machines can learn.

Having settled on the game of checkers for our learning studies, we must, of course, first program the computer to play legal checkers; that is, we must express the rules of the game in machine language and we must arrange for the mechanics of accepting an opponent's moves and of reporting the computer's moves, together with all pertinent data desired by the experimenter. The general methods for doing this were described by Shannon in 1950 as applied to chess rather than checkers. The basic program used in these experiments is quite similar to the program described by Strachey in 1952. The availability of a larger and faster machine (the IBM 704), coupled with many detailed changes in the programming procedure, leads to a fairly interesting game, even without any learning. The basic forms of the program will now be described.

The Basic Checker-playing Program

The computer plays by looking ahead a few moves and by evaluating the resulting board positions much as a human player might do. Board positions are stored by sets of machine words, four words normally being used to represent any particular board position. Thirty-two bit positions (of the 36 available in an IBM 704 word) are, by convention, assigned to the 32 playing squares on the checkerboard, and pieces appearing on these squares are represented by 1's appearing in the assigned bit positions of the corresponding word. "Looking ahead" is prepared for by computing all possible next moves, starting with a given board position. The indicated moves are explored in turn by producing new board-position records corresponding to the conditions after the move in question (the old board positions being saved to facilitate a return to the starting point) and the process can be repeated. This look-ahead procedure is carried several

Initial board position ⟶

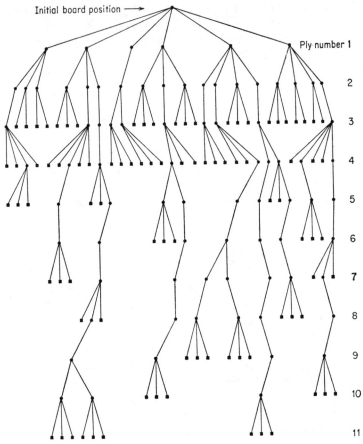

Figure 1. A "tree" of moves which might be investigated during the look-ahead procedure. The actual branchings are much more numerous than those shown, and the "tree" is apt to extend to as many as 20 levels.

moves in advance, as illustrated in Fig. 1. The resulting board positions are then scored in terms of their relative value to the machine.

The standard method of scoring the resulting board positions has been in terms of a linear polynomial. A number of schemes of an abstract sort were tried for evaluating board positions without regard to the usual checker concepts, but none of these was successful.[4] One way of looking at the various terms in the scoring polynomial is that those terms with

[4] One of the more interesting of these was to express a board position in terms of the first and higher moments of the white and black pieces separately about two orthogonal axes on the board. Two such sets of axes were tried, one set being parallel to the sides of the board and the second set being those through the diagonals

numerically small coefficients should measure criteria related as intermediate goals to the criteria measured by the larger terms. The achievement of these intermediate goals indicates that the machine is going in the right direction, such that the larger terms will eventually increase. If the program could look far enough ahead we need only ask, "Is the machine still in the game?"[5] Since it cannot look this far ahead in the usual situation, we must substitute something else, say the piece ratio, and let the machine continue the look-ahead until one side has gained a piece advantage. But even this is not always possible, so we have the program test to see if the machine has gained a positional advantage, et cetera. Numerical measures of these various properties of the board positions are then added together (each with an appropriate coefficient which defines its relative importance) to form the evaluation polynomial.

More specifically, as defined by the rules for checkers, the dominant scoring parameter is the inability for one side or the other to move.[6] Since this can occur but once in any game, it is tested for separately and is not included in the scoring polynomial as tabulated by the computer during play. The next parameter to be considered is the relative piece advantage. It is always assumed that it is to the machine's advantage to reduce the number of the opponent's pieces as compared to its own. A reversal of the sign of this term will, in fact, cause the program to play "giveaway" checkers, and with learning it can only learn to play a better and better giveaway game. Were the sign of this term not known by the programmer it could, of course, be determined by tests, but it must be fixed by the experimenter and, in effect, it is one of the instructions to the machine defining its task. The numerical computation of the piece advantage has been arranged in such a way as to account for the well-known property that it is usually to one's advantage to trade pieces when one is ahead and to avoid trades when behind. Furthermore, it is assumed that kings are more valuable than pieces, the relative weights assigned to them being three to two.[7] This ratio means that the program will trade three men for two kings, or two kings for three men, if by so doing it can obtain some positional advantage.

The choice for the parameters to follow this first term of the scoring polynomial and their coefficients then becomes a matter of concern. Two courses are open—either the experimenter can decide what these subsequent terms are to be, or he can arrange for the program to make the selection. We will discuss the first case in some detail in connection with

[5] This apt phraseology was suggested by John McCarthy.

[6] Not the capture of all the opponent's pieces, as popularly assumed, although all games end in this fashion.

[7] The use of a weight ratio rather than this, conforming more closely to the values assumed by many players, can lead into certain logical complications, as found by Strachey (1952).

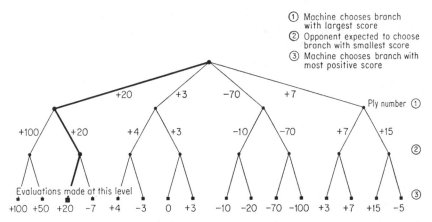

Figure 2. Simplified diagram showing how the evaluations are backed up through the "tree" of possible moves to arrive at the best next move. The evaluation process starts at (3).

the rote-learning studies and leave for a later section the discussion of various program methods of selecting parameters and adjusting their coefficients.

It is not satisfactory to select the initial move which leads to the board position with the highest score, since to reach this position would require the cooperation of the opponent. Instead, an analysis must be made proceeding *backward* from the evaluated board positions through the "tree" of possible moves, each time with consideration of the intent of the side whose move is being examined, assuming that the opponent would always attempt to minimize the machine's score while the machine acts to maximize its score. At each branch point, then, the corresponding board position is given the score of the board position which would result from the most favorable move. Carrying this "minimax" procedure back to the starting point results in the selection of a "best move." The score of the board position at the end of the most likely chain is also brought back, and for learning purposes this score is now assigned to the present board position. This process is shown in Fig. 2. The best move is executed, reported on the console lights, and tabulated by the printer.

The opponent is then permitted to make his move, which can be communicated to the machine either by means of console switches or by means of punched cards. The computer verifies the legality of the opponent's move, rejecting[8] or accepting it, and the process is repeated. When the program can look ahead and predict a win, this fact is reported on the

---

[8] The only departure from complete generality of the game as programmed is that the program requires the opponent to make a permissible move, including the taking of a capture if one is offered. "Huffing" is not permitted.

printer. Similarly, the program concedes when it sees that it is going to lose.

Ply Limitations

Playing-time considerations make it necessary to limit the look-ahead distance to some fairly small value. This distance is defined as the *ply* (a ply of 2 consisting of one proposed move by the machine and the anticipated reply by the opponent). The ply is not fixed but depends upon the dynamics of the situation, and it varies from move to move and from branch to branch during the move analysis. A great many schemes of adjusting the look-ahead distance have been tried at various times, some of them quite complicated. The most effective one, although quite detailed, is simple in concept and is as follows. The program always looks ahead a minimum distance, which for the opening game and without learning is usually set at three moves. At this minimum ply the program will evaluate the board position if none of the following conditions occurs: (1) the next move is a jump, (2) the last move was a jump, or (3) an exchange offer is possible. If any one of these conditions exists, the program continues looking ahead. At a ply of 4 the program will stop and evaluate the resulting board position if conditions (1) and (3) above are not met. At a ply of 5 or greater, the program stops the look-ahead whenever the next ply level does not offer a jump. At a ply of 11 or greater, the program will terminate the look-ahead, even if the next move is to be a jump, should one side at this time be ahead by more than two kings (to prevent the needless exploration of obviously losing or winning sequences). The program stops at a ply of 20 regardless of all conditions (since the memory space for the look-ahead moves is then exhausted) and an adjustment in score is made to allow for the pending jump. Finally, an adjustment is made in the levels of the break points between the different conditions when time is saved through rote learning (see below) and when the total number of pieces on the board falls below an arbitrary number. All break points are determined by single data words which can be changed at any time by manual intervention.

This tying of the ply with board conditions achieves three desired results. In the first place, it permits board evaluations to be made under conditions of relative stability for so-called dead positions, as defined by Turing (Bowden, 1953). Secondly, it causes greater surveillance of those paths which offer better opportunities for gaining or losing an advantage. Finally, since branching is usually seriously restricted by a jump situation, the total number of board positions and moves to be considered is still held down to a reasonable number and is more equitably distributed between the various possible initial moves.

As a practical matter, machine playing time usually has been limited to approximately 30 seconds per move. Elaborate table look-up procedures, fast sorting and searching procedures, and a variety of new programming tricks were developed, and full use was made of all of the resources of the IBM 704 to increase the operating speed as much as possible. One can, of course, set the playing time at any desired value by adjustments of the permitted ply; too small a ply results in a bad game and too large a ply makes the game unduly costly in terms of machine time.

Other Modes of Play

For study purposes the program was written to accommodate several variations of this basic plan. One of these permits the program to play against itself, that is, to play both sides of the game. This mode of play has been found to be especially good during the early stages of learning.

The program can also follow book games presented to it either on cards or on magnetic tape. When operating in this mode, the program decides at each point in the game on its next move in the usual way and reports this proposed move. Instead of actually making this move, the program refers to the stored record of a book game and makes the book move. The program records its evaluation of the two moves, and it also counts and reports the number of possible moves which the program rates as being better than the book move and the number it rates as being poorer. The sides are then reversed and the process is repeated. At the end of a book game a correlation coefficient is computed, relating the machine's indicated moves to those moves adjudged best by the checker masters.[9]

It should be noted that the emphasis throughout all of these studies has been on learning techniques. The temptation to improve the machine's game by giving it standard openings or other man-generated knowledge of playing techniques has been consistently resisted. Even when book games are played, no weight is given to the fact that the moves as listed are presumably the best possible moves under the circumstances.

For demonstration purposes, and also as a means of avoiding lost machine time while an opponent is thinking, it is sometimes convenient to play several simultaneous games against different opponents. With the program in its present form the most convenient number for this purpose has been found to be six, although eight have been played on a number of occasions.

Games may be started with any initial configuration for the board position so that the program may be tested on end games, checker puzzles, et cetera. For nonstandard starting conditions, the program lists the initial

---

[9] This coefficient is defined as $C = (L - H)/(L + H)$, where L is the total number of different legal moves which the machine judged to be poorer than the indicated book moves, and H is the total number which it judged to be better than the book moves.

piece arrangement. From time to time. and at the end of each game, the program also tabulates various bits of statistical information which assist in the evaluation of playing performance.

Numerous other features have also been added to make the program convenient to operate (for details see Appendix A), but these have no direct bearing on the problem of learning, to which we will now turn our attention.

Rote Learning and Its Variants

Perhaps the most elementary type of learning worth discussing would be a form of rote learning in which the program simply saved all of the board positions encountered during play, together with their computed scores. Reference could then be made to this memory record and a certain amount of computing time might be saved. This can hardly be called a very advanced form of learning; nevertheless, if the program then utilizes the saved time to compute further in depth it will improve with time.

Fortunately, the ability to store board information at a ply of 0 and to look up boards at a larger ply provides the possibility of looking much farther in advance than might otherwise be possible. To understand this, consider a very simple case where the look ahead is always terminated at a fixed ply, say 3. Assume further that the program saves only the board positions encountered during the actual play with their associated backed-up scores. Now it is this list of previous board positions that is used to look up board positions while at a ply level of 3 in the subsequent games. If a board position is found, its score has, in effect, already been backed up by three levels, and if it becomes effective in determining the move to be made, it is a 6-ply score rather than a simple 3-ply score. This new initial board position with its 6-ply score is, in turn, saved and it may be encountered in a future game and the score backed up by an additional set of three levels, et cetera. This procedure is illustrated in Fig. 3. The incorporation of this variation, together with the simpler rote-learning feature, results in a fairly powerful learning technique which has been studied in some detail.

Several additional features had to be incorporated into the program before it was practical to embark on learning studies using this storage scheme. In the first place, it was necessary to impart a sense of direction to the program in order to force it to press on toward a win. To illustrate this, consider the situation of two kings against one king, which is a winning combination for practically all variations in board positions. In time, the program can be assumed to have stored all of these variations, each associated with a winning score. Now, if such a situation is encountered, the program will look ahead along all possible paths and each path will

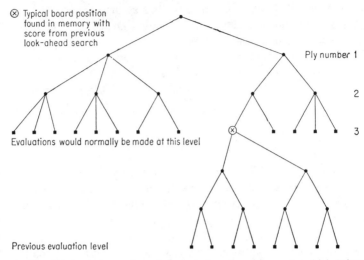

⊗ Typical board position
found in memory with
score from previous
look-ahead search

Ply number 1

2

Evaluations would normally be made at this level   3

Previous evaluation level

Figure 3. Simplified representation of the rote-learning process, in which information saved from a previous game is used to increase the effective ply of the backed-up score.

lead to a winning combination, in spite of the fact that only one of the possible initial moves may be along the direct path toward the win while all of the rest may be wasting time. How is the program to differentiate between these?

A good solution is to keep a record of the ply value of the different board positions at all times and to make a further choice between board positions on this basis. If ahead, the program can be arranged to push directly toward the win while, if behind, it can be arranged to adopt delaying tactics. The most recent method used is to carry the effective ply along with the score by simply decreasing the magnitude of the score a small amount each time it is backed up a ply level during the analyses. If the program is now faced with a choice of board positions whose scores differ only by the ply number, it will automatically make the most advantageous choice, choosing a low-ply alternative if winning and a high-ply alternative if losing. The significance of this concept of a direction sense should not be overlooked. Even without "learning," it is very important. Several of the early attempts at learning failed because the direction sense was not properly taken into account.

Cataloging and Culling Stored Information

Since practical considerations limit the number of board positions which can be saved, and since the time to search through those that are saved can easily become unduly long, one must devise systems (1) to catalog boards that are saved, (2) to delete redundancies, and (3) to discard board positions which are not believed to be of much value. The most effective cataloging system found to date starts by standardizing all board positions, first by reversing the pieces and piece positions if it is a board position in which White is to move, so that all boards are reported as if it were Black's turn to move. This reduces by nearly a factor of two the number of boards which must be saved. Board positions, in which all of the pieces are kings, can be reflected about the diagonals with a possible fourfold reduction in the number which must be saved. A more compact board representation than the one employed during play is also used so as to minimize the storage requirements.

After the board positions are standardized, they are grouped into records on the basis of (1) the number of pieces on the board, (2) the presence or absence of a piece advantage, (3) the side possessing this advantage, (4) the presence or absence of kings on the board, (5) the side having the so-called "move," or opposition advantage, and finally (6) the first moments of the pieces about normal and diagonal axes through the board. During play, newly acquired board positions are saved in the memory until a reasonable number have been accumulated, and they are then merged with those on the "memory tape" and a new memory tape is produced. Board positions within a record are listed in a serial fashion, being sorted with respect to the words which define them. The records are arranged on the tape in the order that they are most likely to be needed during the course of a game; board positions with 12 pieces to a side coming first, et cetera. This method of cataloging is very important because it cuts tape-searching time to a minimum.

Reference must be made, of course, to the board positions already saved, and this is done by reading the correct record into the memory and searching through it by a dichotomous search procedure. Usually five or more records are held in memory at one time, the exact number at any time depending upon the lengths of the particular records in question. Normally, the program calls three or four new records into memory during each new move, making room for them as needed, by discarding the records which have been held the longest.

Two different procedures have been found to be of value in limiting the number of board positions that are saved; one based on the frequency of use, and the second on the ply. To keep track of the frequency of use, an age term is carried along with the score. Each new board position to be saved is arbitrarily assigned an age. When reference is made to a stored board position, either to update its score or to utilize it in the look-ahead procedure, the age recorded for this board position is divided by two. This is called *refreshing*. Offsetting this, each board position is automatically aged by one unit at the memory merge times (normally occurring about once every 20 moves). When the age of any one board position reaches an arbitrary maximum value this board position is expunged from the record. This is a form of *forgetting*. New board positions which remain unused are soon forgotten, while board positions which are used several times in succession will be refreshed to such an extent that they will be remembered even if not used thereafter for a fairly long period of time. This form of refreshing and forgetting was adopted on the basis of reflections as to the frailty of human memories. It has proven to be very effective.

In addition to the limitations imposed by forgetting, it seemed desirable to place a restriction on the maximum size of any one record. Whenever an arbitrary limit is reached, enough of the lowest-ply board positions are automatically culled from the record to bring the size well below the maximum.

Before embarking on a study of the learning capabilities of the system as just described, it was, of course, first necessary to fix the terms and co-efficients in the evaluation polynomial. To do this, a number of different sets of values were tested by playing through a series of book games and computing the move correlation coefficients. These values varied from 0.2 for the poorest polynomial tested, to approximately 0.6 for the one finally adopted. The selected polynomial contained four terms (as contrasted with the use of 16 terms in later experiments). In decreasing order of importance these were: (1) piece advantage, (2) denial of occupancy, (3) mobility, and (4) a hybrid term which combined control of the center and piece advancement.

Rote-learning Tests

After a scoring polynomial was arbitrarily picked, a series of games was played, both self-play and play against many different individuals (several of these being checker masters). Many book games were also followed, some of these being end games. The program learned to play a very good opening game and to recognize most winning and losing end positions many moves in advance, although its midgame play was not greatly improved. This program now qualifies as a rather better-than-average novice, but definitely not as an expert.

At the present time the memory tape contains something over 53,000 board positions (averaging 3.8 words each) which have been selected from a much larger number of positions by means of the culling techniques described. While this is still far from the number which would tax the listing and searching procedures used in the program, rough estimates, based on the frequency with which the saved boards are utilized during normal play (these figures being tabulated automatically), indicate that a library tape containing at least 20 times the present number of board positions would be needed to improve the midgame play significantly. At the present rate of acquisition of new positions this would require an inordinate amount of play and, consequently, of machine time.[10]

The general conclusions which can be drawn from these tests are that:

(1) An effective rote-learning technique must include a procedure to give the program a sense of direction, and it must contain a refined system for cataloging and storing information.

(2) Rote-learning procedures can be used effectively on machines with the data-handling capacity of the IBM 704 if the information which must be saved and searched does not occupy more than, roughly, one million words, and if not more than one hundred or so references need to be made to this information per minute. These figures are, of course, highly dependent upon the exact efficiency of cataloging which can be achieved.

(3) The game of checkers, when played with a simple scoring scheme and with rote learning only, requires more than this number of words for master caliber of play and, as a consequence, is not completely amenable to this treatment on the IBM 704.

(4) A game, such as checkers, is a suitable vehicle for use during the development of learning techniques, and it is a very satisfactory device for demonstrating machine learning procedures to the unbelieving.

Learning Procedure Involving Generalizations

An obvious way to decrease the amount of storage needed to utilize past experience is to generalize on the basis of experience and to save only the generalizations. This should, of course, be a continuous process if it is to be truly effective, and it should involve several levels of abstraction. A start has been made in this direction by having the program select a subset of possible terms for use in the evaluation polynomial and by having the program determine the sign and magnitude of the coefficients which multiply these parameters. At the present time this subset consists of 16 terms chosen from a list of 38 parameters. The piece-advantage term needed to define the task is computed separately and, of course, is not altered by the program.

After a number of relatively unsuccessful attempts to have the program generalize while playing both sides of the game, the program was arranged to act as two different players, for convenience called *Alpha* and *Beta*. Alpha generalizes on its experience after each move by adjusting the coefficients in its evaluation polynomial and by replacing terms which appear to be unimportant by new parameters drawn from a reserve list. Beta, on the contrary, uses the same evaluation polynomial for the dura-

---

[10] This playing-time requirement, while large in terms of cost, would be less than the time which the checker master probably spends to acquire his proficiency.

tion of any one game. Program Alpha is used to play against human opponents, and during self-play Alpha and Beta play each other.

At the end of each self-play game a determination is made of the relative playing ability of Alpha, as compared with Beta, by a neutral portion of the program. If Alpha wins—or is adjudged to be ahead when a game is otherwise terminated—the then current scoring system used by Alpha is given to Beta. If, on the other hand, Beta wins or is ahead, this fact is recorded as a black mark for Alpha. Whenever Alpha receives an arbitrary number of black marks (usually set at three) it is assumed to be on the wrong track, and a fairly drastic and arbitrary change is made in its scoring polynomial (by reducing the coefficient of the leading term to zero). This action is necessary on occasion, since the entire learning process is an attempt to find the highest point in multidimensional scoring space in the presence of many secondary maxima on which the program can become trapped. By manual intervention it is possible to return to some previous condition or make some other change if it becomes apparent that the learning process is not functioning properly. In general, however, the program seeks to extricate itself from traps and to improve more or less continuously.

The capability of the program can be tested at any time by having Alpha play one or more book games (with the learning procedure temporarily immobilized) and by correlating its play with the recommendations of the masters or, more interestingly, by pitting it against a human player.

Polynomial Modification Procedure

If Alpha is to make changes in its scoring polynomial, it must be given some trustworthy criteria for measuring performance. A logical difficulty presents itself, since the only measuring parameter available is this same scoring polynomial that the process is designed to improve. Recourse is had to the peculiar property of the look-ahead procedure, which makes it less important for the scoring polynomial to be particularly good the further ahead the process is continued. This means that one can evaluate the relative change in the positions of two players, when this evaluation is made over a fairly large number of moves, by using a scoring system which is much too gross to be significant on a move-by-move basis.

Perhaps an even better way of looking at the matter is that we are attempting to make the score, calculated for the current board position, look like that calculated for the terminal board position of the chain of moves which most probably will occur during actual play. Of course, if one could develop a perfect system of this sort it would be the equivalent of always looking ahead to the end of the game. The nearer this ideal is approached, the better would be the play.[11]

---

[11] There is a logical fallacy in this argument. The program might save only invariant terms which have nothing to do with goodness of play; for example, it might

In order to obtain a sufficiently large span to make use of this characteristic, Alpha keeps a record of the apparent goodness of its board positions as the game progresses. This record is kept by computing the scoring polynomial for each board position encountered in actual play and by saving this polynomial in its entirety. At the same time, Alpha also computes the backed-up score for all board positions, using the look-ahead procedure described earlier. At each play by Alpha the initial board score, as saved from the previous Alpha move, is compared with the backed-up score for the current position. The difference between these scores, defined as *delta,* is used to check the scoring polynomial. If delta is positive it is reasonable to assume that the initial board evaluation was in error and terms which contributed positively should have been given more weight, while those that contributed negatively should have been given less weight. A converse statement can be made for the case where delta is negative. Presumably, in this case, either the initial board evaluation was incorrect, or a wrong choice of moves was made, and greater weight should have been given to terms making negative contributions, with less weight to positive terms. These changes are not made directly but are brought about in an involved way which will now be described.

A record is kept of the correlation existing between the signs of the individual term contributions in the initial scoring polynomial and the sign of delta. After each play an adjustment is made in the values of the correlation coefficients, due account being taken of the number of times that each particular term has been used and has had a nonzero value. The coefficient for the polynomial term (other than the piece-advantage term) with the then largest correlation coefficient is set at a prescribed maximum value with proportionate values determined for all of the remaining coefficients. Actually, the term coefficients are fixed at integral powers of 2, this power being defined by the ratio of the correlation coefficients. More precisely, if the ratio of two correlation coefficients is equal to or larger than n but less than $n + 1$, where n is an integer, then the ratio of the two term coefficients is set equal to 2^n. This procedure was adopted in order to increase the range in values of the term coefficients. Whenever a correlation-coefficient calculation leads to a negative sign, a corresponding reversal is made in the sign associated with the term itself.

Instabilities

It should be noted that the span of moves over which delta is computed consists of a remembered part and an anticipated portion. During the remembered play, use had been made of Alpha's current scoring polynomial to determine Alpha's moves but not to determine the opponent's moves,

---

count the squares on the checkerboard. The forced inclusion of the piece-advantage term prevents this.

while during the anticipation play the moves for both sides are made using Alpha's scoring polynomial. One is tempted to increase the sensitivity of delta as an indicator of change by increasing the span of the remembered portion. This has been found to be dangerous since the coefficients in the evaluation polynomial and, indeed, the terms themselves, may change between the time of the remembered evaluation and the time at which the anticipation evaluation is made. As a matter of fact, this difficulty is present even for a span of one move pair. It is necessary to recompute the scoring polynomial for a given initial board position after a move has been determined and after the indicated corrections in the scoring polynomial have been made, and to save this score for future comparisons, rather than to save the score used to determine the move. This may seem a trivial point, but its neglect in the initial stages of these experiments led to oscillations quite analogous to the instability induced in electrical circuits by long delays in a feedback loop.

As a means of stabilizing against minor variations in the delta values, an arbitrary minimum value was set, and when delta fell below this minimum for any particular move no change was made in the polynomial. This same minimum value is used to set limits for the initial board evaluation score to decide whether or not it will be assumed to be zero. This minimum is recomputed each time and, normally, has been fixed at the average value of the coefficients for the terms in the currently existing evaluation polynomial.

Still another type of instability can occur whenever a new term is introduced into the scoring polynomial. Obviously, after only a single move the correlation coefficient of this new term will have a magnitude of 1, even though it might go to 0 after the very next move. To prevent violent fluctuations due to this cause, the correlation coefficients for newly introduced terms are computed as if these terms had already been used several times and had been found to have a zero correlation coefficient. This is done by replacing the times-used number in the calculation by an arbitrary number (usually set at 16) until the usage does, in fact, equal this number.

After a term has been in use for some time, quite the opposite action is desired so that the more recent experience can outweigh earlier results. This is achieved, together with a substantial reduction in calculation time, by using powers of 2 in place of the actual times used and by limiting the maximum power that is used. To be specific, at any stage of play defined as the Nth move, corrections to the values of the correlation coefficients C_N are made using 16 for N until N equals 32, whereupon 32 is used until N equals 64, et cetera, using the formula:

$$C_N = C_{N-1} - \frac{C_{N-1} \pm 1}{N}$$

and a value for N larger than 256 is never used.

After a minimum was set for delta it seemed reasonable to attach greater weight to situations leading to large values of delta. Accordingly, two additional categories are defined. If a contribution to delta is made by the first term, meaning that a change has occurred in the piece ratio, the indicated changes in the correlation coefficients are doubled, while if the value of delta is so large as to indicate that an almost sure win or lose will result, the effect on the correlation coefficients is quadrupled.

Term Replacement

Mention has been made several times of the procedure for replacing terms in the scoring polynomial. The program, as it is currently running, contains 38 different terms (in addition to the piece-advantage term), 16 of these being included in the scoring polynomial at any one time and the remaining 22 being kept in reserve. After each move a low-term tally is recorded against that active term which has the lowest correlation coefficient and, at the same time, a test is made to see if this brings its tally count up to some arbitrary limit, usually set at 8. When this limit is reached for any specific term, this term·is transferred to the bottom of the reserve list, and it is replaced by a term from the head of the reserve list. This new term enters the polynomial with zero values for its correlation coefficient, times used, and low-tally count. On the average, then, an active term is replaced once each eight moves and the replaced terms are given another chance after 176 moves. As a check on the effectiveness of this procedure, the program reports on the usage which has accrued against each discarded term. Terms which are repeatedly rejected after a minimum amount of usage can be removed and replaced with completely new terms.

It might be argued that this procedure of having the program select terms for the evaluation polynomial from a supplied list is much too simple and that the program should generate the terms for itself. Unfortunately, no satisfactory scheme for doing this has yet been devised. With a man-generated list one might at least ask that the terms be members of an orthogonal set, assuming that this has some meaning as applied to the evaluation of a checker position. Apparently, no one knows enough about checkers to define such a set. The only practical solution seems to be that of including a relatively large number of possible terms in the hope that all of the contributing parameters get covered somehow, even though in an involved and redundant way. This is not an undesirable state of affairs, however, since it simulates the situation which is likely to exist when an attempt is made to apply similar learning techniques to real-life situations.

Many of the terms in the existing list are related in some vague way to the parameters used by checker experts. Some of the concepts which checker experts appear to use have eluded the writer's attempts at definition, and he has been unable to program them. Some of the terms are quite unrelated to the usual checker lore and have been discovered more or less by accident. The second moment about the diagonal axis through the double corners is an example. Twenty-seven different simple terms are now in use, the rest being combinational terms, as will be described later.

A word might be said about these terms with respect to the exact way in which they are defined and the general procedures used for their evaluation. Each term relates to the relative standings of the two sides, with respect to the parameter in question, and it is numerically equal to the difference between the ratings for the individual sides. A reversal of the sign obviously corresponds to a change of sides. As a further means of insuring symmetry the individual ratings of the respective sides are determined at corresponding times in the play as viewed by the side in question. For example, consider a parameter which relates to the board conditions as left after one side has moved. The rating of Black for such a parameter would be made after Black had moved, and the rating of White would not be made until after White had moved. During anticipation play, these individual ratings are made after each move and saved for future reference. When an evaluation is desired the program takes the differences between the most recent ratings and those made a move earlier. In general, an attempt has been made to define all parameters so that the individual-side ratings are expressible as small positive integers.

Binary Connective Terms

In addition to the simple terms of the type just described, a number of combinational terms have been introduced. Without these terms the scoring polynomial would, of course, be linear. A number of different ways of introducing nonlinear terms have been devised but only one of these has been tested in any detail. This scheme provides terms which have some of the properties of binary logical connectives. Four such terms are formed for each pair of simple terms which are to be related. This is done by making an arbitrary division of the range in values for each of the simple terms and assigning the binary values of 0 and 1 to these ranges. Since most of the simple terms are symmetrical about 0, this is easily done on a sign basis. The new terms are then of the form $A \cdot B$, $A \cdot \bar{B}$, $\bar{A} \cdot B$, and $\bar{A} \cdot \bar{B}$, yielding values either of 0 or 1. These terms are introduced into the scoring polynomial with adjustable coefficients and signs, and are thereafter indistinguishable from the other terms.

As it would require some 1404 such combinational terms to interrelate the 27 simple terms originally used, it was found desirable to limit the actual number of combinational terms used at any one time to a small fraction of these and to introduce new terms only as it became possible to retire older ineffectual terms. The terms actually used are given in Appendix C.

Preliminary Learning-by-generalization Tests

An idea of the learning ability of this procedure can be gained by analyzing an initial test series of 28 games[12] played with the program just described. At the start an arbitrary selection of 16 terms was chosen and all terms were assigned equal weights. During the first 14 games Alpha was assigned the White side, with Beta constrained as to its first move (two cycles of the seven different initial moves). Thereafter, Alpha was assigned Black and White alternately. During this time a total of 29 different terms was discarded and replaced, the majority of these on two different occasions.

Certain other figures obtained during these 28 games are of interest. At frequent intervals the program lists the 12 leading terms in Alpha's scoring polynomial with their correlation coefficients and a running count of the number of times these coefficients have been altered. Based on these samplings, one observes that at least 20 different terms were assigned the largest coefficient at some time or other, some of these alternating with other terms a number of times, and two even reappearing at the top of the list with their signs reversed. While these variations were more violent at the start of the series of games and decreased as time went on, their presence indicated that the learning procedure was still not completely stable. During the first seven games there were at least 14 changes in occupancy at the top of the list involving 10 different terms. Alpha won three of these games and lost four. The quality of the play was extremely poor. During the next seven games there were at least eight changes made in the top listing involving five different terms. Alpha lost the first of these games and won the next six. Quality of play improved steadily but the machine still played rather badly. During Games 15 through 21 there were eight changes in the top listing involving five terms; Alpha winning five games and losing two. Some fairly good amateur players who played the machine during this period agreed that it was "tricky but beatable." During Games 22 through 28 there were at least four changes involving three terms. Alpha won two games and lost five. The program appeared to be approaching a quality of play which caused it to be described as "a better-than-average player." A detailed analysis of these results indicated that the learning procedure did work and that the rate of learning was surprisingly high, but that the learning was quite erratic and none too stable.

Second Series of Tests

Some of the more obvious reasons for this erratic behavior in the first series of tests have been identified. The program was modified in several

---

[12] The games averaged 68 moves (34 to a side) of which approximately 20 caused changes to be made in the scoring polynomial.

respects to improve the situation, and additional tests were made. Four of these modifications are important enough to justify a detailed explanation.

In the first place, the program was frequently fooled by bad play on the part of its opponent. A simple solution was to change the correlation coefficients less drastically when delta was positive than when delta was negative. The procedure finally adopted for the positive delta case was to make corrections to selected terms in the polynomial only. When the scoring polynomial was positive, changes were made to coefficients associated with the negatively contributing terms, and when the polynomial was negative, changes were made to the coefficients associated with positively contributing terms. No changes were made to coefficients associated with terms which happened to be zero. For the negative delta case, changes were made to the coefficients of all contributing terms, just as before.

A second defect seemed to be connected with the too frequent introduction of new terms into the scoring polynomial and the tendency for these new terms to assume dominant positions on the basis of insufficient evidence. This was remedied by the simple expedient of decreasing the rate of introduction of new terms from one every eight moves to one every 32 moves.

The third defect had to do with the complete exclusion from consideration of many of the board positions encountered during play by reason of the minimum limit on delta. This resulted in the misassignment of credit to those board positions which permitted spectacular moves when the credit rightfully belonged to earlier board positions which had permitted the necessary ground-laying moves. Although no precise way has yet been devised to ensure the correct assignment of credit, a very simple expedient was found to be most effective in minimizing the adverse effects of earlier assignments. This expedient was to allow the span of remembered moves, over which delta is computed, to increase until delta exceeded the arbitrary minimum value, and then to apply the corrections to the coefficients as dictated by the terms in the retained polynomial for this earlier board position. In this case, the difficulty which was mentioned in the section on Instabilities in connection with an arbitrary increase in span, does not occur after each correction, since no changes are made in the coefficients of the scoring polynomial as long as delta is below the minimum value. Of course, whenever delta does exceed the minimum value the program must then recompute the initial scoring polynomial for the then current board position and so restart the procedure with a span of a single remembered move pair. This over-all procedure rectifies the defect of assigning credit to a board position that lies too far along the move chain, but it introduces the possibility of assigning credit to a board position that is not far enough along.

As a partial expedient to compensate for this newly introduced danger, a change was made in the initial board evaluation. Instead of evaluating the initial board positions directly, as was done before, a standard but rudimentary tree search (terminated after the first nonjump move) was used. Errors due to impending jump situations were eliminated by this procedure, and because of the greater accuracy of the evaluation it was possible to reduce the minimum delta limit by a small amount.

Finally, to avoid the danger of having Beta adopt Alpha's polynomial as a result of a chance win on Alpha's part (or perhaps a situation in which Alpha had allowed its polynomial to degenerate after an early or midgame advantage had been gained), it was decided to require a majority of wins on Alpha's part before Beta would adopt Alpha's scoring polynomial.

With these modifications, a new series of tests was made. In order to reduce the learning time, the initial selection of terms was made on the basis of the results obtained during the earlier tests, but no attention was paid to their previously assigned weights. In contrast with the earlier erratic behavior, the revised program appeared to be extremely stable, perhaps at the expense of a somewhat lower initial learning rate. The way in which the character of the evaluation polynomial altered as learning progressed is shown in Fig. 4.

The most obvious change in behavior was in regard to the relative number of games won by Alpha and the prevalence of draws. During the first 28 games of the earlier series Alpha won 16 and lost 12. The corresponding figures for the first 28 games of the new series were 18 won by Alpha, and four lost, with six draws. In all cases the games were terminated, if not finished, in 70 moves and a judgment made in terms of the final positions. Unfortunately, these figures are not strictly comparable because of the decreased frequency with which Beta adopted Alpha's polynomial during the second series, both by design and because a programming error immobilized the adoption procedure during part of the tests. Nevertheless, the great decrease in the number of losses and the prevalence of draws seemed to indicate that the learning process was much more stable. Some typical games from this second series are given in Appendix B.

As learning proceeds, it should become harder and harder for Alpha to improve its game, and one would expect the number of wins by Alpha to decrease with time. If secondary maxima in scoring space are encountered, one might even find situations in which Alpha wins less than half of the games. With Beta at such a maximum any minor change in Alpha's polynomial would result in a degradation of its play, and several oscillations about the maximum might occur before Alpha landed at a point which would enable it to beat Beta. Some evidence of this trend is discernible in the play, although many more games will have to be played before it can be observed with certainty.

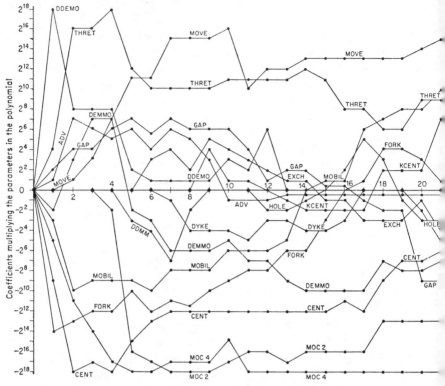

Figure 4. Second series of learning-by-generalization tests. Coefficients assigned by plotted as a function of the number of games played. Two regions of special found that the initial signs of many of the terms had been set incorrectly, and or 32 games.

The tentative conclusions which can be drawn from these tests are:

(1) A simple generalization scheme of the type here used can be an effective learning device for problems amenable to tree-searching procedures.

(2) The memory requirements of such schemes are quite modest and remain fixed with time.

(3) The operating times are also reasonable and remain fixed, independent of the amount of accumulated learning.

(4) Incipient forms of instability in the solution can be expected but, at least for the checker program, these can be dealt with by quite straightforward procedures.

(5) Even with the incomplete and redundant set of parameters which

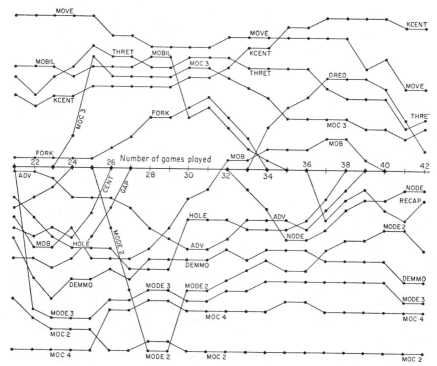

the program to the more significant parameters of the evaluation polynomial
interest might be noted: (1) the situation after 13 or 14 games, when the program
(2) the conditions of relative stability which are beginning to show up after 31

have been used to date, it is possible for the computer to learn to play a
better-than-average game of checkers in a relatively short period of time.

As a final precautionary note, it should be stated that these experiments
have not encompassed a sufficiently large series of games to demonstrate
unambiguously that the learning procedure is completely stable or that
it will necessarily lead to the best possible choice of parameters and coefficients.

Rote Learning vs. Generalization

Some interesting comparisons can be made between the playing style developed by the learning-by-generalization program and that developed by
the earlier rote-learning procedure. The program with rote learning soon

learned to imitate master play during the opening moves. It was always quite poor during the middle game, but it easily learned how to avoid most of the obvious traps during end-game play and could usually drive on toward a win when left with a piece advantage. The program with the generalization procedure has never learned to play in a conventional manner and its openings are apt to be weak. On the other hand, it soon learned to play a good middle game, and with a piece advantage it usually polishes off its opponent in short order. Interestingly enough, after 28 games it had still not learned how to win an end game with two kings against one in a double corner.

Apparently, rote learning is of the greatest help either under conditions when the results of any specific action are long delayed or in those situations where highly specialized techniques are required. Contrasting with this, the generalization procedure is most helpful in situations in which the available permutations of conditions are large in number and when the consequences of any specific action are not long delayed.

Procedures Involving Both Forms of Learning

The next obvious step is to combine the better features of the rote-learning procedure with a generalization scheme. This must be done with some care, since it is not practical to update the previously saved information after every change in the evaluation polynomial. A compromise solution might be to save only a very limited amount of information during the early stages of learning and to increase the amount as warranted by the increasing stability of the evaluation coefficient with learning. For example, the program could be arranged to save only the piece-advantage term at the start. At some stage in the learning process the next term could be added, perhaps when no change had been made in the parameter used for this term during some fairly long period, say for three complete games. If and when the program is able to play an additional period without changes in the next parameter, this could also be added, et cetera. Whenever a change does occur in a parameter previously assumed to be stable, the entire memory tape could be reviewed, all terms involving the changed parameter and those lower on the list could be expunged, and the program could drop back to the earlier condition with respect to its term-saving schedule.

Another solution would be to utilize the generalization scheme alone until it had become fairly stable and to introduce rote learning at this time. It is, of course, perfectly feasible to salvage much of the learning which has been accumulated by both of the programs studied to date. This could be done by appending an abridged form of the present memory tape to the generalization scheme in its present stage of learning and by proceeding from there in accordance with the first solution proposed above.

Future Development

While it is believed that these tests have reached the stage of diminishing returns, some effort might well be expended in an attempt to get the program to generate its own parameters for the evaluation polynomial. Lacking a perfectly general procedure, it might still be possible to generate terms based on theories as proposed by students of the game. This procedure would be at variance with the writer's previous philosophy, but it is highly likely that similar compromises will have to be made when one attempts to apply learning procedures to problems of economic importance.

Conclusions

As a result of these experiments one can say with some certainty that it is now possible to devise learning schemes which will greatly outperform an average person and that such learning schemes may eventually be economically feasible as applied to real-life problems.

Appendix A: Programming Details

Approximate Size of Program

Basic checker-playing routine	1100 instructions
Input, move verification and output	1400 instructions
Game starting and terminating routines	600 instructions
Loaders, table generators, dumping, et cetera	850 instructions
Statistical and analytical routines	700 instructions
Rote-learning routines	1500 instructions
Generalization-learning routines	650 instructions
Tables and constants for basic play	700 words
Working space for basic play	2000 words
Working space for generalization learning	500 words
Working space for rote learning	Balance of memory

Approximate Computation Times

To find all available moves from given board position	2.6 milliseconds
To make a single move and find resulting board position	1.5 milliseconds
To evaluate a board position (4 terms)	2.4 milliseconds
To find score for a saved board position (rote learning)	2.3 milliseconds
To evaluate position (with 16 terms for generalization learning)	7.5 milliseconds

Board Representations

The standard checkerboard numbering system (see Appendix B) is used in communicating with the machine. A modified numbering system is used for internal computations, the numbers shown on the squares in Fig. 5 corresponding to the bit positions in an IBM 704 word. Any given board position is represented by four such words; one word (FA) containing 1's

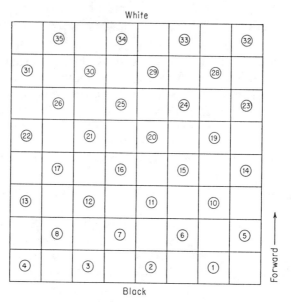

Figure 5. Checkerboard notation for internal computations.

in those bit positions corresponding to squares containing pieces of the color whose turn it is to move and which normally move in a forward direction. To be specific, if it is Black's turn to move (*i.e.*, if Black is "active") *FA* designates the location of all of Black's pieces, both men and kings. Conversely, if White is active, *FA* designates the location of White's kings only, since White's men can only move in the direction arbitrarily called *backward*. The other words designate, respectively: *BA*, backward active pieces; *FP*, forward passive pieces; and *BP*, backward passive pieces.

To conserve space when writing on tape, three words are used to record board positions with kings, and only two words are used for board positions without kings. These are saved in a standardized form, as explained in the text.

Possible moves are designated by five words; one word to indicate by its sign (with the word itself containing other information) whether the moves are jumps or not. (If a jump is available, only jump moves are saved.) The other four words designate the location of those pieces which can move in the four different diagonal directions: *RF*, for right forward; *LF*, for left forward; *LB* for left backward; and *RB*, for right backward, respectively.

By reference to Fig. 5, it will be observed that a right-forward move results in an increase of 4 in the square designation, while a left-forward move results in an increase of 5. Bit positions 9, 18 and 27 do not appear on the board. This notation makes it possible to compute available moves for all pieces simultaneously. Having previously computed a word called *EMPTY,* which contains 1's in locations corresponding to all unoccupied squares, one can compute *RF,* for the normal move case, in four instructions, as listed below (in IBM 704 symbolic language):

CLA	*EMPTY*	(puts word *EMPTY* into the accumulator)
ALS	4	(shifts word to left by 4 positions)
ANA	*FA*	(forms logical AND between *EMPTY* and *FA*)
STO	*RF*	(stores word as newly computed *RF*)

Jump moves are computed by a simple extension of this procedure. Multiple jumps are handled as a sequence of single jumps separated by null-reply moves.

Additional Timesaving Expedients

Bit counting is done by a table look-up procedure in a closed subroutine of 16 executed instructions (408 microseconds). This requires a 256-word table which is generated at the start by a 13-word program. Similar table look-up procedures are used, to turn a word end for end, and to locate the 1's in a word for move reporting.

Multiplications are usually avoided. In several places where multiplication by small integers must be done, it is programmed in terms of shifts and logical operations.

During the look-ahead procedure a complete record is kept of the sequence of board positions currently under investigation. As a result, no computing is needed to retract moves.

Appendix B: Sample Games from the Second Series with Generalization Learning

Typical Openings

The first eight moves of selected games in which Alpha played Black against Beta, showing the way in which different types of play were tried.

G-4	*G-6*	*G-12*	*G-17*	*G-19*	*G-21*	*G-31*	*G-37*	*G-39*	*G-41*	*G-43*
10 14	11 16	11 16	11 16	11 16	11 16	11 16	12 16	11 16	10 14	11 16
24 19	22 18	22 17	24 20	24 20	24 20	23 18	24 20	24 20	24 20	23 19
14 18	16 20	16 20	10 14	7 11	8 11	7 11	8 12	10 15	11 15	16 23
23 14	18 14	17 13	20 11	22 17	28 24	27 23	28 24	20 11	27 24	26 19
9 18	9 18	9 14	8 15	10 14	10 14	16 20	10 14	7 16	7 10	8 11
22 15	23 14	23 18	22 17	17 10	23 18	23 19	23 18	21 17	23 18	22 17
11 18	10 17	14 23	7 11	6 15	14 23	20 27	14 23	6 10	14 23	10 14
21 17	21 14	27 18	17 10	28 24	27 18	31 24	27 18	23 19	26 19	17 10

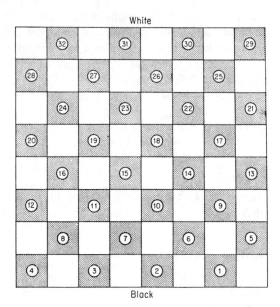

Figure 6. Square designations used in reporting games.

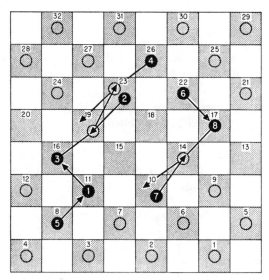

Figure 7. Eight-move opening utilizing generalization learning. (See Appendix B, Game *G-43*.)

Typical Games

Sample games in which Alpha played White against forced Beta openings.

G-1	G-18	G-30	G-40	G-1	G-18	G-30	G-40
12 16	12 16	12 16	10 14	9 13	12 16	9 14	4 8
24 19	24 20	24 20	24 20	1 6	24 20	18 9	1 6
8 12	8 12	8 12	11 15	13 17	16 19	8 11	10 14
22 18	28 24	28 24	27 24	32 27	29 25	15 8	6 10
10 14	10 15	10 14	7 10	16 20	13 17	4 11	14 17
26 22	22 18	22 18	23 18	18 14	10 7	19 15	10 15
16 20	15 22	6 10	14 23	11 15	2 11	11 18	17 21
30 26	25 18	24 19	26 19	6 10	14 10	23 14	32 28
11 16	7 10	1 6	10 14	15 18	19 23	13 17	5 9
28 24	18 14	32 28	19 10	14 9	21 14	9 5	27 24
7 11	10 17	3 8	6 15	Terminated	23 26	12 16	20 27
22 17	21 14	26 22	22 17	manually	10 7	28 24	19 16
3 8	9 18	9 13	2 7		26 30	17 22	12 19
17 10	23 14	18 9	17 10		25 21	6 10	15 22 31
6 15 22	6 9	5 14	7 14		30 26	30 25	9 14
26 17	30 25	22 18	24 19		7 3	1 6	31 26
9 13	9 18	6 9	15 24		11 15	25 21	14 18
17 14	26 23	25 22	28 19		14 10	5 1	28 24
2 7	3 8	2 6	14 17		5 9	21 17	8 11
23 18	23 14	30 25	21 14		10 6	24 20	24 19
16 23	1 6	14 17	9 18		15 19	16 19	21 25
14 10	27 23	21 14 5	25 22		6 1	20 16	30 21
7 14	6 9	6 9	18 25		26 22	17 13	Beta
18 9	14 10	18 15	29 22		1 6	6 2	concedes
5 14	9 13	11 18	5 9		9 13	13 17	
27 18 9	25 21	20 11 2	31 27		20 16	10 6	
20 27	11 15	10 14	1 5		19 23	Beta	
31 24	20 11	22 15	20 16		6 9	concedes	
12 16	15 18	14 17	3 7		23 27		
21 17	23 14	5 1	22 17		16 11		
13 22	8 15	17 21	8 11		22 25		
25 18	24 19	25 22	17 13		11 7		
1 5	15 24	21 25	11 20		25 30		
9 6	32 28	22 18	13 6		7 2		
5 9	24 27	25 30	7 10		27 32		
6 1	31 24	2 6	6 1		70 Move termination		

Appendix C: Evaluation Polynomial Details for Second Series

Method of Computing Terms

The 16 terms called for in the evaluation polynomial are computed, individually, by taking the value of the appropriate parameter, as defined below, for the board position under consideration and subtracting the value of this same parameter computed for the board position just prior to the last move (with the necessary reversal in the definitions of active and passive sides). This difference is then multiplied by the corresponding program-computed coefficient, which can vary between -2^{18} and $+2^{18}$, and credited to the side which was passive on the board position under consideration.

Definitions of Parameters

ADV (Advancement)
The parameter is credited with 1 for each passive man in the 5th and 6th rows (counting in passive's direction) and debited with 1 for each passive man in the 3rd and 4th rows.

APEX (Apex)
The parameter is debited with 1 if there are no kings on the board, if either square 7 or 26 is occupied by an active man, and if neither of these squares is occupied by a passive man.

BACK (Back Row Bridge)
The parameter is credited with 1 if there are no active kings on the board and if the two bridge squares (1 and 3, or 30 and 32) in the back row are occupied by passive pieces.

CENT (Center Control I)
The parameter is credited with 1 for each of the following squares: 11, 12, 15, 16, 20, 21, 24 and 25 which is occupied by a passive man.

CNTR (Center Control II)
The parameter is credited with 1 for each of the following squares: 11, 12, 15, 16, 20, 21, 24 and 25 that is either currently occupied by an active piece or to which an active piece can move.

CORN (Double-corner Credit)
The parameter is credited with 1 if the material credit value for the active side is 6 or less, if the passive side is ahead in material credit, and if the active side can move into one of the double-corner squares.

CRAMP (Cramp)
The parameter is credited with 2 if the passive side occupies the cramping square (13 for Black, and 20 for White) and at least one other nearby square (9 or 14 for Black, and 19 or 20 for White), while certain squares (17, 21, 22 and 25 for Black, and 8, 11, 12 and 16 for White) are all occupied by the active side.

DENY (Denial of Occupancy)
The parameter is credited with 1 for each square defined in MOB if on the next move a piece occupying this square could be captured without an exchange.

DIA (Double Diagonal File)

The parameter is credited with 1 for each passive piece located in the diagonal files terminating in the double-corner squares.

DIAV (Diagonal Moment Value)

The parameter is credited with $\frac{1}{2}$ for each passive piece located on squares 2 removed from the double-corner diagonal files, with 1 for each passive piece located on squares 1 removed from the double-corner files and with $\frac{3}{2}$ for each passive piece in the double-corner files.

DYKE (Dyke)

The parameter is credited with 1 for each string of passive pieces that occupy three adjacent diagonal squares.

EXCH (Exchange)

The parameter is credited with 1 for each square to which the active side may advance a piece and, in so doing, force an exchange.

EXPOS (Exposure)

The parameter is credited with 1 for each passive piece that is flanked along one or the other diagonal by two empty squares.

FORK (Threat of Fork)

The parameter is credited with 1 for each situation in which passive pieces occupy two adjacent squares in one row and in which there are three empty squares so disposed that the active side could, by occupying one of them, threaten a sure capture of one or the other of the two pieces.

GAP (Gap)

The parameter is credited with 1 for each single empty square that separates two passive pieces along a diagonal, or that separates a passive piece from the edge of the board.

GUARD (Back-row Control)

The parameter is credited with 1 if there are no active kings and if either the Bridge or the Triangle of Oreo is occupied by passive pieces.

HOLE (Hole)

The parameter is credited with 1 for each empty square that is surrounded by three or more passive pieces.

KCENT (King Center Control)

The parameter is credited with 1 for each of the following squares: 11, 12, 15, 16, 20, 21, 24 and 25 which is occupied by a passive king.

MOB (Total Mobility)

The parameter is credited with 1 for each square to which the active side could move one or more pieces in the normal fashion, disregarding the fact that jump moves may or may not be available.

MOBIL (Undenied Mobility)
The parameter is credited with the difference between MOB and DENY.

MOVE (Move)
The parameter is credited with 1 if pieces are even with a total piece count (2 for men, and 3 for kings) of less than 24, and if an odd number of pieces are in the move system, defined as those vertical files starting with squares 1, 2, 3 and 4.

NODE (Node)
The parameter is credited with 1 for each passive piece that is surrounded by at least three empty squares.

OREO (Triangle of Oreo)
The parameter is credited with 1 if there are no passive kings and if the Triangle of Oreo (squares 2, 3 and 7 for Black, and squares 26, 30 and 31 for White) is occupied by passive pieces.

POLE (Pole)
The parameter is credited with 1 for each passive man that is completely surrounded by empty squares.

RECAP (Recapture)
This parameter is identical with Exchange, as defined above. (It was introduced to test the effects produced by the random times at which parameters are introduced and deleted from the evaluation polynomial.)

THRET (Threat)
The parameter is credited with 1 for each square to which an active piece may be moved and in so doing threaten the capture of a passive piece on a subsequent move.

Binary Connective Terms

The abbreviations used for the terms of this type which have been employed are listed below, in the order of $A \cdot B$, $A \cdot \bar{B}$ $\bar{A} \cdot B$, and $\bar{A} \cdot \bar{B}$, where A and B are the two respective parameters heading the sublists of abbreviations.

Denial of occupancy—total mobility	Undenied mobility—denial of occupancy	Undenied mobility—center control I
DEMO	MODE 1	MOC 1
DEMMO	MODE 2	MOC 3
DDEMO	MODE 3	MOC 2
DDMM	MODE 4	MOC 4

Evaluation Polynomial (First 12 Terms Only) after 42 Games, during Which a Total of 1,039 Different Sets of Adjustments Were Made to the Terms and Their Coefficients[13]

Term	Correlation coefficient	Sign of coefficient	Power of 2 used as coefficient	Times adjusted
MOC 2	0.45	−	18	84
KCENT	0.40	+	16	127
MOC 4	0.35	−	14	95
MODE 3	0.33	−	13	210
DEMMO	0.27	−	11	132
MOVE	0.19	+	8	91
ADV	0.19	−	8	739
MODE 2	0.19	−	8	55
BACK	0.14	−	6	6
CNTR	0.13	+	5	12
THRET	0.13	+	5	442
MOC 3	0.10	+	4	89

Discarded Terms during 42 Games[13]

Term	Times adjusted before discard	Term	Times adjusted before discard
CORN	0	MODE 1	1
CRAMP	0	CENT	386
GUARD	0	MODE 4	0
EXPOS	162	FORK	400
DDMM	19	MOBIL	707
DYKE	115	POLE	11
MOC 1	1	HOLE	598
EXCH	445	GAP	792
DDEMO	53	MOB	608

[13] An additional 20 games have recently been played. Although some significant changes were noted, the general stabilization of the learning process suggested by Fig. 4 has been confirmed. During this play, 412 more adjustments were made to the terms and their coefficients and 12 additions were made to the list of discarded terms.

Appendix D: Game Played by Mr. R. W. Nealey and the Samuel Checker Program

In the summer of 1962, at the request of the editors of this collection, Dr. Samuel arranged a match between his checker-playing program (on an IBM 7090 computer) and a human checker champion.

Mr. Robert W. Nealey is described in the *IBM Research News* for August, 1962, as "a former Connecticut checkers champion, and one of the nation's foremost players."

The Samuel program bested Mr. Nealey in the game reprinted below. The annotations were made by Dr. Samuel. Mr. Nealey's comments, as quoted by the *IBM Research News,* are as follows:

Our game . . . did have its points. Up to the 31st move, all of our play had been previously published, except where I evaded "the book" several times in a vain effort to throw the computer's timing off. At the 32-27 loser and onwards, all the play is original with us, so far as I have been able to find. It is very interesting to me to note that the computer had to make several star moves in order to get the win, and that I had several opportunities to draw otherwise. That is why I kept the game going. The machine, therefore, played a perfect ending without one misstep. In the matter of the end game, I have not had such competition from any human being since 1954, when I lost my last game.

Nealey (*WHITE*) vs. Samuel Checker Program (*BLACK*)

Date: July 12, 1962
Place: Yorktown, New York
Mr. Nealey was given the option and chose to defend. The Old Fourteenth opening was followed.

11	15		
23	19		
8	11		
22	17		
4	8		
17	13		25-22 would restrict Black's variety of play a little more.
15	18		
24	20		Lee's Old Fourteenth, Var. 9. 11-15 is the trunk move.
9	14		
26	23		Doran's Var. 100 listed as an even game.
10	15		
19	10		
6	15		
28	24		Doran lists 23-19 as giving an easier game for White.
15	19		An aggressive move for Black.
24	15		
5	9		
13	6		
1	19	26	
31	22	15	
11	18		Still in Lee's Var. 9 and Doran's Var. 100.

30	26	This is probably a poor move on Mr. Nealey's part.
8	11	A good reply maintaining control of the center.
25	22	
18	25	
29	22	
11	15	
27	23	
15	19	
23	16	
12	19	
32	27	White makes a losing move.
19	24	The obvious reply, guaranteeing Black a king.
27	23	
24	27	
22	18	
27	31	Black now has his king.
18	9	
31	22	
9	5	
22	26	A delaying move to force White to advance.
23	19	
26	22	
19	16	
22	18	
21	17	
18	23	
17	13	
2	6	Le coup de maitre. A Black win is now certain.
16	11	
7	16	
20	11	
23	19	Le coup mortel

White concedes.

Location of Black pieces-3,6,19K
Location of White pieces-5,11,13.

Machines That Prove Mathematical Theorems

The discovery of proofs for mathematical theorems constitutes intellectual activity of a high order. The learning of mathematical proof techniques is considered by many to be good training in general problem-solving discipline.

Ironically, the elegant proofs that mathematicians present in their scholarly reports and textbooks usually do not provide one with much insight into the actual mental processes of discovery that were used to find the proofs. Occasionally one catches a glimpse of these processes during a classroom lecture by an excellent teacher of mathematics. Such an experience is probably the closest point of contact with the private problem-solving world of the mathematician.

The fascination with mechanical theorem proving for most of the researchers working in this area lies less with the end (the production of theorems, perhaps new and important) than with the means (a thorough understanding of the organization of information processing activity in mathematical discovery). It is felt that understanding these problem-solving processes is an important step toward the programming of more complex and general problem-solving processes for a variety of intellectual tasks. In theorem-proving research, as in the game-playing studies, the simplicity of the formal system allows most of the research effort to be devoted to understanding problem-solving processes rather than to modeling the task environment.

Not all work on mechanical theorem proving is concerned with problem-solving means—the more general problem. Some researchers, notably Wang, are deeply concerned with the end—the production of theorems. They have achieved impressive results using advanced and sophisticated mathematical decision rules.

The Logic Theorist is a computer program which discovers proofs to the theorems in symbolic logic (chapter 2 of the Whitehead-Russell *Principia Mathematica*). It uses proof methods no more advanced than those available to the student just beginning a first course in *Principia*.

The Logic Theorist was programmed by Newell, Shaw, and Simon in early 1956. It was the first heuristic program fully realized on a computer, the first foray by artificial intelligence research into high-order intellectual processes.

It is interesting to note that the Logic Theorist was accompanied by, or gave rise to, another development of great importance to artificial intelligence research and the computer sciences in general: the first list processing computer language. The language was reported by Newell and Shaw in a companion piece to the paper which is reprinted (the piece was called "Programming the Logic Theory Machine," and the language is called Information Processing Language, or IPL).

The work of Gelernter and his associates extends heuristic programming ideas to the proof of theorems in euclidean geometry. His program makes use of heuristic methods where they are most effective, but it also applies more powerful, more direct symbol manipulation processes where these are useful. Of special interest in the geometry proof program is the use of the diagram as a heuristic device in guiding search of the subproblem structure.

The geometry group, too, developed a list processing language for writing their program. Called FORTRAN List Processing Language (FLPL), it combines the ordinary capabilities of FORTRAN (for specifying numerical computations) with certain list processing features.

H. Gelernter and J. R. Hansen are members of the research staff of the IBM Research Laboratory in Yorktown Heights, N.Y. D. W. Loveland is at the Courant Institute, New York, N.Y.

EMPIRICAL EXPLORATIONS WITH THE LOGIC THEORY MACHINE: A CASE STUDY IN HEURISTICS

by Allen Newell, J. C. Shaw, & H. A. Simon

This is a case study in problem-solving, representing part of a program of research on complex information-processing systems. We have specified a system for finding proofs of theorems in elementary symbolic logic, and by programming a computer to these specifications, have obtained empirical data on the problem-solving process in elementary logic. The program is called the Logic Theory Machine (LT); it was devised to learn how it is possible to solve difficult problems such as proving mathematical theorems, discovering scientific laws from data, playing chess, or understanding the meaning of English prose.

The research reported here is aimed at understanding the complex processes (heuristics) that are effective in problem-solving. Hence, we are not interested in methods that guarantee solutions, but which require vast amounts of computation. Rather, we wish to understand how a mathematician, for example, is able to prove a theorem even though he does not know when he starts how, or if, he is going to succeed.

This focuses on the pure theory of problem-research solving (Newell and Simon, 1956a). Previously we specified in detail a program for the Logic Theory Machine; and we shall repeat here only as much of that specification as is needed so that the reader can understand our data. In a companion study (Newell and Shaw, 1957) we consider how computers can be programmed to execute processes of the kinds called for by LT, a problem that is interesting in its own right. Similarly, we postpone to later papers a discussion of the implications of our work for the psychological theory of human thinking and problem-solving. Other areas of application will readily occur to the reader, but here we will limit our attention to the nature of the problem-solving process itself.

Our research strategy in studying complex systems is to specify them in detail, program them for digital computers, and study their behavior empirically by running them with a number of variations and under a variety of conditions. This appears at present the only adequate means to obtain a thorough understanding of their behavior. Although the problem area with which the present system, LT, deals is fairly elementary, it provides a good example of a difficult problem—logic is a subject taught in college courses, and is difficult enough for most humans.

Our data come from a series of programs run on the JOHNNIAC, one of RAND's high-speed digital computers. We will describe the results of these runs, and analyze and interpret their implications for the problem-solving process.

The Logic Theory Machine in Operation

We shall first give a concrete picture of the Logic Theory Machine in operation. LT, ot course, is a program, written for the JOHNNIAC, represented by marks on paper or holes in cards. However, we can think of LT as an actual physical machine and the operation of the program as the behavior of the machine. One can identify LT with JOHNNIAC after the latter has been loaded with the basic program, but before the input of data.

LT's task is to prove theorems in elementary symbolic logic, or more precisely, in the sentential calculus. The sentential calculus is a formalized system of mathematics, consisting of expressions built from combinations of basic symbols. Five of these expressions are taken as axioms, and there are rules of inference for generating new theorems from the axioms and from other theorems. In flavor and form elementary symbolic logic is much like abstract algebra. Normally the variables of the system are interpreted as sentences, and the axioms and rules of inference as formalizations of logical operations, *e.g.*, deduction. However, LT deals with the system as a purely formal mathematics, and we will have no further need of the interpretation. We need to introduce a smattering of the sentential calculus to understand LT's task.

There is postulated a set of *variables* $p, q, r, \ldots A, B, C, \ldots$, with which the sentential calculus deals. These variables can be combined into expressions by means of *connectives*. Given any variable p, we can form the expression "not-p." Given any two variables p and q, we can form the expression "p or q," or the expression "p implies q," where "or" and "implies" are the connectives. There are other connectives, for example "and," but we will not need them here. Once we have formed expressions, these can be further combined into more complicated expressions. For example, we can form:[1]

$$\text{``}(p \text{ implies not-}p) \text{ implies not-}p.\text{''} \tag{2.01}$$

There is also given a set of expressions that are axioms. These are taken to be the universally true expressions from which theorems are to be derived by means of various rules of inference. For the sake of definiteness in our work with LT, we have employed the system of axioms, definitions, and rules that is used in the *Principia Mathematica,* which lists five axioms:

$(p \text{ or } p)$ implies p	(1.2)
p implies $(q \text{ or } p)$	(1.3)
$(p \text{ or } q)$ implies $(q \text{ or } p)$	(1.4)
$[p \text{ or } (q \text{ or } r)]$ implies $[q \text{ or } (p \text{ or } r)]$	(1.5)
$(p \text{ implies } q)$ implies $[(r \text{ or } p) \text{ implies } (r \text{ or } q)].$	(1.6)

Given some true theorems one can derive new theorems by means of three rules of inference: *substitution, replacement, and detachment.*

1. By the rule of substitution, any expression may be substituted for any variable in any theorem, provided the substitution is made throughout the theorem wherever that variable appears. For example, by substitution of "p or q" for "p," in the second axiom we get the new theorem:

$$(p \text{ or } q) \text{ implies } [q \text{ or } (p \text{ or } q)].$$

2. By the rule of replacement, a connective can be replaced by its definition, and *vice versa*, in any of its occurrences. By definition "p implies q" means the same as "not-p or q." Hence the former expression can always be replaced by the latter and *vice versa*. For example from axiom 1.3, by replacing "implies" with "or," we get the new theorem:

$$\text{not-}p \text{ or } (q \text{ or } p).$$

3. By the rule of detachment, if "A" and "A implies B" are theorems, then "B" is a theorem. For example, from:

$$(p \text{ or } p) \text{ implies } p,$$

and $[(p \text{ or } p) \text{ implies } p]$ implies $(p \text{ implies } p),$

we get the new theorem:

$$p \text{ implies } p.$$

Given an expression to prove, one starts from the set of axioms and theorems already proved, and applies the various rules successively until

---

[1] For easy reference we have numbered axioms and theorems to correspond to their numbers in *Principia Mathematica,* 2nd ed., vol. 1, New York: by A. N. Whitehead and B. Russell, 1935.

the desired expression is produced. The proof is the sequence of expressions, each one validly derived from the previous ones, that leads from the axioms and known theorems to the desired expression.

This is all the background in symbolic logic needed to observe LT in operation. LT "understands" expressions in symbolic logic—that is, there is a simple code for punching expressions on cards so they can be fed into the machine. We give LT the five axioms, instructing it that these are theorems it can assume to be true. LT already knows the rules of inference and the definitions—how to substitute, replace, and detach. Next we give LT a single expression, say expression 2.01, and ask LT to find a proof for it. LT works for about 10 seconds and then prints out the following proof:

(*p* implies not-*p*) implies not-*p*	(theorem 2.01, to be proved)
1. (*A* or *A*) implies *A*	(axiom 1.2)
2. (not-*A* or not-*A*) implies not-*A*	(subs. of not-*A* for *A*)
3. (*A* implies not-*A*) implies not-*A*	(repl. of "or" with "implies")
4. (*p* implies not-*p*) implies not-*p*	(subs. of *p* for *A*; *QED*).

Next we ask LT to prove a fairly advanced theorem (Whitehead and Russell, 1935), theorem 2.45; allowing it to use all 38 theorems proved prior to 2.45. After about 12 minutes, LT produces the following proof:

not (*p* or *q*) implies not-*p*	(theorem 2.45, to be proved)
1. *A* implies (*A* or *B*)	(theorem 2.2)
2. *p* implies (*p* or *q*)	(subs. *p* for *A*, *q* for *B* in 1)
3. (*A* implies *B*) implies (not-*B* implies not-*A*)	(theorem 2.16)
4. [*p* implies (*p* or *q*)] implies [not (*p* or *q*) implies not-*p*]	[subs. *p* for *A*, (*p* or *q*) for *B* in 3]
5. not (*p* or *q*) implies not-*p*	(detach right side of 4, using 2; *QED*).

Finally, all the theorems prior to (2.31) are given to LT (a total of 28); and then LT is asked to prove:

$$[p \text{ or } (q \text{ or } r)] \text{ implies } [(p \text{ or } q) \text{ or } r]. \qquad (2.31)$$

LT works for about 23 minutes and then reports that it cannot prove (2.31), that it has exhausted its resources.

Now, what is there in this behavior of LT that needs to be explained? The specific examples given are difficult problems for most humans, and most humans do not know what processes they use to find proofs, if they find them. There is no known simple procedure that will produce such proofs. Various methods exist for verifying whether any given expression is true or false; the best known procedure is the method of truth tables. But these procedures do not produce a proof in the meaning of Whitehead and Russell. One can invent "automatic" procedures for producing proofs. We will look at one briefly later, but these turn out to require computing times of the orders of thousands of years for the proof of (2.45).

We must clarify why such problems are difficult in the first place, and then show what features of LT account for its successes and failures. These questions will occupy the rest of this study.

Problems, Algorithms, and Heuristics

In describing LT, its environment, and its behavior we will make repeated use of three concepts. The first of these is the concept of *problem*. Abstractly, a person is given a problem if he is given a set of possible solutions, and a test for verifying whether a given element of this set is in fact a solution to his problem.

The reason why problems are problems is that the original set of possible solutions given to the problem-solver can be very large, the actual solutions can be dispersed very widely and rarely throughout it, and the cost of obtaining each new element and of testing it can be very expensive. Thus the problem-solver is not really "given" the set of possible solutions; instead he is given some process for generating the elements of that set in some order. This generator has properties of its own, not usually specified in stating the problem; *e.g.,* there is associated with it a certain cost per element produced, it may be possible to change the order in which it produces the elements, and so on. Likewise the verification test has costs and times associated with it. The problem can be solved if these costs are not too large in relation to the time and computing power available for solution.

One very special and valuable property that a generator of solutions sometimes has is a guarantee that if the problem has a solution, the generator will, sooner or later, produce it. We will call a process that has this property for some problem an *algorithm* for that problem. The guarantee provided by an algorithm is not an unmixed blessing, of course, since nothing has been specified about the cost or time required to produce the solutions. For example, a simple algorithm for opening a combination safe is to try all combinations, testing each one to see if it opens the safe. This algorithm is a typical problem-solving process: there is a generator that produces new combinations in some order, and there is a verifier that determines whether each new combination is in fact a solution to the problem. This search process is an algorithm because it is known that *some* combination will open the safe, and because the generator will exhaust all combinations in a finite interval of time. The algorithm is sufficiently expensive, however, that a combination safe can be used to protect valuables even from people who know the algorithm.

A process that *may* solve a given problem, but offers no guarantees of doing so, is called a *heuristic*[2] for that problem. This lack of a guarantee is not an unmixed evil. The cost inflicted by the lack of guarantee depends on what the process costs and what algorithms are available as alternatives. For most run-of-the-mill problems we have only heuristics, but occasionally we have both algorithms and heuristics as alternatives for solving the same problem. Sometimes, as in the problem of finding maxima for simple differentiable functions, everyone uses the algorithm of setting the first derivative equal to zero; no one sets out to examine all the points on the line one by one as if it were possible. Sometimes, as in chess, everyone plays by heuristic, since no one is able to carry out the algorithm of examining all continuations of the game to termination.

The Problem of Proving Theorems in Logic

Finding a proof for a theorem in symbolic logic can be described as selecting an element from a generated set, as shown by Fig. 1. Consider the *set of all possible sequences of logic expressions*—call it E. Certain of these sequences, a very small minority, will be proofs. A proof sequence satisfies the following test:

Each expression in the sequence is either

1. One of the accepted theorems or axioms, or
2. Obtainable from one or two previous expressions in the sequence by application of one of the three rules of inference.

Call the *set of sequences that are proofs P*. Certain of the sequences in E have the *expression to be proved*—call it X, as their final expression. Call this set of sequences T_X. Then, to find a proof of a given theorem X means to select an element of E that belongs to the intersection of P and T_X. The set E is given implicitly by rules for generating new sequences of logic expressions.

The difficulty of proving theorems depends on the scarcity of elements in the intersection of P and T_X, relative to the number of elements in E. Hence, it depends on the cost and speed of the available generators that produce elements of E, and on the cost and speed of making tests that determine whether an element belongs to T_X or P. The difficulty also de-

---

[2] As a noun, "heuristic" is rare and generally means the art of discovery. The adjective "heuristic" is defined by Webster as: serving to discover or find out. It is in this sense that it is used in the phrase "heuristic process" or "heuristic method." For conciseness, we will use "heuristic" as a noun synonymous with "heuristic process." No other English word appears to have this meaning.

pends on whether generators can be found that guarantee that any element they produce automatically satisfies some of the conditions. Finally, as we shall see, the difficulty depends heavily on what heuristics can be found to guide the selection.

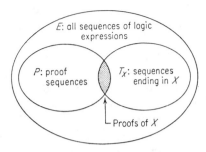

A little reflection, and experience in trying to prove theorems, make it clear that proof sequences for specified theorems are rare indeed. To reveal more precisely why proving

Figure 1. Relationships between E, P, and T_x.

theorems is difficult, we will construct an algorithm for doing this. The algorithm will be based only on the tests and definitions given above, and not on any "deep" inferred properties of symbolic logic. Thus it will reflect the basic nature of theorem proving; that is, its nature prior to building up sophisticated proof techniques. We will call this algorithm the British Museum algorithm, in recognition of the supposed originators of procedures of this type.

The British Museum Algorithm

The algorithm constructs all possible proofs in a systematic manner, checking each time (1) to eliminate duplicates, and (2) to see if the final theorem in the proof coincides with the expression to be proved. With this algorithm the set of one-step proofs is identical with the set of axioms (*i.e.*, each axiom is a one-step proof of itself). The set of n-step proofs is obtained from the set of $(n-1)$-step proofs by making all the permissible substitutions and replacements in the expressions of the $(n-1)$-step proofs, and by making all the permissible detachments of pairs of expressions as permitted by the recursive definition of proof.[3]

Figure 2 shows how the set of n-step proofs increases with n at the very start of the proof-generating process. This enumeration only extends to replacements of "or" with "implies," "implies" with "or," and negation of variables (*e.g.*, "not-p" for "p"). No detachments and no complex substitutions (*e.g.*, "q or r" for "p") are included. No specializations have been made (*e.g.*, substitution of p for q in "p or q"). If we include the specializations, which take three more steps, the algorithm will generate

[3] A number of fussy but not fundamental points must be taken care of in constructing the algorithm. The phrase "all permissible substitutions" needs to be qualified, for there is an infinity of these. Care must be taken not to duplicate expressions that differ only in the names of their variables. We will not go into details here, but simply state that these difficulties can be removed. The essential feature in constructing the algorithm is to allow only one thing to happen in generating each new expression, i.e., one replacement, substitution of "not-p" for "p," etc.

an (estimated) additional 600 theorems, thus providing a set of proofs of 11 steps or less containing almost 1000 theorems, none of them duplicates.

In order to see how this algorithm would provide proofs of specified theorems, we can consider its performance on the sixty-odd theorems of chap. 2 of *Principia*. One theorem (2.01) is obtained in step (4) of the generation, hence is among the first 42 theorems proved. Three more (2.02, 2.03, and 2.04) are obtained in step (6), hence among the first 115. One more (2.05) is obtained in step (8), hence in the first 246. Only one more is included in the first 1000, theorem 2.07. The proofs of all the remainder require complex substitutions or detachment.

We have no way at present to estimate how many proofs must be generated to include proofs of all theorems of chap. 2 of *Principia*. Our best guess is that it might be a hundred million. Moreover, apart from the six theorems listed, there is no reason to suppose that the proofs of these theorems would occur early in the list.

Our information is too poor to estimate more than very roughly the times required to produce such proofs by the algorithm; but we can estimate times of about 16 minutes to do the first 250 theorems of Fig. 2 [*i.e.*, through step (8)] assuming processing times comparable with those in LT. The first part of the algorithm has an additional special property, which holds only to the point where detachment is first used; that no check for duplication is necessary. Thus the time of computing the first few thousand proofs only increases linearly with the number of theorems generated. For the theorems requiring detachments, duplication checks must be made, and the total computing time increases as the square of the number of expressions generated. At this rate it would take hundreds of thousands of years of computation to generate proofs for the theorems in chap. 2.

The nature of the problem of proving theorems is now reasonably clear. When sequences of expressions are produced by a simple and cheap (per element produced) generator, the chance that any particular sequence is the desired proof is exceedingly small. This is true even if the generator produces sequences that always satisfy the most complicated and restrictive of the solution conditions: that each is a proof of something. The set of sequences is so large, and the desired proof

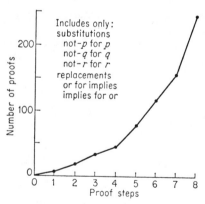

Figure 2. Number of proofs generated by first few steps of British Museum algorithm.

so rare, that no practical amount of computation suffices to find proofs by means of such an algorithm.

The Logic Theory Machine

If LT is to prove any theorems at all it must employ some devices that alter radically the order in which possible proofs are generated, and the way in which they are tested. To accomplish this, LT gives up almost all the guarantees enjoyed by the British Museum algorithm. Its procedures guarantee neither that its proposed sequences are proofs of something, nor that LT will ever find the proof, no matter how much effort is spent. However, they *often* generate the desired proof in a reasonable computing time.

Methods

The major type of heuristic that LT uses we call a *method*. As yet we have no precise definition of a method that distinguishes it from all the other types of routines in LT. Roughly, a method is a reasonably self-contained operation that, if it works, makes a major and permanent contribution toward finding a proof. It is the largest unit of organization in LT, subordinated only to the executive routines necessary to coordinate and select the methods.

THE SUBSTITUTION METHOD

This method seeks a proof for the problem expression by finding an axiom or previously proved theorem that can be transformed, by a series of substitutions for variables and replacements of connectives, into the problem expression.

THE DETACHMENT METHOD

This method attempts, using the rule of detachment, to substitute for the problem expression a new subproblem which, if solved, will provide a proof for the problem expression. Thus, if the problem expression is B, the method of detachment searches for an axiom or theorem of the form "A implies B." If one is found, A is set up as a new subproblem. If A can be proved, then, since "A implies B" is a theorem, B will also be proved.

THE CHAINING METHODS

These methods use the transitivity of the relation of implication to create a new subproblem which, if solved, will provide a proof for the problem expression. Thus, if the problem expression is "a implies c," the method of forward chaining searches for an axiom or theorem of the form "a

implies *b*." If one is found, "*b* implies *c*" is set up as a new subproblem. Chaining backward works analogously: it seeks a theorem of the form "*b* implies *c*," and if one is found, "*a* implies *b*" is set up as a new subproblem.

Each of these methods is an independent unit. They are alternatives to one another, and can be used in sequence, one working on the subproblems generated by another. Each of them produces a major part of a proof. Substitution actually proves theorems, and the other three generate subproblems, which can become the intermediate expressions in a proof sequence.

These methods give no guarantee that they will work. There is no guarantee that a theorem can be found that can be used to carry out a proof by the substitution method, or a theorem that will produce a subproblem by any of the other three methods. Even if a subproblem is generated, there is no guarantee that it is part of the desired proof sequence, or even that it is part of any proof sequence (*e.g.*, it can be false). On the other hand, the generated methods do guarantee that any subproblem generated is part of a sequence of expressions that ends in the desired theorem (this is one of the conditions that a sequence be a proof). The methods also guarantee that each expression of the sequence is derived by the rules of inference from the preceding ones (a second condition of proof). What is not guaranteed is that the beginning of the sequence can be completed with axioms or previously proved theorems.

There is also no guarantee that the combination of the four methods, used in any fashion whatsoever and with unlimited computing effort, comprises a sufficient set of methods to prove all theorems. In fact, we have discovered a theorem [(2.13), "*p* or not-not-not-*p*"] which the four methods of LT cannot prove. All the subproblems generated for (2.13) after a certain point are false, and therefore cannot lead to a proof.

We have yet no general theory to explain why the methods transform LT into an effective problem-solver. That they do, in conjunction with the other mechanisms to be described shortly, will be demonstrated amply in the remainder of this study. Several factors may be involved. First, the methods organize the sequences of individual processing steps into larger units that can be handled as such. Each processing step can be oriented toward the special function it performs in the unit as a whole, and the units can be manipulated and organized as entities by the higher-level routines.

Apart from their "unitizing" effect, the methods that generate subproblems work "backward" from the desired theorem to axioms or known theorems rather than "forward" as did the British Museum algorithm. Since there is only one theorem to be proved, but a number of known true theorems, the efficacy of working backward may be analogous to the ease with which a needle can find its way out of a haystack, compared with the difficulty of someone finding the lone needle in the haystack.

The Executive Routine

In LT the four methods are organized by an executive routine, whose flow diagram is shown in Fig. 3.

1. When a new problem is presented to LT, the substitution method is tried first, using all the axioms and theorems that LT has been told to assume, and that are now stored in a *theorem list*.

2. If substitution fails, the detachment method is tried, and as each new subproblem is created by a successful detachment, an attempt is made to prove the new subproblem by the substitution method. If substitution fails again, the subproblem is added to a *subproblem list*.

3. If detachment fails for all the theorems in the theorem list, the same cycle is repeated with forward chaining, and then with backward chaining: try to create a subproblem; try to prove it by the substitution method; if unsuccessful, put the new subproblem on the list. By the nature of the methods, if the substitution method ever succeeds with a single subproblem, the original theorem is proved.

4. If all the methods have been tried on the original problem and no proof has been produced, the executive routine selects the next untried subproblem from the subproblem list, and makes the same sequence of attempts with it. This process continues until (1) a proof is found, (2) the time allotted for finding a proof is used up, (3) there is no more available memory space in the machine, or (4) no untried problems remain on the subproblem list.

In the three examples cited earlier, the proof of (2.01) [(p implies not-p) implies not-p] was obtained by the substitution method directly, hence did not involve use of the subproblem list.

The proof of (2.45) [not (p or q) implies not-p] was achieved by an application of the detachment method followed by a substitution. This proof required LT to create a subproblem, and to use the substitution method on it. It did not require LT ever to select any sub-

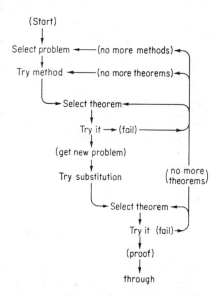

Figure 3. General flow diagram of LT.

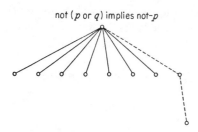

not $(p$ or $q)$ implies not-p

Figure 4. Subproblem tree of proof by LT of (2.45) (all previous theorems available).

problem from the subproblem list, since the substitution was successful. Figure 4 shows the *tree of subproblems* corresponding to the proof of (2.45). The subproblems are given in the form of a downward branching tree. Each node is a subproblem, the original problem being the single node at the top. The lines radiating down from a node lead to the new subproblems generated from the subproblem corresponding to the node. The proof sequence is given by the dashed line; the top link was constructed by the detachment method, and the bottom link by the substitution method. The other links extending down from the original problem lead to other subproblems generated by the detachment method (but not provable by direct substitution) prior to the time LT tried the theorem that leads to the final proof.

LT did not prove theorem 2.31, also mentioned earlier, and gave as its reason that it could think of nothing more to do. This means that LT had considered all subproblems on the subproblem list (there were six in this case) and had no new subproblems to work on. In none of the examples mentioned did LT terminate because of time or space limitations; however, this is the most common result in the cases where LT does not find a proof. Only rarely does LT run out of things to do.

This section has described the organization of LT in terms of methods. We have still to examine in detail why it is that this organization, in connection with the additional mechanisms to be described below, allows LT to prove theorems with a reasonable amount of computing effort.

The Matching Process

The times required to generate proofs for even the simplest theorems by the British Museum algorithm are larger than the times required by LT by factors ranging from five (for one particular theorem) to a hundred and upward. Let us consider an example from the earliest part of the generation, where we have detailed information about the algorithm. The 79th theorem generated by the algorithm (see Fig. 2) is theorem 2.02 of *Principia,* one of the theorems we asked LT to prove. This theorem, "p implies (q implies p)," is generated by the algorithm in about 158 seconds with a sequence of substitutions and replacements; it is proved by LT in about 10 seconds with the method of substitution. The reason for the difference becomes apparent if we focus attention on axiom 1.3, "p implies (q or p)," from which the theorem is derived in either scheme.

Figure 5 shows the tree of proofs of the first twelve theorems obtained from (1.3) by the algorithm. The theorem 2.02 is node (9) on the tree and is obtained by substitution of "not-q" for "q" in axiom 1.3 to reach node (5); and then by replacing the "(not-q or p)" by "(q implies p)" in (5) to get (9). The 9th theorem generated from axiom 1.3 is the 79th generated from the five axioms considered together.

This proof is obtained directly by LT using the following *matching* procedure. We compare the axiom with (9), the expression to be proved:

$$p \text{ implies } (q \text{ or } p) \qquad\qquad (1.3)$$
$$p \text{ implies } (q \text{ implies } p). \qquad\qquad (9)$$

First, by a direct comparison, LT determines that the main connectives are identical. Second, LT determines that the variables to the left of the main connectives are identical. Third, LT determines that the connectives within parentheses on the right-hand sides are different. It is necessary to replace the "or" with "implies," but in order to do this (in accordance with the definition of implies) there must be a negation sign before the variable that precedes the "or." Hence, LT first replaces the "q" on the right-hand side with "not-q" to get the required negation sign, obtaining (5). Now LT can change the "or" to "implies," and determines that the resulting expression is identical with (9).

The matching process allowed LT to proceed directly down the branch from (1) through (5) to (9) without even exploring the other branches. Quantitatively, it looked at only two expressions instead of eight, thus reducing the work of comparison by a factor of four. Actually, the saving is even greater, since the matching procedure does not deal with whole expressions, but with a single pair of elements at a time.

An important source of efficiency in the matching process is that it proceeds componentwise, obtaining at each step a feedback of the results of a substitution or replacement that can be used to guide the next step. This feedback keeps the search on the right branch of the tree of possible ex-

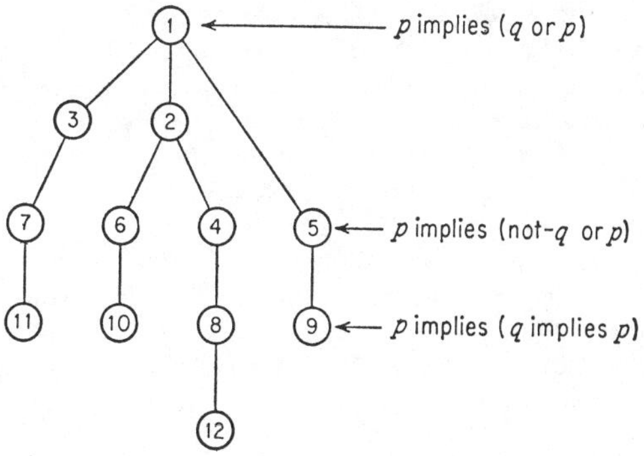

Figure 5. Proof tree of proof 2.02 by British Museum algorithm (using axiom 1.3).

p implies (q or p)

p implies (not-q or p)

p implies (q implies p)

pressions. It is not important for an efficient search that the goal be known from the beginning; it is crucial that hints of "warmer" or "colder" occur as the search proceeds.[4] Closely related to this feedback is the fact that where LT is called on to make a substitution or replacement at any step, it can determine immediately what variable or connective to substitute or replace by direct comparison with the problem expression, and without search.

Thus far we have assumed that LT knows at the beginning that (1.3) is the appropriate axiom to use. Without this information, it would begin matching with each axiom in turn, abandoning it for the next one if the matching should prove impossible. For example, if it tries to match the theorem against axiom 1.2, it determines almost immediately (on the second test) that "p or p" cannot be made into "p" by substitution. Thus, the matching process permits LT to abandon unprofitable lines of search as well as guiding it to correct substitutions and replacements.

MATCHING IN THE SUBSTITUTION METHODS

The matching process is an essential part of the substitution method. Without it, the substitution method is just that part of the British Museum algorithm that uses only replacements and substitutions. With it, LT is able, either directly or in combination with the other methods, to prove many theorems with reasonable effort.

To obtain data on its performance, LT was given the task of proving in sequence the first 52 theorems of *Principia*. In each case, LT was given the axioms plus all the theorems previously proved in chap. 2 as the material from which to work (regardless of whether LT had proved the theorems itself).[5]

Of the 52 theorems, proofs were found for a total 38 (73 per cent). These proofs were obtained by various combinations of methods, but the substitution method was an essential component of all of them. Seventeen of these proofs, almost a half, were accomplished by the substitution method alone. Subjectively evaluated, the theorems that were proved by

[4] The following analogy may be instructive. Changing the symbols in a logic expression until the "right" expression is obtained is like turning the dials on a safe until the right combination is obtained. Suppose two safes, each with ten dials and ten numbers on a dial. The first safe gives a signal (a "click") when any given dial is turned to the correct number; the second safe clicks only when all ten dials are correct. Trial-and-error search will open the first safe, on the average, in 50 trials; the second safe, in five billion trials.

[5] The version of LT used for seeking solutions of the 52 problems included a similarity test (see next section). Since the matching process is more important than the similarity test, we have presented the facts about matching first, using adjusted statistics. A notion of the sample sizes can be gained from Table 1. The sample was limited to the first 52 of the 67 theorems in chap. 2 of *Principia* because of memory limitations of JOHNNIAC.

the substitution method alone have the appearance of "corollaries" of the theorems they are derived from; they occur fairly close to them in the chapter, generally requiring three or fewer attempts at matching per theorem proved (54 attempts for 17 theorems).

The performance of the substitution method on the subproblems is somewhat different, due, we think, to the kind of selectivity implicit in the order of theorems in *Principia*. In 338 attempts at solving subproblems by substitution, there were 21 successes (6.2 per cent). Thus, there was about one chance in three of proving an original problem directly by the substitution method, but only about one chance in 16 of so proving a subproblem generated from the original problem.

MATCHING IN DETACHMENT AND CHAINING

So far the matching process has been considered only as a part of the substitution method, but it is also an essential component of the other three methods. In detachment, for example, a theorem of form "*A* implies *B*" is sought, where *B* is identical with the expression to be proved. The chances of finding such a theorem are negligible unless we allow some modification of *B* to make it match the theorem to be proved. Hence, once a theorem is selected from the theorem list, its right-hand subexpression is matched against the expression to be proved. An analogous procedure is used in the chaining methods.

We can evaluate the performance of the detachment and chaining methods with the same sample of problems used for evaluating the substitution method. However, a successful match with the former three methods generates a subproblem and does not directly prove the theorem. With the detachment method, an average of three new subproblems were generated for each application of the method; with forward chaining the average was 2.7; and with backward chaining the average was 2.2. For all the methods, this represents about one subproblem per $7\frac{1}{2}$ theorems tested (the number of theorems available varied slightly).

As in the case of substitution, when these three methods were applied to the original problem, the chances of success were higher than when they were applied to subproblems. When applied to the original problem, the number of subproblems generated averaged eight to nine; when applied to subproblems derived from the original, the number of subproblems generated fell to an average of two or three.

In handling the first 52 problems in chap. 2 of *Principia*, 17 theorems were proved in one step—that is, in one application of substitution. Nineteen theorems were proved in two steps, 12 by detachment followed by substitution, and seven by chaining forward followed by substitution. Two others were proved in three steps. Hence, 38 theorems were proved in all. There are no two-step proofs by backward chaining, since, for two-step proofs only, if there is a proof by backward chaining, there is also one by forward chaining. In 14 cases LT failed to find a proof. Most of these unsuccessful attempts were terminated by time or space limitations. One of these 14 theorems we know LT cannot prove, and one other we believe it cannot prove. Of the remaining twelve, most of them can be proved by LT if it has sufficient time and memory (see section on subproblems, however).

Similarity Tests and Descriptions

Matching eliminates enough of the trial and error in substitutions and replacements to make LT into a successful problem solver. Matching permeates all of the methods, and without it none of them would be useful within practical amounts of computing effort. However, a large amount of search is still used in finding the correct theorems with which matching works. Returning to the performance of LT in chap. 2, we find that the over-all chances of a particular match being successful are 0.3 per cent for substitution, 13.4 per cent for detachment, 13.8 per cent for forward chaining, and 9.4 per cent for backward chaining.

The amount of search through the theorem list can be reduced by interposing a screening process that will reject any theorem for matching that has low likelihood of success. LT has such a screening device, called the *similarity test*. Two logic expressions are defined to be similar if both their left-hand and right-hand sides are equal, with respect to, (1) the maximum number of *levels* from the main connective to any variable; (2) the number of *distinct* variables; and (3) the number of *variable places*. Speaking intuitively, two logic expressions are "similar" if they look alike, and look alike if they are similar. Consider for example:

$$(p \text{ or } q) \text{ implies } (q \text{ or } p) \qquad (1)$$
$$p \text{ implies } (q \text{ or } p) \qquad (2)$$
$$r \text{ implies } (m \text{ implies } r). \qquad (3)$$

By the definition of similarity, (2) and (3) are similar, but (1) is not similar to either (2) or (3).

In all of the methods LT applies the similarity tests to all expressions to be matched, and only applies the matching routine if the expressions are similar; otherwise it passes on to the next theorem in the theorem list. The similarity test reduces substantially the number of matchings attempted, as the numbers in Table 1 show, and correspondingly raises the probability of a match if the matching is attempted. The effect is particularly strong in substitution, where the similarity test reduces the matchings attempted by a factor of ten, and increases the probability of a successful match by a factor of ten. For the other methods attempted matchings were

TABLE 1   Statistics of Similarity Tests and Matching

Method	Theorems considered	Theorems similar	Theorems matched	Per cent similar of theorems considered	Per cent matched of theorems similar
Substitution	11,298	993	37	8.8	3.7
Detachment	1,591	406	210	25.5	51.7
Chain. forward	869	200	120	23.0	60.0
Chain. backward	673	146	63	21.7	43.2

reduced by a factor of four or five, and the probability of a match increased by the same factor.

These figures reveal a gross, but not necessarily a net, gain in performance through the use of the similarity test. There are two reasons why all the gross gain may not be realized. First, the similarity test is only a heuristic. It offers no guarantee that it will let through only expressions that will subsequently match. The similarity test also offers no guarantee that it will not reject expressions that would match if attempted. The similarity test does not often commit this type of error (corresponding to a type II statistical error), as will be shown later. However, even rare occurrences of such errors can be costly. One example occurs in the proof of theorem 2.07:

$$p \text{ implies } (p \text{ or } p). \tag{2.07}$$

This theorem is proved simply by substituting p for q in axiom 1.3:

$$p \text{ implies } (q \text{ or } p). \tag{1.3}$$

However, the similarity test, because it demands equality in the number of distinct variables on the right-hand side, calls (2.07) and (1.3) dissimilar because (2.07) contains only p while (1.3) contains p and q. LT discovers the proof through chaining forward, where it checks for a direct match before creating the new subproblem, but the proof is about five times as expensive as when the similarity test is omitted.

The second reason why the gross gain will not all be realized is that the similarity test is not costless, and in fact for those theorems which pass the test the cost of the similarity test must be paid in addition to the cost of the matching. We will examine these costs in the next section when we consider the effort LT expends.

Experiments have been carried out with a weaker similarity test, which compares only the number of variable places on both sides of the expression. This test will not commit the particular type II error cited above, and (2.07) is proved by substitution using it. Apart from this, the modification had remarkably little effect on performance. On a sample of ten problems it admitted only 10 per cent more similar theorems and about 10 per cent more subproblems. The reason why the two tests do not differ more radically is that there is a high correlation among the descriptive measures.

Effort in LT

So far we have focused entirely on the performance characteristics of the heuristics in LT, except to point out the tremendous difference between the computing effort required by LT and by the British Museum algorithm. However, it is clear that each additional test, search, description, and the like, has its costs in computing effort as well as its gains in performance. The costs must always be balanced against the performance gains, since there are always alternative heuristics which could be added to the system in place of those being used. In this section we will analyze the computing effort used by LT. The memory space used by the various processes also constitutes a cost, but one that will not be discussed in this study.

MEASURING EFFORTS

LT is written in an interpretive language or pseudocode, which is described in the companion paper to this one. LT is defined in terms of a set of primitive operations, which, in turn, are defined by subroutines in JOHNNIAC machine language. These primitives provide a convenient unit of effort, and all effort measurements will be given in terms of total number of primitives executed. The relative frequencies of the different primitives are reasonably constant, and, therefore, the total number of primitives is an adequate index of effort. The average time per primitive is quite constant at about 30 milliseconds, although for very low totals (less than 1000 primitives) a figure of about 20 milliseconds seems better.

COMPUTING EFFORT AND PERFORMANCE

On *a priori* grounds we would expect the amount of computing effort required to solve a logic problem to be roughly proportional to the total number of theorems examined (*i.e.,* tested for similarity, if there is a similarity routine; or tested for matching, if there is not) by the various methods in the course of solving the problem. In fact, this turns out to be a reasonably good predictor of effort; but the fit to data is much improved if we assign greater weight to theorems considered for detachment and chaining than to theorems considered for substitution.

Actual and predicted efforts are compared below (with the full similarity test included, and excluding theorems proved by substitution) on the assumption that the number of primitives per theorem considered is twice as great for chaining as for substitution, and three times as great for detachment. About 45 primitives are executed per theorem considered with the substitution method (hence 135 with detachment and 90 with chaining). As Table 2 shows, the estimates are generally accurate within a few per cent, except for theorem 2.06, for which the estimate is too low.

TABLE 2   Effort Statistics with
"Precompute Description" Routine

	Total primitives, thousands	
Theorem	Actual	Estimate
2.06	3.2	0.8
2.07	4.3	4.4
2.08	3.5	3.3
2.11	2.2	2.2
2.13	24.5	24.6
2.14	3.3	3.2
2.15	15.8	13.6
2.18	34.1	35.8
2.25	11.1	11.5

There is an additional source of variation not shown in the theorems selected for Table 2. The descriptions used in the similarity test must be computed from the logic expressions. Since the descriptions of the theorems are used over and over again, LT computes these at the start of a problem and stores the values with the theorems, so they do not have to be computed again. However, as the number of theorems increases, the space devoted to storing the precomputed descriptions becomes prohibitive, and LT switches to recomputing them each time it needs them. With recomputation, the problem effort is still roughly proportional to the total number of theorems considered, but now the number of primitives per theorem is around 70 for the substitution method, 210 for detachment, and 140 for chaining.

Our analysis of the effort statistics shows, then, that in the first approximation the effort required to prove a theorem is proportional to the number of theorems that have to be considered before a proof is found; the number of theorems considered is an effort measure for evaluating a heuristic. A good heuristic, by securing the consideration of the "right" theorems early in the proof, reduces the expected number of theorems to be considered before a proof is found.

EVALUATION OF THE SIMILARITY TEST

As we noted in the previous section, to evaluate an improved heuristic, account must be taken of any additional computation that the improvement introduces The net advantage may be less than the gross advantage, or the extra computing effort may actually cancel out the gross gain in selectivity. We are now in a position to evaluate the similarity routines as preselectors of theorems for matching.

A number of theorems were run, first with the full similarity routine, then with the modified similarity routine (which tests only the number of variable places), and finally with no similarity test at all. We also made some comparisons with both precomputed and recomputed descriptions.

When descriptions are precomputed, the computing effort is less with the full similarity test than without it; the factor of saving ranged from 10 to 60 per cent (*e.g.,* 3534/5206 for theorem 2.08). However, if LT must recompute the descriptions every time, the full similarity test is actually more expensive than no similarity test at all (*e.g.,* 26,739/22,914 for theorem 2.45).

The modified similarity test fares somewhat better. For example, in proving (2.45) it requires only 18,035 primitives compared to the 22,914 for no similarity test (see the paragraph above). These comparisons involve recomputed descriptions; we have no figures for precomputed descriptions, but the additional saving appears small since there is much less to compute with the abridged than with the full test.

Thus the similarity test is rather marginal, and does not provide anything like the factors of improvement achieved by the matching process, although we have seen that the performance figures seem to indicate much more substantial gains. The reason for the discrepancy is not difficult to find. In a sense, the matching process consists of two parts. One is a testing part that locates the differences between elements and diagnoses the corrective action to be taken. The other part comprises the processes of substituting and replacing. The latter part is the major expense in a matching that works, but most of this effort is saved when the matching fails. Thus matching turns out to be inexpensive for precisely those expressions that the similarity test excludes.

Subproblems

LT can prove a great many theorems in symbolic logic. However, there are numerous theorems that LT cannot prove, and we may describe LT as having reached a plateau in its problem solving ability.

Figure 6 shows the amount of effort required for the problems LT solved out of the sample of 52. Almost all the proofs that LT found took less than 30,000 primitives of effort. Among the numerous attempts at proofs that went beyond this effort limit, only a few succeeded, and these required a total effort that was very much greater.

The predominance of short proofs is even more striking than the approximate upper limit of 30,000 primitives suggests. The proofs by substitution

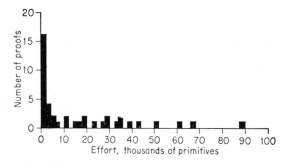

Figure 6. Distribution of LT's proofs by effort. Data include all proofs from attempts on the first 52 theorems in chap. 2 of *Principia*.

—almost half of the total—required about 1000 primitives or less each. The effort required for the longest proof—89,000 primitives—is some 250 times the effort required for the short proofs. We estimate that to prove the 12 additional theorems that we believe LT can prove requires the effort limit to be extended to about a million primitives.

From these data we infer that LT's power as a problem solver is largely restricted to problems of a certain class. While it is logically possible for LT to solve others by large expenditures of effort, major adjustments are needed in the program to extend LT's powers to essentially new classes of problems. We believe that this situation is typical: good heuristics produce differences in performance of large orders of magnitude, but invariably a "plateau" is reached that can be surpassed only with quite different heuristics. These new heuristics will again make differences of orders of magnitude. In this section we shall analyze LT's difficulties with those theorems it cannot prove, with a view to indicating the general type of heuristic that might extend its range of effectiveness.

The Subproblem Tree

Let us examine the proof of theorem 2.17 when all the preceding theorems are available. This is the proof that cost LT 89,000 primitives. It is reproduced below, using chaining as a rule of inference (each chaining could be expanded into two detachments, to conform strictly to the system of *Principia*).

(not-q implies not-p) implies (p-implies q)	(theorem 2.17, to be proved)
1. A implies not-not-A	(theorem 2.12)
2. p implies not-not-p	(subs. p for A in 1)
3. (A implies B) implies [(B implies C) implies (A implies C)]	(theorem 2.06)
4. (p implies not-not-p) implies [(not-not-p implies q) implies (p implies q)]	(subs. p for A, not-not-p for B, q for C in 3)

5. (not-not-*p* implies *q*) implies (*p* im- (det. 4 from 3)
plies *q*)

6. (not-*A* implies *B*) implies (not-*B* (theorem 2.15)
implies *A*)

7. (not-*q* implies not-*p*) implies (not- (subs. *q* for *A*, not-*p* for *B*)
not-*p* implies *q*)

8. (not-*q* implies not-*p*) implies (*p* im- (chain 7 and 5; *QED*)
plies *q*)

The proof is longer than either of the two given earlier. In terms of LT's methods it takes three steps instead of two or one: a forward chaining, a detachment, and a substitution. This leads to the not surprising notion, given human experience, that length of proof is an important variable in determining total effort: short proofs will be easy and long proofs difficult, and difficulty will increase more than proportionately with length of proof. Indeed, all the one-step proofs require 500 to 1500 primitives, while the number of primitives for two-step proofs ranges from 3000 to 50,000. Further, LT has obtained only six proofs longer than two steps, and these require from 10,000 to 90,000 primitives.

The significance of length of proof can be seen by comparing Fig. 7, which gives the proof tree for (2.17), with Fig. 4, which gives the proof tree for (2.45), a two-step proof. In going one step deeper in the case of (2.17), LT had to generate and examine many more subproblems. A comparison of the various statistics of the proofs confirms this statement: the problems are roughly similar in other respects (*e.g.*, in effort per theorem considered); hence the difference in total effort can be attributed largely to the difference in number of subproblems generated.

Let us examine some more evidence for this conclusion. Figure 8 shows the subproblem tree for the proof of (2.27) from the axioms, which is the only four-step proof LT has achieved to date. The tree reveals immediately

(not-*q* implies not-*p*) implies (*p* implies *q*)

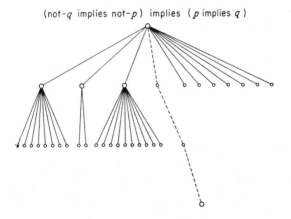

Figure 7. Subproblem tree of proof by LT of (2.17) (all previous theorems available).

why LT was able to find the proof. Instead of branching widely at each point, multiplying rapidly the number of subproblems to be looked at, LT in this case only generates a few subproblems at each point. It thus manages to penetrate to a depth of four steps with a reasonable amount of effort (38,367 primitives). If this tree had branched as the other two did, LT would have had to process about 250 subproblems before arriving at a proof, and the total effort would have been at least 250,000 primitives. The statistics quoted earlier on the effectiveness of subproblem generation support the general hypothesis that the number of subproblems to be examined increases more or less exponentially with the depth of the proof.

The difficulty is that LT uses an algorithmic procedure to govern its generation of subproblems. Apart from a few subproblems excluded by the type II errors of the similarity test, the procedure guarantees that all subproblems that can be generated by detachment and chaining will in fact be obtained (duplications are eliminated). LT also uses an algorithm to determine the order in which it will try to solve subproblems. The subproblems are considered in order of generation, so that a proof will not be missed through failure to consider a subproblem that has been generated.

Because of these systematic principles incorporated in the executive program, and because the methods, applied to a theorem list averaging 30 expressions in length, generate a large number of subproblems, LT must find a rare sequence that leads to a proof by searching through a very large set of such sequences. For proofs of one step, this is no problem at all; for proofs of two steps, the set to be examined is still of reasonable size in relation to the computing power available. For proofs of three steps, the size of the search already presses LT against its computing limits; and if one or two additional steps are added the amount of search required to

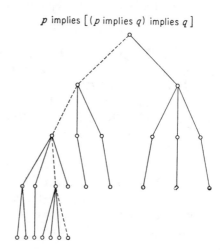

p implies $[(p$ implies $q)$ implies $q]$

Figure 8. Subproblem tree of proof by LT of (2.27) (using the axioms).

find a proof exceeds any amount of computing power that could practically be made available.

The set of subproblems generated by the Logic Theory Machine, however large it may seem, is exceedingly selective and rich in proofs compared with the set through which the British Museum algorithm searches. Hence, the latter algorithm could find proofs in a reasonable time for only the simplest theorems, while proofs for a much larger number are accessible with LT. The line dividing the possible from the impossible for any given problem-solving procedure is relatively sharp; hence a further increase in problem-solving power, comparable to that obtained in passing from the British Museum algorithm to LT, will require a corresponding enrichment of the heuristic.

Modification of the Logic Theory Machine

There are many possible ways to modify LT so that it can find proofs of more than two steps in a way which has reason and insight, instead of by brute force. First, the unit cost of processing subproblems can be substantially reduced so that a given computing effort will handle many more subproblems. (This does not, perhaps, change the "brute force" character of the process, but makes it feasible in terms of effort.) Second, LT can be modified so that it will select for processing only subproblems that have a high probability of leading to a proof. One way to do this is to screen subproblems before they are put on the subproblem list, and eliminate the unlikely ones altogether. Another way is to reduce selectively the number of subproblems generated.

For example, to reduce the number of subproblems generated, we may limit the lists of theorems available for generating them. That this approach may be effective is suggested by the statistics we have already cited, which show that the number of subproblems generated by a method per theorem examined is relatively constant (about one subproblem per seven theorems).

An impression of how the number of available theorems affects the generation of subproblems may be gained by comparing the proof trees of (2.17) (Fig. 7) and (2.27) (Fig. 8). The broad tree for (2.17) was produced with a list of twenty theorems, while the deep tree for (2.27) was produced with a list of only five theorems. The smaller theorem list in the latter case generated fewer subproblems at each application of one of the methods.

Another example of the same point is provided by two proofs of theorem 2.48 obtained with different lists of available theorems. In the one case, (2.48) was proved starting with all prior theorems on the theorem list; in the other case it was proved starting only with the axioms and theorem 2.16. We had conjectured that the proof would be more difficult to obtain under the latter conditions, since a longer proof chain would have to be constructed than under the former. In this we were wrong: with the longer theorem list, LT proved theorem 2.48 in two steps, employing 51,450 primitives of effort. With the shorter list, LT proved the theorem in three steps, but with only 18,558 primitives, one-third as many as before. Examination of the first proof shows that the many "irrelevant" theorems on the list took a great deal of processing effort. The comparison provides a dramatic demonstration of the fact that a problem solver may be encumbered by too much information, just as he may be handicapped by too little.

We have only touched on the possibilities for modifying LT, and have seen some hints in LT's current behavior about their potential effectiveness. All of the avenues mentioned earlier appear to offer worthwhile modifications of the program. We hope to report on these explorations at a later time.

Conclusion

We have provided data on the performance of a complex information processing system that is capable of finding proofs for theorems in elementary symbolic logic. We have used these data to analyze and illustrate the difference between systematic, algorithmic processes, on the one hand, and heuristic, problem-solving processes, on the other. We have shown how heuristics give the program power to solve problems in a reasonable computing time that could be solved algorithmically only in large numbers of years. Finally, we have assessed the limitations of the present program of the Logic Theory Machine and have indicated some of the directions that improvement would have to take to extend its powers to problems at new levels of difficulty.

Our explorations of the Logic Theory Machine represent a step in a program of research on complex information processing systems that is aimed at developing a theory of such systems and applying that theory to such fields as computer programming and human learning and problem-solving.

REALIZATION OF A
GEOMETRY - THEOREM PROVING
MACHINE

by H. Gelernter

Introduction

Few of those who have seen a modern high-speed digital computer digest and transform a mass of data in less time than it takes to follow the process in the mind can suppress a certain amount of speculation concerning the future of such machines. Under the assumption that the computer is operating at the mere threshhold of its capacity in performing the tasks we have thus far delegated to it, a long-range program directed at the problem of "intelligent" behavior and learning in machines has been established at the IBM Research Center in New York (Gelernter and Rochester, 1958). In particular the technique of heuristic programming is under detailed investigation as a means to the end of applying large-scale digital computers to the solution of a difficult class of problems currently considered to be beyond their capabilities; namely those problems that seem to require the agent of human intelligence and ingenuity for their solution. It is difficult to characterize such problems further, except, perhaps, to remark rather vaguely that they generally involve complex decision processes in a potentially infinite and uncontrollable environment.

If, however, we should restrict the universe of problems to those that amount to the discovery of a proof for a theorem in some well-defined formal system, then the distinguishing characteristics of those problems of special interest to us are brought clearly into focus. We should like our machine to be able to prove many of the theorems presented to it in a formal system that is manifestly undecidable. Further, as the machine

134

gains "experience" in proving theorems, we should expect it to be able to solve problems that were earlier beyond its capabilities.

The requirement that a machine should deal with undecidable systems places a fundamental restriction on its modus operandi. Finding a suitable algorithm, the obvious technique for the solution of problems on a digital computer, is no longer acceptable for the simple reason that no such algorithm exists. An exhaustive search for the initial axioms and theorems of the proof, combined with exhaustive development of the proof sequence by systematically applying the rules of transformation until the required proof has been produced, has been shown to be much too time-consuming for so simple a logic as propositional calculus (Newell, Shaw and Simon, 1957a). It is a fortiori out of the question for any of the more interesting logics. A remaining alternative is to have the machine rely upon heuristic methods, as people usually do under similar circumstances.

Heuristic Methods

A heuristic method is a provisional and plausible procedure whose purpose is to discover the solution of a particular problem at hand. The use of heuristic methods by the human mathematician is quite well understood, at least in its less subtle forms. The reader is referred to the excellent two-volume treatise by Prof. G. Polya (1954) for a definitive treatment of heuristics and mathematical discovery. A machine that functioned under the full set of principles indicated by Polya would be a formidable problem-solver in mathematics, and would be well on the way toward satisfying Turing's requirements for a machine able to compete successfully in the "imitation game" (1950). Such a machine, however, lies in the indefinite future, for the art of instructing a computer is yet in too primitive a state to consider translating Polya into machine language. As a representative problem more in keeping with the present state of computer technology, we have selected the discovery of proofs for theorems in elementary euclidean plane geometry in the manner, let us say, of a high-school sophomore. This problem contains in relatively pure form the difficulties we must surmount in order to attain our stated goal. It must be emphasized that although plane geometry will yield to a decision algorithm, the proofs offered by the machine will not be of this nature. The methods developed will be no less valid for problem-solving in systems where no such decision algorithm exists.

Although we have narrowed the scope of our study to include only those machines that deal with formal systems, there is ample justification for such a restriction. First, the concept of a problem is now well defined, as is the concept of a solution for that problem. Second, our ultimate goal stands clearly before us; it is the design of an efficient theorem-prover in some undecidable system. And, finally, just as manipulation of numbers in arithmetic is the fundamental mode of operation in contemporary computers, manipulation of symbols in formal systems is likely to be the fundamental operating mode of the more sophisticated problem-solving computers of the future. It seems clear that while the problems of greatest concern to lay society will be, for the most part, not completely formalizable, they will have to be expressed in some sort of formal system before they can be dealt with by machine.[1]

Our problem, then, is a statement (or string) in some formal logistic system. A solution for the problem will be a sequence of statements, each of which comprises a string of symbols of the alphabet of the system. The last string of the solution will be the problem itself; the first will always be an axiom or previously established theorem of the system. Every other string will be immediately inferable from some set preceding it or will itself be an axiom or previously established theorem.[2] It is the task of the machine to choose from its stock of axioms and theorems the appropriate ones for the base of the proof, and to generate from these the remaining strings necessary to complete the proof.

The problem of theorem-proving is, in a sense, of a particularly simple nature. Once a sequence of expressions is found that passes the test for a proof of the theorem (such a test always exists), one may, so to speak, "close the book" on that problem, provided that no stipulations have been made concerning the elegance required of the proof. But, basing our estimate on the work of Newell, Shaw, and Simon (1957), any computer extant would require times of the order of a thousand years to prove a not uncommon ten-step geometry theorem by exhaustively developing sequences until one emerged that passed the test for a proof. What is clearly called for is a technique for generating sequences with a much higher *a priori* probability of being the solution to the problem than those generated by an exhaustion algorithm.

As did the *Logic Theorist* of Newell, Shaw, and Simon, the geometry machine relies upon the well-known analytic method to achieve this end. By working backward, the machine is assured that every sequence it considers does indeed terminate in the required theorem. This in itself, however, represents no striking improvement over exhaustion without additional heuristics, for the advantages of working backward are purchased at a steep price; each sequence generated, while terminating properly, is no longer guaranteed to be a proof of anything at all. Indeed, most of the strings generated in this way will be false! But it is here that the great

---

[1] For a critique of some attempts to formalize scientific, but nonmathematical theories, see Dunham, Fridshal, and Sward (1959).

[2] The machine will use the deduction theorem to get ⊢ {premises} ⊃ {conclusions} from {premises} ⊢ {conclusions}.

power of the analytic method lies, for if one could find a way of making their falseness manifest, such sequences could be immediately rejected, allowing most of the deadwood to be pruned away from the highly branched problem-solving tree. The set of sequences generated under such a process would contain fewer members by many orders of magnitude by the time the search reached any depth, and the density of possible proofs for the theorem among them would be proportionately greater. It is here, too, that the geometry machine finds the additional theorem-proving power necessary for the complex formal system assigned to it; theorem-proving power that was not necessary, and therefore not sought for in the propositional calculus machine of Newell, Shaw, and Simon (Polya, 1954). Like the human mathematician, the geometry machine makes use of the potent heuristic properties of a diagram to help it distinguish the true from the false sequences. Although the diagram is useful to the machine in other ways as well, the single heuristic "Reject as false any statement that is not valid in the diagram" is sufficient to enable the machine to prove a large class of interesting theorems, some of which contain a certain trivial kind of construction.

Before examining the internal structure of the geometry machine in some detail, we remark on two fundamental, if obvious, principles that must guide the choice of heuristics for any problem-solving machine. A heuristic is, in a very real sense, a filter that is interposed between the solution generator and the solution evaluator for a given class of problems. The first requirement for such a filter is a consequence of the fact that its introduction into the system is never costless. It must, therefore, be sufficiently "nonporous" to result in a net gain in problem-solving efficiency. Secondly, a heuristic will generally remove from consideration a certain number of sequences that are quick and elegant solutions, if not indeed all solutions, to some potential problems within the domain of the problem-solving machine. The filter must, then, be carefully matched to that subclass of problems in the domain containing those that are considered "interesting," and are therefore likely to be posed to the machine. For a given class of heuristics, the balance between these essentially opposing requirements is largely a function of the organization and computing power of the machine, and can under certain rather easily attainable conditions be quite critical. In the case of the *Logic Theorist*[3] experiments with varying "strengths" of a particular heuristic (the similarity test) indicated that the optimum porosity of that heuristic varied markedly with the length of the

[3] The designers of the *Logic Theorist* were not unaware of this heuristic device. In a later version of that machine, they did, in fact, include some syntactic heuristics to reject false subgoals. To use a semantic interpretation of the propositional calculus (a truth table, for example) for this purpose would have reduced the *Logic Theorist* to triviality.

problem and the number of theorems already established in the theorem memory, a consequence of the limited storage capacity of the computer.

The Geometry Machine

With the object of our research program clearly determined, there were a number of specific alternatives to theorem-proving in Euclidean geometry that might have been adopted as a test problem; the evaluation of indefinite integrals, for example, or theorem-proving in the pure functional calculus. The decisive point in favor of geometry was the great heuristic value of the diagram. The creative scientist generally finds his most valuable insights into a problem by considering a model of the formal system in which the problem is couched. In the case of Euclidean geometry, the semantic interpretation is so useful that virtually no one would attempt the proof of a theorem in that system without first drawing a diagram; if not physically, then in the mind's eye. If a calculated effort is made to avoid spurious coincidences in the figure, one is usually safe in generalizing any statement in the formal system that correctly describes the diagram, with the notable exception of those statements concerning inequalities. Further geometry provides illustrative material in treatises and experiments in human problem-solving. It was felt that we could exchange valuable insights with behavioral scientists during the course of our research. In any event, elementary Euclidean geometry is comprehensible to every segment of the scientific community to which we should wish to communicate our results. Finally, it should not be a difficult task to generalize our machine to include the more interesting case of the non-Euclidean geometrics. A program of the same theorem-proving power as our Euclidean theorem-prover should be sufficient to prove a large class of non-obvious theorems in non-Euclidean geometry. A machine furnished with a non-Euclidean diagram (no more difficult to supply than the Euclidean one in suitable analytic form) encounters none of the assault on rationality experienced by a human mathematician searching from some heuristic insight into a theorem by considering a non-Euclidean diagram.

The formalization of geometry must be carried out within the framework of the lower functional calculus. Since we are interested in having the machine produce proofs comparable to those of a high-school student, we have preferred to construct a more or less *ad hoc* system following the scheme of most elementary texts, rather than to adopt as a primitive basis the fundamental axiomatization of Tarski, Hilbert, or Forder. No attempt has been made to provide a formalization that is either complete or non-redundant. If at some later time, the machine is able to prove one axiom from the others, that axiom will be discarded and we shall applaud the elegance displayed by our automaton. With regard to completeness, the

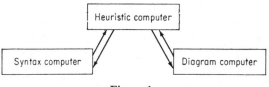

Figure 1.

machine is granted the same privileges enjoyed by the high-school student who is always assuming (*i.e.,* introducing as additional axioms) the truth of a plethora of "obviously self-evident" statements concerning, for example, the ordering properties of points on a line and the intersection properties of lines in a plane. Some of these statements are indeed independent of his original axioms, and must be introduced to complete the system. Most could be derived (but usually with some difficulty) from what he already has. There is nothing essentially wrong with this procedure of extracting assumptions from the model, provided that one is fully aware that this is being done (of course, this is rarely the case for the average student), and it simplifies the proof considerably without invalidating it. The geometry machine explicitly records its assumptions for a given proof. It could, if necessary, minimize the danger that it is proving a specific instance of a given theorem by drawing alternate diagrams to test the generality of its assumptions.

The geometry machine is in reality a particular state configuration of the IBM 704 electronic Data Processing Machine specified by a rather long and complex program written for the computer. Its organization falls naturally into three parts: a *syntax computer* and a *diagram computer* both embedded in an executive routine, which is a *heuristic computer*. The flow of control is indicated in Fig. 1.

Manipulation of the formal system is relegated to the syntax computer, which has within it the equivalent of most of the syntactic heuristics used by the *Logic Theorist*.[4] The diagram computer contains a coordinate representation of the theorem to be established together with a series of routines that produce a qualitative description of the diagram. It is important to point out that although the procedures of analytic geometry are used to generate the description, the only information transmitted to the heuristic computer (there is no direct link between the diagram and the formal system) is of the form: "Segment AB appears to be equal to segment CD in the diagram," or "Triangle ABC does not contain a right angle in the diagram." The behavior of the system would not be changed if the diagram computer were replaced by a device that could draw figures on paper and scan them.

[4] The process of *chaining* as defined by Newell et al. is under the control of the heuristic computer.

The major function of the heuristic computer for our first system, the subject of this report, is to compare strings generated by the syntax computer (working backward) with their interpretation in the diagram, rejecting those sequences that are not supported by the model. In addition to the above, the heuristic computer performs several other tasks. Among these are the organization of the proof-search process and the recognition of the syntactic symmetry of certain classes of strings. The latter function produces behavior equivalent to that of the human mathematician who, when A and B are syntactically symmetric, and both must be established, will merely prove A, and say "Similarly, B." It is an important feature, and is described in detail in an earlier report (Gelernter, 1959a). The procedures above are clearly independent of geometry; they are applicable to any formal system with its corresponding interpretation. The heuristic computer applies some additional semantic heuristics that are not indepedent of geometry. These may be "switched off" so that the behavior of the machine can be observed with and without specific geometry heuristics.

The character of the theorem-proving machine is determined largely by the heuristic computer. Modifications and improvements in the system (the introduction of learning processes, for example) will be made by modifying this part of the program.

Our first system does not "draw" its own initial figure, but is, instead, supplied with the diagram in the form of a list of possible coordinates for the points named in the theorem. This point list is accompanied by another list specifying the points joined by segments. Coordinates are chosen to

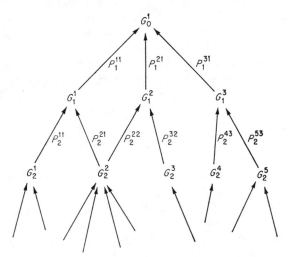

Figure 2. Problem-solving graph. The nodes G_i^α represent subgoals of order i, with α numbering the subgoals of a given order. $P_i^{\alpha\beta}$ is a transformation on G_i^α into G_{i-1}^β.

reflect the greatest possible generality in the figures. Later systems will construct their own interpretation of the premises, but since most problems for high school students are accompanied by a diagram, it was felt that we could dispense with this additional spate of programming at the current stage. When the machine is drawing its own figures, points will be chosen at random, subject to the constraints of the premises.

In working backward, the system generates a problem-solving graph, defined in the following way: Let G_0 be the formal statement to be established by the proof. It will be called the problem goal. If G_i is a formal statement with the property that G_{i-1} may be immediately inferred from G_i, then G_i is said to be a subgoal of order i for the problem. All G_j such that $j < i$ are higher subgoals than G_i, where G_0 is considered to be a subgoal of order zero. The problem-solving graph (Fig. 2) has as nodes the G_i, with each G_i joined to at least one G_{i-1} by a directed link. Each link represents a given transformation from G_i to G_{i-1}. The problem is solved when any G_i can be immediately inferred from the premises and axioms. If, as is generally the case in geometry, a given subgoal is a conjunction of statements, the graph splits at that point, and each parallel subgoal must be separately established. At any given time, the problem-solving graph is a complete representation of the current status of the proof-search process.

The organization of the heuristic computer (which is also the organization of the entire system) is displayed in greatly simplified form in Fig. 3. The diagram and syntax computers are accessible as subroutines to the heuristic computer. In operation, the machine executes the following processes (numbered below to correspond with like-numbered blocks in the flow chart).

1. The diagram is scanned to construct three lists, one containing every segment in the figure, one the angles, and one the triangles. Each element on a list is followed by a sublist describing that element.

2. The initial configuration of the system is set up, with the premises placed on a list of established formulas, and the conclusion on the problem-solving graph as a zero-order subgoal.

3. Definitions of nonprimitive predicates in the premises are added to the list of established formulae.

4. A subgoal to be established (the generating subgoal) is chosen from the problem-solving graph.

5. Appropriate axioms and theorems are selected from the theorem memory and, by working backward, a set of lower subgoals is generated such that if any one of these is established, the generating subgoal may be established by modus ponens and the generating axiom (or theorem). If the generating subgoal was labeled "provisionally fruitless" (see step 8), constructions are attempted (see below, p. 144).

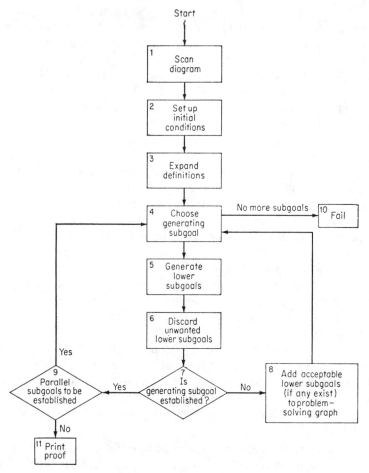

Figure 3. Simplified flow chart for the geometry-theorem proving machine.

6. Subgoals that are not valid in the diagram are rejected, as are those that appear as higher subgoals on the graph (or are syntactically symmetric to some higher subgoal).

7. If any lower subgoal is valid by virtue of its instance on the list of established formulas or if it may be assumed from the diagram, the generating subgoal is established; otherwise—

8. Acceptable nonredundant lower subgoals are added to the graph, and a new subgoal generator is chosen (4). If there are no acceptable lower subgoals and a construction is possible at this point, the generating subgoal is designated as provisionally fruitless. If a construction is not possible, or if the machine has tried and failed to find one, the generating subgoal is designated as fruitless.

9. If the generating subgoal is established, it is added to the list of established formulas, together with all of its higher consequences as determined by the graph. If there are no parallel subgoals remaining to be established, the machine reconstructs the proof from the problem-solving graph and prints it (11).

10. If at any time, every free subgoal on the graph is fruitless, the machine fails, providing it has not previously exhausted its available storage or the patience of the operator.

It is within blocks 4, 5 and 6, where subgoals are chosen, developed, and discarded, that the major heuristics reside. These subprograms represent, if you like, the seat of our artificial intelligence.

Some Early Results

The geometry machine is able to prove many of the theorems within the scope of its ad hoc formal system using the diagram only to indicate which subgoals are probably valid. In this way, the following theorem is proved in less than a minute.[5]

Theorem: A point on the bisector of an angle is equidistant from the sides of the angle (see Fig. 4 in Appendix A).

In less than five minutes, the machine is able to find the attached proof, which requires the construction of an auxiliary segment.

Theorem: In a quadrilateral with one pair of opposite sides equal and parallel, the other pair of sides are equal (see Fig. 5 in Appendix B).

Although the introduction of a new element by the machine is impressive, the construction in this proof is essentially trivial, for the new segment merely joins two already existing points. It was discovered by the following process. In attempting to develop subgoals for the string "AB = CD," the machine could find none that were valid in the diagram. The normal procedure at this point is to seek an alternative path on the problem-solving graph. But when none is available (as was the case here, since the offending string is a zero-order subgoal), the machine reexamines those of the previously rejected subgoals containing instances of predicates for which there was no representation in the diagram. The machine then considers for each one an augmented set of premises such that the

---

[5] In the proofs displayed herein, the nonobvious predicates have the following interpretations:

OPP-SIDE XYUV	Points X and Y are on opposite sides of the line through points U and V.
SAME-SIDE XYUV	Points X and Y are on the same side of the line through points U and V.
PRECEDES XYZ	Points X, Y, and Z are collinear in that order.
COLLINEAR XYZ	Points X, Y, and Z are collinear.

interpretation does contain a representation of the predicate. If the string is valid in the augmented system, and there exist theorems permitting the required additional premises to be derived from the original set, then the string becomes a subgoal in the augmented system. The added premises specify a construction in the diagram that is permitted by virtue of the theorems through which they were derived. Returning to our example, the subgoal "ΔABD ≅ ΔCDB" is generated for the string "AB = CD," but the required triangles are not represented in the diagram until the premise "Segment BD exists" is added. The axiom "Two distinct points determine a segment" justifies the construction.[6] The entire process is a variant of the major heuristic above, and is clearly independent of the particular formal system under consideration. Note, too, that the process is finite, since no new points are introduced into the predicates; the old ones are merely reconsidered.

Our second example illustrates one further point. Although it is clear in the diagram (Fig. 5) that the transversal BD makes alternate interior angles with sides BC and AD, this is a consequence of the theorem "Opposite vertices of a convex quadrilateral fall on opposite sides of the diagonal through the other vertices." That this is not true of a general quadrilateral becomes clear when one considers the outside diagonal of a reflex quadrilateral. A completely rigorous solution, then, requires that one prove the lemma above if it is not already available, and that one demonstrate that the quadrilateral ABCD can only be convex. Rather than do this, the machine makes the usual assumption that the diagonal forms alternate interior angles with the opposite sides of the quadrilateral. Unlike the usual high-school text, however, the assumption is made explicit in the proof.

The theorem-proving system described thus far is adequate for many problems of greater complexity than the ones cited above. However, with a linear increase in the number of individual points mentioned in the premises, the rate of growth of the problem-solving graph increases exponentially and the time required to explore the graph increases correspondingly. If the machine were able to select those among a given set of subgoals that were more likely to lead to a solution, much of the wasted search time could be eliminated. Two specific geometry heuristics have been introduced to enable the machine to do this. The first is a routine that recognizes certain of the subgoals that are usually established in just one step. Identities are in this category, for example, as are equalities between angles that are observed to be vertical angles in the diagram. Such subgoals

[6] Our ad hoc formal system requires that the segments joining the vertices of a triangle be specified, as well as the vertices themselves, to define the triangle. This is necessary in order to avoid the difficulties that would otherwise arise when the theorem names a large number of noncollinear points. If our formal system were a true point geometry, all such constructions would be implicit in the diagram.

are placed on a priority list and developed before any of the others are considered. The second specific heuristic is a routine that assigns a "distance" between each subgoal string and the set of premise strings in some vaguely defined formula space. After those on the priority list have been developed, the next subgoal chosen is that which is "closest" to the premise set in formula space.

It is instructive to examine the machine's behavior in proving complex theorems both with and without the expanded set of semantic heuristics. For the theorem "Two vertices of a triangle are equidistant from the median to the side determined by those vertices," the machine finds a proof in about eight minutes with the basic heuristics alone (see Fig. 6 in Appendix C). The expanded set of heuristics produces a proof in one minute. In addition, the second proof is quite short and to the point, while the first proof meanders blindly about the direct path to the goal before reaching it.

Reflecting the greater efficiency with which the machine attacked the problem in the second trial, only four circuits of the subgoal-generating loop were required compared with twenty-four circuits required without the extended heuristics. Twenty-one intermediate subgoals were generated, compared with sixty-one in the first case, and the problem-solving graph extended to a depth of only three levels, rather than twelve levels for the proof with basic heuristics alone.

For a particular case of a problem taken from a Brooklyn technical high school final examination in plane geometry a solution was found with the extended heuristics in less than five minutes. With the basic heuristics alone, the machine exhausted its working storage in half an hour without having completed the problem. On the other hand, there are problems for which the machine achieves no net gain by applying the additional heuristics. The theorem: "Diagonals of a parallelogram bisect one another" was proved in about three minutes in either mode. The proofs produced in each trial were equivalent, though not the same. A Brooklyn technical high school final examination supplied an example of an intermediate case, where the machine found identical proofs in both modes, but took almost three times as long with the basic heuristics alone (eight minutes, compared with three minutes with extended heuristics). We shall undoubtedly encounter cases for which the application of the extended set will result in a net loss of efficiency, although none has appeared yet in our limited tests.

Conclusion

It is well at this point in our discussion to reemphasize the fact that the object of this research has not been the design of a machine capable of proving theorems in Euclidean plane geometry, or even one able to prove theorems in some undecidable system such as number theory. We are, rather, interested in understanding the use of heuristic methods (or strategies) by machines for the solution of problems that would otherwise be inaccessible to them. Theorem-proving machines in themselves are objects of much interest to mathematicians and logicians, and important work at IBM is being done on this approach by Wang and by Gilmore. Wang (1960a) has written a program for the IBM 704 that is able to prove all theorems in propositional logic offered by Russell and Whitehead in the *Principia Mathematica,* whereas the Logic Theorist could master only about 38 of the 52 theorems appearing in chap. 2 of that volume. Also, the time required by the latter machine was far in excess of that used by the former. Newell, Shaw, and Simon, however, were interested in heuristic methods, whereas Wang, and also Gilmore, whose machine deals with the first order predicate calculus, are searching for algorithms, which, though less than a decision procedure, will produce "interesting" proofs within a reasonable amount of time. Both Wang and Gilmore find that for more complex formal systems, heuristics are required (they prefer the word "strategies") to make their algorithms sufficiently selective to produce, within acceptable bounds on space and time, proofs of any great interest.

The work of Wang and Gilmore is most relevant to a new branch of applied logic first characterized by Wang. He names this discipline "inferential analysis," and defines it to include "treatment of proofs as numerical analysis does calculations" (1960a). The results of inferential analysis are expected to "lead to mechanical checks of new mathematical results," and ultimately "lead to proofs of difficult new theorems by machine." The present author feels that inferential analysis is relevant, too, to the problem of intelligent behavior in machines. An automaton confronted with the real world, however, will certainly have to rely heavily on heuristics, for the unorthodox formal systems describing its environment will probably be far from amenable to the traditional methods of mathematical logic.

In conclusion, we should like to specify the course of this research for the immediate future. The machine described above is purely a problem-solving system. Except for the annexation of new theorems to the list of axioms, its structure is static. A sequence of practice problems given to the machine will not improve its performance unless a usable theorem is among them. Because it is incapable of developing its own structure, the machine will always be limited in the class of problems it can solve by the initial intent of the designer. It seems that the problem of designing a more general problem-solving machine will be enormously greater than that of designing one not so intelligent but with the capacity to learn.

An immediately obvious approach to the problem of introducing learning into the geometry machine is to allow the machine to adjust all of the parameters that determine its specific semantic heuristics, maximizing the predicted utility of those subgoals that prove to be useful in practice. The machine will thus improve the match of its heuristic filters to the class of problems considered interesting enough to be presented to it for solution. Of greater significance would be the introduction of routines enabling the machine to recognize recurring patterns in its proof-search procedure. Once discovered, such a pattern would enable the machine to construct its own heuristics designed to induce a repetition of the pattern in later proofs. For example, the machine might notice that certain classes of premise strings are regularly followed by the same first step in a proof. The heuristic derived from this pattern would search the premises for such strings and perform the first deduction before starting on the problem-solving graph. The difficult subject of abstract pattern recognition must be understood first, however, and the transformation of pattern to effective heuristic is by no means trivial. But whatever approach to learning is considered most worthwhile to explore, the geometry machine should serve as an excellent framework within which the explorations may be pursued.

Appendix A

Premises

Angle ABD equals angle DBC
Segment AD perpendicular segment AB
Segment DC perpendicular segment BC

Definition

Right angle DAB
Right angle DCB

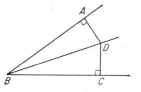

Figure 4.

Syntactic Symmetries

CA, BB, AC, DD

Goals

Segment AD equals segment CD

Solution

Angle ABD equals angle DBC
   Premise
Right angle DAB
   Definition of perpendicular
Right angle DCB
   Definition of perpendicular
Angle BAD equals angle BCD
   All right angles are equal

Segment DB
  Assumption based on diagram
Segment BD equals segment BD
  Identity
Triangle BCD
  Assumption based on diagram
Triangle BAD
  Assumption based on diagram
Triangle ADB congruent triangle CDB
  Side-angle-angle
Segment AD equals segment CD
  Corresponding elements of congruent triangles are equal

Total elapsed time = 0.3200 minute

Appendix B

Premises

Quad-lateral ABCD
Segment BC parallel segment AD
Segment BC equals segment AD

CA	BA	DA
DB	AB	CB
AC	DC	BC
BD	CD	AD

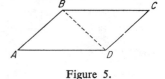

Figure 5.

Goals

Segment AB equals segment CD

I am stuck, elapsed time = 0.88 minute

Construct segment DB
Add premise segment DB
Restart problem

Solution

Segment BC parallel segment AD
  Premise
Opp-side CADB
  Assumption based on diagram
Segment DB
  Premise
Angle ADB equals angle CBD
  Alternate interior angles of parallel lines

Segment BC equals segment AD
   Premise
Segment BD equals segment DB
   Identity
Triangle CDB
   Assumption based on diagram
Triangle ABD
   Assumption based on diagram
Triangle ABD congruent triangle CDB
   Side-angle-side
Segment AB equals segment CD
   Corresponding elements of congruent triangles

Total elapsed time = 4.06 minutes

Appendix C

Premises

Triangle ABC
Precedes BMC
Segment BM equals segment MC
Precedes ADM
Precedes DME
Segment BD perpendicular segment AM
Segment CE perpendicular segment ME

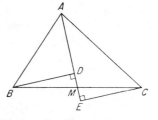

Figure 6.

Definition

Right angle MEC
Right angle BDM
Right angle BDA
Angle BDA equals angle BDM

No syntactic symmetries

Goals

Segment BD equals segment EC

Solution

Precedes BMC
   Premise
Segment EC
   Assumption based on diagram

Angle ECM equals angle BCE
  Same angle
Precedes DME
  Premise
Angle CED equals angle MEC
  Same angle
Right angle BDM
  Definition of perpendicular
Right angle MEC
  Definition of perpendicular
Angle BDM equals angle CEM
  Right angles are equal
Angle CED equals angle BDM
  Angles equal to the same angle are equal
Same side MEDB
  Assumption based on diagram
Same side DACE
  Assumption based on diagram
Collinear EDM
  Ordered collinearity implies collinearity
Precedes ADM
  Premise
Precedes EDA
  Combinatorial properties of ordered collinearity
Collinear EDA
  Ordered collinearity implies collinearity
Angle BDE equals angle AEC
  Different names for equal angles
Precedes EMA
  Combinatorial properties of ordered collinearity
Angle CEM equals angle AEC
  Same angle
Angle BDE equals angle MEC
  Angles equal to the same angle are equal
Angle CED equals angle EDB
  Angles equal to the same angle are equal
Opp side CBED
  Assumption based on diagram
Segment ED
  Assumption based on diagram
Segment EC parallel segment BD
  Segments are parallel if alternate interior angles are equal
Opp side EDCB
  Assumption based on diagram

Segment CB
  Assumption based on diagram
Angle BCE equals angle DBC
  Alternate interior angles of parallel lines
Angle ECM equals angle DBC
  Angles equal to the same angle are equal
Same side CMBD
  Assumption based on diagram
Same side MBEC
  Assumption based on diagram
Collinear CMB
  Ordered collinearity implies collinearity
Angle DBM equals angle BCE
  Different names for equal angles
Angle MBD equals angle MCE
  Angles equal to the same angle are equal
Angle DMB equals angle EMC
  Vertical angles
Segment BM equals segment MC
  Premise
Triangle BDM
  Assumption based on diagram
Triangle CEM
  Assumption based on diagram
Triangle BDM congruent triangle CEM
  Angle-side-angle
Segment BD equals segment EC
  Corresponding elements of congruent triangles

Total elapsed time = 8.08 minutes

WITH BASIC HEURISTICS

Solution

Precedes DME
  Premise
Precedes BMC
  Premise
Angle DMB equals angle EMC
  Vertical angles
Right angle BDM
  Definition of perpendicular
Right angle MEC
  Definition of perpendicular

Angle BDM equals angle CEM
    Right angles are equal
Segment BM equals segment MC
    Premise
Triangle CEM
    Assumption based on diagram
Triangle BDM
    Assumption based on diagram
Triangle BDM congruent triangle CEM
    Side-angle-angle
Segment BD equals segment EC
    Corresponding elements of congruent triangles

Total elapsed time = 1.06 minutes

WITH EXTENDED HEURISTICS

EMPIRICAL EXPLORATIONS
OF THE GEOMETRY -
THEOREM PROVING MACHINE

by H. Gelernter, J. R. Hansen, & D. W. Loveland

Introduction

In early spring, 1959, an IBM 704 computer, with the assistance of a program comprising some 20,000 individual instructions, proved its first theorem in elementary Euclidean plane geometry (Gelernter, 1959*b*). Since that time, the geometry-theorem proving machine (a particular state configuration of the IBM 704 specified by the afore mentioned machine code) has found solutions to a large number of problems[1] taken from high-school textbooks and final examinations in plane geometry. Some of these problems would be considered quite difficult by the average high-school student. In fact, it is doubtful whether any but the brightest students could have produced a solution for any of the latter group when granted the same amount of prior "training" afforded the geometry machine (*i.e.*, the same vocabulary of geometric concepts and the same stock of previously proved theorems).

The research project which had as its consequence the geometry-theorem proving machine was motivated by the desire to learn ways to use modern high-speed digital computers for the solution of a new and difficult class of problems; a class heretofore considered to be beyond the capabilities of a finite-state automaton. In particular, we wished to make our computer perform tasks which are generally considered to require the intervention of human intelligence and ingenuity for their successful completion. The reasons behind our choice of theorem proving in geometry as a representative task are set forth in detail in an earlier study (1958). We

[1] More than fifty proofs are on file at the present time.

only remark here that problem-solving in geometry satisfies our definition of an intellectual activity, while being at the same time especially well suited to the approach we wished to explore. The fact that geometry is decidable is irrelevant for the purpose of our investigation. The methods employed by the machine are suitable as well for the proof of theorems in systems for which no decision algorithm can exist.

We shall not labor the question as to whether our machine is indeed behaving intelligently in performing a task for which humans are credited with intelligence. The psychologists offer us neither aid nor comfort here; they have yet to satisfactorily characterize such behavior in humans, and have rarely considered the abstract concept of intelligence independent of its agent. In the final analysis, people are occasionally observed to do things that may best be described as intelligent, however vague the connotations of the word. These are, in general, tasks involving highly complex decision processes in a potentially infinite and uncontrollable environment. We should be most happy to have our machine duplicate this kind of behavior, whatever label is affixed to it.

Heuristic Programming and the Geometry Machine

The geometry machine is able to discover proofs for a significant number of interesting theorems within the domain of its *ad hoc* formal system (comprising theorems on parallel lines, congruence, and equality and inequality of segments and angles) without resorting to a decision algorithm or exhaustive enumeration of possible proof sequences. Instead, the theorem-proving program relies upon heuristic methods to restrain it from generating proof sequences that do not have a high *a priori* probability of leading to a proof for the theorem in question.

The general problem of heuristic programming has been discussed by Minsky (1959a) and Newell, Shaw, and Simon (1959a). The particular approach pursued by the authors has been described at length in the papers to which we have already referred (Gelernter et al., 1958, 1959b). We shall therefore defer to the presentation of the machine's detailed results in the full study summarized here for a description of how these results were achieved. It should be recorded here, however, that the geometry machine operates principally in the analytic mode (reasoning backward). At each stage of the search for a proof, a goal exists which must be "connected" with the premises for the problem by a bridge of axioms and previously established theorems of lemmas. If the connection cannot be made directly, then a set of "subgoals" is generated and the process is repeated for one of the subgoals. Heuristic rules are used to reject subgoals that are not likely to prove useful, to select one from those remaining to work on, and to choose particular axioms and theorems to use in generating new subgoals. The machine does depart from this procedure in a number of circumstances (in setting up an indirect proof, for example), but these cases account for only a small fraction of the total search time.

The computer program itself was written within the framework of the so-called Newell-Shaw-Simon list memory (1957*b*). In order to ease the task of writing so massive and complex a machine code, a convenient special-purpose list processing language was designed to be compiled by the already available FORTRAN system for the IBM 704 computer (Gelernter et al., 1960*b*). The authors feel that had they not made free use of an intermediate programming language, it is likely that the geometry program could not have been completed.

Summary of Results

Since its initial solo performance, the geometry machine has existed in several different configurations. In its earliest and most primitive form, the system was equipped with a single major semantic heuristic.[2] That first system was, however, able to prove a large number of interesting, though admittedly simple theorems in elementary plane geometry.[3] The heuristic rule in question, which is independent of the particular formal system under consideration, may be described in the following way. All subgoal formulas that are generated at a given stage of the proof search are interpreted in a model of the formal system; in our case, the model is a diagram, a formal semantic interpretation. If the interpreted subgoal is valid in the diagram, it is accepted as a possible step in the proof, provided that it is noncircular (Gelernter, 1959*a*). Otherwise, it is rejected.

As an experiment, a number of attempts were made to prove extremely simple theorems with the latter heuristic "disconnected" from the system (*i.e.*, all noncircular subgoals generated were accepted). In each case, the computer's entire stock of available storage space was quickly exhausted by the initial several hundreds of first level subgoals generated, and, in fact, the machine never finished generating a complete set of first level subgoals. We estimate conservatively that on the average, a number of the order of 1000 subgoals are generated per stage by the decoupled system. If one compares the latter figure with the average of 5 subgoals per stage accepted when the diagram is consulted by the machine, it is easy to see that the use of a diagram is crucial for our system. (Note that the total number of subgoals appearing on the problem-solving graph grows exponentially with the number accepted per stage.)

Since the procedure described above is a heuristic one, errors are oc-

---

[2] A semantic heuristic is one based on an interpretation of the formal system rather than on the structure of the strings within that system.

[3] A number of these proofs are reproduced in Gelernter, 1959*b*.

casionally made in the selection or rejection of formulas as subgoals. The diagram is made available to the machine in coordinate representation to finite precision. Formulas are interpreted by transforming them into an appropriate calculation on the numerical coordinates representing the point variables. For example, to check the validity of a statement concerning the equality of two segments, the length of each segment in the figure is calculated, and they are then compared to a certain preassigned number of decimal places. If, instead, the statement concerned parallel segments, the slopes would be calculated and compared. In a small number of cases, round-off error has propagated beyond the allowed value, so that valid subgoals were rejected, or invalid ones accepted. It is important to point out, however, that in no case could this effect result in a false proof. Where valid subgoals were rejected, the machine found alternate paths to the solution. Where invalid ones were accepted, the machine failed, of course, to establish them within the formal system. In the worst possible case, the interpretation error could prevent the computer from finding any solution at all, but never could it lead to an invalid proof.

It should be clear at this point that the diagram is used only to guide the search for a proof by supplying yes or no answers to questions of the form: "Is segment AB equal to segment CD in the figure?", or "Is angle ABC a right angle in the figure?". There is no direct link between the diagram and the formal system in the geometry machine. The behavior of the machine would not be changed if the coordinate representation were replaced by a device capable of drawing figures on paper and scanning them.

In the basic theorem-proving system described above, after a set of subgoals has been generated, each member of the set is explored in order. The next subgoal in line is not examined until the one preceding it has been followed down to a dead end. Too, in generating the next level for a given subgoal, every applicable theorem available is pressed into service.

This system was soon extended by the introduction of selection heuristics for both subgoals and subgoal-generating theorems. The subgoal selection heuristic assigns a "distance" between each subgoal string and the set of premises in a vaguely defined *ad hoc* formula space. At each stage, the next subgoal selected is that which is "closest" to the premises in formula space. The generator selection routine recognizes certain classes of subgoals that are usually established in one step. For such "urgent" subgoals, the appropriate generator is withdrawn immediately, and an attempt is made for a one-step proof (of that particular subgoal) before generating the full set for that formula.

The extended system is able to prove a number of somewhat more difficult theorems that are beyond the capacity of the basic machine. For those problems within the range of both systems, the former is, on the

average, about three times faster, and
generates about two-thirds the total number of subgoals in half as many subgoal
generation cycles as required by the basic
system. The average depth of the problem-solving graph for the refined system,
about seven to nine levels, is two-thirds
the average depth for the basic system.

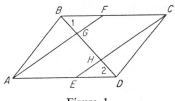

Figure 1.

By the addition of a simple construction routine, the theorem-proving
power of the machine is expanded to include an entirely new class of
problem, hitherto logically unattainable. The routine, called upon only
when all other attempts have failed, allows the machine to join two previously unconnected points in the diagram, and extends the newly created
segment to its intersections with all other segments in the figure. The new
segment, when it intersects previously given ones, introduces new points
into the problem which are named by the machine and become part of the
problem system.

At this stage in its development, the geometry machine was capable of
producing proofs that were quite impressive (Appendix 1).[4] Its performance, however, fell off rapidly as the number of points in the diagram
increased. This effect was due largely to the fact that unlike humans, who
generally identify angles visually by their vertices and rays, the computer
specifies an angle by a predicate on three variables, the vertex and a point
on each ray. Consequently, the equality of angles 1 and 2 in Fig. 1 may be
represented in thirty-six different ways, since each angle has six different
names. Formal rigor demands, too, that the equality of angles ADH and
EDG, for example, be proved rather than taken for granted. It should be
clear that where the condition above exists, the search for a proof quickly
bogs down in a mass of uninteresting detail.

In the current system, the angle problem is solved by allowing the
machine to use the diagram to identify a given angle with its full set of
names, and to assume the equality relationship between different names for
the same angle, as does its human counterpart. The geometry machine in
its present configuration is able to find proofs for theorems of the order of
difficulty represented by the following:

Theorem: If the segment joining the midpoints of the diagonals of a

---

[4] In the proofs appended to this paper, the nonobvious predicates have the following interpretations:

OPP-SIDE XYUV   Points X and Y are on opposite sides of the line through
                 points U and V.
SAME-SIDE XYUV   Points X and Y are on the same side of the line through
                 points U and V.
PRECEDES XYZ   Points X, Y, and Z are collinear in that order.
COLLINEAR XYZ   Points X, Y, and Z are collinear.

trapezoid is extended to intersect a side of the trapezoid, it bisects that side (Appendix 2).

Limitations of the System

It will be immediately evident to those familiar with the properties of formal logistic systems that unless a construction which generates a new point is introduced by the machine, all problems are solved within the framework of a propositional calculus, however complex its structure. Although the machine's present construction routine can and does generate new points, we could not expect our results to be of great interest to logicians until a full set of possible constructions (corresponding to a complete set of existentially quantified axioms) is made available to the system to abet its search for a proof.

An equally serious limitation on the formal generality of the theorem-proving machine is imposed by our method for determining the well-formedness of strings within the logical system. In order to attain the necessary speed and efficiency in processing, well-formed formulas are defined by schema rather than recursively. The kind of statement that can be made in the system is then determined by the schema available to the machine. The practical effect of this loss in generality is to restrict rather severely the freedom with which algebraic statements in geometry may be manipulated.

In addition to the above, there are a number of nonessential bounds on the theorem-proving ability of the machine. These are a consequence of the limited speed and memory capacity of the computer for problems of such highly combinatorial character. Improvements in either of the above will be immediately effective in extending the class of machine-solvable problems in both quantity and difficulty.

Conclusion

The initial goal of our research program in machine intelligence has been attained. If the interrogator were to restrict his probing to the area of theorem-proving in elementary Euclidean plane geometry, our machine could be expected to give an excellent account of itself in competition with a human in Turing's well-known "imitation game" (1950). Of course there are many other problem areas (solving arithmetic problems, for example) where computers have always been able to compete successfully with humans. The significant point is that a knowledgeable interrogator would certainly avoid such areas in his questioning, while he might well (until now, at any rate) introduce a plane geometry problem in a calculated attempt to separate the men from the machines.[5] Although the stage is now set for the argument that any distinct area of human intellectual activity will in the same way succumb to the inexorable logic of electrons, switches, and gates, we defer to our philosopher colleagues for debate on the implications of that contention, at least until the time that computers have been programmed to consider such issues.

There are a number of consequences of our work that are, fortunately, more concrete than that alluded to above. Perhaps the most important are those relating to inferential analysis, a new branch of applied logic first characterized by Wang (1960a). Inferential analysis "treats proofs as numerical analysis does calculations," and is expected to "lead to mechanical checks of new mathematical results" and, more important, "lead to proofs of difficult new theorems by machine." It is expected that our techniques for the manipulation and efficient search of problem-solving trees and our results concerning syntactic symmetry will prove to be useful tools in pursuing the goals of inferential analysis.

Contributions have been made, too, in the area of techniques for computer implementation of complex information processes. Results pertaining to the design and use of intermediate languages for the specification of list manipulation processes have been reported elsewhere (Gelernter et al., 1960b). The latter work indicates clearly the requirements of a digital computer system designed for optimum execution of such list processes. In brief, a list processing computer should possess hardware facilities for:

1. Generalized indirect addressing; specified in the indirectly addressed instruction to arbitrary depth and in arbitrary order from either the left or the right field of a two-address register,

2. Effective address recovery; making available the terminal content of the address register (the final address in a long and complex indirect address chain, for example) as the address field for a subsequent operation,

3. Field logic; a greatly expanded set of interfield operations within a full register sectioned according to some previously established convention, and

4. List search operations; a list equivalent of the conventional table look-up instruction.

The bulk storage input-output requirements for a list processing computer are severe, and are not included in the enumeration above. The system

[5] It may be argued (and undoubtedly, it *will* be argued) that the truly knowledgeable interrogator, cognizant of the decidability of geometry, would certainly avoid this area as well, perhaps preferring the manifestly undecidable parts of the predicate calculus or number theory to effect the distinction between man and machine. We recall here that our methods are independent of the decidability of the formal system, and, in fact, Wang (1960a) and Gilmore (1960) have developed proofs for theorems in the undecidable area of the predicate calculus.

design of a digital computer for the manipulation of list structures will be described in detail in a subsequent paper.

Finally, we consider the implications of our work for the basic problem of machine intelligence. The geometry machine, we feel, offers convincing evidence of the power and fruitfulness of heuristic programming for the solution of problems of a certain class by computer. In our experience, the theorem-proving power of the machine has often been extended by the addition of a single heuristic to a degree equivalent to a three-to-fivefold increase in the speed or storage capacity of the computer.

Our program has proved to be disappointing as a tool for the study of the more elementary trial-and-error types of machine learning, largely because of the rather low rate at which it accumulates experience. It is reasonable to expect, however, that the geometry machine might yet be pressed into service in an investigation of the higher, conceptual types of machine learning, providing that one will someday know how to formulate the problem.

If nothing else, our work offers some qualitative indication of the order of magnitude of difficulty for problems that could be expected to yield to contemporary computer technology. Three years ago, the dominant opinion was that the geometry machine would not exist today. And today, hardly an expert will contest the assertion that machines will be proving interesting theorems in number theory three years hence.

Appendix 1

Premises

Quad-lateral ABCD
Point E midpoint segment AB
Point F midpoint segment AC
Point G midpoint segment CD
Point H midpoint segment BD

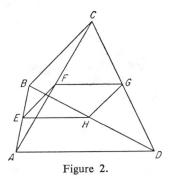

Figure 2.

To Prove

Parallelogram EFGH

Syntactic Symmetries

BA, AB, DC, CD, EE, HF, GG, FH, CA, DB, AC, BD, GE, FF, EG, HH, DA, CB, BC, AD, GE, HF, EG, FH

Proof

Segment DG equals segment GC
    Definition of midpoint

Segment CF equals segment FA
  Definition of midpoint
Triangle DCA
  Assumption based on diagram
Precedes DGC
  Definition of midpoint
Precedes CFA
  Definition of midpoint
Segment GF parallel segment AD
  Segment joining midpoints of sides of triangle is parallel to base
Segment HE parallel segment AD
  Syntactic conjugate
Segment GF parallel segment EH
  Segments parallel to the same segment are parallel
Segment HG parallel segment FE
  Syntactic conjugate
Quad-lateral HGFE
  Assumption based on diagram
Parallelogram EFGH
  Quadrilateral with opposite sides parallel is a parallelogram

Total elapsed time = 1.03 minutes

Appendix 2

Premises

Quad-lateral ABCD
Segment BC parallel segment AD
Point E midpoint segment AC
Point F midpoint segment BD
Precedes MEF
Precedes AMB

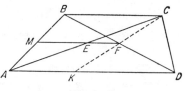

Figure 3.

To prove

Segment MB equals segment MA

No Syntactic Symmetries

I Am Stuck, Elapsed Time = 8.12 Minutes
Construct segment CF
Extend segment CF to intersect segment AD in point K

Add to Premises the Following Statements

Precedes CFK
Collinear AKD

Proof

Segment BC parallel segment AD
  Premise
Collinear AKD
  Premise
Segment KD parallel segment BC
  Segments collinear with parallel segments are parallel
Opp-side KCDB
  Assumption based on diagram
Segment DB
  Assumption based on diagram
Angle KDB equals angle CBD
  Alternate interior angles of parallel lines are equal
Precedes CFK
  Premise
Precedes DFB
  Definition of midpoint
Angle KFD equals angle CFB
  Vertical angles are equal
Segment DF equals segment FB
  Definition of midpoint
Triangle FDK
  Assumption based on diagram
Triangle FBC
  Assumption based on diagram
Triangle FDK congruent triangle FBC
  Two triangles are congruent if angle-side-angle equals angle-side-angle
Segment KF equals segment CF
  Corresponding segments of congruent triangles are equal
Segment CE equals segment EA
  Definition of midpoint
Triangle AKC
  Assumption based on diagram
Precedes CEA
  Definition of midpoint
Segment EF parallel segment AK
  Segment joining midpoints of sides of triangle is parallel to base
Segment EF parallel segment KD
  Segments collinear with parallel segments are parallel
Segment FE parallel segment BC
  Segments parallel to the same segment are parallel

Precedes MEF
  Premise
Collinear MEF
  Ordered collinear points are collinear
Segment FM parallel segment BC
  Segments collinear with parallel segments are parallel
Segment FM parallel segment DA
  Segments parallel to the same segment are parallel
Triangle DBA
  Assumption based on diagram
Precedes AMB
  Premise
Segment MB equals segment MA
  Line parallel to base of triangle bisecting one side bisects other side

Total elapsed time = 30.68 minutes

section 4

Two Important Applications

What good is artificial intelligence research? Can the devices and techniques developed be used in the solution of "real" problems? These are questions which a practical man, an engineer, say, or an operations research analyst, might reasonably ask.

The reports in this section describe heuristic programs which solve complex problems in important areas of application. One program handles integration problems in the elementary calculus. The other handles problems of assembly line balancing in a manufacturing process. The problems have these features in common:

1. Both are problems which are moderately difficult for intelligent human beings with college training.

2. Both are readily attackable by heuristic methods, and these methods closely resemble the methods used by intelligent human beings to solve the problems.

3. It is economically feasible to use programs to solve these problems. In most cases, it would be difficult to hire a man with comparable skill to solve the problems as cheaply. The time required by an IBM 7090 to solve the problems is generally much shorter than would be required by the average human problem-solver skilled in the problem area. This is true in spite of the fact that present-day computers were not designed with heuristic programming applications in mind and hence existing computer languages well suited to heuristic programming use digital computers quite inefficiently.

The assembly line balancing program developed by F. Tonge is an application of heuristic programming to an important management science problem. Balancing an assembly line involves finding an efficient arrangement of workers, tasks, and work stations so as to maximize the rate of assembly or minimize the number of workers needed for a given rate of assembly. More or less "straightforward" procedures for doing this have been devised, but they are generally not practical, since they involve the enumeration of a very large number of "tries"—combinations of the work elements. Tonge's program differs from these in that it employs a variety of line balancing heuristics—"tricks of the trade"—to simplify the constraints, to structure the assignment part of the problem, and to carry out the actual computations.

A significant feature of Tonge's program is its "level-of-aspiration" effort-limiting heuristic. In the line balancing problem, the maximum rate of assembly or the minimum number of workers for a given rate can be computed easily, even though the actual assignment cannot. Tonge's program *does not seek the optimal solution but merely one which is "satisfactory,"* i.e., within some (given) percentage of the calculated optimum. The power of this heuristic derives from the facts that, the closer to optimum one requires the solution to be, the more computing effort is needed to find the solution (as one would expect), and that the relationship is strongly nonlinear.

Slagle's SAINT program handles problems in an area familiar to many of us. By now, the elementary calculus is almost a common language among university graduates. The integration of elementary functions (when the answer is not to be found by rote recall or looking in a table of integrals) is not a trivial intellectual task. Many a college sophomore has stayed up half the night searching for the "key" which would unlock the solution to some complicated integral. The successful human performer is generally considered to have not only a wide repertory of "tricks and transformations" he can apply but also a keen "intuitive feel" concerning which tricks to choose and what sequence to apply them in. Finally, analytic integration of elementary functions constitutes a significant portion of the routine mathematics of modern engineering and natural science.

SAINT is a program for performing analytic integration of elementary functions. It uses the same kinds of "tricks" that are taught to and used by students in elementary calculus courses. In its conception and structure, it is a linear descendant of the Logic Theory machine. As with LT, the SAINT program shows that the behavior vaguely labeled "cleverness" or "keen insight" in human problem-solving is really just the result of the judicious application of certain heuristics for narrowing and guiding the search for solutions.

Fred Tonge is on the faculty of the Graduate School of Industrial Administration, Carnegie Institute of Technology.

James Slagle is a member of the staff of the Lawrence Radiation Laboratory, Livermore, California.

SUMMARY OF A HEURISTIC
LINE BALANCING PROCEDURE

by Fred M. Tonge

1. Introduction

This study describes a heuristic program for assembly line balancing. We employ heuristic methods because the assembly line balancing problem, like many combinatorial problems, has not been solved in a practical sense by advanced mathematical techniques.

Because this approach does not guarantee an optimum solution, the ultimate measure of a heuristic program is whether it provides better solutions more quickly and/or less expensively than other methods. However, at this early stage in the development of heuristic procedures there is still much to be learned about both the specification and the mechanization on a computer of such procedures. The research reported here was undertaken to explore these questions. No special emphasis was placed on producing an economically competitive program; but the results are sufficiently interesting to report.

Here we summarize the heuristic program developed for assembly line balancing and the operating results obtained with that program. A detailed description of the procedure and further comments on this approach to utilizing digital computers are presented elsewhere (Tonge, 1961*a*).

2. Assembly Line Balancing

In many industries (home appliances, automobiles) the product is assembled on a continuous conveyor line. The elemental tasks making up the assembly operation must be assigned to work stations along the line. (For

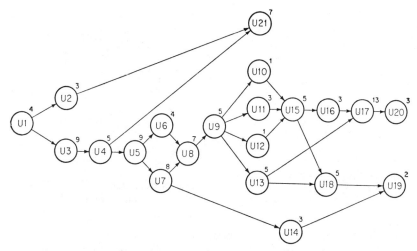

Figure 1. Twenty-one-element problem-directed graph representation.

our purposes, "work station" and "operator" are equivalent.) In the simplest case, each elemental task (also called "task" or "element") is characterized by an operation time per unit of product and a partial ordering relationship with other elemental tasks.

Figure 1 represents one such assembly (taken from Mitchell, 1957). Here, for example, elemental task U5 requires nine time units. It cannot be started until task U4 is completed, and must be completed before either U6 or U7 can be started. The constraint that task U5 must precede task U14 need not be represented explicitly; this information is implied by the sequence U5 → U7 → U14.

In industrial practice the ordering constraints are not explicitly stated. The industrial engineer works directly from bill of material and standard time data for the product and from his own knowledge of manufacturing technology.

A production rate set by management determines the maximum time (cycle time) to be assigned to any work station. That is, hours per shift divided by units per shift determine the maximum time an operator can spend on each unit.

The assembly line balancing problem[1] can be stated as:

Given a production rate (or, equivalently, a cycle time), what is the minimum number of work stations (operators) consistent with the time and ordering constraints of the product?

---

[1] There are, of course, many variants of the balancing problem, introducing such factors as uncertainty of time values, varying operator capabilities, etc. None of these other constraints are treated here.

TABLE 1

Work station	Total time	Elemental tasks
1	18	U1, U3, U4
2	19	U2, U5, U21
3	15	U6, U7, U14
4	17	U8, U9, U10, U11, U12
5	20	U13, U15, U16, U18, U19
6	16	U17, U20

A closely related problem is:

Given some number of men (work stations), what is the maximum production rate consistent with the time and ordering constraints of the product?

We shall consider the first formulation.

More explicitly, then, the assembly line balancing problem concerns a set of elemental tasks such that:

1. each elemental task requires a known operation time per unit of product, independent of when performed;

2. a partial ordering exists among the elemental tasks.

An optimal solution of the problem consists of an assignment of elemental tasks to work stations such that:

1. each elemental task is assigned to one and only one work station;

2. the sum of the times of all elemental tasks assigned to any one station does not exceed some maximum (the cycle time);

3. the stations thus formed can be ordered such that the partial orderings among elemental tasks are not violated;

4. the number of work stations thus formed is minimized.

A minimal work-station solution to the problem of Fig. 1 (given a cycle time of 20) is shown in Table 1.

Actual instances of the assembly line balancing problem are much more complex than the example given here. A representative problem from the appliance industry would contain nearly a hundred elemental tasks. The industrial engineer balancing a line works from a sheet listing the elements and their operation times and from his knowledge of the manufacturing process. In the absence of any formal procedures, he must rely on judicious use of trial-and-error methods to find an acceptable grouping.

3. Exhaustive Procedures for Assembly Line Balancing

Assembly line balancing techniques have received little attention in standard production management literature; most works merely acknowledge that the problem is a common one. However, several management scientists have studied the problem.

Salveson (1955) reviews the industrial setting of the problem and comments on several difficulties associated with line balancing, *e.g.*, determining before solution the minimum number of operators, taking into account variances in operation times. He suggests application of limited combinatorial analysis, but the procedure rests upon previous enumeration of all possible work stations, an enormous task. However, many of Salveson's observations on the nature of the assembly line balancing problem are valid, and this article first brought the problem to the attention of the management science audience.

Jackson (1956) presents an algorithm for systematically enumerating and evaluating possible solutions. Comparisons of this exhaustive method with the heuristic procedure developed here are presented in a later section.

In commenting on Jackson's article, Helgeson and Kwo (1956) suggest an additional criterion—minimizing the variation in work load among stations—in evaluating possible solutions.

Bryton (1954) develops a "convergence" procedure for shifting elements among given work stations so as to increase the maximum attainable production rate. While not directly applicable to the problem stated here, this procedure is useful for equalizing the work load among stations once a solution has been found.

Mitchell (1957) extends Jackson's algorithm to include another common constraint, zoning. By zoning is meant the division of the set of elemental tasks into (possibly overlapping) subsets corresponding to physical constraints on the assembly operation. Zoning of an assembly line may be determined by the position of the product on the conveyor, the layout of the production facility, or both. For example, certain elements may be performed only from the back of the product, or only while it is lying on its side; likewise, some elements may be carried out on a smaller subline joining the main conveyor. The constraint that all elemental tasks assigned to a work station must be in the same zone is added to the definition of a solution.

The methods mentioned above are not practical for large assembly line balancing problems because of their computational requirements. Indeed, no satisfactory general scheme for resolving large combinatorial problems involving partial ordering relations has yet been devised.[2]

4. Heuristic Programs

Webster's New International Dictionary of the English Language, 1959, defines the adjective "heuristic" as "serving to discover or reveal." Thus,

---

[2] However, much unreported research is being done by industrial firms into assembly line balancing and related problems.

by heuristics we mean (after Newell, Shaw, and Simon, 1958*d*) principles or devices that contribute, on the average, to reduction of search in problem-solving activity. The admonitions "Draw a diagram" in geometry, "Reduce everything to sines and cosines" in proving trigonometric identities, or "Always take a check—it may be mate" in chess are all familiar heuristics.

Heuristic problem-solving procedures are procedures organized around such effort-saving devices. A heuristic program is the mechanization on a digital computer of some heuristic procedure. The computer attempts to solve the problem by carrying out the heuristic program. At present this use of digital computers is the only means we have of making explicit the behavior of a complex heuristic procedure in dealing with a large class of problems. The Logic Theorist (Newell, Shaw, and Simon, 1957*a*), the Chess Machine (Newell, Shaw, and Simon, 1958*b*), and the Geometry Machine (Gelernter and Rochester, 1958) are examples of working heuristic programs in other areas.

The distinction between heuristic and non-heuristic problem-solving procedures is often vague. Rather than attempt to specify a rule by which all procedures can be so categorized, we shall cite some common characteristics of existing heuristic procedures:

1. Factorization of the problem into a number of "smaller" problems and subproblems (often through means-end analysis), with a corresponding goal-subgoal organization of behavior. For example, the Chess Machine might realize that it cannot play P-K4 because it would lose an exchange on that square, and consequently sets up the subgoal of first bringing another man to bear on its K4.

2. Use of cues in the environment to determine the particular behavior evoked from a wide set of possible alternatives available to the program. That is, a high degree of interdependence between the specific problem (from a more general class) being considered and the particular problem-solving methods used. Thus, the methods used by the assembly line balancing program for choosing elements to shift between groupings depend on the particular characteristics of those groupings.

3. Use of recursive procedures to bring to bear on subproblems the same repertoire of problem-solving techniques used on the original problem. Thus, the Logic Theorist can use the same "bag of tricks" to prove a derived expression as to prove the initial statement from which the derived expression was produced.

4. No guarantee of a satisfactory solution or, often, of any solution. For example, the Chess Machine, because of time and space limitations, may not be able to consider some promising continuations, including the a postiori optimum one.

Because a heuristic procedure substitutes the effort reduction of its shortcuts for the guaranteed optimal solution of an exhaustive method, the justification of such a program as a problem-solver must be in terms of the number of cases successfully solved and the relative amount of effort involved. In a later section on operating results, the assembly balancing program presented here is compared with several exhaustive procedures.

The set of heuristics outlined here for balancing an assembly line evolved from several sources: discussions with industrial engineers of how they actually balance lines; study of the various papers cited above; explorations with several co-workers, particularly A. Newell, of possible techniques; and finally extensive experimentation with particular instances of the problem.

5. The Assembly Line Balancing Program

This heuristic approach to assembly line balancing is based on simplification—sufficient simplification of a complex combinatorial problem that it becomes solvable (in most cases) by simple, straightforward methods.

Two recursively defined routines form the essence of this procedure.[3] Phase I constructs a hierarchy of increasingly simpler line balancing problems by aggregating groups of elements into a single compound element. Each of these compound elements is itself a member of this same class of line balancing problems, since it is made up of elements requiring a given operation time and among whom partial ordering relationships exist.

Phase II solves a simple (small number of elements) line balancing problem by assigning groups of available workmen to elements and then taking as subproblems those compound elements (simple problems in themselves) which have been assigned more than one man.

This approach requires heuristics for aggregating groups of elements into compound elements, for solving the simplified problems thus created, and for reintroducing the detail of the original problem when the simplified version does not yield a solution.

A third phase of the problem-solving process, utilizing virtually the same heuristics as already required, involves "smoothing" the final work load (assigned time) among work stations. Since the greatest total time assigned any work station limits the speed of the line, a smooth balance answers

[3] Several other strategies could be suggested as bases for heuristic approaches to the problem: (1) division of the problem into relatively independent subproblems, solution of these by optimizing techniques, and combination of the subsolutions by heuristic methods; (2) solution of a problem abstracted from the original by replacing all times with one of a single large or a single small value, and then adjustment of the result to fit actual times; (3) development of stations in an order determined by the density of partial ordering constraints, first building in those regions of the problem where there is least freedom among elements. None of these alternative approaches are considered here in any further detail.

the problem "What is the highest production rate achievable with a given number of men?" That is, since both men and time are measured in discrete units, a *nonsmoothed* optimum solution of the problem "given a production rate, minimize the number of men required" need not be an optimum solution of the dual problem "given a number of men, maximize the production rate."

Thus, the general problem-solving scheme calls for:

Phase I. Repeated application of aggregative procedures, creating a hierarchy of simplified line balancing problems ranging in complexity from the initial problem to one containing a single compound element.

Phase II. Recursive application to these simplified problems of a procedure for assigning men to tasks, down to the level of problems whose component tasks require one man each. When the compound elements making up a problem require more men than are available, these elements are broken up and their components regrouped to require fewer men.

Phase III. Smoothing the resulting balance by transferring tasks among work stations until the distribution of assigned time is as even as possible.

The following sections discuss the heuristics entailed in each of these procedures.

Since this approach does not guarantee an optimum solution to the overall line balancing problem, we must have some notion of a satisfactory solution and accept or reject proposed solutions based on this notion. Also, since the solution of a problem does not guarantee that its subproblems will be solved, whatever process generates solutions must remain active until all subproblems have been solved, ready to generate another solution if necessary. The methods by which these requirements are met are indicated below.

6. Constructing the Hierarchy of Problems

The ordering constraints present in the problem suggest two natural units of aggregation of elements. Either a completely ordered relationship exists between several elements—as U3 must always precede U4 (Fig. 1)—or no ordering is specified—as U10, U11, U12. We adopt the "chain" and the "set" as basic aggregative units in constructing a simplified problem:

I. A group of adjacent elements whose relative order is completely determined, each except the first having a single direct predecessor and each except the last having a single direct follower, can be replaced by a single compound element, called a *chain*.

II. A group of elements whose relative order is completely unspecified, all having the same direct predecessors and followers, can be replaced by a single compound element, called a *set*.

Thus, U10, U11, U12 in Fig. 1 can be replaced by a set V2, and then V2, U15 can be replaced by a chain V3. These aggregations can be indicated on the original problem, as in Fig. 2a. However, it is convenient to represent the aggregations as a branching tree, with each compound element having beneath it the elements of which it is composed.

The tree of compound element V3 is shown in Fig. 2b. Note that the time requirement of a compound element is the sum of the times of its components.

We use the term "chain relationship" to indicate that some ordering (possibly indirect) exists between two elements and "set relationship" to indicate that none exists.

While the solution strategy calls for repeated application of the aggregative operations to yield a hierarchy of simplified problems, these two types of aggregation are not sufficient to completely reduce (to a single compound element) most actual problems. We can proceed by first defining more complex aggregative operations and then, if necessary, removing "troublesome" ordering constraints. Proposed solutions must then be checked to see that these missing constraints are not violated.

The one additional compound element introduced to date is the Z.

III.   A Z is a group of four elements with the two front elements having common predecessors and the other two back elements having common followers. The single direct follower of one front element is one of the back elements; the two direct followers of the other front element are the back elements. The back elements have no other direct predecessors.

An example of a Z and its representation in tree form are given in Figs. 3a and 3b. (Note that there is a canonical order of subelements in the tree representation of the chain and the Z.)

The recursive procedure carrying out this aggregating process may be applied to any assemblage of elements. By an assemblage of elements we

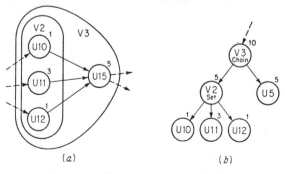

Figure 2. Chain and set aggregations.

here mean those given elements without predecessors within the assemblage (called the front elements) and their direct followers, and their followers' direct followers, and so forth, to and including those elements with no direct followers. Thus, the illustrative problem of Fig. 1 is an assemblage with front element U1.

While there is not space here to present the full details of this procedure, a brief summary follows.

Given an assemblage of elements with a single front element, the routine attempts to create a chain. When an element having several direct followers is encountered, the program first sets up the subproblem of aggregating the assemblage with those several front elements and then applies itself to that problem. (The routine is recursive, so that attempting to solve that subproblem may involve setting up and attempting to solve sub-subproblems and so forth.) If the subproblem is solved successfully, the higher-level problem of creating a chain is continued. If the subproblem fails, or if an element is encountered with direct predecessors outside the assemblage (other than those of the front element), the higher-level problem fails.

Given an assemblage of elements with several front elements, the routine attempts to create a set or, failing that, a Z. If this can be done, the problem becomes one of reducing an assemblage with a single front element. If not, the routine first sets up the independent subproblems of aggregating separate assemblages starting with each of the front elements, and applies itself to each of these subproblems in turn. When these subproblems are concluded, the higher level problem of creating a set or Z is resumed.

Trying to resolve these subproblems independently often reveals complex ordering constraints between them. A Z is then postulated incorporating such constraints. Further constraints that prevent completion of an already postulated Z are relaxed so that the Z can be completed, and the higher level problem is then continued.

Figure 4 is the tree of compound elements constructed by application of this recursive procedure to the problem of Fig. 1. The running commentary of this routine is given in Appendix A; this is a dynamic statement of how

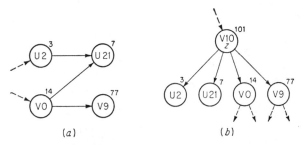

Figure 3. Z aggregations.

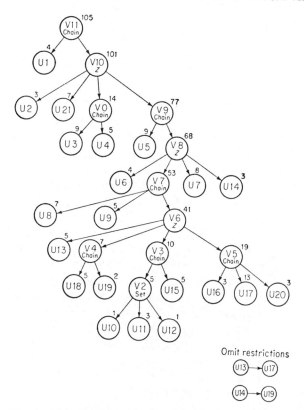

Figure 4. Twenty-one-element problem—Phase I output.

the routine is proceeding. It is instructive to follow through this "protocol" while viewing Figs. 1 and 4. This first phase of the problem-solving process need be carried out only once for a given product (set of constraints). The resulting hierarchy is supplied as an input to the second phase of the process.

7. Grouping Tasks into Work Stations

Inputs to the second phase, grouping tasks into work stations, are: the problem hierarchy as developed in Phase I; a cycle time determined by the required production rate; and a "per cent usable time" supplied as a guide for setting up and accepting potential work stations. Per cent usable time is an estimate (at present made by the user) of how close to the required station the task elements can be grouped. This measure reflects the structure and time values of the particular problem being solved.

The assignment routine consists of a simple recursive procedure for allocating men (work stations) to groups of tasks and a set of procedures for regrouping the tasks when necessary. These regrouping heuristics are described in the following section.

The recursive routine for allocating men to groups of tasks proceeds as follows:

1. An initial estimate is made of the number of men required to meet the given production rate, given a per cent usable time (per cent effectiveness). This number of men is assigned to the "top" compound element, representing a single grouping of all task elements. The recursive routine described in step 2 is then applied to that element. If the routine succeeds, the line has been balanced and Phase II ends. If the routine fails, the number of men assigned to the top element is increased and the procedure repeated.

2. (a) If the element being considered has been assigned more than one man, these available men are allocated among the direct components of the element according to their time requirements. This recursive routine is then applied to each of these component elements in turn. If the routine successfully solves each of the subproblems, then the problem of grouping tasks into work stations is also solved at this level and the routine terminates. If the available men cannot be allocated among the direct components of the element in question—if, considered independently, they require more men than are available—then regrouping procedures are called upon to shift tasks among these groupings so that they are independently solvable. If such a regrouping cannot be found, control is returned to the next higher level, signaling failure to solve the subproblem.

If the recursive routine should fail to handle one of the components below this level and report back failure, excess elements from the failing subproblem are shifted to another grouping or, failing that, the regrouping procedures are activated to produce another set of independent groupings. Again, if solvable subproblems cannot be found, control is returned to the next higher level with a failure signal.

(b) If the element being considered has been assigned a single man, additional elements are added to it if necessary to bring near the maximum allowable size and the grouping is marked as a work station. Control then returns to the next higher level, signaling success.

Thus, this recursive routine, like that of Phase I, deals with examples of a particular class of problems. It solves a problem by setting up within it (and solving in the same way) other "easier" problems of the same class whose solutions can be combined to solve the larger problem also. In particular, Phase I of the line balancing program makes use of natural groupings of the elemental tasks to build up a hierarchy of simplified problems, and Phase II attempts to balance the line using these groupings as complete units, transferring tasks among these groupings only when the simple allocation scheme fails.

8. Regrouping Procedures

Five regrouping procedures—direct transfer, trading, sequential grouping, complete grouping, and exhaustive grouping—are available to the Phase II recursive routine when its simple scheme for allocating available men fails. Which of these regrouping heuristics will be called upon, and in what order, is determined by characteristics of the compound elements being regrouped. These procedures are also used by Phase III of the assembly line balancing program in smoothing a proposed line balance.

All five methods make use of a single recursive routine that scans a given part of the hierarchy of elements (the "problem tree") and generates a sequence of groups of elements lying within certain specifications (maximum total time of group, minimum total time of group, from front or from back). This routine proceeds by building a first group, always taking the largest element acceptable, and then constructs further groups by eliminating from consideration (or breaking down into components, if a compound element) successive elements of that group and applying itself to the remaining elements of the given part of the hierarchy. Thus, if requested to produce groups totaling at least 8 but not more than 16 time units from the back of compound element V6 (see Fig. 4), the routine would generate the sequence (V4, U13, U20), and (U20, U17). The routine generates each element of this sequence as requested, remembering where it is in the sequence to be able to generate the next one.

The first three methods—direct transfer, trading, and sequential grouping—are used to set up independently solvable subproblems which can then be handled by the Phase II recursive routine.

Direct transfer is applied when only two components are involved. This method tries simply to transfer elements from one component to the other and thus reduce the number of men required by a straightforward totaling of whole men.

Thus, if V11 in Fig. 4 had been assigned six men (given a cycle time of 20), the direct transfer procedure would first attempt to shift elements totaling at least 1 but not more than 16 time units from V10 to U1, and would in fact shift V0 (14 time units).

Trading also is applied only to two components, and assumes that direct transfer has been attempted without success. Trading tries to regroup by shifting an element larger than the acceptable limit from one component in exchange for smaller elements (in a set relationship with the first element shifted) from the other component.

An example of this method is cited in the next section.

Sequential grouping is used when there are several components, and attempts to construct an acceptable work station from the front of the given group of components. If the remaining components can be handled by the remaining men available, the method is considered successful. If not, an attempt is made to construct another work station from the back of the component group, and a similar test is made.

Suppose, for example, that V7 in Fig. 4 had been assigned three men (cycle time 20). Since V7 is made up of three components requiring one, one, and three men, regrouping procedures would be evoked. Sequential grouping would first group together U8, U9, and V2 and then, since the remaining component V6 would now total 36 time units, requiring only the two remaining available men, the method would be successful.

The remaining two regrouping procedures, complete grouping and exhaustive grouping, try to completely solve the subproblems remaining. They may be regarded as "last-ditch" methods at any particular level.

Complete grouping attempts, first from the front of the component group and then from the back, to construct work stations until all task elements are grouped. If at any time the method cannot construct a station such that the remaining elements total less than can be handled by the remaining men, the method fails.

Exhaustive grouping generates all possible (independent) first work stations, then all possible following work stations for each of these. This method is, in fact, the exhaustive algorithm suggested by Jackson (1956). Because of the comparatively large amount of effort required to do an exhaustive grouping, this procedure is used only when two men are to be assigned. The method does furnish to the next higher level Phase II routine (on failure) the best groupings it was able to construct from the front

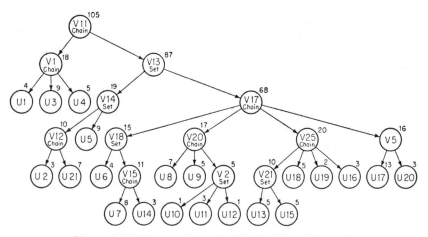

Figure 5. Twenty-one-element problem—Phase II output.

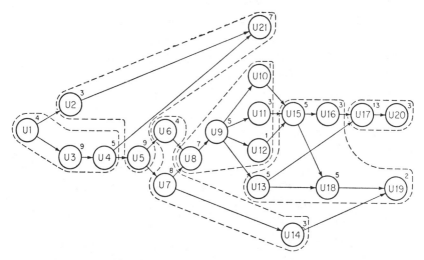

Figure 6. Twenty-one-element problem with stations, cycle time 20.

and the back, as well as which elements were left ungrouped in those solutions.

While these regrouping methods are clearly not foolproof, they have proven satisfactory for all problems attempted to date. Figure 5 shows the problem of Figs. 1 and 4 after the Phase II recursive routine has been applied to it (cycle time 20, 95 per cent usable time), and Fig. 6 pictures the work stations thus created on the original problem. (See also Table 1.) Appendix B lists the protocol produced during this assignment.

9. Smoothing the Resulting Balance

Phase III of the assembly line balancing program seeks to even the distribution of work among work stations by repeatedly reducing the time requirement of the largest work station. Inputs to this phase of the problem are a balanced line in hierarchical representation, such as would be produced by Phase II, and a cycle time. This iterative routine uses the same regrouping heuristics used by the Phase II recursive routine.

The following steps comprise the Phase III procedure:

1. Calculate the least possible time value of the highest station (with the given cycle time). If the largest station's time value is not greater than this bound, no further smoothing is possible and the routine terminates.

2. Given the largest station, consider in turn, in increasing order of size, all "adjacent" (in a set relationship or direct predecessors or followers) stations to that largest station. Try to even the distribution of work between

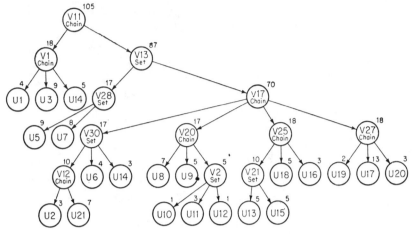

Figure 7. Twenty-one-element problem—Phase III output.

them using the direct transfer heuristic. If successful, return to step 1. If not, go to step 3.

3. Consider again those stations adjacent to the largest station in increasing order of size. Try to reduce the work load of the larger using the trading heuristic. If successful, return to step 1. If not, proceed to step 4.

4. Once again, consider adjacent stations in increasing order of size. For each one, using first direct transfer and then trading, try to make any transfer that reduces the largest station, even if the formerly smaller station is now as large or larger. If some such transfer is found, set up the subproblem of reducing this new larger station and apply this routine to it (excepting that step 4, setting up further subproblems, cannot be used). If successful, return to step 1; if not, the Phase III routine terminates.

The procedure outlined above has not yet been coded (which should be a relatively easy task, as it relies so heavily on already coded routines), but it has been hand-simulated for several cases. The results of this hand simulation for the problem of Figs. 1 and 4 is shown in Fig. 7. The simulated output of this phase of the assembly line balancing program is given in Appendix C.

10. Operating Results

Three sample problems were used in developing and testing this heuristic procedure. These are an 11-element problem taken from Jackson (1956), the 21-element problem used as an example here, taken from the Mitchell (1957), and a 70-element problem representing actual appliance industry

TABLE 2

	Phase I			Phase II			
Problem	Effort IPL instr.	Cycle time	Per cent usable	No. of stations	Per cent idle	Effort	Effort per station $\times 10^3$
11-element	14,478	10	95	5	8	153,075	30.6
21-element	51,386	20	90	6	12	141,868	23.7
		19	95	6	8	143,183	23.8
		14	95	8	6	627,809	78.5
		18	98	6	3	483,458	80.5
		21	100	5	0	760,803	152.2
70-element	207,194	176	93	23	9	2,495,118	108.5

data. While these few cases do not completely test the method's general validity,[4] we can extract some interesting measures of performance in different types of problems.

Data summarizing these problem-solving exercises are given in Table 2. Note the increase in computing effort with problem-size in both Phases I and II. We also observe for the several cases of the 21-element problem an increase in effort per station as per cent idle time decreases. It appears that the amount of effort required to reach a balance depends upon the number of elements in the problem, number of stations desired and the per cent idle time available. Additional experience with actual problems will enable us to develop a method for estimating the effort required in particular cases.

To get some feeling for the effort required by exhaustive algorithms, we also attempted the 11-element problem with only the "exhaustive grouping" method, thus solving the problem using Jackson's algorithm (1956). (This is only a rough comparison, since the algorithm is carried out here using list processes and would benefit more than the heuristic program as a whole from use of matrix representation. Also, since the method is imbedded in the midst of our procedure, some amount of processing not required by that algorithm per se is included in the measure.) Under these conditions the program required about 389,000 IPL instructions to reach a balance, a factor of 2.5 over the heuristic approach. While this difference is not striking in light of the above warnings, the disparity will grow rapidly with increasing problem size.

We also tested Salveson's (1955) linear programming formulation of

[4] It is necessary to test this procedure against other large problems not only to measure its economic efficiency but also to ensure that the heuristics incorporated here have not been unconsciously adapted to meet the requirements of these particular test problems.

the assembly line balancing problem on our 11-element problem, using the RAND Simplex Code. The formulation required 11 equations in 62 unknowns (1 unknown for each possible legal grouping, given a cycle time of 10). This program required 15 iterations (starting from an artificial basis) to reach an optimum solution. As was expected, this answer contained groupings of fractional parts of elements. We must await an operating integer programming code in order to really test a linear programming approach.

The next areas we hope to analyze are (1) the effort saved through incremental changes—that is, starting from a nearby balance as opposed to starting from scratch with each new cycle time—and (2) the usefulness of initially producing balances at a range of interesting production rates, thus providing an approximation to the labor cost function for the assembly operation.

11. Adding the Zoning Constraint

One of the advantages sought from the heuristic approach to complex decision problems is the ability to redefine the problem, adding or deleting restrictions on a solution, with ease. As a specific example, we introduce the zoning restriction treated by Mitchell (1957). Under this restriction

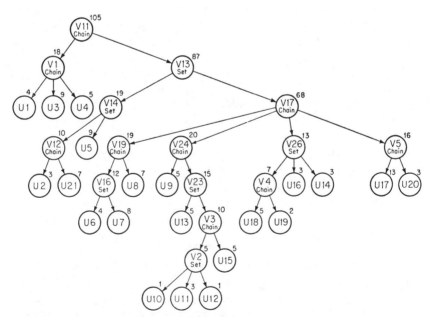

Figure 8. Twenty-one-element problem with zoning constraint—Phase II output.

TABLE 3

Zone	Elemental tasks
1	U1, U2, U3, U4, U5, U7, U8, U21
3	U3, U4, U6, U7, U8, U9, U10, U11, U12, U13, U15, U16, U18
4	U13, U14, U15, U16, U17, U18, U19, U20

each elemental task is assigned to one or more zones reflecting the physical limitations of the production process.

To incorporate this new restriction, the basic grouping generator (see *Regrouping Procedures*) is modified to produce only groupings within a specified zone or zones, and the routine that accepts work stations is modified to reject groups whose elements are not in a common zone. These modifications can be made relatively easily without affecting other parts of the over-all program. These modifications have been hand-simulated for several problems. Table 3 indicates the zoning of elements in the sample problem of Fig. 1. Figure 8 is the result of the modified Phase II operation on that problem (cycle time 20).

12. Mechanizing the Assembly Line Balancing Program

The assembly line balancing program described here is programmed in an interpretative system, IPL-IV, on the RAND Corporation's digital computer, JOHNNIAC. The IPL-IV system uses about 1200 of the JOHNNIAC's 4096 words of high-speed core memory and about 650 words of the 12,288-word auxiliary drum memory. In running the line balancing problem, which makes heavy use of the drum for temporary storage of data, the system interprets at the rate of about 9,000 to 10,000 IPL instructions per minute. While there has been no published account of IPL-IV, the closely related IPL-V for the IBM 650, 704 and 709 is fully documented (Newell and Tonge, 1960c, Newell et al., 1961e).

Why symbol manipulation languages[5] are extremely useful research tools for exploring techniques for problem-solving in complex and ill-structured situations is examined in more detail in another place (Tonge, 1961a). The essential point is that the "parameters" which the problem-solver wishes to vary freely are policies—general principles, rules of thumb, or what have you. The diversity of these principles cannot be anticipated when the problem-solving process begins with the problem of finding a good problem-solving process for the problem at hand. Some system for using the computer is required which frees the problem-solver from making

[5] Such programming languages include the IPL (Information Processing Language) Series (Newell and Tonge, 1960c; Newell et al., 1961e), LISP (McCarthy, 1959), COMIT (Yngve, 1958), and FORTRAN List Processing Language (Gelernter and Rochester, 1958).

early commitments (which he will later regret) about storage allocation, information to be carried, and so forth. This system must allow the user (possibly at the cost of machine speed and storage usage) to state his incompletely formulated problem and method of solution and start experimenting. List structure languages are a first step toward such a system.

The assembly line balancing program itself requires about 6700 machine locations, of which about 6100 are in auxiliary storage. In keeping with our preference for quick results rather than "efficient" operation, the entire structure of the problem was encoded in list form. With a satisfactory program (from the performance standpoint) developed, savings in machine space and speed could be made by encoding some structural information in matrix form. Bryton (1954), Marimont (1959), and others have made interesting contributions in this direction. Such a recoding would require only changing those routines that locate the value of certain properties of elements. The rest of the code is independent and would remain unchanged. Other reductions in operating time can be obtained by recoding in basic machine language certain operations now in interpretive code. Using IPL-V on the 704, it will be possible to implement the program described here at 5 times the speed achieved on the JOHNNIAC. At such speeds (about an hour maximum to balance an appliance line) this approach seems close to economic feasibility in treating some complex industrial decision problems.

13. Final Remarks

The aims of this research have been broader than just trying to produce a method for solving the assembly line balancing problem. We have set out to test the feasibility of a heuristic approach to complex decision-making in a particular industrial area and to examine the use of new computer techniques in implementing such an approach. As always, many interesting questions remain unexplored. But based on the experience reported here, we must conclude that the combination of a heuristic approach and these new methods of computer utilization are useful research tools in complex problem-solving.

Our program is not economically competitive when measured against the dollar per hour cost of line balancing by the industrial engineer. However, a true evaluation of the method must also consider (1) the possibility of fewer men required along the line on the average (a subject not yet fully explored), (2) the value of quick production of balances at a large number of production rates and (3) the value of releasing industrial engineers to do other, more creative analytic work.

Also, our research has indicated that present symbol manipulation languages, while a great advance for these purposes over conventional programming techniques, are still relatively primitive. While it is difficult to conceive preparing this program in a less powerful language than IPL-IV, much effort is required in machine-oriented aspects of communicating the problem-solving procedure to the computer. Further research in this area is needed before the heuristically oriented problem-solver will be free to expend his effort primarily on developing satisfactory problem-solving techniques, using the computer as a tool for spelling out the implications of his procedures.

Appendix A

Phase I—21-Element Problem

1 Propose chain U1
  2 Propose set U2, U3
    3 Propose chain U2
      4 Cannot reduce U2 to U21
    3 Propose chain U3
      4 Define chain V0 = U3, U4
      4 Propose set U5, U21
        5 Cannot reduce U21
    3 Propose Z V0, U2
      4 Propose chain U21
      4 Propose chain U5
        5 Propose set U6, U7
          6 Propose chain U6
            7 Cannot reduce U6 to U8
          6 Propose chain U7
            7 Propose set U8, U14
              8 Cannot reduce U8
          6 Propose Z U7, U6
            7 Delete constraint U14 to U19
            7 Propose chain U8
              8 Define chain V1 = U8, U9
              8 Propose set U10, U11, U12, U13
                9 Define set V2 = U10, U11, U12
                9 Propose chain V2
                  10 Define chain V3 = V2, U15
                  10 Propose set U16, U18
                    11 Cannot reduce U18
                9 Propose chain U13
                  10 Propose set U17, U18
                    11 Cannot reduce U17
                    11 Cannot reduce U18

9 Propose Z U13, V3
    10 Delete constraint U13 to U17
    10 Propose chain U18
        11 Define chain V4 = U18, U19
    10 Propose chain U16
        11 Define chain V5 = U16, U17, U20
    10 Define Z V6 = U13, V4, V3, V5
8 Propose chain V6
8 Define chain V7 = U8, U9, V6
7 Propose chain U14
7 Define Z V8 = U6, V7, U7, U14
5 Propose chain V8
5 Define chain V9 = U5, V8
4 Define Z V10 = U2, U21, V0, V9
2 Propose chain V10
2 Define chain V11 = U1, V10

Appendix B

Phase II—21-Element Problem—Cycle Time 20—PCT Usable 90

1 Consider V11—components U1, V10—6 men available
2 Activate direct transfer
    3 Combine V0, U1
        4 Redefine chain V11 = V1, V13
        4 Define chain V1 = U1, U3, U4
        4 Define chain V12 = U2, U21
        4 Define set V13 = V12, V9
2 Assign 1 man to V1, 5 to V13
    3 Consider V1—components U1, U3, U4—1 man available
        4 Mark V1 as work station—time = 18
    3 Consider V13—components V12, V9—5 men available
        4 Assign 1 man to V12, 4 to V9
            5 Consider V12—components U2, U21—1 man available
                6 Combine U5, V12
                    7 Redefine set V13 = V14, V8
                    7 Define V14 = U5, V12
                6 Mark V14 as work station—time = 19
            5 Consider V8—components U6, V7, U7, U14
                6 Add U14, U6 to waiting list
                6 Assign 3 men to V7, 1 to U7
                    7 Consider U7—1 man available
                        8 Combine U7, U14, U6
                            9 Define set V18 = U6, V15

    9 Define chain V17 = V18, V7
    9 Define chain V15 = U7, U14
    9 Redefine set V13 = V14, V17
  8 Mark V18 as work station—time = 15
7 Consider V7—components U8, U9, V6—3 men available
  8 Activate sequential grouping
    9 Combine U8, U9, V2
      10 Redefine chain V7 = V20, V6
      10 Define V20 = U8, U9, V2
      10 Redefine Z V6 = U13, V4, U15, V5
  8 Assign 1 man to V20, 2 to V6
    9 Consider V20—components U8, U9, V2—1 man available
      10 Mark V20 as work station—time = 17
    9 Consider V6—components U13, V4, U15, V5—2 men available
      10 Activate sequential grouping
        11 Combine U15, U13, V4, U16
          12 Define chain V23 = V25, V5
          12 Define chain V25 = V21, U18, U19, U16
          12 Redefine chain V5 = U17, U20
          12 Define set V21 = U13, U15
          12 Redefine chain V7 = V20, V23
      10 Assign 1 man to V25, 1 to V5
        11 Consider V5—components U17, U20—1 man available
          12 Mark V5 as work station—time = 16
        11 Consider V25—components V21, U18, U19, U16—1 man available
          12 Mark V25 as work station—time = 20
7 Define chain V17 = V18, V20, V25, V5

Appendix C

Phase III—21-Element Problem—Cycle Time 20—PCT Usable 90

1 Least possible high station = $105/6 = 17+ = 18$ time units
1 Consider V25—time = 20
  2 Activate direct transfer, V25 to V5
    3 Combine U19, V5
      4 Redefine chain V17 = V18, V20, V25, V27
      4 Redefine chain V25 = V21, U18, U16
      4 Define chain V27 = U19, U17, U20

1 Consider V14—Time = 19
   2 Activate direct transfer, V14 to V18
   2 Activate direct transfer, V14 to V1
   2 Activate trade, V14 and V18
      3 Combine V14, U7
         4 Redefine set V13 = V28, V17
         4 Redefine set V28 = V12, U5, U7
         4 Redefine set V18 = U6, U14
      3 Combine V12, V18
         4 Redefine set V28 = U5, U7
         4 Redefine chain V17 = V30, V20, V25, V27
         4 Define set V30 = V12, U6, U14

A HEURISTIC PROGRAM THAT SOLVES SYMBOLIC INTEGRATION PROBLEMS IN FRESHMAN CALCULUS

by James R. Slagle

A large high-speed general-purpose digital computer (IBM 7090) was programmed to solve elementary symbolic integration problems at approximately the level of a good college freshman. The program is called SAINT, an acronym for "Symbolic Automatic INTegrator." The SAINT program is written in LISP (McCarthy, 1960), and most of the work reported here is the substance of a doctoral dissertation at the Massachusetts Institute of Technology (Slagle, 1961). This discussion concerns the SAINT program and its performance.

Some typical samples of SAINT's external behavior are given so that the reader may think in concrete terms. Let SAINT read in its card reader an IBM card containing (in a suitable notation) the symbolic integration problem $\int xe^{x^2}\,dx$. In less than a minute and a half, SAINT prints out the answer, $\frac{1}{2}e^{x^2}$. Except where otherwise noted, every problem mentioned in this chapter has been solved by SAINT. Note that SAINT omits the constant of integration, and we, too, shall ignore it throughout our discussion. After working for less than a minute on the problem $\int e^{x^2}\,dx$ (which cannot be integrated in elementary form) SAINT prints out that it cannot solve it.

SAINT performs indefinite integration, also called antidifferentiation. In addition it performs definite and multiple integration when these are trivial extensions of indefinite integration. SAINT handles integrands that represent explicit elementary functions of a real variable which, for the sake of brevity, will be elementary functions. The elementary functions are the functions normally encountered in freshman integral calculus, except that SAINT does not handle hyperbolic notation. The elementary functions are defined recursively as follows:

a. Any constant is an elementary function.

b. The variable is an elementary function.

c. The sum or product of elementary functions is an elementary function.

d. An elementary function raised to an elementary function power is an elementary function.

e. A trigonometric function of an elementary function is an elementary function.

f. A logarithmic or inverse trigonometric function of an elementary function (restricted in range if necessary) is an elementary function.

Currently SAINT uses twenty-six standard forms. It uses eighteen kinds of transformations including integration by parts and various substitution methods (but excluding, among others, the method of partial fractions). Since the SAINT program uses heuristic methods, it is by definition a heuristic program. Although many authors have given many definitions, in this discussion a heuristic method (or simply a heuristic) is a method which helps in discovering a problem's solution by making plausible but fallible guesses as to what is the best thing to do next.

Indefinite Integration Procedure of SAINT

This section describes how SAINT performs indefinite integration. An attempt is made to orient the reader before a detailed description of the procedure is given. The executive organization of SAINT is like that of the Logic Theorist of Newell, Shaw, and Simon (1957). It will help to take a preview of Sec. 14 (especially Fig. 3). The "try for an immediate solution" mentioned twice in Fig. 3 may be described roughly as follows: As soon as a new goal *g* is generated, SAINT uses its straightforward methods in an attempt to achieve it. While doing this, SAINT may add *g* or certain of *g*'s subgoals to the "temporary goal list." If *g* is achieved, an attempt is made to achieve the original goal. Slagle (1961) includes among other things, a full description together with a detailed example and suggestions for future work.

As a concrete example we sketch how SAINT solved

$$\int \frac{x^4}{(1 - x^2)^{5/2}} \, dx$$

in eleven minutes. SAINT's only guess at a first step is to try substitution: $y = \arcsin x$, which transforms the original problem into

$$\int \frac{\sin^4 y}{\cos^4 y} \, dy$$

For the second step SAINT makes three alternative guesses:

A. By trigonometric identities $\int \dfrac{\sin^4 y}{\cos^4 y}\, dy = \int \tan^4 y\, dy$

B. By trigonometric identities $\int \dfrac{\sin^4 y}{\cos^4 y}\, dy = \int \cot^{-4} y\, dy$

C. By substituting $z = \tan(y/z)$ $\int \dfrac{\sin^4 y}{\cos^4 y}\, dy = \int 32\, \dfrac{z^4}{(1+z^2)(1-z^2)^4}\, dz$

SAINT immediately brings the 32 outside of the integral.

After judging that (A) is the easiest of these three problems SAINT guesses the substitution $z = \tan y$, which yields

$$\int \tan^4 y\, dy = \int \frac{z^4}{1+z^2}\, dz$$

SAINT immediately transforms this into

$$\int \left(-1 + z^2 + \frac{1}{1+z^2}\right) dz = -z + \frac{z^3}{3} + \int \frac{dz}{1+z^2}$$

Judging incorrectly that (B) is easier than

$$\int \frac{dz}{1+z^2}$$

SAINT temporarily abandons the latter and goes off on the following tangent. By substituting $z = \cot y$,

$$\int \cot^{-4} y\, dy = \int -\frac{dz}{z^4(1+z^2)} = -\int \frac{dz}{z^4(1+z^2)}$$

Now SAINT judges that

$$\int \frac{dz}{1+z^2}$$

is easy and guesses the substitution, $w = \arctan z$ which yields $\int dw$. Immediately SAINT integrates this, substitutes back and solves the original problem.

$$\int \frac{x^4}{(1-x^2)^{5/2}}\, dx = \arcsin x + \tfrac{1}{3} \tan^3 \arcsin x - \tan \arcsin x$$

The indefinite integration procedure may be described as follows:

1. Goals

In each application of the present procedure, the solutions of certain problems, namely, performing integrations with side conditions, are goals. How goals are generated, manipulated, and achieved is described later. For now, let us limit ourselves to describing what we shall call the "original goal," which consists of the originally given integrand and variable of integration.

2. The Goal List

The original goal is made the first member of a list called the goal list. From time to time new goals may be generated. Each newly generated goal is added to the end of the goal list.

3. Standard Forms

Whenever an integrand of a newly generated goal is of "standard form," that goal is immediately achieved by substitution. An integrand is said to be of standard form when it is a substitution instance of one of a certain set of forms. For example, $\int 2^x\ dx$ is an instance of $\int c^v\ dv = c^v/(\ln\ c)$ and hence has the solution $2^x/(\ln\ 2)$. Currently SAINT uses twenty-six standard forms (Slagle, 1961).

4. Algorithmlike Transformations

Whenever an integrand is found to be not of standard form, it is tested to see if it is amenable to an algorithmlike transformation. By an algorithmlike transformation is meant a transformation which, when applicable, is always or almost always appropriate. For a goal, a transformation is called appropriate if it is the correct next step to bring that goal nearer to achievement. Three of the eight algorithmlike transformations used in SAINT are:

a. Factor constant, i.e.,

$$\int cg(v)\ dv = c\int g(v)\ dv$$

b. Decompose, i.e.,

$$\int \Sigma g_i(v)\ dv = \Sigma \int g_i(v)\ dv$$

c. Linear substitution, i.e., if the integral is of the form

$$\int f(c_1 + c_2 v)\ dv$$

substitute $u = c_1 + c_2 v$, and obtain an integral of the form

$$\int \frac{1}{c_2} f(u)\ du$$

for example, in

$$\int \frac{\cos 3x}{(1 - \sin 3x)^2}\ dx$$

substitute $y = 3x$.

5. The AND-OR Goal Tree

When a heuristic transformation (to be described in Sec. 11) or an algorithmlike transformation is applied to a goal, new goals are generated. These goals, in turn, may generate more goals, and a certain hierarchy is created. Such a hierarchy is conveniently represented by a graph or tree growing downward. To facilitate understanding, the terminology of ordinary and family trees is adopted by analogy, for example pruning, alive, dead, child, parent, descendant, ancestor, etc.

Suppose we have an integration to perform, or more generally, any goal g, which we shall represent graphically by a point. A goal may be transformed into one or more subgoals which may be related to the goal in many ways. This integration procedure incorporates two common relations, namely AND and OR.

a. AND relationship

An AND relationship between a goal and at least two subgoals exists when the achieving of all of the subgoals causes the achieving of the goal. Figure 1 depicts a relationship with three subgoals. The arc joining the three branches denotes the AND relationship.

b. OR relationship

An OR relationship between a goal and its subgoals exists when the achieving of any one of the subgoals causes the achieving of the goal. Examples of this will appear later.

From these two basic relationships, more complicated relationships among goals may be built up; for example, see Fig. 2a and b in Sec. 12.

6. The Temporary Goal List

The first attempt on new goals is performed by the procedures "imsln" ("IMmediate SoLutioN") described in Sec. 13 below. Any goal en-

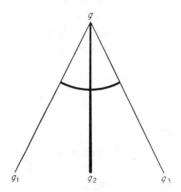

Figure 1. An AND relationship.

countered by imsln which is neither of standard form nor amenable to an algorithmlike transformation is added to the end of the "temporary goal list" (not to be confused with the "goal list") and later transferred to the "heuristic goal list" described in Sec. 10 below. If the goal were added directly to the heuristic goal list rather than to the temporary goal list, time might be wasted by finding the goal's character (cf. Sec. 8).

7. The Role of the Resource Allotment

The resource allotment, or the total amount of work space, is a side condition of the original goal. Before proceeding to apply heuristic transformations, it must be verified that the resource allotment has not been exceeded. If the resource allotment has been exceeded, SAINT reports this fact as its final answer. Although other kinds of resources, for example, time, might also be considered, the only kind of resource allotment handled by SAINT is the total amount of work space. For hand simulation, the work space can be measured by the number of pages or by the number of lines used for the final and all intermediate results.

8. Character of a Goal

When a goal is taken off the temporary goal list its "character" is obtained, that is, an ordered list of "characteristics." A characteristic of a goal is a feature which might be useful either in estimating the cost of attempting its attainment or in selecting appropriate heuristic transformations (see Sec. 11). In SAINT, the character is composed of eleven characteristics of the integrand (Slagle, 1961) including its function type (whether it is a rational function, algebraic function, rational function of sines and cosines, etc.) and its depth. The depth of an integrand is the maximum level of function composition which occurs in that expression:

$$x \text{ is of depth } 0,$$
$$x^2 \text{ is of depth } 1,$$
$$e^{x^2} \text{ is of depth } 2,$$
$$xe^{x^2} \text{ is of depth } 3.$$

As one might guess, this helps get a crude estimate of the problem's difficulty.

9. Relative Cost Estimate

Although other estimates could be tried, for the relative cost estimate of a goal we take simply the depth of its integrand. This makes use of the fact that, ordinarily, the deeper the integrand the more will be the resources needed to investigate that goal.

10. The Heuristic Goal List

A list of goals requiring heuristic transformations, or, more briefly, a heuristic goal list, is an ordered list of those goals which are neither of standard form nor amenable to an algorithmlike transformation. A member of the heuristic goal list is called a heuristic goal. New such goals are inserted in order of increasing relative cost estimate.

11. The Heuristic Transformations

A transformation of a goal is called heuristic when, even though it is applicable and plausible, there is a significant risk that it is not the appropriate next step. A transformation may be inappropriate either because it leads no closer to the solution or because some other transformation would be better. The heuristic transformations are analogous to the methods of detachment, forward chaining and backward chaining in the Logic Theorist of Newell, Shaw, and Simon (1957). The ten types of heuristic transformation (Slagle, 1961) used by SAINT are designed to suggest plausible transformations of the integrand, substitutions, and attempts using the method of integration by parts. Below is given only the most successful heuristic, "substitution for a subexpression whose derivative divides the integrand."

Let $g(v)$ be the integrand. For each nonconstant nonlinear subexpression $s(v)$ such that neither its main connective is MINUS nor is it a product with a constant factor, and such that the number of nonconstant factors of the fraction $g(v)/s'(v)$ (after cancellation) is less than the number of factors of $g(v)$, try substituting $u = s(v)$. Thus, in $xe^{x^2}\,dx$, substitute $u = x^2$. (When SAINT tried this problem it used this heuristic but surprised me by substituting $u = e^{x^2}$, which is somewhat better.)

12. Pruning the Goal Tree

Whenever some goal g has been achieved, the goal tree is pruned, that is, certain closely related goals are automatically achieved and certain other goals, newly rendered superfluous, are killed.

The pruning procedure will be clarified by an example. In Fig. 2a the achieving of g_{221} allows g_{22} to be achieved (since, as indicated by the black dot, g_{222} has already been achieved). In turn, the achieving of g_{22} allows g_2 to be achieved (since there is an OR relationship). Since the achieving of g_2 now has rendered g_{23} superfluous, it is killed. However, another of g_2's children g_{12} is not killed since, through its other parent g_1 it has direct living ancestry to the original goal g. The original goal g cannot be achieved from the achieving of g_2 since there is an AND relationship and g_1 has not yet been achieved. Therefore, the result of the pruning process is as shown

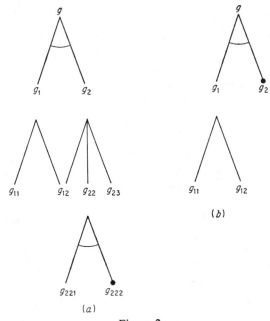

Figure 2.

in Fig. 2*b*. If either g_{11} or g_{12} is later achieved, the original goal could and would be achieved.

13. Trying for an Immediate Solution

As soon as a new goal g is generated, SAINT uses its straightforward methods in an attempt to achieve it. While doing this, SAINT may add g or certain of g's subgoals to the temporary goal list. If g is achieved, an attempt is made to achieve the original goal.

14. Executive Organization

Precisely how all the various elements 1 through 13 are pieced together to form an integration procedure is described below. The original goal is given as a triplet, namely, the integrand, the variable of integration, and the resource allotment. The procedure (see Fig. 3) is as follows:

a. If a try for an immediate solution with the original goal is successful, return with the answer, the actual indefinite integral.

b. If the resource allotment has been exceeded, report failure.

c. Obtain and associate with each goal on the temporary goal list its character and relative cost estimate. Take the goals off the temporary goal list, and insert each one in the heuristic goal list according to its relative cost estimate. If no goals remain on the heuristic goal list, report failure.

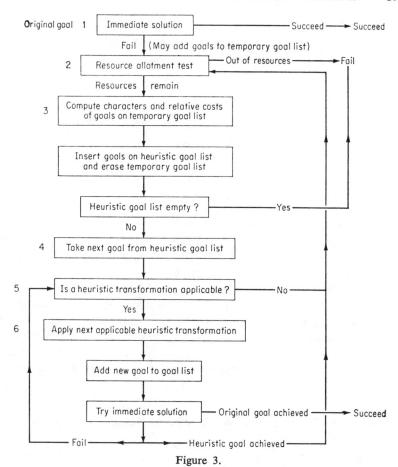

Figure 3.

d. Take the next goal g_i off the heuristic goal list and let it be the goal under consideration in the following inner loop.

e. If no heuristic transformations applicable to g_i remain, go to step *b.*

f. Apply the next heuristic transformation applicable to g_i. As soon as a new goal g is so generated, add it to the goal list, and try for an immediate solution with g. Then there are three cases. If this try achieves the original goal, return with the answer. Failing this, if g_i is achieved, go to step *b.* Otherwise go to step *e.*

Definite Integration Procedure

SAINT can perform some definite integrations by first finding the corresponding indefinite integrals. Thus, for example, for the problem

$$\int_0^3 x \sqrt{x^2 + 16} \, dx$$

SAINT first finds the indefinite integral,

$$\int x \sqrt{x^2 + 16} \, dx = \tfrac{1}{3}(x^2 + 16)^{3/2}$$

SAINT substitutes the limits and obtains the answer $6\tfrac{1}{3}$.

Multiple Integration Procedure

SAINT can perform multiple integration when it can perform the required definite integrations, e.g.,

$$\int_1^1 \int_{y^2}^{2-y^2} dx \, dy$$

Experiments and Findings with SAINT

This section describes some of SAINT's typical observed behavior and how one modification changes its behavior. Slagle (1961) describes other experiments and gives further details. The experiments to measure SAINT's behavior involve 86 problems. Largely for the purposes of debugging, 32 of the problems were selected or constructed by the author, who fully expected SAINT to solve them all. More objectively, the remaining 54 problems were selected from MIT freshman calculus final examinations by the author's assistant, Gerald Shapiro, with instructions to select the more diverse and difficult problems, provided only that the method of partial fractions was not needed for the solution. The measures of behavior that we use are:

1. Power
The power of a version of SAINT refers to the size of the class of problems that it can solve.
2. Time
All the times mentioned refer to the IBM 7090 computer.
3. Number of subgoals and unused subgoals
The original goal is not included in the number of subgoals. An unused subgoal is a subgoal which is not needed in the solution chain.
4. Level
The level of a solution is the maximum level at which a used subgoal occurs in the goal tree during that solution.
5. Heuristic level of a solution
This measure is similar to "level" except that only the goal-tree branches representing heuristic transformations are considered rather than all the branches representing algorithmlike or heuristic transformations.

A. Unmodified SAINT

The SAINT program described in the preceding sections tried to solve all 86 problems selected by the author and Gerald Shapiro. In this attempt, the computer spent about half of its time in reclaiming abandoned memory registers for reuse. Approximately half of the remaining time was spent in pattern recognition, that is, in finding characters and in recognizing when an integrand is of standard form or amenable to an algorithmlike or heuristic transformation. As the author expected, SAINT solved all 32 of his problems. Of the 54 MIT problems, SAINT solved 52 and quickly (in less than a minute) reported failure for the other 2. Both of the failures are excluded from the averages in the table below, which summarizes SAINT's average performance.

SAINT's Average Performance

	Minutes	Subgoals	Unused subgoals	Level	Heuristic level
32 author problems	3.3	6.4	2.0	3.5	1.0
52 MIT problems	2.0	4.7	0.8	2.9	0.8
All 84 problems	2.4	5.3	1.25	3.0	0.9

In this paragraph we complement the tabulation of SAINT's average performance on MIT problems with some examples of SAINT's extreme behavior. For this purpose, only MIT problems are considered since they were selected more objectively. SAINT seemed to find $\int_1^? (dx/x)$ the easiest problem since it generated no subgoals at all and took the least time, namely 0.03 minute. SAINT took the most time, 18 minutes, for

$$\int \frac{\sec^2 t}{1 + \sec^2 t - 3 \tan t} \, dt$$

whose solution ties for the maximum heuristic level of four. The other problem whose SAINT solution has a heuristic level of four is

$$\int \frac{x^4}{(1 - x^2)^{5/2}} \, dx$$

The maximum heuristic level obtained by the unmodified Logic Theorist is two, which occurred for two of 38 solutions (Newell, Shaw, and Simon, 1957a). SAINT generated the most subgoals (18) and had the maximum level (8) for $(\sin x + \cos x)^2 \, dx$. In 37 of the 52 problems, SAINT generated only subgoals that were needed in the solution chain. In this regard, SAINT registered its best performance on one of these 37 problems

$$\int_{5/2}^4 \int_{x(11-2x)}^{4(x-1)(5-x)} dy \, dx$$

for which SAINT generated 16 subgoals, all of which were needed in the solution chain.

B. BSAINT, *i.e.,* SAINT Trying Heuristic Goals in Order of Generation

Instead of trying heuristic goals in order of increasing depth, BSAINT tries heuristic goals merely in the order in which they were generated. In measures of performance including time and the number of unused subgoals, SAINT was better than BSAINT in three of the four problems which caused a difference in behavior.

Main Conclusions

The conclusions are based on experience, namely, the experiments described in the preceding sections and the author's experience concerning the creation, structure, and performance of SAINT. Throughout this section, a parenthesized mention of an experiment is an appeal for support of a conclusion to an experiment described in the previous section.

1. A machine can manifest intelligent problem-solving behavior, that is, behavior which, if performed by people, would be called intelligent (experiment A).

2. A heuristic program can easily include programs for handling an AND-OR goal tree (such as found in SAINT), which is often useful in complex goal-achieving schemes.

3. In SAINT, pattern recognition plays a very important part in three senses.

    a. Pattern recognition consumes much of the program and programming effort.

    b. Pattern recognition is used frequently and with great variety, for instance, in determinations involving standard forms, algorithmlike and heuristic transformations, and relative cost estimates.

    c. Pattern recognition consumes much of the time in solving integration problems (experiment A).

4. The tripartite division of methods into standard forms, algorithmlike transformations, and heuristic transformations is very useful in problem-solving. Standard forms in SAINT and "substitution" in the Logic Theorist may be instances of an "immediately achieve" procedure which seems to be a basic component of a goal-achieving scheme. The input to the procedure is a goal. The output is "no" (the goal is not yet achieved) or one or more of the following three items, namely, "yes," how to achieve the goal, or the achievement of the goal. In each domain, the procedure for immediately achieving a goal must be supplied anew and, since it is a very frequently used procedure, should operate very rapidly. The algorithmlike transformations also seem to be a basic component of a goal-achieving scheme, but this remains to be seen since they are not present in all schemes, for ex-

ample, the Logic Theorist. The organization of SAINT's heuristic transformations (corresponding to that of the Logic Theorist's methods of detachment, forward chaining, and backward chaining) seems to be an often convenient but not a basic component of a goal-achieving scheme.

5. A fourfold increase in SAINT's memory size (now 32,768 registers) could have been readily converted into a hundredfold increase in speed, since the reclaiming of abandoned memory registers for reuse, which now accounts for about half of the running time, would become insignificant and since a compiled program would run about fifty times faster. Much computer time and space could be saved if one computer instruction represented the very frequently used symbol manipulating functions.

6. The present speed of SAINT compares very favorably with the speed of the average college freshman (experiment A). With a now commercially available large high-speed digital computer, such as the IBM 7030 (STRETCH), a compiled but otherwise unimproved SAINT program would run eight hundred times faster, which would far surpass in speed even the most gifted of mathematicians at this task. At present commercial rates, an IBM 7090 SAINT solution of an average MIT final-examination problem costs about fifteen dollars, far more expensive than a human solution. However, a STRETCH SAINT solution would cost only about two dollars or, if compiled, only about four cents. This rapidly decreasing cost trend in computers, not to mention possible improvements in the SAINT program, will result in solutions which are far cheaper by machine than by man.

section 5
Question-answering Machines

Question-answering machines are computer programs that can be interrogated in natural language (with some constraints) for the answers to questions about a universe of discourse. The problem of constructing such machines has both theoretical and practical interest.

From the theoretical point of view, one of the most intriguing pursuits in artificial intelligence research is that of discovering the information processing structure underlying the act of "comprehending" or the process of "understanding." Though some will view the use of these two words with alarm, we use them here invested with their full human meaning. For this is precisely the goal of the researchers themselves. They are engaged in a quest for an information processing theory of an intelligent mechanism capable of "grasping the meaning" of those strings of symbols which are our natural language sentences and questions.

As a practical matter, throughout the entire field of computer applications—in information retrieval applications, in computer-controlled libraries and classrooms, in military command-control applications, in the research toward man-machine cooperative problem-solving, to mention just a few areas—users are feeling acutely the need to communicate with computers more directly, with greater fluidity and facility, than has been possible in the past.

The two reports reprinted in this section describe important initial steps toward these goals. The BASEBALL program of Green, Wolf, Chomsky, and Laughery is, in sportswriters' parlance, a baseball buff, answering certain kinds of queries about baseball "facts and figures" from a stylized baseball "yearbook" stored in the computer's memory. Lindsay's SAD SAM program answers questions about family kinship relations.

The basic differences in approach between the two efforts are as follows:

1. In the BASEBALL project, the "fact library" is stored in the computer memory in advance in a form which makes searching the library relatively easy. In SAD SAM, the kinship relationships between members of the particular family under discussion are not given the program in advance but are input to the program in the form of English sentences. The program, assimilating and analyzing these sentences, constructs an internal "map," or "model," of the familial relationships—an information structure referenced later in answering questions about the family.

2. In BASEBALL, within certain constraints upon the type of question that can be asked and the availability of words in the program's glossary, full-blown English is the language of discourse. In SAD SAM a simplified English (the so-called Basic English system, devised to facilitate English language learning) is the language of discourse.

Both programs, of course, operate within extremely limited fact universes. At this exploratory stage of the research, however, discovery and thorough understanding of possible basic mechanisms for language comprehension would appear to be more important than premature attempts to deal with wide-ranging universes of discourse.

The BASEBALL research was done at Lincoln Laboratory under the direction of Bert Green, who is presently Chairman of the Psychology Department at the Carnegie Institute of Technology.

Alice Wolf is presently a member of the research staff of Bolt, Beranek, and Newman in Cambridge, Massachusetts.

Carol Chomsky is associated with Harvard University.

Kenneth Laughery is a member of the faculty of the University of Buffalo.

Robert Lindsay is a member of the faculty of the Psychology Department, and a member of the staff of the Computer Center, at the University of Texas.

BASEBALL: AN AUTOMATIC QUESTION ANSWERER

by Bert F. Green, Jr., Alice K. Wolf, Carol Chomsky, &
Kenneth Laughery

Introduction

Men typically communicate with computers in a variety of artificial, stylized, unambiguous languages that are better adapted to the machine than to the man. For convenience and speed, many future computer-centered systems will require men to communicate with computers in natural language. The business executive, the military commander, and the scientist need to ask questions of the computer in ordinary English, and to have the computer answer the questions directly. Baseball is a first step toward this goal.

Baseball is a computer program that answers questions posed in ordinary English about data in its store. The program consists of two parts. The linguistic part reads the question from a punched card, analyzes it syntactically, and determines what information is given about the data being requested. The processor searches through the data for the appropriate information, processes the results of the search, and prints the answer.

The program is written in IPL-V (Newell, et al., 1960*e*), an information processing language that uses lists, and hierarchies of lists, called list structures, to represent information. Both the data and the dictionary are list structures, in which items of information are expressed as attribute-value pairs, *e.g.*, Team = Red Sox.

The program operates in the context of baseball data. At present, the data are the month, day, place, teams and scores for each game in the American League for one year. In this limited context, a small vocabulary is sufficient, the data are simple, and the subject matter is familiar.

Some temporary restrictions were placed on the input questions so that the initial program could be relatively straightforward. Questions are limited to a single clause; by prohibiting structures with dependent clauses the syntactic analysis is considerably simplified. Logical connectives, such as *and, or,* and *not,* are prohibited, as are constructions implying relations like *most* and *highest.* Finally, questions involving sequential facts, such as "Did the Red Sox ever win six games *in a row?"* are prohibited. These restrictions are temporary expedients that will be removed in later versions of the program. Moreover, they do not seriously reduce the number of questions that the program is capable of answering. From simple questions such as "Who did the Red Sox lose to on July 5?" to complex questions such as "Did every team play at least once in each park in each month?" lies a vast number of answerable questions.

Specification List

Fundamental to the operation of the baseball program is the concept of the *specification list,* or *spec list.* This list can be viewed as a canonical expression for the meaning of the question; it represents the information contained in the question in the form of attribute-value pairs, *e.g.,* Team = Red Sox. The spec list is generated from the question by the linguistic part of the program, and it governs the operation of the processor. For example, the question "Where did the Red Sox play on July 7?" has the spec list:

$$Place = ?$$
$$Team = Red\ Sox$$
$$Month = July$$
$$Day = 7.$$

Some questions cannot be expressed solely in terms of the main attributes (Month, Day, Place, Team, Score, and Game Serial Number), but require some modification of these attributes. For example, on the spec list of "What teams won 10 games in July?", the attribute Team is modified by Winning, and Game is modified by Number of, yielding

$$Team\ _{(winning)} = ?$$
$$Game\ _{(number\ of)} = 10$$
$$Month = July.$$

Dictionary

The dictionary definitions, which are expressed as attribute-value pairs, are used by the linguistic part of the program in generating the spec list. A complete definition for a word or idiom includes a part of speech, for use in determining phrase structure; a meaning, for use in analyzing content; an indication of whether the entry is a question word, *e.g., who* or *how many;* and an indication of whether a word occurs as part of any stored idiom. Separate dictionaries are kept for words and idioms, an idiom being any contiguous set of words that functions as a unit, having a unique definition.

The meaning of a word can take one of several forms. It may be a main or derived attribute with an associated value. For example, the meaning of the word *Team* is Team = (blank), the meaning of *Red Sox* is Team = Red Sox, and the meaning of *who* is Team = ?. The meaning may designate a subroutine, together with a particular value, as in the case of modifiers such as *winning, any, six,* or *how many.* For example, *winning* has the meaning Subroutine A1 = Winning. The subroutine, which is executed by the content analysis, attaches the modifier Winning to the attribute of the appropriate noun. Some words have more than one meaning; the word *Boston* may mean either Place = Boston or Team = Red Sox. The dictionary entry for such words contains, in addition to each meaning, the designation of a subroutine that selects the appropriate meaning according to the context in which the word is encountered. Finally, some words such as *the, did, play,* etc., have no meaning.

Data

The data are organized in a hierarchical structure, like an outline, with each level containing one or more items of information. Relationships among items are expressed by their occurrence on the same list, or on associated lists. The main heading, or highest level of the structure, is the attribute Month. For each month, the data are further subdivided by place. Below each place under each month is a list of all games played at that place during that month. The complete set of items for one game is found by tracing one path through the hierarchy, *i.e.* one list at each level. Each path contains values for each of six attributes, *e.g.:*

> Month = July
> Place = Boston
>   Day   = 7
>   Game Serial No. = 96
>   (Team = Red Sox, Score = 5)
>   (Team = Yankees, Score = 3)

The parentheses indicate that each Team must be associated with its own score, which is done by placing them together on a sublist.

The processing routines are written to accept any organization of the data. In fact, they will accept a nonparallel organization in which, for example, the data might be as above for all games through July 31, and then organized by place, with month under place, for the rest of the season. The processing routines will also accept a one-level structure in which each game is a list of all attribute-value pairs for that game. The possibility of hierarchical organization was included for generality and potential efficiency. The basic rule is that any one path through the data, including one list at each level, must contain all of the facts for a single game. Also, on every such path, each attribute may occur at most once, unless it occurs on parallel sublists.

Details of the Program

The program is organized into several successive, essentially independent routines, each operating on the output of its predecessor and producing an input for the routine that follows. The linguistic routines include question read-in, dictionary look-up, syntactic analysis, and content analysis. The processing routines include the processor and the responder.

Linguistic Routines

QUESTION READ-IN

A question for the program is read into the computer from punched cards. The question is formed into a sequential list of words.

DICTIONARY LOOK-UP

Each word on the question list is looked up in the word dictionary and its definition copied. Any undefined words are printed out. (In the future, with a direct-entry keyboard, the computer can ask the questioner to define the unknown words in terms of words that it knows, and so augment its vocabulary.) The list is scanned for possible idioms; any contiguous words that form an idiom are replaced by a single entry on the question list, and an associated definition from the idiom dictionary. At this point, each entry on the list has associated with it a definition, including a part of speech, a meaning, and perhaps other indicators.

SYNTAX

The syntactic analysis is based on the parts of speech, which are syntactic categories assigned to words for use by the syntax routine. There are 14 parts of speech and several ambiguity markers.

First, the question is scanned for ambiguities in part of speech, which are resolved in some cases by looking at the adjoining words, and in other cases by inspecting the entire question. For example, the word *score* may be either a noun or a verb; our rule is that, if there is no other main verb in the question, then *score* is a verb, otherwise it is a noun.

Next, the syntactic routine locates and brackets the noun phrases, [□]) and the prepositional and adverbial phrases, (□). The verb is left unbracketed. This routine is patterned after the work of Harris and his associates at the University of Pennsylvania (Harris, 1960). Bracketing proceeds from the end of the question to the beginning. Noun phrases, for example, are bracketed in the following manner: certain parts of speech indicate the end of a noun phrase; within a noun phrase, a part of speech may indicate that the word is within the phrase, or that the word starts the phrase, or that the word is not in the phrase, which means that the previous word started the phrase. Prepositional phrases consist of a preposition immediately preceding a noun phrase. The entire sequence, preposition and noun phrase, is enclosed in prepositional brackets. An example of a bracketed question is shown below:

[How many games] did [the Yankees] play (in [July])?

When the question has been bracketed, any unbracketed preposition is attached to the first noun phrase in the sentence, and prepositional brackets added. For example, "Who did the Red Sox lose to on July 5?" becomes "(To [who]) did [the Red Sox] lose (on [July 5])?"

Following the phrase analysis, the syntax routine determines whether the verb is active or passive and locates its subject and object. Specifically, the verb is passive if and only if the last verb element in the question is a main verb and the preceding verb element is some form of the verb *to be*. For questions with active verbs, if a free noun phrase (one not enclosed in prepositional brackets) is found between two verb elements, it is marked *Subject,* and the first free noun phrase in the question is marked *Object*. Otherwise the first free noun phrase is the subject, the next, if any, is the object. For passive verbs, the first free noun phrase is marked *Object* (since it is the object in the active form of the question) and all prepositional phrases with the preposition *by* have the noun phrase within them marked *Subject*. If there is more than one, the content analysis later chooses among them on the basis of meaning.

Finally, the syntactic analysis checks to see if any of the words is marked as a question word. If not, a signal is set to indicate that the question requires a *yes/no* answer.

CONTENT ANALYSIS

The content analysis uses the dictionary meanings and the results of the syntactic analysis to set up a specification list for the processing program. First any subroutine found in the meaning of any word or idiom in the question is executed. The subroutines are of two basic types; those that deal with the meaning of the word itself and those that in some way change the meaning of another word. The first type chooses the appropriate meaning for a word with multiple meanings, as, for example, the subroutine mentioned above that decides, for names of cities, whether the meaning is Team = A_t or Place = A_p. The second type alters or modifies the attribute or value of an appropriate syntactically related word. For example, one such subroutine puts its value in place of the value of the main noun in its phrase. Thus Team = (blank) in the phrase *each team* becomes Team = each; in the phrase *what team,* it becomes Team = ?. Another modifies the attribute of a main noun. Thus Team = (blank) in the phrase *winning team* becomes Team$_{(winning)}$ = (blank). In the question "Who beat the Yankees on July 4?", this subroutine, found in the meaning of *beat,* modifies the attribute of the subject and object, so that Team = ? and Team = Yankees are rendered Team$_{(winning)}$ = ? and Team$_{(losing)}$ = Yankees. Another subroutine combines these two operations: it both modifies the attribute and changes the value of the main noun. Thus, Game = (blank) in the phrase *six games* becomes Game$_{(number\ of)}$ = 6, and in the phrase *how many games* becomes Game$_{(number\ of)}$ = ?.

After the subroutines have been executed, the question is scanned to consolidate those attribute-value pairs that must be represented on the specification list as a single entry. For example, in "Who was the winning team . . ." Team = ? and Team$_{(winning)}$ = (blank) must be collapsed into Team$_{(winning)}$ = ?. Next, successive scans will create any sublists implied by the syntactic structure of the question. Finally, the composite information for each phrase is entered onto the spec list. Depending on its complexity, each phrase furnishes one or more entries for the list. The resulting spec list is printed in outline form, to provide the questioner with some intermediate feedback.

Processing Routines

PROCESSOR

The specification list indicates to the processor what part of the stored data is relevant for answering the input question. The processor extracts the matching information from the data and produces, for the responder, the answer to the question in the form of a list structure.

The core of the processor is a search routine that attempts to find a match, on each path of a given data structure, for all the attribute-value pairs on the spec list; when a match for the whole spec list is found on a given path, those pairs relevant to the spec list are entered on a *found list.* A particular spec list is considered matched when its attribute has been found on a data path and either the data value is the same as the spec value, or the spec value is ? or *each,* in which case any value of the particular attribute is a match. Matching is not always straightforward. Derived attributes and some modified attributes are functions of a number of attributes on a path and must be computed before the values can be matched. For example, if the spec entry is Home Team = Red Sox, the actual home team for a particular path must be computed from the place and teams on that path before the spec value Red Sox can be matched with the computed data value. Sublists also require special handling because the entries on the sublist must sometimes be considered separately and sometimes as a unit in various permutations.

The found list produced by the search routine is a hierarchical list structure containing one main or derived attribute on each level of each path. Each path on the found list represents the information extracted from one or more paths of the data. For example, for the question "Where did each team play in July?", a single path exists, on the found list, for each team which played in July. On the level below each team, all places in which that team played in July occur on a list that is the value of the attribute Place. Each path on the found list may thus represent a condensation of the information existing on many paths of the search data.

Many input questions contain only one query, as in the question above, *i.e.,* Place = ?. These questions are answered, with no further processing, by the found list produced by one execution of the search routine. Others require simple processing on all occurrences of the queried attribute on the generated found list. The question "In how many places did each team play in July?" requires a count of the places for each team, after the search routine has generated the list of places for each team.

Other questions imply more than one search as well as additional processing. For a spec attribute with the value *every,* a comparison with a list of all possible values for that attribute must be made after the search routine has generated lists of found values for that attribute. Then, since only those found list paths for which all possible values of the attribute exist should remain on the found list as the answer to the question, the search routine, operating on this found list as the data, is again executed. It now generates a new found list containing all the data paths for which all possible values of the attribute were found. Likewise, questions involving a specified number, such as 4 teams, imply a search for *which teams,* a count of the teams found on each path, and a search of the found list for paths containing 4 teams.

In general, a question may contain several implicit or explicit queries. Since these queries must be answered one at a time, several searches, with intermediate processing, are required. The first search operates on the stored data while successive searches operate on the found list generated by the preceding search operation. As an example, consider the question "On how many days in July did eight teams play?" The spec list is

$$Day_{(number\ of)} = ?;$$
$$Month = July;$$
$$Team_{(number\ of)} = 8.$$

On the first pass, the implicit question *which teams* is answered. The spec list for the first search is

$$Day \quad = Each;$$
$$Month = July;$$
$$Team \ = ?.$$

The found data is a list of days in July; for each day there is a list of teams that played on that date. Following this search, the processor counts the teams for each day and associates the count with the attribute Team. On the second search, the spec list is

$$Day \qquad\qquad = ?;$$
$$Month \qquad\quad = July;$$
$$Team_{(number\ of)} = 8.$$

The found data is a list of days in July on which eight teams played. After this pass, the processor counts the days, adds the count to the found list, and is finished.

RESPONDER

No attempt has yet been made to respond in grammatical English sentences. Instead, the final found list is printed in outline form. For questions requiring a yes/no answer, YES is printed along with the found list. If the search routine found no matching data, NO is printed for yes/no questions, and NO DATA for all other cases.

Discussion

The differences between Baseball and both automatic language translation and information retrieval should now be evident. The linguistic part of the Baseball program has as its main goal the understanding of the meaning of the question as embodied in the canonical specification list. Syntax must be considered and ambiguities resolved in order to represent the meaning adequately. Translation programs have a different goal: transforming the input passage from one natural language to another. Meanings must be considered and ambiguities resolved to the extent that they affect the correctness of the final translation. In general, translation programs are concerned more with syntax and less with meaning than the Baseball program.

Baseball differs from most retrieval systems in the nature of its data. Generally the retrieval problem is to locate relevant documents. Each document has an associated set of index numbers describing its content. The retrieval system must find the appropriate index numbers for each input request and then search for all documents bearing those index numbers. The basic problem in such systems is the assignment of index categories. In Baseball, on the other hand, the attributes of the data are very well specified. There is no confusion about them. However, Baseball's derived attributes and modifiers imply a great deal more data processing than most document retrieval programs. (Baseball does bear a close relation with the ACSI-MATIC system discussed by Miller et al. at the 1960 Western Joint Computer Conference.)

The concept of the spec list can be used to define the class of questions that the Baseball program can answer. It can answer all questions whose spec list consists of attribute-value pairs that the program recognizes. The attributes may be modified or derived, and the values may be definite or queries. Any combination of attribute-value pairs constitutes a specification list. Many will be nonsense, but all can be answered. The number of questions in the class is, of course, infinite, because of the numerical values. But even if all numbers are restricted to two digits, the program can answer millions of meaningful questions.

The present program, despite its restrictions, is a very useful communication device. Any complex question that does not meet the restrictions can always be broken up into several simpler questions. The program usually rejects questions it cannot handle, in which case the questioner may rephrase his question. He can also check the printed spec list to see if the computer is on the right track, in case the linguistic program has erred and failed to detect its own error. Finally, he can often judge whether the answer is reasonable.

Next Steps

No important difficulty is expected in augmenting the program to include logical connectives, negatives, and relation words. The inclusion of multiple-clause questions also seems fairly straightforward, if the questioner will mark off for the computer the boundaries of his clauses. The program can then deal with the subordinate clauses one at a time before it deals with the main clause, using existing routines. On the other hand, if the syntax analysis is required to determine the clause boundaries as well as the phrase structure, a much more sophisticated program would be required.

The problem of recognizing and resolving semantic ambiguities remains largely unsolved. Determining what is meant by the question "Did the Red Sox win most of their games in July?" depends on a much larger context than the immediate question. The computer might answer all meaningful versions of the question (we know of five), or might ask the questioner which meaning he intended. In general, the facility for the computer to query the questioner is likely to be the most powerful improvement. This would allow the computer to increase its vocabulary, to resolve ambiguities, and perhaps even to train the questioner in the use of the program.

Considerable pains were taken to keep the program general. Most of the program will remain unchanged and intact in a new context, such as voting records. The processing program will handle data in any sort of hierarchical form, and is indifferent to the attributes used. The syntax program is based entirely on parts of speech, which can easily be assigned to a new set of words for a new context. On the other hand, some of the subroutines contained in the dictionary meanings are certainly specific to baseball; probably each new context would require certain subroutines specific to it. Also, each context might introduce a number of modifiers and derived attributes that would have to be defined in terms of special subroutines for the processor. Hopefully, all such occasions for change have been isolated in a small area of special subroutines, so that the main routines can be unaltered. However, until we have actually switched contexts, we cannot say definitely that we have been successful in producing a general question-answering program.

INFERENTIAL MEMORY
AS THE BASIS OF
MACHINES WHICH UNDERSTAND
NATURAL LANGUAGE

by Robert K. Lindsay

Participants in the search for intelligent machines frequently disagree on a basic question of strategy in their quest. On the one hand there are those who believe that the major obstacles can be overcome by reliance on the computer's infallible memory, electronic speed, and arithmetic capabilities if these capacities are cleverly employed in sophisticated searching and statistical procedures. On the other hand there are those who feel that the problems of meaning and intuition must be somehow resolved before significant progress will be made, and that these problems are not solely a matter of speed and arithmetic. This issue will only be resolved by demonstration, and yet it is of some importance to decide how to allocate our efforts. This report takes the position that immediate, practical applications can derive from the former approach, but the major problems will be solved only by the latter. To mention a single example, the implementation of information retrieval techniques on present-day computers would be a large step forward, even though the techniques thus far considered have largely been conceptually trivial. The automation of libraries and scientific document files could immediately bring about great savings in valuable human time and effort, plus increased accuracy in literature searching. Kehl (1961) is now implementing a retrieval system which searches for certain combinations of key words in a large corpus and yields references to those documents which contain the proper combinations. Luhn (1958) has used a straightforward statistical procedure to extract key sentences from scientific articles, thus yielding useful abstracts of a sort. The use of these two techniques on a large scale would go a long way toward extracting us from the clutches of the information explosion which is so often discussed.

217

And yet it is quite clear that these techniques, whose primary advantages derive from using the great speed of the computer, will not produce intelligent machines, or even produce machines which do simple jobs with the intelligence displayed by a human clerk. For even an unintelligent human does more than count frequencies or search for key words. The human displays intelligent features which are generally summed up by saying that he *understands* the *meaning* of what he hears and reads.

The meaning of meaning and the meaning of understanding have never been adequately explicated when applied to human thought processes. How then can we hope to make them precise enough to enable us to build machines which understand meaning? Before attempting to answer this question, let us attempt to sharpen our intuitions by considering more specifically some examples of things which could be done by machines which understand but which would be beyond the capabilities of machines without this ability.

One of the major problems of the many encompassed by artificial intelligence is that of the mechanical translation of natural languages. Many of the early advocates of mechanical translation felt that high-quality translations could be produced by machines supplied with sufficiently detailed syntactic rules, a large dictionary, and sufficient speed to examine the context of ambiguous words for a few words in each direction. No doubt such machines will be able, when the syntactic rules are discovered, to produce fairly good translations, and yet it should be clear that such machines will never produce truly high-quality translations without the aid of pre-editing and postediting by human translators.

Here is one example of a difficulty. We wish to translate "The boy is in the house" and "The boy is in Paris" into French. In the first instance, the preposition "in" is rendered in French as "dans"; in the second sentence, the same preposition is rendered in French as "à." The human translator makes his decision by knowing that houses enclose people on all sides, while cities do not. This situation could, of course, be handled by marking all nouns with an indicator which tells the machine whether or not the thing denoted can enclose other things. But the hope that all such idiosyncrasies can be handled by such multiplication of stored details is futile. Bar-Hillel (1960) has given an even more perplexing example. We wish to translate the sentences "The pen is in the box" and "The box is in the pen" into French. There is no other context, and no other is needed by a human translator who knows that "pen" in the first sentence must denote a writing instrument and not a fenced enclosure, while the opposite is true in the second sentence. He can thus select the proper French equivalent for each, even though in French a single word does not suffice as it does in English. Once again we must increase the information stored in our machine, this time indicating for each noun those things which it can enclose.

The problem of understanding may be rephrased to state that we must find ways of storing large amounts of such detailed knowledge while keeping the amount of memory capacity required within realizable limits.

Much of the literature on meaning has not been directly connected with this notion, but has been concerned with the problem of denotation: to what things does a symbol refer. Here, however, we are faced with the problem of what a *proposition* means. Osgood (1957) and Mowrer (1954) have attempted to extend notions of association and conditioning to include associations between groups of words rather than single words.

According to Osgood's theory, a word elicits associated internal responses. These responses can be described by their values along certain dimensions, such as active-inactive, good-bad, strong-weak. The meaning of a combination of words is an average of the component values for each of the words taken individually. For example, if "shy" is valued as mildly inactive, mildly bad, and mildly weak, and if "secretary" is valued as being very active, very good, and mildly weak, then "shy secretary" is valued as mildly active, mildly good, and mildly weak.

According to Mowrer's theory, sentences are temporal sequences of words and the internal responses to the first words are conditioned, in the classical sense, to the internal responses to the later words. Thus the sentence "Tom is a thief" conditions the notion of Tom to the notion of thief, where we use the loose term "notion" to indicate that it is not the words themselves, but the internal responses to them which become associated.

In both of these theories, the measure of meaning of a concatenation of words amounts to some sort of combination of the measures for the individual words. It appears that a useful theory must somehow make use of more complicated associative connections than those proposed by either of these two workers. For one thing, Osgood's scheme depends not at all on word order, only on which words are used; Mowrer's scheme depends only on word order, and not upon any other relations. To Osgood, "Tom hit Joe" would have the same meaning as "Joe hit Tom"; to Mowrer, "Tom is a thief" would have the same meaning as "Tom hit a thief."

Intuitively, a concept of meaning must include the notion of implication: what does a proposition imply. This does not mean, that is, imply, logical implication, but merely implication to the individual. Thus the meaning of a proposition is relative to the audience, and this probably is an unavoidable requirement.

Knowing more than one is told is a characteristic of human performance which is present in most behaviors which are called intelligent. We have argued that this characteristic is necessary for machines which are to solve the real problems of information retrieval, language translation, and problem-solving. And furthermore, we must find efficient ways to store implications if we are to develop intelligent machines with finite memory capacities, that is, if we are to develop intelligent machines.

Examples of memory structures with these desired properties immediately come to mind from personal experience. They are often called mental pictures. Gelernter (1959b), for example, has developed a geometry machine whose basic source of intelligence lies in its ability to reject most of the formally possible sequences of proof steps because they "cannot possibly be correct." In effect, the machine constructs a diagram based upon the premises of the theorem to be proved. (Actually, the machine is supplied with such a diagram, although the task of constructing one is, while difficult, not taxing of memory and speed.) The implications of the premises are explicitly contained in this diagram, as are some nonimplications, but most nonimplications are not contained. The machine then merely rejects as possible subgoals (intermediate steps) all things which are not true in the diagram. For example, the premises "Triangle ABC," "AB = BC," "A, D, C collinear," and "AD = DC" are supplied in conjunction with coordinates for each point, such as A(0,0), B(5,5), C(10,0) and D(5,0) (see Fig. 1). The machine will never attempt to prove "triangle ABC congruent to triangle ABD" because this is not true in the diagram, as the machine can determine by calculating their respective perimeters. However, it might try to prove "angle DAB = angle DCB," which is implied by the premises. It may also try to prove "AD = DB" which is true in the diagram, but not implied by the premises. By supplying the machine with a more general diagram, such as by moving B to (5,15) (see Fig. 2), this last *cul de sac* could be avoided.

Such two-dimensional pictures have the properties we desire: they store implications and they do so in compact fashion. They also have a wide

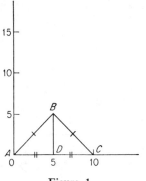

Figure 1.

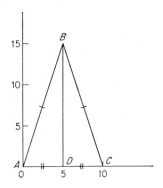

Figure 2.

range of application, few of which, aside from Gelernter's work, have been explored. One further example is provided by Venn diagrams, which are devices which aid logical reasoning. We may represent the proposition "all B are A" by two areas, one completely enclosed by the other, with appropriate labels. If we add a third area, C, according to the same rules to represent the proposition, "all C are B," the resulting diagram contains the implication that "all C are A," since area C must lie wholly within area A. Similar rules can be devised for other propositional forms, as elsewhere discussed by Lindsay (1961). Actually there are simpler schemes for such situations since not all of the properties of euclidian two-dimensional space are required, but, since such representations also handle many other situations, an intelligent machine would achieve some economy by employing such general-purpose representations wherever usable rather than devising special schemes for each case.

So far we have discussed only situations where few difficulties arise. Reasoning does not always obey the rules of logic and geometry, and we quickly encounter additional difficulties when we attempt to handle even simple situations. A program has been written to handle a different class of problems, and the difficulties will become clear as this program is described.

The program to be described parses sentences written in Basic English and makes inferences about kinship relations. To do this it constructs two types of complex structures in the computer memory, one corresponding to a sentence diagram of the sort produced by high-school students, the other corresponding to the familiar family tree. These are represented inside the computer by so-called *list structures*. A list structure is a form of associative memory, wherein each symbol is tagged by an indicator which tells the machine the location of a related symbol. So far this corresponds to the associative bonds which are the basic concept of stimulus-response psychology. However, each symbol may at times refer to a whole string of other, connected symbols, thus producing a hierarchical organization of memory associations. This feature provides much greater flexibility than either the single associations of stimulus-response psychology or the mediated associations which have recently been discussed and seem to be a first step in the direction of generalizing the limited stimulus-response schema.

The Sentence-parsing Program

The grammars of certain languages may be described by rules of replacement, which, if they satisfy certain conditions of simplicity, are called phrase structure rules (see Chomsky, 1957). For example, a simple grammar might consist of the following rules:

1. S   ↔ NP + Pred
2. S   ↔ NP + VP + NP
3. S   ↔ NP + V + NP
4. NP   ↔ They
5. NP   ↔ planes
6. NP   ↔ A + N
7. N   ↔ planes
8. N   ↔ man
9. A   ↔ the
10. A   ↔ flying
11. VP   ↔ Aux + V
12. V   ↔ are
13. V   ↔ flying
14. Aux ↔ are
15. Pred ↔ VP + NP + Ad
16. Ad   ↔ swiftly

These rules may be interpreted as, for example, the twelfth, "When V is encountered in a string of symbols, it may be replaced by 'are,'" or "when 'are' is encountered in a string of words it may be replaced by V." The former interpretation concerns the production of sentences, while the latter concerns the parsing of sentences. Thus we may produce a sentence by beginning with the symbol S and successively applying rules. For example: S → NP + VP + NP → NP + Aux + V +NP → They + Aux + V + NP → They + are + V + NP → They + are + flying + NP → They are flying planes.

Different sequences of rules produce different sentences. With the rules given above, certain sentences can be produced which are ungrammatical within English. For example, we could generate "The man are flying planes." A proper grammar (set of rules) for English would have to rule out such possibilities. This is generally accomplished both by defining rules more narrowly (assuring, for example, that subject agrees with verb) and by introducing certain metarules which specify which sequences of application are legitimate [for two methods of accomplishing this, see Chomsky (1957) and Pendergraft (1961)].

It is also clear that different sequences of rules may produce the same sentences. For example:[1] S → NP + V + NP → NP + V + A + N → They + V + A + N → They + are + A + N → They + are + flying + N → They are flying planes.

Consider now a straightforward parsing technique which might be applied to the sentence "They are flying planes swiftly," using the rules of our example. This sentence has a unique parsing which may be discovered as follows. Find each word or group of words which occurs in the sentence

---

[1] This example is due to Chomsky (1957).

on the right-hand side of one of the rules, and replace it by the symbol which appears on the left-hand side of the rule. Apply the same procedure to the resulting string of symbols. If a symbol or word appears on the right-hand side of more than one rule, form separate strings for each case. Continue until the sequence is reduced to the single symbol S, abandoning paths to which this procedure ceases to apply. Thus we have:

They are flying planes swiftly

1. $NP + V + V + N + Ad$
    can go no farther
2. $NP + V + V + NP + Ad$
    can go no farther
3. $NP + V + A + N + Ad$
    $NP + V + NP + Ad$
    $S + Ad$
    can go no farther
4. $NP + V + A + NP + Ad$
    can go no farther
5. $NP + Aux + A + N + Ad$
    $NP + Aux + NP + Ad$
    can go no farther
6. $NP + Aux + A + NP + Ad$
    can go no farther
7. $NP + Aux + V + N + Ad$
    $NP + VP + N + Ad$
    can go no farther
8. $NP + Aux + V + NP + Ad$
    $NP + VP + NP + Ad$
    8.1. $S + Ad$
            can go no farther
    8.2. $NP + Pred$
            S
            successful parsing

Even after a sufficient number of rules and metarules are supplied so as to eliminate ungrammatical sequences, there will remain, for natural languages, sentences which can be generated by two or more different production sequences. Conversely, any procedure which parses sentences should be able to discover all such sequences. The decision as to which parsing is correct depends upon a context larger than a single sentence and in many cases will also depend upon the meaning of the sentence, including a dependence upon what the various words denote.

However, even if we neglect the problem of selecting which legitimate parsing is correct in a given instance, the problem of discovering *any* legitimate parsing is itself formidable when we deal with the tens of thousands of rules needed to describe a natural language. A complete set of rules is, in fact, so large that none has yet been devised for any natural language, although some have been under study for thousands of years. With even a moderately large number of rules, the parsing procedure described above will generate many possible branches, some of which may continue to be feasible for a long time. In order to discover any parsing in reasonable time and with reasonable effort, it is useful to employ some sort of selection procedure.

The procedure employed in the program to be described here is based upon two assumptions which are psychologically realistic. First, it is assumed that almost all sentences which will be encountered in actual text may be parsed by a procedure which proceeds from left to right, making decisions about the disposition of earlier phrases without considering the entire sentence. This reduces the number of rule combinations which must be searched. Secondly, it is assumed that a very limited amount of memory is available to remember intermediate results during the parsing of even extremely long sentences. This places severe restrictions upon which types of complexity will be analyzed and which types of syntactic structure will not be handled.

The final result of applying the parsing program to a sentence is an associatively organized memory whose structure reflects the interrelations among words, but does not give complete information as to which rules should be applied first to produce the sentence. The sentence diagram for our above example might be drawn as in Fig. 3. Each node in a sentence diagram corresponds to a substructure which has been constructed during the scanning of the sentence.

The sentence-parsing program is provided with a string of words as an input sentence. Each word may be found in a dictionary which indicates

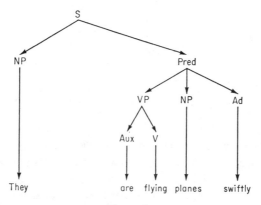

Figure 3.

a series of possible parts of speech which that word may serve as, the series being ordered so as to present the most frequent function first. The machine proceeds in a left-to-right fashion, assuming temporarily that the first word serves its most common function. To each part of speech there corresponds an associative structure which the machine forms. This structure is then temporarily held in memory and the next word is examined. If the structure so created requires the services of an additional word type, the machine continues to search for this type. If the next word serves the purpose, its structure is incorporated with that of the first word so that only a single structure name must be kept in rapid access memory, the remainder of the information being obtainable via the name. If the next word does not serve the desired purpose, its structure is stored separately, and the machine continues to look for words which will complete the structures of each of the words now held in memory. However, the number of structure names which can be held for rapid access is limited to a small total so that the machine must eventually begin to combine its substructures or else forget where it is. Frequently, the machine will be forced to complete a structure even though it has not found what it wants. This results in changing the part of speech designation for one or more words so that the entire sequence will now be compatible. The machine thus proceeds through the sentence, making temporary decisions, storing substructures in its limited rapid access memory, and revising its decisions only when forced to by lack of rapid access memory space or by complete incompatibility of substructures.

Loosely, the machine's behavior can be described as follows. The first word is "the." All right, now I need to find a nounlike word. The second word is "very," so now I need an adjective or adverb. The third word is "big," which is the adjective I needed, so combine these two words into the structure "very big." Now I need a nounlike word. The fourth word is "man," which is the noun needed. Now all words are combined into the structure "(the((very) big)) man." But now we have a subject, so look for a verb. The fifth word is "bit" which can act as the verb, so create the structure "((the((very)big))man) bit." Now another nounlike word or structure could serve as object. The sixth word is "the," so save it to modify a nounlike word; now we have two things saved, both looking for a nounlike word. The final word is "dog" which will serve both needed functions. We now have the complete sentence, whose structure is illustrated in Fig. 4.

In one sense this program is nothing but an algorithm which produces an output for every possible sequence of part-of-speech series inputs. However, if the program were written so as to merely check the input sequence and produce the corresponding output, a serious difficulty would arise. The size of the table required increases exponentially with sentence length,

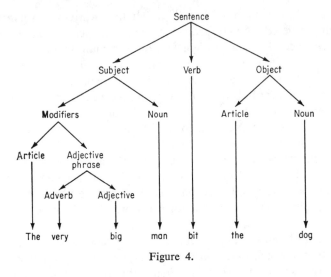

Figure 4.

thus an extremely large table for sentences of even moderate length would be needed. Although the program as it stands is limited in terms of the complexity of the sentences which it can handle, length alone does not contribute to complexity. For example, the program can handle a sentence such as "The big, black, ugly, ferocious, . . . , strong dog bit him," where the number of adjectives which may be inserted in the string is limited only by the memory capacity of the computer. This is possible because all of the adjectives are combined into a single substructure at every step, hence the rapid access memory is never exceeded. Further, the total memory requirements only increase linearly with sentence length. However, sentences which require the construction of an excessive number of substructures will cause the program to fail, even though these sentences are relatively short. Yngve (1961) has described a similar device for *producing* sentences, and argues that the limitations on complexity imposed by limits on rapid access memory capacity explain why certain constructions are not commonly used in natural English and hence are called ungrammatical.

The part-of-speech routines provide a finite set of processes which can handle an infinite number of sentences, in principle. They are superior to the table look-up method for the same reason that a program which computes e^x for any value of x is superior to a table of this function and a look-up program.

Obviously humans must employ some finite set of processes which are used to parse sentences, and obviously each word acts as a stimulus to elicit the corresponding processes. These processes, as in this program, are highly complex, and their decisions are contingent upon which other processes have been initiated before. It is quite consistent with our knowledge of human thought processes to assume that the interaction takes place in the above-described manner, that is, through a small set of rapid access memory locations. However, the adult human undoubtedly has a larger set of processes, which effectively categorize words into more narrow categories than the few part-of-speech designations provided to our program, and these processes are no doubt much more complex.

Another psychologically tenable feature of this program is its left-to-right analysis. Although English grammar may conceivably be more readily analyzed in some other fashion, humans generally proceed from left to right, with only occasional reversals.

The limits of this program are not very well known. It will accept no words not included in Basic English, a system of grammar and a vocabulary of about 1700 English words which was defined by Ogden (1933). (Basic English is simplified English in the sense that anything which is good Basic is good English, but not vice versa.) The program will not accept certain punctuation marks, such as colons, and it does not distinguish between others, such as exclamation points and periods. Also, phrases and clauses in apposition must be indicated by dashes rather than commas. However, the program is not limited to single-clause sentences, nor must the input be a complete sentence. Thus, the program can handle many inputs which appear in actual writing but not in books on grammar. The program always makes a decision, and the result is always a complete structure containing all of the input.

The end result of the application of the program to a sentence is a structure which relates all the words of a sentence. This could be replaced logically by a set of descriptions listing all of these relations, but such a set would be far more elaborate and costly to memory. The syntactic meaning of the sentence is just this structure, wherein relations among words are implicit in its organization.

The Semantic-analysis Program

After the diagram of a sentence is constructed, the program attempts to deal with the meaning of some of the words. First, a list of all nouns is constructed. This list includes not only words which were used as subjects or objects, but also names used as possessive adjectives, such as "Bill's."

At this point, words cease to be considered solely by their syntactic-category membership. The sentence diagram is used as an information store which relates words. Subject-object combinations whose main verb is some form of "to be" are discovered. When such a combination is found, the words are marked "equivalent" by a cross-referencing scheme which indicates that both subject and object refer to the same thing or person. The modifiers of all equivalent nouns are then grouped together.

Next, a search is made for the eight words which Basic English provides to discuss kinship relations: "father," "mother," "brother," "sister," "offspring," "brother-in-law," "sister-in-law," and "married." If any of these relation words occurred in the sentence, their modifiers are examined to discover proper names which appeared as possessive adjectives or objects of a preposition, as would be the case if the original sentence contained phrases of the form "Jane's brother" or "the father of John." Each such proper name is paired with all others associated with the same occurrence of the relation word. By proceeding through the entire collection of words in this fashion, a list of elementary relations is formed. The items on this list are word triplets, two proper nouns, and a relation word which connects them.

Now the family tree is constructed. The computer memory is organized in an associative fashion again, with one computer storage location linked to others. The structure is isomorphic to diagrams such as given in the example below. Each "marriage" is represented by an association between the husband and wife, plus the name of a similar family unit for the parents of the husband, another for the parents of the wife, and the name of a list of offspring of this marriage. If the names of one of the partners, one of their parents, or some of their offspring are not given, places are reserved for these names should they occur in the future. The resulting tree is the same no matter whether the information was explicitly given in the text or merely implied.

By way of illustration, Fig. 5 depicts the memory structure for a simple family tree. The tree is composed of two basic family units, one formed by the marriage of A and B, and the other formed by the marriage of C and D. One of the offspring, E, of the first marriage is married to one of the offspring, F, of the second. It is evident that many relations are described by the tree given. However, it is important to note that the associations are one-way associations. This fact necessitates the addition of the name of the parent family unit at the end of each offspring unit. Thus, given A we may determine that E is one of his offspring by moving only in the direction of the arrows. Given E we may again trace the connection to A by moving only in the direction of the arrows, but this is true only because the family unit associated with E also contains the name of A's family unit. It follows that, given the fact that F (already located in the tree) and G (a name not previously encountered) are siblings, it is not sufficient to add G to the list of A-B offspring (dotted lines) but we must also copy the name of F's parental family unit into the newly constructed family unit of G (dashed lines).

The family tree, or trees, so constructed, are not erased after a single sentence is processed, but continue to grow as additional information is given throughout the passage.

The complexities and many small difficulties which are encountered in even this simple type of relation are indicative of the problem involved in the construction of semantic structures. More instructive, however, are the conceptual problems which arise in attempting to generalize this program to less strictly structured situations. Let us consider two of the most important problems.

It often happens, even when dealing with simple kinship relations, that the order of presentation of the input information has a crucial effect upon the efficiency of memory allocation. For example, if we are first told that X has offspring A, B, C, and D, we must construct an elaborate organization to handle this information, locations such as for the spouse of X being left blank. If we are then told that Y has offspring E, F, G, and H, we must construct another such structure, unrelated to the first. Finally, we may learn that B and H are brothers. This permits (neglecting such complications as multiple marriages) a collapsing of the two structures into a single organization which much more compactly represents the information

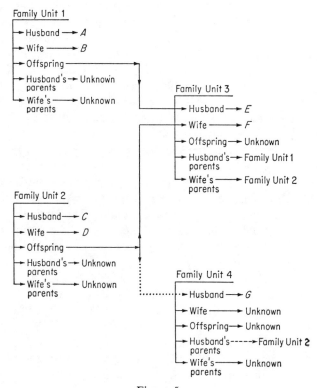

Figure 5.

implied. If we had been fortunate enough to have first learned of B's relation to H (or of X's relation to Y), we would have made much more efficient use of our memory capacity. In the program, the extra structures are "erased," that is, the memory used for them is returned to a common stockpile for use anywhere else it is needed. This is quite handily done with the easily altered computer memory, but a memory which is hard to erase, as the human memory presumably is, could be affected in important ways by such unhappy input sequences.

Nonetheless, an intelligent machine should have the property of being intelligent no matter what the order of its inputs. One aspect of the "aha" phenomenon is just that many formerly unrelated items of information are suddenly brought together by a single additional item, so that many implications suddenly leap out. Educators are beset by the problem of determining optimal orders of presentation of material, but, fortunately for the student, the human mind is capable of seeing connections under nonoptimal conditions.

An even more baffling problem is that of handling what has been called connotative meaning (Lindsay, 1961). Probably more often than not, a set of propositions which make some definite implications contains several subsets which alter the probabilities of other propositions without making any of them definite. Thus the statement that "George voted for Eisenhower and is opposed to medical care for the aged" makes it more likely that George is opposed to the United Nations, though only slightly so. It is quite clear that human cognitive organizations frequently take cognizance of these altered probabilities, perhaps to a greater extent than is reasonable. But how can such implicit connotations be intelligently and efficiently handled?

Let us consider a more concrete example arising in the context of the kinship-relation program. Consider the following sentence: "Joey was playing with his brother Bobby in their Aunt Jane's yard when their mother called them home." Certain definite information is given by this sentence, such as the fact that Joey and Bobby are brothers. Also, it is clear that Jane is either the sister or the sister-in-law of the children's mother, but it is not known definitely which is the case. If previous information has related, say, Joey to many others and Jane to many others, but has not related Joey's relations to Jane's relations, then the given sentence may imply a large number of things and remove the possibilities of a large number of other things. Still other possibilities depend upon knowing the exact relation between Joey's mother and Jane. The problem is to capture in the family-tree structure all of the definite implications, to eliminate all of the things definitely ruled out, indicate the altered probabilities of other relations, and still not make any *definite* assertions about the relation between Joey's mother and Jane.

The structure thus far described is unable to handle even this simple case, since the associations are either there or they are not, and only one connection is permissible. One solution to this problem is to construct several family-tree structures, one for each possibility. This corresponds, for example, to the situation in which a student will draw diagrams of an acute triangle, a right triangle, and an obtuse triangle corresponding to the possible cases for which he wishes to prove a theorem. This solution, however, will work well only when the number of alternatives is small and when the structures are themselves simple. In more complex situations this procedure is too taxing of memory capacity. It is desirable to include the uncertainty within a single structure.

In order to do this, we must allow multiple connections. Thus, in place of every association in our original format we must substitute a list of all the possibilities, and the process which retrieves information must recognize that only one of these can be correct. When nothing at all has been implied, the lists of possibilities will contain an "all" symbol indicating that all things are possible; when something definite is implied later, this "all" symbol is replaced by the proper connection; when several things have been implied, the universal symbol is replaced by a list of the remaining possibilities. We may also need to record a list of connections which are definitely impossible. When nothing has been implied, this list will contain a "none" symbol indicating that no things are impossible.

It is to be noted that a probabilistic connection of the sort frequently hypothesized by psychologists is not appropriate here. That is, we do not want a connection such that a given stimulus will sometimes evoke one association, sometimes another on a probability basis. In the above example, the reader knows *definitely* that either Jane is the sister of Joey's mother *or* is the sister of Joey's father, but not both; no reader would conclude half the time that Jane is the sister of Joey's mother and half the time that she is the sister of Joey's father, altering his decision from time to time.

But we are still faced with two problems. First, it is impossible, or at least impractical, to retain an extremely large number of possibilities; second, it is not clear how we should indicate that some possibilities are more probable than others. The first problem is perhaps solved by humans by not remembering all possibilities; thus humans are unable to remember all possible implications when the set of such possibilities is large. This will no doubt remain a problem for machines as well. We might solve the second problem by ordering the list of probabilities, placing the most likely alternatives first; or perhaps we might decide to associate probabilities with each alternative. In any event, the probabilities so established will determine the weight which is assigned to implications, but will *not* determine the implications which will hold to the exclusion of others. Finally, we can imagine a situation in which the list of possibilities is truncated due to the limited computing capabilities of man or machine, and where subsequently all of the possibilities which remain are eliminated by further information. In this case, the machine, after all, will have to indicate that something is wrong and review previous inputs, this time reselecting possibilities in the light of knowledge of information to follow.

To complete our example, we may present the modified storage format (Fig. 6) which could be used to solve our sample problem.

Finally, we note that we have solved the problem of connotative meaning while retaining our basic device of storing *definite* implications implicitly, but we have resorted to storing *possible* implications explicitly. Techniques for avoiding this listing of possibilities would prove extremely valuable, since as we have seen, requirements on memory capacity increase rapidly when storage is explicit.

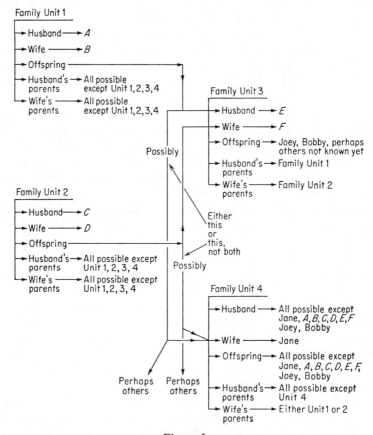

Figure 6.

Summary

It has been argued that the problem of meaning is of major importance in the study of the nature of intelligence, and that a useful definition of meaning must include not only denotation but connotation and implication as well. To handle these important questions it is necessary to study cognitive organizations which are more complex than those upon which most psychological theories are based. A central question is the storage of large numbers of interrelated propositions in a manner which efficiently uses memory capacity. Illustration of these points was given by reference to a computer program which stores syntactic relations and extracts and stores semantic implications of a very limited character. The illustrations put into concrete terms some of the problems which must be resolved before machines of formidable intelligence can be constructed.

section 6

Pattern Recognition

Pattern-recognition research is one of the most difficult areas of artificial intelligence activity to characterize succintly. In its infancy it was concerned with optical character recognition and later, voice recognition. Selfridge has labeled this kind of pattern-recognition work as "eyes and ears for computers." More recently the "pattern-recognition" label has been applied, with much justification, to studies of hypothesis formation by machine, discrimination learning in random nets, perceptual learning in human beings and schemes for inductive inference automata in general. There is a close relationship between the work on pattern recognition and studies of cognitive behavior. It is quite appropriate, therefore, that this material should be placed at the junction of the two major sections of this volume.

Much pattern recognition research has been concerned with programming a computer to recognize that the same name should be given to different manifestations of an object, for example, that short A's, tall A's, fat A's, and skinny A's are all A's. This behavior might be described as elementary perceptual generalization.

The problem becomes one of being able to represent the essence of A-ness in a computer program. For some researchers the computer is a vehicle for testing out their hypotheses about A-ness (perceptual performance). The second example in the Selfridge-Neisser report is a case in point. For others, the computer is a vehicle for generating hypotheses about A-ness (perceptual learning). The Uhr-Vossler piece is an example of this approach.

The work in pattern recognition differs from the work in computer models of verbal learning, hypothesis behavior, and particularly concept formation only in the relatively greater emphasis on complex "central" cognitive processes in the latter work. However the importance of the basic pattern-recognition activity in problem-solving by human beings or computers is well recognized. The principal function of pattern recognition may be characterized as reduction of complex environments. Neither the human being nor the computer can afford to deal with each event as a special case. Suppose, for example, that a performance system has stored some useful "A information." This information about A may be independent of the size or shape of A. If tall A, short A, skinny A, and fat A can all be recognized as A, the stored information can be made available about any particular occurrence of an A. A small set of information structures and processes can be made powerful if there is available a device for recognizing when and where this set is applicable or relevant.

Even if we classify the reports of Feigenbaum, Hunt and Hovland, and Feldman as reports on pattern recognition, we still have collected in this volume only a very small sample of the available work on the subject. This inadequacy is remedied somewhat by the short review in the Uhr-Vossler study and by the discussion in Minsky's review. We regret that space limitations forced the omission of the pioneering work of Selfridge (1955). His report was an early landmark in pattern recognition in particular and artificial intelligence in general. The work of Kochen (1961a, 1961b) is also of great interest and closely related to work in concept formation. We have also omitted reports on pattern recognition in randomly connected nets. We hope that the Bibliography will provide some help to the reader who wants to investigate these and others works on pattern recognition.

Oliver Selfridge is on the staff of the Lincoln Laboratory, Massachusetts Institute of Technology, and Ulric Neisser is a member of the faculty of the Psychology Department, Brandeis University.

Leonard Uhr is on the staff of the Mental Health Research Institute, University of Michigan, and Charles Vossler was a member of the Artificial Intelligence Research Staff of the System Development Corporation, Santa Monica, when this research was done. Vossler is now at Cornell Aeronautical Laboratory, Buffalo, New York.

PATTERN RECOGNITION
BY MACHINE

by Oliver G. Selfridge & Ulric Neisser

Can a machine think? The answer to this old chestnut is certainly "yes": Computers have been made to play chess and checkers, to prove theorems, to solve intricate problems of strategy. Yet the intelligence implied by such activities has an elusive, unnatural quality. It is not based on any orderly development of cognitive skills. In particular, the machines are not well equipped to select from their environment the things, or the relations, they are going to think about.

In this they are sharply distinguished from intelligent living organisms. Every child learns to analyze speech into meaningful patterns long before he can prove any propositions. Computers can find proofs, but they cannot understand the simplest spoken instructions. Even the earliest computers could do arithmetic superbly, but only very recently have they begun to read the written digits that a child recognizes before he learns to add them. Understanding speech and reading print are examples of a basic intellectual skill that can variously be called cognition, abstraction or perception; perhaps the best general term for it is pattern recognition.

Except for their inability to recognize patterns, machines (or, more accurately, the programs that tell machines what to do) have now met most of the classic criteria of intelligence that skeptics have proposed. They *can* outperform their designers: The checker-playing program devised by Arthur L. Samuel of International Business Machines Corporation (1959*a*) usually beats him. They *are* original: The "Logic Theorist," a creation of a group from the Carnegie Institute of Technology and the RAND Corporation [Newell, Simon, and Shaw (1956*a*, 1957*b*)] has found proofs for many of the theorems in *Principia Mathematica*, the

237

monumental work in mathematical logic by A. N. Whitehead and Bertrand Russell (1940). At least one proof is more elegant than the Whitehead-Russell version.

Sensible as they are, the machines are not perceptive. The information they receive must be fed to them one "bit" (a contraction of "binary digit," denoting a unit of information) at a time, up to perhaps millions of bits. Computers do not organize or classify the material in any very subtle or generally applicable way. They perform only highly specialized operations on carefully prepared inputs.

In contrast, a man is continuously exposed to a welter of data from his senses, and abstracts from it the patterns relevant to his activity at the moment. His ability to solve problems, prove theorems and generally run his life depends on this type of perception. We suspect that until programs to perceive patterns can be developed, achievements in mechanical problem-solving will remain isolated technical triumphs.

Developing pattern-recognition programs has proved rather difficult. One reason for the difficulty lies in the nature of the task. A man who abstracts a pattern from a complex of stimuli has essentially classified the possible inputs. But very often the basis of classification is unknown, even to himself; it is too complex to be specified explicitly. Asked to define a pattern, the man does so by example; as a logician might say, ostensively. This letter is A, that person is mother, these speech sounds are a request to pass the salt. The important patterns are defined by experience. Every human being acquires his pattern classes by adapting to a social or environmental consensus—in short, by learning.

In company with workers at various institutions our group at the Lincoln Laboratory of the Massachusetts Institute of Technology has been working on mechanical recognition of patterns. Thus far only a few simple cases have been tackled. We shall discuss two examples. The first one is MAUDE (for Morse Automatic Decoder), a program for translating, or rather transliterating, hand-sent Morse code. This program was developed at the Lincoln Laboratory by a group of workers under the direction of Bernard Gold.

If telegraphers sent ideal Morse, recognition would be easy. The keyings, or "marks," for dashes would be exactly three times as long as the marks for dots; spaces separating the marks within a letter or other character (mark spaces) would be as long as dots; spaces between characters (character spaces), three times as long; spaces separating words (word spaces), seven times as long. Unfortunately human operators do not transmit these ideal intervals. A machine that processed a signal on the assumption that they do would perform very poorly indeed. In an actual message the distinction between dots and dashes is far from clear. There is a great deal of variation among the dots and dashes, and also among the three kinds of space. In fact, when a long message sent by a single operator is analyzed, it frequently turns out that some dots are longer than some dashes, and that some mark spaces are longer than some character spaces. (See Fig. 1.)

With a little practice in receiving code, the average person has no trouble with these irregularities. The patterns of the letters are defined for him in terms of the continuing consensus of experience, and he adapts to them as he listens. Soon he does not hear dots and dashes at all, but perceives the characters as wholes. Exactly how he does so is still obscure, and the mechanism probably varies widely from one operator to another. In any event transliteration is impossible if each mark and space is considered individually. MAUDE therefore uses contextual information, but far less than is available to a trained operator. The machine program knows all the standard Morse characters and a few compound ones, but no syllables or words. A trained operator, on the other hand, hears the characters themselves embedded in a meaningful context.

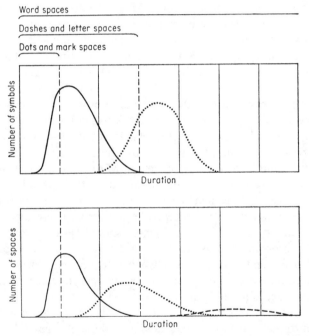

Figure 1. Variability of Morse code sent by a human operator is illustrated in these curves. Upper graph shows range of durations for dots (solid curve) and dashes (dotted curve) in a message. Lower graph gives the same information for spaces between marks within a character (solid curve), spaces between characters (dotted curve) and between words (dashed curve). Ideal durations are shown by brackets at top and vertical broken lines.

Empirically it is easier to distinguish between the two kinds of mark than among the three kinds of space. The main problem for any mechanical Morse translator is to segment the message into its characters by identifying the character spaces. MAUDE begins by assuming that the longest of each six consecutive spaces is a character space (since no Morse character is more than six marks long), and the shortest is a mark space. It is important to note that although the former rule follows logically from the structure of the ideal code, and that the latter seems quite plausible, their effectiveness can be demonstrated only by experiment. In fact the rules fail less than once in 10,000 times.

The decoding process is as follows. (See Fig. 2.) The marks and spaces, received by the machine in the form of electrical pulses, are converted into a sequence of numbers measuring their duration. (For technical reasons these numbers are then converted into their logarithms.) The sequence of durations representing spaces is processed first. The machine examines each group of six (spaces one through six, two through seven, three through eight and so on), recording in each the longest and shortest durations. When this process is complete, about 75 per cent of the character spaces and about 50 per cent of the mark spaces will have been identified.

To classify the remaining spaces a threshold is computed. It is set at the most plausible dividing line between the range of durations in which mark spaces have been found and the range of the identified character spaces. Every unclassified number larger than the threshold is then identified as a character space; every one smaller than the threshold, as a mark space.

Now, by a similar process, the numbers representing marks are identified as dots and dashes. Combining the classified marks and spaces gives a string of tentative segments, separated by character spaces. These are inspected and compared to a set of proper Morse characters stored in the machine. (There are about 50 of these, out of the total of 127 possible sequences of six or fewer marks.) Experience has shown that when one of the tentative segments is not acceptable, it is most likely that one of the supposed mark spaces within the segment should be a character space instead. The program reclassifies the longest space in the segment as a character space and examines the two new characters thus formed. The procedure continues until every segment is an acceptable character, whereupon the message is printed out.

In the course of transmitting a long message, operators usually change speed from time to time. MAUDE adapts to these changes. The computed thresholds are local, moving averages that shift with the general lengthening or shortening of marks and spaces. Thus a mark of a certain duration could be classified as a dot in one part of the message and a dash in another.

MAUDE's error rate is only slightly higher than that of a skilled human

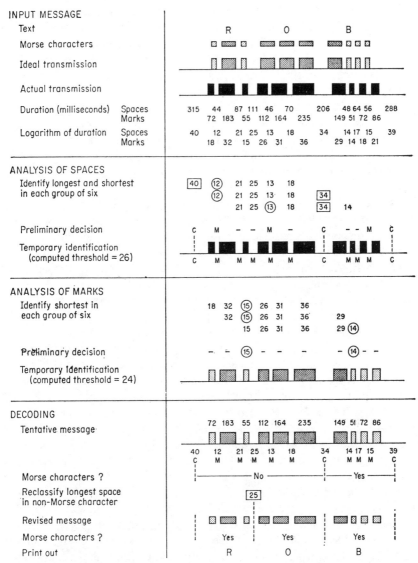

Figure 2. "MAUDE" program described in text, translates Morse code. Marks identified as dots are shown in light color; marks identified as dashes in dark color. Unidentified marks are in black. Character spaces are denoted by C; mark spaces, by M. A circle around a number indicates that it is the smallest in a group; a rectangle means it is the largest. Analysis of spaces and marks proceeds by an examination of successive groups of six throughout the message. The table shows only the first three such groups in each case.

operator. Thus it is at least possible for a machine to recognize patterns even where the basis of classification is variable and not fully specified in advance. Moreover, the program illustrates an important general point. Its success depends on the rules by which the continuous message is divided into appropriate segments. Segmentation seems likely to be a primary problem in all mechanical pattern recognition, particularly in the recognition of speech, since the natural pauses in spoken language do not generally come between words. MAUDE handles the segmentation problems in terms of context, and this will often be appropriate. In other respects MAUDE does not provide an adequate basis for generalizing about pattern recognition. The patterns of Morse code are too easy, and the processing is rather specialized.

Our second example deals with a more challenging problem: the recognition of hand-printed letters of the alphabet. The characters that people print in the ordinary course of filling out forms and questionnaires are surprisingly varied. Gaps abound where continuous lines might be expected; curves and sharp angles appear interchangeably; there is almost every imaginable distortion of slant, shape and size. Even human readers cannot always identify such characters; their error rate is about 3 per cent on randomly selected letters and numbers, seen out of context.

The first step in designing a mechanical reader is to provide it with a means of assimilating the visual data. By nature computers consider information in strings of bits: sequences of zeros and ones recorded in on-off devices. The simplest way to encode a character into such a sequence is to convert it into a sort of halftone by splitting it into a mesh or matrix of squares as fine as may be necessary. Each square is then either black or white—a binary situation that the machine is designed to handle. Making such halftones presents no problem. For example, an image of the letter could be projected on a bank of photocells, with the output of each cell controlling a binary device in the computer. In the experiments to be described here the appropriate digital information from the matrix was recorded on punch cards and was fed into the computer in this form.

Once this sequence of bits has been put in, how shall the program proceed to identify it? Perhaps the most obvious approach is a simple matching scheme, which would evaluate the similarity of the unknown to a series of ideal templates of all the letters, previously stored in digital form in the machine. The sequence of zeros and ones representing the unknown letter would be compared to each template sequence, and the number of matching digits recorded in each case. The highest number of matches would identify the letter.

In its primitive form the scheme would clearly fail. Even if the unknown were identical to the template, slight changes in position, orientation or size could destroy the match completely. (See Fig. 3a.) This difficulty has long been recognized, and in some character-recognition programs it has been met by inserting a level of information-processing ahead of the template-matching procedure. The sample is shifted, rotated and magnified or reduced in order to put it into a standard, or at least a more tractable, form.

Although obviously an improvement over raw matching, such a procedure is still inadequate. What it does is to compare shapes rather successfully. But letters are a good deal more than mere shapes. Even when a sample has been converted to standard size, position and orientation, it may match a wrong template more closely than it matches the right one. (See Fig. 3b.)

Nevertheless the scheme illustrates what we believe to be an important general principle. The critical change was from a program with a single level of operation to a program with two distinctly different levels. The first level shifts, and the second one matches. Such a hierarchical structure is forced on the recognition system by the nature of the entities to be recognized. The letter A is defined by the set of configurations that people call A, and their selections can be described—or imitated—only by a multi-level program.

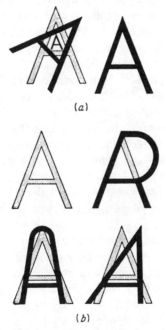

(a)

(b)

Figure 3. (a) Template matching cannot succeed when the unknown letter (color) has the wrong size, orientation, or position. The program must begin by adjusting sample to standard form. (b) Incorrect match may result even when sample (gray) has been converted to standard form. Here R matches A template more closely than do samples of the correct letter.

We have said that letter patterns cannot be described merely as shapes. It appears that they can be specified only in terms of a preponderance of certain *features*. Thus A tends to be thinner at the top than at the bottom; it is roughly concave at the bottom; it usually has two main strokes more vertical than horizontal, one more horizontal than vertical, and so on. All these features taken together characterize A rather more closely than they characterize any other letter. Singly none of them is sufficient. For example, W is also roughly concave at the bottom, and H has a pattern of horizontal and vertical strokes similar to that described for A. Each letter has its own set of probable features, and a successful character recognizer will determine which set is the best fit to an unknown sample.

So far nothing has been said about how the features are to be determined and how the program will use them. The template-matching scheme represents one approach. Its "features," in a sense, are the individual cells of the matrix representing the unknown sample, and its procedure is to match them with corresponding cells in the template. Both features and procedures are determined by the designer. We have seen that this scheme will not succeed. In fact, any system must fail if it tries to specify every detail of a procedure for identifying patterns that are themselves defined only ostensively. A pattern-recognition system must learn. But how much?

At one extreme there have been attempts to make it learn, or generate, everything: the features, the processing, the decision procedure. The initial state of such a system is called a "random net." A large number of on-off computer elements are multiply interconnected in a random way. Each is thus fed by several others. The thresholds of the elements (the number of signals that must be received before the element fires) are then adjusted on the basis of performance. In other words, the system learns by reinforcing some pathways through the net and weakening others.

How far a random net can evolve is controversial. Probably a net can come to act as though it used templates. However, none has yet been shown capable of generating features more sophisticated than those based, like templates, on single matrix cells. Indeed, we do not believe that this is possible.

At present the only way the machine can get an adequate set of features is from a human programmer. The effectiveness of any particular set can be demonstrated only by experiment. In general there is probably safety in numbers. The designer will do well to include all the features he can think of that might plausibly be useful.

A program that does not develop its own features may nevertheless be capable of modifying some subsequent level of the decision procedure, as we shall see. First however, let us consider that procedure itself. There are two fundamentally different possibilities: sequential and parallel processing. In sequential processing the features are inspected in a predetermined order, the outcome of each test determining the next step. Each letter is represented by a unique sequence of binary decisions. To take a simple example, a program to distinguish the letters A, H, V and Y might decide among them on the basis of the presence or absence of three features: a concavity at the top, a crossbar and a vertical line. The sequential process would ask first: "Is there a concavity at the top?" If the answer is no, the sample is A. If the answer is yes, the program asks: "Is there a crossbar?" If yes, the letter is H; if no, then: "Is there a vertical line?" If yes, the letter is Y; if no, V. (See Fig. 4.)

In parallel processing all the questions would be asked at once, and all the answers presented simultaneously to the decision maker. (See Fig. 5.) Different combinations identify the different letters. One might think of the various features as being inspected by little demons, all of whom then shout the answers in concert to a decision-making demon. From this conceit comes the name "Pandemonium" for parallel processing.

Of the two systems the sequential type is the more natural for a machine. Computer programs are sequences of instructions, in which choices or alternatives are usually introduced as "conditional transfers": Follow one set of instructions if a certain number is negative (say) and another set of instructions if it is not. Programs of this kind can be highly efficient, especially in cases where any given decision is almost certain to be right. But in "noisy" situations sequential programs require elaborate checking and backtracking procedures to compensate for erroneous decisions.

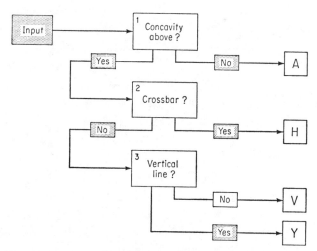

Figure 4. Sequential-processing program for distinguishing four letters, A, H, V and Y, employs three test features: presence or absence of a concavity above, a crossbar, and a vertical line. The tests are applied in order, with each outcome determining the next step.

Parallel processing, on the other hand, need make no special allowance for error and uncertainty.

Furthermore, some features are simply not subject to a reasonable dichotomy. An A very surely has a crossbar, an O very surely has not. But what about B? The most we can say is that it has more of a crossbar than O, and less than A. A Pandemonium program can handle the situation by having the demons shout more or less loudly. In other words, the information flowing through the system need not be binary; it can represent the quantitative preponderance of the various features.

Still another advantage of parallel processing lies in the possibility of making small changes in a network for experimental purposes. In typical sequential programs the only possible changes involve replacing a zero with a one, or vice versa. In parallel ones, on the other hand, the weight given to crossbarness in deciding if the unknown is actually B may be changed by as small an amount as desired. Experimental changes of this kind need not be made by the programmer alone. A program can be designed to alter internal weights as a result of experience and to profit from its mistakes. Such learning is much easier to incorporate into a Pandemonium than into a sequential system, where a change at any point has grave consequences for large parts of the system.

Parallel processing seems to be the human way of handling pattern

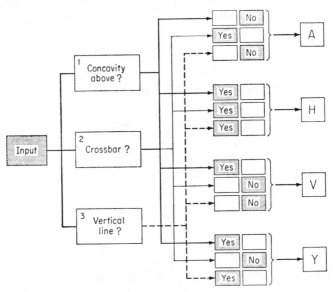

Figure 5. Parallel-processing program uses the same test features as the sequential program in Fig. 4, but applies all tests simultaneously and makes decision on the basis of the combined outcomes. The input is a sample of one of the letters A, H, V and Y.

Figure 6. Hand-printed letter A is processed for recognition by a computer. Original sample is placed on grid and converted to a cellular pattern by completely filling in all squares through which lines pass (top left). The computer then cleans up the sample, filling in gaps (top right) and eliminating isolated cells (botton left). The program tests the pattern for a variety of features. The test illustrated here (bottom right) is for the maximum number of intersections of the sample with all horizontal lines across the grid.

recognition as well. Speech can be understood if all acoustic frequencies above 2000 cycles per second are eliminated, but it can also be understood if those below 2000 are eliminated instead. Depth perception is excellent if both eyes are open and the head is held still; it is also excellent if one eye is open and the head is allowed to move.

A Pandemonium system that learns from experience has been tested by Worthie Doyle of the Lincoln Laboratory. At present it is programmed to identify 10 hand-printed characters, and has been tested on samples of A, E, I, L, M, N, O, R, S and T. The program has six levels: (1) input,

Type of test and designation		Outcome	A	E	I	L	M	N	O	R	S	T
Horizontal and vertical cross-sections	HOMSXC	3	.083	.070			.250	.347	.097	.056		.097
	VEMSXC	3	.073	.339			.040		.008	.194	.258	.089
	HORUNS	2111111		.500						.500		
	VERUNS	2111111						1.000				
Strokes	HORSTR	1	.182	.006	.125	.125	.125	.146	.016	.057	.016	.203
	VERSTR	2	.178	.007			.170	.207	.229	.207		
Edge lengths and ratios	SEDGE	1	.267	.007	.024	.014	.158	.115	.007	.165		.266
	WEDGE	1	.083	.071	.153	.024	.035	.012		.047	.318	.389
	NEDGE	2	.259	.024	.161	.024	.106	.106		.059	.189	.012
	EEDGE	4	.232				.214	.286	.071			
	NO:SOU	4	.513			.309	.205	.077	.107	.128		.077
	EA:WES	1	.055	.400			.018	.036		.163		.018
Profiles	SCUCAV	3	.150	.094	.023	.012	.800	.050	.035	.059	.412	.259
	WESCAV	2	.047	.177	.100	.092	.023	.035	.133	.108	.116	.137
	NORCAV	1	.133	.005	.115	.095	.004		.170	.010	.050	.165
	EASCAV	1	.155	.106		.068	.105	.130	.008	.220	.008	
	SOUBOT	220	.268	.030	.061		.159	.167	.354		.364	.515
	WESBOT	221	.030	.145					.266	.042	.042	.125
	NORBOT	121	.290					.102		.020	.245	.020
	EASBOT	121	.326				.020					
Internal structure	SBOTSG	2	.250	.008	.090	.016	.125	.141	.219	.203	.039	.157
	WBOTSG	1	.161	.076	.111	.099	.108	.121	.063	.081	.045	.159
	NBOTSG	1	.119	.190	.098	.102	.013	.018	.089	.040	.159	.061
	EBOTSG	1	.147	.058		.103	.103	.121	.062	.071	.076	.500
	SOUBEN	20	.198	.143	.011	.022	.333	.167			.022	.241
	WESBEN	10	.169	.180		.135	.121	.132	.011	.099	.247	.045
	NORBEN	10	.211	.012	.012	.118	.079			.146		.188
	EASBEN	10					.176	.106		.176		
Total score			4.579	2.648	1.084	1.358	3.490	3.622	1.945	2.851	2.606	3.823

Figure 7. Recognition program for hand-printed letters applies the 28 feature tests listed by code name at left. Names represent such features as maximum intersection with horizontal line (HOMSXC), concavity facing south (SOUCAV), and so on. Figures in right-hand section are relative probabilities of all letters for each test outcome. The program decides on the letter with the largest total of all probabilities. In the example shown here the decision is for the letter A, with a probability total of 4.579.

248

(2) cleanup, (3) inspection of features, (4) comparison with learned-feature distribution, (5) computation of probabilities and (6) decision. The input is a 1024-cell matrix, 32 on a side. At the second level the sample character is smoothed by filling in isolated gaps and eliminating isolated patches. (See Fig. 6.)

Recognition is based on such features as the relative length of different edges and the maximum number of intersections of the sample with a horizontal line. (The computer "draws" the lines by inspecting every horizontal row in the matrix, and recognizes "intersections" as sequences of ones separated by sequences of zeros.) No single feature is essential to recognition, and various numbers of them have been tried. The particular program shown here uses 28. (See Fig. 7.)

Every letter fed into the machine is tested for each of the features. During the learning phase a number of samples of each of the 10 letters is presented and identified. For every feature the program compiles a table or "census." It tests each sample and enters the outcome under the appropriate letter. When the learning period is finished, the table shows how many times each outcome occurred for each of the 10 letters. Figure 8, which refers to maximum intersections with a horizontal line, represents the experience gained from a total of 330 training samples. It shows, for example, that the outcome (three intersections) occurred 72 times distributed among six A's, five E's, 18 M's, 25 N's, seven O's, four R's, seven T's and no other letters. The other possible outcomes are similarly recorded.

Next the 28 censuses are converted to tables of estimated probabilities,

Letter	Samples	Outcome			
		1	2	3	4
A	39		33	6	
E	46	6	35	5	
I	25	25			
L	24	7	17		
M	24			18	6
N	28		2	25	1
O	34		27	7	
R	33		28	4	1
S	38	8	30		
T	39	10	22	7	
Total	330	56	194	72	8

Figure 8. "CENSUS" represents information learned by letter-recognition program during training period. This table summarizes the outcomes of the test for maximum number of intersections with a horizontal line, applied to a total of 330 identified samples in the learning process.

by dividing each entry by the appropriate total. Thus the outcome—three intersections—comes from an A with a probability of .083 (6/72); an E, with a probability of .070 (5/72), and so on.

Now the system is ready to consider an unknown sample. It carries out the 28 tests and "looks up" each outcome in the corresponding feature census, entering the estimated probabilities in a table. Then the total probabilities are computed for each letter. The final decision is made by choosing the letter with the highest probability.

This program makes only about 10 per cent fewer correct identifications than human readers make—a respectable performance, to be sure. At the same time, the things it cannot do point to the difficulties that still lie ahead. We would emphasize three general problems: segmentation, hierarchical learning and feature generation.

Characters must be fed in one at a time. The program is unable to segment continuous written material. The problem will doubtless be relatively easy to solve for text consisting of separate printed characters, but will be more formidable in the case of cursive script.

The program learns on one level only. The relation between feature presence and character probability is determined by experience; everything else is fixed by the designer. It would certainly be desirable for a character recognizer to use experience for more general improvements: to change its cleanup procedures, alter the way probabilities are combined and refine its decision process. Eventually we look to recognition of words; at this point the program will have to learn a vocabulary so that it can use context in identifying dubious letters. At the moment, however, neither we nor any other designers have any experience with the interaction of several levels of learning.

The most important learning process of all is still untouched: No current program can generate test features of its own. The effectiveness of all of them is forever restricted by the ingenuity or arbitrariness of their programmers. We can barely guess how this restriction might be overcome. Until it is, "artificial intelligence" will remain tainted with artifice.

A PATTERN - RECOGNITION PROGRAM THAT GENERATES, EVALUATES, AND ADJUSTS ITS OWN OPERATORS

by Leonard Uhr & Charles Vossler

Background Review

The typical pattern-recognition program is either elaborately prepro-grammed to process specific arrays of input patterns, or else it has been designed as a *tabula rasa,* with certain abilities to adjust its values, or "learn." The first type often cannot identify large classes of patterns that appear only trivially different to the human eye, but that would com-pletely escape the machine's logic (Bailey and Norrie, 1957; Greanias et al., 1957). The best examples of this type are probably capable of being extended to process new classes of patterns (Grimsdale et al., 1959a; Sherman, 1959). But each such extension would seem to be an *ad hoc* complication where it should be a simplification, and to represent an additional burden of time and energy on both programmer and computer.

The latter type of self-adjusting program does not, at least as yet, appear to possess methods for accumulating experience that are sufficiently powerful to succeed in interesting cases. The random machines show relatively poor identification ability (Rosenblatt, 1958, 1960a). (One ex-ception to this statement appears to be Roberts' modification of Rosen-blatt's Perceptron (Roberts, 1960). But this modification appears to make the Perceptron an essentially nonrandom computer.) The most successful of this type of computer, to date, simply accumulates information or proba-bilities about discrete cells in the input matrix (Baran and Estrin, 1960; Highleyman and Kamentsky, 1960). But this is an unusually weak type of learning (if it should be characterized by that vague epithet at all), and

251

this type of program is bound to fail as soon as, and to the extent that, patterns are allowed to vary.

Several programs compromise by making use of some of the self-adapting and separate operator processing features of the latter type of program, but with powerful built-in operations of the sort used by the first type (Doyle, 1960; Unger, 1959). They appear to have gained in flexibility in writing and modifying programs; but they have not, as yet, given (published) results that indicate that they are any more powerful than the weaker sort of program (*e.g.,* Baran and Estrin) that uses individual cells in the matrix in ways equivalent to their use of "demons" and "operators." A final example of this mixed type of program is the randomly coupled "n-tuple" operator used by Bledsoe and Browning (1959; 1961*a*). In this program, random choice of pairs, quintuples and other tuples of cells in the input matrix is used to compose operators, in an attempt to get around the problems of preanalyzing and preprogramming. This method appears to be guaranteed to have at least as great power as the single cell probability method (Uhr, 1961*b*). But it has not as yet demonstrated this power. And it would, like most of the other programs discussed (or known to the authors) fall down when asked to process patterns which differed very greatly from those with which it had originally "gained experience" by extracting information (Uhr, 1960).

Summary of Program Operation

In summary, the original running pattern recognition program works as follows: Unknown patterns are presented to the computer in discrete form, as a 20×20 matrix of zeros and ones. The program generates and composes operators by one of several random methods, and uses this set of operators to transform the unknown input matrix into a list of characteristics. Or, alternately, the programmer can specify a set of pregenerated operators in which he is interested.

These characteristics are then compared with lists of characteristics in memory, one for each type of pattern previously processed. As a result of similarity tests, the name of the list most similar to the list of characteristics just computed is chosen as the name of the input pattern. The characteristics are then examined by the program and, depending on whether they individually contributed to success or failure in identifying the input, amplifiers for each of these characteristics are then turned up or down. This adjustment of amplifiers leads eventually to discarding operators which produce poor characteristics, as indicated by low amplifier settings, and to their replacement by newly generated operators.

One mode of operation of the present program is to begin with no operators at all. In this case operators are initially generated by the program at a fixed rate until some maximum number of operators is reached. The continual replacement of poor operators by new ones then tends to produce an optimum set of operators for processing the given array of inputs.

Details of Program Operation

The program can be run in a number of ways, and we will present results for some of these. The details of the operation of the program follow.

1. An unknown pattern to be identified is digitized into a 20 × 20 0–1 input matrix (Fig. 1).

2. A rectangular mask is drawn around the input (its sides defined by the leftmost, rightmost, bottommost, and topmost filled cells) (Fig. 2).

3. The input pattern is transformed into four 3-bit characteristics by each of a set of 5 × 5 matrix operators, each cell of which may be visualized as containing either a 0, 1, or blank. These small matrices which measure local characteristics of the pattern are translated, one at a time, across and then down that part of the matrix which lies within the mask. The operator is considered to match the input matrix whenever the 0's and 1's in the operator correspond to identical values in the pattern, and for each match the location of the center cell of the 5 × 5 matrix operator is temporarily recorded (Fig. 3). This information is then summarized and scaled from 0 to 7 to form four 3-bit characteristics for the operator. These represent (1) the number of matches, (2) the average horizontal position of the matches within the rectangular mask, (3) the average

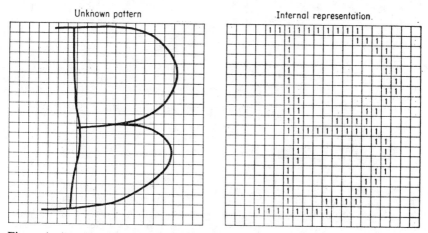

Figure 1. An unknown pattern is input as a 20 × 20 matrix with the cells covered by the pattern represented by "1's" and the other cells by "0's."

vertical position of the matches, and (4) the average value of the square of the radial distance from the center of the mask.

A variable number of operators can be used in any machine run. This can mean either a number preset for that specific run, or a number that begins at zero and expands, under one of the rules described below, up to the maximum. The string of 25 numbers which defines a 5×5 matrix operator can be generated in any of the following ways (Fig. 4):

  a. A preprogrammed string can be fed in by the experimenter.
  b. A random string can be generated; this string can be restricted as to the number of "ones" it will contain, and as to whether these "ones" must be connected in the 5×5 matrix. (We have not actually tested this method as yet.)
  c. A random string can be "extracted" from the present input matrix and modified by the following procedure (which in effect is imitating a certain part of the matrix). The process of inserting blanks

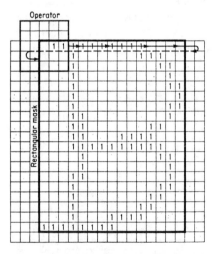

Figure 2. A rectangular mask is drawn around the unknown pattern. Each of the 5×5 matrix "operators" is then translated over the pattern.

Figure 3. The operator at the lower left in the figure is shown in the two positions where it matches the input matrix. An operator gives a positive output each time its "1's" cover "1's" and its "0's" cover "0's" in the unknown pattern.

Operator	Hit	X	Y	R^2
1 1 1 1	A	1	0	4
1 0				
1 0	B	2	4	0
N = 2		2	2	2

in the extracted operator allows for minor distortions in the local characteristics which the operator matches.

(1) A 5×5 matrix is extracted from a random position in the input matrix.

(2) All "zero" cells connected to "one" cells are then replaced by blanks.

(3) Each of the remaining cells, both "zeros" and "ones," is then replaced by a blank with a probability of $\frac{1}{2}$.

(4) Tests are made to ensure that the operator does not have "ones" in the same cells as any other currently used operator or any operator in a list of those recently rejected by the program. If the operator is similar to one of these in this

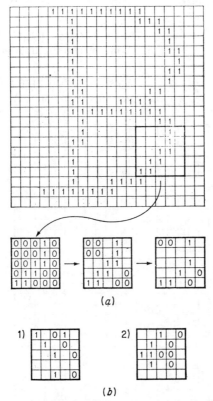

Figure 4. Operators are generated within the 5×5 matrix by either: (a) extraction from the input pattern (random placement of a 5×5 matrix, elimination of "0's" connected to "1's" and elimination of each of the remaining cells with a probability of $\frac{1}{2}$) or (b) by random designation of cells as either "0" or "1" (choose a "1," then place a "0" two cells to its right). In 1) from 3 to 7 "1's" are chosen completely at random, while in 2) the choice is limited to connected cells,

respect a new operator is generated by starting over at'
step 1 (Fig. 5).

4. A second type of operator is also used. This is a combinatorial
operator which specifies one of 16 possible logical or arithmetic operations and two previously calculated characteristics which are to be combined to produce a third characteristic. These operators are generated by
the program by randomly choosing one of the possible operations and the
two characteristics which are to be combined. This random generation
process is improved by generating a set of ten operators, and then pretesting these using the last two examples of each pattern which have been
saved in memory for this purpose. This pretesting is designed to choose
an operator from the set which produces characteristics that tend to be
invariant over examples of the same pattern yet vary between different
patterns.

Since these operators may act upon characteristics produced by previous
operators of the same type, functions of considerable complexity may be
built up.

5. The two types of operators just described produce a list of characteristics by which the program attempts to recognize the unknown input

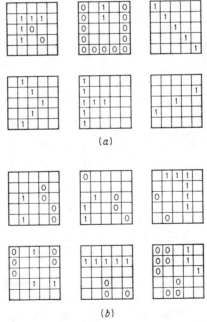

(a)

(b)

Figure 5. (a) Some typical examples of preprogrammed operators are shown.
(b) Six of the operators generated by the program, during a run that reached 94
per cent success on 7 sets of 5 patterns, are shown.

pattern (Fig. 6). At any time the program has stored in memory a similar list of characteristics for each type of pattern which the program has previously encountered. Corresponding to each list of characteristics in memory is a list of 3-bit amplifiers, which gives the current weighting for each characteristic as a number from 0 to 7.

The recognition process proceeds by taking the difference between each of the characteristics for the input pattern and those in the recognition list of the first pattern. These differences are then weighted by the corresponding pattern amplifiers, and then by general amplifiers which represent the average of the pattern amplifiers across all patterns, producing a weighted average difference between the input list and the list in memory. This average difference is multiplied by a final "average difference" amplifier to obtain a "difference score" for the list in memory. When a difference score has been computed for each list in memory, the name of the list with the smallest score is printed as the name of the input pattern (Fig. 7).

6. After each pattern is recognized the program modifies pattern amplifiers in those patterns which have difference scores less than or only slightly above the difference score for the correct pattern (Fig. 8). This means that the program will tend to concentrate on the difficult discrimination problems, since amplifiers are adjusted only in those patterns which appear similar to the correct pattern in terms of the difference scores and therefore make identification of the input difficult. The correct pattern is compared with each of the similar patterns in turn. Each characteristic in the memory lists for a pair of patterns is examined individually, and a determination is made as to whether the correct pattern would have been chosen if the choice had been made on the basis of this characteristic alone. If this one characteristic would have identified the correct pattern, then the corresponding amplifier is turned up by one. If it would have identified the wrong pattern then the amplifier is turned down by one. If no information is given by the characteristic, for example, if it is the same

Pattern Name	Operator 1				Operator 2				Characteristic			
	N	X	Y	R²	N	X	Y	R²	...	m-2	m-1	m
?	2	2	2	2	2	3	1	6	...	6	7	4
A	3	3	4	1	4	0	1	1	...	1	2	3
B	2	2	3	2	3	3	2	5	...	4	7	5
C	4	5	6	5	1	0	0	4	...	2	1	7

(Matrix operators span Operator 1 and Operator 2; Combinatorial operators span Characteristic.)

Figure 6. Operator outputs are listed for the unknown pattern in the same format as in lists stored in memory.

for both patterns, then the amplifier is turned down with a probability of
⅛. If the pattern compared with the correct pattern had the higher difference score then the amplifiers are adjusted only in that pattern. Otherwise, amplifiers are adjusted in both patterns. This means that if several
patterns obtained lower scores than the correct pattern then the amplifiers
in the correct pattern will be drastically changed, since they will change
when compared with each of these patterns.

The list of characteristics in memory for the pattern just processed is
then modified. The first time a pattern is encountered its list of computed
characteristics is simply stored in memory along with its name. On the
second encounter of a pattern each of the characteristics in memory is
replaced by the new characteristic with a probability of ½. For the third
and following encounters each characteristic is replaced by the new value
with a probability of ¼. Since about ¼ of the characteristics will be
changing each time, after several examples of a pattern have been processed, the list of characteristics in memory will tend to be more similar
to the characteristics of the last patterns processed than to those processed

PATTERN *A*

Characteristics (A)	:	3	3	4	1	4 ... 3
Input (?)	:	2	2	2	2	2 ... 4
Difference |A−?|	:	1	1	2	1	2 ... 1
Pattern amplifiers	:	2	3	1	2	0 ... 3
General amplifiers	:	3	3	1	1	0 ... 3
Diff. X amplifiers	:	6	9	2	2	0 ... 9

Weighted av. diff.	Av. diff. amplifier	Diff. score
$\frac{28}{27} = 1.04$	61	63

PATTERN *B*

Characteristics (B)	:	2	2	3	2	3 ... 5
Input (?)	:	2	2	2	2	2 ... 4
Difference |B−?|	:	0	0	1	0	1 ... 1
Pattern amplifiers	:	4	3	2	3	2 ... 2
General amplifiers	:	3	3	1	1	0 ... 3
Diff. X amplifiers	:	0	0	2	0	0 ... 6

Weighted av. diff.	Av. diff. amplifier	Diff. score
$\frac{8}{32} = 0.25$	60	15

Figure 7. Differences are obtained between the characteristics for the input pattern and each list of characteristics in memory. These differences are then weighted
by the product of the "general amplifiers" and "pattern amplifiers," giving a
weighted average difference for each list in memory. When multiplied by corresponding "average difference amplifiers," the weighted average differences give
"difference scores" for each pattern in memory. The name of the pattern with the
smallest "difference score" is chosen as the name of the input.

earlier. However, to the extent that the learning process is able to produce operators giving invariant characteristics for a single pattern, the list of characteristics will be representative of all the examples processed. The reason for not simply using the average value for each characteristic is that this would require saving in memory more than the 3 bits otherwise needed for each characteristic, as well as saving an indication of the number of times each characteristic had been calculated for each pattern.

An alternate scheme which we tried involved saving the highest and lowest values obtained by each characteristic, and averaging these to obtain a mean value with which to compare the input. This worked quite well in all our test runs, which used a few samples of each pattern. But there is the possibility that with large numbers of examples of a pattern, all the characteristics will eventually have very large ranges; that is, the lower bounds will tend to be 0 and the upper bounds will tend to be 7.

7. The average difference amplifiers which are used in the final step of the recognition process provide only coarse adjustments. These amplifiers are initially set to some fixed value, *e.g.*, 60, and are then adjusted for the same pairs of patterns as the pattern amplifiers. The amplifier for the correct pattern is turned down by N if there are N incorrect patterns, and the amplifier for each of the similar patterns is turned up by one.

8. The general characteristic amplifiers are now computed by averaging the pattern amplifiers across all patterns. These indicate the general value of each characteristic in the recognition process and form the basis for the construction of success counts which control the replacement of operators. Since the combinatorial operators combine characteristics to produce other characteristics, the success count should reflect both the value of a charac-

RIGHT LIST

Difference	:	1	4	2	3 ... 4
Amplifiers	:	4	3	2	3 ... 1
Adjusted	:	+1	0	+1	−1 ... −1
	:	+1	−1	−1	−1 ... +1
New total	:	6	2	2	1 ... 1

1st WRONG LIST

Difference	:	2	4	5	2 ... 2
Amplifiers	:	2	3	1	4 ... 3
Adjusted	:	+1	0	+1	−1 ... −1
New total	:	3	3	2	3 ... 2

2d WRONG LIST

Difference	:	3	1	1	2 ... 5
Amplifiers	:	1	2	2	1 ... 1
Adjusted	:	+1	−1	−1	−1 ... +1
New total	:	2	1	1	0 ... 2

Figure 8. The pattern amplifiers for certain lists are adjusted to *increase* weightings of individual characteristics that gave differences in the right direction, and to *decrease* weightings that gave differences in the wrong direction.

teristic in the recognition process and the importance of this characteristic in aiding the creation of other, possibly important characteristics.

9. This success count is formed by first storing the value of the general characteristic amplifier corresponding to each characteristic in a table for success counts. Then starting with the last combinatorial operator and working back through the list of these operators, $\frac{1}{2}$ the value of the success count for the characteristic corresponding to the operator is added to the success counts of the two characteristics which the operator combines. Finally, two times the general characteristic amplifier setting is added to each success count.

10. Whenever a new operator is generated, the characteristics produced by the operator are computed for each of the possible patterns using the last example of each pattern, which has been saved in the computer memory. These newly calculated characteristics are then inserted into the list of characteristics for their respective patterns. At the same time the pattern amplifier settings for each of these new characteristics are set to 1 so that the characteristic will have very little weight in computing a difference score until it has been turned up as a function of proved ability at differentiation. Since the general amplifier for a characteristic is simply the average of the pattern amplifiers, it will also be 1 for the new characteristic. The success count of a new characteristic which is not combined to produce other characteristics is then 3 and this value will tend to increase if the operator proves to be valuable. On the other hand if a success count drops below 3 (or in the case of a matrix operator, if the average value of the success counts of its four characteristics drops below 3) the operator is rejected and a new operator is generated to take its place.

The pattern amplifiers play a crucial part both by aiding directly in the recognition process and by providing the information which ultimately determines the generation of new operators to replace poor ones. Since the adjustment of these amplifiers is made selectively, based on their individual success or failure in distinguishing pairs of patterns where confusion is likely, the operators rejected by the program will tend to be those which are not useful in making the more difficult discrimination. Also, because amplifiers are usually changed more drastically when the computer makes an incorrect guess, the 5×5 matrix operators will have a higher probability of being extracted from unrecognized patterns. Although the rules governing the learning process seem rather arbitrary in many cases, and it is difficult to describe their effects quantitatively, qualitative effects, such as this ability to concentrate on difficult problems, are fairly easy to show. The description of the program's operation shows that the emphasis is not so much on the design of a specific problem-solving code as it is on the design of a program which, at least in part, will construct such a problem-solving code as a result of experience.

It is interesting to note that the memory of the program exists in at least three different places: (1) in the lists of characteristics in memory, (2) in the settings of the various amplifiers, and (3) in the set of operators in use by the program. While the lists of characteristics bear some direct relationship to the individual patterns processed by the program, the values of the amplifiers and the set of operators in use by the program depend in a more complex way on the whole set of patterns processed by the program, and on the program's success or failure in recognizing these patterns. The learning in the first case, which involves simply storing characteristics in memory, is merely "memorization" or "learning by rote." In the second case, the learning is more subtle for it involves the program's own analysis of its ability to deal with its environment, and its attempt to improve this ability.

Test Results of Original Program

The original program was written for the IBM 709 and required about 2000 machine instructions. The time required to process a single character was about 25 seconds when 5 different patterns were used and 40 seconds when each character had to be compared with ten possible patterns in memory. While such times are not excessive, they are large enough to make it impractical to run extremely large test cases.

In several early runs which we made, 48 preprogrammed matrix operators were used. These were designed to measure such things as straight and curved lines, the ends of vertical and horizontal strokes, and various other features. The program was tested using seven different sets of the five hand-printed characters A, B, C, D, and E. These involved a fair amount of distortion, and variation in size, but were not rotated to any great extent.

The program's performance on the last three or four sets in a run varied from about 70% to 80% depending on various changes which were made to the rules governing the learning process.

One run was made using the individual cells of the input matrix as first level operators, building up higher-level combinatorial operators on these. This gave little better than 30% success. Finally, this version of the program was tested without any preprogrammed operators, the program achieved 97% on known and 70% on unknown examples of a ten-letter alphabet. It also showed ability to recognize simple drawings of objects.

Test Results of Revised Program

The original program was modified, chiefly to increase its running speed, and secondarily to simplify some of its logic. In order to make use of logical machine instructions on the 709, all characteristics and their ampli-

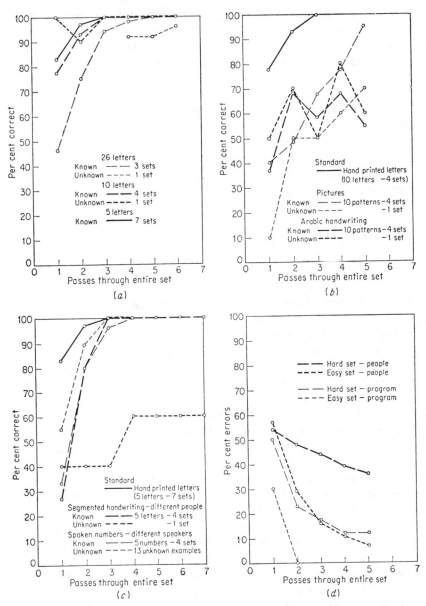

Figure 9. (a) Results of the computer simulation program. Hand-printed alphabetic patterns. Per cent correct on several sets of a 26-pattern, a 10-pattern, and a 5-pattern array. The program was tested on both known and unknown sets of patterns. (b) Results with two additional 10-pattern arrays: (1) line drawings of pictures (different examples of each of 5 faces and 5 objects), (2) arabic handwriting (written by the same person). The program was tested on both known

fiers were reduced to 1-bit values. The revised program stores nine one-bit values for each operator—whether it hit at least once in each of nine parts of the matrix. Operators are weighted either 1 (to be used) or 0 (not to be used), referring to the characteristics they give for each pattern stored in memory. Operators are eliminated when they have given wrong outputs on the last n example for which the program as a whole has been wrong. The "general amplifiers" have been eliminated. These changes effected an increase of speed by a factor of about 40. Thus this program takes about 1 second per example for a 10-pattern alphabet on the 709, and less than .2 second on the 7090. This program is probably weaker than the original program, since it has virtually no range within which to search for a good set of weightings for its operators. But its increased speed led to its use for the bulk of our tests on this version of the program.

The speeded up program has been tested on several different types of input patterns, as shown in Fig. 9. In most cases, results were quite similar on both "known" examples (that is, examples the program had previously processed and hence had learned from) and "unknown" examples (that is, different from the ones used in learning, and also produced by different people). Figure 9a shows results for several different sizes of pattern arrays, all of hand-printed capital letters, printed by different people. These results show relatively little decrease in the program's abilities as the array size is increased, at least up to the 26-letter alphabet. Thus, on the sixth pass through the 26-letter alphabet the program was 100% correct on known patterns and 96% correct on unknown patterns.

Figure 9b presents results for two 10-pattern arrays. These were: (1) line drawings of cartoon faces and simple objects (such as shoes and pliers), each copied from a different picture, as found in cartoon strips and mail-order catalogs (Fig. 10 presents some examples of the cartoons), and (2) handwritten arabic letters, written by the same person. The program achieved 95% success on known and 70% success on unknown pictures, and 60% success on known and 55% success on unknown arabic letters (segmented handwriting) in the fifth pass. Figure 9c presents results from two 5-pattern arrays: (1) digitized and degraded sound spectrograms of speech (the numbers "zero," "one," "two," "three," and "four," as spoken by different speakers) (Uhr and Vossler, 1961d), and (2) segmented lower-case handwriting, written by different people. The

---

and unknown sets of patterns. (c) Results with two additional 5-pattern arrays: (i) spoken numerals (spoken by different people), (ii) segmented handwriting (written by different people). The program was tested on both known and unknown sets of patterns. (d) Results from a comparison experiment. Per cent errors for the program and mean per cent errors for human subjects (from 6 to 10 subjects per point) on one hard and one easy set of "meaningless" patterns. Both sets contained five variant examples of each of five patterns.

program achieved 100% success on both known and unknown spoken numerals by the fourth pass, and 100% success on known handwriting by the third pass. It achieved 60% success on the unknown handwriting, but it is likely that it would have improved further on these inputs if it had been given more opportunity to learn (once it achieves 100% success on known patterns it does not benefit appreciably from subsequent learning experiences).

Finally, the program's performance was compared with the performance of human subjects on sets of "meaningless" patterns. This sort of pattern minimizes the effects of the human being's lifetime of experience and resulting associative context. Figure 9d presents results from two such experiments, in both of which the program performed appreciably better than did any of the human subjects. Three additional experiments previously reported in the psychological literature were replicated. In all cases the program performed at a higher level than did the human subjects (Uhr, Vossler, and Uleman, 1962).

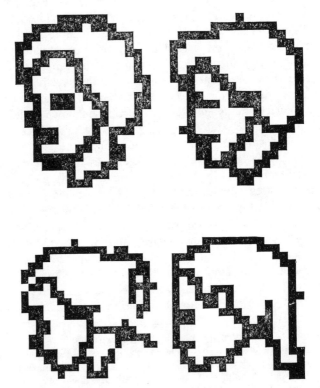

Figure 10. Two examples of each of two cartoon faces as presented to the simulation program (digitized by hand into a 20 × 20 matrix, after optical projection from the newspaper original).

This program was also tested for its ability to handle continuous patterns such as handwritten words and spoken sentences. Simple additional subroutines were written to allow it to input matrices any number of columns long, to make very primitive tentative segmentations (in every nth column, n usually around 7, and in columns with fewer than two filled cells), and to decide among the various alternatives at the various different tentative segmentation points. The program reached 100% correct performance when asked to segment and recognize the words, or alternatively the phonemes, in the simple sentence "Did Dad say before," spoken by different people.

On the handwritten sequences "pattern one," "pattern two," "pattern three" (written by different people), the program reached about 60% success in recognizing the letters. These tests do not in any adequate way sample the range of problems to be encountered with such stimuli. But they give some indication that the program is capable of at least beginning to handle continuous inputs. And it should be relatively easy to improve upon this performance by adding more sophisticated segmenting methods and a straightforward method (such as the use of letter n-tuple frequencies in the language) for making use of contextual information.

Discussion

When this program is given a neurophysiological interpretation, or a neural, net analog, it can be seen to embody relatively weak, plausible, and "natural-looking" assumptions. The 5×5 matrix operator is equivalent to a 5×5 net of input retinal cones or photocells converging on a single output, with "ones" denoting excitatory and "zeros" denoting inhibitory connections, and the threshold for firing the output unit set at the sum of the "ones." Each translation step of the operator matrix over the larger matrix gives a sequential simulation of the parallel placement of many of these simple neural net operators throughout the matrix. Each different operator, then, is the equivalent of an additional connection pattern between input cones, firing onto a new output unit that computes the output for that operation. This is all quite plausible for the retina as known anatomically, with a single matrix of cones in parallel that feed into several layers of neurons. Evidence for excitatory and inhibitory connections is also strong (Hartline, 1938). And there is even beginning to be evidence of several types of simple net operators that exist in parallel iterated form throughout the retinal matrix [four of these as determined by Lettvin, Maturana, McCulloch, and Pitts in the frog (1959); and probably even more as determined by Hubel and Wiesel in the cat (1959)].

It would seem, however, that the known physiological constraints and the plausible geometric constraints on operators would suggest fewer than the 40-odd operators that we have used [or than the 30-odd used by Doyle (1960) or the 75 used by Bledsoe and Browning (1959) ignoring the fact that they cannot be so easily interpreted neurophysiologically]. For example, straight-line and sharp-curve operators would seem to be more plausible in terms of the ease of connection and the importance of the information to which they respond. A possible operator that might overcome this problem, with which we are now working, is a simple differencing operator that will, by means of several additional layers of operations, first delineate contour and then compute successively higher order differences, and hence straightness, slope and curvature, for the unknown pattern. This operator appears to be equivalent to a simple net of excitatory and inhibitory elements (Uhr and Vossler, 1961a).

This, then, suggests that the mapping part of the program would be effected by two layers of parallel basic units in a neuron netlike arrangement. The matching part might similarly be performed by storing the previously mapped lists in a parallel memory and sweeping the input list, now mapped into the same standard format, through these lists. Finally, the amplifiers can be interpreted as threshold values as to when the differences thus computed lead to an output. The specific pattern characteristic amplifier would be an additional single unit layer lying right behind the memory list; the interpretation of the general amplifiers might be made in terms of chemical gradients, but is more obscure.

Thus a suitable parallel computer would perform all of the operations of this program in from three to ten serial steps. This is a somewhat greater depth than those programs, such as Selfridge's (1959) and Rosenblatt's (1958), that attempt to remain true to this aspect of the visual nervous system. But it is well within the limits, and actually closer to the specifications, of that system. It also takes into consideration the very precise (and amazing) point-to-point and nearness relations that are seen in the visual system, both between several spots on the retina or any particular neural layer, and from retina to cortex (Sperry, 1951). It also is using operators that seem more plausible in terms of neural interconnections—again, in the living system, heavily biased toward nearness.

The size of the over-all input matrix has also been chosen with the requirements of pattern perception in mind. Good psychophysical data show clearly that when patterns of the complexity of alphanumeric letters are presented to the human eye, recognition is just as sure and quick no matter how small the retinal cone mosaic, until the pattern subtends a mosaic of about the 20×20 size, at which time recognition begins to fall off, in both speed and accuracy, until a 10×10 mosaic is reached, at which point the pattern cannot be resolved at all. This further suggests something about the size of the basic operator, when we consider that most letters are composed of loops and strokes that are on the order of $\frac{1}{2}$ or $\frac{1}{4}$ of the whole. For our present purposes, the advantage of the 5×5 operator was not only its plausibility but also the fact that it cuts down to a workable size the space within which to generate random operators of the sort we are using when we permute through all possible combinations of the matrix. Again, with the constraint that these random operators be connected, it becomes a more powerful geometry- and topology-sensitive operator, and also a simulation of a more plausible neural net.

Finally, psychophysical evidence also strongly suggests that the resolving power of the human perceptual mechanism is on the order of only two or three bits worth of differentiation as to dimensions of pattern characteristics—things such as length, slope, and curvature (Alluisi, 1957; Miller, 1956b; Uhr, 1959b). This, again, suggests a 5×5 matrix as a minimum matrix that is capable of making these resolutions.

The specifications for and methods used by living systems, and especially the human visual system, suggest certain design possibilities for a pattern-recognition computer; but they certainly do not suggest the only possibilities. Nor should they be slavishly imitated. They should, however, be examined seriously, for the living pattern recognizers are the only successful systems that we know of today. Nor does it seem that the sort of use we have been making of these human specifications will impose any fundamental limitation on a program such as this, one that generates and adjusts its own operators. We have, in fact, already found the program making a different, and, apparently, more powerful, choice of operators than the choice suggested to us by the psychophysiological data and conjectures we have just described. The program's "learning" methods can now depend both on built-in connections (maturation) and on the inputs that need to be learned. The program will develop differently as a function of different input sets. It appears to be capable of extracting and successfully using information from these sets. This would seem to be as completely adaptive—being adaptive to inputs—as a computer or organism can be expected to be.

This sort of design would seem to have some applicability to a variety of more "intelligent" machines. The program replaces the programmer-analyst by a programmed operator that first generates operators that make effective enough use of the unknown input space, and then makes use of feedback as to the success of these new operators in mapping unknown inputs in order to increase their effectiveness. Thus neither programmer nor program needs to know anything specific about the problem ahead of time. The program performs, as part of its natural routine, the data collection, analysis, and inference that is typically left to the programmer. This would be a foolish waste of time for a problem that had already been analyzed. But pattern recognition, and many other problems of machine intelligence, have not been sufficiently analyzed. The different pattern-recognition programs are, themselves, attempts to make this analysis. As long as pattern recognition remains in the experimental stage (as it must do until it is effectively solved), a program of this sort would seem to be the most convenient and flexible format for running what is, in effect, a continuing series of experiments upon whose results continuing modifications of theories are made. This becomes an extremely interesting process for the biologist or psychologist, especially to the extent that the program can be interpreted either physiologically or functionally, or at the least does not violate any known data. For the experimentation and concomitant theory building and modification being undertaken today is rapidly building what appears to us to be the first relatively firm and meaningful theoretical structure—for pattern, or form, perception—for the science of "higher mental processes."

Self-generation of operators, by the various methods employed in this program, may also suggest approaches toward solving a wide variety of pattern-recognition and pattern-extraction problems. Thus there is some hope that relatively powerful operators are being extracted and generated as a result of experience with and feedback from the program's quasi-experimental analysis on the body of data that is available to it—its inputs and the consequences of its actions. Further, the level of power of these operators, and the serial ordering of operators can also be placed under similar control. Thus operators need not be overly simple or random to be machine-chosen; nor preprogrammed to be powerful. Rather, they can arise from the problem, and thus be sensitive to the problem, and to changes in the problem.

part 2
Simulation of
Cognitive Processes

The research reported in Part 2 is concerned with the construction of computer models of the information processes underlying human thought. While the major aim of the research reported in Part 1 is the programming of computers to perform intellectual tasks, the work reported here is concerned with the programming of computers to perform intellectual tasks in the same way that persons perform these tasks. An example may be helpful in clarifying the distinction between artificial intelligence research and simulation of cognitive processes research. An artificial intelligence researcher interested in programming a computer to play chess would be happy only if his program played good chess, preferably better chess than the best human player. However, the researcher interested in simulating the chess-playing behavior of a given individual would be unhappy if his program played chess better (or worse) than that individual, for this researcher wants his program to make the same moves as the human player, regardless of whether these moves are good, bad, or indifferent.

Why Program Computers To Do Tasks the Way People Do Them?

Researchers program computers to behave like people to further their understanding of, *i.e.*, their ability to predict, certain phenomena of human behavior. The computer program is a model which represents the researcher's hypotheses about the information processes underlying the behavior. The program is run on a computer to generate the predictions of the model. These predictions are compared with actual human behavior. There are usually some discrepancies between prediction and behavior, and the model is revised to reduce these discrepancies. Then the entire process is repeated. Eventually the researcher hopes to obtain a model which will be a good predictor of the relevant behavior. As he continues to test his model and to improve it, the researcher gains confidence in the belief that this model represents the processes underlying the behavioral phenomena he is studying.

This overview of the procedure of researchers using computer models to study human thought processes indicates that these workers use the same procedure that all scientists use. The only difference involves the representation of the model as a computer program and the use of the computer to determine the predictions of the model.

What Are the Advantages of Representing Models of Human Thought as Computer Programs?

The researcher may represent a model of human behavior in any of a number of different ways. Perhaps the most common representation is natural language, *i.e.,* the language in which we usually communicate, be it English, French, German, Russian, or Sanskrit. If we were to specify a model of a chess player in natural language, the description of the model might begin as follows:

> Before making a move, the player checks to see if his king or queen is in danger. . . .

A model of a chess player might also be represented in the language of mathematics.

A third possibility is the representation of the model as a program for a digital computer.

The selection of a medium for model construction depends on the characteristics of the medium, the characteristics of the model, and the resources of the model builder. Natural language is an extremely flexible medium, and perhaps any conceivable model can be represented in natural language. Moreover models represented in natural language are generally easy to communicate to others. However, these statements about ease of representation and communication must be qualified for extremely complex models. Perhaps the most serious failing of natural language as a medium for model construction is the difficulty of rigorously determining the predictions of a model expressed in this medium. This is true because, in expressing ourselves in natural language, we use ambiguous words; *e.g.,* in the example of a statement in a natural language description of a model used on page 270, what does "checks" mean? What does "danger" mean?

Many of the models expressed in conventional mathematics can be analyzed in a rigorous fashion. If the mathematics is known to the model builder or can be discovered by him, he will be able to determine the implications of his model. If the mathematical techniques for solving certain equation systems are not known or available to the model builder, he is in no better a position than if he had only a natural language model. The effect of this last condition is to constrain the model builder to consider only that class of models for which he knows solutions are available. Unfortunately this constraint may have a spurious effect on the model builder; *e.g.,* he may oversimplify a complex situation. In general, many of the mathematical models of human behavior are elegant and simple. Sometimes, the constraints of the mathematical medium force unfortunate compromises upon the model and reduce its ability to predict.

The most recently developed medium for model construction is the digital computer program. The computer program has several important advantages as a medium for model construction. One of these is the wide range of models that can be represented as computer programs. Effective constraints on the size and complexity of the models which can be represented are so few and slight that they can be disregarded in most cases. The only real constraint on the model builder is that his statements be unambiguous and complete. For example, before the statement about the chess model given on page 270 could be programmed, the meaning of the words "checks" and "danger" would have to be specified. This constraint should be considered a blessing rather than a limitation, for it forces a refreshing rigor on builders of models of human thought processes. Despite the freedom given to the model builder in constructing computer models, he retains the ability to make a rigorous determination of the implications of the model. For the computer can execute the program and determine the behavior of the program in particular situations.

The construction of computer models has been facilitated by the development of computer languages that relieve the programmer from the burdens of the microprogramming associated with machine languages. The development of powerful algebraic languages like FORTRAN and the various dialects of ALGOL are one class of these higher-order computer languages. A second class of languages are the list processing languages—IPL, FLPL, LISP, and COMIT—which have been developed for work in artificial intelligence and simulation of cognitive processes. These list processing languages provide dynamic storage allocation and many other features which simplify the programming task.

What Is the Information Processing Level of Explanation?

In constructing the models described in the reports in Part 2, the researchers had to make several choices. One is the behavior which they want to predict. All the reports are focused on human thought processes. A second choice is the medium for model construction. All the models described in this part are represented as computer programs. A third choice that must be made is the level of explanation of the model. In all the reports, the researchers chose an information processing level of explanation.

A particular phenomenon may be explained at any one of several different levels. In the present context, this statement means that human thought processes can be explained in terms of electrical and chemical processes which take place in the brain, in terms of the organization of the neurons of the brain, or in terms of information processes. At first glance, explanations at each of these levels may appear to be quite different, for we have not yet been able to develop an integrated theory of thinking which will simultaneously account for all that takes place in the way of electrical, chemical, organizational, and informational processes. Hopefully one day all these levels of explanation will be integrated, and the relationships between them will be established. Until that day, perhaps the wisest course is for investigators to continue to work in parallel, taking time out occasionally to compare notes, for there is not one best level of explanation. One can evaluate the models proposed at any level only by their ability to predict behavior. Models at any of these levels of explanation of human thought can be formulated as computer programs, and computers have been used to study neurons, neural organization, and information processes (see the Bibliography).

The reports in Part 2 explain human thinking processes at an information processing or symbol manipulation level. The basic premise of this approach is that complex thinking processes are built up of elementary symbol manipulation processes. A fundamental set of these elementary processes might be the following: read a symbol, write a symbol, copy a symbol, erase a symbol, and compare two symbols. Another basic facility that is required is the ability to take different courses of action depending on the outcome of the compare operation. If two symbols are compared and found to be identical, the information processing system will take one course of action, *i.e.,* execute one set of elementary processes. If the symbols are different, the system will execute another set of processes.

The goal of the researcher is to find an ordered sequence of these basic processes which when provided with suitable information will produce behavior indistinguishable from the behavior produced by human beings when they are provided with comparable information. The "ordered sequence of these basic processes" is the "model" that we have referred to previously. Thus an information processing model of a chess player would consist of a sequence of these basic processes. We could provide this model with suitable initial information, *e.g.*, a chess problem, and with the aid of a computer determine the predictions of the model.

How are Information Processing Models of Human Thought Determined?

While there is no prescribed procedure for creating information processing models of thought, nevertheless the researchers whose work is reported in Part 2 all had to do certain things in the process of obtaining their models. We now list the major steps involved in the creation of such a model.

The researcher begins with an interest in a certain area of human behavior, *e.g.*, problem-solving, game playing, learning. He then usually focuses on behavior in a specific task, *e.g.*, solving logic problems, playing chess, learning nonsense syllables. The particular task may be selected because the researcher is interested in the task for its own sake or because he has some idea about how people behave in that particular task. In order to construct a preliminary model of behavior in the task, the researcher needs an idea or ideas about behavior in the task. The idea may come from observing behavior, from asking people what they are doing while performing the task, or from cogitating on what type of device would be required to perform the task. The next step is to construct a model, *i.e.*, write a program for a computer, embodying this idea. In the course of this activity, the researcher realizes the inadequacy of his original idea(s). He discovers that he needs more information. To get this information he may have to reanalyze old data or run new experiments. Thus the researcher encounters one of the advantages of computer models —the requirement for completeness and precision. After many changes and revisions of the initial program, the model is finally completed.

The researcher then provides the model with the same task given to human subjects, *i.e.*, a chess problem, a logic problem, a list of nonsense syllables. The program is then run with this information. In effect, the model may be considered as an artificial subject participating in a replication of the experiment that was performed with human beings. The behavior of the program, *e.g.*, the chess moves, the steps in the solution of the logic problem, the responses in the learning task, is then compared with the behavior of the subject. Where possible, the processes which led to the overt behavior are also compared.

How Are Computer Models of Human Thought Processes Tested?

The actual comparison or test procedure depends on whether the model represents a particular individual or a generalized or idealized individual (see the article by Feigenbaum, pp. 299–300). The verbal learning model of Feigenbaum, the concept learning model of Hunt and Hovland, and the social behavior model of the Gullahorns are models of generalized or idealized individuals. The relevant comparisons here, and the comparisons that these authors make, are between the behavior of their models and the behavior of typical individuals.

The models of Newell and Simon, Clarkson, and Feldman are models of specific individuals. The relevant comparisons here are between the detailed choices of the individual subject and the detailed choices of the model. These comparisons involve many problems. None of these problems is new or unique to computer models, but they are highlighted by the types of comparisons made with these models of individual behavior. One of these problems is parameter estimation. Another problem involves the relationship between successive predictions of the model. The prediction of the model at time t depends on the behavior of the model at $t-1$, $t-2$, $t-3$, and/or other decisions of the model. If the model makes a decision different from that of the subject at one point in time, the discrepancy may lead to further discrepancies or spurious agreements. Thus, if the model of a chess player makes a first move different from that of the player, we would hardly expect the second moves to agree. To eliminate this difficulty, some investigators (see the article by Feldman) have selected the strategy of "setting the model back on the track" after each decision. In the chess example, this would mean that after the model makes its first move, the move is compared with the first move of the human player. If the moves are the same, the opponent's move is made; and the model proceeds to its second move. If the first move of the model and the first move of the player differ, the discrepancy is noted; and the model's move is replaced by the subject's move before the play continues. This setting-back-on-the-track strategy attempts to eliminate the dependencies involved and makes each decision of the model as independent as possible of the previous decisions of the model. Such a procedure allows a better evaluation of the performance of the model than a comparison procedure which permits errors to beget errors (or spurious correct decisions). Unfortunately it is not always possible to implement a set-back-on-the-track procedure, either because the intermediate information is not available (as it is in chess or the binary choice experiment) or because it is difficult to set the model back on the track, as, for example, in GPS.

What Are Some of the Unsolved Problems of Simulation of Cognitive Processes Research?

The problems of simulation of cognitive processes research are of two types. The substantive problems are those areas of human cognition about which we know very little. The problems listed above of learning heuristics, of inductive inference, and of using natural language are three good examples of areas in which our knowledge of human thought processes is pitifully small. These are areas which will attract much interest in the near future.

The procedural or methodological problems of the simulation of cognitive processes technique represent a second class of problems. Three of these problems are readily apparent:

1. Testing models and estimating parameters. Models are seldom entirely wrong, and researchers seldom reject models completely. The more common procedure is to try to identify the sources of error in the model and correct the model (Grant, 1962). Since computer models are so large and complex, techniques for identifying sources of error are extremely important. The efficient utilization of the available information on human thought processes is very important.

2. Experimentation. Much of the simulation of cognitive processes work has been identified with the use of a protocol obtained by asking the subject to think aloud. Work needs to be done on this and other ways for obtaining information about thought processes (Blum, 1961). Some work has been done and more needs to be done on the determination of the effects of having the subject think aloud (Colby, 1960; Gagne, 1962). Ingenious procedures must be developed to make explicit the thought processes of the subject. One such procedure is the use of artificial languages for problem statements (Wickelgren and Cohen, 1962). Much additional work is needed in all these areas.

3. Program organization and representation. We have repeatedly stated that the expression of models as computer programs allows considerable flexibility in statement. This assertion is true. However, as models and programs increase in size and complexity, the organization of these programs creates serious problems. Higher-order programming languages and list-processing languages in particular solve some of these problems, but many problems remain (Newell, 1962).

How Will the Computer Affect the Study of Cognitive Processes?

The effects of the modern digital computer on the study of human thought processes will be twofold. On the one hand the researchers in artificial intelligence want to understand how human beings perform all sorts of intelligent tasks. Thus computers will be contributing to the demand for more knowledge of human thought processes. On the other hand, the computer has become the basis of a powerful method for studying human thought processes, and so the computer will contribute to the supply of understanding of human cognitive processes. The supply of knowledge about human thought will never catch up with the demand. But the forecast for progress in research in human cognitive processes is most encouraging.

section 1
Problem-solving

The study of human problem-solving behavior has had a fascination for many persons since the time of the Greeks. With the advent of the modern digital computer and the ability to represent complex problem-solving models as computer programs and to study these models by executing the programs, the study of problem-solving behavior has received new impetus.

The authors of the following report and their colleague, J. C. Shaw, are three of the pioneers in the use of computer models of human problem-solving behavior. The psychological significance of their work on the General Problem Solving program (GPS) derives from their success in creating a model whose behavior in solving logic problems is strikingly similar to human behavior on these same problems. In the report reprinted here, the behavior of a variant of GPS on a problem is compared with the behavior of a human subject on the same problem. In other reports, the behavior of other variants of GPS has been compared with the behavior of other subjects, with equally good results.

While each person behaves somewhat differently, practically all the individuals that have been tested by Newell and Simon and their associates in the logic task display a common set of basic processes involving the use of means-ends type of analysis. Although other investigators (notably Duncker, 1945) have reported the use of means-ends analysis by subjects solving problems, Newell, Shaw, and Simon have rigorously specified means-ends analysis and implemented this problem-solving scheme on a computer. With their computer model, they have been able to perform a wide variety of experimentation with the scheme.

In addition to the means-ends technique, some subjects make use of another powerful method, which has been called "planning." A subject using a planning method abstracts or simplifies a complex problem. He then solves the simpler problem and uses the information obtained in the solution of the simpler problem in the solution of the original complex problem. This technique has also been included in GPS and is more fully described in another report (Newell, Shaw, and Simon, 1959a).

GPS is more than a model of human behavior in logic problems. A deliberate effort has been made in GPS to partition the "general" part of the program—mostly concerned with mean-ends analysis—from the problem-specific part of the program—generally referred to as the "task environment." With the general part of GPS and appropriate task environments, computers can be programmed to solve trigonometric identities (Newell, Shaw, and Simon, 1959a), balance assembly lines (Tonge, 1960, 1961a), and compile computer programs (Simon, 1961c).

GPS, A PROGRAM THAT
SIMULATES HUMAN THOUGHT

by Allen Newell & H. A. Simon

This article is concerned with the psychology of human thinking. It sets forth a theory to explain how some humans try to solve some simple formal problems. The research from which the theory emerged is intimately related to the field of information processing and the construction of intelligent automata, and the theory is expressed in the form of a computer program. The rapid technical advances in the art of programming digital computers to do sophisticated tasks have made such a theory feasible.

It is often argued that a careful line must be drawn between the attempt to *accomplish* with machines the same tasks that humans perform, and the attempt to *simulate* the processes humans actually use to accomplish these tasks. The program discussed in the report, GPS (General Problem Solver), maximally confuses the two approaches—with mutual benefit. GPS has previously been described as an attempt to build a problem-solving program (Newell, Shaw, and Simon, 1959a, 1960a), and in our own research it remains a major vehicle for exploring the area of artificial intelligence. Simultaneously, variants of GPS provide simulations of human behavior (Newell and Simon, 1961a). It is this latter aspect—the use of GPS as a theory of human problem-solving—that we want to focus on exclusively here, with special attention to the relation between the theory and the data.

As a context for the discussion that is to follow, let us make some brief comments on some history of psychology. At the beginning of this century the prevailing thesis in psychology was Associationism. It was an atomistic doctrine, which postulated a theory of hard little elements, either sensations or ideas, that became hooked or associated together without modifica-

279

tion. It was a mechanistic doctrine, with simple fixed laws of contiguity in time and space to account for the formation of new associations. Those were its assumptions. Behavior proceeded by the stream of associations: Each association produced its successors, and acquired new attachments with the sensations arriving from the environment.

In the first decade of the century a reaction developed to this doctrine through the work of the Wurzburg school. Rejecting the notion of a completely self-determining stream of associations, it introduced the task (*Aufgabe*) as a necessary factor in describing the process of thinking. The task gave direction to thought. A noteworthy innovation of the Wurzburg school was the use of systematic introspection to shed light on the thinking process and the contents of consciousness. The result was a blend of mechanics and phenomenalism, which gave rise in turn to two divergent antitheses, Behaviorism and the Gestalt movement.

The behavioristic reaction insisted that introspection was a highly unstable, subjective procedure, whose futility was amply demonstrated in the controversy on imageless thought. Behaviorism reformulated the task of psychology as one of explaining the response of organisms as a function of the stimuli impinging upon them and measuring both objectively. However, Behaviorism accepted, and indeed reinforced, the mechanistic assumption that the connections between stimulus and response were formed and maintained as simple, determinate functions of the environment.

The Gestalt reaction took an opposite turn. It rejected the mechanistic nature of the associationist doctrine but maintained the value of phenomenal observation. In many ways it continued the Wurzburg school's insistence that thinking was more than association—thinking has direction given to it by the task or by the set of the subject. Gestalt psychology elaborated this doctrine in genuinely new ways in terms of holistic principles of organization.

Today psychology lives in a state of relatively stable tension between the poles of Behaviorism and Gestalt psychology. All of us have internalized the major lessons of both: We treat skeptically the subjective elements in our experiments and agree that all notions must eventually be made operational by means of behavioral measures. We also recognize that a human being is a tremendously complex, organized system, and that the simple schemes of modern behavioristic psychology seem hardly to reflect this at all.

An Experimental Situation

In this context, then, consider the following situation. A human subject, a student in engineering in an American college, sits in front of a blackboard on which are written the following expressions:

$$(R \supset \sim P) \cdot (\sim R \supset Q) \quad | \quad \sim (\sim Q \cdot P)$$

This is a problem in elementary symbolic logic, but the student does not know it. He does know that he has twelve rules for manipulating expressions containing letters connected by "dots" ($\cdot$), "wedges" ($\vee$), "horseshoes" ($\supset$), and "tildes" ($\sim$), which stand respectively for "and," "or," "implies," and "not." These rules, given in Fig. 1, show that expressions of certain forms (at the tails of the arrows) can be transformed into expressions of somewhat different form (at the heads of the arrows). (Double arrows indicate transformations can take place in either direc-

Objects are formed by building up expressions from letters (P, Q, R, . . .) and connectives $\cdot$ (dot), V (wedge), $\supset$ (horseshoe), and $\sim$ (tilde). Examples are P, $\sim$Q, P V Q, $\sim$(R $\supset$ S)$\cdot$ $\sim$P; $\sim\sim$P is equivalent to P throughout. Twelve rules exist for transforming expressions (where A, B, and C may be any expressions or subexpressions):

R 1. A $\cdot$ B $\rightarrow$ B $\cdot$ A A V B $\rightarrow$ B V A	R 8. A $\cdot$ B $\rightarrow$ A Applies to main A $\cdot$ B $\rightarrow$ B expression only.
R 2. A $\supset$ B $\rightarrow$ $\sim$ B $\supset$ $\sim$ A	R 9. A $\rightarrow$ A V X Applies to main expression only.
R 3. A $\cdot$ A $\longleftrightarrow$ A A V A $\longleftrightarrow$ A	R 10. $\left. \begin{array}{c} A \\ B \end{array} \right\} \rightarrow$ A $\cdot$ B A and B are two main expressions.
R 4. A $\cdot$ (B $\cdot$ C) $\longleftrightarrow$ (A $\cdot$ B) $\cdot$ C A V (B V C) $\longleftrightarrow$ (A V B) V C	R 11. $\left. \begin{array}{c} A \\ A \supset B \end{array} \right\} \rightarrow$ B A and A $\supset$ B are two main expressions.
R 5. A V B $\longleftrightarrow$ $\sim$($\sim$A $\cdot$ $\sim$B)	R 12. $\left. \begin{array}{c} A \supset B \\ B \supset C \end{array} \right\} \rightarrow$ A $\supset$ C A $\supset$ B and B $\supset$ C are two main ex- pressions.
R 6. A $\supset$ B $\longleftrightarrow$ $\sim$ A V B	
R 7. A $\cdot$ (B V C) $\longleftrightarrow$ (A $\cdot$ B) V (A $\cdot$ C) A V (B $\cdot$ C) $\longleftrightarrow$ (A V B) $\cdot$ (A V C)	

Example, showing subject's entire course of solution on problem:

1.	(R $\supset$ $\sim$ P) $\cdot$ ($\sim$ R $\supset$ Q)	$\sim$ ($\sim$ Q $\cdot$ P)
2.	($\sim$R V $\sim$P) $\cdot$ (R V Q)	Rule 6 applied to left and right of 1.
3.	($\sim$R V $\sim$P) $\cdot$ ($\sim$ R $\supset$ Q)	Rule 6 applied to left of 1.
4.	R $\supset$ $\sim$P	Rule 8 applied to 1.
5.	$\sim$R V $\sim$P	Rule 6 applied to 4.
6.	$\sim$R $\supset$ Q	Rule 8 applied to 1.
7.	R V Q	Rule 6 applied to 6.
8.	($\sim$R V $\sim$P) $\cdot$ (R V Q)	Rule 10 applied to 5. and 7.
9.	P $\supset$ $\sim$ R	Rule 2 applied to 4.
10.	$\sim$Q $\supset$ R	Rule 2 applied to 6.
11.	P $\supset$ Q	Rule 12 applied to 6. and 9.
12.	$\sim$P V Q	Rule 6 applied to 11.
13.	$\sim$(P $\cdot$ $\sim$Q)	Rule 5 applied to 12.
14.	$\sim$($\sim$Q $\cdot$ P)	Rule 1 applied to 13. QED.

Figure 1. The task of symbolic logic.

Well, looking at the left hand side of the equation, first we want to eliminate one of the sides by using rule 8. It appears too complicated to work with first. Now — no, — no, I can't do that because I will be eliminating either the Q or the P in that total expression. I won't do that at first. Now I'm looking for a way to get rid of the horseshoe inside the two brackets that appear on the left and right sides of the equation. And I don't see it. Yeh, if you apply rule 6 to both sides of the equation, from there I'm going to see if I can apply rule 7.

Experimenter writes: 2. $(\sim R \vee \sim P) \cdot (R \vee Q)$

I can almost apply rule 7, but one R needs a tilde. So I'll have to look for another rule. I'm going to see if I can change that R to a tilde R. As a matter of fact, I should have used rule 6 on only the left hand side of the equation. So use rule 6, but only on the left hand side.

Experimenter writes: 3. $(\sim R \vee \sim P) \cdot (\sim R \supset Q)$

Now I'll apply rule 7 as it is expressed. Both — excuse me, excuse me, it can't be done because of the horseshoe. So — now I'm looking — scanning the rules here for a second, and seeing if I can change the R to a $\sim$R in the second equation, but I don't see any way of doing it. (Sigh.) I'm just sort of lost for a second.

Figure 2. Subject's protocol on first part of problem.

tion.) The subject has practiced applying the rules, but he has previously done only one other problem like this. The experimenter has instructed him that his problem is to obtain the expression in the upper right corner from the expression in the upper left corner using the twelve rules. At any time the subject can request the experimenter to apply one of the rules to an expression that is already on the blackboard. If the transformation is legal, the experimenter writes down the new expression in the left-hand column, with the name of the rule in the right-hand column beside it. The subject's actual course of solution is shown beneath the rules in Fig. 1.

The subject was also asked to talk aloud as he worked; his comments were recorded and then transcribed into a "protocol,"—*i.e.*, a verbatim record of all that he or the experimenter said during the experiment. The initial section of this subject's protocol is reproduced in Fig. 2.

The Problem of Explanation

It is now proposed that the protocol of Fig. 2 constitutes data about human behavior that are to be explained by a psychological theory. But what are we to make of this? Are we back to the introspections of the Wurzburgers? And how are we to extract information from the behavior of a single subject when we have not defined the operational measures we wish to consider?

There is little difficulty in viewing this situation through behavioristic eyes. The verbal utterances of the subject are as much behavior as would be his arm movements or galvanic skin responses. The subject was not introspecting; he was simply emitting a continuous stream of verbal behavior while solving the problem. Our task is to find a model of the human problem-solver that explains the salient features of this stream of behavior. This stream contains not only the subject's extemporaneous comments, but also his commands to the experimenter, which determine whether he solves the problem or not.

Although this way of viewing the behavior answers the questions stated above, it raises some of its own. How is one to deal with such variable behavior? Isn't language behavior considered among the most complex human behavior? How does one make reliable inferences from a single sample of data on a single subject?

The answers to these questions rest upon the recent, striking advances that have been made in computers, computer programming and artificial intelligence. We have learned that a computer is a general manipulator of symbols—not just a manipulator of numbers. Basically, a computer is a transformer of patterns. By suitable devices, most notably its addressing logic, these patterns can be given all the essential characteristics of linguistic symbols. They can be copied and formed into expressions. We have known this abstractly since Turing's work in the mid-thirties, but it is only recently that computers have become powerful enough to let us actually explore the capabilities of complex symbol manipulating systems.

For our purpose here, the most important branch of these explorations is the attempt to construct programs that solve tasks requiring intelligence. Considerable success has already been attained (Gelernter, 1959b; Kilburn et al., 1959; Minsky, 1961a; Newell, Shaw, and Simon, 1957a, 1958b; Samuel, 1959a; Tonge, 1960). These accomplishments form a body of ideas and techniques that allow a new approach to the building of psychological theories. (Much of the work on artificial intelligence, especially our own, has been partly motivated by concern for psychology; hence, the resulting rapprochement is not entirely coincidental.)

We may then conceive of an intelligent program that manipulates symbols in the same way that our subject does—by taking as inputs the symbolic logic expressions, and producing as ouputs a sequence of rule applications that coincides with the subject's. If we observed this program in operation, it would be considering various rules and evaluating various expressions, the same sorts of things we see expressed in the protocol of the subject. If the fit of such a program were close enough to the overt behavior of our human subject—*i.e.,* to the protocol—then it would constitute a good theory of the subject's problem-solving.

Conceptually the matter is perfectly straightforward. A program prescribes in abstract terms (expressed in some programming language) how a set of symbols in a memory is to be transformed through time. It is completely analogous to a set of difference equations that prescribes the transformation of a set of numbers through time. Given enough information about an individual, a program could be written that would describe the symbolic behavior of that individual. Each individual would be described by a different program, and those aspects of human problem-solving that are not idiosyncratic would emerge as the common structure and content of the programs of many individuals.

But is it possible to write programs that do the kinds of manipulation that humans do? Given a specific protocol, such as the one of Fig. 2, is it possible to induct the program of the subject? How well does a program fit the data? The remainder of the report will be devoted to answering some of these questions by means of the single example already presented. We will consider only how GPS behaves on the first part of the problem, and we will compare it in detail with the subject's behavior as revealed in the protocol. This will shed considerable light on how far we can consider programs as theories of human problem-solving.

The GPS Program

We will only briefly recapitulate the GPS program, since our description will add little to what has already been published (Newell, Shaw, and Simon, 1959a, 1960a). GPS deals with a task environment consisting of *objects* which can be transformed by various *operators;* it detects *differences* between objects; and it organizes the information about the task environment into *goals.* Each goal is a collection of information that defines what constitutes goal attainment, makes available the various kinds of information relevant to attaining the goal, and relates the information to other goals. There are three types of goals:

Transform object A into object B,
Reduce difference D between object A and object B,
Apply operator Q to object A.

For the task of symbolic logic, the objects are logic expressions; the operators are the twelve rules (actually the specific variants of them); and the differences are expressions like "change connective" or "add a term." Thus the objects and operators are given by the task; whereas the differences are something GPS brings to the problem. They represent the ways of relating operators to their respective effects upon objects.

Basically, the GPS program is a way of achieving a goal by setting up subgoals whose attainment leads to the attainment of the initial goal. GPS has various schemes, called methods, for doing this. Three crucial methods are presented in Fig 3, one method associated with each goal type.

Thus, to transform an object A into an object B, the objects are first matched—put into correspondence and compared element by element. If the match reveals a difference, D, between the two objects, then a subgoal is set up to reduce this difference. If this subgoal is attained, a new object, A', is produced which (hopefully) no longer has the difference D when compared with object B. Then a new subgoal is created to transform A' into B. If the transformation succeeds, the entire goal has been attained in two steps: from A to A' and from A' to B.

If the goal is to reduce the difference between two objects, the first step is to find an operator that is relevant to this difference. Relevance here

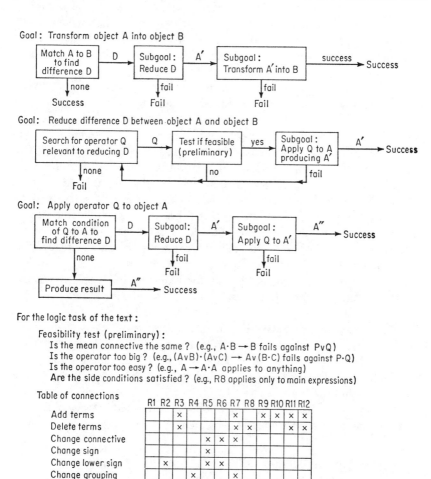

Goal: Transform object A into object B

Goal: Reduce difference D between object A and object B

Goal: Apply operator Q to object A

For the logic task of the text :

Feasibility test (preliminary) :
 Is the mean connective the same ? (e.g., A·B → B fails against PvQ)
 Is the operator too big ? (e.g., (AvB)·(AvC) → Av(B·C) fails against P·Q)
 Is the operator too easy ? (e.g., A → A·A applies to anything)
 Are the side conditions satisfied ? (e.g., R8 applies only to main expressions)

Table of connections

	R1	R2	R3	R4	R5	R6	R7	R8	R9	R10	R11	R12
Add terms			x				x		x	x	x	x
Delete terms			x				x	x			x	x
Change connective					x	x	x					
Change sign						x						
Change lower sign		x				x	x					
Change grouping				x				x				
Change position	x	x										

x means some variant of the rule is relevant. GPS will pick the appropriate variant.

Figure 3. Methods for GPS.

means that the operator affects objects with respect to the difference. Operationally, relevance can be determined by applying the matching process already used to the input and output forms of the operators, due account being taken of variables. The results can be summarized in a table of connections, as shown in Fig. 3, which lists for each difference the operators that are relevant to it. This table also lists the differences that GPS recognizes. [This set is somewhat different from the one given in Newell, Shaw, and Simon (1959a); it corresponds to the program we will deal with in this report.] If a relevant operator, Q, is found, it is subjected to a preliminary test of feasibility, one version of which is given in Fig. 3. If the operator passes this test, a subgoal is set up to apply the operator to the object. If the operator is successfully applied, a new object, A', is produced which is a modification of the original one in the direction of reducing the difference. (Of course, other modifications may also have occurred which nullify the usefulness of the new object.)

If the goal is to apply an operator, the first step is to see if the conditions of the operator are satisfied. The preliminary test above by no means guarantees this. If the conditions are satisfied, then the output, A, can be generated. If the conditions are not satisfied, then some difference, D, has been detected and a subgoal is created to reduce this difference, just as with the transform goal. Similarly, if a modified object, A', is obtained, a new subgoal is formed to try to apply the operator to this new object.

These methods form a recursive system that generates a tree of subgoals in attempting to attain a given goal. For every new difficulty that is encountered a new subgoal is created to overcome this difficulty. GPS has a number of tests it applies to keep the expansion of this goal tree from proceeding in unprofitable directions. The most important of these is a test which is applied to new subgoals for reducing differences. GPS contains an ordering of the differences, so that some differences are considered easier than others. This ordering is given by the table of connections in Fig. 3, which lists the most difficult differences first. GPS will not try a subgoal if it is harder than one of its supergoals. It will also not try a goal if it follows an easier goal. That is, GPS insists on working on the hard differences first and expects to find easier ones as it goes along. The other tests that GPS applies involve external limits (*e.g.,* a limit on the total depth of a goal tree it will tolerate) and whether new objects or goals are identical to ones already generated.

GPS on the Problem

The description we have just given is adequate to verify the reasonableness, although not the detail, of a trace of GPS's behavior on a specific problem. (In particular we have not described how the two-line rules, R10 through R12, are handled, since they do not enter into the protocol we are examining.) In Fig. 4, we give the trace on the initial part of problem D1. Indentation is used to indicate the relation of a subgoal to a goal. Although the methods are not shown, they can clearly be inferred from the goals that occur.

The initial problem is to transform L1 into L0. Matching L1 to L0 reveals that there are R's in L1 and no R's in L0. This difference leads to the formulation of a reduce goal, which for readability has been given its functional name, *Delete*. The attempt to reach this goal leads to a search for rules which finds rule 8. Since there are two forms of rule 8, both of which are admissible, GPS chooses the first. (Variants of rules are not indicated, but can be inferred easily from the trace.) Since rule 8 is

```
L0   ~(~Q·P)
L1   (R⊃~P)·(~R⊃Q)

GOAL 1  TRANSFORM L1 INTO L0
        GOAL 2  DELETE R FROM L1
                GOAL 3  APPLY R8 TO L1
                        PRODUCES L2  R⊃~P

        GOAL 4  TRANSFORM L2 INTO L0
                GOAL 5  ADD Q TO L2
                        REJECT

        GOAL 2
                GOAL 6  APPLY R8 TO L1
                        PRODUCES L3  ~R⊃Q

        GOAL 7  TRANSFORM L3 INTO L0
                GOAL 8  ADD P TO L3
                        REJECT

        GOAL 2
                GOAL 9  APPLY R7 TO L1
                        GOAL 10  CHANGE CONNECTIVE TO V IN LEFT L1
                                 GOAL 11  APPLY R6 TO LEFT L1
                                          PRODUCES L4  (~R V ~P)·(~R⊃Q)

                        GOAL 12  APPLY R7 TO L4
                                 GOAL 13  CHANGE CONNECTIVE TO V IN RIGHT L4
                                          GOAL 14  APPLY R6 TO RIGHT L4
                                                   PRODUCES L5  (~R V ~P)·(R V Q)

                        GOAL 15  APPLY R7 TO L5
                                 GOAL 16  CHANGE SIGN OF LEFT RIGHT L5
                                          GOAL 17  APPLY R6 TO RIGHT L5
                                                   PRODUCES L6  (~R V ~P)·(~R⊃Q)

                        GOAL 18  APPLY R7 TO L6
                                 GOAL 19  CHANGE CONNECTIVE TO V
                                          IN RIGHT L6
                                          REJECT

                        GOAL 16
                                 NOTHING MORE

                        GOAL 13
                                 NOTHING MORE

                        GOAL 10
                                 NOTHING MORE
```

Figure 4. Trace of GPS on first part of problem.

applicable, a new object, L2, is produced. Following the method for transform goals, at the next step a new goal has been generated: to transform L2 into L0. This in turn leads to another reduce goal: to restore a Q to L2. But this goal is rejected by the evaluation, since adding a term is more difficult than deleting a term. GPS then returns to goal 2 and seeks another rule which will delete terms. This time it finds the other form of rule 8 and goes through a similar excursion, ending with the rejection of goal 8.

Returning again to goal 2 to find another rule for deleting terms, GPS obtains rule 7. It selects the variant $(A \lor B) \cdot (A \lor C) \to A \lor (B \cdot C)$, since only this one both decreases terms and has a dot as its main connective. Rule 7 is not immediately applicable; GPS first discovers that there is a difference of connective in the left subexpression, and then that there is one in the right subexpression. In both cases it finds and applies rule 6 to change the connective from horseshoe to wedge, obtaining successively L4 and L5. But the new expression reveals a difference in sign, which leads again to rule 6—that is, to the same rule as before, but perceived as accomplishing a different function. Rule 6 produces L6, which happens to be identical with L4 although GPS does not notice the identity here. This leads, in goal 19, to the difference in connective being redetected; whereupon the goal is finally rejected as representing no progress over goal 13. Further attempts to find alternative ways to change signs or connectives fail to yield anything. This ends the episode.

Comparison of the GPS Trace with the Protocol

We now have a highly detailed trace of what GPS did. What can we find in the subject's protocol that either confirms or refutes the assertion that this program is a detailed model of the symbol manipulations the subject is carrying out? What sort of correspondence can we expect? The program does not provide us with an English language output that can be put into one-one correspondence with the words of the subject. We have not even given GPS a goal to "do the task and talk at the same time," which would be a necessary reformulation if we were to attempt a correspondence in such detail. On the other hand, the trace, backed up by our knowledge of how it was generated, does provide a complete record of all the task content that was considered by GPS, and the order in which it was taken up. Hence, we should expect to find every feature of the protocol that concerns the task mirrored in an essential way in the program trace. The converse is not true, since many things concerning the task surely occurred without the subject's commenting on them (or even being aware of them). Thus, our test of correspondence is one-sided but exacting.

Let us start with the first sentence of the subject's protocol (Fig. 2):

> *Well, looking at the left-hand side of the equation, first we want to eliminate one of the sides by using rule 8.*

We see here a desire to decrease L1 or eliminate something from it, and the selection of rule 8 as the means to do this. This stands in direct correspondence with goals 1, 2, and 3 of the trace.

Let us skip to the third and fourth sentences:

> *Now—no,—no, I can't do that because I will be eliminating either the Q or the P in that total expression. I won't do that at first.*

We see here a direct expression of the covert application of rule 8, the subsequent comparison of the resulting expression with LO, and the rejection of this course of action because it deletes a letter that is required in the final expression. It would be hard to find a set of words that expressed these ideas more clearly. Conversely, if the mechanism of the program (or something essentially similar to it) were not operating, it would be hard to explain why the subject uttered the remarks that he did.

One discrepancy is quite clear. The subject handled both forms of rule 8 together, at least as far as his comment is concerned. GPS, on the other hand, took a separate cycle of consideration for each form. Possibly the subject followed the program covertly and simply reported the two results together. However, we would feel that the fit was better if GPS had proceeded something as follows:

```
GOAL 2 DELETE R FROM L1
    GOAL 3 APPLY R8 TO L1
        PRODUCES L2 R ⊃ ~P OR ~R ⊃ Q

GOAL 4 TRANSFORM L2 INTO LO
    GOAL 5 ADD Q TO R ⊃ ~P OR ADD P TO ~R ⊃ Q
        REJECT
```

We will consider further evidence on this point later.

Let us return to the second sentence, which we skipped over:

> *It appears too complicated to work with first.*

Nothing in the program is in simple correspondence with this statement, though it is easy to imagine some possible explanations. For example, this could merely be an expression of the matching—of the fact that L1 is such a big expression that the subject cannot absorb all its detail. There is not enough data locally to determine what part of the trace should correspond to this statement, so the sentence must stand as an unexplained element of the subject's behavior.

Now let us consider the next few sentences of the protocol:

Now I'm looking for a way to get rid of the horseshoe inside the two brackets that appear on the left and right side of the equation. And I don't see it. Yeh, if you apply rule 6 to both sides of the equation, from there I'm going to see if I can apply rule 7.

This is in direct correspondence with goals 9 through 14 of the trace. The comment at the end makes it clear that applying rule 7 is the main concern and that changing connectives is required in order to accomplish this. Further, the protocol shows clearly that rule 6 was selected as the means. All three rule selections provide some confirmation that a preliminary test for feasibility was made by the subject—as by GPS—in the reduce goal method. If there was not selection on the main connective, why wasn't rule 5 selected instead of rule 6? Or why wasn't the $(A \cdot B) \lor (A \cdot C) \to A \cdot (B \lor C)$ form of rule 7 selected?

However, there is a discrepancy between trace and protocol, for the subject handles both applications of rule 6 simultaneously, (and apparently was also handling the two differences simultaneously); whereas GPS handles them sequentially. This is similar to the discrepancy noted earlier in handling rule 8. Since we now have two examples of parallel processing, it is likely that there is a real difference on this score. Again, we would feel better if GPS proceeded somewhat as follows:

```
GOAL 9 APPLY R7 TO L1
   GOAL 10 CHANGE CONNECTIVE TO V IN LEFT L1 AND RIGHT L1
      GOAL 11 APPLY R6 TO LEFT L1 AND RIGHT L1
         PRODUCES L5  (~R V ~P) · (R V Q)
```

A common feature of both these discrepancies is that forming the compound expressions does not complicate the methods in any essential way. Thus, in the case involving rule 8, the two results stem from the same input form, and require only the single match. In the case involving rule 7, a single search was made for a rule and the rule applied to both parts simultaneously, just as if only a single unit was involved.

There are two aspects in which the protocol provides information that the program is not equipped to explain. First, the subject handled the application of rule 8 covertly but commanded the experimenter to make the applications of rule 6 on the board. The version of GPS used here did not make any distinction between internal and external actions. To this extent it fails to be an adequate model. The overt-covert distinction has consequences that run throughout a problem, since expressions on the blackboard have very different memory characteristics from expressions generated only in the head. Second, this version of GPS does not simulate the search process sufficiently well to provide a correspondent to "And I don't see it. Yeh, . . .". This requires providing a facsimile of the rule sheet, and distinguishing search on the sheet from searches in the memory.

The next few sentences read:

> *I can almost apply rule 7, but one R needs a tilde. So I'll have to look for another rule. I'm going to see if I can change that R to a tilde R.*

Again the trace and the protocol agree on the difference that is seen. They also agree that this difference was not attended to earlier, even though it was present. Some fine structure of the data also agrees with the trace. The right-hand R is taken as having the difference (R to $\sim$ R) rather than the left-hand one, although either is possible. This preference arises in the program (and presumably in the subject) from the language habit of working from left to right. It is not without consequences, however, since it determines whether the subject goes to work on the left side or the right side of the expression; hence, it can affect the entire course of events for quite a while. Similarly, in the rule 8 episode the subject apparently worked from left to right and from top to bottom in order to arrive at "Q or P" rather than "P or Q." This may seem like concern with excessively detailed features of the protocol, yet those details support the contention that what is going on inside the human system is quite akin to the symbol manipulations going on inside GPS.

The next portion of the protocol is:

> *As a matter of fact, I should have used rule 6 on only the left-hand side of the equation. So use 6, but only on the left-hand side.*

Here we have a strong departure from the GPS trace, although, curiously enough, the trace and the protocol end up at the same spot, $(\sim R \vee \sim P) \cdot (\sim R \supset Q)$. Both the subject and GPS found rule 6 as the appropriate one to change signs. At this point GPS simply applied the rule to the current expression; whereas the subject went back and corrected the previous application. Nothing exists in the program that corresponds to this. The most direct explanation is that the application of rule 6 in the inverse direction is perceived by the subject as undoing the previous application of rule 6. After following out this line of reasoning, he then takes the simpler (and less foolish-appearing) alternative, which is to correct the original action.

The final segment of the protocol reads:

> *Now I'll apply rule 7 as it is expressed. Both—excuse me, excuse me, it can't be done because of the horseshoe. So—now I'm looking— scanning the rules here for a second, and seeing if I can change the R to ~R in the second equation, but I don't see any way of doing it. (Sigh). I'm just sort of lost for a second.*

The trace and the protocol are again in good agreement. This is one of the few self-correcting errors we have encountered. The protocol records the futile search for additional operators to affect the differences of sign and connective, always with negative results. The final comment of mild despair can be interpreted as reflecting the impact of several successive failures.

Summary of the Fit of the Trace to the Protocol

Let us take stock of the agreements and disagreements between the trace and the protocol. The program provides a complete explanation of the subject's task behavior with five exceptions of varying degrees of seriousness.

There are two aspects in which GPS is unprepared to simulate the subject's behavior: in distinguishing between the internal and external worlds, and in an adequate representation of the spaces in which the search for rules takes place. Both of these are generalized deficiencies that can be remedied. It will remain to be seen how well GPS can then explain data about these aspects of behavior.

The subject handles certain sets of items in parallel by using compound expressions; whereas GPS handles all items one at a time. In the example examined here, no striking differences in problem solving occur as a result, but larger discrepancies could arise under other conditions. It is fairly clear how GPS could be extended to incorporate this feature.

There are two cases in which nothing corresponds in the program to some clear task-oriented behavior in the protocol. One of these, the early comment about "complication," seems to be mostly a case of insufficient information. The program is making numerous comparisons and evaluations which could give rise to comments of the type in question. Thus this error does not seem too serious. The other case, involving the "should have . . ." passage, does seem serious. It clearly implies a mechanism (maybe a whole set of them) that is not in GPS. Adding the mechanism required to handle this one passage could significantly increase the total capabilities of the program. For example, there might be no reasonable way to accomplish this except to provide GPS with a little continuous hindsight about its past actions.

An additional general caution must be suggested. The quantity of data is not large considering the size and complexity of the program. This implies that there are many degrees of freedom available to fit the program to the data. More important, we have no good way to assess how many relevant degrees of freedom a program possesses, and thus to know how easy it is to fit alternative programs. All we do know is that numerous minor modifications could certainly be made, but that no one has proposed any major alternative theories that provide anything like a comparably detailed explanation of human problem-solving data.

It would help if we knew something of how idiosyncratic the program was. We have discussed it here only in relation to one sample of data for one subject. We know enough about subjects on logic problems to assert that the same mechanisms show up repeatedly, but we cannot discuss these data here in detail. In addition, several recent investigations more generally support the concept of information processing theories of human thinking (Bruner et al., 1956; Feigenbaum, 1961a; Feldman, 1961a; Hovland and Hunt, 1960; Miller et al., 1960).

Conclusion

We have been concerned in this report with showing that the techniques that have emerged for constructing sophisticated problem-solving programs also provide us with new, strong tools for constructing theories of human thinking. They allow us to merge the rigor and objectivity associated with Behaviorism with the wealth of data and complex behavior associated with the Gestalt movement. To this end their key feature is not that they provide a general framework for understanding problem-solving behavior (although they do that, too), but that they finally reveal with great clarity that the free behavior of a reasonably intelligent human can be understood as the product of a complex but finite and determinate set of laws. Although we know this only for small fragments of behavior, the depth of the explanation is striking.

section 2

Verbal Learning and Concept Learning

One of the principal topics in the study of human thinking has been learning—the process by which behavior is modified over time. Human learning has been studied in an experimental situation in which the subject is presented with a pair of items, one of which is called a *stimulus* and the other a *response*. After seeing a list of such pairs, the subject is presented with only the stimulus member of a pair and asked to reply with the response member of the pair. After his reply, the correct response is indicated. A large number of variations of this basic experiment have been explored in an effort to study the learning process.

In a popular verbal learning experiment, both the stimulus and the response are unique, three-letter nonsense syllables. To study learning in this experiment, investigators have varied the number of nonsense syllables to be learned, the degree of similarity between the syllables, the number and order of lists learned in a given experiment, the speed of presentation of the material, and other aspects of the experimental situation. The experimenters have been interested in the effect of these variations on the length of time and the number of repetitions required to learn a list, the number of errors made, and the ability to retain the list. In his model of verbal learning behavior, Feigenbaum offers a model of the information processing activity underlying human discrimination and association learning. His model accounts for many of the phenomena observed in these experiments. The basic processes of the model create a network of tests, or discriminators, which distinguish items from each other. Other processes store associative cues which link stimuli with responses.

In a typical concept learning experiment, the subject is also presented with a series of stimuli and a series of associated responses. The stimuli may be geometric figures, nonsense syllables, numbers, etc. There are usually only two responses, *e.g.,* "yes" or "no," and these responses are associated with certain characteristics of the stimuli. While the principal task in the standard verbal learning experiment is to distinguish each stimulus so that the appropriate response may be associated with it, the principal task in the concept learning experiment is to find what each class of stimuli has in common with the other classes. To test his understanding of the concept, the subject may be asked to state the concept and/or produce the appropriate response to some additional stimuli. As in the verbal learning experiments, a large number of variations of this basic concept learning experiment have been conducted.

In the second article in this section, Hunt and Hovland present an information processing model which is consistent with many of the phenomena observed in these experiments.

Learning is of interest not only to psychologists studying human behavior but also to artificial intelligence researchers interested in improving the performance of computer programs. The interested reader is referred to the discussion of Minsky (pages 425 to 435), to Samuel's description of his work on learning with his checkers program (pages 71 to 105), and to the report of Newell, Shaw, and Simon on the Logic Theorist (pages 109 to 133). Feigenbaum and Simon (1961*b*) have discussed some of the implications for artificial intelligence of the verbal learning model described in this section. Hunt (1962) has constructed some other models of concept formation which are relevant to artificial intelligence.

Edward Feigenbaum is a member of the faculty of the School of Business Administration, University of California at Berkeley.

E. B. Hunt is a lecturer in psychology, University of Sydney, Sydney, Australia.

The late C. I. Hovland was Sterling Professor of Psychology at Yale University.

THE SIMULATION OF
VERBAL LEARNING BEHAVIOR

by Edward A. Feigenbaum

The purpose of this report is to describe in detail an information processing model of elementary human symbolic learning processes. This model is realized by a computer program called the Elementary Perceiver and Memorizer (EPAM).

The EPAM program is the precise statement of an information processing theory of verbal learning that provides an alternative to other verbal learning theories which have been proposed.[1] It is the result of an attempt to state quite precisely a parsimonious and plausible mechanism sufficient to account for the rote learning of nonsense syllables. The critical evaluation of EPAM must ultimately depend not upon the interest which it may have as a learning machine, but upon its ability to explain and predict the phenomena of verbal learning.

I should like to preface my discussion of the simulation of verbal learning with some brief remarks about the class of information processing models of which EPAM is a member.

a. These are models of mental processes, not brain hardware. They are *psychological* models of mental function. No physiological or neurological assumptions are made, nor is any attempt made to explain information processes in terms of more elementary neural processes.

b. These models conceive of the brain as an *information processor* with sense organs as input channels, effector organs as output devices, and with internal programs for testing, comparing, analyzing, rearranging, and storing information.

---

[1] Examples of quantitative (or quasi-quantitative) theories of verbal learning are those of Hull et al. (1940), Gibson, (1940), and Atkinson (1954).

297

c. The central processing mechanism is assumed to be serial; *i.e.,* capable of doing only one (or a very few) things at a time.

d. These models use as a basic unit the *information symbol; i.e.,* a pattern of bits which is assumed to be the brain's internal representation of environmental data.

e. These models are essentially *deterministic,* not probabilistic. Random variables play no fundamental role in them.

The Basic Experiment

Early in the history of psychology, the psychologist invented an experiment to simplify the study of human verbal learning. This "simple" experiment is the rote memorization of nonsense syllables in associate pairs or serial lists.

The items to be memorized are generally three-letter words having consonant letters on each end and a vowel in the middle. Nonsense syllables are chosen in such a way that the three-letter combinations have no ordinary English meaning. For example, CAT is not a nonsense syllable, but XUM is.[2]

In one basic variation, the rote memory experiment is performed as follows:

a. A set of nonsense syllables is chosen and the syllables are paired, making, let us say, 12 pairs.

b. A subject is seated in front of a viewing apparatus and the syllables are shown to him, one pair at a time.

c. First, the left-hand member of the pair (*stimulus item*) is shown. The subject tries to say the second member of the pair (*response item*).

d. After a short interval, the response item is exposed so that both stimulus and response items are simultaneously in view.

e. After a few seconds, the cycle repeats itself with a new pair of syllables. This continues until all pairs have been presented (a *trial*).

f. Trials are repeated, usually until the subject is able to give the correct response to each stimulus. There is a relatively short time interval between trials.

g. For successive trials the syllables are reordered randomly. This style of carrying out the experiment is called *paired-associates presentation.*

The other basic variant of the experiment is called *serial-anticipation presentation.* The nonsense syllables (say, 10 or 12 items) are arranged

[2] People will defy an experimenter's most rigorous attempt to keep the nonsense syllables association-free. Lists of nonsense syllables have been prepared, ordering syllables on the basis of their so-called "association value," in order to permit the experimenter to control "meaningfulness."

in a serial list, the order of which is not changed on successive trials. When he is shown the nth syllable, the subject is to respond with the $(n + 1)$st syllable. A few seconds later, the $(n + 1)$st syllable is shown and the subject is to respond with the $(n + 2)$d syllable, and so on. The experiment terminates when the subject is able to correctly anticipate all of the syllables.

Numerous variations on this experimental theme have been performed.[3] The phenomena of rote learning are well studied, stable, and reproducible. For example, in the typical behavioral output of a subject, one finds:

   a. Failures to respond to a stimulus are more numerous than overt errors.

   b. Overt errors are generally attributable to confusion by the subject between similar stimuli or similar responses.

   c. Associations which are given correctly over a number of trials some-times are then forgotten, only to reappear and later disappear again. This phenomenon has been called oscillation.[4]

   d. If a list *x* of syllables or syllable pairs is learned to the criterion; then a list *y* is similarly learned; and finally retention of list *x* is tested; the subject's ability to give. the correct *x* responses is degraded by the inter-polated learning. The degradation is called retroactive inhibition. The overt errors made in the retest trial are generally intrusions from the list *y*. The phenomenon disappears rapidly. Usually after the first retest trial, list *x* has been relearned back to criterion.

   e. As one makes the stimulus syllables more and more similar, learning takes more trials.

The Information Processing Model

This section describes the processes and structures of EPAM.

EPAM is not a model for a particular subject. In this respect it is to be contrasted with the binary choice models of particular subjects which Feldman describes (1961*a*). The fact is that individual differences play only a small part in the results of the basic experiment described above.

It is asserted that there are certain elementary information processes which an individual must perform if he is to discriminate, memorize and associate verbal items, and that these information processes participate in all the cognitive activity of all individuals.[5]

It is clear that EPAM does not yet embody a complete set of such

[3] For an extended treatment of this subject, see Hovland, *Human Learning and Retention* in Stevens (1951).

[4] By Hull (1935). Actually he called it "oscillation at the threshold of recall," reflecting his theoretical point of view.

[5] Some information processing models are conceived as models of the mental

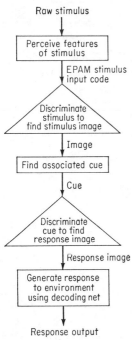

Figure 1. EPAM performance process for producing the response associated with a stimulus.

processes. It is equally clear that the processes EPAM has now are essential and basic.

OVERVIEW: PERFORMANCE AND LEARNING

Conceptually, EPAM can be broken down into two subsystems, a performance system and a learning system. In the performance mode, EPAM produces responses to stimulus items. In the learning mode, EPAM learns to discriminate and associate items.

The performance system is the simpler of the two. It is sketched in Fig. 1. When a stimulus is noticed, a *perceptual process* encodes it, producing an internal representation (an *input code*). A *discriminator* sorts the input code in a *discrimination net* (a tree of tests and branches) to find a stored *image* of the stimulus. A response *cue* associated with the image is found, and fed to the discriminator. The discriminator sorts the cue in the net and finds the response image, the stored form of the response. The response image is then decoded by a *response generator* letter by letter in another discrimination net into a form suitable for output. The response is then produced as output.

The processes of the learning system are more complex. The discrimination learning process builds discriminations by growing the net of tests and branches. The association process builds associations between images by storing response cues with stimulus images. These processes will be described fully in due course.

---

function of particular subjects; *e.g.,* Feldman's Binary Choice Model (1959). Others treat the general subject as EPAM does. Still others are mixed in conception, asserting that certain of the processes of the model are common for all subjects while other processes may vary from subject to subject; *e.g.,* the General Problem Solver of Newell, Shaw, and Simon (1959*a*). Alternatively, information processing models may also be categorized according to how much of the processing is "hard core" (*i.e.,* necessary and invariant) as opposed to "strategic" (*i.e.,* the result of strategy choice by control processes). I suggest the obvious: that models of strategies for information processing will tend to be models of particular subjects. As exemplars, Lindsay's Reading Machine (1960), a "hard-core" model, treats the general subject; Wickelgren's model of the conservative focusing strategy in concept attainment (Wickelgren, 1962; Bruner, Goodnow, and Austin, 1956), a pure strategy model, can predict only the behavior of particular subjects.

The succeeding sections on the information processing model give a detailed description of the processes and structures of both systems.

INPUT TO EPAM: INTERNAL REPRESENTATIONS OF EXTERNAL DATA

The following are the assumptions about the symbolic input process when a nonsense syllable is presented to the learner. A *perceptual system* receives the raw external information and codes it into *internal symbols*. These internal symbols contain descriptive information about features of external stimuli. For unfamiliar 3-letter nonsense symbols, it is assumed that the coding is done in terms of the individual letters, for these letters are familiar and are well-learned units for the adult subject.[6] The end result of the perception process is an internal representation of the nonsense syllable—a list of internal symbols (*i.e.,* a list of lists of bits) containing descriptive information about the letters of the nonsense syllable. Using Minsky's terminology (1961*a*), this is the "character" of the nonsense syllable.

I have not actually programmed this perception process. For purposes of this simulation, I have assigned coded representations for the various letters of the alphabet based on 15 different geometrical features of letters. For purposes of exploring and testing the model, at present all that is really needed of the input codes is:

a. that the dimensions of a letter code be related in some reasonable way to features of real letters.

b. that the letter codes be highly redundant, that is, include many more dimensions than is necessary to discriminate the letters of the alphabet.

To summarize, the internal representation of a nonsense syllable is a list of lists of bits, each sublist of bits being a highly redundant code for a letter of the syllable.

Given a sequence of such inputs, the essence of the learner's problem is twofold: first, to *discriminate* each code from the others already learned, so that differential response can be made; second, to *associate* information about a "response" syllable with the information about a "stimulus" syllable so that the response can be retrieved if the stimulus is presented.

DISCRIMINATING AND MEMORIZING: GROWING TREES OF IMAGES

I shall deal with structure first and reserve my discussion of process for a moment.

Discrimination Net. The primary information structure in EPAM is the

---

[6] The basic perception mechanism I have in mind is much the same as that of Selfridge (1955) and Dinneen (1955), whose computer program scanned letters and perceived simple topological features of these letters.

discrimination net. It embodies in its structure at any moment all of the discrimination learning that has taken place up to a given time. As an information structure it is no more than a familiar friend: a sorting tree or decoding network. Figure 2 shows a small net. At the terminals of the net are lists called *image lists,* in which symbolic information can be stored. At the nodes of the net are stored programs, called *tests,* which examine characteristics of an input code and signal branch left or branch right. On each image list will be found a list of symbols called the *image.* An image is a partial or total copy of an input code. I shall use these names in the following description of net processes.

Net Interpreter. The discrimination net is examined and altered by a number of processes, most important of which is the *net interpreter.* The net interpreter sorts an input code in the net and produces the image list associated with that input code. *This retrieval process is the essence of a purely associative memory: the stimulus information itself leads to the retrieval of the information associated with that stimulus.* The net interpreter is a very simple process. It finds the test in the topmost node of the tree and executes this program. The resulting signal tells it to branch left or branch right to find the succeeding test. It executes this, tests its branches again, and repeats the cycle until a terminal is found. The name of the image list is produced, and the process terminates. This is the discriminator of the performance system which sorts items in a static net.

Discrimination Learning. The discrimination learning process of the learning system grows the net. Initially we give the learning system no discrimination net but only a set of simple processes for growing nets and storing new images at the terminals.

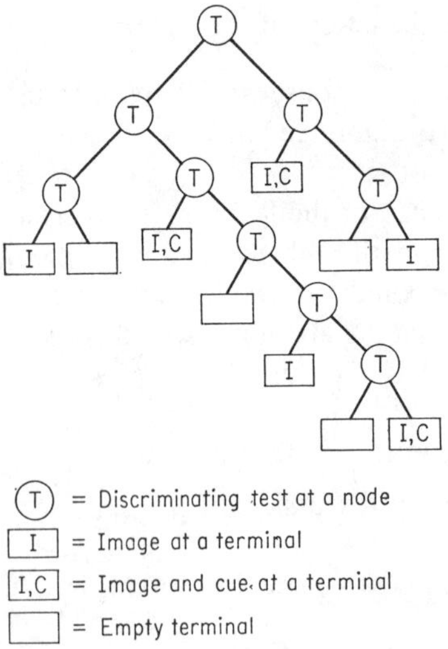

To understand how the discrimination and memorization processes work, let us examine in detail a concrete example from the learning of nonsense syllables. Suppose that the first stimulus-response associate pair on a list has been learned. (Ignore for the moment the question of how the association link is actually formed.) Suppose that the first syllable pair was DAX-JIR. The discrimination net at this point has the simple two-branch structure shown in Fig. 3. Because the syllables differ in their first letter, Test 1 will probably be

(T) = Discriminating test at a node
[I] = Image at a terminal
[I,C] = Image and cue at a terminal
[ ] = Empty terminal

Figure 2. A Typical EPAM discrimination net.

a test of some characteristic on which the letters D and J differ. No more tests are necessary at this point.

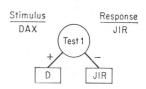

Figure 3. Discrimination net after the learning of the first two items. Cues are not shown. Condition: no redundant tests added. Test 1 is a first-letter test.

Notice that the image of JIR which is stored is a full image. Full response images must be stored—to provide the information for *producing* the response; but only partial stimulus images need be stored—to provide the information for *recognizing* the stimulus. How much stimulus image information is required the learning system determines for itself as it grows its discrimination net, and makes errors which it diagnoses as inadequate discrimination.

To pursue our simple example, suppose that the next syllable pair to be learned is PIB-JUK. There are no storage terminals in the net, as it stands, for the two new items. In other words, the net does not have the discriminative capability to contain more than two items. The input code for PIB is sorted by the net interpreter. Assume that Test 1 sorts it down the plus branch of Fig. 3. As there are differences between the incumbent image (with first letter D) and the new code (with first letter P) an attempt to store an image of PIB at this terminal would destroy the information previously stored there.

Clearly what is needed is the ability to discriminate further. A match for differences between the incumbent image and the challenging code is performed. When a difference is found, a new test is created to discriminate upon this difference. The new test is placed in the net at the point of failure to discriminate, an image of the new item is created, and both images—incumbent and new—are stored in terminals along their appropriate branches of the new test, and the conflict is resolved.[7] The net as it now stands is shown in Fig. 4. Test 2 is seen to discriminate on some difference between the letters P and D.

The input code for JUK is now sorted by the net interpreter. Since Test

[7] With the processes just described, the discrimination net would be grown each time a new item was to be added to the memory. But from an informational processing standpoint, the matching and net-growing processes are the most time-consuming in the system. In general, with little additional effort, more than one difference can be detected, and more than one discriminating test can be added to the net. Each redundant test placed in the net gives one "empty" image list. At some future time, if an item is sorted to this empty image list, an image can be stored without growing the net. There is a happy medium between small nets which must be grown all the time and large nets replete with redundant tests and a wasteful surplus of empty image lists. Experimentation with this "structural parameter" has been done and it has been found that for this study one or two redundant tests per growth represents the happy medium. However, I would not care to speak of the generality of this particular result.

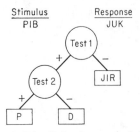

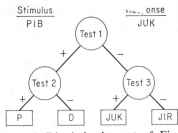

Figure 4. Discrimination net of Fig. 3 after the learning of stimulus item, PIB. Test 2 is a first-letter test.

Figure 5. Discrimination net of Fig. 4 after the learning of the response item, JUK. Test 3 is a third-letter test.

1 cannot detect the difference between the input codes for JUK and JIR (under our previous assumption), JUK is sorted to the terminal containing the image of JIR. The match for differences takes place. Of course, there are no first-letter differences. But there are differences between the incumbent image and the new code in the second and third letters.

Noticing Order. In which letter should the matching process next scan for differences? In a serial machine like EPAM, this scanning must take place in some order. This order need not be arbitrarily determined and fixed. It can be made variable and adaptive. To this end EPAM has a *noticing order for letters of syllables,* which prescribes at any moment a letter-scanning sequence for the matching process. Because it is observed that subjects generally consider end letters before middle letters, the noticing order is initialized as follows: first letter, third letter, second letter. When a particular letter being scanned yields a difference, this letter is promoted up one position on the noticing order. Hence, letter positions relatively rich in differences quickly get priority in the scanning. In our example, because no first-letter differences were found between the image of JIR and code for JUK, the third letters are scanned and a difference is found (between R and K). A test is created to capitalize on this third-letter difference and the net is grown as before. The result is shown in Fig. 5. The noticing order is updated; third letter, promoted up one, is at the head.

Learning of subsequent items proceeds in the same way, and we shall not pursue the example further.

ASSOCIATING IMAGES: RETRIEVAL USING CUES

The discrimination net and its interpreter associate codes of external objects with internal image lists and images. But the basic rote learning experiment requires that stimulus information somehow lead to response information and a response. The discrimination net concept can be used for the association of internal images with each other (*i.e.,* response with stimulus) with very little addition to the basic mechanism.

An association between a stimulus image and a response image is accomplished by storing with the stimulus image some of the coded information about the response. This information is called *the cue*. A cue is of the same form as an input code, but generally contains far less information than an input code. A cue to an associated image can be stored in the discrimination net by the net interpreter to retrieve the associated image. If, for example, in the net of Fig. 3 we had stored with the stimulus image the letter J as a cue to the response JIR, then sorting this cue would have correctly retrieved the response image. *An EPAM internal association is built by storing with the stimulus image information sufficient to retrieve the response image from the net at the moment of association.*

The association process determines how much information is sufficient by trial and error. The noticing order for letters is consulted, and the first-priority letter is added to the cue. The cue is then sorted by the net interpreter and a response image is produced. It might be the wrong response image; for if a test seeks information which the cue does not contain, the interpreter branches left or right randomly (with equal probabilities) at this test.[8] During association, the selection of the wrong response is immediately detectable (by a matching process) because the response input code is available. The next-priority letter is added to the cue and the process repeats until the correct response image is retrieved. The association is then considered complete.

Note two important possibilities. First, by the process just described, a cue which is really not adequate to guarantee retrieval of the response image may by happenstance give the correct response image selection during association. This "luck" usually gives rise to response errors at a later time.

Second, suppose that the association building process does its job thoroughly. The cue which it builds is sufficient to retrieve the response image *at one particular time,* the time at which the two items were associated. If, at some future time, the net is grown to encompass new images being added to the memory, then a cue which previously was sufficient to correctly retrieve a response image may no longer be sufficient to retrieve that response image. In EPAM, association links are "dated," and ever vulnerable to interruption by further learning. Responses may be "unlearned" or "forgotten" temporarily, not because the response information has been destroyed in the memory, but because the information has been temporarily lost in a growing network. If an association failure of this type can be detected through feedback from the environmental or ex-

---

[8] This is the only use of a random variable in EPAM. We do not like it. We use it only because we have not yet discovered a plausible and satisfying adaptive mechanism for making the decision. The random mechanism does, however, give better results than the go-one-way-all-the-time mechanism which has also been used.

perimental situation, then the trouble is easily remedied by adding additional response information to the cue. If not, then the response may be more or less permanently lost in the net. The significance of this phenomenon will perhaps be more easily appreciated in the discussion of results of the EPAM simulation.

RESPONDING: INTERNAL AND EXTERNAL

A conceptual distinction is made between the process by which EPAM selects an internal response image and the process by which it converts this image into an output to the environment.

Response Retrieval. A stimulus item is presented. This stimulus input code is sorted in the discrimination net to retrieve the image list, in which the cue is found. The cue is sorted in the net to retrieve another image list containing the proposed response image. If there is no cue, or if on either sorting pass an empty image list is selected, no response is made.

Response Generation. For purposes of response generation, there is a fixed discrimination net (decoding net), assumed already learned, which transforms letter codes of internal images into output form. The response image is decoded letter by letter by the net interpreter in the decoding net for letters.

THE ORGANIZATION OF THE LEARNING TASK

The learning of nonsense symbols by the processes heretofore described takes time. EPAM is a serial machine. Therefore, the individual items must be dealt with in some sequence. This sequence is not arbitrarily prescribed. It is the result of higher order executive processes whose function is to control EPAM's focus of attention. These *macroprocesses,* as they are called, will not be described or discussed here. A full exposition of them is available in a paper by Feigenbaum and Simon (1962).

Stating the Model Precisely: Computer Program for EPAM

The EPAM model has been realized as a program in Information Processing Language V (Newell et al., 1961*e*) and is currently being run both on the Berkeley 7090 and the RAND 7090. Descriptive information on the computer realization, and also the complete IPL-V program and data structures for EPAM (as it stood in October, 1959) are given in an earlier work by the author (1959).

IPL-V, a list processing language, was well suited as a language for the EPAM model for these key reasons:

a. The IPL-V basic processes deal explicitly and directly with list *structures.* The various information structures in EPAM (e.g., discrimination net, image list) are handled most easily as list structures. Indeed, the discrimination is, virtually by definition, a list structure of a simple type.

b. It is useful in some places, and necessary in others, to store with some symbols information descriptive of these symbols. IPL-V's description list and description list processes are a good answer to this need.

c. The facility with which hierarchies of subroutine control can be written in IPL-V makes easy and uncomplicated the programming of the kind of complex control sequence which EPAM uses.

Empirical Explorations with EPAM

The procedure for exploring the behavior of EPAM is straightforward. We have written an "Experimenter" program and we give to this program the particular conditions of that experiment as input at the beginning of an experiment. The Experimenter routine then puts EPAM *qua* subject through its paces in that particular experiment. The complete record of stimuli presented and responses made is printed out, as is the final net. Any other information about the processing or the state of the EPAM memory can also be printed out.

A number of simulations of the basic paired-associate and serial-anticipation experiments have been run. Simulations of other classical experiments in the rote learning of nonsense syllables have also been run. The complete results of these simulation experiments and a comparison between EPAM's behavior and the reported behavior of human subjects will be the subject of a later report. However, some brief examples here will give an indication of results expected and met.

A. STIMULUS AND RESPONSE GENERALIZATION

These are psychological terms used to describe the following phenomenon. If X and X' are similar stimuli, and Y is the correct response to the presentation of X; then if Y is given in response to the presentation of X', this is called stimulus generalization. Likewise, if Y and Y' are similar responses, and Y' is given in response to the presentation of X, this is called response generalization. Generalization is common to the behavior of all subjects, and is found in the behavior of EPAM. It is a consequence of the responding process and the structure of the discrimination net. For those "stimuli" are similar in the EPAM memory whose input codes are sorted to the same terminal; and one "response" is similar to another if the one is stored in the same local area of the net as the other (and hence response error may occur when response cue information is insufficient).

B. OSCILLATION AND RETROACTIVE INHIBITION

We have described these phenomena in an earlier section.

Oscillation and retroactive inhibition appear in EPAM's behavior as consequences of simple mechanisms for discrimination, discrimination learning, and association. They were in no sense "designed into" the behavior. The appearance of rather complex phenomena such as these gives one a little more confidence in the credibility of the basic assumptions of the model.

These two phenomena are discussed together here because in EPAM they have the same origin. As items are learned over time, the discrimination net grows to encompass the new alternatives. Growing the net means adding new tests, which in turn means that more information will be examined in all objects being sorted. An important class of sorted objects is the set of cues. Cue information sufficient at one moment for a firm association may be insufficient at a later moment. As described above, this may lead to response failure. The failure is caused entirely by the ordinary process of learning new items. In the case of oscillation, the new items are items within a single list being learned. In the case of retroactive inhibition, the new items are items of the second list being learned in the same discrimination net. In both cases the reason for the response failure is the same. According to this explanation, the phenomena are first cousins (a hypothesis which has not been widely considered by psychologists).

In the EPAM model, the term *interference* is no longer merely descriptive—it has a precise and operational meaning. The process by which later learning interferes with earlier learning is completely specified.

C. FORGETTING

The usual explanations of forgetting use in one way or another the simple and appealing idea that stored information is physically destroyed in the brain over time (*e.g.,* the decay of a "memory trace," or the overwriting of old information by new information, as in a computer memory). Such explanations have never dealt adequately with the commonplace observation that all of us can remember, under certain conditions, detailed and seemingly unimportant information after very long time periods have elapsed. An alternative explanation, not so easily visualized, is that forgetting occurs not because of information destruction but because learned material gets lost and inaccessible in a large and growing association network.

EPAM forgets seemingly well-learned responses. This forgetting occurs as a direct consequence of later learning by the learning processes. Furthermore, forgetting is only temporary: lost associations can be reconstructed by storing more cue information. EPAM provides a mechanism for explaining the forgetting phenomenon in the absence of any information loss. As far as we know, it is the first concrete demonstration of this type of forgetting in a learning machine.

Conclusion: A Look Ahead

Verification of an information processing theory is obtained by simulating many different experiments and by comparing in detail specific qualitative and quantitative features of real behavior with the behavior of the simulation. To date, H. A. Simon and I have run a number of simulated experiments. As we explore verbal learning further, more of these will be necessary.

We have been experimenting with a variety of "sense modes" for EPAM, corresponding to "visual" input and "written" output, "auditory" input and "oral" output, "muscular" inputs and outputs. To each mode corresponds a perceptual input coding scheme, and a discrimination net. Associations across nets, as well as the familiar associations within nets, are now possible. Internal transformations between representations in different modes are possible. Thus, EPAM can "sound" in the "mind's ear" what it "sees" in the "mind's eye," just as all of us do so easily. We have been teaching EPAM to read by association, much as one teaches a small child beginning reading. We have only begun to explore this new addition.

The EPAM model has pointed up a failure shared by all existing theories of rote learning (including the present EPAM). It is the problem of whether association takes place between symbols or between tokens of these symbols. For example, EPAM cannot learn a serial list in which the same item occurs twice. It cannot distinguish between the first and second occurrence of the item. To resolve the problem we have formulated (and are testing) processes for building, storing, and responding from chains of token associations (Feigenbaum and Simon, 1962).

PROGRAMMING A MODEL OF
HUMAN CONCEPT FORMULATION

by Earl B. Hunt & Carl I. Hovland

What is a concept? Ordinarily usage is not precise. The English "the concept of force," "the concept of massive retaliation," and "concept of dogs" are all permissible. Church (1956) has offered a definition which has been accepted, implicitly, by psychologists who perform "concept learning" experiments. Church's argument is that any given symbol (or *name*) can be attached to the members of a set of objects. For any arbitrary object there exists a rule concerning the description of the object, a rule which can be used to decide whether or not the object is a member of the set of objects to which the name applies. The decision rule is the concept of the name, the set of objects is the denotation of the name.

In a typical concept learning experiment the subject is confronted with a series of stimuli which are given a particular name and another series of stimuli which are either given another particular name, or a series of different names. Thus the first set might be called "dogs" and the second either "not-dogs" or "cats, wolves, sheep, etc." Thus some routines are necessary to classify the instances to correspond to the names assigned by the experimenter. These are our ordering routines. Sometimes the various stimuli given one name have certain common characteristics, *e.g.,* all the positive instances may have three triangles. At other times there are no common relating elements, but there are common relationships, *e.g.* all the positive instances may have the same size of upper figure as lower figure, although the figures may be large, medium or small sized in each row. A machine routine may be required to describe relations between basic stimulus elements. So we must have description routines in a simulation. Finally, different types of stimulus sets may be organized differently in

310

terms of different types of logical connectives. Sometimes the concept involves the joint presence of two or more characteristics. Such concepts are referred to as conjunctive concepts (*e.g.,* large red figure). Other concepts involve the presence of different subsets of characteristics. These are disjunctive concepts, *e.g.,* red *or* large figures. Different ways of defining the form of an answer are provided by a set of solution routines.

The program must be capable of simulating a variety of conditions under which experiments have been performed. As illustrations of some of the variations, or manipulations, which must be simulated the following may be mentioned.

The number and complexity of the stimuli may vary from study to study. The speed of presentation of new stimuli can be altered. The instances may be left in view or the subject may be forced to rely on his memory. Different concept learning problems can be compared along such dimensions as: logical complexity of the correct answer, number of relevant vs. number of irrelevant dimensions, order of presentation of problems of different types, and presentation of information by positive or negative instances.

The subject may make a variety of responses during the experiment. Subjects may describe, verbally, their intermediate and final hypotheses concerning the characteristics of the concept. These responses may give us clues as to the nature of the individual's information processing procedures. As such, they constitute accessory measures used in our simulation studies. The time taken to develop an answer under various experimental conditions is also a useful response measure. The errors that subjects make in subsequent identifications of stimulus names can be analyzed. The more objective records are to be preferred, and our major goal is to predict these by computer simulation.

In order to develop a theoretical explanation of concept learning we have accepted the "black box" analogy. We have attempted to write a computer program which, when given as input coded representations of the stimuli, will give as output coded responses that can be used to predict the responses of a human subject. Accurate prediction of the responses, not the development of a good hypothesis developer, nor, solely, the reproduction of previously obtained protocols, is our goal. We are not concerned with the processes specific to the task of categorizing geometric patterns. These are used as stimuli because they are convenient and because they represent stimuli which can be described in terms of previously discriminated stimuli. Hopefully we shall be able to make conclusions about concept learning processes irrespective of the particular form of the stimuli.

Reports of our psychological experimental work have been, and are being, made in separate publications. This report will be concerned with the programming details of our concept learning model. This model has been completed, debugged, and used to simulate several experiments. After describing the model we shall indicate the result of some simulations and discuss the modifications of the model which have been indicated.

The concept learning program is a list processing language program written for the IBM 709-7090 data processing systems. The original programs were written in Information Processing Language V (IPL-V), the interpreter list processing language developed by Newell, Shaw, and Simon (Newell, 1961e). Partly for local administrative reasons, we are in the process of converting our programs to LISP, a list processing language developed by McCarthy (1960). We do not have sufficient experience with LISP to compare the two languages for our type of problem. As the basic logic of the LISP and IPL-V programs are the same, no distinction will be made between them.

Description of the Program

The program consists of two blocks of data, specified by the programmer at the beginning of each run, and five subsystems for data processing. At the beginning of a simulation the programmer specifies a sequence of problems, a set of parameters, and a set of lists. The last two represent the capabilities of the artificial subject. The problem data remains constant throughout the run, the specifications of the subject may be changed by the program.

Problems are presented by describing instances, the denotations of names (classes), and the conditions of presentation to be used. This takes the form of specification of memory requirements, number of stimuli presented at a single time, etc. All the conditions used to describe a problem are specified in the property list of the symbol naming the problem.

Each instance (*i.e.,* object to be categorized) is represented by a symbol whose property list specifies the symbol's class membership, and, by a list of pairs, the dimensions and values which constitute a formal description of the object. For instance, in our previous example, a large, red triangle would contain the following pairs on its description list: (class name- "alpha"), (size-large), (color-red), (shape-triangle). The formal description list constitutes the most molecular information about objects which is made available to the program. Higher-order, working descriptions based upon relations between elements of the formal description may be developed by the program.

Dimensions represent the manner in which objects are free to vary. We have utilized a "dimensional analysis" of objects which specifies a finite universe with a built-in structure to describe objects (cf. Hovland, 1952). Dimensions are also organized into "dimension sets," or groupings. These groupings represent subsets of the set of all dimensions which will be considered together during recognition and answer development.

The "subject" specifications fall into two broad categories; numerical parameters and initial settings used to control the program. They will be discussed as they enter into the action of the model.

Figure 1 specifies the channels of communications between the various subsystems in the model. There are two major groups of subsystems. The first, as indicated in Fig. 1, is the recognition and memory system. Its task is to acquire information from the formal description of presented instances and to retain this information for later processing by the answer development and checking group.

By examining the property list of the problem, the program determines the conditions of presentation of stimuli. If these conditions would not require memorization by a human subject (*i.e.,* if instances are presented to the subject and left in view) the name of each instance, together with its entire formal description, is added to internal memory as the instance is presented. We do not maintain that subjects see all of a complex instance at the time it is presented. However, when the conditions of presentation are such that he can always reexamine the instance we see no reason for using a special recognition program.

If an instance is shown only once, and then removed, the subject can only store the information which he receives at the time the instance is presented. Here a special "recognition" program is needed. We have a rather primitive method for reading instances into memory in our present model. Included in the initial specification of the artificial subject is a list of dimension sets. Sets are read in the order in which they are placed on the list. During a particular problem our program reads, at every presentation of an instance, all dimension sets which have ever been read. If this provides sufficient information with which to discriminate the current in-

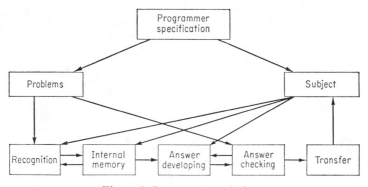

Figure 1. Program control chart.

stance from previous instances, the reading process terminates. If sufficient information is not presented, a new dimension set is read, and the discrimination test reapplied. New dimension sets are added until either all dimension sets have been used or discrimination from previously presented instances is possible. When the read program is terminated the appropriate description (some part of the formal description) is entered into internal memory.

For problems in which a requirement for memory exists, a limited occupancy model of human memory is employed (cf. Hunt, 1960a). The subject parameters specify a certain number of storage cells. These are set aside for representational memory of instances. Each new instance is stored, at random, in one of the cells. The previous content, if any, is lost. Thus, the probability that the artificial subject has a given instance available decreases as the number of intervening instances increases. We consider this model a crude approximation to human memory, although it has been shown to be useful in predicting the probability of utilization of information in certain cases.

Figure 1 represents the very indirect tie between recognition memory and answer developing checking units in the present system. It may be that this is not the most effective arrangement. Schemes for joining the subsystems may be considered in a later model.

The "heart" of the model is the answer development subsystem. Its internal procedure is depicted in Fig. 2. The answer developing section finds binary decision rules for distinguishing between the denotation of one name and its complement. In doing so it restricts its attention to one dimension set at a time. Dimension sets are selected in the order specified by the current description of the artificial subject. If an answer already exists which involves a particular dimension set, that set will be ignored in answer

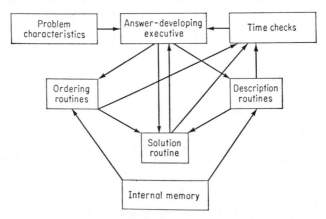

Figure 2. Answer-developing procedure.

development. The "executive routine" of the answer developing system is entered when a dimension set is found for which no answer is currently available. The plan followed by the executive routine is to prepare an *execution list* containing the names of three routines which will be executed in the order specified by the *execution list*. The contents of internal memory are used as output for the first and second of the three routines. They, in turn, provide the output for the third (last) routine of the execution list. Successful completion of the third routine results in a tentative concept definition.

The executive routine selects routines for the execution list from three reference lists. These are initially specified by the programmer as part of the subject's description list. They may be changed during execution of a simulation.

The first reference list contains the names of *ordering routines*. Each of these routines splits the instances on internal memory into two sets, working positive and working negative instances. The two categories are mutually exclusive and exhaustive of all instances in memory. In the simulations we have tried thus far three ordering routines are provided. One places in the "working positive" set all instances which are members of a class which has been indicated, by the programmer, as the class for which a concept is to be found. The second currently available routine reverses this procedure, placing the same instances in the working negative set. (If the programmer has indicated that there are several classes of equal importance the class name of the most recently presented instance is used by these two routines.) The third ordering routine defines as "working positives" all those instances which have the class name of the smallest set that is represented in internal memory, provided that there are at least two instances in the set.

Another reference list contains the name of routines which produce a working description of the instances in memory. These routines attach to each instance in internal memory a description based on a transformation of that part of the formal description included in the current dimension set. We have dealt with two description routines. One simply copies the necessary dimensions and values from the formal description to the working description. The other routine defines new dimensions based upon the relation between values of the dimensions of a formal description. The following rules are used to generate the working description:

1. A new dimension is defined for any pair of (source) dimensions whose values are numerical quantities on the same scale. For a particular instance the value of the new dimension is EQUAL, GREATER, or LESS, depending on the comparison of the values of the original pair of dimensions on that instance.

2. A new dimension is defined for any pair of source dimensions on the formal description list if, over the entire set of instances in memory, the two source dimensions share a common value. (The common value need not appear on both dimensions in the same instance.) The value of the new dimension is, for a particular instance, either SAME or DIFFERENT, depending on a comparison of the value of the original dimensions on the instance in question.

In actual programming, the ordering and description routines are applied serially. They are functionally parallel; the output of one does not affect the output of the other. They both provide output to the solution routine. This consists of all instances in internal memory, recategorized and re-described. The solution routine attempts to define a method for discriminating between working positive and working negative instances. The discrimination is always stated as a definition of the working positive instances, even though these may be members of the complement of the class for which the program is trying to define a concept.

At present the model contains three solution routines. The first two are suited for handling conjunctive concept learning problems (problems in which the answer can be stated using only the logical connective *and*). The third is a conditional procedure which is slower, more complex, and of greater generality.

The two "conjunctive" routines both, as their first operation, list those dimensions which have only one value over the entire set of working positive instances. If this list does not exist no conjunctive definition of the working positive instances exists. If the list does exist, it is handled somewhat differently by the two routines. The first conjunctive routine searches through each of the dimensions to find if one of them *never* has the same value on the negative instances as it does on all positive instances. The second routine examines all negative instances to see whether any negative instance has the entire conjunction of dimension-value pairs which are common to all positive instances. The routine returns an answer if no such instance can be found. Thus either routine, when it succeeds, defines a conjunctive concept that can be used for the instances in internal storage.

The third solution routine, the conditional routine, is a recursive function which, if slightly modified, would give the artificial subject the capability of answering any concept learning problem. As it currently stands, it provides the capability of solving disjunctive concept learning problems of limited complexity.

The conditional routine first identifies the dimension-value pair which is most frequently found on positive instances. It then generates two sublists of working positives and working negatives, all of which contain this pair. The first conjunctive routine is applied to the two sublists. If it succeeds, it returns with an answer which can be applied to any future instance, which has the appropriate dimension-value pair. If it happens that the conditional routine generates only a sublist of positive instances, the answer is the value of the single dimension being considered. If the dimension-value pair does not occur on a future instance, the class membership of this instance is indeterminate.

If an answer is not generated in this manner, or if there remain unclassified instances, the conditional routine is repeated, omitting dimension-value pairs previously considered *and* any instances which have been classified. The result of the application of the conditional and conjunctive routines constitute a second "conditional" answer. This procedure is repeated until all instances in internal memory have been classified or until all dimensions have been considered. The result is a classification rule composed of a chain of statements about simple conjunctive answers and the rules under which they apply (*e.g.,* red triangle, green circle). The chain of statements may be of any length, but each statement must contain only two dimension-value pairs. We could have removed this restriction by applying the second conjunctive rule instead of the first. We could also have permitted an *n*th-level conditional rule by applying the conditional routine, recursively, to the sublists until all instances were classified. The resulting procedure would generate a rule for all concept learning problems. It would not necessarily be the most compact statement of the correct rule. It could degenerate into a description of particular instances.

When the executive routine selects an execution list it is, in effect, applying a template for an answer to a particular problem. If the problem has an answer which involves the relevant features abstracted by the ordering and description routines, operating on a particular dimension set, and if the answer is of a particular logical type, there exists an execution list which will find it.

The manner in which our first model changes its template is also indicated in Fig. 2. Initially the dimension set is selected. The first execution list is then selected from the reference lists contained in the subject description. The first execution list always uses the routines which are at the top of each reference list. If the execution list cannot obtain an answer, the description or solution routine (alternately) is replaced until the original execution list is reconstructed. When this happens a new ordering routine is chosen. The alternation of description and solution routines is repeated until, again, an execution list is repeated. At this point a new ordering routine is selected. When there are no more ordering routines the dimension set is replaced, using the next dimension set on the subject's list of order of noticing dimension sets. The process ends whenever either, an answer is developed, all dimension sets are examined, *or,* when the allotted time is exceeded. How this is instrumented will be described presently.

During a particular problem the order of dimension sets remains constant. However, during the time when an answer is being developed, the reference lists for description and solution routines may be temporarily altered. This is done by moving a symbol from first to last place on its reference list whenever it is removed from an execution list. One of the ways in which we can simulate individual differences is to change the initial order of routines on the reference lists.

As we have indicated, there is a "time-checking" mechanism which may interrupt the answer development process. Associated with each routine on a reference list is an index number. These numbers are specified by the programmer as part of the initial data. The programmer also specifies, as part of the problem data, a number which represents the time that the artificial subject has to develop an answer. Depending on the presentation conditions, this may represent the time he is permitted to spend on the entire problem or the time between stimulus presentations. Every time a routine on an execution list is applied, its index number is subtracted from a time signal which was, originally, set equal to the allowable time number. When the time signal reaches zero, answer developing is halted (possibly with the reference lists for description and solution rearranged) and control is returned from the executive solution routine to a higher level.

The index number associated with each routine can be thought of as an "effort" number, the cost of a particular information processing routine to the subject. Success in any problem depends on a complex interaction between the rules for rearrangement of order of routines on reference lists, the value of the index number, and the value of the allowable time number. One of our more fascinating research tasks is the unraveling of this relation.

The model, as presently programmed, has an independent check on time. Whenever a new instance is presented it is examined to see if its class membership agrees with that predicted for it by currently active answers. If the new instance does not agree, or (in the case of conditional answers) if no class membership is predicted for that instance, the answer development routine will be entered. If correct prediction occurs the answer development section is entered *only* if a "slow" rate of stimulus presentation is specified in the problem description.

Whenever an answer is developed the dimension set and execution list used are stored on its description list. When a problem is solved (*i.e.* after all instances have been presented), those dimension sets which have been associated with an answer, and those routines which have appeared on successful lists, are moved to the head of their respective reference lists. Thus, the characteristics of the subject which were originally specified by the programmer have been modified by the program.

The transfer procedure has an interesting psychological implication. Our artificial subject shows positive or negative transfer only when the preceding problem is solved. Also, transfer is almost entirely dependent upon the form of the immediately preceding problem. We do not know whether or not this is true of human problem-solving.

Simulations and Evaluations

The model was not conceived *in vacuo*. Previous, unprogrammed models (Hovland and Hunt, 1960) had been considered for some time. In addition, we gathered protocols from Yale undergraduates who attempted to solve a "concept learning" problem which had three logically correct answers; a disjunction, a conjunction, and a relation. (This problem has been described previously (Hunt and Hovland, 1960) and some data on its difficulty was available.) All three conditions of presentation were given to each subject. The model we have just presented gave the best over-all "postdiction" of response of any model we could devise. In fitting it we altered the order and identity of symbols on reference lists, but otherwise kept the model constant. Since each subject solved three problems, we were able to make some tests of our transfer procedures and thus do not rely too heavily upon prespecified orders. The results of our match were generally encouraging. However, they cannot be taken as validating evidence since the protocols were used to develop the program.

Some more encouraging evidence came when the artificial subject attempted a series of problems used by Shepard, Hovland and Jenkins (1961). This was a completely separate study. Human subjects were asked to find categorizing rules for each of the six possible types of splits of eight instances, each describable by one of two values on three dimensions, into two sets of four each. Human subjects could solve, quite rapidly, a problem in which all relevant information could be derived from a single dimension. So could our artificial subject. Both human and artificial intelligence found a problem consisting of a "string" of two conditional statements (*e.g.* big and red, or small and white) easy. In a third case, humans and the artificial subject were unable to develop a workable rule for the authors' "Type VI" classification, in which the answer requires either description of each instance or a rather subtle rule about alternation of values. Humans did better than the artificial subject in one situation. When the correct answer could be stated as a simple rule with one exception, our program finds the problem difficult. Humans find it hard, but not nearly as hard as the "Type VI" problem. The results of this simulation, and particularly the discrepancy just mentioned, forced us to consider alternate recursions in the conditional solution routine.

A somewhat similar, unpublished, experiment was performed by Hunt and H. H. Wells. Here the five commonly used logical connectives between two elements provided the answer. A "Truth table" was constructed and presented to subjects in geometric form. For example, the connective "p *and* q" might be represented by "red and star." The five problems were presented in five orders, each subject solving all five problems in one of the orders. Simulation and analysis of this experiment has not been completed at the time of this writing, however, we have some preliminary results. There is good general agreement between our simulation routines and *some* protocols. Both the computer model and the subjects are sensitive to the order in which problems are presented, but their reactions are not as similar as we would like. A new transfer procedure is needed. In an experiment which is not directly related to simulation, Wells is studying the manner in which human subjects learn methods of solution for disjunctive problems. We hope that his experiments will provide some clues about the nature of the transfer procedures we should include in our model.

We do not claim to have presented a complete explanation of concept learning! Certainly others will agree with us. In programming the model we made many decisions with little theoretical or empirical justification. Some of these are certain to be wrong. But which ones?

We shall probably have to change our routines for memory and recognition. Some of the known phenomena of memory cannot be reproduced by a simple occupancy model. For instance, the effect of stimulus similarity upon memory cannot be represented. Our model has an all-or-none aspect in its interference features. An intervening instance either completely eliminates the record of a previous instance or does not affect it at all. This does not seem to be the final answer to the problem of memory in concept learning.

Two alternative memory systems are being considered. One system retains and extends the limited occupancy model. Instead of storing one "code word" (actually, a list structure), representing all known information about an instance, on a single occupancy list, several code words would be stored in several occupancy lists. Each of these code words would represent a particular type of information about some part of the instance in question. Storage of each code word would be independent on each occupancy list. Code words referring to the same instance would reference each other's locations. When information from memory was required a picture of each instance would be reconstructed from the cross-referencing system. However, since intervening instances would be storing instances independently on each occupancy list, some of the code words might be replaced. The extent of this replacement would depend upon the similarity between the instance to be recalled and the stimuli which followed its presentation. This system would be sensitive to stimulus similarity effects.

Alternately, we could use an associationist memory system. Instead of trying to remember units of information directly we would build "associations" between names and stimulus features. This is the logic of the technique used by many learning theorists in psychology. Machinery to realize such a memory has been extensively investigated by Rosenblatt (1958, 1959). There is also some similarity between this approach and the classification mechanisms based upon Selfridge's "Pandemonium" scheme (Selfridge and Neisser, 1960). To adopt such a memory system would require changing the entire logic of our model. Association schemes generally contain, in themselves, a mechanism for concept learning. It also seems that they require some sort of gradient of generalization. Recent experiments (Shepard and Chang, 1961a; Shepard et al., 1961b) indicate that, in concept learning, the tendency to code stimuli symbolically plays a greater role than generalization based upon stimulus similarity. For these reasons we have, tentatively, rejected an associationist memory mechanism.

In the present model we subject the formal description of an instance to two transformations. When an instance is presented, the dimensions of the formal description are sampled to determine what information is to be placed in memory. At some later time, that part of the formal description which is in memory is retransformed to provide a working description. The two procedures could be combined if the description routine currently at the head of the description routine reference list were to be applied directly to an instance before it entered memory.

Such a procedure would have advantages in saving storage space. Instead of having to have two separate locations, for working and permanent description, in the internal memory, only one description need be stored. But we pay for saving this space by losing information. By definition, any working description can be derived from the formal description. All working descriptions cannot be derived from each other. For instance, if we know that an instance contained two figures of the same color, we do not know what that color is. As a result, our artificial subject's ability to utilize a particular description routine at time t would depend very much upon the description routines used previously.

The role of "set" at time of presentation as a determinant of later memory characteristics needs more extensive investigation. Some experiments (Lawrence and Coles, 1954; Lawrence and LaBerge, 1956), suggest that "set" is a function of how memory is searched rather than how items enter into memory. Also, there exists a rather contradictory literature on "latent learning," a term used to describe experiments in which animals, trained to respond to cue A in the presence of cue B, which is irrelevant to the animal's current need, learn more rapidly a later response to cue B. From present experimental results it is not obvious how stimulus recognition and answer development procedures should be connected in a concept learning simulation.

Procedures for representing transfer may not be represented adequately in the present model. Transfer is defined as the effect of previous problem-solving experience upon solution of the problem with which the subject is faced at the time of the test. We decided to work first with a simple method of representing transfer, in which the subject tries whatever worked last time. A principal result of the simulation of the Hunt and Wells work on logical connectives has been a demonstration that a new transfer procedure is needed.

In the tradition of classical learning theory, we could attach a modifiable numerical index to each routine on a reference list. This index could be used to determine the probability that a routine would be selected. This method of representing learning is probably the most common. The principal objection to it is that it implies the existence of "counters in the head" and, essentially, makes our program a digital simulation of an analog system.

The alternative to association indices is a new method of ordinal rearrangement of routines on a reference list. The problem with ordinary rearrangements is that they did not permit us to specify a variable distance between routines on a list. Suppose we consider each concept learning problem as a contest between routines on the same reference list. The one that finds a place on a successful execution list is victorious. How many times must the routine in position n "win" before it gains the next highest position? Should it jump positions? As we have indicated, some research relative to this topic is being conducted.

Conceivably, we may have to change our entire method of transfer. At present our model records answers, with associated information about useful routines. We could attach to routines information about problems on which they had been useful. We would then have to develop some way for the artificial subject to extract, rapidly, key features of a problem while the answer is being developed. Routines would be examined to see what, in the light of past experience, was their probable usefulness on this sort of problem.

Closely related to the problem of transfer is the problem of response selection during learning. Our present model rearranges its order of response selection after a problem is solved. During a problem, response selection is controlled by time parameters which are independent of program control. No use is made of intermediate computations in selecting the next item to be placed on an execution list. In an alternate model this might be the controlling factor. The means-end analysis of the Logic Theorist (Newell and Shaw, 1957b) uses intermediate calculations heavily. Amarel (1960) has proposed a computer model for an area very similar to ours in which intermediate computations exert control on answer development.

Our simulation work, and analysis of experimental data, has convinced us that some method of making the choice of one item on an execution list dependent upon the product of execution of previously selected routines is desirable. What is not clear is the optimum amount of dependency. Bartlett (1958) has presented an analog, in an entirely different context, which may clarify the problem. He compared problem-solving and thinking to motor skills responses, such as serving in tennis. There are certain points at which a chain of responses can be altered; in between these points a series of acts will be executed without interruption. Our problem, experimentally, is to identify the responses and choice points.

We feel that the principal use of our model, so far, has not been in the generating of an explanation of concept learning so much as it has been in indicating the type of new experimental data needed. We have had to be very specific in our thoughts as we programmed this model. As a result, we have reached some conclusions about the kind of experiments that need to be done. It may well be that the typical concept learning experiment confuses three processes; memory, recognition, and symbolic problem-solving. It is not clear whether or not these should be treated as part of a unitary "concept learning" act. They can be programmed separately. In addition we have become concerned with questions of transfer, the effect of the subject's current hypothesis upon his later retention of information, and the effect of time pressure upon information processing. A real awareness of these problems has been a major outcome of programming a concept learning model.

Comparisons with Related Work

Viewed formally, our problem is closely related to models of pattern recognition. Programming either a pattern recognizer or a concept learner involves the development of a mechanism which operates on a specified stimulus universe to map stimuli from predetermined subsets into particular responses. Because of this mathematical identity, at least one critic (Keller, 1961) has suggested that problems of this sort should be treated together, without "psychologizing" or "neurologizing." While this may be useful in developing theorems about a canonical form of categorization, it may not be an appropriate strategy for simulation studies. In particular, our approach is quite different from that of the pattern recognition studies with which we are familiar.

The most striking difference is in the manner in which we precode the stimuli. Pattern recognizers usually accept stimuli coded into projections on a grid. The result is a string of bits, each bit representing the presence or absence of illumination of some part of the grid. The same representation could be used for a temporal pattern. Each bit would stand for the presence or absence of some stimulus feature.

We presuppose the existence of a dimension and value coding (Hovland, 1952) and deal with perceptual aspects which are readily verbalizable. A pattern recognizer develops its own code. Any coding scheme developed by a pattern recognizer will be specific to the stimuli used (visual vs. auditory, etc.). Since we are interested in the manipulation of coded elements we avoid this problem by *fiat* in our programming and by explicit instructions to our subjects in our experimental work.

Our model is also different from most pattern recognizers in the processes it uses. Pattern recognizers, at least as developed by Selfridge and his co-workers (Selfridge and Neisser 1958, 1959), and by Rosenblatt (1960), are basically parallel processing devices which utilize a large number of redundant, error-prone tests. Our program is a serial processor which tries to develop a single, perhaps complex, error-free classification test. We do not see any incompatibility in the two approaches. Our program deals with the simulation of a symbolic process. That the two problems are formally similar does not mean that they are realized in the same way by problem-solvers.

In principle, there would be no objection to utilizing a pattern recognizer to provide the input to the concept learner. The combined system could develop its own dimensions and values and then operate upon them. In practice, such a scheme is undoubtedly premature. But it is a long-range goal.

The concept learning problem has been attacked directly in two previously mentioned studies, by Kochen (1961a) and Amarel (1960). Kochen restricted his program to solution of "concepts" based upon a conjunctive rule involving stimuli specified by strings of bits. His program consisted of executing algorithms upon the information about the universe of objects which was available *at any one time,* in memory. The program also contained features for making random guesses about the correct concept. These guesses could be weighed for "confidence," using an index which satisfied Polya's (1954) postulates for plausible reasoning. One of Kochen's (1954) findings, based on Monte Carlo runs of his system, was that changes in the value of the confidence index could be used to estimate the probability that an answer was correct before a proof of the answer was available.

Amarel (1960) proposed a machine that could generate routines to map arguments to values in symbolic logic. The key feature of his proposal, one we might well adopt, is his use of intermediate results to "monitor" future answer development.

Neither Kochen nor Amarel were directly concerned with simulation of human performance. This difference in goals, and features of programming, are the major differences between our work and theirs.

Superficially, our program is similar to the list processing programs written by the Carnegie Institute of Technology–RAND Corporation group headed by Newell, Shaw, and Simon, and McCarthy (McCarthy, 1960) and his associates at MIT. In particular, the work of Feigenbaum (1959), at RAND, is related to ours. He developed a program to simulate paired-associates learning. As part of his program he included a routine for selective recognition of stimulus features. As more experience with the stimulus universe was provided, more features were read into the system to enable it to make finer discriminations. The logic of Feigenbaum's recognizing system, and in particular its capability for dropping stimulus features which are not useful in discrimination, could be incorporated into our program.

Our present program, although running now, is in no sense complete. Almost every new simulation has indicated ways in which it could be improved. We intend to continue to investigate concept learning by use of an information processing model. But we do wish to add a word of caution. Neither our model, nor any other, has generated a large number of new experiments. This is a traditional test of the utility of a scientific model, and it is going to have to be met by us and by others interested in this field. We do not feel that the utility of computer programming models in psychology has been proven or disproven. The jury is still **out.** We, of course, hope that a favorable verdict will be returned.

section 3

Decision-making under Uncertainty

A large number of decisions are made under conditions of uncertainty, *i.e.,* where the decision-maker does not know the consequences of his alternatives. The commander sending his troops into battle is faced with such a decision problem. The book publisher deciding how many copies of a book to print is in a similar situation. Economists, mathematicians, and statisticians have studied how people "should" behave in these situations, while behavioral scientists have studied how people do behave in these situations. The two articles in this section are in the latter category. In both of them, the computer is used in the construction of information processing models of the behavior of individual decision-makers in uncertain situations.

Feldman reports a study of behavior in the binary choice experiment. In this experiment the subject is asked to predict which of two events will occur on each of a series of trials. With the aid of data obtained from students "thinking aloud" in the binary choice experiment, Feldman has been able to construct models of the cognitive processes underlying binary choice behavior. These models represent the hypothesis-testing behavior that subjects exhibit in these experiments. One of these models and the associated protocol are presented in the following article.

Clarkson has chosen to study human behavior in portfolio selection. He has studied how an investment officer in a bank selects a portfolio of stocks for a trust fund, given the legal constraints involved, the goals of the trust, and the conditions of the market,

Clarkson's analysis of the behavior of this decision-maker has enabled him to construct a computer program which, in test cases, has been able to make very accurate predictions of the trust officer's behavior. In four test cases, the model selects 29 stocks—the same number as the trust officer—and correctly predicts the number of different stocks in each portfolio. The model does very well on the number of shares of each stock, too. Of the 29 selections, there are only five cases in which the model selected a stock different from the stock selected by the trust officer. These results certainly indicate that Clarkson's model is an excellent predictor of the trust officer's behavior.

The implications of both these models extend beyond the particular decision situations in which they were developed. Feldman's work indicates that what appears to be a simple problem is treated by the subject as a very complex situation. The hypothesis-testing procedure which the subject uses is quite similar to the behavior of the researcher studying the subject. The subject is looking for patterns in the event series, and the experimenter is looking for patterns in the subject's behavior. Both are trying to induce the regularity which they both believe does exist. Clarkson's model furnishes important support for a problem-solving model of human decision-making that depicts a decision-maker of limited rationality using a limited memory and a rather small set of rules of thumb. Neither the subject in the binary choice experiment nor the trust investment officer are following the accepted strategies for "rational" behavior in their environments. Detailed analyses such as Feldman and Clarkson have done provide useful information on how people behave in particular decision situations and suggest explanations of behavior in other situations.

Julian Feldman is a member of the faculty of the School of Business Administration, University of California, Berkeley.

Geoffrey Clarkson is a member of the faculty of the School of Industrial Management, Massachusetts Institute of Technology.

SIMULATION OF BEHAVIOR IN THE BINARY CHOICE EXPERIMENT

by *Julian Feldman*

Introduction

Modern, high-speed digital computers have been used to simulate large, complex systems in order to facilitate the study of these systems. One of these systems that has been studied with the aid of computer simulation is man. The present report describes another addition to the growing list of efforts to study human thinking processes by simulating these processes on a computer. The research summarized here has been concerned with simulating the behavior of individual subjects in the binary choice experiment (Feldman, 1959). The first section contains a description of the experiment. An overview of the model is given in the second section. The model for a particular subject is described in some detail in the third section.

The Binary Choice Experiment

In the binary choice experiment, the subject is asked to predict which of two events, E_1 or E_2, will occur on each of a series of trials. After the subject makes a prediction, he is told which event actually occurred. The sequence of events is usually determined by some random mechanism, e.g., a table of random numbers. One and only one event occurs on each trial. The events may be flashes of light or symbols on a deck of cards. The subject is usually asked to make as many correct predictions as he can.

In the research reported here, the experiment described in the preceding paragraph was modified by asking the subject to "think aloud"—to give his reasons for making a prediction as well as the prediction itself. The

329

subject's remarks were recorded. The subject was instructed to "think aloud" in order to obtain more information on the processing that the subject was doing. This technique has been used in some of the classical investigations of problem-solving behavior (Duncker, 1945; Heidbreder, 1924) and in other computer simulation studies of thinking (Clarkson and Simon, 1960; Newell and Simon, 1959d). A comparison of the behavior of subjects in the binary choice experiment who did "think aloud" with the behavior of subjects who did not "think aloud" did not reveal any major differences (Feldman, 1959). The events in the present experiment were the symbols "plus" and "check." "Check" occurred on 142 of 200 trials and "plus" on the remaining 58 trials. The symbols were recorded on a numbered deck of 3-inch $\times$ 5-inch cards. After the subject made his prediction for trial t, he was shown card t which contained a "plus" or "check." While the subject was predicting the event of trial t, he could only see the event of trial t-1. A transcription of the tape recording of the remarks of subject DH and the experimenter, the author, in an hour-long binary choice experiment is presented in the Appendix. In the Appendix and the rest of this report, the symbols "plus" and "check" are represented by "P" and "C" respectively. The transcription will be referred to as a protocol.

The Basic Model

To simulate the behavior of an individual subject in the binary choice experiment, a model of the subject's behavior must be formulated as a computer program. If the program is then allowed to predict the same event series as the subject has predicted, the behavior of the program— the predictions and the reasons—can be compared to the behavior of the subject. If the program's behavior is a reasonable facsimile of the subject's behavior, the program is at least a sufficient explanation of the subject's behavior. The level of explanation is really determined by the subject's statements. No attempt is made to go beyond these to more basic processes, e.g., neurological or chemical, of human behavior. Thus, the model is an attempt to specify the relationship between the reasons or hypotheses that the subject offers for his predictions and the preceding hypotheses, predictions, and events. The subject is depicted as actively proposing hypotheses about the structure of the event series. These hypotheses are tested by using them to predict events. If the prediction of the event is correct, the hypothesis is usually retained. If the prediction of the event is wrong, a new hypothesis is generally proposed.

The Model for DH

The model for each subject is based on a detailed examination of the protocol and some conjectures about human behavior. Perhaps the best thing to do at this point is to describe in some detail a model for the subject, DH, whose protocol appears in the Appendix.

The Hypotheses

This model proposes two types of hypotheses about the event series. The first type of hypothesis is a pattern of events. The model has a repertoire of nine patterns:

progression of C's
progression of P's
single alternation
2 C's and 1 P
1 C   and 2 P's
2 P's and 2 C's
3 P's and 3 C's
4 P's and 4 C's
4 P's and 3 C's

The model can propose that the event series is behaving according to one of these patterns and use the pattern hypothesis to predict the event of a given trial, t. The predictions of the first two patterns—progression of C's and progression of P's—for trial t are independent of the events preceding trial t. The predictions of the other patterns (the alternation patterns) are dependent on these preceding events. Thus, if the subject proposes the pattern "single alternation" for trial t and the event of trial t − 1 was a C, the prediction for trial t is a P. In order to facilitate the determination of the prediction of an alternation pattern for trial t, the patterns are coded as sorting nets. For example, the pattern "2 C's and 1 P" is represented in the following fashion:

Is event t − 1 a C?
No—Predict C for trial t.
Yes—Is event t − 2 a C?
No—Predict C for trial t.
Yes—Predict P for trial t.

The second type of hypothesis that the model can propose is an anti-pattern or guess-opposite hypothesis. For example, the model can propose that the event of trial t will be the opposite of that predicted by a given pattern. This type of hypothesis is the model's representation of the notion of "gambler's fallacy"—the reason people predict "tails" after a coin falls "heads" seven times in a row.

The most general form of hypothesis has two components: a pattern component and a guess-opposite component. The prediction of the hypothesis is obtained by finding the prediction of the pattern component. If the hypothesis has a guess-opposite component, then the prediction of the hypothesis is the opposite of the pattern prediction. If the hypothesis does not have a guess-opposite component, then the prediction of the hypothesis is the prediction of the pattern component. Thus, while the prediction of the pattern hypothesis "progression of C's" is always a C, the prediction of the hypothesis "guess-opposite-progression-of-C's" is always a P.

The Basic Cycle

The basic cycle of the model is as follows: The model uses an hypothesis to predict the event of trial t. The event is then presented. The model in Phase One "explains" the event of trial t with an explanation hypothesis. In Phase Two a prediction hypothesis for trial $t + 1$ is formed. The model uses this prediction hypothesis to predict trial $t + 1$. The event of trial $t + 1$ is presented, and the cycle continues.

Phase One

The basic motivation for this phase of the model is that the model must "explain" each event. An acceptable explanation is an hypothesis that could have predicted the event. The processing of Phase One is represented in the flow chart of Fig. 1.

The processing to determine the explanation hypothesis for trial t begins by testing whether the pattern component of the prediction hypothesis for trial t could have predicted the event of trial t correctly. If the pattern component could have predicted correctly, the pattern component is the explanation hypothesis. If the pattern component could not have predicted correctly, the pattern-change mechanism is evoked. Thus if the prediction hypothesis for trial t contained only a pattern component and the hypothesis predicted correctly, the explanation hypothesis for trial t is the prediction hypothesis for trial t. If the prediction hypothesis for trial t contained a guess-opposite component and the hypothesis predicted correctly, the pattern-change mechanism is evoked because the pattern component could not have predicted the event correctly by itself. If the

A. COULD THE PATTERN COMPONENT OF THE PREDICTION-HYPOTHESIS FOR TRIAL T HAVE PREDICTED THE EVENT OF TRIAL T CORRECTLY?
B. YES—EXPLANATION-HYPOTHESIS FOR TRIAL T IS THE PATTERN COMPONENT OF THE PREDICTION-HYPOTHESIS FOR TRIAL T.
C. NO—EVOKE PATTERNS THAT COULD HAVE PREDICTED THE EVENTS OF TRIALS T AND T-1 CORRECTLY. THE PATTERN OF THE PREDICTION-HYPOTHESIS FOR TRIAL T IS EVOKED IF IT COULD HAVE PREDICTED CORRECTLY THE EVENTS OF TRIAL T-1, T-2, AND T-3.
D. SELECT FROM THE SET OF EVOKED PATTERNS THAT PATTERN THAT HAS BEEN SELECTED MOST OFTEN ON PRECEDING TRIALS.
E. IS THE SELECTED PATTERN THE PATTERN COMPONENT OF THE PREDICTION-HYPOTHESIS FOR TRIAL T?
F. YES—EXPLANATION-HYPOTHESIS FOR TRIAL T IS THROW ME OFF THE SELECTED PATTERN.
G. NO—EXPLANATION-HYPOTHESIS FOR TRIAL T IS THE SELECTED PATTERN.

Figure 1. Phase One of binary choice model for DH.

prediction hypothesis for trial t was a guess-opposite hypothesis and it predicted incorrectly, the pattern component of the prediction-hypothesis becomes the explanation hypothesis for trial t. The motivation here is really quite simple although the explanation may sound involved. If, in this binary situation, the hypothesis that a pattern will change leads to an incorrect prediction, the pattern must have persisted; and the pattern is an acceptable explanation of the event. If the hypothesis that a pattern will change leads to a correct prediction, the pattern obviously did not persist; and the possibility of a new pattern is considered.

The pattern-change mechanism is evoked on trial t if the pattern component of the prediction hypothesis for trial t is unable to predict the event of trial t. The pattern-change mechanism consists of two parts. The first part evokes a subset of the nine patterns listed above. The second part of the pattern-change mechanism selects a single pattern out of the evoked set. A pattern is evoked, *i.e.,* considered as a possible explanation of the event of trial t, if the pattern can predict the events of trials t and t — 1. The pattern of the prediction hypothesis for trial t, *i.e.,* the pattern that cannot predict event t, is included in the evoked set if it can predict events t — 1, t — 2, and t — 3. Of the patterns that are evoked, the pattern that has been selected most often on prior trials is selected as the pattern component of the explanation hypothesis. If the pattern component of the prediction hypothesis for trial t is selected, then the explanation hypothesis is an antipattern hypothesis which is the model's interpretation of the subject's hypothesis "you have thrown me off the pattern" (cf. trial 9 of the protocol in the Appendix). The model interprets event t as an attempt to "throw me off" when the following three conditions are met: (1) the pattern is unable to predict the event of trial t; (2) the pattern is able to predict at least the three consecutive events of trials t — 1, t — 2, and t — 3; and (3) the pattern is also the most frequently selected of those patterns that are evoked.

Phase Two

While Phase One is concerned mainly with the processing of the pattern component of the hypothesis, Phase Two is concerned with the processing of the guess-opposite component. Phase Two is represented in the flow chart of Fig. 2.

If the prediction hypothesis for trial t contained a guess-opposite component, the guess-opposite component is processed in a fashion quite analogous to the processing of the pattern component in Phase One. If the antipattern prediction hypothesis for trial t predicted the event of trial t correctly, the guess-opposite component is retained, and the prediction hypothesis for trial t + 1 is guess-opposite-the-pattern-of-the-explanation-hypothesis. If the antipattern prediction hypothesis for trial t predicted

H. DID THE PREDICTION-HYPOTHESIS FOR TRIAL T CONTAIN A GUESS-
    OPPOSITE COMPONENT?
    I. YES—DID THE PREDICTION-HYPOTHESIS FOR TRIAL T PREDICT
        THE EVENT OF TRIAL T CORRECTLY?
        J. YES—PREDICTION-HYPOTHESIS FOR TRIAL T+1 IS GUESS-
            OPPOSITE THE PATTERN COMPONENT OF THE EXPLANATION-
            HYPOTHESIS FOR TRIAL T.
        K. NO—DID THE PREDICTION HYPOTHESIS FOR TRIALS T–1 AND
            T–2 CONTAIN GUESS-OPPOSITE COMPONENTS AND WERE THE
            PREDICTIONS OF THE EVENTS OF THESE TRIALS CORRECT?
            L. YES—PREDICTION-HYPOTHESIS FOR TRIAL T+1 IS GUESS-
                OPPOSITE THE EXPLANATION-HYPOTHESIS FOR TRIAL T.
            M. NO—PREDICTION-HYPOTHESIS FOR TRIAL T+1 IS THE
                EXPLANATION-HYPOTHESIS FOR TRIAL T.
    N. WILL THE EXPLANATION-HYPOTHESIS FOR TRIAL T CONTINUE?
        (SEE TEXT FOR AN EXPLANATION OF THIS TEST.)
        O. YES—PREDICTION-HYPOTHESIS FOR TRIAL T+1 IS THE
            EXPLANATION-HYPOTHESIS FOR TRIAL T.
        P. NO—PREDICTION-HYPOTHESIS FOR TRIAL T+1 IS GUESS-
            OPPOSITE THE EXPLANATION-HYPOTHESIS FOR TRIAL T.
Q. PREDICT EVENT FOR TRIAL T+1.

Figure 2. Phase Two of binary choice model for DH.

the event of trial t incorrectly, the guess-opposite component is considered for retention in a fashion analogous to the "throw-me-off" consideration for patterns. If the prediction hypotheses for trial t — 1 and t — 2 had guess-opposite components and these hypotheses predicted correctly, then the guess-opposite component is retained for the prediction hypothesis of trial t + 1. If these conditions are not fulfilled, the guess-opposite component is dropped; and the prediction hypothesis for trial t + 1 is the explanation hypothesis for trial t.

If the prediction hypothesis for trial t did not contain a guess-opposite component, the model considers whether or not the guess-opposite component should be introduced on trial t + 1. The model makes this decision on the basis of its past experience. It determines the number of consecutive events including and preceding the event of trial t that can be predicted by the explanation hypothesis for trial t. This number will be called N_1. Then the model searches its memory backward from the last trial included in N_1 to find a trial for which the explanation hypothesis was the same as the explanation hypothesis for trial t. Then the model determines the number of contiguous events including, preceding, and following this prior occurrence of the explanation hypothesis of trial t that can be predicted by this hypothesis. This number will be called N_2. If $N_2 = N_1$, the model decides that the explanation hypothesis for trial t will not be the prediction-hypothesis for trial t + 1. The prediction hypothesis for trial t + 1 becomes guess-opposite-the-explanation-hypothesis for trial t. If $N_2 > N_1$, the model decides that the explanation hypothesis for trial t will be the prediction hypothesis for trial t + 1. If $N_1 > N_2$, the model decides that this prior occurrence of the explanation hypothesis for trial t is really not pertinent and continues to search its memory for an occurrence of the explanation hypothesis where $N_2 \geqq N_1$. If no such occurrence can be found, the prediction hypothesis for trial t + 1 is the explanation hypothesis for trial t.

Predicting with the Models

Models of individual behavior like the one described for DH can be used to predict the same series of binary events that the subject was asked to predict. The predictions and hypotheses of the model—the model's protocol—can then be compared to the subject's protocol. The model does not speak idiomatic English, and so the comparison is made between the machine's protocol and a suitably coded version of the subject's protocol.

```
A. COULD THE PATTERN COMPONENT OF THE PREDICTION-HYPOTHESIS
   FOR TRIAL T HAVE PREDICTED THE EVENT OF TRIAL T CORRECTLY?
B. YES—EXPLANATION-HYPOTHESIS FOR TRIAL T IS THE PATTERN
   COMPONENT OF THE PREDICTION-HYPOTHESIS FOR TRIAL T.
         *  1. DID SUBJECT'S EXPLANATION-HYPOTHESIS
         *        FOR TRIAL T CONTAIN PATTERN COMPONENT
         *        OF THE PREDICTION-HYPOTHESIS FOR TRIAL T?      120
         *        YES—GO TO 6.                                   117
         *        NO—ERROR—FAILURE TO EVOKE PATTERN-
         *        CHANGE MECHANISM. GO TO C.                       3
C. NO—EVOKE PATTERNS THAT COULD HAVE PREDICTED THE EVENTS
   OF TRIALS T AND T-1 CORRECTLY. THE PATTERN OF THE
   PREDICTION-HYPOTHESIS FOR TRIAL T IS EVOKED IF IT COULD
   HAVE PREDICTED CORRECTLY THE EVENTS OF TRIALS T-1, T-2,
   AND T-3.
         *  2. WAS THE PATTERN OF THE SUBJECT'S EXPLANATION-
         *        HYPOTHESIS FOR TRIAL T EVOKED?                  78
         *        YES—GO TO D.                                    61
         *        NO—ERROR—FAILURE TO EVOKE PATTERN.
         *        ADD SUBJECT'S PATTERN TO EVOKED SET
         *        AND CONTINUE.                                   17
D. SELECT FROM THE SET OF EVOKED PATTERNS THAT PATTERN THAT
   HAS BEEN SELECTED MOST OFTEN ON PRECEDING TRIALS.
         *  3. WAS THE PATTERN OF THE SUBJECT'S EXPLA-
         *        NATION-HYPOTHESIS FOR TRIAL T SELECTED?         78
         *        YES—GO TO E.                                    64
         *        NO—ERROR—FAILURE TO SELECT PATTERN.
         *        REPLACE INCORRECT PATTERN WITH SUBJECT'S
         *        PATTERN AND CONTINUE.                           14
E. IS THE SELECTED PATTERN THE PATTERN COMPONENT OF THE
   PREDICTION-HYPOTHESIS FOR TRIAL T?
F. YES—EXPLANATION-HYPOTHESIS FOR TRIAL T IS THROW ME OFF
   THE SELECTED PATTERN.
         *  4. DID SUBJECT'S EXPLANATION-HYPOTHESIS
         *        FOR TRIAL T CONTAIN THROW-ME-OFF?               27
         *        YES— GO TO H.                                   26
         *        NO—ERROR—INCORRECT EVOCATION OF
         *        THROW-ME-OFF. DELETE THROW-ME-OFF
         *        AND GO TO H.                                     1
G. NO—EXPLANATION-HYPOTHESIS FOR TRIAL T IS THE
   SELECTED PATTERN.
         *  5. DID SUBJECT'S EXPLANATION-HYPOTHESIS
         *        FOR TRIAL T CONTAIN THROW-ME-OFF?               51
         *        YES—ERROR—FAILURE TO EVOKE THROW-ME-
         *        OFF. INSERT THROW-ME-OFF AND GO TO H.            3
         *        NO—GO TO H.                                     48
         *  6. DID SUBJECT'S EXPLANATION-HYPOTHESIS
         *        FOR TRIAL T CONTAIN THROW-ME-OFF?              117
         *        YES—ERROR—FAILURE TO EVOKE THROW-ME-
         *        OFF. INSERT THROW-ME-OFF AND GO TO H.            3
         *        NO—GO TO H.                                    114
```

Figure 3. Summary of behavior of Phase One of binary choice model for DH adapted for conditional prediction.

H. DID THE PREDICTION-HYPOTHESIS FOR TRIAL T CONTAIN A GUESS-OPPOSITE COMPONENT?

    I. YES—DID THE PREDICTION-HYPOTHESIS FOR TRIAL T PREDICT THE EVENT OF TRIAL T CORRECTLY?

        J. YES—PREDICTION-HYPOTHESIS FOR TRIAL T+1 IS GUESS-OPPOSITE THE PATTERN COMPONENT OF THE EXPLANATION-HYPOTHESIS FOR TRIAL T.

            * 7. DID SUBJECT'S PREDICTION-HYPOTHESIS
            *   FOR TRIAL T+1 CONTAIN GUESS-OPPOSITE
            *   COMPONENT?   6
            *   YES—GO TO 12.   5
            *   NO—ERROR—INCORRECT RETENTION OF
            *   GUESS-OPPOSITE COMPONENT. DELETE
            *   GUESS-OPPOSITE AND GO TO 12.   1

    K. NO—DID THE PREDICTION HYPOTHESIS FOR TRIALS T-1 AND T-2 CONTAIN GUESS-OPPOSITE COMPONENTS AND WERE THE PREDICTIONS OF THE EVENTS OF THESE TRIALS CORRECT?

        L. YES—PREDICTION-HYPOTHESIS FOR TRIAL T+1 IS GUESS-OPPOSITE THE EXPLANATION-HYPOTHESIS FOR TRIAL T.

            * 8. DID SUBJECT'S PREDICTION-HYPOTHESIS
            *   FOR TRIAL T+1 CONTAIN GUESS-OPPOSITE
            *   COMPONENT?   2
            *   YES—GO TO 12.   2
            *   NO—ERROR—INCORRECT RETENTION OF
            *   GUESS-OPPOSITE COMPONENT. DELETE
            *   GUESS-OPPOSITE AND GO TO 12.   0

        M. NO—PREDICTION-HYPOTHESIS FOR TRIAL T+1 IS THE EXPLANATION-HYPOTHESIS FOR TRIAL T.

            * 9. DID SUBJECT'S PREDICTION-HYPOTHESIS
            *   FOR TRIAL T+1 CONTAIN GUESS-OPPOSITE
            *   COMPONENT?   12
            *   YES—ERROR—FAILURE TO KEEP GUESS-
            *   OPPOSITE COMPONENT. INSERT GUESS-
            *   OPPOSITE AND GO TO 12.   1
            *   NO—GO TO 12.   11

N. WILL THE EXPLANATION-HYPOTHESIS FOR TRIAL T CONTINUE? (SEE TEXT FOR AN EXPLANATION OF THIS TEST.)

    O. YES—PREDICTION-HYPOTHESIS FOR TRIAL T+1 IS THE EXPLANATION-HYPOTHESIS FOR TRIAL T.

        *10. DID SUBJECT'S PREDICTION-HYPOTHESIS
        *   FOR TRIAL T+1 CONTAIN GUESS-OPPOSITE
        *   COMPONENT?   136
        *   YES—ERROR—FAILURE TO EVOKE GUESS-
        *   OPPOSITE COMPONENT. INSERT GUESS-
        *   OPPOSITE AND GO TO 12.   10
        *   NO—GO TO 12.   126

    P. NO—PREDICTION-HYPOTHESIS FOR TRIAL T+1 IS GUESS-OPPOSITE THE EXPLANATION-HYPOTHESIS FOR TRIAL T.

        *11. DID SUBJECT'S PREDICTION-HYPOTHESIS
        *   FOR TRIAL T+1 CONTAIN GUESS-OPPOSITE
        *   COMPONENT?   39
        *   YES—GO TO 12.   2
        *   NO—ERROR—INCORRECT SELECTION OF
        *   GUESS-OPPOSITE. DELETE GUESS-OPPOSITE
        *   AND CONTINUE.   37
        *12. WAS PATTERN OF SUBJECT'S EXPLANATION-
        *   HYPOTHESIS FOR TRIAL T THE SAME AS
        *   THE PATTERN OF THE SUBJECT'S PREDICTION-
        *   HYPOTHESIS FOR TRIAL T+1?   195
        *   YES—GO TO Q.   192
        *   NO—ERROR—FAILURE TO CHANGE PATTERN.
        *   INSERT SUBJECT'S PATTERN IN PREDICTION-
        *   HYPOTHESIS FOR TRIAL T+1 AND CONTINUE.   3

Q. PREDICT EVENT FOR TRIAL T+1.

        *13. DID SUBJECT PREDICT SAME EVENT?   195
        *   YES—GO TO A.   193
        *   NO—ERROR—INCORRECT PREDICTION.
        *   CORRECT AND GO TO A.   2

Figure 4. Summary of behavior of Phase Two of binary choice model for DH adapted for conditional prediction.

The model's protocol can be generated by presenting the model with the events in the same way the subject was presented with the events in the binary choice experiment; or the computer can take the experimenter's role, too, if suitable precautions are taken to prevent the model from peeking. However, this straightforward method of simulating the subject's behavior raises difficulties. These difficulties are identical to those of getting a chess or checker program to play a book game (Newell, Shaw and Simon, 1959c; Samuel 1959a). Because the decision of the chess or checker program at move m depends on its decisions at the preceding moves, m — 1, m — 2, . . . , such a program, when it is playing a book game, must be "set back on the track" if its move deviates from the book move. The program and the book must have the same history if the program is to have a fair chance to make the same decision as that made in the book game. This "setting back on the track" may involve resetting a large number of parameters as well as changing the move itself. Elsewhere, I have called this "setting-back-on-the-track" technique *conditional prediction*. The prediction of the model is conditional on the preceding decisions of the model being·the same as those of the subject it is trying to predict (Feldman, 1962).

The application of the conditional prediction technique to binary choice models such as the one described above for the subject DH involves (1) comparing the program's behavior and the subject's behavior at every possible point, (2) recording the differences between the behaviors, and (3) imposing the subject's decision on the model where necessary. A type of monitor system is imposed on the program to perform these functions. The model for DH with the conditional prediction system controls is represented in Figs. 3 and 4. An example will help clarify these figures. In Fig. 3, after each decision by the model to keep the pattern of the prediction hypothesis for trial t for the explanation hypothesis for trial t (B), this decision is compared to the subject's decision (1). If the model's decision was different from that of the subject, control is transferred to the pattern-change mechanism (3 trials). If the model's decision was the same as that of the subject, control is transferred to another part of the monitor (117 trials). Figures 3 and 4 only contain the results for 195 trials because the model began at trial 6.

Conclusions

Deficiencies of the Models

The model for DH and the similar models that have been constructed to simulate the behavior of two other subjects in the binary choice experiment (Feldman, 1959) are deficient in several respects. First of all, the comparison of the behavior of the model to that behavior of the subject from which the model was developed is, of course, not a very good test of the model. This type of comparison only yields some indication of the adequacy of the model and its components. Comparison of the behavior of the model to sequences of behavior of the subject not used in constructing the model awaits correction of some of the deficiencies mentioned below.

The segment of the model which has the highest number of errors relative to the number of times it is used is the guess-opposite segment (see Fig. 4). The subject certainly exhibits this type of behavior, but the model does not very often predict "guess opposite" when the subject does.

The pattern-change segment has a better error record, but it raises another issue. This segment is actually a selection device. A pattern is selected from the list of patterns that the subject uses. A more elegant pattern-change mechanism would generate a pattern out of the preceding sequence of events and some basic concepts. One of these concepts might be that patterns with equal numbers of P's and C's are preferred to alternation patterns with unequal numbers of P's and C's, all other things being equal.

The models have no mechanisms for making perceptual errors—"seeing" one symbol when another has occurred. Examination of the protocol of DH (Appendix) indicates that he does sometimes think that a C is a P (*e.g.,* trial 196).

The models do not have a sufficiently rich repertoire of hypotheses. Subjects entertain more types of hypotheses about the event series than the two types, pattern and antipattern used in the model for DH. Some subjects entertain more sophisticated hypotheses. For example, one subject was able to detect the fact that a series of events was randomized in blocks of ten trials, *i.e.,* the series had 7 P's and 3 C's in each block of ten trials.

Some evidence also exists that when suitably motivated by money, some subjects in a binary choice experiment will predict the most frequent event on each trial. Models for these subjects require statements of the conditions under which subjects abandon testing other hypotheses or at least abandon testing hypotheses by using them to predict events. Hypotheses could still be considered and tested without using them to predict events.

Contributions of the Models

The consequences of computer simulation for the study of human behavior have been discussed at some length in several places, and I have made a limited statement of my views on this matter in another place (Feldman, 1962). It will suffice then to discuss some of the implications of the work reported here for our understanding of behavior. The computer models of binary choice behavior are relatively simple computer programs; however, they are relatively complex psychological models. A widely accepted view of binary choice behavior has been the idea of verbal conditioning embodied in the stochastic learning model. In its simplest form, this model says the subject's probability of predicting E_1 or E_2 in the binary choice experiment is an exponentially weighted moving average over preceding events. The verbal conditioning model is hardly consistent with the hypothesis-testing behavior exhibited by DH and a dozen other subjects for whom I have protocols. Protocols of group behavior in the binary choice experiment made available to me by David G. Hays are also consistent with the general idea of hypothesis-testing. Other inadequacies of the verbal conditioning model and evidence for hypothesis-testing models have been discussed elsewhere (Feldman, 1959).

The computer has provided the exponents of hypothesis-testing models of behavior with the means for studying and testing these complex models. Oversimplified explanations of human behavior can no longer be justified on the grounds that the means for studying complex models do not exist. Hopefully, the use of computers to simulate human behavior can extend man's intellect by helping him study his own behavior.

Appendix: Protocol of Subject DH[1]

(All right, now I'll read the instructions to you. I'm going to show you a series of symbols. They will either be a P symbol or a C symbol. Before each word I'll give the signal NOW. When you hear the signal NOW, tell me what symbol you expect will occur on the next trial and why you selected that symbol. That's the purpose of the tape recorder. Take your time. After you have given me your guess, I will show you the correct symbol. Your goal is to anticipate each word as accurately as you can. Please . . . Well, do you have any questions?) Primarily, I just guess whether it'll be a P or a C. (That's it.) But this explaining why I think so. It can be little more than—I think it'll be this, I guess, I have a feeling. How more involved can it be than that? (Well, whatever reasons you have. If those are the only reasons that occur to you as you go thru this, those will be the only reasons. Maybe they won't. OK, we'll try a few and then if you have any questions . . .)

(Now what do you expect the first symbol will be?) P. (OK, the 1st symbol is a C.)
(OK, now what do you expect the 2d symbol will be?) It'll be a P. (Why?) It's pictured in my mind. (OK, the 2d symbol is a C.)
I'll say a C. (Why?) Primarily this time because I'm trying to outguess you. (OK, the 3d symbol is a C.)
(What do you say for the 4th symbol?) I'll say C again. (Why?) This

time I feel it'll be a C. (The 4th symbol is a C. When you give your answer, if you say, "I think the 5th one will be something," it'll be easier to check the tape against the answer sheet.)

(What do you think the 5th one will be?) The 5th one will be a P. (Why is that?) I feel it'll be a P, that's all. (The 5th one is a C.)

(What do you think the 6th one will be?) The 6th one will be a C because you've been giving me C's all along, and I don't think this progression will end. (The 6th one is a C.)

(What do you think the 7th one will be?) The 7th one will be a C because I don't think the progression will be broken. (OK, the 7th one was a C.)

The 8th one will be a C for the same reason. You won't break the progression. (OK, the 8th one is a P.)

(What do you think the 9th one will be?) The 9th one will be a C. (Why is that?) I think that you just gave me the P to throw me off and you'll continue the progression. (The 9th one is a C. Oh, one thing, can you see these cards?) Yes. (Can you see me writing?) No, I can't. (OK.) I'm not looking. (Well, you can look at these cards. I want you to see I'm not picking these out of my head. This set has been predetermined.)

All right. This one will be a P. The 10th one will be a P. (Why is that?) I feel that the progression will start to mix up now. (The 10th one is a C.)

(What do you think the 11th one will be?) The 11th one will be a C. You're continuing the progression. (The 11th one is a C.)

(What do you think the 12th one will be?) The 12th one will be a C because you're continuing the progression. (The 12th one is a P.)

The 13th one will be a C. The 12th one was a P. You were trying to throw me off. The progression will continue. (The 13th one is a P.)

The 14th one will be a P. You're beginning a new progression with P's. (The 14th one is a P.)

The 15th one will be a P. You're still continuing the progression. (The 15th one is a P.)

(What about the 16th one?) The 16th one will be a C. . . . to throw me off now. (The 16th one is a C.)

The 17th one will be a C. You're going to see if I'll revert to the progression of P's. (The 17th one is a C.)

The 18th one will be a P. You're going to break this progression of C's. (The 18th one is a C.)

The 19th one will be a P. You're going to get off this progression of C's. (The 19th one is a P.)

The 20th one will be a P. You're going to try to throw me off trying to make me think that all—think you're going back to the other progression which I'm confused about now. I don't remember what the last one was—C, I believe. (The 20th one is a P.)

The 21st one will be a C. You won't continue with the progression of P's. (The 21st one is a P.)

The 22d one is a C. You're doing this so that I might think the P progression will continue. (The 22d one is a C.)

The 23d one will be a C. You're trying to make me think that the next one will be a P—going back to the old progression. (The 23d one is a C.)

The 24th one will be a C. You're going to continue the progression of C's. (The 24th one was a C.)

The 25th one is a C. You're still going to continue the progression of C's. (The 25th one is a C.)

The 26th one is still a C. You'll continue the progression. (The 26th one is a C.)

The 27th one is a P. You'll break the progression now. (The 27th one is a C.)

The 28th one will be a P. You're going to break the progression now. (The 28th one is a C.)

The 29th one is a C. You're continuing the progression. (The 29th one is a C.)

The 30th is a C. You'll still continue the progression. (The 30th is a C.)

The 31st is a C. You'll continue the progression. (The 31st is a C.)

The 32d is a C. You'll still continue the progression. (The 32d is a P.)

The 33d is a C. You gave me a P last time to throw me off. (The 33d is a C.)

The 34th is a C. You'll continue the progression. (The 34th is a C.)

The 35th is a P. You're going to throw me off the progression. (The 35th is a C.)

The 36th is a C. You'll continue the progression. (The 36th is a C.)

The 37th is a C. You'll continue the progression. (The 37th is a C.)

The 38th is a C. You'll continue the progression. (The 38th is a C.)

The 39th is a C. You'll continue the progression. (The 39th is a C.)

The 40th is a C. You'll continue the progression. (The 40th is a C.)

The 41st is a C. You'll continue the progression. (The 41st is a C.)

The 42d is a C. You'll continue the progression. (The 42d is a C.)

The 43d is a C. You'll still continue the progression. (The 43d is a C.)

The 44th is a C. You'll still continue the progression. (The 44th is a C.)

The 45th is a C. You'll still continue the progression. (The 45th is a C.)

The 46th is a C. You'll still continue the progression. (The 46th is a C.)

The 47th will be a P. You'll now break the progression. (The 47th is a C.)

The 48th will be a C. You'll go back to the old progression. (The 48th is a C.)

The 49th is a C. You'll continue the progression. (The 49th is a C.)

The 50th is a C. You'll continue the progression. (The 50th is a P.)

The 51st will be a C. You gave me the P to throw me off. (The 51st is a P.)

The 52d is a P. You've begun a progression of P's. (The 52d is a C.)

The 53d is a P. You gave me a C to throw me off. (The 53d is a C.)

The 54th is a C. You'll continue the progression of C's. (The 54th is a C.)

The 55th is a C. You'll still continue the progression. (The 55th is a C.)

The 56th is a C. You'll continue the progression. (The 56th is a P.)

57 is a P. The P will throw me off the progression thinking you had tried to throw me off the C progression with your last P. (57 you said was a P?) P. (57 was a C.)

58 is a C. You began a progression of C's. (58 is a P.)

59 is a C. You're still trying to throw me off with the C's. (59 is a P.)

60 will be a P. You're beginning a progression of P's. (60 is a C.)

61 is a P. You're zigzagging between P's and C's. (61 is a P.)

62 is a C. You'll continue the oscillation. (62 is a C.)

63 is a C—rather 63 is a P because of the oscillation pattern. (63 is a P.)

64 is a C because of the oscillation pattern. (64 is a C.)

65 is a P because of the oscillation pattern. (65 is a C.)

66 is a C. You've begun a progression of C's. (66 is a P.)

67 will be a C. You're oscillating again. (67 is a C.)

68 is a C. You're having a different type of oscillation—2 C's between a P. (68 is a P.)

69 is a C. You're oscillating with C's and P's. (69 is a C.)

70 will be a P. It's the alternate symbol. (70 is a P.)

71 will be a C because of the oscillation sequence. (71 is a C.)

72 will be a P because of the oscillation sequence. (72 is a C.)

73 will be a C. You've begun a new progression of C's. (73 is a C.)

74 is a C. You're continuing the progression. (74 is a C.)

75 is a C. You're still continuing with the progression. (75 is a C.)

76 is still a C. You're continuing with the progression. (76 is a C.)

77 is a C. You're still continuing with the progression. (77 is a C.)

78 is a C. The progression is continuing. (78 is a P.)

79 is a C. The P is to throw me off. The progression continues. (79 is a C.)

80 is a C. The progression will continue. (80 is a C.)

81 is a C. The progression continues. (81 is a P.)

82 will be a C. You're alternating now with C's and P's. (82 is a P.)

83 is a P. You've begun a progression of P's. (83 is a C.)

84 will be a C. The P's were given to throw me off. (84 is a P.)

85 will be a P. You've begun a new alternating sequence. (85 is a P.)

86 will be a C. You're following with a C and 2 P's. Another C will come. (86 is a C.)

87 will be a P. You'll follow the same sequence. (87 is a C.)

88 will be a P. You've begun a sequence of 2 C's and a P. (88 is a C.)

89 is a C. You've begun a new progression of C's. (89 is a C.)

90 is a C. You'll continue the progression. (90 is a C.)

91 is a C. The progression continues. (91 is a C.)

92 is a C. The progression continues. (92 is a P.)

93 is a P. The P's given to me previously to make me think that the progression was being broken and that you would revert to it after the P. The next one will be a P. (93 is a C.)

94 will be a C. You've gone back to the C progression. (94 you say now is a C.) 94 is a C. (OK, 94 is a C.)

95 is a C. You've begun a progression of C's. (95 is a P.)

96 will be a C. You're alternating now with C's and P's. (96 is a P.)

97 is a C. You've begun a progression of a C and 2 P's. (97 is a P.)

98 is a P. You've begun a progression of P's. (98 is a C.)

99 is a C. You've begun a progression of 3 P's and 3 C's. You've already had the 3 P's. 98 (sic) will be a C. (That was . . . 99 is going to be a C. You said. 99 is a C.)

(What's 100?) 100 will be a C. It follows the progression. (100 is a C.)

101 will still be a C. Continue the progression of 3 P's and 3 C's. (101 is a C.)

102 will be a C. You've begun a progression of C's. (102 is a C.)

103 is a C. You'll continue the progression of C's. (103 is a C.)

104 is a C. You'll continue with the progression. (104 is a C.)

105 will be a C. You'll continue the progression. (105 is a C.)

106 will be a P. You'll break the progression now. (106 was a C.)

107 will be a C. You'll continue the progression. (107 was a P.)

108 will be a C. You gave me the P to throw me off. The progression will continue. (108 is a C.)

109 will be a C. You'll continue the progression. (109 was a P.)

110 will be a C. You're alternating with C's and P's. (110 is a C.)

111 will be a P. You'll continue the alternation. (111 was a P.)

112 will be a C. You'll continue the alternation. (112 was a P.)

113 will be a C. You've begun a progression of a C and 2 P's. (113 is a P.)

114 will be a P. You've begun a progression of P's. (114 is a P.)

115 will be a P. You'll continue the progression. (115 is a C.)

116 will be a P. The C was given to throw me off. (116 is a C.)

117 is a C. You've begun a progression of 4 P's and 4 C's. (117 is a P.)

118 will be a P. The progression has changed from 4 P's and 4 C's to 4 P's and 3 C's. (118 is a C.)

119 will be a P. You're alternating with C's and P's. (119 is a C.)

120 will be a C. You're continuing the progression. (120 is a P.)

121 will be a P. You have a progression of 2 C's and 2 P's. (121 is a P.)

122 will be a C. You'll continue this progression of 2 and 2. (122 is a C.)

123 will be a C. You're continuing the progression. (Of what?) Of 2 C's and 2 P's. (123 is a C.)

124 will be a C. You've begun a progression of C's. (124 is a C.)

124 (sic) will be a C. You're continuing the progression. (125 is a C.)

126 will be a C. You're continuing the progression. (126 is a P.)

127 will be a C. You gave me the P to throw me off. (127 is a P.)

128 will be a P. You've begun a progression of P's. (128 is a C.)

129 will be a C. You've begun a progression of 2 P's and 2 C's. (129 was a C.)

130 will be a C. You've begun a progression of C's. (130 is a P.)

131 will be a P. You're continuing the progression of 2 P's and 2 C's. (131 is a C.)

132 will be a P. You're alternating the signs now. (132 is a C.)

133 will be a C. You've begun a sequence of C's. (133 is a C.)

134 will be a C. You're continuing the sequence. (134 is a C.)

135 is a C. You're continuing with the progression. (135 is a P.)

136 will be a P. You've begun . . . you're trying to throw me off now with a 2d P. Think there would be only one P. (136 is a C.)

137 is a C. You're going to continue with the progression of C's. (137 is a C.)

138 is a C. You'll continue the progression. (138 is a C.)

139 is a C. You'll continue the progression. (139 is a P.)

140 is a C. The P was given to throw me off. (140 is a P.)

141 is a C. You gave me the 2 C's (sic) for the same reason as the previous time you had given me the 2 C's 'er 2 P's . . . (141 is a C.)

142 is a C. You'll continue with the progression. (142 is a C.)

143 is a C. You'll continue with the progression. (143 is a C.)

144 is a C. You'll continue with the progression. (144 is a C.)

145 is a P. You'll break the progression. (145 is a C.)

146 is a C. You'll continue the progression. (146 is a C.)

147 is a C. You'll continue the progression. (147 is a C.)

148 is a C. You'll continue the progression. (148 is a C.)

149 is a C. You'll continue the progression. (149 is a C.)

150 is a C. You'll still continue the progression. (150 is a C.)

151 is a C. You'll still continue the progression. (151 is a C.)

152 will be a P. You'll break the progression. (152 is a C.)

153 is a C. You'll continue the progression. (153 is a P.)

154 is a C. You've broken the progression and you'll revert to it now. (154 is a C.)

155 is a C. You'll continue the progression. (155 is a P.)

156 is a C. You're alternating with P's and C's. (156 is a C.)

157 is a C. The alternation of P's and C's was to throw me off the progression of C's. The C progression will continue. (157 is a P.)

158 is a C. You're still going back to C sequence. (158 is a C.)

159 is a C. You're still going to continue this sequence. (159 is a P.)

160 is a C. You have an alternating sequence of P's and C's. (160 is a C.)

161 will be a P. You'll continue to alternate. (161 is a P.)

162 will be a C. You'll continue this oscillation. (162 is a P.)

163 will be a C. You'll continue the alternation. (163 is a C.)

164 will be a P. You'll continue the alternation. (164 is a C.)

165 will be a P. You'll go back to the alternation. (165 is a C.)

166 will be a C. You've begun a sequence of C's. (166 is a C.)

167 will be a C. You've begun a sequence of C's. (167 is a P.)

168 will be a P. You've begun a sequence of 2 C's and 2 P's. (168 is a C.)

169 is a C. The previous P's were given to throw me off. You'll continue the sequence of C's. (169 is a C.)

170 will be a C. You'll continue the sequence. (170 is a P.)

171 will be a P. You'll begin a sequence of P's. (171 is a P.)

172 will be a C. You'll revert to the C's. (172 is a C.)

173 will be a C. You're alternating with 2 P's and 2 C's. (173 is a P.)

174 will be a C. The alternation is a C and a P. (174 is a C.)

175 will be a P. You'll continue this alternation. (175 is a C.)

176 will be a C. You've begun a sequence of C's. (176 is a P.)

177 will be a C. You'll continue with the progression of C's. (177 is a P.)

178 will be a C. You've begun a progression of 2 P's and 2 C's. (What did you say 178 was?) A C. (178 is a C.)

179 will be a C. You'll continue with another C to complete the sequence of 2 P's and 2 C's. (179 is a C.)

180 will be a P. You'll continue this sequence. (180 is a C.)

181 is a C. You've begun a sequence of C's. (181 is a C.)

182 is a C. You'll continue the sequence. (182 is a C.)

183 is a C. You'll continue the sequence. (183 is a P.)

184 will be a C. The P was given to throw me off. (184 is a C.)

185 is a C. You'll continue the sequence of C's. (185 is a C.)

186 will be a C. You'll continue the sequence. (186 is a C.)

187 will be a C. You'll continue the sequence. (187 is a C.)

188 is a C. You'll continue the sequence. (188 is a C.)

189 is a C. You'll continue the sequence. (189 is a P.)

190 will be a C. The P was given to throw me off. (190 is a C.)

191 will be a C. The double P (sic) was given to throw me off a little more. (191 is a C.)

192 is a C. You've . . . been giving me a sequence of 2 P's and 2 C's. (192 is a C.)

192 (sic) is a P. You're continuing the sequence of 2 P's and 2 C's. (193 is a C.)

194 is a C. You've begun a sequence of C's. (194 is a C.)

195 is a C. You'll continue the sequence. (195 is a P.)

196 will be a P. You have a sequence here of inserting 2 P's. (196 is a C.)

197 is a C. The P was given to throw me off. (197 is a C.)

198 will be a C. You'll continue the sequence. (198 is a C.)

199 is a C. You'll continue the sequence. (199 is a C.)

200 will be a C. You'll continue the sequence. (200 is a C.)

A MODEL OF THE
TRUST INVESTMENT PROCESS

by Geoffrey P. E. Clarkson

The object of this study is the investment of trust funds held by banks in the United States—funds that currently amount to nearly $60 billions. The purpose of our model is to simulate the process employed in the investment of trust funds in common stocks. When making a decision a trust officer in a bank is confronted with a large assortment of information. Information abounds on the operation of firms and the market valuation of their stocks, and published reports make predictions about the future state of the general economy and stock market. When an investor acts in an agency or fiduciary capacity, legal restrictions and the desires of his client must also be considered. These factors, when evaluated and combined into an investment program, ultimately result in a decision to buy specific quantities of particular stocks and bonds. Thus, an investor choosing a portfolio is processing information: he sorts the useful from the irrelevant, and decides which parts of the total information flow are most important.

The investment process is a problem in decision-making under uncertainty. Our model, written as a computer program, simulates the procedures used in choosing investment policies for particular accounts, in evaluating the alternatives presented by the market, and in selecting the required portfolios. The analysis is based on the operations at a medium-sized national bank[1] and the decision-maker of our model is the trust investment officer.[2] We require our simulation model to select portfolios

---

[1] The trust assets of this bank are approximately equal to the average for all national banks.

[2] It should be noted that our model reflects the behavior of one investor and hence

using the same information that is available to the trust officer at the time his decisions are made.

Postulates and Data for the Model

Since our model is a theory of individual decision-making behavior, the method of analysis is based on the theory of human problem-solving (Newell, Shaw, and Simon, 1958a). In keeping with the postulates of this theory, the main postulates for the analysis of the investment decision process are that there exist:

1. A *memory* that contains lists of industries each of which has a list of companies associated with it. The memory also contains information associated with the general economy, industries, and individual companies.[3]

2. *Search* and *selection* procedures that perform the task of searching the lists of information stored in memory, selecting those bits that have the required attributes, regrouping the selected items of information into new lists, and performing algebraic operations when necessary. These procedures function in a manner similar to a clerk who prepares lists of stocks suitable for current investment by scanning a master list.

3. A *set of rules* or criteria that guide the decision-making process by stipulating when and how each decision process is to be used. The set of rules constitutes the structure of the decision processes for an individual investor. It might be compared to the "rules of thumb" of the traditional "expert," but there is an important difference—namely, the set of rules must be defined unambiguously.

In common with other problem-solving programs, the processes are used iteratively and recursively. Lists of industries and companies are searched for particular attributes; sublists are created, searched and divided again. For example, to obtain a high growth portfolio, the list of companies stored in memory is searched to obtain securities with the desired characteristics. Additional criteria are employed to narrow (or expand) this list. Further search and testing against desired criteria yields the specific selection of stocks to buy.

Like the investor it simulates, the program stores the final result (list)

may not describe the general case. The implications of this study for more general theories of investment are discussed in Clarkson (1962), chap. 8.

[3] Investors categorize companies by industry. Not all investors may associate identical companies with a given industry, but the process of classification by industry remains invariant as the primary basis for listing companies in the memory. The information associated with each company also varies among investors, but each may be represented as having a list of attributes with their values stored in memory, *e.g.* growth rate, dividend rate, price earnings ratio, expected earnings, expected yield, etc.

for future use. If the same problem reoccurs, the entire process need not be repeated. The list may be judged by present criteria, accepted, adapted to meet new conditions, or completely rejected. In the latter event the program would renew search and selection activity until a new list had been formed.

To define a model of trust investment behavior within this general framework we require the basic rules (operations) used in making a decision to purchase particular securities. To obtain these data, trust departments of several local banks are studied by interviewing departmental officers and by observing behavior at committee meetings called to review past and future decisions. Attention was then focused on an investment officer who was chiefly responsible for all decisions relevant to the choice of portfolios within a particular bank. The history of several accounts were examined and naïve behavioral models were constructed to help uncover these decision processes that appeared to be invariant among accounts.

In an attempt to confirm or refute these hypotheses, the trust officer was asked to permit "protocols" to be made of his decision processes.[4] These protocols recorded the trust officer's decision processes for accounts that arose in the course of his work. The decisions made during those problem sessions determined the particular securities that were purchased for those accounts.

Close inspection of the protocols revealed that many of the decisions pertaining to the formulation of expectations, and the evaluation of industries, companies and stocks were made before the selection of a particular portfolio began. In an attempt to discover how these prior decisions were made a new approach was taken. The trust officer was asked to read articles from financial journals and analysts' reports, to which he subscribed, and comment on the ideas, forecasts, facts, etc., presented in the articles. Protocols of these thought processes were more successful in that they revealed many of the decision processes subsumed in the earlier transcripts

On the basis of these data and analytic techniques, a model was constructed. The model considers the problem of investing the funds of new accounts in common stocks. It does not directly consider the problem of allocating the funds among bonds, preferreds, and common stocks. The trust investment model is stated in terms of a computer model and is presented in the next section.[5]

<hr>

[4] A "protocol" is a transcript of the verbalized thought and actions of a subject when the subject has been instructed to think or problem-solve aloud. Thus, the transcript is a record of the subject's thought processes while engaged in making a decision. Since a protocol is a detailed description of what a person does it avoids some of the problems inherent in interview and questionnaire techniques that ask the subject to state his reasons for behaving as he does. For further discussion see Newell, Shaw, Simon (1958a).

[5] The program is written in Information Processing Language V (Newell, 1961e).

The trust investment process can be divided into three parts: (a) the analysis and selection of a list of stocks suitable for current investment—the "A" List, (b) the formulation of an investment policy, and (c) the selection of a portfolio. Each of these sections can be also broken down into a number of subsections (see Fig. 1).

The process of selecting a current list of stocks [step (a)] entails an analysis of individual companies as well as an appreciation of the factors affecting their respective industries and the economy as a whole. The problem of formulating an investment policy [step (b)] involves a process that translates the information on the beneficiary or client into an investment goal that will yield the desired combination of income and/or appreciation. This process requires the trust investor to consider such things as the effect of taxes on the stream of income generated by the portfolio as well as the stability of that stream. The actual selection of a portfolio [step (c)] follows directly from steps (a) and (b). While the selection

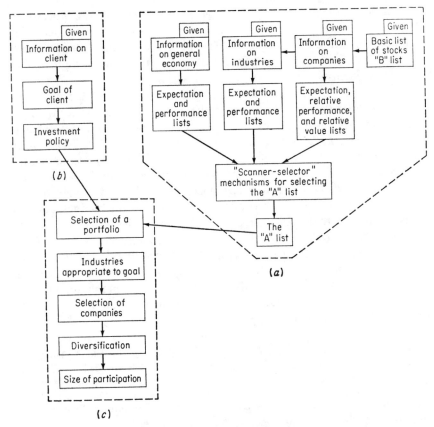

Figure 1. Structure of decision process.

procedure contains rules on diversification and on how to determine the size of participations, the essence of the process lies in carrying the prior analysis to its logical conclusion.

In presenting this model of trust investment behavior, we shall follow the outline of the process given in Fig. 1 so that each subsection as well as the interrelations can stand by themselves for critical appraisal.

Having outlined the investment process and the method of analysis used in constructing the model, the only question that needs to be examined before proceeding with a description of the model is the effect of the organization and the fiduciary relation on the trust investment process.[6]

Since banks are responsible for all investments made in their name, elaborate procedures are set up to review and approve all investment decisions.[7] Also, the necessity of being able to justify their investment decisions in a court of law has led trust investors to create a set of criteria with which to judge the quality of any given portfolio or investment. For all practical purposes these criteria can be reduced essentially to one maxim: A security is of investment quality *if and only if* it is being bought or is being held by other leading trust institutions.[8] Clearly, this maxim is circular in nature and if strictly true would preclude change. However, the smaller the bank the truer the maxim, which implies that innovations must come from the larger banks acting by themselves or in small groups. If innovations do not occur very frequently, the maxim then asserts that the general list of stocks that are considered suitable for trust investment will remain fairly stable over time. The addition of a further observation, namely, that trust investors eschew taking losses, *i.e.,* selling stocks whose prices have fallen below the purchase price, allows an even stronger prediction to be made. The basic list of stocks—the "B" List—that are considered to be suitable for trust investment by a particular bank will remain fairly stable over time, any changes being in the form of additions. Thus, for any given trust investor, the basic list of stocks from which he can choose is given to him by the historical record. At any particular point in time an investor selects stocks from a subset of his basic list. This subset

[6] As we are principally concerned with the investment of trust funds for individual accounts, the important constraints are those that are imposed on the investor by the banking institution and the fiduciary relation with the client.

[7] "All investments of trust funds shall be made, retained or disposed of only with the approval of the Trust Committee. . . . The Trust Committee shall, at least once during each period of twelve months, review all the assets held in or for each fiduciary account to determine their safety and current value and the advisability of retaining or disposing of them." Excerpt from the *Trust Manual* of a National Bank.

It is interesting to note that this Trust Committee is appointed by the Board of Directors and is composed of the President, the Vice-President in charge of investments, the Vice-President in charge of trusts, and other officials.

[8] By a simple substitution of words this maxim can roughly be applied to the composition of portfolios, *i.e.* the ratio of common stock to bonds and preferred stocks.

is a proper subset of the "B" List and is defined by a concept of relative valuation. As expectations, prices, yields, and other metrics change with time, so does the content of this subset which is called the "A" List.

Hence, institutional constraints reduce the problem of determining the list of stocks from which, at a given point in time, an investor actually chooses—the "A" List—to one of "stocks" and "flows." Since the "stocks" change slowly with time the model assumes them to be given and takes as part of its goal the analysis and prediction of the "flows."

1. Selection of the Current List of Stocks—The "A" List

In this section we shall present the data and the mechanisms that the model uses to evaluate and select the stocks for the "A" List. Unlike the model's processes for steps (*b*) and (*c*), the mechanisms described in this section are not intended to be a reproduction of the analytic procedures used by the trust officer each time he selects a new portfolio. To reproduce

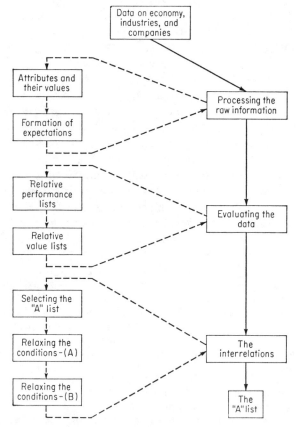

Figure 2. Selecting the "A" List.

only those procedures would require us to ignore all the data on each company that he has collected and processed in preceding years. To take the historical data into account, the model must employ a set of mechanisms that generate the same sorts of measures and comparative data that the trust officer actually employs when he is selecting a portfolio. Clearly, the trust investor (unlike the model) does not evaluate all companies at one time. But, our object is to use that set of mechanisms that yield the right kind of data and measures of performance. Thus, the processes described in this section should not be viewed as a complete simulation of what the trust officer does prior to each portfolio selection, but rather as an approximation of the processes he has used over the years in order to build up a set of measures by which the performance of a company can be judged. Our success in this respect will be tested later on.

In order to describe the processes that are involved in the selection of the "A" List it is necessary, at first, to treat some of the mechanisms as though they were independent of each other. While this is not in fact the case, the ways in which they are interrelated will be discussed after the data processing mechanisms have been described. To facilitate this explication a flow chart of the selection procedure is presented in Fig. 2.

1A. PROCESSING THE RAW INFORMATION

Although the information used to derive the current list of stocks is classified into three main categories, e.g., general economy, industry, and company, the processes by which the information is handled are roughly the same. Differences occur in the content of the information processed and the manner in which interrelations are formed, but the basic structure of the sorting and evaluating processes remains the same.

For each category there is a set of attributes that correspond to the important variables in that category. For example, for all companies the set of attributes consists of sales, earnings, cash flow per share, profit margin, working capital, price earnings ratio, dividend payout ratio, dividends per share, dividend yield, and prices. The values of these attributes are their numerical values, and these are determined by the information which is fed into the model. Since the values will reflect the changes that occur in economy, industry and company variables those that change frequently are readily distinguished from those that do not. Those that change infrequently with time reflect the general trend of the economy, industry, or company, while the others indicate those attributes that are more sensitive to short-run fluctuations. The mechanisms that derive these values are the same in all cases, and it is to these processes that attention is now directed.

1A1. Determination of Attributes and Their Values. All information, except that dealing with economy or industry forecasts, is fed into the model in numerical form. These data consist of the historical values of each attribute in the system for the last ten years.[9] The data are entered in the form of lists, and from these basic lists the model generates, for each attribute, three additional lists. The first of these lists contains the mean of the ten historical values. The second contains a set of nine values which record the rate of increase (or decrease) of each value in the historical record over the value immediately proceeding it. The third of these lists contains the average rate of change of the values for the entire ten year period. For each attribute, then, the model contains the four following lists of information:

(i) *Current Value.* This list contains the last ten annual values of each attribute arranged chronologically so that the most recent is at the head of the list.

(ii) *Ten-year Average.* Each time a new value is added to (i) a new average of the ten values is placed on this list. Thus, this list contains a ten year moving average of the values in (i).

(iii) *Recent Changes.* This list contains the rate of increase (or decrease) of each value in the Current Value List over the value immediately below it. Thus, if the values of the Current Value List are called x_i, where $i = 1, 2, \ldots , 10$, then the Recent Change List will have nine entries whose values will equal:

$$\frac{x_i - x_{i+1}}{x_{i+1}} \quad \text{where } i = 1, 2, \ldots , 9$$

(iv) *Average Rate of Change.* This list contains the average rate of change of the values on list (i) for the entire ten year period. Like list (ii), this is revised every time there is a new entry on the Current Value List.

Hence, the basic information which is given to the model is processed so that it is expressed in terms of rates of change and/or ratios which are directly comparable throughout the system.

1A2. The Formation of Expectations. Information on forecasts is fed into the model in two different forms. Forecasts for economy and industry attributes are converted for input into a three-valued scale "above," "below," or "equal to." The entry is based on the published predictions that the value for a given attribute is going to rise, fall, or stay the same over the next interval of time. Numerical data is not used in an attempt to avoid the chaos of averaging the array of forecasts found in financial literature.

For the analysis of company performance, however, numerical forecasts

[9] The attributes themselves are taken as given. They were derived by an analysis of trust investors' decision processes and by observing which variables are considered important by investment services.

The data for economy and industry attributes was taken from *Moody's Industrials, Review of Current Business,* and *Statistical Abstracts,* while data for company attributes was taken from the *Value Line Investment Survey.*

are needed, and in a further effort to avoid conflicting opinions all forecasts for company attributes are taken from the *Value Line Investment Survey.*

All forecast attributes have the current forecasts as their only value. Previous forecasts are not kept and the model takes each forecast at face value without making any attempt to judge its "goodness" or "record of success." This procedure may not be too realistic as it ignores the effects of personal preferences on perception. But, the model is not equipped to handle "second guessing" and other judgmental modifications and the information is assumed to be reliable. Before discussing the role of expectations in our model, it is necessary to mention some further behavioral characteristics of trust investors.

By and large, trust investment is long-term investment. As previously noted, trust investors do not engage in trading stocks for their clients, but look to the long-term growth of the economy and the market to justify their investments. This is not to say that they remain aloof from daily, monthly, or yearly fluctuations, but rather that their emphasis is on the analysis of industries and their respective companies. Their basic belief is that the market will eventually recognize a company's "true value." Hence, in general, trust investors analyze companies and not the market.

Clearly changes in the market do affect investor behavior, but the effects are more in keeping with a feedback mechanism than one where the investor acts on the basis of his own market forecasts. Thus, attributes containing forecasted information are included in this model, but they receive different amounts of attention depending on whether the attributes belong to the economy, industries, or specific companies. Since the content of the Expectation Lists varies as well as the form, these lists are described in turn.

(i) *Economy and Industry Expectation Lists.* For each attribute in both of these categories the Expectation Lists contain two entries. The first is the forecasted value for that attribute converted into the input form of "above," "below," or "equal to." The second is the first value on the Recent Change List—namely, the rate of change of that attribute for last year—converted into the same three-valued scale.[10] Hence Economy and Industry Expectation Lists contain pairs of "aboves," "belows," or "equals to" which under two possible sets of conditions will form a pattern of only "aboves" or "belows."

(ii) *Company Expectation Lists.* Expectation Lists exist for five of the ten company attributes.[11] These Expectation Lists contain one or two entries all of which are in numerical form. These entries are derived from

[10] In this case the three-valued scale is recording whether the rate of change for this attribute last year was positive, negative or zero.

[11] The five attributes which have forecasted values are: sales, earnings per share, cash flow per share, profit margin, and dividends per share.

the twelve-month and three- to five-year forecasts recorded in the model for these attributes. The first entry is on all Expectation Lists and is obtained by converting the twelve-month forecast into an expected rate of change. The second entry exists only for sales and earnings per share Expectation Lists and is obtained by converting the three- to five-year forecast into an expected average rate of change.

1B. EVALUATING THE DATA

Logically this section should contain all the procedures of evaluation used in this model. However, in order to simplify the problem of describing the actual mechanisms, the processes of evaluation have been divided into two parts. Those that pertain to the information within each major category, *i.e.,* economy, industry, and company, are examined here; those that involve the interrelations between these sections are discussed in Sec. 1c.

The model evaluates the data by creating two main lists: the Relative Performance List, and the Relative Value List. As these processes are described in some detail it is worth pausing for a moment to make a list of the information already gathered for each attribute of each company:

(i)   A list of the last ten values of the attribute
(ii) The mean of these ten values
(iii) A list of the rates of change of these values
(iv) The mean of these rates of change
(v)   For relevant attributes an Expectation List that contains the expected rate of change for the coming year and, in the case of the sales and the earnings per share attributes, the expected average rate of change for the next three to five years

Attention has been drawn to this information as the processes of evaluation use these data as inputs.

1B1. The Relative Performance List. In order to determine the relative performance of each company within its given industry a list is made for *each* of the basic lists for *each attribute* of the mean for that attribute for *each company.* Hence, for each attribute there is now a list of means each of which belongs to a particular company within a given industry. The average of this list of means is taken so that we now have a distribution of means for a given attribute, plus the mean of that distribution. The deviation of each mean from the distribution mean is calculated as a percentage deviation and is then converted into the three-valued scale "above," "below," or "equal to." These per cent deviations from the distribution mean are recorded on the Relative Performance List of each attribute.

To classify this process further let a_{ij} represent the class of all company attribute means where:

$i = 1, 2, \ldots, n$ represents the number of attributes for each company
$j = 1, 2, \ldots, m$ represents the number of companies for each industry

$$\text{Then the matrix } A_{n,m} = \begin{bmatrix} a_{11} & a_{12} & \cdots & a_{1m} \\ a_{21} & a_{22} & \cdots & a_{2m} \\ \cdot & & & \\ \cdot & & & \\ \cdot & & & \\ a_{n1} & a_{n2} & \cdots & a_{nm} \end{bmatrix}$$

is the row-by-row array of means for each attribute, for all companies within a given industry. The mean of the distribution of means for attribute i is given by:

$$\bar{a}_i = \frac{1}{m} \sum_{j=1}^{m} a_{ij}$$

The list of all such means forms the vector

$$\bar{A}_n = \begin{bmatrix} \bar{a}_1 \\ \bar{a}_2 \\ \cdot \\ \cdot \\ \cdot \\ \bar{a}_n \end{bmatrix}$$

To determine the deviations of each a_{ij} from its respective mean $\bar{a}_i$ the model takes the difference $(a_{ij} - \bar{a}_i)$ as a per cent of $\bar{a}_i$. Hence, the deviations for each attribute for all companies are given by the row-by-row array:

$$\begin{bmatrix} \dfrac{a_{11} - \bar{a}_1}{\bar{a}_1}, & \dfrac{a_{12} - \bar{a}_1}{\bar{a}_1}, & \cdots, & \dfrac{a_{1m} - \bar{a}_1}{\bar{a}_1} \\ \dfrac{a_{21} - \bar{a}_2}{\bar{a}_2}, & \dfrac{a_{22} - \bar{a}_2}{\bar{a}_2}, & \cdots, & \dfrac{a_{2m} - \bar{a}_2}{\bar{a}_2} \\ \cdot & & & \\ \cdot & & & \\ \dfrac{a_{n1} - \bar{a}_n}{\bar{a}_n}, & \dfrac{a_{n2} - \bar{a}_n}{\bar{a}_n}, & \cdots, & \dfrac{a_{nm} - \bar{a}_n}{\bar{a}_n} \end{bmatrix}$$

These percentage deviations are then converted into the three-valued scale "above," "below," or "equal to" where the base for the comparison is given by a five per cent boundary level either side of the distribution mean $\bar{a}_i$. Thus for the relevant[12] attribute there is a Relative Performance List on which is recorded:

[12] All Relative Performance Lists contain items (i) and (ii). Lists for attributes cash flow per share and profit margin contain items (i), (ii) and (iii). While lists for sales, earnings per share, and dividends per share attributes contain all four items.

(*i*) The mean value over the last ten years as well as whether this mean is "above," "below," or "equal to" the mean for this attribute for the other companies in this industry.

(*ii*) The mean rate of growth over the last ten years as well as whether this mean is "above," "below," or "equal to" the population mean for this attribute.

(*iii*) The expected rate of growth over the coming twelve months as well as whether this expected rate of growth is "above," "below," or "equal to" the mean of the population of expected rates of growth.

(*iv*) The mean, expected rate of growth over the next three to five years as well as whether this mean rate of growth is "above," "below," or "equal to" the mean of the population of mean, expected rates of growth.

1B2. The Relative Value List. Having described the procedures that determine the Relative Performance of each company within its industry, we will now examine the set of processes that determine the Relative Value of each company's stock.

As noted above each company has an attribute that records a three- to five-year forecast of its earnings per share. Although this is only an estimate, the figure is assumed to be reliable and is used, for each company to form a price earnings ratio of the forecasted earnings. As the model already contains the values for the current price earnings ratio and the historical mean of the prices earnings multiple for that company, the entries for the Relative Value List are as follows: The first consists of the difference between the mean price earnings ratio and the price earnings ratio of the forecasted earnings. This difference is taken as a per cent of the mean and is recorded as "above," "below," or "equal to" the historical mean. The second entry consists of the difference between the historical mean and the current price earnings ratio. As before, this difference is taken as a per cent of the historical mean and is recorded as "above," "below," or "equal to." To clarify this process, let:

P = current market price
E = expected earnings per share for the current year
E^* = forecasted earnings per share three to five years from now
$\bar{P}/E^*$ = ten year average of price earnings ratio

Then for each company the calculations are as follows, the results of each being recorded as "above," "below," or "equal to."

(i) $$\frac{(\bar{P}/E) - (P/E^*)}{\bar{P}/E}$$

(ii) $$\frac{(\bar{P}/E) - (P/E)}{\bar{P}/E}$$

The Relative Value List contains these results, plus their value on the three point scale in the order that they are produced. Thus, for each company the Relative Value List is a pair of "aboves," "belows," or "equals to" which under two possible conditions will form a pattern of only A "aboves" or "belows."

1C. THE INTERRELATIONS

Up to now we have described the mechanisms which process the data as though they were independent of each other. While this is true to a certain extent, these mechanisms are related by the processes that select the stocks suitable for current investment. In order to present these interrelations in as orderly fashion as possible, we will first examine the processes that select the "A" List under simplified conditions. By relaxing these conditions we will be able to examine the complexities as they occur.

To facilitate the exposition it is necessary to assign names to the two values which appear on the Relative Value List. Hence, if we let:

$$x = \frac{\bar{P}}{E} - \frac{P}{E^*} \quad \text{and} \quad y = \frac{\bar{P}}{E} - \frac{P}{E}$$

we can, in the future, refer to the values of x and y of the Relative Value List.

1C1. Selecting the "A" List. For simplicity, we shall first assume that all Economy and Industry Expectation Lists have both of their values reading "above." For such a condition to hold, the economy would have to be in the middle of a roaring boom. But ignoring this implication for a moment, we can now examine the basic operations of the selection mechanism which is composed of two parts:

(i) *The Scanner.* This mechanism examines each Economy and Industry Expectation List in turn and notes the values of adjacent pairs. In this case all adjacent pairs have the same value, *i.e.,* "above." Hence, having completed its search and finding such perfect accord the Scanner halts and the Selector takes over.

(ii) *The Selector.* Under such ideal conditions the selection process consists of searching through the Relative Value Lists of all companies and placing on the "A" List those companies whose Relative Values are recorded as:

$$(x) = \text{"above," or "equal to"}$$
$$(y) = \text{"above," "equal to," or "below"}$$

1C2. Relaxing the Conditions—A. Throughout this discussion it must be remembered that information is fed into the various categories, i.e., economy, industry, and company, at different intervals of time. Although these intervals may be chosen to suit any particular set of requirements, we have assumed the following time lags: Information on economy and industry attributes is fed in quarterly while company attributes are adjusted monthly.

Given these time differentials we will now examine the effects of adding new information, to the respective categories, in the order in which they are assumed to occur.

(i) After a change in prices or earnings per share the information is processed as per Secs. 1A and 1B above, and new values are placed on the Relative Value List. The Scanner then proceeds to check the Economy and Industry Expectation Lists and finding them unchanged initiates the selection procedure. The Selector examines the "A" List first and removes from it any companies whose entries on their Relative Lists have changed to:

$$(x) = \text{"below"}$$

The Selector then proceeds to the remaining list of companies and places on the "A" List all companies whose entries on their Relative Value List now record:

$$(x) = \text{"above" or "equal to"}$$

(ii) At the end of each quarter, new information is entered into the model on economy and industry attributes and, when relevant, on company attributes as well. Whenever new information is fed in it is processed immediately, as per Secs. 1A and 1B, and the attention of the Scanner is directed toward that category which received the new information. When more than one category receives new information, the Scanner always goes to the most general category first, e.g., economy or industry, and then proceeds down through the categories noticing and recording changes as it goes. At this point changes in the Economy and Industry Expectation Lists are translated into one of two values, "hold" or "delete hold." These values are placed on the Relative Value List. Companies which were previously on the "A" List are not taken off the list. They are left there until the new information on the companies themselves decides the issue of whether they should stay on the list or not.

1C3. Relaxing the Conditions—B. In order to examine all the operations of the Scanner and the Selector, changes in the forecasted values of the Economy and Industry Expectation Lists will be divided into three categories:

(i) *Forecasted Value Falls below Recent Change Value.* As noted earlier, the function of the Scanner is to examine the Economy and Industry Expectation Lists of all the attributes that have received new information. In this case let us assume that information has been entered into the model which forecasts a leveling off in capital spending, while at the same time the most recent change in this index is still rising. Given this change the Scanner will first proceed to the capital spending Expectation List. Noticing that the other economic Expectation Lists are unchanged the Scanner will descend a level and create a list of the capital intensive industries. The Scanner then examines the changes that have occurred in the Industry Expectation Lists. Since the forecasts for some of these industries will also have fallen or leveled off, the list of affected industries is reduced to that set whose forecasts have been lowered.[13]

The Selector then takes over and scans the list created by the Scanner and searches the "A" List for companies belonging to those industries. All such companies are subjected to the following test:

(a) Mark all companies "hold" which have entry (x) on the Relative Value List recorded as "equal to."

If the forecasts for the other economic attributes fall, the Scanner searches all industry Expectation Lists for corresponding changes, makes a list of those industries whose forecasted values have fallen and presents this list to the Selector which applies the same set of tests as before.

(ii) *Recent Change Value Falls Below Forecasted Value.* In this case the functions of the Scanner and Selector are essentially the same as in (i) except that the Selector applies one extra test.

If economic indices have turned down the performance of some industries and companies will also have turned down. This means that basic changes in company evaluations may be taking place at the same time. However, since these changes are completed first the function of the Scanner is still to create a list of the affected industries, and of the Selector to apply the following tests to those companies on the "A" List which belong to the affected industries.

(a) Mark all companies "hold" which have entry (x) on the Relative Value List recorded as "equal to."

(β) Mark all companies "hold" which have entry (y) on the Relative Value List recorded as "below."

(iii) *Forecasted Values and Recent Change Values Both Turn Down.* Under these conditions, although the Scanner performs in the same manner, a change occurs in the tests applied by the Selector. Instead of testing the companies presented to it by the Scanner on the basis of the tests given above, the Selector makes the following more rigorous tests:

[13] The assumption here is that the forecasts for total capital spending cannot change without a corresponding change in one or all of the capital intensive industries. The only exception to this rule is the Construction Industry which is also included on the list of industries to be examined if there is a fall in the expected level of capital spending.

(γ) Remove all companies from the "A" List which have entry (x) on the Relative Value List recorded as "equal to."

(β) Mark all companies "hold" which have entry (y) on the Relative Value List recorded as "below."

Clearly, the three categories of forecast changes are not mutually exclusive and at any given point in time one would not expect to find the model in one particular category but rather in some combination of the three. This situation in no way changes the functions of the Scanner and Selector; it merely requires them to take each category in turn and perform the required operations sequentially.

When forecast and recent change values are moving up, instead of down as described above, the testing procedures of the Selector are reversed. Instead of marking companies with "hold" and removing them from the "A" List, a "hold" is replaced by a "delete hold" and companies are restored to the "A" List.

The Formulation of an Investment Policy

By and large, trust investors formulate investment policies for two types of funds: (1) large trust funds, *e.g.,* Common Trust Funds (excluding Pension and similar types of funds, and (2) individual trust accounts.

As we are primarily interested in the investment decisions pertaining to the latter set of accounts, the model does not consider the problem of investing the funds of Common Trust Funds. The decision on whether to invest an account in a Fund or not, however, is relevant to the decision process. Although the rules governing this process are not explicitly included in the model—that is, the model is only concerned with investing the funds of individual accounts—a brief discussion of these rules is included here.

2A. COMMON TRUST FUNDS

As the cost of management per dollar invested is much lower in Common Trust Funds than in individual accounts, banks prefer to invest small accounts in their funds. In order to persuade clients to participate in these funds, banks are forced to make the funds' goals explicit. In practice these funds have goals which range from an emphasis on capital appreciation to stability of principal with emphasis on current income.

As the legal restriction governing the investment of Common Trust Funds have ben discussed elsewhere (Clarkson, 1962), the rules outlined here pertain only to the decision on whether to invest the assets of individual accounts in one of these funds.

(*a*) All "legal"[14] trusts are eligible for investment in a Common Trust Fund. Accounts which are not legal trusts and/or whose beneficiaries have waived legal requirements are not so invested.

(*b*) All legal trusts that have assets of less than K dollars are automatically placed in a Common Trust Fund.[15]

(*c*) Legal trusts greater than K dollars may or may not be placed in a Common Trust Fund. As noted before, no account may participate for more than $100,000. Thus, in the range between K dollars and $100,000 the decision will be determined by the degree of correspondence between the goals of the account and the expected results of the Common Trust Fund.

2B. INDIVIDUAL TRUST ACCOUNTS

In order to determine a client's goal, the investment officer has two main sources of information: an administrative officer's interview with the client, and the written record. The former provides the investor with some subjective impressions of the client and the latter with a copy of the legal instrument (often a will) setting up the trust. In most cases this document contains information about the beneficiary, the investment powers of the bank, what is to be done with the principal, the desired amount of income, etc. The instrument also contains information about the beneficiary's age, marital status, number and age of dependents, place of legal residence, income-tax bracket, and status and age of future beneficiaries if any.

Armed with this data, the investment officer must now decide on an investment policy for the account. This policy must lie somewhere along the continuum between the extremes of growth and income and the process that determines it is as follows:

---

[14] " 'Legal investment' statutes fall into two general categories: (1) those that restrict all or part of the investments to specific investments or specific classes of investments, and (2) those that limit investment in non-legal securities to a given percentage of the account or fund. The statutory limitations on investment in non-legal securities range from 30 percent to 50 percent of the market value (in one state, inventory value) of the fund." Survey of Common Trust Funds, 1959, *Federal Reserve Bulletin*, May, 1960, p. 480.

Pennsylvania belongs in the first category and "legal" stocks are defined by law (Act No. 340, 1951) as those securities which, if preferred stocks have paid dividends for sixteen years and which, if common stocks have had positive earnings and have paid dividends in twelve out of the last sixteen years. A list of securities meeting these requirements is prepared by the Pennsylvania Bankers Association. (*Corporate Securities Considered Legal Investments for Trust Funds in the State of Pennsylvania*, Trust Division, Pennsylvania Bankers Association, October, 1960).

Many people when setting up the trust relation specifically waive these investment restrictions. Thus, "legal" refers to situations in which the investment officer must comply with these investment restrictions.

[15] To protect this Bank's anonymity, the precise dollar figures are not revealed. Nationally, the average Common Trust Fund participation is approximately $23,000. *Federal Reserve Bulletin*, May, 1960, p. 481.

(1) *The Scanner.* Information on the client is fed into the model in the form of a list which contains the following attributes: (i) The desired amount of growth, (ii) The desired amount of income, (iii) Whether current income is sufficient for the client's needs, (iv) The desired amount of stability of income and principal, (v) Income-tax bracket, (vi) Client's profession, (vii) Client's place of legal residence, (viii) Whether trust is revocable or not, and (ix) Whether trust is legal or not. The function of the Scanner is to proceed through the first six of these attributes testing for the value of each in turn.[16] The tests consist of classifying the values of attributes (i), (ii), (iv), (v), and (vi) on the basis of whether they are below a median value or not. The criteria for these tests are given to the model in advance and the Scanner converts the values of the attribute into a two-valued scale—"Low," or "Not Low"—which correspond to being below or not below the particular criterion. Attributes (iii) and (vii) are scaled on a "Yes," "No" basis.

The results of these tests are placed on a list so that for each client there is a particular pattern of test answers. Thus for a client in the legal profession, who is a resident of Pennsylvania and has a large current income, a high tax bracket, and desires to build an estate to provide for his retirement, the pattern generated by the Scanner would read: (i) "~ Low," (ii) "Low," (iii) "Yes," (iv) "Low," (v) "~ Low," (vi) "~ Low," (vii) "Yes."

(2) *The Selector.* The function of the Selector is to take the list generated by the Scanner and convert it into the appropriate investment policy. Clearly, the number of possible combinations of growth and income is large. But, in practice they can be characterized in the following manner:[17]

(i) *Growth Account.* In these accounts assets are expected to appreciate at an average rate of 10% per year over a ten-year period. Income is not stressed and fluctuations in principal are tolerated.

(ii) *Growth and Income Account.* Here assets are expected to appreciate at 5–6% per year, while dividend yield should approach 2–3% per year.

(iii) *Income and Growth.* In this type of account assets are only expected to appreciate at 3–4% per year. The desired dividend yield is 3–4% per year and the stability of the income stream is stressed.

(iv) *Income Account.* Here the size and stability of the income streams are stressed with the expected dividend yield being

[16] Attributes (viii) and (ix) are used by the portfolio-selection process.
[17] It should be noted that the figures used here are in no way fixed and will in fact vary with changing market conditions.

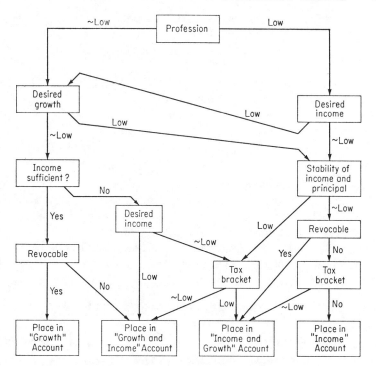

Figure 3. Selector for investment policy.

4–6% per year. In this type of account growth (capital appreciation) is not stressed.

The Selector chooses an investment policy for a particular client by applying a set of tests to the pattern of answers given to the Selector by the Scanner. The flow chart for this procedure is given in Fig. 3, and essentially consists of applying different sets of tests depending on the type of pattern derived by the Scanner. Thus, the Selector chooses the appropriate investment policy by correctly identifying the pattern of answers that is presented to it.

The Selection of a Portfolio

To facilitate the explanation of the selection procedures it is worth-while interrupting the discussion for a moment to outline the information that is on hand prior to choosing a set of stocks for a particular portfolio.

(a) A list of stocks, the "A" List, which contains those stocks that are judged to be suitable for current investment. These stocks are categorized by industry.

(*b*) For each company on the "A" List there is a Relative Value List, a set of Relative Performance Lists, as well as historical, current, and forecasted information on sales, earnings, dividend yield, and other attributes.

(*c*) A list of information on the client for whom this portfolio is to be selected. This list includes the information discussed in the second section as well as an attribute that records the sum of money which is to be invested in common stocks.

(*d*) An investment policy that was chosen for this client as outlined above.

Given this information, the selection of a portfolio is essentially a process of mapping the set of industries and companies in (*a*) onto the investment policy in (*d*). This process yields a subset of industries and their respective companies that is reduced to a particular set of stocks for a portfolio by the addition of the information in (*b*) and (*c*), and the application of a set of tests based on this information. The actual processes governing this selection procedure are as follows:

3A. SELECTION OF INDUSTRIES APPROPRIATE TO THE INVESTMENT POLICY

Despite the large overlap between the characteristics of various industries, the investment officer associates a set of industries with each goal. As this association depends on the characteristics of the goal as well as the general characteristics of the companies within each industry, the particular set of industries associated with a given goal may include some of the industries which are associated with other goals. For example, some industries contain companies which vary only slightly in their individual characteristics, *e.g.*, banks, or utilities, while others, like oils, are more heterogeneous and appear on several lists. As the investment officer's classification of an industry's characteristics change very slowly with time, no attempt was made to determine how these attitudes and associations were developed. Instead, these lists were derived by direct questioning and examination of the investment officer's behavior. The model, then, takes these lists as given and by searching through the "A" List derives, for each goal, a list of those industries and companies that are on the "A" List. Thus, for each goal there is now a list of industries whose companies are both currently acceptable as well as suited to the investment performance desired from the portfolio.

3B. SELECTION OF COMPANIES

Once the list of industries has been generated, the companies on this list are selected for participation by the application of still another Scanner-Selector mechanism.

In this case the Scanner and the Selector have two separate functions. The first is to check the list of information on the client and see if the trust is a legal trust and/or whether the client is a resident of Pennsylvania [attributes (ix) and (vii)]. If either or both are the case the Selector applies one or both of the following two tests:

(i) If the trust is a true fiduciary relation all the companies on the given list that do not have legal status in Pennsylvania are rejected.

(ii) If the client is a resident of Pennsylvania, all the companies that are subject to property tax in Pennsylvania are rejected.

Having eliminated all companies that do not meet the only two absolute criteria the model then takes the remaining list of companies and applies to it the set of tests that are associated with each investment policy.

The Scanner performs the task of ordering the companies in each industry on the basis of the dominant attribute of the investment policy. For example, if an Income Portfolio was being selected the Scanner would rank order the companies in each industry on the basis of yield. The Selector takes the first company from the industry that is at the head of this list and applies a set of tests to it.

The tests consist of a series of binary decisions on the performance and expectations of important attributes. As the importance of particular attributes depends on the investment policy that is being applied, the series of tests varies with each investment goal.

The set of tests is qualitative in nature and is applied, in turn, to the companies within each industry. Unless the value of some attribute is very much out of line with what it should be, the Selector will accept the first company that is processed. If for some reason the first company does not pass the tests, the Selector moves on to the second company and repeats the process. If no company from that industry is able to pass through the set of tests, the Selector moves on to the next industry. If after processing all the industries funds remain to be invested, the Selector returns to the first industry from which no selection was made and recommences processing. This time processing begins at that test that immediately proceeds the spot where the Selector stopped on the first run through. As soon as a company is selected the Scanner and Selector move on to the next industry.

To further clarify this process, consider the set of tests which the Selector applies in order to choose growth portfolios (see Fig. 4). As can be seen from the flow chart, the tests are grouped in hierarchies. Thus, if Company A passes Test 3 it will go directly to Test 5. But, if it does not pass Test 5, it must pass Tests 6, 7, and 8, before it can be accepted back into the mainstream of tests. If no company from a particular industry succeeds in being accepted, and the Selector returns to it in order

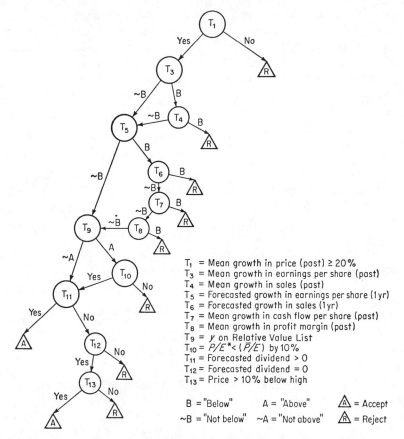

Figure 4. Growth-portfolio discrimination net.

to recommence testing, then this testing would occur in the following way. If company A was first rejected at Test 6, the Selector would now begin testing at Test 7. In this particular case, testing might continue until a company was selected. However, as each Discrimination Net has a test that all participations must meet, it is entirely possible for the model to reject all companies within a given industry.

3C. DIVERSIFICATION

Diversification is achieved by insisting that all accounts participate in at least *five* industries, and that participation in stocks be limited, in general, to *one* per industry. When the portfolio includes bonds and preferred stocks, each $10,000 invested in bonds or preferreds is taken to be equivalent to a participation in one industry. Hence, for an account of $50,000 with $20,000 invested in government bonds, the model would require that the remaining funds be invested in at least three industries.[18]

3D. SIZE OF PARTICIPATION

The number of shares to be purchased of each company that is selected for participation is determined by the "Share Selector." The essence of this process is given by the following rules:

(1) The total funds to be invested in common stocks are divided by the number of participations desired.[19] This produces the average number of dollars to be invested in each company.

(2) To determine the number of shares to be purchased, the average number of dollars to be invested in each company is divided by the price of the particular company's stock. This figure is always rounded to the nearest multiple of five, and whenever the funds available for each participation permit it, round lots, *e.g.,* 100 shares, are purchased.

Clearly, this selection process can only continue as long as there are funds remaining for investment. When the funds have been used up, the selection process stops, and the stocks that have been chosen become the required portfolio.

Testing the Model

In order to test the model's ability to reproduce the behavior of the trust investor—*i.e.,* to simulate the trust investment process—the model was required to select portfolios for a particular set of actual trust accounts. In particular, stock-exchange and other data were fed into the computer to cover the first and third quarters of 1960. The running program was then presented with data on four of the bank's new clients, for whom the trust investor had selected portfolios during the same two quarters, and the program was required to generate its portfolios for these accounts. The portfolios are presented in Figs. 5 and 6, along with the selections made by the trust officer for the same accounts. The generated portfolios were then compared with other portfolios generated by various random and naïve models. The results of these tests indicate that the trust

---

[18] As can be seen from the above, the investment officer's "rule of thumb" seeks to spread risk by diversification. But as Markowitz has shown (H. Markowitz, *Portfolio Selection,* p. 109, New York, 1959) when the returns on securities are correlated, this may not be accomplished if the amount invested for the client is relatively small.

[19] For accounts of $50,000 or less the usual number of participations is five, each $10,000 of bonds and preferreds counting as one. For accounts greater than $50,000 the minimum number is usually five as approximately $10,000 is invested in each participation.

Simulation of Account 1, 1/8/60
Growth Account
Funds available for investment: $22,000

The *program* selected:
  60 General American Transportation
  50 Dow Chemical
  10 I.B.M.
  60 Merck and Company
  45 Owens Corning Fiberglass

The *Trust Officer* selected:
  30 Corning Glass
  50 Dow Chemical
  10 I.B.M.
  50 Merck and Company
  50 Owens Corning Fiberglass

Simulation of Account 2, 6/10/60
Income and Growth Account
Funds available for investment: $37,500

The *program* selected:
  100 American Can Co.
  100 Continental Insurance
  100 Equitable Gas Co.
  100 Duquesne Light Co.
  100 Libbey Owens Ford
  100 International Harvester
  100 Philadelphia Electric
  100 Phillips Petroleum
  100 Socony Mobil

The *Trust Officer* selected:
  100 American Can Co.
  100 Continental Insurance
  100 Equitable Gas Co.
  100 General Public Utilities
  100 Libbey Owens Ford
  50 National Lead
  100 Philadelphia Electric
  100 Phillips Petroleum
  100 Socony Mobil

Figure 5. Comparison of portfolios selected by the model and by a trust officer: Accounts 1 and 2.

Simulation of Account 3, 7/8/60
Income and Growth Account
Funds available for investment: $31,000

The *program* selected:
  100 American Can Co.
  100 Continental Insurance
  100 Duquesne Light
  100 Equitable Gas
  100 Pennsylvania Power and Light
  100 International Harvester
  100 Libbey Owens Ford
  100 Socony Mobil Oil

The *Trust Officer* selected:
  100 American Can Co.
  100 Continental Insurance
  100 Duquesne Light
  100 Equitable Gas
  100 General Public Utilities
  100 International Harvester
  100 Libbey Owens Ford
  100 Socony Mobil Oil

Simulation of Account 4, 8/26/60
Income Account
Funds available for investment: $28,000

The *program* selected:
  100 American Can Co.
  100 Continental Insurance
  100 Duquesne Light
  100 Equitable Gas
  100 Pennsylvania Power and Light
  100 International Harvester
  100 Phillips Petroleum

The *Trust Officer* selected:
  100 American Can Co.
  100 Continental Insurance
  100 Duquesne Light
  100 Equitable Gas
  100 General Public Utilities
  100 International Harvester
  100 Phillips Petroleum

Figure 6. Comparison of portfolios selected by the model and by a trust officer: Accounts 3 and 4.

investment program selected a greater proportion of correct securities than did any one of the alternative models.

To obtain additional confirmation, the testing process was carried one step further—that is, the processes by which the portfolios are generated were submitted to empirical test. The test consisted of comparing the stream of output of the trust investment model to the recorded decision behavior of the trust investor. This test was applied to several of the mechanisms incorporated in the model. While it is not possible to state that all the processes were unequivocally confirmed, the evidence strongly supports the hypothesis that the model's mechanisms capture a considerable portion of the trust investment process.

section 4
Social Behavior

In recent years much empirical work has been done in the field of social behavior, particularly in the area of small group experiments. This work has provided us with much information about the effects of a wide range of variables on group behavior.

More recently, work has been done on models of group behavior. This work has been in part based on the empirical studies, but it has also contributed to the direction of the empirical work. The models have been formulated in ordinary verbal terms, and more recently in mathematical forms—differential equations and Markov processes.

The empirical work and the mathematical models have been very interesting and stimulating. However, there have been many complaints about the simplicity and paucity of the mathematical models. One reply to this sort of criticism has been the creation of computer models.

The charge to students of social behavior to look to the computer model as a useful technique was given by Bales in his paper on "Small Group Theory and Research" (1959). Bales took as the sociologist's goal the prediction of behavior in natural settings as opposed to the prediction in highly controlled laboratory situations. To accomplish this goal, Bales believes that what is required is a synthesis of "large numbers of variables in highly complex conditional relationships to one another." And he goes on to say that the computer is the tool that can aid in the attainment of such a model.

This charge has been taken up by Bales and his associates, who are pursuing a research program directed toward developing computer models of group behavior (Bales, 1959); by McPhee, who has developed a computer model of voting behavior (1961); and by John and Jeanne Gullahorn, who have developed a computer model of social interaction. The following article by the Gullahorns is a report of their work prepared especially for this collection.

John Gullahorn is a member of the faculty of the Department of Sociology and Anthropology at Michigan State University. Jeanne Gullahorn is a graduate student at the same institution. They are also consultants to the Artificial Intelligence Section, System Development Corporation.

A COMPUTER MODEL OF
ELEMENTARY SOCIAL BEHAVIOR

by John T. Gullahorn & Jeanne E. Gullahorn

Ten years ago the social psychologist Solomon Asch observed, "To act in the social field requires a knowledge of social facts—of persons and groups. To take our place with others we must perceive each other's existence and reach a measure of comprehension of one another's needs, emotions and thoughts" (1952, p. 139). In recent years the traditions of psychoanalysis, field theory, and symbolic interaction have generated many insightful explorations of how individuals perceive and cognize the human environment. A radical departure from these relatively intuitive approaches has recently appeared in George Homans' *Social Behavior,* which incorporates principles from two self-consciously rigorous disciplines—classical economics and behavioral psychology (1961). In our opinion the work represents one of the most provocative explanations of human response in interpersonal situations yet published, and we have selected Homans' treatise as a model for research concerning individual reactions in relatively simple social interaction. At present our efforts are directed primarily toward building and refining a statement of the model of elementary social behavior in the form of a computer program written in Information Processing Language (Newell, 1961*e*). In addition to enhancing the clarity and precision of the model, we hope such a representation will ultimately contribute to the goal of naturalistic prediction of behavior in small groups.

Before proceeding to a discussion of the program itself let us consider briefly Homans' treatment of elementary social behavior, that is, of "face-to-face contact between individuals, in which the reward each gets from the behavior of the others is relatively direct and immediate" (1961, p. 7). His model envisages human behavior as a function of its payoff; in amount

375

and kind, an individual's responses depend on the amount and quality of reward and punishment his actions elicit.

To illustrate the application of the propositions he advances to explain social exchange, Homans uses Blau's description of interpersonal behavior in a bureaucracy (1955). Sixteen agents holding the same title were employed in this federal office. The men varied in competence, and as expected the more skilled received more requests for assistance from their co-workers. In analyzing the social economics of such consultations, Blau and Homans regard the interaction as an exchange of values: both participants benefited, but both had to pay a price. The agent requesting help usually was rewarded by being enabled to do a better job; however, he paid the cost of implicitly admitting his inferiority to a colleague who by title was supposedly his equal. The consultant, on the other hand, gained prestige; however, he incurred the cost of time taken from his own work.

We have used this relatively simple interaction sequence between two hypothetical agents, whom we have named Ted and George, to begin actualizing in a computer program the dynamic implications of Homans' explanatory propositions as they relate to the decision processes of individuals involved in social exchange. The program, entitled HOMUNCULUS, now is running for interactions between two persons; but we are still in the stage of writing additional routines to introduce refinements into the basic model. The simulation appears to have verisimilitude, but its verity has not yet been tested against actual social interaction.

The Program

In planning the program of our model we first had to make explicit our conception of a person as an information processing organism. That is, in order to behave according to the principles set forth in Homans' explanatory propositions a person must be "programmed" to do at least the following: He must be able to receive stimuli, recognize stimuli, store stimuli in memory, and compare and contrast stimuli; he must be able to emit activities, differentiate reward and punishment, associate a stimulus situation with a response, and associate a response with a reinforcement; and, on the basis of past experience, he must be able to predict the probability of reward resulting from each response he contemplates. In social situations he must be able to differentiate among other members of a group, evaluate a social stimulus in terms of the specific person emitting it, and select his response accordingly so as to elicit a positive reaction in turn.

Once we had outlined some of the basic qualities necessary for a programmed social being, we then faced the practical problem of how to get such a creature into the computer. Fortunately, IPL-V is ideally suited to the solution of this task. Since it is a list processing language, both data and routines are written in the form of lists. Very complex information can be handled efficiently through the use of list structures, or hierarchies of lists containing as many sublists as desirable, and of description lists which associate with any symbol a list of its attributes and their values. A person thus is represented in our program as a list structure containing a large number of description lists. Among the data included in the list structure of a person are such items as his identity, his abilities, his relative and absolute positions in various social groups, his image lists of his reference groups, and his image lists of other group members.

The flow chart depicted in Figs. 1 through 3 represents our interpretation of the processes involved in operationalizing Homans' propositions for elementary social behavior. The interaction sequence we have programmed begins with an agent, Ted, emitting to his colleague, George, a symbol which represents a request for help in completing a job assignment. Let us postpone discussion of Proposition 5 (P5, Box I in the flow diagram) and begin with Proposition 1 (P1, Box IV) and consider only the positive branches in the diagram so that each proposition can be described briefly in sequence. Our programmed statement of Homans' propositions specifies the symbol manipulating processes which enable George to decide what action he will emit in response to Ted's request.

Proposition 1

Homans' first explanatory proposition concerns the influence of stimulus and response generalization:

> *If in the recent past the occurrence of a particular stimulus-situation has been the occasion on which a man's activity has been rewarded, then the more similar the present stimulus-situation is to the past one, the more likely he is to emit the activity, or some similar activity, now* (1961, p. 53).

In translating the proposition into computer routines enacting decision processes, we found it necessary to consider in sequence two aspects of the "stimulus-situation." To begin with we hypothesized that our agent, George, would react in a relatively global manner to the general situation itself. Thus our interpretation of the initial information processing implied by Proposition 1 (see P1, Box IV in Fig. 1) involves George's considering whether AR (the activity received—in this example, a request for help) is a general stimulus situation in which his responses (AE's, or activities emitted) have been rewarded. In executing this process one routine representing a retrieval function of our programmed agent (George) searches

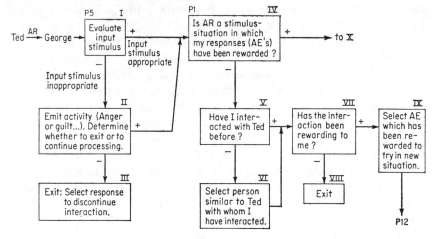

Figure 1.

a memory list of reinforced stimulus situations to determine whether the present input is among them.

Taking the positive branch of the flow diagram and thus assuming that George has found that responding to a request for help has led to reward in the past, let us proceed to his next consideration, depicted in Box X of the flow chart in Fig. 2. George now must determine whether his responses to a request for help have been rewarded by Ted, the person currently introducing the situation.

In order to check on past interactions with Ted, George must search deeper into his memory structure. We noted that the list structure of an individual includes a list in which he stores his image of every person within the group. One routine locates the image list, finds the sublist on it which describes George's previous interactions with Ted, determines whether he has received the present stimulus from Ted before, and if so whether his repsonses to it have generally been rewarded by Ted. In the case we are discussing, George discovers that in the past his responses to requests for assistance have been reinforced by Ted.

Having determined that the stimulus situation has been a rewarding occasion and that Ted has been an agent of reinforcement, George now must consider response alternatives. If he has interacted in similar situations with Ted and has emitted several different activities which Ted has rewarded (*e.g.,* solved Ted's problem, referred Ted to a helpful source or to an expert on the problem in question), then George must choose among these possible reactions to Ted's request. In our program George selects up to three activities from a memory list of responses Ted has rewarded

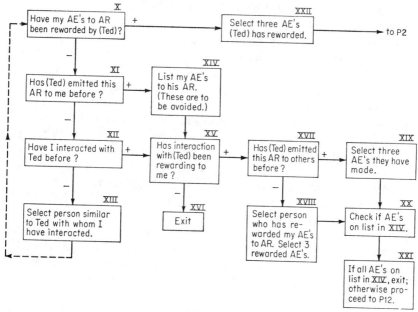

Figure 2.

(Box XXII, Fig. 2) and then proceeds to process further information regarding these contemplated activities.

Proposition 2

Homans' second proposition deals with the positive influence of the frequency and recency of reinforcement:

> The more often within a given period of time a man's activity rewards the activity of another, the more often the other will emit the activity (1961, p. 54).

Reformulating this proposition for computer simulation posed a number of problems. It would have been relatively simple merely to set a counter for each reinforced response and then retrieve the desired information regarding reward frequency. However, we felt this procedure would not adequately simulate human information processing systems. Of course, people do avail themselves of precise measurement scales and use various cultural artifacts—such as computers—to increase their accuracy. But in making estimates concerning frequencies and values of rewards ensuing from everyday social interaction, people seem to use a less refined means of measurement. In programming this proposition, therefore, we devised a rather crude five-point ordinal scale for reward frequency, ranging from an estimate that a response was "nearly always rewarded," through a judgment that it was "rewarded about half the time," to an assessment that it was "almost never rewarded."

At present we are experimenting with different means of manipulating this scale. One routine we have written increases the ordinal scale value for the reward frequency after three reinforcements of the response. This procedure, however, is not completely satisfactory. Indeed, one may argue that estimates of reward frequency are not necessarily independent of the emotional salience of the reinforcement. When HOMUNCULUS has reached the stage of simulating small group behavior in controlled conditions, it should be possible to test various approximations of human judgments of reward frequencies from social interaction and to select the routines which simulate the actual behavior most accurately.

When the processing for this proposition is completed (P2, Box XXIII, Fig. 3), George has a rough estimate of the frequency with which Ted has rewarded each of the activities he is considering in response to Ted's current request for help. Homans' Proposition 2, taken alone, would lead to the expectation that George would then merely emit the most frequently rewarded response alternative. But other information must be processed before a decision is reached.

Perhaps here we should indicate how the program keeps all this material in immediate memory for George. Up to one hundred named private storage cells are assigned for this purpose, and instructions in each routine specify which cells it is to use for storing its findings. At present George is using about fifty of these cells. In addition, important information available to all group participants—for example, what could be seen and heard during the last five interactions—is kept in named public storage cells.

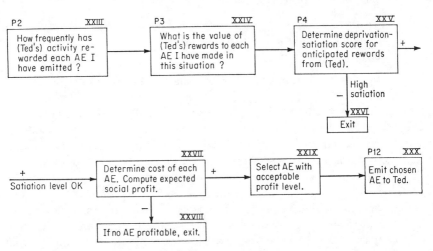

Figure 3.

Proposition 3

Among the other relevant factors that must be considered in selecting an activity to emit is the value of the anticipated reward. Homans' third general position states.

> *The more valuable to a man a unit of the activity another gives him, the more often he will emit activity rewarded by the activity of the other* (1961, p. 55).

Assessing the value of an activity is somewhat more complicated than estimating the frequency with which it occurs. Value has two components —one relatively constant and the other, which we shall discuss in Proposition 4, relatively variable for the periods of time involved in the simple interactions comprising elementary social behavior. The value component referred to in Proposition 3 concerns an individual's rank ordering of the subjective reward attendant on receiving one activity rather than another. With reference to our example, we might predict that George would find warm social approval involving Ted's complimenting him in front of colleagues to be more "valuable" than a halfhearted response of "Hmm, thanks," or an annoyed retort, "Well, sorry I bothered you."

At this point in our program, therefore, we have what game programmers term a "look-ahead." In considering Ted's request, George has "in mind" three responses he recalls Ted's having rewarded in the past, and he has estimated the frequency with which Ted has reinforced each response. Now he must consider more carefully the particular reward he expects Ted to give to each response so that he may determine the inherent worth of each anticipated reward (P3, Box XXIV, Fig. 3). Taking in turn each activity George is contemplating, the routines executing this proposition retrieve the responses Ted previously has made to each, determine which one he is likely to emit now, and search description lists to find the subjective value of the reward for George.

Proposition 4

Homans' fourth proposition deals with the other component of value— the deprivation-satiation aspect, or the marginal utility of a given unit of activity.

> *The more often a man has in the recent past received a rewarding activity from another, the less valuable any further unit of that activity becomes to him* (1961, p. 55).

In contrast to the relatively constant intrinsic satisfaction aspect of value, the deprivation-satiation component varies over a range of possible rankings. Taking into account the amount of an activity a person has received, we note that he "values" that activity more when he has been deprived of it than he does when he is in a state of relative gratification. Thus, while social approval may be highly rewarding to an individual, if in the recent past he has received a great deal of this generalized reinforcer then he is not likely to be so interested at the moment in receiving more.

In processing the information necessary for completion of this stage of the program, George must evaluate his relative deprivation with reference to the rewards he anticipates from Ted. George now has in immediately available memory a record of each activity he is contemplating, and stored with each activity is various information about it, including the response he expects Ted to make to it. The routines which execute Proposition 4 search the description lists of each of the anticipated rewards to determine the degree of George's current deprivation or satiation with respect to them. A deprivation-satiation score based on a simple ordinal scale is stored as the value of a special attribute on the description list of each activity. In executing Proposition 5, which we shall discuss later, routines update the deprivation-satiation score whenever an activity is received.

With the information retrieved thus far George has an estimate of the relative frequency with which Ted has rewarded each activity he is considering emitting. Furthermore, he has predicted Ted's reaction to each of the projected actions and has determined how rewarding each of these anticipated reactions is to him, personally, as well as how deprived or satiated he currently feels with respect to each of these expected rewards. At this point, therefore, George can rank his contemplated responses in terms of their expected payoff. But he is not yet ready to emit the highest ranked action.

Another important consideration is the cost of the proposed response. Homans defines the cost of an activity as the value of the reward obtainable through an alternative activity, forgone in emitting the given one. In our example, George must forgo working on his own assignment if he takes time to assist Ted; therefore George must determine the relative reward value of this alternative activity. To do this he follows a procedure analogous to that just described, processing information concerning the frequency of past reinforcement and the value of the anticipated reward ensuing from this activity as well as his relative satiation with the reward. Then he can compare the over-all expected reward from his contemplated response to Ted with the anticipated reward from continuing with his own work, and he can compute what Homans terms the psychic profit—the reward of an activity less its cost.

Let us suppose George tentatively is planning to give Ted direct assistance on his problem because in the past Ted has praised him for this activity, and social approval is a reinforcement George values highly and

one for which he feels relative deprivation at present. But let us also suppose that George has an important assignment to complete, and that taking
time from it might detract from the quality of his work and thus lessen
the approval he anticipates from his boss for a good job. In this case
George would incur a loss rather than a profit in helping Ted directly;
therefore he will continue processing to see whether one of the other
activities he was contemplating might yield a profit. In this illustration,
George probably will decide that referring Ted to another source will net
him a profit, since he expects some approval for this activity (albeit less
than he would get from directly assisting Ted), and he will incur a very
small cost in terms of time taken from his own work.

Having selected what he expects to be a socially profitable activity,
George emits that response to Ted. At this point our program cycles, and
the activity George has emitted becomes the activity Ted has received.
Now Ted must process information in order to select an appropriate and
profitable response to George.

Proposition 5

Distributive justice, the subject of Homan's fifth proposition, is perhaps the most complex of the concepts involved in the explanation
of elementary social behavior. At the very least it requires consideration of information at another level—that of social norms or accepted
expectations for behavior within a group. Through repetition of interaction situations within a group, certain behavior patterns become sta-
bilized so that expectations develop regarding what constitutes justice
in the distribution of rewards and costs between persons. The greater a
man's costs in a given interaction, the greater his rewards ought to be.
But the implications of distributive justice go even further, taking into
account a person's investments in an interaction—for example, his
seniority, skill, experience, age, and sex. The greater the investment a person makes in an interaction, the greater the net profit he has a right to expect. Thus according to the principle of distributive justice it is consen-
sually expected that certain antecedent costs and investments should have
as consequents certain types and degrees of reinforcement.

Homans states the related proposition as follows:

> The more to a man's disadvantage the rule of distributive justice
> fails of realization, the more likely he is to display the emotional
> behavior we call anger (1961, p. 75).

More is included, however, for if a man receives rewards beyond those
to which he considers himself entitled, he is likely to experience guilt
feelings.

Translating this proposition into computer routines posed some of the most interesting problems we have yet encountered in working with HOMUNCULUS. In effect, the list structures of our agents had to be programmed to have consciences, and they had to include a repertoire of appropriate anger responses.

In essence, our programmed interpretation of this proposition asks whether a stimulus activity is appropriate in the given circumstances (P5, Box I, Fig. 1). If so, then the person receiving it can process it as George did Ted's request, which he considered appropriate. If, however, the stimulus activity is judged inappropriate, then more complex behavior results. To illustrate this let us shift to a description of the interactions between George and Tom, another worker in the same agency.

It is an accepted office norm that a worker who asks for help should do so openly in a manner acknowledging the superiority of his consultant with respect to the given problem. Tom, however, has been seeking aid from George in a rather devious manner, coming to George with "an interesting problem" and saying he would like to see whether George arrives at the same solution as he. This has occurred three times in the recent past, and on each occasion, Tom has greeted George's suggested solution with the comment, "Yes, you reached the same conclusions I did." George decides Tom is violating the norms of fair exchange by evading the cost of thanking him for his assistance and conceding his superiority. The fourth time Tom presents him with an interesting problem George angrily responds, "Look, why don't you do your own work!"

This description, of course, does not answer the question of how the computer is programmed to behave in such an all-too-human way. George is programmed to treat time spent solving a problem presented by another worker as being help to that person for which recognition and social approval are due. When his colleague responds to his efforts with an unrewarding confirmation that he arrived at the same conclusion, George finds this input inappropriate in terms of his expectations regarding distributive justice. Therefore, routines processing Proposition 5 change George's image list of Tom so that next time he expects greater recognition and thanks than normal to atone for the present evasion. After three repetitions of this interaction sequence the discrepancy between Tom's behavior and George's expectations will be so great that when George evaluates Tom's response he will plant a signal in his image list of Tom indicating that interacting with him is not rewarding because Tom violates group norms.

The next time Tom asks for an opinion after this warning signal has been set, George will respond by displaying anger or by storing up aggression to be expressed against someone else. In the computer program an anger response involves emitting behavior punitive to another person. But before actively punishing Tom, George will first assess the consequences to himself of such behavior. In one possible interaction sequence, if George finds that Tom is in favor with George's own boss, he may suppress his aggression at the moment and then release it the next time he interacts with a subordinate.

The routines processing the negative branch of Proposition 5 (Box II, Fig. 1), thus not only modify image lists but also use some of the routines from the other propositions to evaluate the probable consequences of direct anger responses. Depending on the outcome of this processing, the program either proceeds to Proposition 1 or the interaction is terminated.

Conclusions

Like other behavioral scientists who are expressing their theories in IPL-V in order to learn about human processes by simulating them on a digital computer, we are reducing complex social behavior to symbol-manipulating processes. Even in this brief outline of our program it should be obvious that we, too, have found IPL-V particularly appropriate for operationalizing our model. We have already noted the flexibility afforded by organizing information in lists and list structures and the elegant simplicity yet powerful efficiency provided by utilizing description lists for storing information concerning certain symbols. In addition, the relative ease of organizing routines in hierarchial structures greatly facilitates the sequential processing of information involving numerous conditional subroutines. There has not been time to explore the negative branches of our flow diagram except for Proposition 5; however, the general processes should be apparent.

In contrast to the more purely cognitive models of behavior, e.g., Feigenbaum (1959) and Feldman (1959), our model focuses on individual decision-making in social interaction where normative considerations must be processed in the interplay of reciprocal rewards and punishments. HOMUNCULUS is neither a completely general model, like Feïgenbaum's Elementary Perceiver and Memorizer, nor is it specific to particular subjects, like Feldman's simulation of binary choice behavior. Rather, the program blends the two approaches. The information processing involved in the routines is common for all simulated subjects; however, each list structure describing a group participant is highly specific; consequently, individual idiosyncracies and recent past histories determine whether certain subroutines will be executed and what their outputs will be in specific interaction sequences.

With reference to underlying assumptions, however, our model shares several characteristics with those programmed by Feigenbaum and Feldman. Like their models, HOMUNCULUS emphasizes nonnumerical processes and is essentially deterministic rather than probabilistic. In addition, the decision-making processing is assumed to be serial—that is, we consider a person capable of doing only a limited number of things at one time. Furthermore, our model conceives of a person as an hypothesis testing, information processing organism capable of receiving, analyzing, reconstructing, and storing information. HOMUNCULUS is an attempt to explicate in a way not possible with verbal theory the ability of a person engaged in normal social interaction to evaluate the context of behavior, retrieve information necessary to project alternative plans of action, and—before actually committing himself overtly—to select the conditions under which he will emit one activity rather than another.

part 3

Survey of Approaches and Attitudes

It has been said that the best method of presentation is to tell the audience what you are going to say; say it; and then tell the audience what you have said. The first two parts of this injunction have been fulfilled, and only the last part remains to be carried out. We have chosen to conclude this volume with Armer's review, "Attitudes toward Intelligent Machines," and Minsky's review, "Steps toward Artificial Intelligence." We would be presumptuous if we were to review at length these two excellent pieces, and so we shall ask the reader to pause for only two short introductory paragraphs.

Attitudes toward intelligent behavior by computers have been influenced by lack of knowledge and understanding of the work which has taken place and by preconceived notions of what constitutes proof of intelligence. This volume has provided the reader with reports of the current state of the art in research on machine intelligence. Armer provides a review and analysis of preconceived notions concerning machine intelligence. His report is based on a survey of the literature and on his own observations in the United States and the USSR. Although Armer himself has been associated with much of the work reported in this volume, he presents an appealing middle-of-the-road position on the question, "Can computers think?"

The final article in this volume is Minsky's thoughtful review of the trials, errors, and successes of artificial intelligence research. Minsky attempts to supply the field with structure and to state the problems that remain to be solved. This is a unique and important report and is required reading for a thorough understanding of the field.

Paul Armer is head of the Computer Sciences Department of the RAND Corporation.

Marvin Minsky is Associate Professor of Electrical Engineering at Massachusetts Institute of Technology.

ATTITUDES TOWARD
INTELLIGENT MACHINES

by Paul Armer

> "A BIRD IS AN INSTRUMENT WORKING ACCORDING TO MATH-
> EMATICAL LAW, WHICH INSTRUMENT IT IS WITHIN THE CA-
> PACITY OF MAN TO REPRODUCE WITH ALL ITS MOVEMENTS."
> *Leonardo da Vinci (1452–1519)*

This is an attempt to analyze attitudes and arguments brought forth by questions like "Can machines think?" and "Can machines exhibit intelligence?" Its purpose is to improve the climate which surrounds research in the field of machine or artificial intelligence. Its goal is not to convince those who answer the above questions negatively that they are wrong (although an attempt will be made to refute some of the negative arguments) but that they should be tolerant of research investigating these questions. The negative attitudes existent today tend to inhibit such research (MacGowan, 1960).[1]

History

Before examining the current arguments and attitudes toward artificial intelligence, let us look at some of the history of this discussion, for these questions have been around for a long time.

Samuel Butler (1835–1902), in *Erewhon and Erewhon Revisited* (1933), concocted a civil war between the "machinists" and the "anti-machinists." (Victory, incidentally, went to the "anti-machinists.") Butler stated "there is no security against the ultimate development of mechanical consciousness in the fact of machines possessing little consciousness now" and speculated that the time might come when "man shall become to the

---

[1] Almost an entire book, *Computers and Common Sense, The Myth of Thinking Machines,* has been devoted to condemning artificial intelligence research (Taube, 1961). Readers who have been exposed to this book should refer to reviews of it by Richard Laing (1962) and Walter R. Reitman (1962), particularly the former.

machines what the horse and dog are to us." Discussion of this topic apparently took place in Babbage's time (1792–1871), for the Countess of Lovelace commented on it, negatively, in her writings on Babbage's efforts (Bowden, 1953). The topic came into prominence in the late 1940's when Babbage's dreams became a reality with the completion of the first large digital computers. When the popular press applied the term "giant brains" to these machines, computer builders and users, myself included, immediately arose to the defense of the human intellect. We hastened to proclaim that computers did not "think"; they only did arithmetic quite rapidly.

A. M. Turing, who earlier had written one of the most important papers in the computer field on the universality of machines (1936, 1937), published in 1950 a paper entitled, "Computing Machinery and Intelligence." In it he circumvented the problem of properly defining the words "machine" and "thinking" and examined instead the question of a game wherein an interrogator, who can communicate with a human and a machine via teletype, but does not know which is which, is to decide which is the machine. This is now known throughout the computer field as "Turing's Test."

Discussion of machine intelligence died down (but not out) in the early and mid-1950's but has come back in the last several years stronger than ever before. In fact, it has recently invaded the pages of *Science* (MacGowan, 1960; Wiener, 1960; Taube, 1960; Samuel, 1960*b*).

A Way of Thinking about Thinking

Before beginning an examination of the negative arguments, allow me to introduce a concept which will aid in discussing these arguments and which may help resolve some of the semantic difficulties associated with discussions of "Can machines think?" Like Turing, I avoid defining "to think." Instead, observe that thinking is a continuum, an n-dimensional continuum. This notion is certainly not new, for it has existed since man first compared his mental abilities with another man's, and it is implicit in all of the positive arguments on machine intelligence. Psychologists long ago developed "intelligence quotient" as a yardstick in this continuum, and their concept of "factors" is indicative of the n-dimensionality of the continuum of intelligence. The use of the one-dimensional "I.Q." is obviously an oversimplification of reality. Although the concept of an n-dimensional continuum for intelligence is not new, and although it is implicit in many discussions of artificial intelligence, it is rarely stated explicitly.

An analogy may be drawn with the continuum of the ability to transport. With respect to speed in transporting people from New York to Los Angeles, the jet airplane of today outshines all other existing transportation vehicles. But it does not compare favorably, costwise, with ships for transporting newsprint from British Columbia to California. Existing commercial jet transports cannot transport people from one lake to another. A Cadillac may be the most comfortable vehicle to transport people short distances over a good network of roads, but it is hardly a substitute for the jeep in the environment of ground warfare—the jeep's forte is versatility and flexibility. In this dimension, in the continuum of the ability to transport, man outshines the jeep, for man can go where jeeps cannot, just as the jeep can go where Cadillacs cannot. But men cannot carry the load that a jeep can nor can men move with the speed of the jeep.

Similarly, comparisons can be made between men and machines in the continuum of thinking. If there is objection to the use of the word "thinking," then "ability to process information" or some similar term can be used. But it must be admitted that there exists some continuum of behavior in which men and machines coexist and in which they can be compared. (See Fig. 1.)

An n-dimensional continuum is difficult to draw when n is large, so let's examine a two-dimensional one, realizing that reality is far from being that simple. With respect to raw speed, machines outdo men, but when it comes to the sophistication of the information processes available, machines look pretty poor. This dimension deserves further discussion. While the repertoire of today's machines is quite simple—a few basic arithmetic operations and comparisons—man's information processes are very complex. Let me illustrate this point with the following incident. We have all had the experience of trying to recall the name of a person we have once met. On a particular occasion Dr. Willis Ware and I were both trying to recall an individual's name. We recounted to one another his physical characteristics, where he worked, what he did, etc. But his name eluded us. After some time, I turned to Dr. Ware and said, "His name begins with a 'Z'." At which point he snapped his fingers and correctly said, "That's it, it's Frizell!"

Now, of course, the basic question is "Can the machines' capabilities in this dimension be improved?" Let me turn the question around—Is there any evidence that they cannot? I know of none. In fact, over the last decade I think impressive progress has been made. It's easy to underestimate the advances, for "intelligence" is a slippery concept. As Marvin Minsky put it, "You regard an action as intelligent until you understand it. In explaining, you explain away" (1959a).

Today's computers, even with their

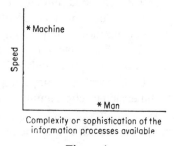

Figure 1

limited capability in the sophistication dimension, have had tremendous impact on science and technology. Accomplishments of the last decade in the fields of nuclear energy, missiles and space would have been impossible without computers. If we can push the capabilities of computers[2] further out in the sophistication dimension, won't they have an even greater impact? *In this context then, the goal of research on artificial intelligence can be stated—it is simply an attempt to push machine behavior further out into this continuum.*

It is irrelevant whether or not there may exist some upper bound above which machines cannot go in this continuum. Even if such a boundary exists, there is no evidence that it is located close to the position occupied by today's machines. Is it not possible that we might one day understand the logical processes which went on in Dr. Ware's head and then mechanize them on a machine? We obviously will not achieve such a goal unless someone believes that it is possible and tries to do it. One does not have to believe that the boundary is nonexistent in order to try; one need only believe that the boundary is much further out than the position occupied by today's machines.

Intelligent Machines and Today's Digital Computer

A common attitude toward today's computers is that such machines are strictly arithmetic devices. While it is true that machines were first built to carry out repetitive arithmetic operations, they are capable of other, nonnumeric tasks. The essence of the computer is the manipulation of symbols—it is only a historical accident that the first application involved numeric symbols. This incorrect notion of the computer as a strictly numeric device results in the inability of many to conceive of the computer as a device exhibiting intelligent behavior, since this would require that the process be reduced to a numerical one. The reaction of many people to statements about intelligent behavior by machines seems to indicate that they take such statements to imply complete functional equivalence between the machine and the human brain. Since this complete functional equivalence does not exist, such people believe they have thereby debunked intelligent machines. Their argument is hollow since this equivalence was never implied. Intelligent behavior on the part of a machine no more implies complete functional equivalence between machine and brain than flying by an airplane implies complete functional equivalence between plane and bird.

The concept of comparing the behavior of men and machines in an n-dimensional continuum recognizes differences as well as similarities.

[2] I make no distinction here between the attributes of the computer and those of the program which controls the computer.

For example, a common argument against machine intelligence is that the brain is a living thing—the machine is not. In our continuum we simply recognize the dimension of living and note that machines and men occupy different positions in this dimension.

While I do believe that today's digital computers can exhibit intelligent behavior, I do not hold that the intelligent machines of the 1970's will necessarily resemble today's machines, either functionally or physically. In particular, in my desire to see machines pushed further out in the continuum of intelligence, my interests in the dimension of speed are very minor; the organizational aspects (sophistication of the information processes) are obviously much more important. Likewise, I hold no brief for the strictly digital approach; a combination of analog and digital equipment may prove to be better. I do not mean to disown the digital computer, for it will be a most important tool in the endeavor to advance in our continuum.

Some of the Negative Arguments

1. The Argument of Invidious Comparison

Considering the behavior of men and machines in the context of intelligence being a multidimensional continuum, an argument that a machine cannot play chess because "it could only operate on standard-size pieces and could not recognize as chessmen the innumerable pieces of different design which the human player recognizes and moves around quite simply" (Taube, 1960) is like saying that the Wright brothers' airplane could not fly because it could not fly nonstop from Los Angeles to New York nor could it land in a tree like a bird. Why must the test of intelligence be that the machine achieve identically the same point in the continuum as man? Is the test of flying the achievement of the same point in the continuum of flying as that reached by a bird?

2. The Argument of Superexcellence

Many of the negativists[3] seem to say that the only evidence of machine intelligence they will accept is an achievement in our continuum seldom achieved by man. For example, they belittle efforts at musical composition by machine because the present output compares miserably with that of Mozart or Chopin. How many *men* can produce music that compares favorably? The ultimate argument of this kind occurred at a recent meeting in England, during which a discussant stated that he would not accept the fact that machines could think until one proved the famous

[3] The terms "negativists" and "positivists" are used in this report to classify those who do not and those who do, respectively, believe machines can exhibit intelligent behavior. Of course, variations of degree exist.

conjecture of Fermat, better known as Fermat's last theorem. By this logic one concludes that, to this date, no man has been capable of thinking, since the conjecture remains unproven.

3. The Argument by Definition

There are many variations of this type of argument. For example, some negativists want to include in their definition of intelligent behavior the requirement that it be carried out by a living organism. With such a definition, machines do not behave intelligently. However, there does still exist machine behavior which can be compared with human behavior. To conclude that research on the simulation of such human behavior with a machine is wrong, as some have done, because the machine is not living, is like concluding that research on the simulation of the functions of the human heart with an artificial heart is wrong because the artificial organ is not a living one.

4. The Argument by Stipulation

An examination of the arguments advanced by the negativists reveals that many of them are not arguments at all, but only statements. They dismiss the notion out of hand, saying things like, "Let's settle this once and for all, machines cannot think!" or "A computer is not a giant brain, in spite of what some of the Sunday supplements and science fiction writers would have you believe. It is a remarkably fast and phenomenally accurate moron" (Andree, 1958).

5. The Argument by False Attribution

Typical of this type of argument is the following:

> The Manchester machine which was set to solve chess problems presumably proceeded by this method, namely by reviewing all the possible consequences of all possible moves. This, incidentally, reveals all the strength and weakness of the mechanism. It can review far more numerous possibilities in a given time than can a human being, but it has to review all possibilities. The human player can view the board as a whole and intuitively reject a number of possibilities. The machine cannot do either of these (Hugh-Jones, 1956).

The statements about machine behavior in the above quotation are simply not true. While it is true that some of the early approaches to chess-playing machines were in the nature of attempts to review *all* possibilities in limited depth (Kister *et al.*, 1957), this is not the only way in which the problem can be approached. The chess-playing routine of Newell, Shaw, and Simon (1958b) does *not* examine all possibilities. And those which it does consider it examines in varying detail. The routine rejects moves which appear to be worthless; it selects moves which appear to be good ones and examines them in depth to ascertain that they are indeed good. An earlier routine developed by this same team to prove theorems in logic (Newell, Shaw and Simon, 1957a) did not examine all possible proofs—to do so with today's computers would literally take endless time. Rather, the routine searched through the maze of possible proofs for ones which looked promising and investigated them. It relied on knowing which approaches had worked before. Most of those who scoff about research on artificial intelligence turn out to be unaware of the details of what is going on in such research today; it is little wonder that they frequently make erroneous statements about the field.

6. The Argument by False Extrapolation

This class of argument is typified by extrapolations based on assumptions that machine properties are invariant. For example:

> The human memory is a filing system that has a far greater capacity than that of the largest thinking machine built. A mechanical brain that had as many tubes or relays as the human brain has nerve cells (some ten billion) would not fit into the Empire State Building, and would require the entire output of Niagara Falls to supply the power and the Niagara River to cool it. Moreover, such a computer could operate but a fraction of a second at a time before several thousand of its tubes would fail and have to be replaced (Troll, 1954).

The point is tied to the vacuum tube (the article was written in 1954) and has therefore already been weakened by the appearance of the transistor, which requires less space and power and is considerably more reliable than the vacuum tube. An offsetting development is that the estimate of the number of nerve cells is undoubtedly too low. However, on the horizon are construction techniques involving the use of evaporated films, where the details of the machine will not be visible under an optical microscope (Shoulders, 1960). It seems reasonable to expect that it will be possible with these techniques to house in one cubic foot of space the same number of logical elements as exist in the human brain. Power requirements will be trivial.

7. The Obedient Slave Argument

One often hears statements like "The machine can only do what it is told to do." People who advance this obedient slave argument would seem to be thinking that they are countering others who have pointed to a large conglomeration of unconnected transistors, resistors and electronic components, and said "It thinks." Certainly man is involved in machine intelligence—so are parents and teachers in human intelligence. Do we deny flying to an airplane because a man is piloting it or even to an unmanned flight because a man designed it?

The negativists who say "the machine can only do what it is told to do" overlook the fact that they have not qualified their statement as to what is the limit of what the machine can be told to do. What evidence exists concerning the location of that limit? Might it not become possible to tell a machine to learn to do a given task, a task usually considered to require intelligence? Many of the tasks being accomplished with computers today were not considered possible ten years ago.

Recent Computer Tasks and Milestones

The mounting list of tasks which can now be carried out on a computer but which we normally consider requiring intelligence when performed by humans, includes such things as:

Proving theorems in logic and plane geometry (Newell, Shaw and Simon, 1957a; Gelernter, 1960a)

Playing checkers and chess (Samuel, 1959; Newell, Shaw and Simon, 1958b)

Assembly line balancing (Tonge, 1961a)

Composing music (Hiller and Isaacson, 1959)

Designing motors (Goodwin, 1958)

Recognition of manual Morse code (Gold, 1959)

Solving calculus problems (Slagle, 1961)

The collection of capabilities which have been ascribed solely to humans in the past is being slowly chipped away by the application of computers. Space precludes going further into the evidence for machine intelligence; this topic is well covered in the articles previously cited and in other papers (Newell, Shaw and Simon, 1956; Milligan, 1959; Minsky, 1961a). Such evidence is, of course, the basis for many of the arguments advanced by the positivists.

To prove that machines *today* do *not* exhibit intelligence, it is only necessary to define a lower bound in our continuum which is above the behavior exhibited by the machines and then say that behavior above that bound is intelligent and below it is not intelligent. This is a variant of the proof by definition. Many who use this gambit have been redefining the lower bound so that it is continually above what machines can do today. For example, we find

> Perhaps the most flexible concept is that any mental process which can be adequately reproduced by automatic systems is not thinking (Meszar, 1953).

This redefinition may not be done consciously. A skill which seems highly intelligent in others becomes much less impressive to us when we acquire that skill ourselves. It would be useful to have at hand some milestones for the future. Turing's test is one such milestone (1950) but additional ones are needed. To this end a clearly defined task is required which is, at present, in the exclusive domain of humans (and therefore incontestably "thinking") but which may eventually yield to accomplishment by machines.

Rivalry Between Man and Machines

There is a strong personal factor in the attitude of many negativists. I'm sure it was a major factor in my being a negativist ten years ago. To concede that machines can exhibit intelligence is to admit that man has a rival in an area previously held to be within the sole province of man. To illustrate this point, let me quote from a letter received at RAND:

> . . . *semantics may have a lot to do with the degree of enthusiasm for supporting research in this area (artificial intelligence). Subjectively, the terms "intelligent machine" or "thinking machine" disturb me and even seem a bit threatening: I am a human being, and therefore "intelligent" and these inhuman devices are going to compete with me and may even beat me out. On the other hand, if the very same black boxes were labelled "problem solver," or even "adaptive problem solver," they would seem much more friendly, capable of helping me in the most effective way to do things that I want to do better, but, best of all, I'd still be the boss. This observation is wholly subjective and emotional. . . .*

Another explanation of why some negativists feel the way they do is related to what might be called the "sins of the positivists." Exaggerated claims of accomplishments, particularly from the publicity departments of computer manufacturers, have resulted in such a strong reaction within the scientific community that many swing too far in the opposite direction.

Da Vinci and Flying

At this point allow me to paraphrase the quotation of da Vinci's, with which this paper was begun, and also, with the benefit of hindsight, expand on it somewhat. Thus, he might have said:

> *When men understood the natural laws which govern the flight of a bird, man will be able to build a flying machine.*

While it is true that man wasted a good deal of time and effort trying to build a flying machine that flapped its wings like a bird, the important point is that it was the understanding of the law of aerodynamic lift (even though the understanding was quite imperfect at first) over an airfoil which enabled men to build flying machines. A bird isn't sustained in the air by the hand of God—natural laws govern its flight. Similarly, natural laws govern what went on in Dr. Ware's head when he produced "Frizell" from my erroneous but related clue. Thus, I see no reason why we won't be able to duplicate in hardware the very powerful processes of association which the human brain has, once we understand them. And if man gained an understanding of the processes of aerodynamics, may he not also obtain an understanding of the information processes of the human brain?

There are other facets to this analogy with flight; it, too, is a continuum, and some once thought that the speed of sound represented a boundary beyond which flight was impossible.

Approaches to the Problem of Building an Intelligent Machine

This topic can perhaps be expounded best with another analogy. Suppose we are given a device which we know exhibits intelligent behavior because we have observed it in action. We would like to build a machine which approaches it in capability (or better yet, exceeds it). We bring in a group of men to study the basic components of the device to understand how they work. These men apply pulses to subsets of the leads, and observe what each component does; they try to understand why the device behaves as it does in terms of basic physics and chemistry. They also seek to learn how these components function in subassemblies.

A second group of men approach the problem from the point of view that the device is a "black box" which they are not able to open. This group observes that some of the appendages of the device are obviously input devices while others are output devices. They observe the device in operation and attempt to theorize how it works. They proceed on the basis that it will not be necessary that the machine they are to construct have the same basic components as exist in the device under study. They believe that if they can understand the logical operation of the existing device, they can duplicate its logic in their own machine, using components they understand and can make.

This second group makes conjectures about the logical construction of the device and tries these conjectures out on a computer which they have at hand. These theories are very crude at first and do not mirror the behavior of the "black box" very well, but over time the resemblance improves.

Because we learned a lesson from the effort spent on attempting to build a flying machine that flapped its wings, we set a third group to work studying "intelligence and information processing" per se and building up a science in the area.

There is much common ground among the three groups and they keep each other posted on results to date. Furthermore, they all use computers to aid them in their research. The groups combine their know-how along the way to build better computers (low-I.Q. intelligent machines) on which to try out their conjectures. Eventually, the three groups "come together in the middle" and build a machine which is almost as capable as our model. They then turn to the task of building an even better one.

In the real-life situation of studying the human brain, the first group, studying components and assemblies thereof, is represented by physiological work. The second, or "black-box" group, is represented by psychological efforts to explain human mental activity. This analogy represents, I believe, a plausible scenario for the way things might go in trying to understand the human mind.

Russian Attitudes

Our examination thus far has been Western in origin; in view of the impact that achievement of the goals of research on artificial intelligence would have on the technological posture of the United States vis-à-vis the Soviet Union, it might be interesting to look at Soviet attitudes toward intelligent machines. As one might suspect, Soviet attitudes have been quite similar to Western ones. Positivists and negativists exist, and each camp advances the same sort of arguments as their Western counterparts. For example, there are negativists who advance the obedient slave argument. Academician S. A. Lebedev, head of the Institute of Precise Mechanics and Computational Techniques and host to the U.S. Exchange Delegation in Computers which visited the USSR in the last two weeks of May, 1959 (of which I was a member), on two occasions dismissed my questions concerning his attitude toward intelligent machines with the statement "Machines can do no more than they are instructed to do."

Their literature is filled with discussions of comparisons between men and machines. In 1961, an entire book, *Philosophical Problems of Cybernetics* (1961), was published on this topic. It was obvious from the questions asked of our delegation by the Russians about Western attitudes that it is a hotly debated issue. In the USSR, research on artificial intelligence is a part of cybernetics, the term coined by Wiener (1948) and now a household word in the Soviet Union. Cybernetics is also used as an umbrella term for research in automatic control, automation, computers, programming, information retrieval, language translation, etc. It is universally recognized as an area related to both men and machines, and the requirement for an interdisciplinary (engineering, mathematics, computing, biology, psychology, physiology, physics, chemistry, linguistics, etc.) approach to such research is also recognized.

As in the West, the use of the term "giant brains" in the late 1940's resulted in a massive revulsion among the Soviet scientific community, and universal rush to the defense of the human mind. The degree of the revulsion was such that several Soviet writers have blamed it for the fact that Russia presently lags the U.S. in the digital-computer field (Shaginyan, 1959). One finds frequent references in the Russian literature to the existence of a negative attitude toward cybernetics, and to the persistence of this attitude for a period of about ten years.

Soviet literature on cybernetics frequently gives credit to Wiener, von Neumann, and other Westerners for pioneering the field. It also contains many references to the work of Pavlov and mixes in much political discussion of communism vs. capitalism, and even of Marx and Lenin. For example, we have:

> *Karl Marx was the first to make use implicitly and anticipatingly of cybernetical ways of thought, or to express it more pointedly, Karl Marx was the first cybernetician!* . . . (Klaus, 1960).

There are some strong positivists in the USSR. For example, I. A. Poletayev has stated "nothing except prejudice and superstition allow one to deny with assurance today the possibility that the machine will pass, in the end, that limit beyond which consciousness begins" (1958). Other strong positivists include S. L. Sobolev (an Academician and a well-known mathematician) and A. A. Lyapunov (1960). We also find:

> *. . . Thus, the perfecting of computer machines involuntarily leads us to the need to create a model of the brain. . . . Also, one of the most effective methods of studying intra-cerebral processes involve experiments carried out in electrical models of the brain. . . .*
>
> *But cybernetics has its critics too. These are skeptics. One can find them among scientists and among ordinary citizens, at times also among administrative personnel. These skeptics reject this branch of science and deny it the right of existence. . . . In rejecting this science, they generally state that the very thought of comparing a machine to a human being is an insult* (Moiseyev, 1960).

The majority of Soviet workers appear to recognize (implicitly, at least) the continuum discussed in this report, and argue that while there does exist an upper bound above which machines cannot go, it is not possible to determine the location of that bound. For example:

> *As a result we arrive at the conclusion that a machine can perform all the intellectual human functions which can be formalized . . . .*
> *But what can be formalized? . . . Upon brief reflection we con-*

clude that it is impossible in principle to answer this question (Kolman, 1960).

Where Do the Russians Stand?

First of all, let us look at what they are doing in those disciplines upon which research in artificial intelligence depends: computing devices, mathematics, psychology, and physiology. With respect to computers, I can speak with firsthand knowledge, for, as mentioned earlier, I spent two weeks in 1959 visiting Soviet computer installations. In my opinion, they are somewhat behind us in the actual construction of machines, particularly with respect to input/output equipment and to numbers of machines (Ware, 1960; Feigenbaum, 1961c). However, there is nothing fundamentally lacking in their state of the art. The quantity of machines is not as important to research as an offhand comparison of numbers of machines might indicate, since none of their machines is devoted to such things as social-security records, subscription fulfillment, or airline reservations. In assessing a comparison of this kind, one always wonders how much of the iceberg we do not see. When visiting the IBM plant in California, Khrushchev said about computers, ". . . for the time being we're keeping them a secret."

The Russians started work on computers after we did, but they have certainly narrowed the gap. Furthermore, they are giving high priority to the computing field. In their announcement concerning the decentralization of responsibility for research, an exception was made for computers, along with fusion, space activities, high-temperature metallurgical research, and certain areas of chemistry; these research areas remained centralized under the cognizance of the Academy of Sciences. Of course, the Russians are interested in spurring the computer field for reasons other than intelligent machine research. There is no reason to believe that future Russian research on intelligent machines need be hampered by the computer tools available to them, although machine time is in short supply today.

In mathematics the Russians have had an outstanding reputation for many decades. In computer mathematics I have no doubts that, in general, they excel the West. One of the things which impressed our delegation, and other delegations before ours (Carr *et al.,* 1959), was the number of outstanding mathematicians now working in the computer field. Unfortunately, many U.S. mathematicians view computers as a glorified slide rule of interest only to engineers, or as an expensive sorting device of interest to businessmen with clerical problems.

Since psychological research on mental processes and neurophysiological research on structure and activity of the brain both play a vital suggestive role in the attempt to construct intelligent machines, progress by the Soviets in these disciplines is of considerable interest. Although psychology was severely inhibited during the Stalin era, a renaissance of impressive proportions has taken place within the last decade. Physiology, less inhibited in the previous era, is in even better shape. The best available evidence indicates that Russian neurophysiology is dynamic, innovative, and up to date. The researchers are competent and generally sophisticated; their laboratories are modern and well equipped.

The Soviets have demonstrated a knack for focusing talent and resources on important applied problems. I believe that the Soviets regard artificial intelligence as one such problem area, and that the best of modern Soviet psychology and neurophysiology will be recruited into the search for solutions. With respect to physiological research, the following is of interest:

> *Essentially, we (the Western World) have not found the physiochemical principles of neural activity, whereas the Russians have not seriously sought them. However, the current 7-year plan for physiology as presented in a recent editorial by D. A. Biriukev in the Sechenov Physiological Journal of the USSR calls for precisely this goal* (Freeman, 1960).

A recent visitor of the USSR reports that Soviet physiologists appear to be under pressure to produce explanations for human behavior which can be incorporated into machines. He further reports that their work is apparently under security wraps.

Russian Emphasis on Artificial Intelligence Research

I went to the Soviet Union convinced they were putting a great deal of emphasis on research in artificial intelligence. Possibly this predisposition influenced what I thought I saw. I also want to emphasize that *I was impressed, not by any substantive results, but by their apparent conviction that this was an important research area.*

In one institute, in response to my question about the problem of simulating the brain with a computer, I was told "It is considered *the* number one problem." The emphasis on "the" was the speaker's; the statement was made in English. At another institute, when Professor L. I. Gutenmacher, head of the Laboratory for Electrical Modeling, told us that the charter of his laboratory was the modeling of human mental processes, I asked him if he had difficulty obtaining financial support for such exotic research. His response was "No, not at all; the President of the Academy of Sciences is convinced that this is an important field for research." There is evidence that he has been given ample support. I was told that his laboratory, which was formerly (and still is ostensibly) a part of the Institute of Scientific Information, had all the status of an institute, being separately funded and reporting directly to the Presidium of the Academy of Sciences. Gutenmacher's laboratory is apparently responsible for mechanizing the functions of the Institute of Scientific Information, which is a large, centralized, information retrieval system for scientific information from all over the world.

Despite much effort, our delegation was unable to visit Gutenmacher's laboratory. To my knowledge, no Westerner has done so; in fact none had met Gutenmacher before our delegation. Some in the U.S. have concluded from this denial of entry to his laboratory that there was nothing to be shown. However, its work may be classified, as Khrushchev indicated. But whether or not anything is being accomplished is not pertinent to the point that the President of the Soviet Academy of Sciences, a man with much power and resources, believes that modeling human mental activities is possible, that he recognizes the importance of research in this field, and that he is devoting considerable resources to this end.

What are some of the other indications about Soviet attitudes toward research on intelligent machines? As previously mentioned, cybernetics is a household word in Russia. Much is being written on the subject, in journals and in the popular press. There appears to be an effort in the popular writings to legitimatize such research as being in harmony with communism. For example, recall the earlier quote about Marx (Klaus, 1960).

With respect to professional writing on machine intelligence, a journal entitled *Problems of Cybernetics* was started in 1958; seven hard-cover volumes have appeared to date (Lyapunov, 1960, 1961). Since 1955, seminars on cybernetics have been held at the University of Moscow. These seminars are aimed at bringing together scientists from various disciplines. Similarly, the editors of *Problems of Cybernetics* state that their aim "is the unification of the scientific interests of those working in different fields of science concerned with cybernetics."

There seems to be widespread recognition for the necessity of an interdisciplinary approach to problems of cybernetics. Article after article appeals to personnel from the various disciplines to get together. How much effect these appeals and seminars have is unknown. During our visit to the Soviet Union, we were told that some 500 physicists had been transferred to the biological sciences. We talked with I. M. Gelfand, a world-famous mathematician now working in the physiological field. He began studying the brain but switched to the heart, which he believes to be much simpler. With knowledge gained from studying the heart, he will return to the study of the brain. We were also told that other mathematicians were working on psychological and physiological problems.

Within the Soviet Academy of Sciences, there exists a "Scientific Council on Cybernetics." This council is headed by A. I. Berg and apparently reports directly to the Presidium of the Academy (Berg, 1960). To my knowledge, there is no evidence of any effect this council may be having in coordinating, controlling, or encouraging research in cybernetics. Outside of Moscow, individual researchers appear to operate entirely on their own, with little communication with other such researchers, and with only meager support. However, one does occasionally encounter references to the formation of new groups and laboratories for such work.

There is some evidence that machine time (until recently in critically short supply) has been made available for work in this area. *Moscow News* of August 12, 1961, has an article on musical composition and medical diagnosis on a computer while the issue of September 2, 1961, discusses chess playing by machines and the deciphering of ancient Mayan manuscripts.

In closing this topic, a quotation which appeared in the February, 1959, issue of *Fortune* is pertinent. Frank Pace, Jr., then president of General Dynamics Corporation, in warning us not to overlook nor be surprised by Russia's capacity to concentrate in specific areas, said:

> *If the area has real military or psychological value to them, they'll put massive concentration on it, and achieve results all out of proportion to the general level of their technical ability.*

The Importance of Research in Artificial Intelligence

I have indicated my feeling that research aimed at pushing machines further out in the continuum of intelligence is very important. Today's computers are helping advance the frontiers of man's knowledge in many fields; computers now pervade almost all scientific disciplines. (The fact that they pervade the field of research on intelligent machines means that such research will feed on itself.) The use of computers in research has been a key factor in the explosion of knowledge we have witnessed in the last decade. Their contribution to date has stemmed largely from their speed in doing arithmetic and the reliability with which they do it. As we move out in the continuum of possibilities, new dimensions and contributions will become important. A machine which retrieves information from a large store by complex associative processes like those inherent in Willis Ware's output of "Frizell," but which exceeds Dr. Ware in speed, reliability, and memory capacity, would be crucial in aiding scientists to cope with the flood of research results presently inundating science.

The large amount of money spent on machines today is evidence of the value placed on the computers' abilities along the dimensions of speed and reliability. If the machine's capabilities can be extended in additional dimensions, would it not be of great importance? Suppose that the boundary (if it exists at all) beyond which machines cannot go lies fairly close to the human brain in the dimension related to the sophistication of the information processing techniques used. Since it is known that the machine can exceed the human in speed and reliability, and probably in amount of memory, such a machine would approach the status of being "super-human." Of course, this is speculation; the boundary may be much lower.

We have been examining the question of the technological importance of research in artificial intelligence in the context of advancing the frontiers of knowledge for the sake of technological and scientific advancement. In such a context, there is little cause for any concern or action; progress in the field is being made at a fairly rapid pace in this country. However, since we are engaged in a technological race with the USSR, action becomes important, particularly since, in my opinion, the Russians appear to be putting much more emphasis on research in artificial intelligence than we are. Even if the Russians were not competing in this particular event of the "technological Olympics," it is an event well worth the running in that we will learn more about man and in that better machines will contribute to advancing the frontiers of knowledge in almost every discipline.

Timing

Before closing, a comment on the question "when?" It is one thing to say it is possible to push machine capabilities way out in the continuum of intelligence, but it is another thing to say when. It was over four hundred years from da Vinci to the Wright brothers. But the sands of time in the scientific world have been flowing much more rapidly of late. Advances now made in a decade compare with earlier steps which took a century. Few would have believed in 1950 that man would hit the moon with a rocket within ten years. Gutenmacher, when told recently of the Simon and Newell prediction that a machine would be chess champion within ten years (Newell and Simon, 1958d) said that he thought the prediction conservative; it would happen sooner.

Conclusion

It is hoped that the definition of research on artificial intelligence as an effort to push machines further out in the continuum of intelligent behavior will reduce some of the semantic difficulties surrounding discussions of such research. I feel that such research is very important to our country and that we must expand our efforts therein. To do so implies that more researchers from the related disciplines are needed. The success of our efforts will depend on how well we do in bringing the various disciplines together and on the number of well-qualified scientists who are attracted to this research area.

STEPS TOWARD
ARTIFICIAL INTELLIGENCE

by Marvin Minsky

Introduction

A visitor to our planet might be puzzled about the role of computers in our technology. On the one hand, he would read and hear all about wonderful "mechanical brains" baffling their creators with prodigious intellectual performance. And he (or it) would be warned that these machines must be restrained, lest they overwhelm us by might, persuasion, or even by the revelation of truths too terrible to be borne. On the other hand, our visitor would find the machines being denounced, on all sides, for their slavish obedience, unimaginative literal interpretations, and incapacity for innovation or initiative; in short, for their inhuman dullness.

Our visitor might remain puzzled if he set out to find, and judge for himself, these monsters. For he would find only a few machines (mostly "general-purpose" computers, programmed for the moment to behave according to some specification) doing things that might claim any real intellectual status. Some would be proving mathematical theorems of rather undistinguished character. A few machines might be playing certain games, occasionally defeating their designers. Some might be distinguishing between hand-printed letters. Is this enough to justify so much interest, let alone deep concern? I believe that it is; that we are on the threshold of an era that will be strongly influenced, and quite possibly dominated, by intelligent problem-solving machines. But our purpose is not to guess about what the future may bring; it is only to try to describe and explain what seem now to be our first steps toward the construction of "artificial intelligence."

Along with the development of general-purpose computers, the past few years have seen an increase in effort toward the discovery and mechanization of problem-solving processes. Quite a number of papers have appeared describing theories or actual computer programs concerned with game playing, theorem proving, pattern recognition, and other domains which would seem to require some intelligence. The literature does not include any general discussion of the outstanding problems of this field.

In this article, an attempt will be made to separate out, analyze, and find the relations between some of these problems. Analysis will be supported with enough examples from the literature to serve the introductory function of a review article, but there remains much relevant work not described here. This report is highly compressed, and therefore, cannot begin to discuss all these matters in the available space.

There is, of course, no generally accepted theory of "intelligence"; the analysis is our own and may be controversial. We regret that we cannot give full personal acknowledgments here—suffice it to say that we have discussed these matters with almost every one of the cited authors.

It is convenient to divide the problems into five main areas: Search, Pattern Recognition, Learning, Planning, and Induction; these comprise the main divisions of the report. Let us summarize, the entire argument very briefly:

A computer can do, in a sense, only what it is told to do. But even when we do not know exactly how to solve a certain problem, we may program a machine to *Search* through some large space of solution attempts. Unfortunately, when we write a straightforward program for such a search, we usually find the resulting process to be enormously inefficient. With *Pattern Recognition* techniques, efficiency can be greatly improved by restricting the machine to use its methods only on the kind of attempts for which they are appropriate. And with *Learning,* efficiency is further improved by directing Search in accord with earlier experiences. By actually analyzing the situation, using what we call *Planning* methods, the machine may obtain a really fundamental improvement by replacing the originally given Search by a much smaller, more appropriate exploration. Finally, in the section on *Induction,* we consider some rather more global concepts of how one might obtain intelligent machine behavior.

I. The Problem of Search[1]

If, for a given problem, we have a means for checking a proposed solution, then we can solve the problem by testing all possible answers. But this

---

[1] The adjective "heuristic," as used here and widely in the literature, means *related to improving problem-solving performance;* as a noun it is also used in regard to any method or trick used to improve the efficiency of a problem-solving system. A

always takes much too long to be of practical interest. Any device that can reduce this search may be of value. If we can detect relative improvement, then "hill-climbing" (Sec. I-B) may be feasible, but its use requires some structural knowledge of the search space. And unless this structure meets certain conditions, hill-climbing may do more harm than good.

When we talk of problem-solving in what follows we will usually suppose that all the problems to be solved are initially *well defined* (McCarthy, 1956). By this we mean that with each problem we are given some systematic way to decide when a proposed solution is acceptable. Most of the experimental work discussed here is concerned with such well-defined problems as are met in theorem-proving, or in games with precise rules for play and scoring.

In one sense all such problems are trivial. For if there exists a solution to such a problem, that solution can be found eventually by any blind exhaustive process which searches through all possibilities. And it is usually not difficult to mechanize or program such a search.

But for any problem worthy of the name, the search through all possibilities will be too inefficient for practical use. And on the other hand, systems like chess, or nontrivial parts of mathematics, are too complicated for complete analysis. Without complete analysis, there must always remain some core of search, or "trial and error." So we need to find techniques through which the results of *incomplete analysis* can be used to make the search more efficient. The necessity for this is simply overwhelming: a search of all the paths through the game of checkers involves some 10^{40} move choices (Samuel, 1959a), in chess, some 10^{120} (Shannon, in Newman, 1956). If we organized all the particles in our galaxy into some kind of parallel computer operating at the frequency of hard cosmic rays, the latter computation would still take impossibly long; we cannot expect improvements in "hardware" alone to solve all our problems! Certainly we must use whatever we know in advance to guide the trial generator. And we must also be able to make use of results obtained along the way.[2,3]

"heuristic program," to be considered successful, must work well on a variety of problems, and may often be excused if it fails on some. We often find it worthwhile to introduce a heuristic method which happens to cause occasional failures, if there is an over-all improvement in performance. But imperfect methods are not necessarily heuristic, nor vice versa. Hence "heuristic" should not be regarded as opposite to "foolproof"; this has caused some confusion in the literature.

[2] McCarthy (1956) has discussed the enumeration problem from a recursive-function-theory point of view. This incomplete but suggestive paper proposes, among other things, that "the enumeration of partial recursive functions should give an early place to compositions of functions that have already appeared."

I regard this as an important notion, especially in the light of Shannon's results (1949) on two-terminal switching circuits—that the "average" n-variable switching

A. Relative Improvement, Hill-climbing, and Heuristic Connections

A problem can hardly come to interest us if we have no background of information about it. We usually have some basis, however flimsy, for detecting *improvement;* some trials will be judged more successful than others. Suppose, for example, that we have a *comparator* which selects as the better, one from any pair of trial outcomes. Now the comparator cannot, alone, serve to make a problem well defined. No goal is defined. But if the comparator-defined relation between trials is "transitive" (*i.e,* if *A dominates B* and *B dominates C* implies that *A dominates C*), then we can at least define "progress," and ask our machine, given a time limit, to do the best it can.

But it is essential to observe that a comparator by itself, however shrewd, cannot alone give any improvement over exhaustive search. The comparator gives us information about partial success, to be sure. But we need also some way of using this information to direct the pattern of search in promising directions; to select new trial points which are in some sense "like," or "similar to," or "in the same direction as" those which have given the best previous results. To do this we need some additional structure on the search space. This structure need not bear much resemblance to the ordinary spatial notion of direction, or that of distance, but it must somehow tie together points which are heuristically related.

We will call such a structure a *heuristic connection*. We introduce this term for informal use only—that is why our definition is itself so informal. But we need it. Many publications have been marred by the misuse, for this purpose, of precise mathematical terms, *e.g., metric* and *topological.* The term "connection," with its variety of dictionary meanings, seems just the word to designate a relation without commitment as to the exact nature of the relation.

An important and simple kind of heuristic connection is that defined when a space has coordinates (or parameters) and there is also defined a numerical "success function" E which is a reasonably smooth function of the coordinates. Here we can use local optimization or *hill-climbing* methods.

---

function requires about $2^n/n$ contacts. This disaster does not usually strike when we construct "interesting" large machines, presumably because they are based on composition of functions already found useful. One should not overlook the pioneering paper of Newell (1955), and Samuel's discussion of the minimaxing process in (1959*a*).

[3] In 1952 and especially in 1956, Ashby has an excellent discussion of the search problem. (However, I am not convinced of the usefulness of his notion of "ultrastability," which seems to be little more than the property of a machine to search until something stops it.)

B. Hill-climbing

Suppose that we are given a black-box machine with inputs $\lambda_1, \ldots, \lambda_n$ and an output $E(\lambda_1, \ldots, \lambda_n)$. We wish to maximize E by adjusting the input values. But we are not given any mathematical description of the function E; hence we cannot use differentiation or related methods. The obvious approach is to explore locally about a point, finding the direction of steepest ascent. One moves a certain distance in that direction and repeats the process until improvement ceases. If the hill is smooth this may be done, approximately, by estimating the gradient component $\partial E / \partial \lambda_i$ separately for each coordinate λ_i. There are more sophisticated approaches (one may use noise added to each variable, and correlate the output with each input, see Fig. 1), but this is the general idea. It is a fundamental technique, and we see it always in the background of far more complex systems. Heuristically, its great virtue is this: the sampling effort (for determining the direction of the gradient) grows, in a sense, only linearly with the number of parameters. So if we can solve, by such a method, a certain kind of problem involving many parameters, then the addition of more parameters of the same kind ought not cause an inordinate increase in difficulty. We are particularly interested in problem-solving methods which can be so extended to more difficult problems. Alas, most interesting systems which involve combinational operations usually grow exponentially more difficult as we add variables.

A great variety of hill-climbing systems have been studied under the names of "adaptive" or "self-optimizing" servomechanisms.

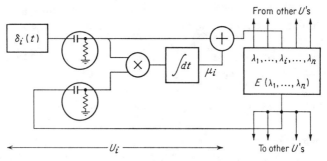

Figure 1. "Multiple simultaneous optimizers" search for a (local) maximum value of some function $E(\lambda_1, \ldots, \lambda_n)$ of several parameters. Each unit U_i independently "jitters" its parameter λ_i, perhaps randomly, by adding a variation $\delta_i(t)$ to a current mean value μ_i. The changes in the quantities δ_i and E are correlated, and the result is used to (slowly) change μ_i. The filters are to move d-c components. This simultaneous technique, really a form of coherent detection, usually has an advantage over methods dealing separately and sequentially with each parameter. [Cf. the discussion of "informative feedback" in Wiener (1948, pp. 133ff.).]

C. Troubles with Hill-climbing

Obviously, the gradient-following hill-climber would be trapped if it should reach a *local peak* which is not a true or satisfactory optimum. It must then be forced to try larger steps or changes.

It is often supposed that this false-peak problem is the chief obstacle to machine learning by this method. This certainly can be troublesome. But for really difficult problems, it seems to us that usually the more fundamental problem lies in finding any significant peak at all. Unfortunately the known E functions for difficult problems often exhibit what we have called (Minsky and Selfridge, 1960) the *"Mesa Phenomenon"* in which a small change in a parameter usually leads to either no change in performance or to a large change in performance. The space is thus composed primarily of flat regions or "mesas." Any tendency of the trial generator to make small steps then results in much aimless wandering without compensating information gains. A profitable search in such a space requires steps so large that hill-climbing is essentially ruled out. The problem-solver must find other methods; hill-climbing might still be feasible with a different heuristic connection.

Certainly, in our own intellectual behavior we rarely solve a tricky problem by a steady climb toward success. I doubt that in any one simple mechanism, *e.g.,* hill-climbing, will we find the means to build an efficient and general problem-solving machine. Probably, an intelligent machine will require a variety of different mechanisms. These will be arranged in hierarchies, and in even more complex, perhaps recursive, structures. And perhaps what amounts to straightforward hill-climbing on one level may sometimes appear (on a lower level) as the sudden jumps of "insight."

II. The Problem of Pattern Recognition

In order not to try all possibilities, a resourceful machine must classify problem situations into categories associated with the domains of effectiveness of the machine's different methods. These pattern-recognition methods must extract the heuristically significant features of the objects in question. The simplest methods simply match the objects against standards or prototypes. More powerful "property-list" methods subject each object to a sequence of tests, each detecting some *property* of heuristic importance. These properties have to be invariant under commonly encountered forms of distortion. Two important problems arise here—inventing new useful properties, and combining many properties to form a recognition system. For complex problems, such methods will have to be augmented by facilities for subdividing complex objects and describing the complex relations between their parts.

Any powerful heuristic program is bound to contain a variety of different methods and techniques. At each step of the problem-solving process the machine will have to decide what aspect of the problem to work on, and then which method to use. A choice must be made, for we usually cannot afford to try all the possibilities. In order to deal with a goal or a problem, that is, to choose an appropriate method, we have to recognize what kind of thing it is. Thus the need to choose among actions compels us to provide the machine with classification techniques, or means of evolving them. It is of overwhelming importance that the machine have classification techniques which are realistic. But "realistic" can be defined only with respect to the environments to be encountered by the machine, and with respect to the methods available to it. Distinctions which cannot be exploited are not worth recognizing. And methods are usually worthless without classification schemes which can help decide when they are applicable.

A. Teleological Requirements of Classification

The useful classifications are those which match the goals and methods of the machine. The objects grouped together in the classifications should have something of heuristic value in common; they should be "similar" in a useful sense; they should depend on relevant or essential features. We should not be surprised, then, to find ourselves using inverse or teleological expressions to define the classes. We really do want to have a grip on "the class of objects which can be transformed into a result of form Y," that is, the class of objects which will satisfy some goal. One should be wary of the familiar injunction against using teleological language in science. While it is true that talking of goals in some contexts may dispose us towards certain kinds of animistic explanations, this need not be a bad thing in the field of problem-solving; it is hard to see how one can solve problems without thoughts of purposes. The real difficulty with teleological definitions is technical, not philosophical, and arises when they have to be used and not just mentioned. One obviously cannot afford to use for classification a method which actually requires waiting for some remote outcome, if one needs the classification precisely for deciding whether to try out that method. So, in practice, the ideal teleological definitions often have to be replaced by practical approximations, usually with some risk of error; that is, the definitions have to be made *heuristically effective,* or economically usable. This is of great importance. (We can think of "heuristic effectiveness" as contrasted to the ordinary mathematical notion of "effectiveness" which distinguishes those definitions which can be realized at all by machine, regardless of efficiency.)

B. Patterns and Descriptions

It is usually necessary to have ways of assigning *names*—symbolic expressions—to the defined classes. The structure of the names will have a crucial influence on the mental world of the machine, for it determines what kinds of things can be conveniently thought about. There are a variety of ways to assign names. The simplest schemes use what we will call *conventional* (or *proper*) names; here, arbitrary symbols are assigned to classes. But we will also want to use complex *descriptions* or *computed names;* these are constructed for classes by processes which *depend on the class definitions.* To be useful, these should reflect some of the structure of the things they designate, abstracted in a manner relevant to the problem area. The notion of description merges smoothly into the more complex notion of *model;* as we think of it, a model is a sort of active description. It is a thing whose form reflects some of the structure of the thing represented, but which also has some of the character of a working machine.

In Sec. III we will consider "learning" systems. The behavior of those systems can be made to change in reasonable ways depending on what happened to them in the past. But by themselves, the simple learning systems are useful only in recurrent situations; they cannot cope with any significant novelty. Nontrivial performance is obtained only when learning systems are supplemented with classification or pattern-recognition methods of some inductive ability. For the variety of objects encountered in a nontrivial search is so enormous that we cannot depend on recurrence, and the mere accumulation of records of past experience can have only limited value. Pattern Recognition, by providing a heuristic connection which links the old to the new, can make learning broadly useful.

What is a "pattern"? We often use the term teleologically to mean a set of objects which can in some (useful) way be treated alike. For each problem area we must ask, "What patterns would be useful for a machine working on such problems?"

The problems of *visual* pattern recognition have received much attention in recent years and most of our examples are from this area.

C. Prototype-derived Patterns

The problem of reading *printed* characters is a clearcut instance of a situation in which the classification is based ultimately on a fixed set of "prototypes"—*e.g.,* the dies from which the type font was made. The individual marks on the printed page may show the results of many distortions. Some distortions are rather systematic: change in size, position, orientation. Some are of the nature of noise: blurring, grain, low contrast, etc.

If the noise is not too severe, we may be able to manage the identification by what we call a *normalization and template-matching* process. We first remove the differences related to size and position—that is, we *normalize* the input figure. One may do this, for example, by constructing a similar figure inscribed in a certain fixed triangle (see Fig. 2); or one may transform the figure to obtain a certain fixed center of gravity and a unit second central moment. [There is an additional problem with rotational

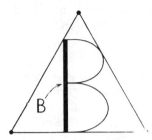

Figure 2. A simple normalization technique. If an object is expanded uniformly, without rotation, until it touches all three sides of a triangle, the resulting figure will be unique, and pattern recognition can proceed without concern about relative size and position.

equivalence where it is not easy to avoid all ambiguities. One does not want to equate "6" and "9." For that matter, one does not want to equate $(0,o)$, or (X,x) or the o's in x_o and x^o, so that there may be context dependency involved.] Once normalized, the unknown figure can be compared with *templates* for the prototypes and, by means of some measure of *matching*, choose the best fitting template. Each "matching criterion" will be sensitive to particular forms of noise and distortion, and so will each normalization procedure. The inscribing or boxing method may be sensitive to small specks, while the moment method will be especially sensitive to smearing, at least for thin-line figures, etc. The choice of a matching criterion must depend on the kinds of noise and transformations commonly encountered.

Still, for many problems we may get acceptable results by using straightforward correlation methods.

When the class of equivalence transformations is very large, *e.g.*, when local stretching and distortion are present, there will be difficulty in finding a uniform normalization method. Instead, one may have to consider a process of adjusting locally for best fit to the template. (While measuring the matching, one could "jitter" the figure locally; if an improvement were found the process could be repeated using a slightly different change, etc.) There is usually no practical possibility of applying to the figure *all* of the admissible transformations. And to recognize the *topological* equivalence of pairs such as those in Fig. 3 is likely beyond any practical kind of iterative local-improvement or hill-climbing matching procedure. (Such recognitions can be mechanized, though, by methods which follow lines, detect vertices, and build up a *description* in the form, say, of a vertex-connection table.)

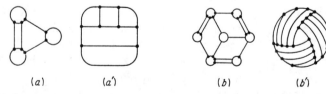

(a)   (a')   (b)   (b')

Figure 3. The figures A, A' and B, B' are topologically equivalent pairs. Lengths have been distorted in an arbitrary manner, but the connectivity relations between corresponding points have been preserved. In Sherman (1959) and Haller (1959) we find computer programs which can deal with such equivalences.

The template-matching scheme, with its normalization and direct comparison and matching criterion, is just too limited in conception to be of much use in more difficult problems. If the transformation set is large, normalization, or "fitting," may be impractical, especially if there is no adequate heuristic connection on the space of transformations. Furthermore, for each defined pattern, the system has to be presented with a prototype. But if one has in mind a fairly abstract class, one may simply be unable to represent its essential features with one or a very few concrete examples. How could one represent with a single prototype the class of figures which have an even number of disconnected parts? Clearly, the template system has negligible descriptive power. The property-list system frees us from some of these limitations.

D. Property Lists and "Characters"

We define a *property* to be a two-valued function which divides figures into two classes; a figure is said to have or not have the property according to whether the function's value is 1 or 0. Given a number N of distinction properties, we could define as many as 2^n subclasses by their set intersections and, hence, as many as 2^{2^n} *patterns* by combining the properties with AND's and OR's. Thus, if we have three properties, *rectilinear, connected,* and *cyclic,* there are eight subclasses (and 256 patterns) defined by their intersections (see Fig. 4).

If the given properties are placed in a fixed order then we can represent any of these elementary regions by a vector, or string of digits. The vector so assigned to each figure will be called the *Character* of that figure (with respect to the sequence of properties in question). [In "Some Aspects of Heuristic Programming and Artificial Intelligence" (1959a), we use the

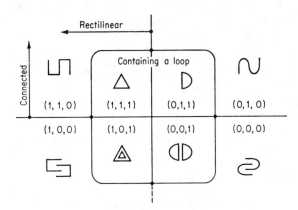

Figure 4. The eight regions represent all the possible configurations of values of the three properties "rectilinear," "connected," "containing a loop." Each region contains a representative figure, and its associated binary "Character" sequence.

term *characteristic* for a property without restriction to 2 values.] Thus a square has the Character (1,1,1) and a circle the Character (0,1,1) for the given sequence of properties.

For many problems one can use such Characters as names for categories and as primitive elements with which to define an adequate set of patterns. Characters are more than conventional names. They are instead very rudimentary forms of description (having the form of the simplest symbolic expression—the *list*) whose structure provides some information about the designated classes. This is a step, albeit a small one, beyond the template method; the Characters are not simple instances of the patterns, and the properties may themselves be very abstract. Finding a good set of properties is the major concern of many heuristic programs.

E. Invariant Properties

One of the prime requirements of a good property is that it be invariant under the commonly encountered equivalence transformations. Thus for visual Pattern Recognition we would usually want the object identification to be independent of uniform changes in size and position. In their pioneering paper Pitts and McCulloch (1947) describe a general technique for forming invariant properties from noninvariant ones, assuming that the transformation space has a certain (group) structure. The idea behind their mathematical argument is this: suppose that we have a function P of figures, and suppose that for a given figure F we define $[F] = \{F_1, F_2, \ldots\}$ to be the set of all figures equivalent to F under the given set of transformations; further, define $P[F]$ to be the set $\{P(F_1), P(F_2), \ldots\}$ of values of P on those figures. Finally, define $P^*[F]$ to be AVERAGE $(P[F])$. Then we have a new property P^* whose values are independent of the selection of F from an equivalence class defined by the transformations. We have to be sure that when different representatives are chosen from a class the collection $[F]$ will always be the same in each case. In the case of continuous transformation spaces, there will have to be a *measure* or the equivalent associated with the set $[F]$ with respect to which the operation AVERAGE is defined, say, as an integration.[4]

This method is proposed (Pitts and McCulloch, 1947) as a neurophysiological model for pitch-invariant hearing and size-invariant visual

[4] In the case studied in Pitts and McCulloch (1947) the transformation space is a *group* with a uniquely defined measure: the set $[F]$ can be computed without repetitions by scanning through the application of all the transforms T_α to the given figure so that the invariant property can be defined by

$$P^*(F) = \int_{\alpha \in G} P(T_\alpha(F)) \, d\mu$$

where G is the group and μ the measure. By substituting $T_\beta(F)$ for F in this, one can see that the result is independent of choice of β since we obtain the same integral over $G\beta^{-1} = G$.

recognition (supplemented with visual centering mechanisms). This model is discussed also by Wiener.[5] Practical application is probably limited to one-dimensional groups and analog scanning devices.

In much recent work this problem is avoided by using properties already invariant under these transformations. Thus a property might count the number of connected components in a picture—this is invariant under size and position. Or a property may count the number of vertical lines in a picture—this is invariant under size and position (but not rotation).

F. Generating Properties

The problem of generating useful properties has been discussed by Selfridge (1955); we shall summarize his approach. The machine is given, at the start, a few basic transformations $A_1, \ldots, A_n$, each of which transforms, in some significant way, each figure into another figure. A_1 might, for example, remove all points *not on a boundary* of a solid region; A_2 might leave only *vertex* points; A_3 might *fill up hollow regions*, etc. (see Fig. 5). Each sequence $A_{i1}A_{i2} \ldots A_{ik}$ of these forms a new transformation, so that there is available an infinite variety. We provide the machine also with one or more "terminal" operations which convert a picture into a number, so that any sequence of the elementary transformations, followed by a terminal operation, defines a property. [Dineen (1955) describes how these processes were programmed in a digital computer.] We can start with a few short sequences, perhaps chosen randomly. Selfridge describes how the machine might learn new useful properties.

We now feed the machine A's and O's telling the machine each time which letter it is. Beside each sequence under the two letters, the machine builds up distribution functions from the results of applying the sequences to the image. Now, since the sequences were chosen completely randomly, it may well be that most of the sequences have very flat distribution functions; that is, they [provide] no information,

[5] See pp. 160ff. of Wiener (1948).

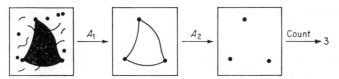

Figure 5. An arbitrary sequence of picture transformations, followed by a numerical-valued function, can be used as a *property* function for pictures. A_1 removes all points which are not at the edge of a solid region. A_2 leaves only vertex points—at which an arc suddenly changes direction. The function C simply counts the number of points remaining in the picture. All remarks in the text could be generalized to apply to properties like A_1A_2C, which can have more than two values.

and the sequences are therefore [by definition] not significant. Let it discard these and pick some others. Sooner or later, however, some sequences will prove significant; that is, their distribution functions will peak up somewhere. What the machine does now is to build up new sequences like the significant ones. This is the important point. If it merely chose sequences at random it might take a very long while indeed to find the best sequences. But with some successful sequences, or partly successful ones, to guide it, we hope that the process will be much quicker. The crucial question remains: how do we build up sequences "like" other sequences, but not identical? As of now we think we shall merely build sequences from the transition frequencies of the significant sequences. We shall build up a matrix of transition frequencies from the significant ones, and use those as transition probabilities with which to choose new sequences.

We do not claim that this method is necessarily a very good way of choosing sequences—only that it should do better than not using at all the knowledge of what kind of sequences has worked. It has seemed to us that this is the crucial point of learning.[6]

It would indeed be remarkable if this failed to yield properties more useful than would be obtained from completely random sequence selection. The generating problem is discussed further in Minsky (1956a). Newell, Shaw, and Simon (1960b) describe more deliberate, less statistical, techniques that might be used to discover sets of properties appropriate to a given problem area. One may think of the Selfridge proposal as a system which uses a finite-state language to describe its properties. Solomonoff (1957, 1960) proposes some techniques for discovering common features of a set of expressions, *e.g.*, of the descriptions of those properties of already established utility; the methods can then be applied to generate new properties with the same common features. I consider the lines of attack in Selfridge (1955), Newell, Shaw and Simon (1960a), and Solomonoff (1960, 1958), although still incomplete, to be of the greatest importance.

G. Combining Properties

One cannot expect easily to find a *small* set of properties which will be just right for a problem area. It is usually much easier to find a large set of properties each of which provides a little useful information. Then one is faced with the problem of finding a way to combine them to make the desired distinctions. The simplest method is to choose, for each class, a typical character (a particular sequence of property values) and then to use some matching procedure, *e.g.*, counting the numbers of agreements and disagreements, to compare an unknown with these chosen "Character

[6] See p. 93 of Selfridge (1955).

prototypes." The linear weighting scheme described just below is a slight generalization on this. Such methods treat the properties as more or less independent evidence for and against propositions; more general procedures (about which we have yet little practical information) must account also for nonlinear relations between properties, *i.e.*, must contain weighting terms for joint subsets of property values.

1. "BAYES NETS" FOR COMBINING INDEPENDENT PROPERTIES

We consider a single experiment in which an object is placed in front of a property-list machine. Each property E_i will have a value, 0 or 1. Suppose that there has been defined some set of "object classes" F_j, and that we want to use the outcome of this experiment to decide in which of these classes the object belongs.

Assume that the situation is basically probabilistic, and that we know the probability p_{ij} that, if the object is in class F_j then the ith property E_i will have value 1. Assume further that these properties are independent; that is, even given F_j, knowledge of the value of E_i tells us nothing more about the value of a different E_k in the same experiment. (This is a strong condition—see below.) Let ϕ_j be the absolute probability that an object is in class F_j. Finally, for this experiment define V to be the particular set of i's for which the E_i's are 1. Then this V represents the Character of the object. From the definition of conditional probability, we have

$$\Pr(F_j,V) = \Pr(V) \cdot \Pr(F_j|V) = \Pr(F_j) \cdot \Pr(V|F_j)$$

Given the Character V, we want to guess which F_j has occurred (with the least chance of being wrong—the so-called *maximum likelihood* estimate); that is, for which j is $\Pr(F_j|V)$ the largest? Since in the above $\Pr(V)$ does not depend on j, we have only to calcuate for which j is

$$\Pr(F_j) \cdot \Pr(V|F_j) = \phi_j \Pr(V|F_j)$$

the largest. Hence, by our independence hypothesis, we have to maximize

$$\phi_j \cdot \prod_{i \in V} p_{ij} \cdot \prod_{i \in \bar{V}} q_{ij} = \phi_j \prod_{i \in V} \frac{p_{ij}}{q_{ij}} \cdot \prod_{\text{all } i} q_{ij} \tag{1}$$

These "maximum-likelihood" decisions can be made (Fig. 6) by a simple network device.[7]

---

[7] At the cost of an additional network layer, we may also account for the possible cost g_{jk} that would be incurred if we were to assign to F_k a figure really in class F_j; in this case the minimum cost decision is given by the k for which

$$\sum_j g_{jk}\phi_j \prod_{i \in V} p_{ij} \prod_{i \in \bar{V}} q_{ij}$$

is the least. $\bar{V}$ is the complement set to V. q_{ij} is $(1 - p_{ij})$.

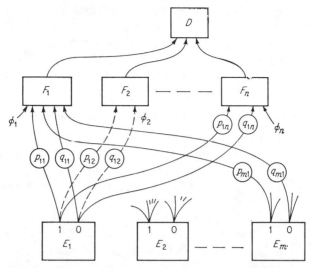

Figure 6. "Net" model for maximum-likelihood decisions based on linear weightings of property values. The input data are examined by each "property filter" E_i. Each E_i has "0" and "1" output channels, one of which is excited by each input. These outputs are weighted by the corresponding p_{ij}'s, as shown in the text. The resulting signals are multiplied in the F_j units, each of which "collects evidence" for a particular figure class. [We could have used here log (p_{ij}), and *added* at the F_j units.] The final decision is made by the topmost unit D, who merely chooses that F_j with the largest score. Note that the logarithm of the coefficient p_{ij}/q_{ij} in the second expression of (1) can be construed as the "weight of the evidence" of E_i in favor of F_j. [See also Papert (1961) and Rosenblatt (1958).]

These nets resemble the general schematic diagrams proposed in the "Pandemonium" model of Selfridge (1959) (see his fig. 3). It is proposed there that some intellectual processes might be carried out by a hierarchy of simultaneously functioning submachines suggestively called "demons." Each unit is set to detect certain patterns in the activity of others and the output of each unit announces the degree of confidence of that unit that it sees what it is looking for. Our E_i units are Selfridge's "data demons." Our units F_j are his "cognitive demons"; each collects from the abstracted data evidence for a specific proposition. The topmost "decision demon" D responds to that one in the multitude below it whose shriek is the loudest.[8]

It is quite easy to add to this "Bayes network model" a mechanism which will enable it to *learn* the optimal connection weightings. Imagine that, after each event, the machine is told which F_j has occurred; we could implement this by sending back a signal along the connections leading to that F_j unit. Suppose that the connection for p_{ij} (or q_{ij}) contains a two-terminal device (or "synapse") which stores a number w_{ij}. Whenever the joint event $(F_j, E_i = 1)$ occurs, we modify w_{ij} by replacing it by

[8] See also the report in Selfridge and Neisser (1960).

$(w_{ij} + 1)\theta$, where θ is a factor slightly less than unity. And when the joint event $(F_j, E_i = 0)$ occurs, we decrement w_{ij} by replacing it with $(w_{ij})\theta$. It is not difficult to show that the expected values of the w_{ij}'s will become proportional to the p_{ij}'s [and, in fact, approach $p_{ij}[\theta/(1 - \theta)]$]. Hence, the machine tends to learn the optimal weighting on the basis of experience. (One must put in a similar mechanism for estimating the ϕ_j's.) The variance of the normalized weight $w_{ij}[(1 - \theta)/\theta]$ approaches $[(1 - \theta)/(1 + \theta)]p_{ij}q_{ij}$. Thus a small value for θ means rapid learning but is associated with a large variance, hence, with low reliability. Choosing θ close to unity means slow, but reliable, learning. θ is really a sort of memory decay constant, and its choice must be determined by the noise and stability of the environment—much noise requires long averaging times, while a changing environment requires fast adaptation. The two requirements are, of course, incompatible and the decision has to be based on an economic compromise.[9]

2. POSSIBILITIES OF USING RANDOM NETS FOR BAYES DECISIONS

The nets of Fig. 6 are very orderly in structure. Is all this structure necessary? Certainly if there were a great many properties, *each of which provided very little marginal information,* some of them would not be missed. Then one might expect good results with a mere sampling of all the possible connection paths w_{ij}. And one might thus, *in this special situation,* use a random connection net.

The two-layer nets here resemble those of the "Perceptron" proposal of Rosenblatt (1958). In the latter, there is an additional level of connections coming directly from randomly selected points of a "retina." Here the properties, the devices which abstract the visual input data, are simple functions which add some inputs, subtract others, and detect whether the result exceeds a threshold. Equation (1), we think, illustrates what is of value in this scheme. It does seem clear that a maximum-likelihood type of analysis of the output of the property functions can be handled by such nets. But these nets, with their simple, randomly generated, connections can probably never achieve recognition of such patterns as "the class of figures having two separated parts," and they cannot even achieve the effect of template recognition without size and position normalization (unless sample figures have been presented previously in essentially all sizes and positions). For the chances are extremely small of finding, by random methods, enough properties usefully correlated with patterns appreciably more abstract than those of the prototype-derived kind. And these networks can really only separate out (by weighting) information in the individual input properties; they cannot extract further information present in nonadditive form. The "Perceptron" class of machines have facilities neither for obtaining better-than-chance properties nor for assembling

[9] See also Minsky and Selfridge (1960), and Papert (1961).

better-than-additive combinations of those it gets from random construction.[10]

For recognizing *normalized* printed or hand-printed characters, single-point properties do surprisingly well (Highleyman and Kamentsky, 1960); this amounts to just "averaging" many samples. Bledsoe and Browning (1959) claim good results with point-pair properties. Roberts (1960) describes a series of experiments in this general area. Doyle (1959) without normalization but with quite sophisticated properties obtains excellent results; his properties are already substantially size- and position-invariant. A general review of Doyle's work and other pattern-recognition experiments will be found in Selfridge and Neisser (1960).

For the complex discrimination, *e.g.,* between one and two connected objects, the property problem is very serious, especially for long wiggly objects such as are handled by Kirsch (1957). Here some kind of recursive processing is required and combinations of simple properties would almost certainly fail even with large nets and long training.

We should not leave the discussion of some decision net models without noting their important limitations. The hypothesis that, for given j, the p_{ij} represent independent events, is a very strong condition indeed. Without this hypothesis we could still construct maximum-likelihood nets, but we would need an additional layer of cells to represent all of the joint events V; that is, we would need to know all the $\Pr(F_j|V)$. This gives a general (but trivial) solution, but requires 2^n cells for n properties, which is completely impractical for large systems. What is required is a system which computes some sampling of all the joint conditional probabilities, and uses these to estimate others when needed. The work of Uttley (1956, 1959) bears on this problem, but his proposed and experimental devices do not yet clearly show how to avoid exponential growth.[11]

H. Articulation and Attention—Limitations of the Property-list Method

Because of its fixed size, the property-list scheme is limited (for any given set of properties) in the detail of the distinctions it can make. Its ability to deal with a compound scene containing several objects is critically weak, and its direct extensions are unwieldy and unnatural. If a machine can recognize a chair and a table, it surely should be able to tell us that "there is a chair and a table." To an extent, we can invent properties which allow some capacity for superposition of object Characters.[12] But there is no way to escape the information limit.

---

[10] See also Roberts (1960), Papert (1961), and Hawkins (1958). We can find nothing resembling an analysis [see (1) above] in Rosenblatt (1958) or his subsequent publications.

[11] See also Papert (1961).

[12] Cf. Mooers' technique of Zatocoding (1956*a*, 1956*b*).

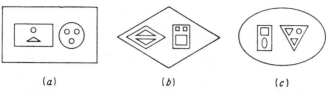

Figure 7. The picture (a) is first described verbally in the text. Then, by introducing notation for the relations "inside of," "to the left of" and "above," we construct a symbolic description. Such descriptions can be formed and manipulated by machines. By abstracting out of the complex relation between the parts of the figure we can use the same formula to describe the related pictures (b) and (c), changing only the list of primitive parts. It is up to the programmer to decide at just what level of complexity a part of a picture should be considered "primitive"; this will depend on what the description is to be used for. We could further divide the drawings into vertices, lines, and arcs. Obviously, for some applications the relations would need more metrical information, e.g., specification of lengths or angles.

What is required is clearly (1) a *list (of whatever length is necessary)* of the primitive objects in the scene and (2) a statement about the relations among them. Thus we say of Fig. 7a, "A rectangle (1) contains two subfigures disposed horizontally. The part on the left is a rectangle (2) which contains two subfigures disposed vertically; the upper a circle (3) and the lower a triangle (4). The part on the right . . . etc." Such a description entails an ability to separate or "articulate" the scene into parts. (Note that in this example the articulation is essentially *recursive;* the figure is first divided into two parts; then each part is described using the same machinery.) We can formalize this kind of description in an expression language whose fundamental grammatical form is a pair (R,L) whose first member R names a *relation* and whose second member L is an *ordered list* $(x_1, x_2, \ldots, x_n)$ of the objects or subfigures which bear that relation to one another. We obtain the required flexibility by allowing the members of the list L to contain not only the names of "elementary" figures but also "subexpressions" of the form (R,L) designating complex subfigures. Then our scene above may be described by the expression

$$[\odot, (\square, (\rightarrow, \{(\odot, (\square, (\downarrow, (\bigcirc, \triangle)))), (\odot, (\bigcirc, (\triangledown, (\bigcirc, \quad \bigcirc, \bigcirc)))))\}))]$$

where $(\odot, (x,y))$ means that y is contained in x; $(\rightarrow, (x,y))$ means that y is to the right of x; $(\downarrow, (x,y))$ means that y is below x, and $(\triangle, (x,y,z))$ means that y is to the right of x and z is underneath and between them. The symbols $\square$, $\bigcirc$, and $\triangle$ represent the indicated kinds of primitive geometric objects. This expression-pair description language may be regarded as a simple kind of "list-structure" language. Powerful computer techniques have been developed, originally by Newell, Shaw and Simon, for manipulating symbolic expressions in such languages for purposes of heuristic programming. (See the remarks at the end of Sec. IV. If some of the members of a list are themselves lists, they must be surrounded by exterior parentheses, and this accounts for the accumulation of parentheses.)

It may be desirable to construct descriptions in which the complex relation is extracted, *e.g.*, so that we have an expression of the form *FG* where *F* is an expression which at once denotes the composite relation between all the primitive parts listed in *G*. A complication arises in connection with the "binding" of variables, *i.e.*, in specifying the manner in which the elements of *G* participate in the relation *F*. This can be handled in general by the "λ" notation (McCarthy, 1960) but here we can just use integers to order the variables.

For the given example, we could describe the relational part *F* by an expression

$$\odot(1,\rightarrow(\odot(2,\downarrow(3,4)),\odot(5,\triangledown(6,7,8))))$$

in which we now use a "functional notation"; "($\odot$, (x,y))" is replaced by "$\odot$ (x,y)," etc., making for better readability. To obtain the desired description, this expression has to be applied to an ordered list of primitive objects, which in this case is ($\Box,\Box,\bigcirc,\triangle,\bigcirc,\bigcirc.\bigcirc,\bigcirc$). This composite functional form allows us to abstract the composite relation. By changing only the object list we can obtain descriptions also of the objects in Fig. 7*b* and *c*.

The important thing about such "articular" descriptions is that they can be obtained by *repeated application of a fixed set of pattern-recognition techniques.* Thus we can obtain *arbitrarily complex* descriptions from a fixed complexity classification mechanism. The new element required in the mechanism (beside the capacity to manipulate the list structures) is the ability to articulate—to "attend fully" to a selected part of the picture and bring all one's resources to bear on that part. In efficient problem-solving programs, we will not usually complete such a description in a single operation. Instead, the depth or detail of description will be under the control of other processes. These will reach deeper, or look more carefully, only when they have to, *e.g.,* when the presently available description is inadequate for a current goal. The author, together with L. Hodes, is working on pattern-recognition schemes using articular descriptions. By manipulating the formal descriptions we can deal with overlapping and incomplete figures, and several other problems of the "Gestalt" type.

It seems likely that as machines are turned toward more difficult problem areas, *passive* classification systems will become less adequate, and we may have to turn toward schemes which are based more on internally generated hypotheses, perhaps "error-controlled" along the lines proposed by MacKay (1956).

Space requires us to terminate this discussion of pattern-recognition and description. Among the important works not reviewed here should be mentioned those of Bomba (1959) and Grimsdale et al. (1959), which involve elements of description, Unger (1959) and Holland (1960) for parallel processing schemes, Hebb (1949) who is concerned with physiological description models, and the work of the Gestalt psychologists, notably Kohler (1947), who have certainly raised, if not solved, a number of important questions. Sherman (1959), Haller (1959) and others have completed programs using line-tracing operations for topological classification. The papers of Selfridge (1955, 1956) have been a major influence on work in this general area.

See also Kirsch et al. (1957) for discussion of a number of interesting computer image processing techniques, and see Minot (1959) and Stevens (1957) for reviews of the reading machine and related problems. One should also examine some biological work, e.g., Tinbergen (1951) to see instances in which some discriminations which seem, at first glance very complicated are explained on the basis of a few apparently simple properties arranged in simple decision trees.

III. Learning Systems

In order to solve a new problem, one should first try using methods similar to those that have worked on similar problems. To implement this "basic learning heuristic" one must generalize on past experience, and one way to do this is to use success-reinforced decision models. These learning systems are shown to be averaging devices. Using devices which learn also which events are associated with reinforcement, i.e., reward, we can build more autonomous "secondary reinforcement" systems. In applying such methods to complex problems, one encounters a serious difficulty—in distributing credit for success of a complex strategy among the many decisions that were involved. This problem can be managed by arranging for local reinforcement of partial goals within a hierarchy, and by grading the training sequence of problems to parallel a process of maturation of the machine's resources.

In order to solve a new problem one uses what might be called the basic learning heuristic—first try using methods similar to those which have worked, in the past, on similar problems. We want our machines, too, to benefit from their past experience. Since we cannot expect new situations to be precisely the same as old ones, any useful learning will have to involve generalization techniques. There are too many notions associated with "learning" to justify defining the term precisely. But we may be sure that any useful learning system will have to use records of the past as *evidence for more general propositions;* it must thus entail some commitment or other about "inductive inference." (See Sec. V*B.*) Perhaps the simplest way of generalizing about a set of entities is through constructing a new one which is an "ideal," or rather, a typical member of that set; the usual way to do this is to smooth away variation by some sort of averaging technique. And indeed we find that most of the *simple* learning devices do incorporate some averaging technique—often that of averaging some sort of product, thus obtaining a sort of correlation. We shall discuss this family of devices here, and some more abstract schemes in Sec. V.

A. Reinforcement

A reinforcement process is one in which some aspects of the behavior of a system are caused to become more (or less) prominent in the future as a consequence of the application of a "reinforcement operator" Z. This operator is required to affect only those aspects of behavior for which instances have actually occurred recently.

The analogy is with "reward" or "extinction" (not punishment) in animal behavior. The important thing about this kind of process is that it is "operant" [a term of Skinner (1953)]; the reinforcement operator does not initiate behavior, but merely selects that which the Trainer likes from that which has occurred. Such a system must then contain a device M which generates a variety of behavior (say, in interacting with some environment) and a Trainer who makes critical judgments in applying the available reinforcement operators. (See Fig. 8.)

Let us consider a very simple reinforcement model. Suppose that on each presentation of a stimulus S an animal has to make a choice, *e.g.,* to

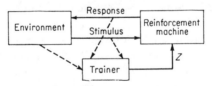

Figure 8. Parts of an "operant reinforcement" learning system. In response to a stimulus from the environment, the machine makes one of several possible responses. It remembers what decisions were made in choosing this response. Shortly thereafter, the Trainer sends to the machine positive or negative reinforcement (reward) signal; this increases or decreases the tendency to make the same decisions in the future. Note that the Trainer need not know how to solve problems, but only how to detect success or failure, or relative improvement; his function is selective. The Trainer might be connected to observe the actual stimulus-response activity, or, in a more interesting kind of system, just some function of the state of the environment.

turn left or right, and that its probability of turning right, at the nth trial, is p_n. Suppose that *we* want it to turn right. Whenever it does this we might "reward" it by applying the operator Z_+;

$$p_{n+1} = Z_+(p_n) = \theta p_n + (1 - \theta) \qquad 0 < \theta < 1$$

which moves p a fraction $(1 - \theta)$ of the way toward unity.[13] If we dislike what it does we apply negative reinforcement,

$$p_{n+1} = Z_-(p_n) = \theta p_n$$

moving p the same fraction of the way toward 0. Some theory of such "linear" learning operators, generalized to several stimuli and responses, will be found in Bush and Mosteller (1955). We can show that the learning result is an average weighted by an exponentially-decaying time factor: Let Z_n be ± 1 according to whether the nth event is rewarded or extinguished and replace p_n by $c_n = 2p_n - 1$ so that $-1 \le c_n \le 1$, as for a correlation coefficient. Then (with $c_0 = 0$) we obtain by induction

$$c_{n+1} = (1 - \theta) \sum_{i=0}^{n} \theta^{n-i} Z_i$$

and since

$$\frac{1}{1 - \theta} \approx \sum_{0}^{n} \theta^{n-i}$$

we can write this as

$$c_{n+1} \approx \frac{\Sigma \theta^{n-i} Z_i}{\Sigma \theta^{n-i}} \tag{1}$$

If the term Z_i is regarded as a product of (i) how the creature responded and (ii) which kind of reinforcement was given, then c_n is a kind of correlation function (with the decay weighting) of the joint behavior of these quantities. The ordinary, uniformly weighted average has the same general form but with time-dependent θ:

$$c_{n+1} = \left(1 - \frac{1}{N}\right) c_n + \frac{1}{N} Z_n \tag{2}$$

In (1) we have again the situation described in Sec. IIG1; a small value of θ gives fast learning, and the possibility of quick adaptation to a changing environment. A near-unity value of θ gives slow learning, but also smooths away uncertainties due to noise. As noted in Sec. IIG1, the response distribution comes to approximate the probabilities of rewards of the alternative responses. (The importance of this phenomenon has, I think, been overrated; it is certainly not an especially rational strategy. One reasonable alternative is that of computing the numbers p_{ij} as indi-

[13] Properly, the reinforcement functions should depend both on the p's and on the previous reaction—reward should decrease p if our animal has just turned to the left. The notation in the literature is also somewhat confusing in this regard.

cated, but actually playing at each trial the "most likely" choice. Except in the presence of a hostile opponent, there is usually no reason to play a "mixed" strategy.[14])

In Samuel's coefficient-optimizing program (1959b) [see Sec. IIIC1], there is a most ingenious compromise between the exponential and the uniform averaging methods: the value of N in (2) above begins at 16 and so remains until $n = 16$, then N is 32 until $n = 32$, and so on until $n = 256$. Thereafter N remains fixed at 256. This nicely prevents violent fluctuations in c_n at the start, approaches the uniform weighting for a while, and finally approaches the exponentially weighted correlation, all in a manner that requires very little computation effort! Samuel's program is at present the outstanding example of a game-playing program which matches average human ability, and its success (in real time) is attributed to a wealth of such elegancies, both in heuristics and in programming.

The problem of extinction or "unlearning" is especially critical for complex, hierarchical, learning. For, once a generalization about the past has been made, one is likely to build upon it. Thus, one may come to select certain properties as important and begin to use them in the characterization of experience, perhaps storing one's memories in terms of them. If later it is discovered that some other properties would serve better, then one must face the problem of translating, or abandoning, the records based on the older system. This may be a very high price to pay. One does not easily give up an old way of looking at things, if the better one demands much effort and experience to be useful. Thus the *training sequences* on which our machines will spend their infancies, so to speak, must be chosen very shrewdly to insure that early abstractions will provide a good foundation for later difficult problems.

Incidentally, in spite of the space given here for their exposition, I am not convinced that such "incremental" or "statistical" learning schemes should play a central role in our models. They will certainly continue to appear as components of our programs but, I think, mainly by default. The more intelligent one is, the more often he should be able to learn from an experience something rather definite; *e.g.,* to reject or accept a hypothesis, or to change a goal. (The obvious exception is that of a truly statistical environment in which averaging is inescapable. But the heart of problem-solving is always, we think, the combinatorial part that gives rise to searches, and we should usually be able to regard the complexities caused by "noise" as mere annoyances, however irritating they may be.) In this connection we can refer to the discussion of memory in Miller, Galanter and Pribram (1960).[15] This seems to be the first major work

---

[14] The question of just how often one should play a strategy different from the estimated optimum, in order to gain information, is an underlying problem in many fields. See, *e.g.,* Shubik (1960).

[15] See especially chap. 10.

in psychology to show the influence of work in the artificial intelligence area, and its programme is generally quite sophisticated.

B. Secondary Reinforcement and Expectation Models

The simple reinforcement system is limited by its dependence on the Trainer. If the Trainer can detect only the *solution* of a problem, then we may encounter "mesa" phenomena which will limit performance on difficult problems. (See Sec. IC.) One way to escape this is to have the machine learn to generalize on what the Trainer does. Then, in difficult problems, it may be able to give itself partial reinforcements along the way, *e.g.,* upon the solution of relevant subproblems. The machine in Fig. 9 has some such ability. The new unit U is a device that learns which external stimuli are strongly correlated with the various reinforcement signals, and responds to such stimuli by reproducing the corresponding reinforcement signals. (The device U is *not* itself a reinforcement learning device; it is more like a "Pavlovian" conditioning device, treating the Z signals as "unconditioned" stimuli and the S signals as conditioned stimuli.) The heuristic idea is that any signal from the environment which in the past has been well correlated with (say) positive reinforcement is likely to be an indication that something good has just happened. If the training on early problems was such that this is realistic, then the system eventually should be able to detach itself from the Trainer, and become autonomous. If we further permit "chaining" of the "secondary reinforcers," *e.g.,* by admitting the connection shown as a dotted line in Fig. 9, the scheme becomes quite powerful, in principle. There are obvious pitfalls in admitting

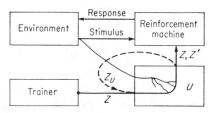

Figure 9. An additional device U gives the machine of Fig. 8 the ability to learn which signals from the environment have been associated with reinforcement. The primary reinforcement signals Z are routed through U. By a Pavlovian conditioning process (not described here), external signals come to produce reinforcement signals like those that have frequently succeeded them in the past. Such signals might be abstract, *e.g.,* verbal encouragement. If the "secondary reinforcement" signals are allowed, in turn, to acquire further external associations (through, *e.g.,* a channel Z_U as shown) the machine might come to be able to handle chains of subproblems. But something must be done to stabilize the system against the positive symbolic feedback loop formed by the path Z_U. The profound difficulty presented by this stabilization problem may be reflected in the fact that, in lower animals, it is very difficult to demonstrate such chaining effects.

such a degree of autonomy; the values of the system may drift to a "non-adaptive" condition.

C. Prediction and Expectation

The evaluation unit U is supposed to acquire an ability to tell whether a situation is good or bad. This evaluation could be applied to *imaginary* situations as well as to real ones. If we could estimate the consequences of a proposed action (without its actual execution), we could use U to evaluate the (estimated) resulting situation. This could help in reducing the effort in search, and we would have in effect a machine with some ability to look ahead, or *plan*. In order to do this we need an additional device P which, given the description of a situation and an action, will predict a description of the likely result. (We will discuss schemes for doing this in Sec. IVC.) The device P might be constructed along the lines of a reinforcement learning device. In such a system the required reinforcement signals would have a very attractive character. For the machine must reinforce P positively when the *actual outcome resembles that which was predicted*—accurate expectations are rewarded. If we could further add a premium to reinforcement of those predictions which have a novel aspect, we might expect to discern behavior motivated by a sort of curiosity. In the reinforcement of mechanisms for confirmed novel expectations (or new explanations) we may find the key to simulation of intellectual motivation.[16]

SAMUEL'S PROGRAM FOR CHECKERS

In Samuel's "generalization learning" program for the game of checkers (1959a) we find a novel heuristic technique which could be regarded as a simple example of the "expectation reinforcement" notion. Let us review very briefly the situation in playing two-person board games of this kind. As noted by Shannon (1956) such games are in principle finite, and a best strategy can be found by following out all possible continuations—if he goes there I can go there, or there, etc.—and then "backing up" or "minimaxing" from the terminal positions, won, lost, or drawn. But in practice the full exploration of the resulting colossal "move tree" is out of the question. No doubt, some exploration will always be necessary for such games. But the tree must be pruned. We might simply put a limit on depth of exploration—the number of moves and replies. We might also limit the number of alternatives explored from each position—this requires some heuristics for selection of "plausible moves."[17] Now, if the backing-up technique is still to be used (with the incomplete move tree) one has to

[16] See also chap. 6 of Minsky (1954).

[17] See the discussion of Bernstein (1958) and the more extensive review and discussion in the very suggestive paper of Newell, Shaw and Simon (1958b).

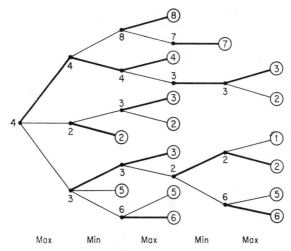

Figure 10. "Backing up" the static evaluations of proposed moves in a game tree. From the vertex at the left, representing the present position in a board game, radiate three branches, representing the *player's* proposed moves. Each of these might be countered by a variety of *opponent* moves, and so on. According to some program, a finite tree is generated. Then the worth to the player of each terminal board position is estimated (see text). If the opponent has the same values, he will choose to minimize the score, while the player will always try to maximize. The heavy lines show how this minimaxing process backs up until a choice is determined for the present position.

The full tree for chess has the order of 10^{120} branches—beyond the reach of any man or computer. There is a fundamental heuristic exchange between the effectiveness of the evaluation function and the extent of the tree. A very weak evaluation (*e.g.,* one which just compares the players' values of pieces) would yield a devastating game if the machine could explore all continuations out to, say, 20 levels. But only 6 levels, roughly within the range of our presently largest computers, would probably not give a brilliant game; less exhaustive strategies, perhaps along the lines of Newell, Shaw, and Simon (1958*b*), would be more profitable.

substitute for the absolute "win, lose, or draw" criterion some other "static" way of evaluating nonterminal positions.[18] (See Fig. 10.) Perhaps the simplest scheme is to use a weighted sum of some selected set of "property" functions of the positions—mobility, advancement, center control, and the like. This is done in Samuel's program, and in most of its predecessors. Associated with this is a multiple-simultaneous-optimizer method for discovering a good coefficient assignment (using the correlation technique noted in Sec. III*A*). But the source of reinforcement signals in

[18] In some problems the backing-up process can be handled in closed analytic form so that one may be able to use such methods as Bellman's "Dynamic Programming" (1957). Freimer (1960) gives some examples for which limited "look-ahead" doesn't work.

Samuel (1959a) is novel. One cannot afford to play out one or more entire games for each single learning step. Samuel measures instead *for each move* the difference between what the evaluation function yields *directly* of a position and what it *predicts* on the basis of an extensive continuation exploration, *i.e.,* backing up. The sign of this error, "Delta," is used for reinforcement; thus the system may learn something at *each move*.[19]

D. The Basic Credit-assignment Problem for Complex Reinforcement Learning Systems

In playing a complex game such as chess or checkers, or in writing a computer program, one has a definite success criterion—the game is won or lost. But in the course of play, each ultimate success (or failure) is associated with a vast number of internal decisions. If the run is successful, how can we assign credit for the success among the multitude of decisions? As Newell noted,

> *It is extremely doubtful whether there is enough information in "win, lose, or draw" when referred to the whole play of the game to permit any learning at all over available time scales. . . . For learning to take place, each play of the game must yield much more information. This is . . . achieved by breaking the problem into components. The unit of success is the goal. If a goal is achieved, its subgoals are reinforced; if not they are inhibited. (Actually, what is reinforced is the transformation rule that provided the subgoal.) . . . This also is true of the other kinds of structure: every tactic that is created provides information about the success or failure of tactic search rules; every opponent's action provides information about success or failure of likelihood inferences; and so on. The amount of information relevant to learning increases directly with the number of mechanisms in the chess-playing machine.*[20]

We are in complete agreement with Newell on this approach to the problem.[21]

It is my impression that many workers in the area of "self-organizing" systems and "random neural nets" do not feel the urgency of this prob-

[19] It should be noted that Samuel (1959a) describes also a rather successful checker-playing program based on recording and retrieving information about positions encountered in the past, a less abstract way of exploiting past experience. Samuel's work is notable in the variety of experiments that were performed, with and without various heuristics. This gives an unusual opportunity to really find out how different heuristic methods compare. More workers should choose (other things being equal) problems for which such variations are practicable.

[20] See p. 108 of Newell (1955).

[21] See also the discussion in Samuel (p. 22, 1959a) on assigning credit for a change in "Delta."

lem. Suppose that one million decisions are involved in a complex task (such as winning a chess game). Could we assign to each decision element one-millionth of the credit for the completed task? In certain special situations we can do just this—*e.g.,* in the machines of Rosenblatt (1958), Roberts (1960), and Farley and Clark (1954), etc., where the connections being reinforced are to a sufficient degree independent. But the problem-solving ability is correspondingly weak.

For more complex problems, with decisions in hierarchies (rather than summed on the same level) and with increments small enough to assure probable convergence, the running times would become fantastic. For complex problems we will have to define "success" in some rich local sense. Some of the difficulty may be evaded by using carefully graded "training sequences" as described in the following section.

FRIEDBERG'S PROGRAM-WRITING PROGRAM

An important example of comparative failure in this credit-assignment matter is provided by the program of Friedberg (1958, 1959) to solve program-writing problems. ·The problem here is to write programs for a (simulated) very simple digital computer. A simple problem is assigned, *e.g.,* "compute the AND of two bits in storage and put the result in an assigned location." A generating device produces a random (64-instruction) program. The program is run and its success or failure is noted. The success information is used to reinforce *individual instructions* (in fixed locations) so that each success tends to increase the chance that the instructions of successful programs will appear in later trials. (We lack space for details of how this is done.) Thus the program tries to find "good" instructions, more or less independently, for each location in program memory. The machine did learn to solve some extremely simple problems. But it took of the order of 1000 times longer than pure chance would expect. In part II of Friedberg *et al.* (1959), this failure is discussed, and attributed in part to what we called (Sec. IC) the "Mesa phenomenon." In changing just one instruction at a time the machine had not taken large enough steps in its search through program space.

The second paper goes on to discuss a sequence of modifications in the program generator and its reinforcement operators. With these, and with some "priming" (starting the machine off on the right track with some useful instructions), the system came to be only a little worse than chance. Friedberg *et al.* (1959) conclude that with these improvements "the generally superior performance of those machines with a success-number reinforcement mechanism over those without does serve to indicate that such a mechanism can provide a basis for constructing a learning machine." I disagree with this conclusion. It seems to me that each of the "improvements" can be interpreted as serving only to increase the step size of the search, that is, the randomness of the mechanism; this helps to avoid the Mesa phenomenon and thus approach chance behavior. But it certainly does not show that the "learning mechanism" is working—one would want at least to see some better-than-chance results before arguing this point. The trouble, it seems, is with credit-assignment. The credit for a working program can only be assigned to functional groups of instructions, *e.g.*, subroutines, and as these operate in hierarchies we should not expect individual instruction reinforcement to work well.[22] It seems surprising that it was not recognized in Friedberg *et al.* (1959) that the doubts raised earlier were probably justified! In the last section of Friedberg *et al.* (1959) we see some real success obtained by breaking the problem into parts and solving them sequentially. (This successful demonstration using division into subproblems does not use any reinforcement mechanism at all.) Some experiments of similar nature are reported in Kilburn, Grimsdale and Sumner (1959).

It is my conviction that no scheme for learning, or for pattern recognition, can have very general utility unless there are provisions for recursive, or at least hierarchical, use of previous results. We cannot expect a learning system to come to handle very hard problems without preparing it with a reasonably graded sequence of problems of growing difficulty. The first problem must be one which can be solved in reasonable time with the initial resources. The next must be capable of solution in reasonable time by using reasonably simple and accessible combinations of methods developed in the first, and so on. The only alternatives to this use of an adequate "training sequence" are (1) advanced resources, given initially, or (2) the fantastic exploratory processes found perhaps only in the history of organic evolution.[23] And even there, if we accept the general view of Darlington (1958) who emphasizes the heuristic aspects of genetic systems, we must have developed early (in, *e.g.*, the phenomena of meiosis and crossing-over) quite highly specialized mechanisms providing for the segregation of groupings related to solutions of subproblems. Recently, much effort has been devoted to the construction of training sequences in connection with programming "teaching machines." Naturally, the psychological literature abounds with theories of how complex behavior is built

[22] See the introduction to Friedberg (1958) for a thoughtful discussion of the plausibility of the scheme.

[23] It should, however, be possible to construct learning mechanisms which can select for themselves reasonably good training sequences (from an always complex environment) by prearranging a relatively slow development (or "maturation") of the system's facilities. This might be done by prearranging that sequence of goals attempted by the primary Trainer match reasonably well, at each stage, the complexity of performance mechanically available to the pattern-recognition and other parts of the system. One might be able to do much of this by simply limiting the depth of hierarchical activity, perhaps only later permitting limited recursive activity.

up from simpler. In our own area, perhaps the work of Solomonoff (1957), while overly cryptic, shows the most thorough consideration of this dependency on *training sequences*.

IV. Problem-solving and Planning

The solution, by machine, of really complex problems will require a variety of administration facilities. During the course of solving a problem, one becomes involved with a large assembly of interrelated subproblems. From these, at each stage, a very few must be chosen for investigation. This decision must be based on (1) estimates of relative difficulties and (2) estimates of centrality of the different candidates for attention. Following subproblem selection (for which several heuristic methods are proposed), one must choose methods appropriate to the selected problems. But for really difficult problems, even these step-by-step heuristics for reducing search will fail, and the machine must have resources for analyzing the problem structure in the large—in short, for "planning." A number of schemes for planning are discussed, among them the use of models —analogous, semantic, and abstract. Certain abstract models, "Character-Algebras," can be constructed by the machine itself, on the basis of experience or analysis. For concreteness, the discussion begins with a description of a simple but significant system (LT) which encounters some of these problems.

A. The "Logic Theory" Program of Newell, Shaw and Simon

It is not surprising that the testing grounds for early work on mechanical problem-solving have usually been areas of mathematics, or games, in which the rules are defined with absolute clarity. The "Logic Theory" machine of Newell and Simon (1956a, 1957a), called "LT" below, was a first attempt to prove theorems in logic, by frankly heuristic methods. Although the program was not by human standards a brilliant success (and did not surpass its designers), it stands as a landmark both in heuristic programming and also in the development of modern automatic programming.

The problem domain here is that of discovering proofs in the Russell-Whitehead system for the propositional calculus. That system is given as a set of (five) axioms and (three) rules of inference; the latter specify how certain transformations can be applied to produce new theorems from old theorems and axioms.

The LT program is centered around the idea of "working backward" to find a proof. Given a theorem T to be proved, LT searches among the axioms and previously established theorems for one from which T can be deduced by a single application of one of three simple "Methods" (which embody the given rules of inference). If one is found, the problem is solved. Or the search might fail completely. But finally, the search may yield one or more "problems" which are usually propositions from which T may be deduced directly. If one of these can, in turn, be proved a theorem the main problem will be solved. (The situation is actually slightly more complex.) Each such subproblem is adjoined to the "subproblem list" (after a limited preliminary attempt) and LT works around to it later. The full power of LT, such as it is, can be applied to each subproblem, for LT can use itself as a subroutine in a recursive fashion.

The heuristic technique of working backward yields something of a teleological process, and LT is a forerunner of more complex systems which construct hierarchies of goals and subgoals. Even so, the basic administrative structure of the program is no more than a nested set of searches through lists in memory. We shall first outline this structure and then mention a few heuristics that were used in attempts to improve performance.

1. Take the next problem from problem list.
   (If there are no more problems, EXIT with total failure.)
2. Choose the next of the three basic Methods.
   (If no more methods, go to 1.)
3. Choose the next member of the list of axioms and previous theorems.
   (If no more, go to 2.)
   Then apply the Method to the problem, using the chosen theorem or axiom.
   If problem is solved, EXIT with complete proof.
   If no result, go to 3.
   If new subproblem arises, go to 4.
4. Try the special (substitution) Method on the subproblem.
   If problem is solved, EXIT with complete proof.
   If no result, put the subproblem *at the end* of the problem list and go to 3.

Among the heuristics that were studied were (1) a *similarity test* to reduce the work in step 4 (which includes another search through the theorem list), (2) a *simplicity test* to select apparently easier problems from the problem list, and (3) a *strong nonprovability test* to remove from the problem list expressions which are probably false and hence not provable. In a series of experiments "learning" was used to find which earlier theorems had been most useful and should be given priority in step 3. We cannot review the effects of these changes in detail. Of interest was the balance between the extra cost for administration of certain heuristics and the resultant search reduction; this balance was quite delicate in some cases when computer memory became saturated. The system seemed to be quite sensitive to the training sequence—the order in which problems were given. And some heuristics which gave no significant over-all improvement did nevertheless affect the class of solvable problems. Curiously enough, the general efficiency of LT was not greatly improved by any or all of these devices. But all this practical experience is reflected in the design of the much more sophisticated "GPS" system described briefly in Sec. IVD2.

Wang (1960) has criticized the LT project on the grounds that there exist, as he and others have shown, mechanized proof methods which, for the particular run of problems considered, use far less machine effort than does LT and which have the advantage that they will ultimately find a proof for any provable proposition. (LT does not have this exhaustive "decision procedure" character and can fail ever to find proofs for some theorems.) The authors of "Empirical Explorations of the Logic Theory Machine," perhaps unaware of the existence of even moderately efficient exhaustive methods, supported their arguments by comparison with a particularly inefficient exhaustive procedure. Nevertheless, I feel that some of Wang's criticisms are misdirected. He does not seem to recognize that the authors of LT are not so much interested in proving these theorems as they are in the general problem of solving difficult problems. The combinatorial system of Russell and Whitehead (with which LT deals) is far less simple and elegant than the system used by Wang.[24] [Note, *e.g.,* the emphasis in Newell, Shaw and Simon (1958a, 1958b).] Wang's problems, while *logically* equivalent, are *formally* much simpler. His methods do not include any facilities for using previous results (hence they are sure to degrade rapidly at a certain level of problem complexity), while LT is fundamentally oriented around this problem. Finally, because of the very effectiveness of Wang's method on the *particular* set of theorems in question, he simply did not have to face the fundamental heuristic problem of *when to decide to give up on a line of attack.* Thus the formidable performance of his program (1960) perhaps diverted his attention from heuristic problems that must again spring up when real mathematics is ultimately encountered.

This is not meant as a rejection of the importance of Wang's work and discussion. He and others working on "mechanical mathematics" have discovered that there are proof procedures which are much more efficient than has been suspected. Such work will unquestionably help in constructing intelligent machines, and these procedures will certainly be preferred, when available, to "unreliable heuristic methods." Wang, Davis and

---

[24] Wang's procedure (1960a), too, works backward, and can be regarded as a generalization of the method of "falsification" for deciding truth-functional tautology. In Wang (1960b) and its unpublished sequel, he introduces more powerful methods (for much more difficult problems).

Putnam, and several others are now pushing these new techniques into the far more challenging domain of theorem proving in the predicate calculus (for which exhaustive decision procedures are no longer available). We have no space to discuss this area,[25] but it seems clear that a program to solve real mathematical problems will have to combine the mathematical sophistication of Wang with the heuristic sophistication of Newell, Shaw and Simon.[26]

B. Heuristics for Subproblem Selection

In designing a problem-solving system, the programmer often comes equipped with a set of more or less distinct "Methods"—his real task is to find an efficient way for the program to decide where and when the different methods are to be used.

Methods which do not dispose of a problem may still transform it to create new problems or subproblems. Hence, during the course of solving one problem we may become involved with a large assembly of interrelated subproblems. A "parallel" computer, yet to be conceived, might work on many at a time. But even the parallel machine must have procedures to allocate its resources because it cannot simultaneously apply all its methods to all the problems. We shall divide this administrative problem into two parts: the selection of those subproblem(s) which seem most critical, attractive, or otherwise immediate, and, in the next section, the choice of which method to apply to the selected problem.

In the basic program for LT (Sec. IVA), subproblem selection is very simple. New problems are examined briefly and (if not solved at once) are placed at the end of the (linear) problem list. The main program proceeds along this list (step 1), attacking the problems in the order of their generation. More powerful systems will have to be more judicious (both in generation and selection of problems) for only thus can excessive branching be restrained.[27] In more complex systems we can expect to consider for each subproblem, at least these two aspects: (1) its apparent "centrality"—how will its solution promote the main goal, and (2) its apparent "difficulty"—how much effort is it liable to consume. We need heuristic methods to estimate each of these quantities and, further, to

[25] See Davis and Putnam (1960), and Wang (1960b).

[26] All these efforts are directed toward the reduction of search effort. In that sense they are all heuristic programs. Since practically no one still uses "heuristic" in a sense opposed to "algorithmic," serious workers might do well to avoid pointless argument on this score. The real problem is to find methods which significantly delay the apparently inevitable exponential growth of search trees.

[27] Note that the simple scheme of LT has the property that each generated problem will eventually get attention, even if several are created in a step 3. If one were to turn *full* attention to each problem, as generated, one might never return to alternate branches.

select accordingly one of the problems and allocate to it some reasonable quantity of effort.[28] Little enough is known about these matters, and so it is not entirely for lack of space that the following remarks are somewhat cryptic.

Imagine that the problems and their relations are arranged to form some kind of directed-graph structure (Minsky, 1956b; Newell and Simon, 1956b; Gelernter and Rochester, 1958). The main problem is to establish a "valid" path between two initially distinguished nodes. Generation of new problems is represented by the addition of new, not-yet-valid paths, or by the insertion of new nodes in old paths. Then problems are represented by not-yet-valid paths, and "centrality" by location in the structure. Associate with each connection, quantities describing its current validity state (solved, plausible, doubtful, etc.) and its current estimated difficulty.

1. GLOBAL METHODS

The most general problem-selection methods are "global"—at each step they look over the entire structure. There is one such simple scheme which works well on at least one rather degenerate interpretation of our problem graph. This is based on an electrical analogy suggested to us by a machine designed by Shannon [related to one described in Shannon (1955) which describes quite a variety of interesting game-playing and learning machines] to play a variant of the game marketed as "Hex" (and known among mathematicians as "Nash"). The initial board position can be represented as a certain network of resistors. (See Fig. 11.) One player's goal is to construct a *short-circuit* path between two given boundaries; the opponent tries to open the circuit between them. Each move consists of shorting (or opening), irreversibly, one of the remaining resistors. Shannon's machine applies a potential between the boundaries and selects that resistor which carries the largest current. Very roughly speaking, this resistor is likely to be most critical because changing it will have the largest effect on the resistance of the net and, hence, in the goal direction of shorting (or opening) the circuit. And although this argument is not perfect, nor is this a perfect model of the real combinatorial situation, the machine does play extremely well. (It can make unsound moves in certain artificial situations, but no one seems to have been able to force this during a game.)

The use of such a global method for problem selection requires that the available "difficulty estimates" for related subproblems be arranged to

[28] One will want to see if the considered problem is the same as one already considered, or very similar. See the discussion in Gelernter and Rochester (1958). This problem might be handled more generally by simply *remembering* the (Characters of) problems that have been attacked, and checking new ones against this memory, *e.g.*, by methods of Mooers (1956), looking more closely if there seems to be a match.

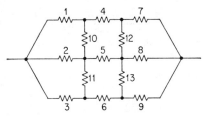

Figure 11. This board game (due to C. E. Shannon) is played on a network of equal resistors. The first player's goal is to open the circuit between the end points; the second player's goal is to short the circuit. A move consists of opening or shortening a resistor. If the first player begins by opening resistor 1, the second player might counter by shorting resistor 4, following the strategy described in the text. The remaining move pairs (if *both* players use that strategy) would be (5, 8) (9, 13) (12, 10 or 2) (2 or 10 *win*). In this game the first player should be able to force a win, and the maximum-current strategy seems always to do so, even on larger networks.

combine in roughly the manner of resistance values. Also, we could regard this machine as using an "analog model" for "planning." (See Sec. IVD.)[29]

2. LOCAL, AND "HEREDITARY," METHODS

The prospect of having to study at each step the whole problem structure is discouraging, especially since the structure usually changes only slightly after each attempt. One naturally looks for methods which merely *update* or modify a small fragment of the stored record. Between the extremes of the "first-come-first-served" problem-list method and the full global-survey methods, lie a variety of compromise techniques. Perhaps the most attractive of these are what we will call the *Inheritance* methods—essentially recursive devices.

In an Inheritance method, the effort assigned to a subproblem is determined only by its immediate ancestry; at the time each problem is created it is assigned a certain total quantity Q of time or effort. When a problem is later split into subproblems, such quantities are assigned to them by some local process which *depends only on their relative merits and on what remains of Q.* Thus the centrality problem is managed implicitly. Such schemes are quite easy to program, especially with the new programming systems such as IPL (Newell and Tonge, 1960c) and LISP (McCarthy, 1960) (which are themselves based on certain hereditary or recursive operations). Special cases of the Inheritance method arise when one can get along with a simple all-or-none Q, *e.g.*, a "stop condition"—this yields the

[29] A variety of combinatorial methods will be matched against the network-analogy opponent in a program being completed by R. Silver, Lincoln Laboratory, MIT, Lexington, Mass.

exploratory method called "backtracking" by Golumb (1961). The decoding procedure of Wozencraft (1961) is another important variety of Inheritance method.

In the complex exploration process proposed for chess by Newell, Shaw, and Simon (1958b) we have a form of Inheritance method with a *non-numerical stop condition*. Here, the subproblems inherit *sets of goals to be achieved*. This teleological control has to be administered by an additional goal-selection system and is further complicated by a global (but reasonably simple) stop rule of the back-up variety (Sec. IIIC). (*Note:* we are identifying here the move-tree-limitation problem with that of problem selection.) Even though extensive experimental results are not yet available, we feel that the scheme of Newell, Shaw, and Simon (1958b) deserves careful study by anyone planning serious work in this area. It shows only the beginning of the complexity sure to come in our development of intelligent machines.[30]

C. "Character-Method" Machines

Once a problem is selected, we must decide which method to try first. This depends on our ability to classify or characterize problems. We first compute the Character of our problem (by using some pattern recognition technique) and then consult a "Character-Method" table or other device which is supposed to tell us which method(s) are most effective on problems of that Character. This information might be built up from experience, given initially by the programmer, deduced from "advice" (McCarthy, 1959), or obtained as the solution to some other problem, as suggested in the GPS proposal (Newell, Shaw and Simon, 1959a). In any case, this part of the machine's behavior, regarded from the outside, can be treated as a sort of stimulus-response, or "table look-up," activity.

If the Characters (or descriptions) have too wide a variety of values, there will be a serious problem of filling a Character-Method table. One might then have to reduce the detail of information, *e.g.,* by using only a few important properties. Thus the *Differences* of GPS (see Sec. IVD2) describe no more than is necessary to define a single goal, and a priority scheme selects just one of these to characterize the situation. Gelernter and Rochester (1958) suggest using a property-weighting scheme, a special case of the "Bayes net" described in Sec. IIG.

D. Planning

Ordinarily one can solve a complicated problem only by dividing it into a number of parts, each of which can be attacked by a smaller search (or be further divided). Generally speaking, a successful division will reduce

---

[30] Some further discussion of this question may be found in Slagle (1961).

the search time not by a mere fraction, but by a *fractional exponent*. In a graph with 10 branches descending from each node, a 20-step search might involve 10^{20} trials, which is out of the question, while the insertion of just four *lemmas* or *sequential subgoals* might reduce the search to only 5×10^4 trials, which is within reason for machine exploration. Thus it will be worth a relatively enormous effort to find such "islands" in the solution of complex problems.[31] Note that even if one encountered, say, 10^6 failures of such procedures before success, one would still have gained a factor of perhaps 10^{10} in over-all trial reduction! *Thus practically any ability at all to "plan," or "analyze," a problem will be profitable,* if the problem is difficult. It is safe to say that all simple, unitary, notions of how to build an intelligent machine will fail, rather sharply, for some modest level of problem difficulty. Only schemes which actively pursue an analysis toward obtaining a set of *sequential goals* can be expected to extend smoothly into increasingly complex problem domains.

Perhaps the most straightforward concept of planning is that of using a *simplified model* of the problem situation. Suppose that there is available, for a given problem, some other problem of "essentially the same character" but with less detail and complexity. Then we could proceed first to solve the simpler problem. Suppose, also, that this is done using a second set of methods, which are also simpler, but in some correspondence with those for the original. *The solution to the simpler problem can then be used as a "plan" for the harder one.* Perhaps each step will have to be expanded in detail. But the multiple searches will *add, not multiply,* in the total search time. The situation would be ideal if the model were, mathematically, a *homomorphism* of the original. But even without such perfection the model solution should be a valuable guide. In mathematics one's proof procedures usually run along these lines: one first assumes, *e.g.,* that integrals and limits always converge, in the planning stage. Once the outline is completed, in this simpleminded model of mathematics, then one goes back to try to "make rigorous" the steps of the proof, *i.e.,* to replace them by chains of argument using genuine rules of inference. And even if the plan fails, it may be possible to patch it by replacing just a few of its steps.

Another aid to planning is the *semantic,* as opposed to the homomorphic, model (Minsky, 1956a, 1959a). Here we may have an *interpretation* of the current problem within another system, not necessarily simpler, but with which we are more familiar and have already more powerful methods. Thus, in connection with a plan for the proof of a theorem, we will want to know whether the proposed lemmas, or islands in the proof, are actually *true;* if not, the plan will surely fail. We can often easily tell if a proposition is true by looking at an interpretation. Thus the truth of a

---

[31] See sec. 10 of Ashby (1956).

proposition from plane geometry can be supposed, at least with great reliability, by actual measurement of a few constructed drawings (or the analytic geometry equivalent). The geometry machine of Gelernter and Rochester (1958, 1959) uses such a semantic model with excellent results; it follows closely the lines proposed in Minsky (1956a).

1. THE "CHARACTER-ALGEBRA" MODEL

Planning with the aid of a model is of the greatest value in reducing search. Can we construct machines which find their own models? I believe the following will provide a general, straightforward way to construct certain kinds of useful, abstract models. The critical requirement is that we be able to compile a "Character-Method Matrix" (in addition to the simple Character-Method table in Sec. IVC). *The CM matrix is an array of entries which predict with some reliability what will happen when methods are applied to problems.* Both of the matrix dimensions are indexed by problem Characters; if there is a method *which usually transforms problems of character C_i into problems of character C_j* then let the matrix entry C_{ij} be the name of that method (or a list of such methods). If there is no such method the corresponding entry is null.

Now suppose that there is no entry for C_{ij}—meaning that we have no *direct* way to transform a problem of type C_i into one of type C_j. Multiply the matrix by itself. If the new matrix has a non-null (i,j) entry then there must be a sequence of *two* methods which effects the desired transformation. If that fails, we may try higher powers. Note that [if we put unity for the (i,i) terms] we can reach the 2^n matrix power with just n multiplications. We don't need to define the symbolic multiplication operation; one may instead use arithmetic entries—putting *unity for any non-null entry* and zero for any null entry in the original matrix. This yields a simple connection, or flow diagram, matrix, and its nth power tells us something about its set of paths of length 2^n.[32] [Once a non-null entry is discovered, there exist efficient ways to find the corresponding sequences of methods. The problem is really just that of finding paths through a maze, and the method of Moore (1959) would be quite efficient. Almost any problem can be converted into a problem of finding a chain between two terminal expressions in some formal system.] If the Characters are taken to be abstract representations of the problem expressions, this "Character-Algebra" model can be as abstract as are the available pattern-recognition facilities. See Minsky (1956a, 1959a).

The critical problem in using the Character-Algebra model for planning is, of course, the *prediction reliability of the matrix entries*. One cannot expect the Character of a result to be strictly determined by the Character of the original and the method used. And the reliability of the pre-

[32] See, *e.g.*, Hohn, Seshu, and Aufenkamp (1957).

dictions will, in any case, deteriorate rapidly as the matrix power is raised. But, as we have noted, any plan at all is so much better than none that the system should do very much better than exhaustive search, even with quite poor prediction quality.

This matrix formulation is obviously only a special case of the character planning idea. More generally, one will have descriptions, rather than fixed characters, and one must then have more general methods to calculate from a description what is likely to happen when a method is applied.

2. CHARACTERS AND DIFFERENCES

In the GPS (General Problem Solver) proposal of Newell, Shaw, and Simon (1959a, 1960a) we find a slightly different framework: they use a notion of Difference between two problems (or expressions) where we speak of the Character of a single problem. These views are equivalent if we take our problems to be links or connections between expressions. But this notion of Difference (as the Character of a pair) does lend itself more smoothly to teleological reasoning. For what is the goal defined by a problem but to *reduce the "difference" between the present state and the desired state?* The underlying structure of GPS is precisely what we have called a "Character-Method Machine" in which each kind of Difference is associated in a table with one or more methods which are known to "reduce" that Difference. Since the characterization here depends always on (1) the current problem expression and (2) the desired end result, it is reasonable to think, as its authors suggest, of GPS as using "means-end" analysis.

To illustrate the use of Differences, we shall review an example (Newell, Shaw, and Simon, 1960a). The problem, in elementary propositional calculus, is to prove that from $S \wedge (- P \supset Q)$ we can deduce $(Q \vee P) \wedge S$. The program looks at both of these expressions with a recursive *matching* process which branches out from the main connectives. The first Difference it encounters is that S occurs on different sides of the main connective "$\wedge$." It therefore looks in the Difference-Method table under the heading "change position." It discovers there a method which uses the theorem $(A \wedge B) \equiv (B \wedge A)$ which is obviously useful for removing, or "reducing," differences of position. GPS applies this method, obtaining $(- P \supset Q) \wedge S$. GPS now asks what is the Difference between this new expression and the goal. This time the matching procedure gets down into the connectives inside the left-hand members and finds a Difference between the connectives "$\supset$" and "$\vee$." It now looks in the CM table under the heading "Change Connective" and discovers the appropriate method using $(- A \supset B) \equiv (A \vee B)$. It applies this method, obtaining $(P \vee Q) \wedge S$. In the final cycle, the difference-evaluating procedure discovers the need for a "change position" inside the left member, and applies a method using $(A \vee B) \equiv (B \vee A)$. This completes the solution of the problem.[33]

Evidently, the success of this "means-end" analysis in reducing general search will depend on the degree of specificity that can be written into the Difference-Method table—basically the same requirement for an effective Character-Algebra.

It may be possible to *plan* using Differences, as well. One might imagine a "Difference-Algebra" in which the predictions have the form $D = D' D''$. One must construct accordingly a difference-factorization algebra for discovering longer chains $D = D_1 \cdots D_n$ and corresponding method plans. We should note that one *cannot* expect to use such planning methods with such primitive Differences as are discussed in Newell, Shaw, and Simon (1960a); for these cannot form an adequate Difference-Algebra (or Character-Algebra). Unless the characterizing expressions have many levels of descriptive detail, the matrix powers will too swiftly become degenerate. This degeneracy will ultimately limit the capacity of any formal planning device.

One may think of the general planning heuristic as embodied in a recursive process of the following form. Suppose we have a problem P:

1. Form a plan for problem P.
2. Select first (next) step of the plan.
   (If no more steps, exit with "success.")
3. Try the suggested method(s):
   Success: return to (b), *i.e.,* try next step in the plan.
   Failure: return to (a), *i.e.,* form new plan, or perhaps change current plan to avoid this step.
   Problem judged too difficult: *Apply this entire procedure to the problem of the current step.*

Observe that such a program schema is essentially recursive; it uses itself as a subroutine (explicitly, in the last step) in such a way that its current state has to be stored, and restored when it returns control to itself.[34]

---

[33] Compare this with the "matching" process described in Newell and Simon (1956). The notions of "Character," "Character-Algebra," etc., originate in Minsky (1956) but seem useful in describing parts of the "GPS" system of Newell and Simon (1956) and Newell, Shaw, and Simon (1960a). The latter contains much additional material we cannot survey here. Essentially, GPS is to be self-applied to the problem of discovering sets of Differences appropriate for given problem areas. This notion of "bootstrapping"—applying a problem-solving system to the task of improving some of its own methods—is old and familiar, but in Newell, Shaw, and Simon (1960a) we find perhaps the first specific proposal about how such an advance might be realized.

[34] This violates, for example, the restrictions on "DO loops" in programming systems such as FORTRAN. Convenient techniques for programming such processes were developed by Newell, Shaw and Simon (1960b); the program state variables

Miller, Galanter and Pribram[35] discuss possible analogies between human problem-solving and some heuristic planning schemes. It seems certain that, for at least a few years, there will be a close association between theories of human behavior and attempts to increase the intellectual capacities of machines. But, in the long run, we must be prepared to discover profitable lines of heuristic programming which do not deliberately imitate human characteristics.[36]

V. Induction and Models

A. Intelligence

In all of this discussion we have not come to grips with anything we can isolate as "intelligence." We have discussed only heuristics, shortcuts, and classification techniques. Is there something missing? I am confident that sooner or later we will be able to assemble programs of great problem-solving ability from complex combinations of heuristic devices—multiple optimizers, pattern-recognition tricks, planning algebras, recursive administration procedures, and the like. In no one of these will we find the

---

are stored in "pushdown lists" and both the program and the data are stored in the form of "list structures." Gelernter (1959) extended FORTRAN to manage some of this. McCarthy has extended these notions in LISP (1960) to permit *explicit* recursive definitions of programs in a language based on recursive functions of symbolic expressions; here the management of program state variables is fully automatic. See also Orchard-Hays (1960).

[35] See chaps. 12 and 13 of Miller, Galanter, and Pribram (1960).

[36] Limitations of space preclude detailed discussion here of theories of self-organizing neural nets, and other models based on brain analogies. [Several of these are described or cited in *Proceedings of a Symposium on Mechanisation of Thought Processes,* London: H. M. Stationery Office, 1959, and *Self Organizing Systems,* M. T. Yovitts and S. Cameron (eds.), New York: Pergamon Press, 1960.] This omission is not too serious, I feel, in connection with the subject of heuristic programming, because the motivation and methods of the two areas seem so different. Up to the present time, at least, research on neural-net models has been concerned mainly with the attempt to show that certain rather simple heuristic processes, *e.g.,* reinforcement learning, or property-list pattern recognition, can be realized or evolved by collections of simple elements without very highly organized interconnections. Work on heuristic programming is characterized quite differently by the search for new, more powerful heuristics for solving very complex problems, and by very little concern for what hardware (neuronal or otherwise) would minimally suffice for its realization. In short, the work on "nets" is concerned with how far one can get with a small initial endowment; the work on "artificial intelligence" is concerned with using all we know to build the most powerful systems that we can. It is my expectation that, in problem-solving power, the (allegedly brainlike) minimal-structure systems will never threaten to compete with their more deliberately designed contemporaries; nevertheless, their study should prove profitable in the development of component elements and subsystems to be used in the construction of the more systematically conceived machines.

seat of intelligence. Should we ask what intelligence "really is"? My own view is that this is more of an aesthetic question, or one of sense of dignity, than a technical matter! To me "intelligence" seems to denote little more than the complex of performances which we happen to respect, but do not understand. So it is, usually, with the question of "depth" in mathematics. Once the proof of a theorem is really understood its content seems to become trivial. (Still, there may remain a sense of wonder about how the proof was discovered.)

Programmers, too, know that there is never any "heart" in a program. There are high-level routines in each program, but all they do is dictate that "if such and such, then transfer to such and such a subroutine." And when we look at the low-level subroutines, which "actually do the work," we find senseless loops and sequences of trivial operations, merely carrying out the dictates of their superiors. The intelligence in such a system seems to be as intangible as becomes the meaning of a single common word when it is thoughtfully pronounced over and over again.

But we should not let our inability to discern a locus of intelligence lead us to conclude that programmed computers therefore cannot think. For it may be so with *man*, as with *machine,* that, when we understand finally the structure and program, the feeling of mystery (and self-approbation) will weaken.[37] We find similar views concerning "creativity" in Newell, Shaw, and Simon (1958c). The view expressed by Rosenbloom (1951) that minds (or brains) can transcend machines is based, apparently, on an erroneous interpretation of the meaning of the "unsolvability theorems" of Godel.[38]

[37] See Minsky (1956, 1959).

[38] On problems of volition we are in general agreement with McCulloch (1954) that our *freedom of will* "presumably means no more than that we can distinguish between what we intend (*i.e.,* our *plan*), and some intervention in our action." See also MacKay (1959) and [the] references; we are, however, unconvinced by his eulogization of "analog" devices. Concerning the "mind-brain" problem, one should consider the arguments of Craik (1952), Hayek (1952), and Pask (1959). Among the active leaders in modern heuristic programming, perhaps only Samuel (1960b) has taken a strong position against the idea of machines thinking. His argument, based on the fact that reliable computers do only that which they are instructed to do, has a basic flaw; it does not follow that the programmer therefore has full knowledge (and therefore full responsibility and credit for) what will ensue. For certainly the programmer may set up an evolutionary system whose limitations are for him unclear and possibly incomprehensible. No better does the mathematician know all the consequences of a proposed set of axioms. Surely a machine has to *be* in order to perform. But we cannot assign all the credit to its programmer if the operation of a system comes to reveal structures not recognizable or anticipated by the programmer. While we have not yet seen much in the way of intelligent activity in machines, Samuel's arguments (circular in that they are based on the presumption that machines do not have minds) do not assure us against this. Turing (1956) gives a very knowledgeable discussion of such matters.

B. Inductive Inference

Let us pose now for our machines, a variety of problems more challenging than any ordinary game or mathematical puzzle. Suppose that we want a machine which, when embedded for a time in a complex environment or "universe," will essay to produce a description of that world—to discover its regularities or laws of nature. We might ask it to predict what will happen next. We might ask it to predict what would be the likely consequences of a certain action or experiment. Or we might ask it to formulate the laws governing some class of events. In any case, our task is to equip our machine with *inductive ability*—with methods which it can use to construct general statements about events beyond its recorded experience. Now, there can be no system for inductive inference that will work well in all possible universes. But given a universe, or an ensemble of universes, and a criterion of success, this (epistemological) problem for machines becomes technical rather than philosophical. There is quite a literature concerning this subject, but we shall discuss only one approach which currently seems to us the most promising; this is what we might call the "grammatical induction" schemes of Solomonoff (1957, 1958, 1959a), based partly on work of Chomsky and Miller (1957b, 1958).

We will take *language* to mean the set of expressions formed from some given set of primitive symbols or expressions, by the repeated application of some given set of rules; the primitive expressions plus the rules is the *grammar* of the language. Most induction problems can be framed as problems in the *discovery of grammars*. Suppose, for instance, that a machine's prior experience is summarized by a large collection of statements, some labelled "good" and some "bad" by some critical device. How could we generate selectively more good statements? The trick is to find some relatively simple (formal) language in which the good statements are grammatical, and in which the bad ones are not. Given such a language, we can use it to generate more statements, and presumably these will tend to be more like the good ones. The heuristic argument is that if we can find a relatively simple way to separate the two sets, the discovered rule is likely to be useful beyond the immediate experience. If the extension fails to be consistent with new data, one might be able to make small changes in the rules and, generally, one may be able to use many ordinary problem-solving methods for this task.

The problem of finding an efficient grammar is much the same as that of finding efficient *encodings,* or programs, for machines; in each case, one needs to discover the important regularities in the data, and exploit the regularities by making shrewd *abbreviations*. The possible importance of Solomonoff's work (1960) is that, despite some obvious defects, it may point the way toward systematic mathematical ways to explore this discovery problem. He considers the class of all programs (for a given general-purpose computer) which will produce a certain given output (the body of data in question). Most such programs, if allowed to continue, will add to that body of data. By properly weighting these programs, perhaps by length, we can obtain corresponding weights for the different possible continuations, and thus a basis for prediction. If this prediction is to be of any interest, it will be necessary to show some independence of the given computer; it is not yet clear precisely what form such a result will take.

C. Models of Oneself

If a creature can answer a question about a hypothetical experiment, without actually performing that experiment, then the answer must have been obtained from some submachine inside the creature. The output of that submachine (representing a correct answer) as well as the input (representing the question) must be coded descriptions of the corresponding external events or event classes. Seen through this pair of encoding and decoding channels, the internal submachine acts like the environment, and so it has the character of a "model." The inductive inference problem may then be regarded as the problem of constructing such a model.

To the extent that the creature's actions affect the environment, this internal model of the world will need to include some representation of the creature itself. If one asks the creature "why did you decide to do such and such" (or if it asks this of itself), any answer must come from the internal model. Thus the evidence of introspection itself is liable to be based ultimately on the processes used in constructing one's image of one's self. Speculation on the form of such a model leads to the amusing prediction that intelligent machines may be reluctant to believe that they are *just* machines. The argument is this: our own self-models have a substantially "dual" character; there is a part concerned with the physical or mechanical environment—with the behavior of inanimate objects—and there is a part concerned with social and psychological matters. It is precisely because we have not yet developed a satisfactory mechanical theory of mental activity that we have to keep these areas apart. We could not give up this division even if we wished to—until we find a unified model to replace it. Now, when we ask such a creature what sort of being it is, it cannot simply answer "directly"; it must inspect its model(s). And it must answer by saying that it seems to be a dual thing—which appears to have two parts—a "mind" and a "body." Thus, even the robot, unless equipped with a satisfactory theory of artificial intelligence, would have to maintain a dualistic opinion on this matter.[39]

[39] There is a certain problem of infinite regression in the notion of a machine

Conclusion

In attempting to combine a survey of work on "artificial intelligence" with a summary of our own views, we could not mention every relevant project and publication. Some important omissions are in the area of "brain models"; the early work of Farley and Clark (1954) [also Farley's paper in Yovitts and Cameron (1960), often unknowingly duplicated, and the work of Rochester (1956) and Milner (1960)]. The work of Lettvin *et al.* (1959) is related to the theories in Selfridge (1959). We did not touch at all on the problems of logic and language, and of information retrieval, which must be faced when action is to be based on the contents of large memories; see, *e.g.,* McCarthy (1959). We have not discussed the basic results in mathematical logic which bear on the question of what can be done by machines. There are entire literatures we have hardly even sampled—the bold pioneering work of Rashevsky (c. 1929) and his later co-workers (Rashevsky, 1960); Theories of Learning, *e.g.,* Gorn (1959); Theory of Games, *e.g.,* Shubik (1960); and Psychology, *e.g.,* Bruner *et al.* (1956). And everyone should know the work of Polya (1945, 1954) on how to solve problems. We can hope only to have transmitted the flavor of some of the more ambitious projects *directly* concerned with getting machines to take over a larger portion of problem-solving tasks.

One last remark: we have discussed here only work concerned with more or less self-contained problem-solving programs. But as this is written, we are at last beginning to see vigorous activity in the direction of constructing usable *time-sharing* or *multiprogramming* computing systems. With these systems, it will at last become economical to match human beings in real time with really large machines. This means that we can work toward programming what will be, in effect, "thinking aids." In the years to come, we expect that these man-machine systems will share, and perhaps for a time be dominant, in our advance toward the development of "artificial intelligence."

---

having a *good* model of itself: of course, the nested models must lose detail and finally vanish. But the argument, *e.g.,* of Hayek (see 8.69 and 8.79, 1952) that we cannot "fully comprehend the unitary order" (of our own minds) ignores the power of recursive description as well as Turing's demonstration that (with sufficient external writing space) a "general-purpose" machine can answer any question about a description of itself that any larger machine could answer.

part 4
Bibliography

A SELECTED DESCRIPTOR-INDEXED BIBLIOGRAPHY TO THE LITERATURE ON ARTIFICIAL INTELLIGENCE

by Marvin Minsky

This listing is intended as an introduction to the literature on Artificial Intelligence—*i.e.,* to the literature dealing with the problem of making machines behave intelligently. We have divided this area into categories and cross-indexed the references accordingly. Large bibliographies without some classification facility are next to useless. This particular field is still young, but there are already many instances in which workers have wasted much time in rediscovering (for better or for worse) schemes already reported. In the last year or two this problem has become worse, and in such a situation just about any information is better than none.

This bibliography is intended to serve just that purpose—to present some information about this literature. The selection was confined mainly to publications directly concerned with construction of artificial problem-solving systems. Many peripheral areas are omitted completely or represented only by a few citations. The classification system is not particularly accurate. The descriptive categories that we have selected do not always permit very sharp distinctions and not always useful ones. There are surely many errors in the assignments of papers to the categories, both for those I have not read, and for those which I did not fully understand. I have seen, or discussed with the authors, about half of the papers. Of about half the remainder, I felt qualified to guess about the contents on other grounds. On most of the remainder I guessed anyway and may have missed entirely.

The meanings of the descriptors—the names of the categories—are not given here in any detail, because the present state of the art will not bear standardization. The terms do assume understanding of the main

453

points discussed in my paper (1961*a*), which is readily available. Obviously, there is much ambiguity in the assignments, *e.g.,* between *learning* and *inductive inference.* In most cases I did *not* assign papers to all competing categories, so that the searcher may have to look in several reasonable listings to find full coverage. Not all of the original papers were retrieved for bibliographic checking. This bibliography should therefore not be used as a base for other compilations without checking all the references carefully. Our purpose was to make available a guide, and not to do all the work necessary for inclusiveness or accuracy. Many erroneous citations, propagated from one bibliography to another over the years, are corrected here, but others have surely been introduced; I have noticed this already in pirated editions of this compilation.

The selection was made on two bases. Papers *directly* concerned with design, construction, and use of problem-solving machinery were admitted more or less indiscriminately; papers in relevant mathematical, psychological and physiological domains were selected more critically to represent entry points to those literatures. A number of clearly relevant areas were omitted almost entirely, and a few remarks on this selection follow. No attempt was made to be comprehensive; in most cases we give only a recent sample for each author. There is very little on the foreign literature; except for England, the foreign literature has been weak until very recently, probably because this field simply does not develop without the testing of models by digital computation. I might remark, at this point, that I do not regard the literature in this field as a substantial source of buried treasures of good ideas; the major problems have not yet been generally recognized and challenged. But there are certainly a great many bad ideas about, and it will pay the worker to be able to recognize them quickly. My own preferences are outlined clearly enough in Minsky, 1961*a.*

Automata Theory, Switching Theory, Recursive Function Theory, Logic

We have included only a few, fairly basic papers. What is needed is a theory of computation and a theory of hierarchies within the computable functions. Neither is available today in satisfactory form. We have included quite a few papers concerned with the problem of proving theorems by machine; these are all concerned with heuristic problems, although the authors may not always choose so to look at things. We have also included several references to the question of reliable computation with unreliable elements (stemming from Von Neumann, 1956); while this question is not directly connected with the artificial intelligence problem, it will surely be important in the realization of these ideas. Similarly with theory of probabilistic machines; here the literature is still rather thin. We neglect the very large literature on minimization of automata and switching circuits, although there are many useful heuristic methods therein.

Language, Mechanical Translation

A number of references to natural and formal languages are included; this area is highly relevant and much more could be adjoined. No references at all are included for Mechanical Translation, even though we feel that this work is important; Oettinger's compilation[1] with 645 entries will serve the purpose.

Information Theory, Coding Theory, Statistical Decision Theory

Only a few references are given. Although coding and decision problems are fundamental to us, we cannot yet say what is relevant.

Neurophysiology and Physiological Psychology

These will someday show how the brain works, and already quite a bit is known about the *Psychology of Problem-solving;* we have tried to include a good many citations of outstanding work in these areas. We have not included much on learning in lower animals; it is our conviction that if one's goal is to build machines to solve difficult problems, it will not help for one to become preoccupied with the mechanics of systems which do not solve very difficult problems. We have omitted the entire area of *Adaptive Servomechanisms* as being similar in nature, but our omission of *Operations Research* is due only to unfamiliarity; we are sure that this is a valuable source of heuristic analysis and technique; likewise for *Information Retrieval.* One area which certainly deserves a larger representation is that of theories of *Inductive Inference;* the philosophical literature contains a great deal on this subject.

The present collection is a revision of the document listed below as Minsky, 1961c. The original collection was based on my own files, the collection of Alice M. Pierce,[2] a listing by Allen Newell,[3] and listings of Russell Kirsch,[4] Simmons and Simmons,[5] and the afore-mentioned collec-

[1] A. G. Oettinger, Bibliography of Mathematical Linguistics and Automatic Translation, Cambridge, Mass., Computation Laboratory, Department of Linguistics, Division of Engineering and Applied Physics, Harvard University, September, 1959. 645 entries, many Soviet.

[2] A. M. Pierce, A Concise Bibliography of the Literature on Artificial Intelligence, Bedford, Mass.: Communication Sciences Laboratory, Electronic Research Directorate AFCRC-TN-59-773, ARDC, USAF, September, 1959.

[3] Allen Newell, Bibliography GI-506, March, 1958. Unpublished.

[4] R. A. Kirsch, Bibliography for NBS Graduate Course 204–204, Washington, D.C.: Data Processing Systems Division, National Bureau of Standards, September, 1959–April, 1960. Effective computational processes with finite and infinite machines.

[5] P. L. Simmons and R. F. Simmons, The Simulation of Cognitive Processes: An Annotated Bibliography, Santa Monica, Calif., System Development Corp., *IRE Transactions on Electronic Computers,* September, 1962, **EC-10:** 462–483. 498 references with informative annotations and subject index. Many Soviet references.

tion of Oettinger.[6] I expect to publish one more revision; the relevant literature now numbers perhaps 2000 papers. A bibliography of that size, without descriptors, would be completely useless, and even our type of index is approaching its limit of practical application. The "citation-index" method appears to be useless here. The only hope is that as the most profitable lines of thought emerge more clearly, we will be able to become more selective.

[6] *Op. cit.*

DESCRIPTOR INDEX

A descriptor is represented by a capital letter and a subscript. The letters indicate main divisions, and the subscripts represent a further breakdown. Following each descriptor, we list those citations in the Bibliography which are associated with that particular descriptor.

A: Mathematical Theory of Computers and Automata

Berkeley 1949

A_1 Finite-state Machines; Mathematical Theory

Ashby 1952a, 1956a, 1959; Babcock 1960b; Burks and Wang 1957; Burks 1959; Culbertson 1952, 1956; Hohn, Seshu, and Aufenkamp 1957; Holland 1959; Keller 1961; Kleene 1956; McCulloch and Pitts 1943; McNaughton 1961; Minsky 1959b; Moore 1956a; Mullin 1959; Murray 1955; Von Neumann 1951, 1956; Rabin and Scott 1959; Shannon 1954; Unger 1958

A_2 Logical Network Theory

Babcock 1960b; Burks 1959; Copi, Elgot, and Wright 1958; George 1956; Gill 1960; Holland 1958; Kleene 1956; McCulloch and Pitts 1943; McNaughton 1961; Minsky 1954a, 1956a, 1959b; Mullin 1959; Shannon 1949b; Tarjan 1958; Von Foerster 1959

A_3 Switching Theory

Calderwood and Porter 1958; McNaughton 1961; Moore and Shannon 1956b; Mullin 1959; Shannon 1949b

A_4 Infinite Memory (Turing) Machines

Burks and Wang 1957; Chomsky 1959b; Davis 1958; Kleene 1952; De Leeuw, Moore, Shannon, and Shapiro 1956; Lofgren 1958; McNaughton 1961; Minsky 1961d; Von Neumann 1951; Rabin and Scott 1959; Rogers 1959; Shannon 1956; Solomonoff 1960; Turing 1936; Wang 1957

A_5 Infinite Structure (Growing) Machines

Burks and Wang 1957; Burks 1959, 1960; Holland 1959, 1960, 1962; McNaughton 1961; Von Neumann 1951

A_6 Probabilistic Machine Theory

Ashby 1951; Blum and McCulloch 1960a; Cowan 1960a, 1960b; Culbertson 1952, 1956; Good 1959; Householder and Landahl 1945; Landahl, Mc-

457

Culloch, and Pitts 1943; De Leeuw, Moore, Shannon, and Shapiro 1956; Mackay 1949; McCulloch 1957*b*, 1959*a*, 1960; McNaughton 1961; Minsky 1954*a*, 1962; Moore and Shannon 1956*b*; Von Neumann 1951; Solomonoff 1960; Verbeek 1960*a*, 1960*b*; Wang 1957

A$_7$ Computability and Recursive Function Theory

Church 1936; Davis 1958; Davis and Putnam 1959; Godel 1931; Holland 1959; Kleene 1935, 1952; De Leeuw, Moore, Shannon, and Shapiro 1956; McCarthy 1956, 1960; McNaughton 1961; Minsky 1961*d*; Post 1943; Rabin and Scott 1959; Rogers 1959, 1960; Turing 1936

A$_8$ Theory of Computation

Bledsoe 1961*b*; Burks 1960; Carr 1958; McCarthy 1960, 1961; McNaughton 1961

B: Computer Structures

Berkeley 1949

B$_1$ Conventional Digital Computers

Andree 1958; Babbage (see appendixes in Bowden 1953); Oettinger 1952; Prywes and Gray 1962; Shannon 1954; Shoulders 1960; Ware 1960

B$_2$ Parallel Computers

Babcock 1960*b*, 1961; Blum and McCulloch 1960*a*; Burks 1959, 1960; Chow 1957; Cowan 1960*b*; Holland 1960, 1962; McCulloch 1951*b*; Nash 1954; Newell 1960*b*; Selfridge 1959; Shoulders 1960; Unger 1958, 1959; Uttley 1956*a*, 1959*b*; Verbeek 1960*a*, 1960*b*; Von Foerster 1959

B$_3$ Reliability through Redundancy of Components

Allanson 1956*b*; Blum and McCulloch 1960*a*; Blum 1960*b*; Cowan 1960*a*, 1960*b*; Elias 1958; Kochen 1959; Landahl, McCulloch, and Pitts 1943; Lofgren 1958, 1962; McCulloch 1957*b*, 1959*a*, 1960; Moore and Shannon 1956*b*; Von Neumann 1951, 1956, 1958; Verbeek 1960*a*, 1960*b*

B$_4$ Random "Neural Nets"

Allanson 1956*a*; Ashby 1950*a*; Babcock 1960*b*; Barus 1959; Cadwallader-Cohen *et al.* 1961; Clark and Farley 1955; Farley and Clark 1954; Good 1959; Hawkins 1961; Hebb 1949; Keller 1961; Milner 1957, 1960, 1961*a*; Minsky 1954*a*, 1959*a*; Minsky and Selfridge 1960; Pask 1959, 1960*b*; Rapoport 1948; Rochester, Holland, Haibt, and Duda 1956; Rosenblatt 1958*a*, 1958*b*, 1959*b*, 1960*a*; Uttley 1954, 1955, 1959*b*; Von Foerster 1959

B$_5$ Allegedly Brainlike Computers

Angyan 1959; Babcock 1960*a*; Balescu 1956; Coupling 1950; Crichton and Holland 1959; Harmon 1959; Harmon, Levinson, and Van Bergeijk 1962*a*;

Hebb 1949; Keller 1961; Milner 1957; Minsky 1954a, 1956b; Rashevsky 1940, 1960; Rosenblatt 1958a, 1958b, 1959b, 1960a, 1962; Russell 1957; Uttley 1954, 1959b

B₆   Neural Nets, Not Necessarily Random in Structure

Allanson 1956b; Babcock 1960a, 1960b, 1961; Barus 1959; Van Bergeijk and Harmon 1960; Bledsoe and Browning 1959; Bledsoe 1961a; Blum 1960b; Burks 1959, 1960; Copi, Elgot, and Wright 1958; Cowan 1960a, 1960b; Culbertson 1950, 1952, 1956; Farley and Clark 1954, 1960b; George 1956; Good 1958; Greene 1959a; Harmon 1959; Harmon, Levinson and Van Bergeijk 1962a; Harmon 1962b; Hawkins 1961; Holland 1958, 1959; Householder and Landahl 1945; Kamentsky 1959; Kleene 1956; Kudielka and Lucas 1961; Landahl, McCulloch, and Pitts 1943; Landahl 1962; Levinson and Harmon 1962; Mackay 1956b; Malin 1961; McCulloch and Pitts 1943; McCulloch 1945, 1957b, 1959a, 1960; Milner 1957, 1960, 1961a; Minsky 1954a, 1956a, 1956b, 1959b, 1962; Mullin 1959; Von Neumann 1956; Rapoport 1948; Rapoport and Shimbel 1949; Rashevsky 1940, 1960; Rochester, Holland, Haibt, and Duda 1956; Selfridge 1948; Sholl and Uttley 1953; Swallow and Weston 1959; Tarjan 1958; Uttley 1954, 1956a, 1959b; Von Foerster 1959; Von Foerster and Zopf 1961; Walter 1954; Wiener and Rosenbleuth 1946; Willis 1959

C: Search Problems[7]

Ashby 1945, 1948, 1956a, 1958b; Bledsoe 1961c, 1961d; Bremermann 1958; Coupling 1950; Holland 1962; Martens 1959; Minsky 1954b, 1961a; Newell 1960b; Polanyi 1957; Russell 1957; Von Foerster and Zopf 1961

C₁   Enumerative Algorithms, Decision Procedures

Ashby 1952a; Bellman 1957; Chomsky 1959b; Davis 1958; Dunham, Fridshal, and Sward 1959; Highleyman 1961b; McCarthy 1956; Minsky 1962; Newell, Shaw, and Simon 1958b, 1958c; Pervin 1959; Prawitz, Prawitz, and Vogera 1960; Pringle 1951; Quine 1955; Wang 1960a

C₂   Imperfect Searches Involving Failure, as Opposed to Decision Procedures

Davis and Putnam 1959, 1960; Gilmore 1959, 1960; Newell and Simon 1956a; Newell, Shaw, and Simon 1957a, 1958b, 1958c; Wang 1960a

C₃   Discussion of Efficiency Problems for Large Searches

Arnold 1959; Ashby 1952a, 1956b; Bledsoe 1961c; Davis and Putnam 1959, 1960; Friedberg 1958; Friedberg, Dunham, and North 1959; Howland, Minsky, and Selfridge 1959; Mackay 1961b; McCarthy 1956; Minsky and Selfridge 1960; Newell, Shaw, and Simon 1957a; Papert 1961; Prywes and Gray 1962; Samuel 1959a; Willis 1960

[7] These categories are particularly hard to separate.

C₄   Heuristics for Reducing Search Magnitude

Arnold 1959; Ashby 1952a, 1956b; Bellman 1957; Mackay 1956b; Tonge 1960

C₅   Partition of Problems into Subproblems

Arnold 1959; Ashby 1952a, 1956b; Bellman 1957; Bledsoe 1961c; Darlington 1958; Friedberg, Dunham, and North 1959; Holland 1962; Spiegelthal 1960; Tonge 1960; Wang 1960a; Willis 1960

C₆   Sequential Improvement Schemes

Andrew 1958, 1959a; Ashby 1956b, 1959; Barus 1959; Bellman 1957; Darlington 1958; Gabor, Wilby, and Woodcock 1961; Holland 1962; Mackay 1959a; Minsky 1954b; Minsky and Selfridge 1960; Prywes and Gray 1962; Selfridge 1956; Tonge 1960

C₇   Problems of Local Peaks, and the Mesa Phenomenon

Campaigne 1959; Darlington 1958; Friedberg 1958; Friedberg, Dunham, and North 1959; Howland, Minsky, and Selfridge 1959; Minsky 1954b; Minsky and Selfridge 1960

C₈   Hill-climbing; Multiple Simultaneous Optimization

Andrew 1958, 1959a; Arnold 1959; Eykhoff 1960; Friedberg 1958; Friedberg, Dunham, and North 1959; Gabor, Wilby, and Woodcock 1961; Highleyman 1961b; Howland, Minsky, and Selfridge 1959; Kailath 1961; Kilburn, Grimsdale, and Summer 1959; Loveland 1958; Minsky 1954b; Minsky and Selfridge 1960; Selfridge 1956, 1959; Widrow 1959

C₉   Discussion of Randomness and Creativity

Cadwallader-Cohen *et al.*, 1961; Campbell 1956, 1960; Cohen 1962; Coupling 1950; Kilburn, Grimsdale, and Summer 1959; Mackay 1949; Minsky 1956b

D: Pattern Recognition and Perception

Van Bergeijk and Harmon 1960; Deutsch 1955; Householder and Landahl 1945; Miller and Chomsky 1957a; Pierce 1961; Rashevsky 1945b; Shepard and Chang 1961a; Sholl and Uttley 1953; Singer 1961; Taylor 1959a; Uhr and Vossler 1961a; Uhr 1961b; Wiener 1949b

D₁   General Discussion, Reviews

Attneave 1954; Babcock 1960b, 1961; Barlow 1959; Clark and Farley 1955; Culbertson 1948; Dineen 1955; Estavan 1959; Farley, Frishkopf, Clark, and

Gilmore 1957; Farley 1960a; Gold 1959; Green 1957; Greene 1959a; Hebb 1958; Kalin 1960; Kirsch, Cahn, Ray, and Urban 1957; Koffka 1935; Kohler 1929; Mackay 1956b; Marill and Green 1960; Marill 1961b; Minot 1959; Minsky 1959a, 1961a; Pitts 1955; Rashevsky 1940, 1960; Selfridge 1955, 1956; Selfridge and Neisser 1960; Sperry 1952; Stevens 1957, 1961a; Sutherland 1959; Unger 1959; Uttley 1954, 1956b; Von Foerster 1959; Wulfeck and Taylor 1957

D_2, D_3 Discussion of Matching Criteria

Attneave 1954; Clark and Farley 1955; Denes and Mathews 1960; Duncker 1945; Estes 1960; Farley 1960a; Frankel 1959; Fry and Denes 1959; Glantz 1960; Highleyman 1961a, 1962; Hughes and Halle 1959; Jakowatz, Shuey, and White 1960; Mattson 1959; McLachlan 1958; Papert 1961; Selfridge 1955, 1956; Selfridge and Neisser 1960; Sprick and Ganzhorn 1959; Steinbuch 1958a; Stevens 1957; Taylor 1959; Wada et al. 1959

D_4 Property-list or Character-vector Schemes

Babcock 1961; Bledsoe and Browning 1959; Bledsoe 1961a; Dimond 1957; Dineen 1955; Doyle 1960; Duncker 1945; Feigenbaum and Simon 1961b; Frishkopf and Harmon 1961; Lewis 1962; McLachlan 1958; Minot 1959; Minsky 1956b; Papert 1961; Samuel 1959a; Selfridge 1955, 1956; Slagle 1961; Steinbuch 1958a; Stevens 1961a

D_5 Schemes Involving Articulation, Recursion, Attention; Division into Parts

Attneave 1954; Balescu 1956; Baneiji 1960; Barnett 1958; Bomba 1959; Canaday 1962; Eden and Halle 1961; Frishkopf and Harmon 1961; Grimsdale, Sumner, Tunis, and Kilburn 1959a; Haller 1959; Harris 1951; Hebb 1949, 1958; Hughes and Halle 1959; Ladefoged 1959; Mackay 1950; Miller 1962; Minsky 1959a, 1961b; Mooers 1951a; Sherman 1959; Stevens 1961a; Uhr 1959a; Unger 1959

D_6 Human Visual Perception

Adrian 1946; Allport 1955; Attneave 1954, 1955; Broadbent 1958; Campbell 1958; Farley 1960a; Freiberger and Murphy 1961; Gibson 1929, 1950; Green 1959; Hake and Hyman 1953; Harmon, Levinson, and Van Bergeijk 1962a; Hayek 1952; Hebb 1949; Householder 1943; Julesz 1960a, 1960b, 1962a; Koffka 1935; Kohler 1929, 1951; Lawrence and Coles 1954; Lawrence and La Berge 1956; Mackay 1960b, 1961c; Marshall and Talbot 1942; Miller 1956b; Neisser 1959a, 1959b, 1960; Pitts and McCulloch 1947; Roberts 1962; Scott and Williams 1959; Selfridge and Neisser 1960; Stevens 1951; Sutherland 1959; Uhr 1960

D_7 Nonvisual Perception, Especially Speech Recognition Machines

Bauman and Licklider 1954; Byrnes, Gold, and Kemball 1958; David 1955, 1958a; David, Matthews, and McDonald 1958b; David 1961; Davis, Biddulph, and Balashek 1953; Denes and Mathews 1960; Fatehchand 1960; Forgie and Forgie 1959; Fry and Denes 1953, 1959; Harmon 1959; Harmon, Levinson, and Van Bergeijk 1962a; Hughes and Halle 1959; Ladefoged 1959; Marill 1961b; Miller 1958; Petrick 1961a; Pierce and David 1958; Shultz 1957; Steinbuch 1958b; Stevens 1951; Wiener 1950b

D₈   Picture Transformations, Especially Local Homogeneous (Kernel)

Attneave 1954; Babcock 1960b; Bomba 1959; Buell 1961; David 1961; Dineen 1955; Elias *et al.* 1952; Kalin 1960; Kirsch, Cahn, Ray, and Urban 1957; Landahl 1962; Minot 1959; Selfridge 1955, 1956; Sherman 1959; Stevens 1961a, 1961b; Unger 1958, 1959

D₉   Pattern Recognition as a Statistical Decision Problem

Chow 1957; Doyle 1960; Estes 1960; Farley 1960a; Frankel 1959; Hawkins 1961; Highleyman 1961b; Marill and Green 1960; Minsky and Selfridge 1960; Papert 1961; Rosenblatt 1958a, 1958b, 1959a, 1959b, 1960a, 1962; Sebestyen 1960, 1961; Stevens 1961a; Uhr 1961b; Unger 1958; Uttley 1954, 1956a, 1956b, 1956c, 1959a, 1959b; Wiener 1949a

D₁₀   Character-reading Machines, Printed Text or Handwritten

Bailey and Norrie 1957; Baran and Estrin 1960; Barus 1959; Bledsoe and Browning 1959; Bledsoe 1961a; Bomba 1959; Broido 1958; Chow 1957; Dimond 1957; Doyle 1960; Eden 1962; Eldredge 1957; Flores 1958; Frankel 1959; Freiberger and Murphy 1961; Frishkopf and Harmon 1961; Glauberman 1959; Greanias, Hoppel, Cloomok, and Osborn 1957a; Greanias and Hill 1957b; Grimsdale, Sumner, Tunis, and Kilburn 1959a; Haller 1959; Heasly 1959; Highleyman and Kamentsky 1959a, 1959b, 1960; Highleyman 1961a, 1962; Kamentsky 1959; Kazmierczak 1959; Leimer 1962; Marill and Green 1960; Mattson 1959; Minot 1959; Pahl and Johnson 1959; Roberts 1960; Rosenblatt 1958a; Selfridge and Neisser 1960; Sherman 1959; Sprick and Ganzhorn 1959; Steinbuch 1958a; Stevens 1957, 1961a; Taylor 1959; Uhr 1959a; Unger 1959; Wada *et al.* 1959

D₁₁   Discovery of Useful Properties for Distinguishing Patterns

Babcock 1960b, 1961; Banerji 1960; Bruner, Goodnow, and Austin 1956; Buell 1961; David 1961; Denes and Mathews 1960; Deutsch 1955; Freiberger and Murphy 1961; Gill 1959; Glantz 1960; Golomb 1960; Heasly 1959; Hubel and Wiesel 1959, 1962; Hughes and Halle 1959; Julesz 1962a; Kazmierczak 1959; Kirsch, Cahn, Ray, and Urban 1957; Lettvin, Maturana, McCulloch, and Pitts 1959; Mackay 1956b; Marill 1961b; Mattson 1959; McLachlan 1958; Minot 1959; Minsky 1956b, 1959a; Minsky and Selfridge 1960; Newell, Shaw, and Simon 1960a; Papert 1961; Sebestyen 1960, 1961; Selfridge 1955, 1956, 1959; Solomonoff 1957; Sprick and Ganzhorn 1959; Stevens 1961b; Uhr 1959a, 1960; Uhr and Vossler 1961c; Von Foerster and Zopf 1961; Watson 1959

D₁₂   Transformation-invariant Properties Not Requiring Prenormalization

Babcock 1960*b*, 1961; Bomba 1959; Buell 1961; Deutsch 1955; Doyle 1960; Harmon 1960*a*, 1960*b*; Hu 1962; Hubel and Wiesel 1959, 1962; Kalin 1960; Lettvin, Maturana, McCulloch, and Pitts, 1959; McCulloch 1951*b*; Minot 1960; Pitts and McCulloch 1947; Roberts 1960; Rosenblatt 1960*a*; Selfridge and Neisser 1960; Stevens 1961*a*, 1961*b*; Wiener 1948

D₁₃   Discrimination by Use of Weighted Sums of Relatively Simple Properties

Bledsoe and Browning 1959; Bledsoe 1961*a*; Braverman 1959; Chow 1957; Denes and Mathews 1960; Doyle 1960; Gamba 1961; Hawkins 1961; Joseph 1960; Keller 1961; Marill and Green 1960; Mattson 1959; Minsky and Selfridge 1960; Murray 1959, 1961; Roberts 1960; Rosenblatt 1958*a*, 1958*b*, 1959*a*, 1959*b*, 1960*a*, 1962; Selfridge 1959; Taylor 1959; Turing 1953; Uttley 1954, 1956*c*, 1959*b*; Wada *et al.* 1959; Willis 1959

D₁₄   Systems Using Hierarchies of Recognition Devices

Canaday 1962; Denes and Mathews 1960; Hubel and Wiesel 1959, 1962; Ladefoged 1959; Lettvin, Maturana, McCulloch, and Pitts 1959; Miller, Galanter, and Pribram 1960; Miller 1962; Minsky 1962; Neisser 1959*a*, 1959*b*, 1960; Rosenblatt 1962; Russell 1957; Selfridge 1959; Selfridge and Neisser 1960; Tinbergen 1951; Uttley 1954, 1956*b*, 1956*c*, 1959*b*

E: Learning Systems

General discussion: Andrew 1959*a*, 1959*b*; Ashby 1948, 1956*a*; Bledsoe 1961*d*; Carr 1958; Chomsky and Miller 1957*b*; Culbertson 1950; Deutsch 1956; Eldredge 1957; Estavan 1959; Feigenbaum and Simon 1961*b*; Feigenbaum 1961*c*; George 1959*b*; Greene 1959*b*; Gyr 1960; Holland 1962; Hull 1943, 1952; Kochen and Levy 1956; Mackay 1961*b*; Minsky 1961*a*; Newell and Simon 1962; Pask 1959, 1960*b*, 1961; Richards 1951, 1952; Rosenblatt 1962; Russell 1957; Shimbel 1950; Singer 1961; Sluckin 1954; Stevens 1951; Turing 1950; Von Foerster and Zopf 1961; Weir 1958; Wyckoff 1954

E₁   Animal Learning Behavior

Deese 1952; Hebb 1958, 1961; Hilgard 1956; Hull 1935; Landahl 1962; Minsky 1956*b*; Skinner 1961; Sutherland 1959; Thorpe 1956; Tinbergen 1951; Watson 1959; Zemanek, Kretz, and Angyan 1960

E₂   Human Learning Behavior

Allport 1955; Bush and Estes 1959; Chomsky 1959*a*; Deese 1952; Feigenbaum and Simon 1961*b*; Gibson 1940; Green 1959; Hebb 1958, 1961; Hilgard 1956; Kochen 1958*a*; Miller, Galanter, and Pribram 1960; Newell and Simon 1962; Pask and Von Foerster 1960c; Shepard and Chang 1961a; Simon 1961b; Skinner 1953, 1957, 1961

E₃ Reinforcement (Reward, Extinction)

Barus 1959; Bush and Mosteller 1955; Bush and Estes 1959; Campaigne 1959; Chomsky 1959a; Clark and Farley 1955; Coupling 1950; Estes 1950; Farley and Clark 1954; Friedberg 1958; Friedberg, Dunham, and North 1959; George 1957; Good 1958; Gorn 1959; Keller 1961; Kilburn, Grimsdale, and Summer 1959; Kirsch 1954; Landahl 1962; Loveland 1958; Mattson 1959; Milner 1957, 1960; Minsky 1954a, 1956b; Minsky and Selfridge 1960; Oettinger 1952; Papert 1961; Roberts 1960; Rosenblatt 1958a, 1958b, 1959a; Samuel 1959a; Selfridge 1959; Skinner 1957, 1961; Wiener 1948; Willis 1959

E₄ Correlation Computations

Arnold 1959; Eykhoff 1960; Friedberg 1958; Friedberg, Dunham, and North 1959; Jakowatz, Shuey, and White 1960; Kac 1962; Kailath 1961; Kilburn, Grimsdale, and Summer 1959; Mattson 1959; McLachlan 1958; Minsky and Selfridge 1960; Newell 1955; Rosenblatt 1959a; Samuel 1959a; Steinbuch 1961; Watson 1959

E₅ Association, Nonreinforcement Learning Ideas

Barus 1959; Feigenbaum 1959, 1961a; Feigenbaum and Simon 1961b; Furst 1949; Hayek 1952; Hebb 1949, 1958; Lashley 1951; Milner 1957, 1960; Prywes and Gray 1962; Stevens 1959; Uttley 1956a, 1956b, 1956c, 1959a, 1959b

E₆ Confirmation of Internally Generated Hypotheses

Banerji 1960; Bledsoe and Browning 1959; Bledsoe 1961a; Chomsky 1959a; Feldman 1959, 1961a; Feldman, Tonge, and Kanter 1961b; Koffka 1935; Kohler 1929; Mackay 1961b; Minsky 1961b; Newell 1955; Newell, Shaw, and Simon 1960a; Papert 1961; Solomonoff 1957, 1959a

E₇ "Adaptation," Adjustment of Internal Parameters

Angyan 1959; Ashby 1947a, 1952a, 1959; Bellman and Kalaba 1958; Cadwallader-Cohen et al. 1961; Campbell 1956; Coupling 1950; Darlington 1958; Eykhoff 1960; Kac 1962; Pask and Von Foerster 1960c; Stevens 1961a; Uhr and Vossler 1961a

E₈ "Conditioning"

Angyan 1959; Braines, Napalkov, and Shreider 1959a; Householder and Landahl 1945; Landahl 1962; Von Neumann 1956; Pitts 1943; Rashevsky 1940, 1960; Walter 1950, 1951; Zemanek, Kretz, and Angyan 1960

E₉ Statistical Learning Theories

Ashby 1945; Atkinson 1954; Bemer 1959; Bush and Mosteller 1955; Bush and Estes 1959; Estes 1950; Farley 1960a; Foulkes 1959; Galanter and

Miller 1960; Gamba 1961; George 1957; Gorn 1959; Joseph 1960; Landahl 1962; Minsky 1962; Murray 1959, 1961; Oettinger 1952; Pask and Von Foerster 1960a; Rapoport 1956; Selfridge 1955, 1956; Uttley 1956a, 1956b, 1959a; White 1959; Widrow 1959

E_{10} "Rote Learning," Literal Storage of Records

Feigenbaum and Simon 1961b; Martens 1959; Samuel 1959a; Shannon 1952, 1955; Tinbergen 1951; Wallace 1952

F: Planning Schemes

General discussion: Galanter and Gerstenhaber 1956; Galton 1883; Gyr 1960; Kochen and Levy 1956; Minsky 1961a, 1961b; Newell 1955; Pask 1961; Rosenblatt 1960a

F_1 Internal Models of the World

Bremermann 1958; Craik 1952; Mackay 1956a, 1956b, 1961b; Minsky 1954a, 1956b

F_2 Prediction of Effects of Contemplated Action

George 1956; Koffka 1935; Kohler 1929; Mackay 1956a, 1956b, 1960a; Milner 1960; Minsky 1954a, 1956b

F_3 Use of Semantic Models

Gelernter and Rochester 1958; Gelernter 1959b; Gelernter, Hansen, and Loveland 1960a; Mackay 1949, 1959a; Minsky 1956b, 1956c, 1959a, 1961b

F_4 Use of Simplified, Possibly Homomorphic, Models

Ashby 1956b; Bremermann 1958; Hartmanis 1961; Kochen and Levy 1956; Minsky 1956b, 1959a; Newell, Shaw, and Simon 1960a; Shannon 1955; Tonge 1960

F_5 Construction of Internal Abstract Models

Mackay 1961b; Minsky 1956b, 1959a, 1961b; Newell, Shaw, and Simon 1960a

F_6 Human Planning Strategies

Cohen 1962; De Groot 1946; Greene 1959c; Luce and Raiffa 1957; Miller, Galanter, and Pribram 1960; Von Neumann and Morgenstern 1947; Pask and Von Foerster 1960a; Polya 1954, 1954a; Shannon 1950a, 1950b; Simon 1957

G: Problem-solving

Ashby 1956a; Bartlett 1958; Boring 1946; Feigenbaum 1961c; Feldman 1962; Galanter and Gerstenhaber 1956; Galton 1883; Greene 1959b; Gyr

1960; Minsky 1961*a*; Newell 1960*b*; Newell and Simon 1961*b*, 1961*c*, 1961*d*, 1962; Pask and Von Foerster 1960*c*; Pask 1961; Polanyi 1957; Simon 1961*a*; Stevens 1951; Tonge 1960

G₁ Administration Problem for Heuristic Programming

Bellman and Brock 1960*b*; Gelernter 1959*a*; Minsky 1956*b*, 1956*c*, 1959*a*, 1962; Newell, Shaw, and Simon 1957*a*, 1959*a*, 1960*a*; Reitman 1959, 1961; Slagle 1961

G₂ Search-tree Termination with Static Evaluation Function (Game Playing)

Bellman 1957; Bernstein *et al.* 1958*a*; Bernstein and Roberts 1958*b*; Freimer 1960; Kister, Stein, Ulam, Walden, and Wells 1957; Newell 1955; Newell, Shaw, and Simon 1958*b*; Samuel 1959*a*; Shannon 1950*a*, 1950*b*; Stein and Ulam 1957; Turing 1953; Wiener 1948

G₃ Explicit Use of Goals and Subgoals

Bellman 1957; Berstein *et al.* 1958*a*; Bernstein and Roberts 1958*b*; Churchman and Ackoff 1950*a*; De Groot 1946; Gelernter 1959*a*; McCarthy 1959; McCulloch 1955*c*; Miller, Galanter, and Pribram 1960; Minsky 1954*a*, 1956*b*; Newell 1955; Newell, Shaw, and Simon 1958*a*, 1958*b*, 1958*c*; Newell and Simon 1961*b*, 1961*c*, 1961*d*; Selfridge 1956; Shannon 1950*a*, 1950*b*; Simon 1961*b*; Spiegelthal 1960

G₄ Human Problem-solving (Psychological Literature)

Boring 1955; Bruner, Goodnow, and Austin 1956; Campbell 1958; Chomsky 1959*a*; Clarkson and Simon 1960; De Groot 1946; Duncan 1959; Feldman 1959, 1961*a*; Feldman, Tonge, and Kanter 1961*b*; Galanter and Miller 1960; Ghiselin 1952; Hadamard 1945; Hebb 1958; Heidbreder 1924; Hovland 1952; Humphrey 1951; John and Miller 1957; Johnson 1955; Katona 1940; Kochen and Levy 1956; Koffka 1935; Kohler 1929; Licklider 1960; Linsky 1952; Luchins 1942; Miller 1956*b*; Miller and Chomsky 1957*a*; Moore and Anderson 1954*a*, 1954*b*; Newell, Shaw, and Simon 1957*a*, 1958*a*, 1958*b*, 1958*c*, 1959*a*, 1960*a*; Newell and Simon 1961*b*, 1961*c*, 1961*d*, 1962; Piaget 1926, 1950, 1954; Poincare 1954; Polya 1954, 1954*a*; Rappaport 1951; Robinson 1957; Simon and Newell 1956*a*; Simon 1957, 1961*a*, 1961*b*; Vinacke 1962; Wertheimer 1945

G₅ The Effect of Different Training Sequences

Birch 1945; Boring 1955; Friedberg 1958; Friedberg, Dunham, and North 1959; Galanter 1959; Katona 1940; Kochen 1958*a*; Luchins 1942; Minsky 1959*a*; Newell, Shaw, and Simon 1958*a*, 1958*b*, 1958*c*; Piaget 1926; Polya 1954, 1954*a*; Russell 1956; Simon 1956*b*; Skinner 1953, 1961; Solomonoff 1957

G₆   Reasoning and Discovery, Human

Birch 1945; Boring 1955; Bruner, Goodnow, and Austin 1956; Campbell 1960; Deutsch 1954, 1956; Ghiselin 1952; Hebb 1949, 1958; Hovland 1952; Luchins 1942; Miller, Galanter, and Pribram 1960; Newell, Shaw, and Simon 1958a, 1958c, 1959a, 1960a; Newell and Simon 1961b, 1961c, 1961d; Polanyi 1957; Rashevsky 1945b, 1946; Robinson 1957

G₇   Theorem Proving by Machine

Copi and Beard 1959; Davis and Putnam 1959, 1960; Dunham, Fridshal, and Sward 1959; Gelernter and Rochester 1958; Gelernter 1959a, 1959b; Gelernter, Hansen, and Loveland 1960a; Gilmore 1959, 1960; Kleene 1952; McCarthy 1961; Minsky 1956b, 1956c, 1959a, 1962; Newell and Simon 1956a; Newell, Shaw, and Simon 1957a, 1959a, 1960a; Newell and Simon 1961b, 1961c, 1961d; Poincare 1954; Polya 1954a; Prawitz, Prawitz, and Vogera 1960; Quine 1955; Robinson 1957; Slagle 1961; Wang 1960a, 1960b, 1961

G₈   Use of Deductive Logic in Problem-solving

Church 1956; Copi and Beard 1959; Dunham, Fridshal, and Sward 1959; Gardner 1952, 1958; Gilmore 1959, 1960; Malin 1961; McCallum and Smith 1951; McCarthy 1959; Minsky 1961b; Moore and Anderson 1954a; Newell and Simon 1956a; Newell, Shaw, and Simon 1957a, 1959a, 1960a; Peirce 1887; Rashevsky 1945b, 1946

G₉   Program-writing or Sequential-action Problems

Amarel 1960; Campaigne 1959; Friedberg 1958; Friedberg, Dunham, and North 1959; Kilburn, Grimsdale, and Summer 1959; McCarthy 1959; Newell, Shaw, and Simon 1960a; Simon 1961c

G₁₀   Character-Method Selection Machines

Gelernter and Rochester 1958; Gelernter 1959b; Gelernter, Hansen, and Loveland 1960a; Minsky 1956b, 1959a; Newell, Shaw, and Simon 1959a, 1960a; Slagle 1961

H: Languages

Ashby 1956a; Feigenbaum 1961c; Stevens 1951

H₁   Natural Languages

Bar-Hillel 1960, 1962; Bloomfield 1933; Ceccato 1956; Chomsky 1953, 1955, 1956, 1957a; Chomsky and Miller 1957b, 1958; Chomsky 1959a; Gold 1959; Green 1961a; Harris 1951, 1960; Lindsay 1960, 1961, 1962a, 1962b; Mandelbrot 1953; McCulloch 1952; Miller 1951; Newell and Simon 1962; Ogden 1933; Pendergraft 1961; Pierce and David 1958; Sapir 1939;

Shannon and Weaver 1949a; Skinner 1957, 1961, 1961; Wiener 1950b; Williams 1956; Yngve 1956, 1961

H₂   Formal Languages

Carr 1958; Chomsky 1953, 1955, 1956, 1957a; Chomsky and Miller 1957b, 1958; Chomsky 1959b, 1959c; Copi, Elgot, and Wright 1958; Davis 1958; Gibson 1929; Green 1961a; Harris 1951; Kleene 1952, 1956; Levien 1962; Miller 1951; Newell and Simon 1956a; Newell and Shaw 1957b; Newell, Shaw, and Simon 1959a, 1960a; Ogden 1933; Post 1943; Prywes and Gray 1962; Rosenbloom 1950; Solomonoff 1958, 1959a, 1959b; Wang 1960a; Williams 1956; Yngve 1961

H₃   Programming Language Systems

Andree 1958; Backus 1959; Bemer 1959; Carr 1958; David 1961; Ernst 1962; Gorn 1957; Green 1961a; Holland 1960; Mathews 1961; McCarthy 1960; Newell and Shaw 1957b; Newell, Shaw, and Simon 1958a, 1959a, 1960a; Newell 1960b; Newell and Tonge 1960c; Orchard-Hays 1961; Petrick 1961b; Reitman 1961; Rochester 1953; Rochester, Goldberg, and Edwards 1959; Shaw, Newell, Simon, and Ellis 1958; Unger 1958, 1959

H₄   Symbol-manipulation Programming Systems

Carr 1958; Craik 1952; Eden and Halle 1961; Fredkin 1960; Gelernter and Rochester 1958; Gelernter 1959a; Gelernter, Hansen, and Gerberich 1960b; Green 1959, 1961a, 1961b; Hiller and Isaacson 1959a; Kahrimanian 1953; McCarthy 1959, 1960; Miller, Minker, Reed, and Shindle 1960; Newell and Simon 1956a; Newell and Shaw 1957b; Newell, Shaw, and Simon 1958a, 1958b, 1958c, 1959a, 1960a; Newell and Tonge 1960c; Newell 1961e; Orchard-Hays 1961; Petrick 1961b; Rochester, Goldberg, and Edwards 1959; Shaw, Newell, Simon, and Ellis 1958; Slagle 1961; Strachey 1952; Tonge 1960; Williams 1956; Yngve 1956

H₅   Role of Language in Thinking and Communication

Bar-Hillel and Carnap 1953a, 1953b; Bar-Hillel 1955a, 1955b; Bloomfield 1933; Broadbent 1958; Campbell 1958; Cherry 1952, 1957; Chomsky 1959a; Hoviland 1952; Koffka 1935; Kohler 1929; Lashley 1951; Lenneberg 1956; Linsky 1952; Mackay 1954a, 1956c, 1961a; *Miller* 1951; Miller and Selfridge 1956a; Minsky 1961b; Mooers 1956a, 1956b, 1959; Mowrer 1954; Newell 1955; Osgood, Suci, and Tannenbaum 1957; Pask 1960b; Pierce 1961; Rothstein 1954; Ryle 1949; Sapir 1939; Selfridge 1956; Skinner 1957

H₆   Language and Coding for Models

Burks 1960; Chomsky and Miller 1957b; Craik 1952; Lindsay 1960, 1961, 1962a, 1962b; Mackay 1949, 1961a; Mandelbrot 1953; Mooers 1956a, 1956b; Von Neumann 1958; Newell 1955; Newell, Shaw, and Simon 1960a; Newman 1959

H₇ Information Theory and Coding Theory

Alluisi 1957; Attneave 1954, 1955; Bar-Hillel and Carnap 1953a, 1953b; Bar-Hillel 1955a, 1955b; Barlow 1959; Brillouin 1951; Cherry 1952, 1957; Cohen 1962; Cowan 1960a, 1960b; Elias 1958; Frankel 1959; Heasly 1959; Jackson 1950; Jacobson 1959; Mackay 1950, 1953, 1956c, 1959a, 1961a, 1961b; Mandelbrot 1953; Miller 1956a, 1956b, 1956c; Pierce 1961; Rapoport 1956; Rothstein 1954; Scott and Williams 1959; Shannon and Weaver 1949a; Shannon 1949b; Sluckin 1958; Wiener 1948; Wozencraft and Horstein 1960

I: Inductive Inference Machines

Ashby 1956a; Gyr 1960; Russell 1957

I₁ Conditional Probability

Andrew 1959a, 1959b, 1961; Barlow 1959; Brooks, Hopkins, Neumann, and Wright 1957; Cohen 1962; Foulkes 1959; Fry and Denes 1959; Good 1961a; Hagelbarger 1955; Hake and Hyman 1953; Hiller and Isaacson 1959a; Jakowatz, Shuey, and White 1960; Kemeny 1955b; Kudielka and Lucas 1961; Luce and Raiffa 1957; Mackay 1956b, 1959a; Minsky 1956b, 1962; Polya 1954, 1954a; Popper 1960; Selfridge 1955, 1956; Shannon 1955; Sluckin 1958; Solomonoff 1960; Uttley 1956a, 1956b, 1956c, 1959a, 1959b; Watanabe 1960; White 1959; Wiener 1949a; Zemanek, Kretz, and Angyan 1960

I₂ Grammatical Induction; Abstracting the Form of a Set of Formal Expressions

Brooks, Hopkins, Neumann, and Wright 1957; Chomsky 1959a; Miller and Chomsky 1957a; Minsky 1956b, 1959a, 1961a, 1962; Newell and Simon 1956a; Newman 1959; Selfridge 1955, 1956; Solomonoff 1958, 1959a, 1959b, 1960; Uhr and Vossler 1961c

I₃ Abbreviative Encoding

Andrew 1961; Martens 1959; Pierce 1961; Rosenblatt 1960a; Selfridge 1956; Shannon and Weaver 1949a; Solomonoff 1958, 1959a

I₄ Hypothesis Formation and Confirmation

Amarel 1960; Bruner, Goodnow, and Austin 1956; Chomsky and Miller 1957b; Good 1958; Hovland and Hunt 1960, 1961; Hunt 1960a; Hunt and Hovland 1960b; Kochen 1958a; Mackay 1956a, 1956b, 1961b; Miller and Chomsky 1957a; Neisser 1960; Newell, Shaw, and Simon 1960a; Popper 1960; Solomonoff 1958, 1959a; Uhr and Vossler 1961c; Watanabe 1960; Weir 1958

I₅   Theories of Inductive Inference

Good 1961a; Hayek 1952; Luce and Raiffa 1957; Minsky 1962; Polya 1954, 1954a; Popper 1960; Ryle 1949; Solomonoff 1960; Somenzi 1956; Watanabe 1960

I₆   Simplicity and Induction

Burge 1958; Good 1961a; Goodman 1951, 1958; Kemeny 1953, 1955c; McCarthy 1956; McCulloch 1951b; Minsky 1959a, 1962; Popper 1960; Shannon 1949b; Solomonoff 1957, 1959a, 1960

J: Heuristics

Darlington 1958; Feigenbaum 1961c; Friedberg 1958; Gyr 1960; Malin 1961

J₁   Discussion of Heuristics for Machine Solution of Problems

Ashby 1956b; Berstein *et al.* 1958a; Bernstein and Roberts 1958b; Bouricius and Keller 1959; Friedberg, Dunham, and North 1959; Gelernter 1959b; Gelernter, Hansen, and Loveland 1960a; Gilmore 1959, 1960; Holland 1959; Kister, Stein, Ulam, Walden, and Wells 1957; Miller, Galanter, and Pribram 1960; Minsky 1956b, 1956c, 1961a, 1961b, 1962; Newell 1955; Newell and Simon 1956a; Newell, Shaw, and Simon 1957a, 1958a, 1958b, 1958c, 1959a, 1960a; Newell 1960b; Reitman 1959, 1961; Selfridge 1956; Simon 1961a; Slagle 1961; Solomonoff 1957; Stein and Ulam 1957; Tonge 1960; Turing 1953; Wang 1960a; Wozencraft and Horstein 1960; Martens 1959

J₂   Discussion of Human Problem-solving Heuristics

Ashby 1956b; Bernstein *et al.* 1958a; Bouricius and Keller 1959; Campbell 1960; Chomsky 1959a; De Groot 1946; Duncan 1959; Good 1958; Greene 1959c; Hadamard 1945; Humphrey 1951; Johnson 1955; Kochen 1958a; McCarthy 1956; McCulloch 1955c; Miller, Galanter, and Pribram 1960; Newell 1955; Newell and Simon 1956a; Newell, Shaw, and Simon 1957a, 1958a, 1958b, 1958c, 1959a, 1960a; Newell 1960b; Newell and Simon 1961b, 1961c, 1961d, 1962; Poincare 1954; Polanyi 1957; Polya 1954, 1954a; Reitman 1959, 1961; Simon 1961a, 1961b; Slagle 1961; Tonge 1960; Vinacke 1962; Wang 1960a

K: Theories of Brain Function

Eccles 1953; Householder 1943; Pask 1961; Uhr and Vossler 1961a; Wiener 1948; Young 1956

K₁   Connection or Path Reinforcement, Synaptic Facilitation

Andrew 1959a; Babcock 1960a; Barus 1959; Farley and Clark 1954; Good 1962; Hebb 1949, 1958; Landahl 1962; Minsky 1954a; Rosenblatt 1958a, 1958b, 1962; Willis 1959

K₂   Cell-Assembly Theories

Barus 1959; Clark and Farley 1955; Good 1962; Hebb 1949, 1958; Milner 1957, 1960, 1961*a*, 1961*b*; Minsky 1954*a*; Minsky and Selfridge 1960; Rochester, Holland, Haibt, and Duda 1956; Selfridge 1959

K₃   Other Neurophysiological Models

Angyan 1959; Ashby 1946; Babcock 1960*a*; Barlow 1959; Coburn 1951, 1952; Culbertson 1948; Goldstein 1960; Harmon 1959; Harmon, Levinson, and Van Bergeijk 1962*a*; Hartline 1938; Hebb 1949; Hubel and Wiesel 1959, 1962; Kalin 1960; Kohler 1951; Kubie 1930, 1941; Landahl 1962; Lashley 1942, 1951; Lettvin, Maturana, McCulloch, and Pitts 1959; Marshall and Talbot 1942; McCulloch 1960; Milner 1957, 1960, 1961*a*, 1961*b*; Minsky 1954*a*; Penfield and Rasmussen 1950; Pfeiffer 1955; Pierce and David 1958; Pitts and McCulloch 1947; Precker 1954; Pribram 1959; Rashevsky 1940, 1945*a*, 1946, 1960; Reitman 1959; Rosenblatt 1962; Shimbel 1950; Sholl and Uttley 1953; Sholl 1956; Sperry 1951; Sutherland 1959; Taylor 1956; Uttley 1954, 1955, 1959*b*; Von Foerster 1949; Wall and Melzak 1962; Walter 1953; Wechsler 1960; Young 1956; Zemanek, Kretz, and Angyan 1960

K₄   Comparing Machines and Brains

Ashby 1947*a*; Bremermann 1958; Broadbent 1954; Crozier 1951; Good 1959, 1962; Mackay 1949, 1951, 1952, 1954*b*, 1960*b*, 1962; McCulloch 1949*a*; McCulloch and Pfeiffer 1949*b*; McCulloch 1951*b*, 1955*a*, 1957*a*; Miller, Galanter, and Pribram 1960; Milligan 1959; Von Neumann 1951, 1958; Newell and Simon 1961*b*, 1961*c*, 1961*d*; Pfeiffer 1955; Pitts 1955; Quastler 1957; Sperry 1952; Spilsbury 1952; Taube 1961; Walter 1950, 1951

L: Epistemological Questions

Boring 1946; Craik 1952; Culbertson 1950; Deutsch 1951; Good 1961*b*; Kattsoff 1954; Kemeny 1955*a*; Mackay 1951, 1952, 1954*b*; McCulloch 1945; McCulloch and Pfeiffer 1949*b*; McCulloch 1951*b*, 1955*a*, 1957*a*; Minsky 1961*a*; Newell and Simon 1961*b*, 1961*c*, 1961*d*; Pask 1960*b*; Pask and Von Foerster 1960*c*; Pask 1961; Pitts 1955; Popper 1960; Rosenblueth, Wiener, and Bigelow 1943; Rosenblueth and Wiener 1950; Ryle 1949; Scriben 1953; Turing 1950; Wiener 1948; Wisdom 1952; Young 1956

L₁   What Can a Machine Know?

Booth 1960; Hayek 1952; McCulloch and Pitts 1943; McCulloch 1954; Pask 1959; Skinner 1961; Taube 1961; Turing 1936

L₂   Can Machines Think? Nature of Intelligence

Armer 1961; Ashby 1961*a*; Balescu 1956; Coupling 1950; Good 1959; Kelly and Selfridge 1962; Laing 1962; Lionnais 1957; Mackay 1949, 1962; Mc-

Culloch 1954, 1955c; Minsky 1959a; Moiseyev 1960; Newell, Shaw, and Simon 1957a; Reitman 1962; Rogers 1960; Rosenbloom 1950; Ross 1933; Samuel 1960b; Simon 1961b; Somenzi 1956; Taube 1960; Troll 1954; Turing 1950; Wang 1957, 1960a; Wechsler 1958, 1960; Wilkes 1953, 1956; Williams 1960; Wright 1959

L₃   Free Will in Man and Machines

Boring 1957; Mackay 1960a, 1962; McCulloch 1954; Russell 1940; Samuel 1960b; Skinner 1961; Turing 1950

L₄   The Mind-Brain Problem

Adrian 1946; Brain 1959; Eccles 1953; Feigl 1959; Gerard 1946; Good 1962; Hayek 1952; Laslett 1950; Mackay 1960a, 1962; Mays 1952; Meszar 1953; Ryle 1949; Skinner 1961; Sperry 1952; Thomson and Sluckin 1954b; Turing 1950

M: Memory and Information Retrieval

Ashby and Riguet 1961b; Fredkin 1960; Newell, Shaw, and Simon 1958c; Rosenblatt 1958b; Stevens 1951; Wechsler 1960; Young 1956

M₁   Retrieval of Relevant Information

Attneave 1954; Bar-Hillel 1962; Brillouin 1951; Bush 1945; Feigenbaum 1959, 1961a; Feigenbaum and Simon 1961b; Furst 1949; Green 1961a; Kehl, Horty, Bacon, and Mitchell 1961; Luhn 1958, 1959; Miller, Galanter, and Pribram 1960; Minsky 1961b; Mooers 1956a, 1956b, 1959; Newell, Shaw, and Simon 1957a; Paycha 1959; Prywes and Gray 1962; Ray and Kirsch 1957; Samuel 1959a, 1959b; Simmons 1940; Solomonoff 1959b; Stevens 1959; Willis 1959

M₂   Reasoning about Stored Information

Green 1961a; Lindsay 1961, 1962a, 1962b; Luhn 1957; McCallum and Smith 1951; McCarthy 1959; Minsky 1961b; Mooers 1951b, 1956b, 1959; Newell, Shaw, and Simon 1958a, 1958b; Paycha 1959; Stevens 1959; Watanabe 1960

M₃   Human Memory, Psychological Literature

Attneave 1954, 1955; Broadbent 1954; Campbell 1958; Duncan 1959; Ernst 1962; Estes 1960; Feigenbaum and Simon 1961b, 1962; Furst 1949; Gibson 1929; Good 1958; Hebb 1958; Kitona 1940; Kochen 1958a; Kubie 1930, 1941; Lawrence and Coles 1954; Lawrence and La Berge 1956; McCulloch 1954; Miller 1956a, 1956b, 1957b; Miller, Galanter, and Pribram 1960; Spilsbury 1952; Von Foerster 1949

N: Servomechanisms and Stability Mechanisms, Cybernetics

Ashby 1948, 1956a; Belenesku 1958; Berkeley 1949; Braines, Napalkov, and Svechinskii 1959b; Bremermann 1958; Couffignal 1959; Feigenbaum 1961c; Gabor 1954; Kemeny 1955a; Kolman 1960; De Latil 1953; Lyapunov 1960; Mays 1956; Moiseyev 1960; Newman 1958; Pask 1958; Pask and Von Foerster 1960c; Pask 1961; Rapoport and Shimbel 1949; Rashevsky 1940, 1960; Rothstein 1954; Russell 1957; Shaginyan 1959; Sluckin 1954; Sobolev, Kitor, and Lyapunov 1958; Sutherland, Mugglin, and Sutherland 1958; Tsien 1954; Weber 1949; Wiener 1958; Wisdom 1951

N_1 Adaptive Control Systems

Andrew 1961; Ashby 1958b; Bellman and Kalaba 1958, 1959a, 1960a; Braines, Napalkov, and Shreider 1959a; Eykhoff 1960; Freimer 1959; George 1959a; Jakowatz, Shuey, and White 1960; De Latil 1956; Pitts and McCulloch 1947; Reich and Ernst 1960; Russell 1957; Widrow 1959; Wiener 1948

N_2 Teleological Mechanisms

Andrew 1959a; Ashby 1952a, 1959; Churchman and Ackoff 1950a; Deutsch 1951; Elsasser 1958; Klaus 1961; Mackay 1960b; Rosenblueth, Wiener, and Bigelow 1943; Rosenblueth and Wiener 1950; Schutzenberger 1954; Wiener 1948

N_3 Automation, Machines, and Society

Ackoff 1955; Beer 1956b; Diebold 1952; George 1959a; Hugh-Jones 1956; De Latil 1956; Mehl 1959; Merriman, Wass, and Gill 1959; Shubik 1960b; Wiener 1948, 1950a, 1960

N_4 Cybernetics and Psychiatry, Society, etc.

Ashby 1954; Berg 1960; Kochen and Levy 1956; Kubie 1930, 1941; Lettvin and Pitts 1943; McCulloch 1953; Sutro 1959; Thomson and Sluckin 1954a; Weinberg 1951; Wiener 1948

N_5 "Self-organizing" Systems

Ashby 1947b, 1952a; Babcock 1960b; Braines and Napalkov 1960; Pask 1959; Pask and Von Foerster 1960a; Pask 1960b, 1962; Von Foerster 1949, 1959, 1960

N_6 Homeostasis and Stability

Ashby 1946, 1947a, 1950a, 1952a, 1953, 1956b, 1958b, 1959, 1962; Cadwallader-Cohen et al. 1961; Elsasser 1958; George 1957; De Latil 1956; Pask and Von Foerster 1960a; Verbeek 1960a; Von Foerster 1949; Wall and Melzak 1962; Weber 1949; Wiener 1948

N_7 Social Organizations

Ackoff 1959; Asch 1952; Beer 1956b, 1957, 1961; Blau 1955; Cohen and Cyert 1961; Cyert, Feigenbaum, and March 1959; Davis 1958; Gullahorn and Gullahorn 1962; Homans 1961; Rome and Rome 1959

P: Some Special Categories

Kudielka and Lucas 1961

P_1 Theory of Games (after Von Neumann, 1947)

Ackoff 1959; Blackwell and Girshick 1954; Galanter and Gerstenhaber 1956; George 1957; Luce and Raiffa 1957; Von Neumann and Morgenstern 1947; Pask and Von Foerster 1960a, 1960c; Shubik 1960a, 1960b; White 1959

P_2 Statistical Decision Theory

Ackoff 1959, 1962; Adey 1959; Blackwell and Girshick 1954; Galanter and Gerstenhaber 1956; Gold 1959; Highleyman 1961b; Kochen 1958a; Luce and Raiffa 1957; Marill and Green 1960; Shubik 1960a, 1960b; Simon 1956b; Wald 1950

P_3 Man-Machine Interaction

Bemer 1959; Bush 1945; Craik 1947; Estavan 1959; Galanter 1959; Licklider 1960; Pask and Von Foerster 1960c; Taube 1959; Yntema and Torgerson 1961

P_4 Self-reproducing Machines

Burks 1959, 1960; Holland 1962; Jacobson 1958; Kemeny 1955a; Lofgren 1958, 1961, 1962; Moore 1956c; Von Neumann 1951, 1958; Penrose 1959a, 1959b

P_5 Game Playing

Ashby 1952b; Bernstein *et al.* 1958a; Bernstein and Roberts 1958b; Byard 1950; De Groot 1946; Good 1959; Hagelbarger 1955; Haldane 1952; Jackson 1960; Kirsch 1954; Kister, Stein, Ulam, Walden, and Wells 1957; Koppel 1952; Luce and Raiffa 1957; Martens 1959; McCulloch 1955c; Michie 1961; Newell 1955; Newell, Shaw, and Simon 1958b, 1959c; Pask and Von Foerster 1960a; Pervin 1959; Prinz 1952; Richards 1951, 1952; Samuel 1959a, 1960a; Selfridge 1956; Shannon 1950a, 1950b, 1955; Stein and Ulam 1957; Strachey 1952; Turing 1953; White 1959; Wiener 1948

P_6 Music Writing

Brooks, Hopkins, Neumann, and Wright 1957; David 1961; Hiller and Isaacson 1959a; Hiller 1959b; Kassler 1961; Mathews 1961; Reitman 1961

P₇ Maze Learning

Coupling 1950; Minsky 1954*b*; Moore 1959; Pfeiffer 1952; Shannon 1952; Wallace 1952

P₈ Industrial Applications

Beer 1956*a*, 1956*b*; Blau 1955; Clarkson and Meltzer 1960; Clarkson 1962; Cohen 1960; Cyert, Feigenbaum, and March 1959; Helgeson and Kwo 1956; Jackson 1956; Mitchell 1957; Shubik 1960*a*, 1960*b*

Further Categories

An attempt was made to classify the papers by broader types. This was done hastily and is particularly subject to error. These categories are designated by two-digit numbers.

1. Program status:
    11. No machine experiment involved.
    12. Program for general-purpose computer.
    13. Experiment involving special-purpose hardware.
    14. Uses special programming system.
    15. For practical application.
    16. Psychological experiment.
2. Technical domain:
    21. Mathematical.
    22. Psychological.
    23. (Neuro) Physiological.
    24. Philosophical.
3. Paper type:
    31. Review article.
    32. With extensive bibliography.
    33. Proposed experiment.
    34. Report of experiment.
    35. Tutorial.
    36. General discussion.

BIBLIOGRAPHY

The citations are given in the conventional form except for the inclusion of additional information (e.g., volume *and* number) where it might be useful. Following the citations is the list of descriptors, sometimes in order of importance, but not always. Following the descriptors are occasionally found lists of citations, indicating other papers reporting closely related work. The references to the future are particularly useful, and we regret not including more of this ancestral structure.

When several citations occur in the same published volume, the volume is cited only as one or two bracketed letters, *e.g.*, "in [AD]." The listing of such volumes, useful in itself, is found at the end of the Bibliography. That collection would serve well as a beginning for a library on artificial intelligence.

Ackoff, R. L., 1955. Automatic management: A forecast and its educational implications, *Management Science,* 2(1): 55–60. N_3.

———, 1959. Games, decisions and organizations, *General Systems,* 4: 145–150. P_1, P_2, N_7.

———, 1962. *Scientific Method: Optimizing Applied Research Decisions,* New York: Wiley. P_2.

Adey, W. R., 1959. "Instrumentation of Nervous System for Studies of Behavior," presented at the 14th Annual Meeting of the American Rocket Society. P_2.

Adrian, E. D., 1946. The physicial background of perception, *The Wayneflete Lectures,* New York: Oxford. D_6, K, L_4.

Allanson, J. T., 1956a. Some properties of a randomly connected neural network, in [I], chap. 30. B_4.

———, 1956b. The reliability of neurons, in [F]. B_6, B_3.

Allport, F. H., 1955. *Theories of Perception and the Concept of Structure,* New York: Wiley. D_6, E_2, K; 31, 36.

Alluisi, E. A., 1957. Conditions affecting the amount of information in absolute judgments, *Psychological Review,* 64: 97–103. H_1.

Amarel, S., 1960. An approach to automatic theory formation, in [W]. I_4, G_9, G_{11}.

Andree, R. V., 1958. *Programming the IBM 650 Magnetic Drum Computer and Data Processing Machine,* New York: Holt.

Andrew, A. M., 1958. Machines which learn, *New Scientist,* Nov. 27, 4: 1383. C_6, C_8; 36.

———, 1959a. Learning machines, in [N], pp. 475–505. C_6, C_8, E, I_1, K_1, N_2; 13, 36.

———, 1959b. Conditional probability computer, in [N], pp. 945–946. E, I_1; 34.

———, 1960. Learning in a non-digital environment, in [AG].

———, 1961. A self-optimizing system of coding, in [X]. I_1, I_3, N_1; 13, 34.

Angyan, A. J., 1959. Machina reproductrix, an analogue model to demonstrate some aspects of neural adaptation, in [N], **2:**933–943. B_5, E_7, E_8, K_3; 13, 22, 34, 36.

Arin, E. I. See Feigenbaum, 1961c.

Armer, P., 1961. Attitudes toward intelligent machines, in [S]. L_2; 32.

Arnold, R. F., 1959. A compiler capable of learning, in [Q], pp. 137–143. C_3, C_4, C_5, C_8, E_4; 12, 33.

Asch, S. E., 1952. *Social Psychology,* New York: Prentice-Hall. N_1.

Ashby, W. R., 1945. The physical origin of adaptation by trial and error, *Journal of General Psychology,* **32:**13–25. C, E_9.

———, 1946. The behavioral properties of systems in equilibrium, dynamics of the cerebral cortex, *American Journal of Psychology,* **59:**682–686. K_3, N_6.

———, 1947a. The nervous system as a physical machine: with special reference to the origin of adaptive behavior, *Mind,* **56:**1–16. K_4, E_7, N_6.

———, 1947b. Principles of the self-organizing dynamic system, *Journal of General Psychology,* **37:**125–128. N_5.

———, 1948. Design for a brain, *Electronic Engineering,* **20:**379–383. C, N, E.

———, 1950a. The stability of a randomly assembled nerve network, *Electroencephalography and Clinical Neurophysiology,* **2:**471–482. B_4, N_6.

———, 1950b. The cerebral mechanisms of intelligent behavior, in *Perspectives in Neuropsychiatry* (D. Richter, ed.), London.

———, 1951. Statistical machinery, *Thales,* **7**(1):1–3. A_6.

———, 1952a. *Design for a Brain,* New York: Wiley (rev. ed. 1960). N_6, A_1, C_1, C_3, C_4, C_5, E_7, N_5, N_2; 21, 35, 13, 34.

———, 1952b. Can a mechanical chess player outplay its designer? *British Journal of Philosophy of Science,* **3:**44–57. P_5.

———, 1953. Homeostasis, in [B], 9th Conference, pp. 73–108. N_6.

———, 1954. The application of cybernetics to psychiatry, *Journal of Mental Science,* **100:**114–124. N_4.

———, 1956a. *An Introduction to Cybernetics,* New York: Wiley. A_1, C, E, G, H, I, N; 35.

———, 1956b. Design for an intelligence amplifier, in [G], pp. 215–234. C_3, C_4, C_5, C_8, N_6, F_4, J_1, J_2; 13 ("Homeostat").

———, 1958a. Cybernetics, *Recent Progress in Psychiatry,* **3:**94–117.

———, 1958b. Requisite variety and its implications for the control of complex systems, *Cybernetica,* **1:**83–99. C, N_1, N_6.

———, 1959. The mechanism of habituation, in [N], pp. 95–113. A_1, C_6, E_7, N_2, N_6; 21.

———, 1960a. The brain as regulator, *Nature,* **186:**413.

———, 1960b. Computers and decision making, *New Scientist,* **7:**746.

———, 1961a. What is an intelligent machine? in [Z], pp. 278–280. L_2.

——— and Riguet, J., 1961b. The avoidance of over-writing in self-organizing systems, *Journal of Theoretical Biology,* **1:**431–439. M.

————, 1962. Principles of the self-organizing system, in [W], pp. 255–278. N₆.

Atkinson, R. C., 1954. *An Analysis of Rote Serial Learning in Terms of a Statistical Model,* doctoral dissertation, Indiana University. E₉.

Attneave, F., 1954. Some informational aspects of visual perception, *Psychological Review,* November, **61**(3):183–193. D₆, D₁, D₂, D₅, D₈, H₇, M₁, M₃; 16.

————, 1955. Symmetry, information, and memory for patterns, *American Journal of Psychology,* **68**:209–222. D₆, H₇, M₃.

Babbage, C. See appendixes in Bowden 1953.

Babcock, M. L., 1960*a. Reorganization by Adaptive Automation,* Technical Report 1, Contract Nonr 1834(21), Electrical Engineering Research Laboratory, Engineering Experiment Station, University of Illinois, Urbana, Ill. B₅, B₆, K₁, K₃; 13, 34, 23, 36.

———— et al., 1960*b. Some Principles of Pre-organization in Self-organizing Systems,* Technical Report 2, Contract Nonr 1834(21), Electrical Engineering Research Laboratory, Engineering Experiment Station, University of Illinois, Urbana, Ill. D₁, A₁, B₆, D₂, D₁₁, D₁₂, B₂, A₂, B₄, N₅; 21.

————, 1961. Some physiology of automata, in [Z], pp. 291–293. B₂, B₆, D₁, D₄, D₁₁, D₁₂; 13, 34.

Backus, J. W., 1959. Automatic programming: properties and performance of FORTRAN systems I and II, in [N], pp. 233–248. H₃; 15.

Bailey, C. E. G., and Norrie, C. O., 1957. Automatic reading of typed or printed characters, *British Institute of Radio Engineering Convention on Electronics in Automation.* D₁₀.

Bales, R. F., 1959. Small-group theory and research, in *Sociology Today* (Merton, Broom, and Cottrell, eds.), New York: Basic Books.

Balescu, I., 1956. Future possibilities and limitations in reproducing brain mechanism by electronic machines, *Review of Science and Sociology* (*Bucharest*), **1**(2):45. B₅, L₂.

Banerji, R. B., 1960. *An Information-processing Program for Object Recognition,* Department of Engineering Administration, Case Institute of Technology, Cleveland, Ohio, unpublished. D₅, D₁₁, E₆.

Baran, P., and Estrin, G., 1960. An adaptive character reader, *IRE Wescon, Convention Records,* **4**(4):29–41. D₁₀.

Bar-Hillel, Y., and Carnap, R., 1953*a.* Semantic information, *British Journal of Philosophy of Science,* **4**:127. H₇, H₈.

———— and ————, 1953*b. An Outline of the Theory of Semantic Information,* Technical Report 247, Research Laboratory of Electronics, Massachusetts Institute of Technology, Cambridge, Mass. H₅, H₇.

————, 1955*a.* An examination of information theory, *Philosophy of Science,* **22**:86–105. H₅, H₇.

————, 1955*b.* Semantic information and its measures, Transactions of the 10th Macy Conference on Cybernetics (Von Foerster, ed.) in [B], pp. 33–48. H₈, H₇.

————, 1960. The present status of automatic translation of languages, in

Advances in Computers, (F. L. Alt, ed.), vol. 1, New York: Academic Press.

————, 1962. Theoretical aspects of the mechanization of literature searching, in *Digitale Informationswandler* (W. Hoffman, ed.), pp. 406–443, Brunswick, Germany: Friedr. Vieweg & Zohn. H₁.

Barlow, H. B., 1959. Sensory mechanisms, the reduction of redundancy and intelligence, in [N], 2:537–574. H₇, D₁, K₃; 13, (I₁) 34, 36.

Barnett, M. P., 1958. *Digitized Description Processing; Part I: Elementary Considerations,* N.R.L., Department of Chemistry, University of Wisconsin, Madison, ASTIA Document AD 153312. D₅.

Bartlett, F. C., 1958. *Thinking,* New York: Basic Books. G.

Barus, C., 1959. *Machine Learning and Pattern Recognition,* Progress Report, National Science Foundation Grant G-5945, Swarthmore College, Swarthmore, Pa. C₆, K₂, B₄, B₆, E₃, D₁₀, E₅, K₁; 21, 33, 36.

————, 1961. *A Scheme for Recognizing Patterns from an Unspecified Class,* Progress Report, National Science Foundation, Grant G-5945, Swarthmore College, Swarthmore, Pa.

Bauman, R. H., and Licklider, J. C. R., 1954. An electronic word recognizer, *Journal of the Acoustical Society of America,* **26**:137. D₇.

Beer, S., 1956. Operational research and cybernetics, in [F], pp. 29–45. N, P₈.

————, 1956b. The impact of cybernetics on the concept of industrial organization, in [F], pp. 535–554. N₃, N₇, P₈.

————, 1957. The scope for operational research in industry, *Institute for Production Engineers Journal,* May, **16**(2). N₇.

————, 1961. *Cybernetics and Management,* London: English Universities Press, 1957, 1960; New York: Wiley, 1961. N₇.

Belenesku, I. N., 1958. Cybernetics and some problems of physiology and psychology, *Voprosy Filos.,* **11**:153, 1957; *Psyshological Abstracta* 3472. N; 22, 23.

Bellman, R., 1957. *Dynamic Programming,* Princeton, N.J.: Princeton University Press. C₁, C₄, C₅, C₆, G₂, G₃; 21.

———— and Kalaba, R., 1958. On communication processes involving learning and random duration, *IRE National Convention Record,* (4)**6**:16–21. E₇, N₁.

———— and ————, 1959a. On adaptive control processes, *IRE National Convention Record,* (4)**7**:3–11; also in *IRE Transactions on Automatic Control,* **AC-4**:1–9, 1959. N₁.

———— and ————, 1960a. Dynamic programming and adaptive processes: mathematical foundations, *IRE Transactions on Automatic Control,* **AC-5**:5–10. N₁.

———— and Brock, P., 1960b. On the concepts of a problem and problem-solving, *American Mathematical Monthly,* February, **67**(2):119–134. G₁.

Bemer, R. W., 1959. A checklist of intelligence for programming systems, *Communications of the ACM,* March, **2**(3):8–13. E₆, H₃, P₃.

Berg, A. I., 1960. Cybernetics and society, *Economic Gazette;* translated in *The Soviet Review,* New York: International Arts and Sciences Press, 1960. N₄.

van Bergeijk, W. A., and Harmon, L. D., 1960. What good are artificial neurons? in [S], pp. 395–406. B₆, D.

Berkeley, E. C., 1949. *Giant Brains, or Machines That Think,* New York: Wiley. A, B, N; 35.

Bernstein, A. et al., 1958a. A chess-playing program for the IBM 704 computer, *Proceedings of the Western Joint Computer Conference* (WJCC), pp. 157–159. P₅, G₂, G₃, J₁, J₂; 12, 34, 36. (Kister, 1957; Newell, 1958b).

——— and Roberts, M. deV. 1958b. Computer vs. chess-player, *Scientific American,* June, **198**:96–105. P₅, G₂, G₃, J₁, J₂; 12, 34, 36.

Birch, H. G., 1945. The relation of previous experience to insightful problem solving, *Journal of Comparative Psychology,* **38**:367. G₅, G₆.

Blackwell, D., and Girshick, M. A., 1954. *Theory of Games and Statistical Decisions,* New York: Wiley. P₁, P₂.

Blau, P. M., 1955. *The Dynamics of Bureaucracy,* Chicago: University of Chicago Press. N₇, P₈.

Bledsoe, W. W., and Browning, I., 1959. Pattern recognition and reading by machine, in [Q], pp. 225–232. D₁₀, D₁₃, D₄, B₆, E₆; 12, 34. (Highleyman, 1960, 1961a, 1962; Bledsoe, 1961a.)

———, 1961a. Further results on the N-tuple character recognition method, *IRE Transactions on Electronic Computers,* March, **EC-10**(1):96. D₁₀, D₁₃, D₄, B₆, E₆; 34.

———, 1961b. A basic limitation on the speed of digital computers, *IRE Transactions on Electronic Computers,* September, **EC-10**(3). A₈. (Bremermann, 1962.)

———, 1961c. *Lethally Dependent Genes Using Instant Selection,* Panoramic Research Publication, Palo Alto, Calif., PRI-2. C, E.

———, 1961d. *The Use of Biological Concepts in the Analytical Study of Systems,* Panoramic Research Publication, Palo Alto, Calif., PRI-2. C, E.

Bloomfield, L., 1933. *Language,* New York: Holt. H₁, H₅; 36.

Blum, G. S., 1961. *A Model of the Mind,* New York: Wiley.

Blum, M., and McCulloch, W. S., 1960a. On parallel computation, Research Laboratory of Electronics, Massachusetts Institute of Technology, *Quarterly Progress Report,* January, (56):194–195. B₂, B₃, A₆.

———, 1960b. Properties of a neuron with many inputs, in [S]. B₆, B₃. See also paper in [W].

Bomba, J. S., 1959. Alpha-numeric character recognition using local operations, in [Q], pp. 218–224. D₈, D₁₀, D₁₂, D₅; 12, 34.

Booth, A. D., 1960. How much can machines learn? *Automatic Data Processing,* February, **2**(2):22–26. L₁.

Boring, E. G., 1946. Mind and mechanism, *American Journal of Psychology,* **59**(2):173–192. L, G.

———, 1955. Dual role of the *Zeitgeist* in scientific creativity, *Scientific Monthly,* February, **80**(2):101–106. G₄, G₅, G₆.

———, 1957. When is human behavior predetermined? *Scientific Monthly,* April, **84**(4):189–196. L₃.

Borko, H., 1962. *Computer Applications in the Social Sciences,* Englewood Cliffs. N.J.: Prentice Hall.

Bouricius, W. G., and Keller, J. M., 1959. Simulation of human problem-solving, in [P], pp. 116–119. J₁, J₂; 12, 34, 36.

Bowden, B. V. (ed.), 1953. *Faster than Thought,* New York: Pitman. A, B₁, P₈, P₅ (chap. 25), Chapter 1 and appendix have historical material on Babbage's computers.

Brain, W. R., 1951. *Mind, Perception, and Science,* Oxford: Blackwell Scientific Publications. L₄.

Braines, S. N., Napalkov, A. V., and Shreider, Iu. A., 1959a. Analysis of the working principles of some self-adjusting systems in engineering and biology, in [R]. N₁, E₈.

——, ——, and Svechinskii, V. B., 1959b. *Problems of Neuro-cybernetics,* published in the USSR, 1959. Available from the U.S. Joint Publications Research Service, Office of Technical Services, Department of Commerce, Washington, D.C. N.

—— and ——, 1960. *Certain Problems in the Theory of Self-organizing Systems,* Joint Publications Research Service Report 2177-N, U.S. Department of Commerce, Washington, D.C. N₅.

Braverman, E. M., 1959. Certain problems in the design of machines which classify objects according to an identifying feature which is not specified a priori, *Automatica Telemekhanika,* October, **21**(10):1375–1386. D₁₃. (Rosenblatt 1958a).

Bremermann, H. J., 1958. *The Evolution of Intelligence: The Nervous System as a Model of its Environment,* Technical Report 1, (July), Contract Nonr 477(17), Project NR-043-200, Mathematics Department, University of California, Berkeley, Calif. F₄, F₁, C, K₄, N; 21.

Brenner, W. C., Schinzinger, R., and Suarez, R. M., 1956. Application of high speed electronic computers to generator design problems, AIEE Conference Paper 56-940. 15.

Brillouin, L., 1951. Information theory and most efficient codings for communication or memory devices, *Journal of Applied Physics,* **22**:1808–1811. M₁, H₇.

Broadbent, D. E., 1954. A mechanical model for human attention and immediate memory, *Psychological Review,* **64**:205. M₃, K₄.

——, 1958. *Perception and Communication,* London: Pergamon Press. D₆, H₅.

Broido, D., 1958. Recent work on reading machines for data processing, *Automation Progress,* **4**:183–224. D₁₀; 31.

Brooks, F. P., Hopkins, A. L., Neumann, P. G., and Wright, W. V., 1957. An experiment in musical composition, *IRE Transactions on Electronic Computers,* September, **EC-2** (3), 175–182. P₆, I₁, I₂; 12, 34.

Bruner, J. S., Goodnow, J. J., and Austin, G. A., 1956. *A Study of Thinking,* New York: Wiley. G₄, G₆, D₁₁, I₄; 16, 34, 36.

—— et al., 1957. *Contemporary Approaches to Cognition,* Cambridge, Mass.: Harvard. 22, 35, 36.

Bryton, B., 1954. *Balancing of a Continuous Production Line,* unpublished master of science thesis, Northwestern University, Evanston, Ill. (Tonge, 1960.)

Buell, D. N., 1961. Chrysler optical processing scanner (COPS), *Proceedings of the 1961 Eastern Joint Computer Conference* (EJCC), **20**:352–370, published as *Computers, a Key to Total Systems Control.* D_8, D_{11}, D_{12}.

Burge, W. H., 1958. Sorting, trees, and measures of order, *Information and Control,* **1**:181–197. I_6.

Burks, A. W., and Wang, H., 1957. The logic of automata, *Journal of the Association for Computing Machinery,* April, July, (1,2) **4**:193–218, 279–292. A_1, A_4, A_5; 21, 31, 36.

————, 1959. Logic of fixed and growing automata, *Proceedings of an International Symposium on the Theory of Switching,* in *Annals of the Computation Laboratory,* vol. 29, pp. 147, Cambridge, Mass: Harvard. A_1, A_2, A_5, B_2, B_6, P_4; 21, 35, 36.

————, 1960. Computation, behavior, and structure, in [U], pp. 282–311. A_5, A_8, B_2, B_6, H_6, P_4; 36.

Bush, R. R., and Mosteller, F., 1955. *Stochastic Models for Learning,* New York: Wiley. E_3, E_9; 21, 35, 36.

———— and Estes, W. K. (eds.), 1959. *Studies in Mathematical Learning Theory,* Stanford, Calif.: Stanford. E_9, E_3, E_2; 16, 31, 35, 36.

Bush, V., 1945. As we may think, *Atlantic Monthly,* July, **176**: 101. M_1, P_3.

Butler, S., 1865. *Erewhon,* chaps. 23–25, *The Book of the Machines,* London.

————, 1933. *Erewhon and Erewhon Revisited,* Modern Library No. 136, New York: Random House.

Byard, S., 1950. Robots which play games, *Penguin Scientific News,* **20**:82. P_5.

Byrnes, B., Gold, B., and Kemball, C., 1958. *Some Results of the MAUDE Program,* Lincoln Laboratory Group Report 34-72, Massachusetts Institute of Technology; hand keyed Morse Code machine (Gold, 1959; Selfridge, 1960.) D_7.

Cadwallader-Cohen et al., 1961 (V. A. Vyssotsky). The Chaostron: an important advance in learning machines, *IRE Professional Group in Information Theory Newsletter* 19, April. N_6, B_4, C_9, E_7; 11, 12, 13, 32 (hoax).

Calderwood, J. H., and Porter, A., 1958. Pattern recognition in the synthesis of complex switching systems, *Journal of Electronics and Control,* May, **4**:466–480. A_3; 15.

Campaigne, H., 1959. Some experiments in machine learning, in [P], pp. 173–175. G_9, C_7, E_3; 12, 34.

Campbell, D. T., 1956. Adaptive behavior from random response, *Behavioral Science,* **1**:105–110. C_9, E_7.

————, 1958. Systematic error on the part of human links in communication systems, *Information and Control,* September, **1**(4):334–369. G_4, M_3, D_6, H_5; 22, 31, 32, 36.

————, 1960. Blind variation and selective survival as a general strategy in knowledge-processes, in [U], pp. 205–231. C_9, J_2, G_6; 32, 36.

Canaday, R. H., 1962. *The Description of Overlapping Figures,* unpublished master-of-science thesis in Electrical Engineering, Massachusetts Institute of Technology. D_5, D_{14}; 14 (LISP), 12, 34.

Carr, J. W., III, 1958. Languages, logic, learning, and computers, *Computers and Automation*, April, **7**(4):21–26. A_8, H_2, H_3, H_4, E; 35.

———— et al., 1959. A visit to computation centers in the Soviet Union, *Communications of the Association for Computing Machinery*.

Ceccato, S., 1956. La machine qui pense et qui parle, in [F], pp. 288–299. H_1.

Cherry, C. C., 1952. The communication of information, *American Scientist*, **40**:640–664. H_7, H_5.

————, 1957. *On Human Communication*, New York: Wiley. H_5, H_7; 21, 22, 31, 35, 36.

Chomsky, A. N., 1953. Systems of syntactic analysis, *Journal of Symbolic Logic*, **18**(3):242–265. H_1, H_2.

————, 1955. Logical syntax and semantics: their linguistic relevance, *Language*, **31**:36–45. H_1, H_2.

————, 1956. Three Models for the Description of Language, Proceedings of a Symposium on Information Theory, *IRE Transactions on Information Theory*, September, **IT-2**(3):113–124. H_2, H_1.

————, 1957a. *Syntactic Structures*, The Hague, The Netherlands: Uitgverij Mouton, H_2, H_1; 36.

———— and Miller, G. A., 1957b. *Pattern Conception*, AFCRC, Technical Note Report AFCRCRTN-57-57, Astia Document 110076, Bedford, Mass. E, I_4, H_2, H_6, H_1; 34.

———— and Miller, G. A., 1958. Finite state languages, *Information and Control*, **1**(3):91–112. H_2, H_1.

————, 1959a. Review of B. F. Skinner's "Verbal Behavior," *Language*, **35**:26–58. I_2, H_1, E_2, E_3, E_6, G_4, G_5, H_5, J_2; 31, 32, 36 (Skinner, 1957).

————, 1959b. On certain formal properties of grammars, *Information and Control*, June, **2**:137. C_1, A_4, H_2; 21.

————, 1959c. A note on phrase structure grammars, *Information and Control*, December, **2**:393–395. H_2.

Chow, C. K., 1957. Optimum character recognition system using decision functions, *IRE WESCON Convention Record*, pt. 4, pp. 121–129; also in *IRE Transactions on Electronic Computers*, **EC-6**(4):247–254. D_{13}, D_{10}, D_9, B_2; 21, 36 (Flores, 1958).

————, 1959. Comments on optimum character recognition system, *IRE Transactions*, June, **PGEC-8**:230. (Chow, 1957).

Church, A., 1936. An unsolvable problem of elementary number theory, *American Journal of Mathematics*, **58**:345–363. A_7.

————, 1956. *Introduction to Mathematical Logic, I*, Princeton, N.J.: Princeton University Press. G_8.

Churchman, C. W., and Ackoff, R. L., 1950a. Purposive behavior and cybernetics, *Social Forces*, **29**:32–39. G_3, N_2.

———— and ————, 1950b. *Methods of Inquiry*, St. Louis: Educational Publishers.

Clark, W. A., and Farley, B. G., 1955. Generalization of pattern-recognition in a self-organizing system, in [E], p. 86. B₄, D₁, D₃, E₃, K₁; 12, 24, 36 (Farley, 1954).

Clarkson, G. P. E., and Simon, H. A., 1960. Simulation of individual and group behavior, *American Economic Review,* **50**:920–932. G₄.

———— and Meltzer, A. H., 1960. Portfolio selection: a heuristic approach, *Journal of Finance,* **15**(4). P₈; 34.

————, 1962. *Portfolio Selection: A Simulation of Trust Investment,* Englewood Cliffs, N.J.: Prentice-Hall. P₈.

Coburn, H. E., 1951. The brain analogy, *Psychological Review,* **58**:155–178. K₃.

————, 1952. The brain analogy: A discussion, *Psychological Review,* **59**:453. K₃.

Cohen, J., 1962. Information theory and music, *Behavioral Science,* April, **7**(2). H₇, I₁, F₆, C₉; 22, 31, 32, 36.

Cohen, K. J., 1960. *Computer Models of the Shoe, Leather, Hide Sequence,* Englewood Cliffs, N.J.: Prentice-Hall, P₈.

———— and Cyert, R. M., 1961. Computer models and dynamic economics, *Quarterly Journal of Economics,* **75**(1). N₇.

Colby, K. M., 1960. Experiments on the effects of an observer's presence on the Imago System during psychoanalytic free-association, *Behavioral Science,* **5**:216–232.

Copi, I. M., Elgot, C. C., and Wright, J. B., 1958. Realization of events by logical nets, *Journal of Association for Computing Machinery,* **5**:181–196. A₂, B₆, H₂; 21 (Kleene, 1956).

———— and Beard, R. W., 1959. *Programming an Idealized General-purpose Computer to Decide Questions of Truth and Falsehood,* Report 2144-402-T. Willow Run Laboratories, University of Michigan, Ypsilanti. G₇, G₈.

Couffignal, L., 1959. Les machines semantiques, in [F], pp. 129–138. N.

Coupling, J. J., 1950. (J. R. Pierce, 1950) How to build a thinking machine, *Astounding Science Fiction,* August. E₃, E₇, B₅, C, C₉, L₂, P₇.

Cowan, J., 1960*a*. Many-valued logics and reliable automata, in [W]. A₆, B₃, B₆, H₇.

————, 1960*b*. Towards a proper logic for parallel computation in the presence of noise, in [S]. A₆, B₃, B₆, H₇, B₂.

Craik, K. J. W., 1947. Theory of the human operator in control systems, *British Journal of Psychology,* **38**:56. P₃.

————, 1952. *The Nature of Explanation,* New York: Cambridge. F₁, H₄, H₆, L; 24, 36 (preface dated 1943).

Crichton, J. W., and Holland, J. H., 1959. *A New Method of Simulating the Central Nervous System Using an Automatic Digital Computer,* Report 2144-1195-M, Willow Run Laboratories, University of Michigan, Ypsilanti. B₅; 14.

Crozier, W. J., 1951. Physiology and computation devices, *Proceedings of the Second Symposium on Large-scale Digital Calculating Machines,* Cambridge, Mass.: Harvard. K₄.

Culbertson, J. T., 1948. A device for optic nerve conduction and form perception, *Bulletin of Mathematical Biophysics,* **10**:31, 97. D₁, K₃.

————, 1950. *Consciousness and Behavior,* Dubuque, Iowa: Wm. C. Brown. L, E. A, B₆.

————, 1952. *Hypothetical Robots and the Problem of Neuroeconomy,* Report P-296, RAND Corporation, Santa Monica, Calif. a A₁, A₆, B₆.

————, 1956. Some uneconomical robots, in [G], pp. 99–116. A₁, A₆, B₆.

————, 1957. Robots and automata: A short history, *Computers and Automation,* 6:32. 31, 32.

Cyert, R. M., Feigenbaum, E. A., and March, J. G., 1959. Models in a behavioral theory of the firm, *Behavioral Science,* April, 4:81–95. N₇, P₈.

Darlington, C. D., 1958. *The Evolution of Genetics,* New York: Basic Books. C₅, C₆, C₇, E₇, J.

David, E. E., 1955. Ears for computers, *Scientific American,* February, 192: 92. D₇; 13, 34, 36.

————, 1958a. Artificial auditory recognition in telephony, *IBM Journal of Research and Development,* October, 2:294. D₇.

————, Matthews, M. V., and McDonald, H. S., 1958b. Description and results of experiments with speech using digital computer simulation, *IRE WESCON Convention Record,* (7)2:3–10. D₇; 12, 34.

————, 1961. Digital simulation in research on human communication, *Proceedings of the IRE,* January, 49:319–328. D₇, D₈, P₆, H₃, D₁₁.

Davies, D. W., 1959. Mechanization of thought processes, *Nature,* January, 183:225–226. (Review of [N].)

Davis, K. H., Biddulph, R., and Balashek, S., 1953. Automatic recognition of spoken digits, in [K]. D₇; 13 ("Audrey"), 34.

Davis, M., 1958. *Computability and Unsolvability,* New York: McGraw-Hill. A₇, A₄, C₁, H₂; 21, 31, 32, 35, 36.

———— and Putnam, H., 1959. *A Computational Proof Procedure,* AFOSR TR 59-124, Rensselaer Polytechnical Institution, Troy, N.Y. C₂, C₃, A₇, G₇; 12, 21, 32, 33.

———— and ————, 1960. A computing procedure for qualification, *Journal of the Association for Computing Machinery,* July, 7(2). C₂, C₃, G₇; 12, 32, 33. (Less complete version of [1959].)

Davis, R. C., 1958. The domain of homeostasis, *Psychological Review,* 62:8–13. 31 [N₆], 36.

Deese, J., 1952. *The Psychology of Learning,* New York: McGraw-Hill. E₁, E₂; 22, 35, 36, 32, 31.

DeGroot, A. D., 1946. *Het Denken van den Schaker,* Amsterdam, The Netherlands. F₆, G₃, G₄ (chess), P₅, J₂.

Denes, P., and Mathews, M. V., 1960. Spoken digit recognition using time-frequency pattern matching, *Journal of the Acoustical Society of America,* November, 32(11):1450–1455. D₂, D₃, D₇, D₁₁, D₁₃, D₁₄.

Deutsch, J. A., 1953. A new type of behavior theory. *British Journal of Psychology,* 44:304.

————, 1954. A machine with insight, *Quarterly Journal of Experimental Psychology,* February 6:6–11. G₆.

————, 1955. A theory of shape recognition, *British Journal of Psychology,* February, (1) 46:30–37. D, D₁₁, D₁₂ (Stevens 1961b).

————, 1956. A theory of insight, reasoning, and latent learning, *British Journal of Psychology*, **47**:115. G₆, E.

Deutsch, K. W., 1951. Mechanism, teleology, and mind, *Philosophical and Phenomenological Research*, **12**:185–222. N₂, L.

Diebold, J., 1952. *Automation: The Advent of the Automatic Factory*, Princeton, N.J.: Van Nostrand. N₃.

Dimond, T. L., 1957. Devices for reading handwritten characters, *Proceedings of the Eastern Joint Computer Conference* (EJCC), pp. 232–237. D₁₀, D₄; 13.

Dinneen, G. P., 1955. Programming pattern recognition, in [E], pp. 94–100. D₁, D₄, D₈; 12, 34 (Selfridge 1955).

Doyle, W., 1960. Recognition of sloppy hand-printed characters, in [V], pp. 133–142. D₁₃, D₁₂, D₁₀, D₄, D₉; 12, 34 (Selfridge 1960).

Duncan, C. P., 1959. Recent research on human problem solving, *Psychological Bulletin*, November, **56**(6):397–429. G₄, J₂, M₃; 22, 31, 32, 36.

Duncker, K., 1945. On problem solving, *Psychological Monographs*, **58**(270). D₄, D₃; 16, 22, 34, 36.

Dunham, B., Fridshal, R., and Sward, G. L., 1959. A nonheuristic program for proving elementary logical theorems, in [R], pp. 282–285. C₁, G₇, G₈; 12, 21, 34.

Eccles, J. C., 1953. *The Neurophysiological Basis of the Mind: The Principles of Neurophysiology*, New York: Oxford. K, L₄; 23, 36.

Eden, M., and Halle, M., 1961. Characterization of cursive writing, in [X]. D₅, H₄; 34.

————, 1962. Handwriting and pattern recognition, in [AA], pp. 160–166. D₁₀.

Eldredge, K., 1957. Teaching machines how to read, *Stanford Research Institute Journal*, May, **1**. D₁₀, E.

Elias, P. et al., 1952. Fourier treatment of optical processes, *Journal of the Optical Society of America*, February, **42**:127. D₈; 21, 35, 36.

————, 1958. Computation in the presence of noise, *IBM Journal of Research and Development*, May, October, **2**:346. H₇, B₃; 21.

Elsasser, W. H., 1958. *Physical Foundations of Biology*, New York: Pergamon Press. N₂, N₆.

Ernst, H. A., 1962. *MH-1. A Computer-operated Mechanical Hand*, dissertation Ph.D., E. E. Massachusetts Institute of Technology, 1961; presented at the Western Joint Computer Conference (WJCC), May, 1962. H₃, M₃; 13, 12, 34.

Estavan, D., 1959. *Pattern Recognition, Machine Learning, and Automated Teaching*, Report SP-70, System Development Corporation, Santa Monica, Calif. D₁, E, P₃.

Estes, W. K., 1950. Toward a statistical theory of learning, *Psychological Review*, **57**:94–107. E₉, E₃; 21.

————, 1960. Statistical models for recognition and recall of stimulus patterns by human observers, in [U]. M₃, D₃, D₉; 16, 34, 36.

Eykhoff, P., 1960. *Optimizing Control and Process Parameter Estimation*, unpublished dissertation, University of California, Berkeley. N₁, E₄, E₇, C₈.

Farley, B. G., and Clark, W. A., 1954. Simulation of self-organizing system by a digital computer, *IRE Transactions on Information Theory,* September, **PGIT-4:**76–84. B₆, B₄, E₃, K₁; 21, 34 (Clark 1955).

————, Frishkopf, L. S., Clark, W. A., and Gilmore, J. T., 1957. *Computer Techniques for the Study of Patterns in the Electroencephalogram,* Technical Report 165, Lincoln Laboratory, Massachusetts Institute of Technology, Lexington, Mass. D₁; 12, 34, 36.

————, 1960a. Self-organizing models for learned perception, in [U]. D₁, D₃, D₆, D₉, E₉; 36.

———— and Clark, W. A., 1960b. Activity in networks of neuronlike elements, in [X]. B₆; 12, 34.

Fatechand, R., 1960. Machine recognition of spoken words, *Advances in Computers,* **1:**193–229 (F. Alt, ed.), New York: Academic. D₇.

Feigenbaum, E., 1959. *An Information Processing Theory of Verbal Learning,* P-1817, October, Santa Monica, Calif. RAND Corporation, M₁, E₅.

————, 1961a. The simulation of verbal learning behavior. *Proceedings of the Western Joint Computer Conference* (WJCC), **19:**121–132. M₁, E₅.

———— and Simon, H. A., 1961b. Forgetting in an associative memory, *Proceedings of the Association Computing Machinery National Conference* (ACM), **16:**2C2–2C5. D₄, E, E₂, E₁₀, M₁, M₃, E₅.

————, 1961c. Soviet cybernetics and computer sciences, 1960, *Communications of the Association for Computing Machinery* (ACM), December, **4:** 566–579. (*Note:* This is an outstanding summary of the status of artificial intelligence in the USSR as seen by a visitor. It contains a detailed report of the work of Arin, E. I. See also Carr, 1959.) E, G, H, J, N; 31.

———— and Simon, H. A., 1962. A theory of the serial position effect, *British Journal of Psychology,* August, **53:**307–320. (CIP Working Paper 14, Graduate School of Industrial Administration, Carnegie Institute of Technology, Pittsburgh.) M₃.

Feigl, H., 1959. Philosophical embarrassments of psychology, *American Psychologist,* March, **14:**115–128. L₄.

Feldman, J., 1959. *An Analysis of Predictive Behavior in a Two-choice Situation,* unpublished doctoral dissertation, Carnegie Institute of Technology, Pittsburgh, Pa. E₆, G₄.

————, 1961a. Simulation of behavior in the binary choice experiment, in [Z], pp. 133–144. E₆, G₄.

————, Tonge, F., and Kanter, H., 1961b. *Empirical Explorations of a Hypothesis-testing Model of Binary Choice Behavior,* SP-546, System Development Corporation. E₆, G₄.

————, 1962. Computer simulation of cognitive processes, in *Computer Applications in the Behavioral Sciences* (H. Borko, ed.), Englewood Cliffs, N.J.: Prentice-Hall. G.

Flores, I., 1958. An optimum character-recognition system using decision functions, *IRE Transactions on Electronic Computers,* June, **EC-7:**180. (Chow, 1957). D₁₀.

Foerster, See Von Foerster.

Forgie, J. W., and Forgie, C. D., 1959. Results obtained from an auditory-recognition computer program, *Journal of the Acoustical Society of America*, November, 31:1480–1484. D₇; 12, 34.

Foulkes, J. D., 1959. A class of machines which determine the statistical structure of a sequence of characters, *WESCON Convention Record*, (4)3:66–73. I₁, E₉.

Frankel, S., 1959. Information-theoretic aspects of character reading, in [R], pp. 248–251. D₃, D₁₀, D₉, H₇.

Fredkin, E., 1960. Trie memory, in [T]. H₄, M.

Freiberger, H., and Murphy, E., 1961. Reading machines for the blind, *IRE Transactions on Human Factors in Electronics*, March, 2(1):8–20. D₁₀, D₆, D₁₁; 31, 32.

Freimer, M., 1959. A dynamic programming approach to adaptive control processes, *IRE Transactions on Automatic Control*, November, AC-4:10–15. N₁.

———, 1960. *Topics in Dynamic Programming, II*, Lincoln Laboratory Report 52-G-0020, Massachusetts Institute of Technology, Lexington, Mass.; Massachusetts Institute of Technology Hayden Library No. H-82. See especially Secs. I–E. G₂; 21.

Friedberg, R. M., 1958. A learning machine, part I, *IBM Journal of Research and Development*, January, 2:2–13. E₃, E₄, C₃, C₇, C₈, G₉, G₅, J; 12, 34 (Arnold, 1959; Campaigne, 1959; Kilburn, 1959).

———, Dunham, B., and North, J. H., 1959. A learning machine, part II, *IBM Journal of Research and Development*, June, 3:282–287. E₃, E₄, C₃, C₅, C₇, C₈, G₉, G₅, J₁; 21, 34, 36.

Frishkopf, L. S., and Harmon, L. D., 1961. Machine reading of cursive script, in [X], pp. 300–316. D₄, D₅, D₁₀; 12, 13, 34, 33, 36.

Fry, D. B., and Denes, P., 1953. Experiments in mechanical speech recognition, in [K], pp. 206–212; in [I]. D₇; 34.

——— and ———, 1959. An analogue of the speech recognition process, in [N], 1:377–395. D₇, D₂, D₃, I₁; 33.

Furst, B., 1949. *Stop Forgetting!* New York: Garden City. M₁, M₃, E₅; 22, 35.

Gabor, D., 1954. Communication theory and cybernetics, *IRE Transactions on Circuit Theory*, December, CT-1:19–31. N.

———, Wilby, W. P., and Woodcock, R., 1961. A self-optimizing nonlinear filter, predictor and simulator, in [X]. C₆, C₈; 13.

Gagne, R. M., and Smith, E. C., Jr. A study of the effects of verbalization on problem solving, *Journal of Experimental Psychology*, 63:218–227.

Galanter, E., and Gerstenhaber, M., 1956. On thought: The extrinsic theory, *Psychological Review*, 63:218–227. F, G, P₁, P₂; 22, 36.

——— (ed.), 1959. *Automatic Teaching*, New York: Wiley. P₃, G₅.

——— and Miller, G. A., 1960. Some comments on stochastic models and psychological theories, *Mathematical Methods in the Social Sciences, 1959* (Arrow, Karlin, and Suppes, eds.), Stanford: Stanford University Press. E₄, G₄.

Galton, F., 1883. *Inquiries into Human Faculty and Development*, N.Y.: Macmillan. F, G; 16, 22, 34, 36.

Gamba, A., 1961. Optimum performance of learning machines, in [Y], p. 349 (letter). D₁₃, E₉.

Gardner, M., 1952. Logic machines, *Scientific American,* **186**(3):68. G$_8$; 13, 31, 35.

————, 1958. *Logic Machines and Diagrams,* New York: McGraw-Hill. G$_8$; 13, 31, 35.

Gelernter, H., and Rochester, N., 1958. Intelligent behavior in problem-solving machines, *IBM Journal of Research and Development,* **2**(4):336–345. G$_7$ (Geometry), G$_{10}$, F$_3$, H$_4$, J$_1$; 14, 33, 36 (Minsky, 1956).

————, 1959a. A note on syntactic symmetry and the manipulation of formal systems by machine, *Information and Control,* April, **2**:80–89. G$_1$, G$_3$, H$_4$, G$_7$ (Geometry); 21, 36.

————, 1959b. Realization of a geometry theorem-proving machine, in [R], pp. 273–282. G$_7$ (Geometry), G$_{10}$, F$_3$, J$_1$; 14, 15, 34, 36 (Minsky, 1956).

————, Hansen, J. R., and Loveland, D. W., 1960a. Empirical exploration of the geometry theorem machine, in [V], pp. 143–147. G$_7$ (Geometry), G$_{10}$, F$_3$, J$_1$; 14, 34, 36.

————, ————, and Gerberich, C. L., 1960b. A FORTRAN-compiled list-processing language, *Journal of the Association for Computing Machinery* (ACM), April, **7**:87–101. H$_3$ (FLPL), H$_4$; 14, 15, 34 (Newell, 1957b; McCarthy, 1960; Green, 1961b).

George, F. H., 1956. Logical networks and behavior, *Bulletin of Mathematical Biophysics,* **18**:337. A$_2$, B$_6$, F$_2$.

————, 1957. Logical networks and probability, *Bulletin of Mathematical Biophysics,* **19**:187. E$_3$, E$_5$, N$_6$, P$_1$.

————, 1959a. *Automation, Cybernetics, and Society,* New York: Philosophical Library. N$_1$, N$_3$; 35.

————, 1959b. Inductive machines and the problem of learning, *Cybernetica,* **2**:109–126. I, E.

Gerard, R. W., 1946. The biological basis of imagination, *Scientific Monthly,* June, **62**:477. L$_4$.

Ghiselin, K. (ed.), 1952. *The Creative Process,* Berkeley, Calif.: University of California Press. G$_4$, G$_6$, 22.

Gibson, E. J., 1940. A systematic application of the concepts of generalization and differentiation to verbal learning, *Psychological Review,* **47**:196–229. E$_2$.

Gibson, J. J., 1929. The reproduction of visually perceived forms, *Journal of Experimental Psychology,* **12**:1–39. D$_6$, H$_2$, M$_3$; 16, 22, 34.

————, 1950. *The Perception of the Visual World,* Boston: Houghton Mifflin. D$_6$; 35.

Gill, A., 1959. Minimum-scan pattern recognition, *IRE Transactions on Information Theory,* June, **IT-5**(1):52–58. D$_{11}$; 21.

————, 1960. Analysis of nets by numerical methods, *Journal of the Association for Computing Machinery* (ACM), July, **7**(2):251–254. A$_2$; 21.

Gilmore, P. C., 1959. A program for the production of proofs for theorems derivable within the first order predicate calculus from axioms, in [R], pp. 265–273. G$_7$, G$_8$, C$_2$, J$_1$; 33a, 34.

————, 1960. A proof method for quantification theory: its justification and realization, *IBM Journal of Research and Development*, January, 4(1): 28–35. G_7, G_8, C_2, J_1; 21, 34, 38 (176).

Glantz, H. T., 1960. On the recognition of information with a digital computer, *Journal of the Association for Computing Machinery* (ACM), April, 4 (2):178–188. D_3, D_{11}.

Glauberman, M. H., 1959. Character recognition for business machines, *Electronics*, February, 29:132–136. D_{10}.

Gödel, K., 1931. Uber formal unentscheidbare Sätze der Principia Mathematica und verwandter Systeme, I, *Monatshefte für Mathematica und Physics*, pp. 173–189. A_7.

Gold, B., 1959. Machine recognition of hand-sent Morse code, *IRE Transactions on Information Theory*, March, IT-5:17–24. D_1, P_2, H_1; 12, 13, 34 (Brynes, 1958; Selfridge, 1960).

Goldstein, M. H., 1960. A statistical model for interpreting neuroelectric responses, *Information and Control*, 3:1–17. K_3.

Golomb, S., 1960. A mathematical theory of discrete classification, in [X] D_{11}; 21, 35.

Good, I. J., 1958. How much science can you have at your finger-tips? *IBM Journal of Research and Development*, October, 2(4):282–288. M_3, J_2, B_6, E_3, I_4.

———, 1959. Could a machine make probability judgments? *Computers and Automation*, 8(1):14–16,(2):24–26. L_2, A_6, P_5, B_4, K_4.

———, 1961a. Weight of evidence and false target probabilities, in [X]. I_1, I_5, I_6.

———, 1961b. A causal calculus, *British Journal of Philosophy of Science*, 11, 12:305–318, 43–51. L.

———, 1962. The mind-body problem, or could an android feel pain? *Theories of the Mind*, Urbana: Glencoe Free Press. L_4, K_2, K_4, K_1.

Goodman, N., 1951. *The Structure of Appearance*, Cambridge, Mass.: Harvard. I_6; 24.

———, 1954. *Fact, Fiction and Forecast*, Cambridge, Mass.: Harvard.

———, 1958. The test of simplicity, *Science*, 128:1064–1069. I_6.

Goodwin, G. L., 1958. Digital computers tap out designs for large motors . . . fast, *Power*, April. 12, 15.

———, 1959. Machine recognition of hand sent Morse code, *IRE Transactions on Information Theory*.

Gorn, S., 1957. Standardized programming methods and universal coding, *Journal of the Association for Computing Machinery* (ACM), July, 4: 254. H_3.

———, 1959. On the mechanical simulation of learning and habit-forming, *Information and Control*, 2(3):226–259. E_3, E_9, 21, 36.

Grant, D. A., 1962. Testing the Null Hypothesis and the strategy and tactics of investigating theoretical models, *Psychological Review*, 69:54.

Greanias, E. C., Hoppel, C. J., Cloomok, M., and Osborn, J. S., 1957a. Design of logic for recognition of printed characters by simulation, *IBM Journal of Research and Development*, 1(1):8–18. D_{10}; 12, 34.

——— and Hill, J. Y. M., 1957b. Considerations in the design of characte** recognition devices, *1957 IRE National Convention Record,* pt. 4, pp. 119–126. D₁₀.

Green, B. F., 1957. The use of high-speed digital computers in studies on form recognition, in Wolfeck, 1957. D₁; 31, 32.

———, 1959. Non-computational uses of digital computers, *Behavioral Science,* 4:164–167. D₆, E₂, H₁; 31.

———, 1961*a*. Baseball: an automatic question-answerer, in [Z]. M₁, H₁, M₂, H₂, H₄, H₃; 12, 14 (IPL), 34.

———, 1961*b*. Computer languages for symbol manipulation, in [AF], pp. 3–8; reprinted in *IRE Transactions on Elec. Computer,* Oct. 10 (no. 4) 729–735. H₄, H₃ (Newell, 1957*b*, 1960*c*; Gelernter, 1960*b*; McCarthy, 1960).

Greene, P. H., 1959*a*. Networks for pattern perception, *Proceedings of the National Electronics Conference,* **15.** D₁, B₆.

———, 1959*b*. Problem-solving and learning machines, *Behavioral Science,* 4:249–250. E, G.

———, 1959*c*. An approach to computers that perceive, learn, and reason, in [P], pp. 181–186. F₆, J₂; 22, 24, 32, 36.

———, 1960. A suggested model for information representation in a computer that perceives, learns and reasons, in [V], pp. 151–164. D₅, D₁₁, D₉, D₃, F.

Grimsdale, R. L., Sumner, F. H., Tunis, C. J., and Kilburn, T., 1959*a*. A system for the automatic recognition of patterns, *Proceedings of the Institute of Electrical Engineers,* March, (B)**106**(26):215. D₅, D₁₀; 12, 34.

———, 1959*b*. Automatic pattern recognition, *Wireless World,* November, **65:**499–501. 38(199).

Gullahorn, J., and Gullahorn, J., 1962. *Homunculus: A Simulation of Social Interaction,* Michigan State University, East Lansing, Mich. N₇.

Gutenmacher, L. I., 1959. The information machine problem, *Izvestiia,* Apr. 1.

Gyr, J. W., 1960. An investigation into, and speculations about, the formal nature of a problem-solving process, *Behavioral Science,* January, 5(1): 39–59. E, F, G, I, J.

Hadamard, J., 1945. *The Psychology of Invention in the Mathematical Field,* Princeton, N.J.: Princeton University Press. G₄, J₂.

Hagelbarger, D. W., 1955. SEER, a sequence extrapolation robot, *IRE Transactions on Electronic Computers,* March, **EC-5**(1):1–7. P₅, I₁; 13 (Kirsch, 1954; Shannon, 1955).

Hake, H. W., and Hyman, R., 1953. Perception of the statistical structure of a random series of binary symbols, *Journal of Experimental Psychology,* **45:**64. I₁, D₆.

Haldane, J. B. S., 1952. The mechanical chess player, *British Journal of Philosophy of Science,* 3:189. P₅.

Halle, M., and Stevens, K., 1962. Speech recognition: A model and a program for research, in [AA], pp. 155–159.

Haller, N., 1959. *Line Tracing for Character Recognition,* MSEE thesis, Massachusetts Institute of Technology, Cambridge, Mass. D₅, D₁₀.

Harmon, L. D., 1959. Artificial neuron, *Science,* Apr. 10, **129:**962–963. B₆, B₅, K₃, D₇; 13, 34, 23.

————, 1960a. A line-drawing recognizer, in [V], pp. 351–364. D₁₁, D₁₂; 13.

————, 1960b. Line-drawing pattern recognizer, *Electronics,* Sept. 2, pp. 39–43.

————, 1961a. Neural analogs, *Proceedings of the IRE,* **49**(8):1316–1317.

————, Levinson, J., and van Bergeijk, W. A., 1962a. Analog models of neural mechanisms, in [AA], pp. 107–112. B₅, B₆, D₆, D₇, K₃, Bib.

————, 1962b. Studies with artificial neurons, I: Properties and functions of an artificial neuron, *Kybernetik,* in press. B₆.

Harris, Z. S., 1951. *Methods in Structural Linguistics,* Chicago: University of Chicago Press, H₁, H₂, D₅.

————, 1960. Project summary, in *Current Research and Development in Scientific Documentation,* No. 6, National Science Foundation, May, pp. 52–53. H₁.

Hartline, H. K., 1938. The response of single optic nerve fibers of the vertebrate eye to illumination of the retina, *American Journal of Physiology,* **121**:400–415. K₃.

Hartmanis, J., 1961. Task simplification and learning devices, in [X]. F₄.

Hartree, D. R., 1949. *Calculating Instruments and Machines,* Urbana, Ill.: University of Illinois Press.

Hawkins, J. K., 1961. Self-organizing systems—a review and commentary, in [Y], pp. 31–48. B₆, B₄, D₁₃, D₉; 31, 32, 35.

Hayek, F. A., 1952. *The Sensory Order,* Chicago: University of Chicago Press. L₄, L₁, I₅, D₆, E₅; 24, 22, 36.

Heasly, C. C., Jr., 1959. Some communications aspects of character-sensing systems, in [P], pp. 176–180. D₁₀, D₁₁, H₇.

Hebb, D. O., 1949. *The Organization of Behavior,* New York: Wiley. B₄, B₅, D₆, E₅, D₅, G₆, K₁, K₂, K₃; 11, 22, 23, 36, 31 (Milner, 1957; Rochester, 1956; Allport, 1955).

————, 1958. *Textbook of Psychology,* Philadelphia: Saunders. D₁, D₅, E₁, E₂, E₅, G₄, K₁, K₂, M₃.

————, 1961. Distinctive features of learning in the higher animal, in [AC₂]. E₁, E₂.

Heidbreder, E., 1924. An experimental study of thinking, *Archives of Psychology,* **11**(73):5–175. G₄.

Helgeson, W. B., and Kwo, T. T., 1956. Letter to the Editor, *Management Science,* **3.**

Heymann, H., Jr., 1959. The USSR in the technological race, RAND Corporation Paper P-1754, Santa Monica, Calif.

Highleyman, W. K., and Kamentsky, L. A., 1959a. Pattern recognition (perception) machine, *Behavioral Science,* **4**:248. D₁₀; 13, 34.

———— and ————, 1959b. A generalized scanner for pattern and character recognition studies, in [P], pp. 291–294. D₁₀; 13, 15, 34.

———— and ————, 1960. Comments on a character recognition method of Bledsoe and Browning, *IRE Transactions on Electronic Computers,* June, **BC-9**:163. D₁₀, D₃; 12, 34.

————, 1961a. Further comments on the N-tuple pattern recognition method,

IRE Transactions on Electronic Computers, March, **EC-10**(1):97. D₃, D₁₆ (Bledsoe, 1959; Highleyman, 1960).

————, 1961*b. Linear Decision Functions with Application to Pattern Recognition,* unpublished doctoral dissertation, Brooklyn Polytechnic Institute. D₉, P₂; 12, 15, 21, 34; C₁ C₈.

————, 1962. The design and analysis of pattern recognition experiments, *Bell System Technical Journal,* March, **41**(2):723–744. D₃, D₁₀. (Discusses Bledsoe, 1959; Bomba, 1959; Doyle, 1960; Frischkopf, 1960; Marill, 1960; Sebestyen, 1961, and others.)

Hilgard, E. R., 1956. *Theories of Learning,* New York: Appleton-Century-Crofts. E₁ E₂; 31, 32, 35.

Hiller, L. A., Jr., and Isaacson, L. M., 1959*a. Experimental Music,* New York: McGraw-Hill. P₆, I₁, H₁; 12, 34, 36.

————, 1959*b. Computer music, *Scientific American,* December, **201**:109–120. P₆.

Hohn, F. E., Seshu, S., and Aufenkamp, D. D., 1957. The theory of nets, *IRE Transactions on Electronic Computers,* September, **EC-3**(3):154–161. A₁; 21, 32.

Holland, J. H., 1958. Cycles and automaton behavior, notes from course, *Advanced Theory of the Logical Design of Digital Computers,* Summer Session, University of Michigan, Ann Arbor. A₂, B₆.

————, 1959. *Survey of Automata Theory,* Report 2900-52-R, 1959, Willow Run Laboratories, University of Michigan, Ypsilanti. A₇, A₁, B₆, A₅, J₁; 21, 32, 35, 36.

————, 1960. Iterative circuit computers, in [V], pp. 259–266. B₂, A₅, H₃; 21, 36.

————, 1962. Outline for a logical theory of adaptive systems. *Journal of the Association for Computing Machinery* (ACM), July, (3):297–314. P₄, A₅, B₂, C, C₅, C₆, E.

Homans, G. C., 1961. *Social Behavior: Its Elementary Forms,* New York: Harcourt, Brace & World. N₁.

Householder, A. S., 1943. A theory of the induced size effect, *Bulletin of Mathematical Biophysics,* **5**:155. D₆, K.

———— and Landahl, H. D., 1945. *Mathematical Biophysics of the Central Nervous System,* Bloomington, Ind.: Principia Press. B₆, D, E₈, A₆; 21, 31, 32, 36 (Rashevsky, 1940).

Hovland, C. I., 1952. A "communication analysis" of concept learning, *Psychological Review,* November, **59**:461–472. G₆, G₄, H₅; 22.

———— and Hunt, E. B., 1960. The computer simulation of concept attainment, *Behavioral Science,* **5**:265–267. F₄.

———— and ————, 1961. Programming a model of human concept formation, in [Z], pp. 145–155. F₄.

Howland, B., Minsky, M. L., and Selfridge, O. G., 1959. *Hill-climbing: Some Remarks on Multiple Simultaneous Optimization,* Group Report 54-15, Lincoln Laboratory, Massachusetts Institute of Technology, Lexington, Mass. C₈, C₇, C₃; 12, 13, 21, 34, 36.

Hu, M. K., 1962. Visual pattern recognition by moment invariants, in [AA], pp. 179–187. D_{12}.

Hubel, D. H., and Wiesel, T. N., 1959. Receptive fields of single neurons in the cat's striate cortex, *Journal of Physiology*, **148**:574–591. K_3, D_{11}, D_{12}, D_{14}; 23, 34, 36 (Lettvin, 1959).

—— and ——, 1962. Receptive fields, binocular interaction and functional architecture in the cat's visual cortex, *Journal of Physiology*, **160**:106–154. K_3, D_{11}, D_{12}, D_{14}; 23, 34, 36.

Hugh-Jones, E. M., 1956. Automation today, in *Automation in Theory and Practice*, Oxford. N_3.

Hughes, G. W., and Halle, M., 1959. On the recognition of speech by machine, in [R], pp. 252–256. D_5, D_7, D_{11}, D_3; 12, 34, 36.

Hull, C. L., 1935. The influence of caffeine and other factors on certain phenomena of rote learning, *Journal of General Psychology*, **13**:249–273. E_1.

——, Hovland, C. I., Ross, R. T., Hall, M., Perkins, D. T., and Fitch, F. B., 1940. *Mathematico-Deductive Theory of Rote Learning*, New Haven, Conn.: Yale University Press.

——, 1943. *Principles of Behavior*, New York: Appleton-Century-Crofts. E.

——, 1952. *A Behavioral System*, New Haven, Conn.: Yale University Press. E.

Humphrey, G., 1951. *Thinking*, New York: Wiley, J_2, G_4; 22, 36.

Hunt, E. B., 1960a. *An Experimental Analysis and Computer Simulation of the Role of Memory in Concept Learning*, unpublished Ph.D. dissertation, Yale University. I_4.

—— and Hovland, C. I., 1960b. Orders of consideration of different types of concepts, *Journal of Experimental Psychology*, **59**:220–225. I_4.

——, 1962. *Concept Formation: An Information Processing Problem*, New York: Wiley.

Jackson, J. R., 1956. A computing procedure for a line balancing problem, *Management Science*, April, **2**(3):261–271. P_8.

Jackson, R. F., 1960. "A Bridge-playing Program," presented at the National Conference of the Association for Computing Machinery, Paper 89; abstract appeared in *Communications of the ACM*, July, 398; full paper never published. P_5 (Bridge).

Jackson, W. (ed.), 1950. *Proceedings of a Symposium on Information Theory*, London: Ministry of Supply. (This seems to be known as the *1st London Symposium on Information Theory*. Our references [K], [I], and [X] are apparently continuations of a sequence, although the title of [K] is somewhat inconsistent with this.) H_7.

Jacobson, H., 1958. On models of reproduction, *American Scientist*, September, **46**(3):255–284. P_4.

——, 1959. The informational content of mechanisms and circuits, *Information and Control*, September, **2**(B):285–296. H_7.

Jakowatz, C. V., Shuey, R. L., and White, G. M., 1960. Adaptive waveform recognition, in [X]. N_1, E_4, D_3 I_1; 12, 13, 34.

Jefferson, G., 1949. The mind of mechanical man, Lister Oration for 1949, *British Medical Journal*, **1**:1105–1121.

John, E. R., and Miller, J. G., 1957. The acquisition and application of information in the problem-solving process, *Behavioral Science*, October, **2**(4):291–300. G_4; 22 [Gyr, 1960].

Johnson, D. M., 1955. *The Psychology of Thought and Judgement*, New York: Harper & Row. G_4, J_2; 22.

Joseph, R. D., 1960. *Contributions to Perception Theory*, Cornell Aeronautical Laboratory Report VG-1196-G-7, June 15. P_{13}, E_9.

Julesz, B., 1960a. Binocular depth perception and pattern recognition, in [X], pp. 212–224. D_6; 12, 16, 34.

———, 1960b. Binocular depth perception of computer-generated patterns, *Bell System Technical Journal*, September, **39**:1125–1161. D_6.

———, 1962a. Visual pattern discrimination, in [AA], pp. 84–91. D_6, D_{11}; 12, 16, 21, 22, 34 (Toward the Automation of Binary Depth Perception).

——— and Miller, J. E., 1962b. Automatic stereoscopic presentation of functions of two variables, *Bell System Technical Journal*, March, **40**(2):663–676.

Kac, M., 1962. A note on learning signal detection, in [AA], pp. 126–128. E_4, E_7.

Kahrimanian, H. G., 1953. *Analytic Differentiation by a Digital Computer*, unpublished M.A. thesis, Temple University, Philadelphia, Pa. H_4; 12, 34.

Kailath, T., 1961. Optimum receivers for randomly varying channels, in [X]. C_8, E_4; 21.

Kalin, T. A., 1960. *Some Metric Considerations in Pattern Recognition*, Research Laboratory of Electronics, Massachusetts Institute of Technology, Cambridge, Mass. D_1, D_{12}, D_8, K_3; 21, 36.

Kamentsky, L. A., 1959. Pattern and character recognition systems—picture processing by nets of neuron-like elements, in [P], pp. 304–309. B_6, D_{19}; 12, 34.

Kassler, M., 1961. The decision of Arnold Schoenberg's twelve-note system and related systems, Library of Congress Catalog Card No. 61-18855. P_6; 21, 11, 32.

Katona, G., 1940. *Organizing and Memorizing*, New York: Columbia. G_4, G_5, M_3; 16, 34, 36.

Kattsoff, L. O., 1954. Brains, thinking, and machines, *Methodos*, **6**(24):279. L.

Kazmierczak, H., 1959. The potential field as an aid to character recognition, in [R], pp. 244–247. D_{11}, D_{19}; 13, 34.

Kehl, W. B., Horty, J. F., Bacon, C. R. T., and Mitchell, D. S., 1961. An information retrieval language for legal studies, *Communications of the Association for Computing Machinery*, **4**(9):380–389. M_1.

Keller, H. B., 1961. Finite automata, pattern recognition and perceptrons. *Journal of the Association for Computing Machinery*, January, **8**(1):1–20. A_1, B_4, B_5, D_{13}, E_3 (Rosenblatt, 1958a).

Kelly, J. L., and Selfridge, O. G., 1962. Sophistication in computers: A disagreement, in [AA], pp. 78–**80**.

Kemeny, J. G., 1953. The use of simplicity in induction, *Philosophical Review*, **62**:391–408. I₆.

———, 1955a. Man viewed as a machine, *Scientific American*, April, **192**:58–67. 36; L, N, P₄.

———, 1955b. Fair bets and inductive probabilities, *Journal of Symbolic Logic*, **20**:263–273. I₁.

———, 1955c. Two measures of complexity, *Journal of Philosophy*, November, **52**:722–733. I₆.

Kilburn, T., Grimsdale, R. L., and Summer, F. H., 1959. Experiments in machine learning and thinking, in [R]. G₉, C₉, C₈, E₃, E₄; 12, 34 (Friedberg, 1958).

Kirsch, R. A., 1954. Experiments with a Computer Learning Routine, *Bureau of Standards Computer Seminar Notes: July;* see NBS publication *Computer Development (SEAC and DYSEAC) at the National Bureau of Standards,* 1955. E₃, P₅ (Penny Matching); 12, 34 (Hagelbarger, 1955).

———, Cahn, L., Ray, L. C., and Urban, G. H., 1957. Experiments with processing pictorial information with a digital computer, *Proceedings of the Eastern Joint Computer Conference* (EJCC), pp. 221–229. D₁, D₈, D₁₁; 12, 13, 34, 36.

Kister, J., Stein, P., Ulam, S., Walden, W., and Wells, M., 1957. Experiments in chess, *Journal of the Association for Computing Machinery* (ACM), April, **4**(2):174–177. P₅, G₂ (Chess), J₁; 12, 34 (X, Stein, 1957).

Klaus, G., 1961. Relationship of causality and teleology from the cybernetics viewpoint, *German (East) Journal of Philosophy*, **8**(10) 1960; Joint Publications Research Service Report 8374, 1961, U.S. Department of Commerce, Washington, D.C. N₂.

Kleene, S. C., 1935. General recursive functions of natural numbers, *American Journal of Mathematics*, **57**:153–157, 219–244. A₇.

———, 1952. *Introduction to Metamathematics*, Princeton, N.J.: Van Nostrand. A₄, A₇, H₂, G₇; 21, 32, 35.

———, 1956. Representation of events in nerve nets and finite automata, in [G], pp. 3–41. A₂, A₁, B₆, H₂; 21, 36 (McCulloch, 1943; Copi, 1958).

Klein, S., and Simmons, R. F., 1963. A computational approach to grammatical coding of English words, *Journal of the ACM*, **10**:334–347.

Kochen, M., Levy, M. J., Jr., 1956. The logical nature of an action scheme. *Behavioral Science*, October, **1**(4):265–289. G₄, F, E, F₄, N₄; 22.

———, 1957. Group behavior of robots, *Computers and Automation*, **6**(3):16–21, 48.

———, 1958a. The acquisition and utilization of information in problem solving and thinking. *Information and Control*, **1**(3):267–288. E₂, I₄, J₂, P₂, M₃, G₅; 11, 22, 34, 16, 36, 21.

———, 1958b. Organized systems with discrete information transfer, *General Systems Yearbook*, **2**:30–47.

———, 1959. Extension of Moore-Shannon model for relay circuits, *IBM Journal of Research and Development*, **3**(2):169–186. B₃.

———, 1961a. Experimental study of 'hypothesis formation' by computer, in [X]. I₄, J₂, J₁, C₄, C₆, D₄, D₁₁; 21, 32.

————, 1961b. An experimental program for the selection of "disjunctive hypotheses," in [Z], pp. 571–578.

Koffka, K., 1935. *Principles of Gestalt Psychology,* New York: Harcourt, Brace & World. D_1, D_6, E_6, F_2, G_4, H_5; 22, 35.

Kohler, W., 1929. *Gestalt Psychology,* New York: Liveright. D_1, D_6, E_6, F_2, G_4, H_5; 22, 35, 36.

————, 1951. Relational determination in perception, in [C], pp. 200–243. D_6, K_3.

Kolman, E., 1960. *Cybernetics,* Joint Publications Research Service Report 5002, U.S. Department of Commerce, Washington, D.C. N.

Koppel, H., 1952. Digital computer plays NIM, *Electronics,* November, **25:** 155. P_5 (NIM); 12.

Krieger, F. J., 1959. *Future Science and Technology of the USSR,* RAND Corporation Paper P-1647, Santa Monica, Calif.

Kubie, L. S., 1930. Theoretical application to some neurological problems of properties of excitation waves which move in closed circuits, *Brain,* July, **53:**166. K_3, M_3, N_4; 22, 21, 36.

————, 1941. Repetitive core of neurosis, *Psychoanalysis Quarterly,* January, **10:**77. K_3, M_3, N_4; 22, 21, 36.

Kudielka, V., and Lucas, P., 1961. Lerneprogramme am "Mailufterl," in [AE], pp. 125–143. B_6, I_1, P (Willis, 1959; Steinbuch, 1961; Uttley, 1959a, 1959b).

Ladefoged, P., 1959. The perception of speech, in [N], pp. 397–415. D_5, D_7, D_{14}; 11, 22, 36, 32.

Laing, R., 1962. Book review, *Computers and Common Sense* by M. Taube, in *Behavioral Science,* April, **7**(2):238–240. L_2.

Landahl, H. D., McCulloch, W. S., and Pitts, W., 1943. A statistical consequence of the logical calculus of nervous nets, *Bulletin of Mathematical Biophysics,* **5:**135. B_6, B_3, A_6.

————, 1962. Mathematical theory of the central nervous system (Rashevsky, ed.), *Mathematical Theories of Biological Phenomena, Annals of the New York Academy of Science,* March 2, **96**(art. 4):1056–1070. B_6, E_1, E_3, E_8, E_9, K_1, K_3, D_8 (Color).

Lashley, K. S., 1942. The problem of cerebral organization in behavior (Cattell), *Biological Symposia,* **7:**302. K_3.

————, 1951. The problem of serial order in behavior, in [C], pp. 112–146. K_3, E_5, H_5; 23, 36.

Laslett, P. (ed.), 1950. *The Physical Basis of Mind,* New York: Macmillan. L_4.

de Latil, P., 1953. *Introduction à la Cybernétique; le Pensée Artificielle,* Paris, France: Gallimard. N; 35.

————, 1956. *Thinking by Machine,* Boston, Mass.: Houghton-Mifflin. N_1, N_3, N_6; 13, 12, 31, 35 (Ashby, 1952a; Walter, 1951).

Lawrence, D. H., and Coles, G. R., 1954. Accuracy of Recognition with alternatives before and after the stimulus, *Journal of Experimental Psychology,* **47:**208–214. D_6, M_3.

———— and LaBerge, D. L., 1956. The relationship between recognition accuracy and order of reporting stimulus dimensions, *Journal of Experimental Psychology*, **51**:12–18. D₆, M₃.

de Leeuw, K., Moore, E. F., Shannon, C. E., and Shapiro, N., 1956. Computability by probabilistic machine, in [G], pp. 183–212. A₆, A₇, A₄; 21.

Leimer, J. J., 1962. Design factors in the development of an optical character recognition machine, in [AA], pp. 167–170. D₁₀.

Lenneberg, E. H., 1956. *An Empirical Investigation into the Relation Between Language and Cognition,* unpublished thesis, Harvard University, Cambridge, Mass. H₅.

Lettvin, J. Y., and Pitts, W., 1943. A mathematical theory of the affective psychoses, *Bulletin of Mathematical Biophysics,* **5**:139. N₄.

——, Maturana, H., McCulloch, W. S., and Pitts, W., 1959. What the frog's eye tells the frog's brain, *Proceedings of the IRE,* November, **47**:1940–1951. K₃, D₁₁, D₁₂, D₁₄; 23, 34, 36 (Hubel, 1962).

Levien, R. E., 1962. *Studies in the Theory of Computational Algorithms; I. Formalization Computability, Representation, and Analysis Problems,* RAND Corporation Report RM-3007; Ph.D. thesis, Applied Mathematics, Harvard University, Cambridge, Mass. H₂.

Levinson, J., and Harmon, L. D., 1962. Studies with artificial neurons, III: Mechanisms of flicker-fusion, *Kybernetik,* in press. B₆.

Lewis, P. M., II, 1962. The characteristic selection problem in recognition systems, in [AA], pp. 171–179. D₄.

Licklider, J. C. R., 1960. Man-computer symbiosis. *IRE Transactions on Human Factors in Electronics,* **1**(1):4–11. P₃, G₄; 36.

Lindsay, R. K., 1960. *The Reading Machine Problem,* CIP Working Paper 33, Graduate School of Industrial Administration, Carnegie Institute of Technology, Pittsburgh, Pa. H₁, H₆.

——, 1961. *Toward the Development of Machines Which Comprehend,* unpublished dissertation, Carnegie Institute of Technology, Pittsburgh, Pa. H₁, H₆, M₂.

——, 1962. Information processing theory, in *Symposium on Information Storage and Neural Control,* 10th Annual Meeting of the Houston Neurological Society (W. S. Fields and W. Abbot, eds.), to be published. H₁, H₆, M₂.

——, 1962. A program for parsing sentences and making inferences about kinship relations, *Proceedings of Western Management Science Conference on Simulation* (A. Hoggatt, ed.), to be published. H₁, H₆, M₂ (Green, 1961a).

Linsky, L. (ed.), 1952. *Semantics and the Philosophy of Language,* Urbana: University of Illinois Press. H₅, G₄.

Lionnais, F. L., 1957. *L'imitation de la Pensée Creatrice par les Machines,* Paris, France: Université de Paris. L₂.

Löfgren, L., 1958. Automata of high capacity and methods of increasing their reliability by redundancy, *Information and Control,* **1**:127; also in [F], p. 493, 1956. B₃, A₄, P₄.

——, 1961. *Kinematic and Tesselation Models of Self-repair,* Technical

Report 8, Contract Nonr 1834(21), Electrical Engineering Research Laboratory, Engineering Experiment Station, University of Illinois, Urbana, Ill. P_4.

————, 1962. Self-repair as the limit for automatic error correction, in [W], pp. 181–228. B_3, P_4.

Lovelace, (Countess) A. A., 1842. Translator's notes to an article on Babbage's Analytical Engine, *Scientific Memoirs,* **3**:691–731 (R. Taylor, ed.); see also writings reprinted in appendix to Bowden, 1953.

Loveland, D. W., 1958. *Heuristic Approximation,* unpublished M.S. thesis, Massachusetts Institute of Technology, Cambridge, Mass. C_8, E_3; 12, 34.

Luce, R. D., and Raiffa, H., 1957. *Games and Decisions,* New York: Wiley. P_1, P_2, F_6, P_5, I_1, I_5; 35, 32, 21.

Luchins, A. S., 1942. Mechanization in problem-solving, *Psychological Monographs,* **54**(6):248. G_4, G_5, G_6; 22, 34.

Luhn, H. P., 1957. A statistical approach to mechanized encoding and searching of literary information, *IBM Journal of Research and Development,* **1**(4):309–317. M_2; 12, 34.

————, 1958. The automatic creation of literature abstracts, *IBM Journal of Research and Development,* **2**(2):159. M_1; 12, 34.

————, 1959. *Potentialities of Auto-encoding of Scientific Literature,* IBM Research Center, Yorktown Heights, N.Y. M_1.

Lyapunov, A. A., and Sobolev, S. L., 1958. Cybernetics and natural science, *Problems of Philosophy,* No. 5, in OTS-61-11565.

———— (ed.), 1960. *Problems of Cybernetics* (translated by Nadler et al., from Russian edition of 1958), New York: Pergamon Press. N.

MacGowan, R. A., 1960. Letter to the Editor, *Science,* July 22.

MacKay, D. M., 1949. On the combination of digital and analogical techniques in the design of analytical engines, mimeographed; reprinted as an appendix, pp. 53–65, in [N], 1959. C_9, A_6, H_6, K_4, L_2, F_3; 36.

————, 1950. Quantal aspects of scientific information, *Philosophy Magazine,* **41**:289; also in Jackson, 1950. H_7, D_5.

————, 1951. Mind-like behaviour in artifacts, *British Journal of Philosophy of Science,* **2**:105–121. L, K_4.

————, 1952. Mentality in machines, *Proceedings of the Aristotelian Society,* **26**, suppl. pp. 61–86; contains also Spilsbury, 1952, and Wisdom, 1952. L, K_4.

————, 1953. Generators of information, in [K], pp. 475–485. H_7.

————, 1954a. Operational aspects of some fundamental concepts of human communication, *Syntheses* (the Netherlands) **9**:182–194. H_5.

————, 1954b. Comparing the brain with machines, *American Scientist,* April, **42**:261–268. K_4, L.

————, 1956a. Towards an information-flow model of human behavior, *British Journal of Philosophy,* February, (1)**47**:30–43. I_4, F_1, F_2.

————, 1956b. The epistemological problem for automata, in [C], pp. 235–251. F_2, D_1, D_{11}, I_1, I_4, C_4, B_6, I_1; 13, 36.

————, 1956c. The place of "meaning" in the theory of information, in [I], pp. 215–225. H_5, H_7 (MacKay, 1959, 1954a; [X]).

————, 1957. Brain and will, *The Listener,* May 9, 16; also in *Faith and Thought,* **90**:103–115 (1958).

————, 1959a. Operational aspects of intellect, in [N], pp. 39–54. I₁, H₇, C₆, F₃.

————, 1960a. On the logical indeterminacy of a free choice, *Mind,* **63**:31–40. F₂, L₃, L₄.

————, 1960b. Theoretical models of space perception, in [AG]. D₆, K₄, N₂ (MacKay, 1956a).

————, 1961a. The informational analysis of questions and commands, in [X]. H₅, H₆, H₇.

————, 1961b. Information and learning, in [AE], pp. 40–49. C₃, E, E₆, F₁, F₅, H₇, I₄ (MacKay, 1956a, 1956b, 1959a).

————, 1961c. The visual effects of non-redundant stimulation, *Nature,* Nov. 25, **192**:739–740. D₆.

————, 1962. The use of behavioural language to refer to mechanical processes, *British Journal of Philosophy of Science,* in press. K₄, L₂, L₃, L₄.

Malin, D., 1961. CONTRANS: Conceptual though random net simulation, *Proceedings of the Eastern Joint Computer Conference* (EJCC), pp. 124–234; published as *Computers: Key to Total Systems Control,* AFIPS, **20,** New York: Macmillan. G₈, B₆, J; 33.

Mandelbrot, B., 1953. An informal theory of the structure of language based on theory of statistical matching of messages and coding, in [K]. H₁, H₆, H₇.

Marill, T., and Green, D. M., 1960. Statistical recognition functions and the design of pattern recognizers, *IRE Transactions on Electronic Computers,* December, **EC-9**(4):472–477. D₉, D₁₀, D₁₃, P₂, D₁; 12, 21, 34.

————, 1961a. Progress in artificial intelligence, editorial in [AF], p. 2. 36.

————, 1961b. Automatic recognition of speech, in [AF], pp. 34–38. D₁, D₇, D₁₁; 31, 32, 35.

Marimont, R. B., 1959. A new method of checking the consistency of precedence matrices, *Journal of the Association for Computing Machinery* (ACM), April, **6**(2): 164–171. G₁₁.

Marshall, W. H., and Talbot, S. A., 1942. Recent evidence for neural mechanisms in vision, in *Visual Mechanisms* (H. Kluver, ed.), Tempe, Ariz.: Cattell. D₆, K₃; 23.

Martens, H. H., 1959. Two notes on machine "learning," *Information and Control,* December, **2**(4):364–379. C, E₁₀, I₃, J₁, P₅.

Marzocco, F. N., and Bartram, P. R., 1962. Statistical learning models for behavior of an artificial organism, in *Biological Prototypes and Synthetic Systems,* vol. 1, New York: Plenum.

Mathews, M. V., 1961. An acoustic compiler for music and psychological stimuli, *Bell System Technical Journal,* May, **40**:677–694. H₃, P₆; 14.

Mattson, R. L., 1959. A self-organizing logical system, in [Q], pp. 212–217. D₁₃, D₃, D₁₁, D₁₀, E₃, E₄; 12, 34.

Mays, W., 1952. Mindlike behavior in artefacts and the concept of mind, *British Journal of Philosophy of Science,* **3**:191. L₄.

————, 1956. Cybernetic models and thought processes, in [F], p. 103. N.

McCallum, D., and Smith, J. B., 1951. Mechanized reasoning, *Electronic Engineering*, **23**:126–133; see also p. 458. M₂, G₈.

McCarthy, J., 1956. The inversion of functions defined by Turing machines, in [G], pp. 177–181. J₂, C₁, C₃, I₆, A₇; 11, 21, 36.

———, 1959. Programs with common sense, in [N], pp. 75–84. J₁, M₂, G₃, G₉, H₄, G₈; 33.

———, 1960. Recursive functions of symbolic expressions, in [T], pp. 184–195. H₃ (LISP), A₇, A₈, H₄; 15, 36.

———, 1961. A basis for a mathematical theory of computation, in [Z]. A₈, G₇; 38 (282).

McCulloch, W. S., and Pitts, W., 1943. A logical calculus of the ideas immanent in nervous activity, *Bulletin of Mathematical Biophysics*, **5**:115–137. A₂, A₁, B₆, L₁; 21.

———, 1945. A heterarchy of values determined by the topology of nervous nets, *Bulletin of Mathematical Biophysics*, **7**:89–93. B₆, L; 21.

———, 1949a. The brain as a computing machine, *Electrical Engineering*, June; **68**(6):492. K₄; 35.

——— and Pfeiffer, J., 1949b. Digital computers called brains, *Scientific Monthly*, **69**:368–376. K₄, L; 35.

———, 1950. Machines that know and want, in *Brain and Behavior, a Symposium* (Halstead, ed.); *Comparative Psychology Monographs* 20 (No. 1), Berkeley, Calif.: University of California Press.

———, 1951a. Dans l'Antre du Metaphysicien, *Thales*, **7**:37–49, Paris: Presses Université de France.

———, 1951b. Why the mind is in the head, in [C], pp. 42–74. K₄, B₂, I₆, D₁₂, L; 36.

———, 1952. *Finality and Form*, Springfield, Ill.: Charles C Thomas. H₁.

———, 1953. *The Past of a Delusion*, Chicago: Chicago Literary Club. N₄.

———, 1954. Through the den of the metaphysician, *British Journal of Philosophy of Science*, **5**:18–31. L₁, M₃, L₃, L₂; 36. Less complete version of 1951a.

———, 1955a. Mysterium iniquitatis of sinful men aspiring into the place of God, *Scientific Monthly*, January, **80**:35–39. L, K₄.

———, 1955b. Symposium: The design of machines to simulate the behavior of the human brain, in [J].

———, 1955c. Towards some circuitry of ethical robots, *Acta Biotheoretica*, **11**:147. P₅, L₂, J₁, G₃.

———, 1957a. Biological computers, *IRE Transactions on Electronic Computers*, September, **EC-6**(3):190–192. K₄, L.

———, 1957b. The stability of biological systems, in *Homeostatic Mechanisms: Brookhaven Symposia in Biology*, **10**:207–215. B₃, B₆, A₆.

———, 1959a. Agathe Tyche—of nervous nets—the lucky reckoners, in [N], pp. 613–625. B₆, B₃, A₆; 21, 37 (1957b).

———, 1959b. *Where Is Fancy Bred? Bicentennial Conference on Experimental Psychiatry*, University of Pittsburgh. 36.

———, 1960. The reliability of biological systems, in [U], pp. 264–281. B₆, B₃, A₆, K₃; 21, 37 (1959a).

McLachlan, D., Jr., 1958. Description mechanics, *Information and Control,* **1**(3):240–266. D₄, D₁₁, E₄, D₃; 11.

McNaughton, R., 1961. The theory of automata, a survey, *Advances in Computers,* 2:379–421. A₁, A₂, A₃, A₄, A₅, A₆, A₇, A₈.

McPhee, W. N., 1961. Note on a campaign simulator, *Public Opinion Quarterly,* Summer, **25**:184–193.

Mehl, L., 1959. Automation in the legal world, in [N], **2**:755. N₃.

Merriman, J., Wass, D. W. G., and Gill, S., 1959. To what extent can administration be mechanized? in [N], **2**:809. N₃.

Meszar, J., 1953. Switching systems as mechanized brains, *Bell Telephone Laboratories Record,* February. L₅ ("Machines can't think").

Michie, D., 1961. Trial and error, *Penguin Science Library,* no. 2, pp. 129–145. P₅.

Miller, G. A., 1951. *Language and Communication,* New York: McGraw-Hill. H₅, H₁, H₂; 22, 21, 35.

———— and Selfridge, J. A., 1956*a*. Verbal context and the recall of meaningful material, *American Journal of Psychology,* **63**:176. M₃, H₅.

————, 1956*b*. The magical number seven, *Psychological Review,* **63**:81. D₆, M₃, H₇, G₄; 34, 36.

————, 1956*c*. Information and memory, *Scientific American,* **195**(2):42–46. M₃, H₇; 36.

————, 1956*d*. Human memory and the storage of information, *IRE Transactions on Information Theory,* **IT-2**(3):129–137.

———— and Chomsky, A. N., 1957*a*. *Pattern Conception,* Report AFCRC-TN-57-57, ASTIA Document AD-110076, Cambridge Research Center. I₂, I₄, D, G₄.

————, 1957*b*. A note on the remarkable memory of man, *IRE Transactions on Electronic Computers,* September, **EC-6**:194–195. M₃.

————, 1958. Speech and communication, *Journal of the Acoustical Society of America,* **30**(5):397–398. D₇; 36.

————, Galanter, E., and Pribram, K., 1960. *Plans and the Structure of Behavior,* New York: Holt. F₆, J₂, J₁, D₁₄, G₃, E₂, M₃, M₁, G₆, K₄; 36, 31, 32.

————, 1962. Decision units in the perception of speech, in [AA], pp. 81–83. D₅, D₁₄.

Miller, L., Minker, J., Reed., W. G., and Shindle, W. E., 1960. A multilevel file structure for information processing, *Proceedings of the Western Joint Computer Conference* (WJCC), **17**:53–59. H₄.

Milligan, M., 1959. Machines are smarter than I am! *Data Processing Digest,* October. K₄.

Milner, P. M., 1957. The cell-assembly: Mark II, *Psychological Review,* **64**:242. K₂, K₃, B₄, B₅, B₆, E₅, E₃; 23, 22 (Hebb, 1949).

————, 1960. Learning in neural systems, in [U]. K₂, K₃, B₄, B₆, E₅, F₂; 11, 23, 22, 34.

————, 1961*a*. A neural mechanism for the immediate recall of sequences, *Kybernetik,* 1:76–81. B₄, B₆, K₂, N₃.

————, 1961*b*. The application of physiology to learning theory, Symposium,

Current Trends in Psychological Theory, Pittsburgh: University of Pittsburgh Press. K₂, K₃.

Minot, O. N., 1959. *Automatic Devices for Recognition of Visible Two-dimensional Patterns: A Survey of the Field,* Report TM-364, June 25, U.S. Navy Electronics Laboratory, San Diego, Calif. D₁₁, D₁, D₁₀, D₈, D₄; 31, 32, 36, 13, 15.

————, 1960. *Counting and Outlining of "Two-dimensional" Patterns by Digital Computer,* Technical Memorandum TM-414, Aug. 4, U.S. Navy Electronics Laboratory, San Diego, Calif. D₁₂.

Minsky, M. L., 1954a. *Neural Nets and the Brain Model Problem,* unpublished Ph.D. dissertation, Princeton University; available from University Microfilms, Ann Arbor, Mich. A₂, B₆, E₃, B₄ (SNARC), B₅, A₆, F₂, F₁, G₃, K₁, K₂, K₃; (13, 34) 33, 36.

————, 1954b. *Discrete Selection Processes,* Report 1954-494-03-21, Navy Contract Nonr-494(03), Tufts College, Medford, Mass. C, C₆, C₇, C₈, P₇.

————, 1956a. Some universal elements for finite automata, in [G]. A₂, B₆.

————, 1956b. *Heuristic Aspects of the Artificial Intelligence Problem,* Group Report 34-55, ASTIA Document AD 236885 (MIT Hayden Library No. H-58), Lincoln Laboratories, Massachusetts Institute of Technology, Lexington, Mass. G₁, G₁₀, G₇, G₃, F₁, F₂, F₃, F₄, F₅, J₁, D₄, D₁₁, I₁, I₂, B₅, B₆, C₉, E₁, E₃.

————, 1956c. *Notes on the Geometry Problem, I and II,* Artificial Intelligence Project, Dartmouth College, Hanover, Vt., August, mimeographed. F₃, G₁, G₇, J₁.

————, 1957. Learning systems and artificial intelligence, in *Applications of Logic to Advanced Digital Computer Programming,* Ann Arbor, Mich.: University of Michigan Press.

————, 1959a. Some methods of heuristic programming and artificial intelligence, in [N], pp. 3–36. L₂, G₁, D₁, D₅, G₁₀, G₅, F₃, F₄, F₅, G₇, D₁₁, I₆, I₂, B₄; 37 (1956b).

————, 1959b. *Physical Machines and Their Abstract Counterparts,* Group Report 54-4, March, Lincoln Laboratories, Massachusetts Institute of Technology, Lexington, Mass. A₁, A₂, B₆; 35.

———— and Selfridge, O. G., 1960. Learning in random nets, in [X]; ASTIA Document AD-238220. D₁₃, D₉, D₁₁, C₃, C₆, C₇, C₈, B₄, E₃, E₄, K₂.

————, 1961a. Steps toward artificial intelligence, in [Y], pp. 8–30. C, D₁, E, F, G, I₂, J₁, L; 36, 25, 32, 31. Some of the descriptor terminology of this bibliography comes from this paper.

————, 1961b. Descriptive languages and problem solving, in [Z], pp. 215–218. D₅, E₆, F, F₃, F₅, G₈, H₅, J₁, M₁, M₂.

————, 1961c. A selected descriptor-indexed bibliography to the literature on artificial intelligence, in [AF]. The present bibliography is a revised version of this reference.

————, 1961d. Recursive unsolvability of Post's problem of "Tag," *Annals of Mathematics.* A₄, A₇ (Post, 1943; Rabin, 1959; Wang, 1957).

————, 1962. Problems of formulation in the artificial intelligence area, *Proceedings of a Symposium on Mathematical Problems in Biology,*

American Mathematical Society. A_6, B_8, C_1, D_{14}, E_0, G_1, G_7, I_1, I_2, I_5, I_6, J_1.

Mitchell, J., 1957. *A Computational Procedure for Balancing Zoned Assembly Lines,* Research Report 6-94801-1-R3, Westinghouse Research Laboratories, Pittsburgh, Pa. P_8.

Moiseyev, K., 1960. *Man and the "Thinking" Machine,* Joint Publications Research Service Report 2200-N, U.S. Department of Commerce, Washington, D.C. L_2, N.

Mooers, C. N., 1951a. Ciphering chemical formulas—the Zatopleg system, *Zator Technical Bulletin* 59, Zator Co., Cambridge, Mass. (Ray, 1957), D_5.

———, 1951b. ZATOCODING applied to mechanical organization of knowledge, *American Documentation,* **2**(1):20. M_1.

———, 1956a. ZATOCODING and developments in information retrieval, *Aslib Proceedings,* **8**(1):3–22. M_1, H_5, H_6.

———, 1956b. Information retrieval on structured content, in [I], pp. 212–234. M_1, M_2, H_5, H_6.

———, 1959. Some mathematical fundamentals of the use of symbols in information retrieval, in [R]. M_2, M_1, H_5.

Moore, E. F., 1956a. Gedanken-experiments on sequential machines, in [G], pp. 129–156. A_1.

——— and Shannon, C. E., 1956b. Reliable circuits using less reliable relays, *Journal of the Franklin Institute,* **262**:191–208, 281–297. B_3, A_3, A_6; 21.

———, 1956c. Artificial living plants, *Scientific American,* October, **195**:118–122. P_4.

———, 1959. On the shortest path through a maze, *Proceedings of an International Symposium on Switching Theory,* in *Annals of the Computation Laboratory,* Cambridge, Mass.: Harvard, vols. 29, 30. P_7.

Moore, O. K., and Anderson, S. B., 1954a. Modern logic and tasks for experiments on problem solving behavior, *Journal of Psychology,* **38**:151–160. G_4, G_8.

——— and ———, 1954b. Search behavior in individual and group problem solving, *American Sociological Review,* **19**(6):702–714. G_4.

Mowrer, O. H., 1954. The psychologist looks at language, *American Psychologist,* **9**(10):660–694. H_5.

Mullin, A. A., 1959. Some mathematical aspects of the analysis and synthesis of biological computers, in [O], pp. 1–18. B_6, A_1, A_2, A_3.

Murray, A. E., 1959. A review of the perceptron program, *Proceedings of the National Electronics Conference,* **15**. D_{13}, E_9.

———, 1961. Perceptron applications in photo interpretation, *Photogrammetric Engineering,* September, pp. 627–637. D_{13}, E_9.

Murray, F. J., 1955. Mechanisms and robots, *Journal of the Association for Computing Machinery* (ACM) **2**:61–82. A_1.

Nash, J. F., 1954. *Parallel Control,* Monograph RM-1361, ASTIA Document AD-86392, RAND Corporation, Santa Monica, Calif. B_2.

Neisser, U., 1959a. *A Preliminary Study of Human Pattern-Recognition,* Group Report 34-75, Lincoln Laboratories, Massachusetts Institute of Technology, Lexington, Mass. D_{14}, D_6.

———, 1959b. *Hierarchies in Pattern Recognition,* Report 54-G-0009, Lincoln

Laboratories, Massachusetts Institute of Technology, Lexington, Mass. D₆, D₁₄; 16, 34.

———, 1960. *A Theory of Cognitive Processes,* Group Report 54-19, Lincoln Laboratories, Massachusetts Institute of Technology, Lexington, Mass. D₁₄, D₆, I₄; 16, 34, 36.

von Neumann, J., and Morgenstern, O., 1947. *Theory of Games and Economic Behavior,* Princeton, N.J.: Princeton. P₁, F₆.

———, 1951. The general and logical theory of automata, in [C], pp. 1–31; also reprinted in [H], p. 2070, 1956. A₁, A₄, A₅, A₆, B₃, P₄, K₄.

———, 1956. Probabilistic logics and the synthesis of reliable organisms from unreliable components, in [G], pp. 43–98. B₃, B₆, A₁, E₅; 21, 36.

———, 1958. *The Computer and the Brain,* New Haven, Conn.: Yale University Press. K₄, B₃, P₄, H₆.

Newell, A., 1955. The chess machine, in [E], pp. 101–108. J₁, J₂, P₅ (Chess), G₂, G₃, H₅, H₆, F, E₄, E₆; 33.

——— and Simon, H. A., 1956a. The logic theory machine, *IRE Transactions on Information Theory,* IT-2(3):61–79. J₁, J₂, C₂, G₇, G₈, I₂, H₄, H₂; 14 (IPL), 34, 36.

——— and ———, 1956b. *Problem-solving in Humans and Computers,* RAND Corporation Paper P-987, Santa Monica, Calif.

———, Shaw, J. C., and Simon, H. A., 1957a. Empirical explorations of the logic theory machine, *Proceedings of the Western Joint Computer Conference* (WJCC), pp. 218–239. G₁, G₄, L₂, G₈, G₇, C₂, J₁, J₂, M₁, C₃; 12, 14, 34, 36.

——— and ———, 1957b. Programming the logic theory machine, *Proceedings of the Western Joint Computer Conference* (WJCC), pp. 230–240. H₂, H₃, H₄; 12, 14, 15.

———, ———, and Simon, H. A., 1958a. Elements of a theory of human problem-solving, *Psychological Review,* March, 65:151–166. G₆, G₄, H₄, M₂, H₃, G₅, J₁, J₂, G₃; 23, 36.

———, ———, and ———, 1958b. Chess-playing programs and the problem of complexity, *IBM Journal of Research and Development,* 2(4):320–335. G₂, G₄, P₅, C₁, C₂, H₄, M₂, G₅, J₁, J₂, G₃; 23, 36 (P₅; 31) (Turing, 1953; Kister, 1957; Bernstein, 1958a; Samuel, 1960).

———, ———, and ———, 1958c. *The Processes of Creative Thinking,* RAND Corporation Paper P-1320, Santa Monica, Calif. G₆, G₄, G₅, C₁, C₂, H₄, M, J₁, J₂, G₃.

——— and Simon, H. A., 1958d. Heuristic problem-solving: The next advance in operations research, *Journal of the Operations Research Society of America,* 6(1).

———, Shaw, J. C., and Simon, H. A., 1959a. Report on a general problem-solving program, in [R], pp. 256–264. G₁, G₁₀, G₄, G₆, H₄, H₂, H₃, G₇, G₈, J₁, J₂; 33, 36.

———, ———, and ———, 1959b. A general problem-solving program for a computer, *Computers and Automation,* 8(7):10–16.

———, ———, and ———, 1959c. *Report on the Play of Chess Player I-5 of a Book Game of Morphy vs. Duke Karl of Brunswick and Count*

Isouard, CIP Working Paper 21, Graduate School of Industrial Administration, Cargenie Institute of Technology. P₅ (Chess).

——, Shaw, J. C., and Simon, H. A., 1960*a*. A variety of intelligent learning in a general problem solver, in [U], pp. 153–189. D₁₁, G₁, G₄, G₆, H₄, H₂, H₃, H₆, G₇, G₈, G₉, F₄, F₅, G₁₀, E₆, I₄, J₁, J₂; 34, 33.

——, 1960*b*. On programming a highly parallel machine to be an intelligent technician, in [V], pp. 267–282. J₁, J₂, B₂, G, H₃, C (Holland, 1960).

—— and Tonge, F. M., 1960*c*. An introduction to information processing language IPL-V, in [T], pp. 205–211. H₃, H₄; 15, 35 (Shaw, 1959).

—— and Simon, H. A., 1961*a*. GPS—a program that simulates human problem-solving, in [AE].

—— and ——, 1961*b*. The simulation of human thought, in *Current Trends in Psychological Theory,* Pittsburgh, Pa.: The University of Pittsburgh Press, pp. 152–179. G, G₃, G₄, G₆, G₇, J₂, K₄, L.

—— and ——, 1961*c*. GPS, a program that simulates human thought, in *Lernende Automaten* (H. Billing, ed.), Munich: R. Oldenbourg KG, 109–124. G, G₃, G₄, G₆, G₇, J₂, K₄, L.

—— and ——, 1961*d*. Computer simulation of human thinking, *Science,* Dec. 22, **134**(3495):2011–2017. G, G₃, G₄, G₆, G₇, J₂, K₄, L.

—— (ed.), 1961*e*. *Information Processing Language V Manual,* Englewood Cliffs, N.J.; Prentice-Hall. H₄.

—— and Simon, H. A., 1962*a*. Computer simulation of human thinking and problem-solving, in [AD], pp. 94–133; reprinted in *Computers and Automation,* **10**:18–19ff. (April, 1961) and in *Datamation,* nos. 6, 7, 1961. E, E₂, G, G₄, H₁, J₂.

——, 1962*b*. Some problems of basic organization in problem-solving programs, in *Self-organizing Systems—1962* (M. Yovitts, G. T. Jacobi, and G. D. Goldstein, eds.), New York: Spartan.

Newman, E. A., 1958. Machines that try to think, *Control,* December, **1**:294–295. N; 31.

——, 1959. An analysis of non-mathematical data processing, in [N], pp. 863–876. I₁, I₂, H₆; 36.

Oettinger, A. G., 1952. Programming a digital computer to learn, *Philosophical Magazine,* **43**:1243–1262; reprinted in *Methodos,* **11,** 1959. An incomplete version appeared in the *Proceedings of the Association for Computing Machinery* (ACM), September, 1952. E₃, E₆, B₁; 12, 34, 36, 32.

Ogden, C. K., 1933. *Basic English: An Introduction with Rules and Grammar,* 4th ed., London: Kegan Paul, Trench, Trubner & Co. H₁, H₂.

Orchard-Hays, W., 1961. The evolution of programming systems, in [Y], pp. 283–295. H₃, H₄; 31, 32, 35.

Osgood, C. E., Suci, G., and Tannenbaum, P., 1957. *The Measurement of Meaning,* Urbana, Ill.: University of Illinois Press. H₅.

Pahl, P. M., and Johnson, D. L., 1959. Pattern recognition in an electronic reader, *Trend,* July, **11**:16–21. D₁₀.

Papert, S., 1961. Some mathematical models of learning, in [X]. D₄, D₃, D₉, E₃, E₆, D₁₁, C₃; 21, 33.

Pask, G., 1958. Organic control and the cybernetic method, *Cybernetica*, 1(3):155–173. N; 11, 24, 36.

——, 1959. Physical analogues to the growth of a concept, in [N], 2:877–928. L$_1$, B$_4$, E, N$_5$; 13, 24, 34.

—— and Von Foerster, H., 1960a. A proposed evolutionary model, in [W]. E$_9$, F$_6$, P$_1$, P$_5$, N$_5$, N$_6$; 16, 31, 35.

——, 1960b. The natural history of networks, in [U], pp. 232–263. L, B$_4$, E, H$_5$, N$_5$; 13, 24, 34.

—— and Von Foerster, H., 1960c. A predictive model for self-organizing systems, *Cybernetica*, 3(4):258–300 (1960), 4(1):20–55 (1961). E$_2$, E$_7$, G, L, N, P$_1$, P$_3$; 21, 24, 33, 36.

——, 1961. *An Approach to Cybernetics*, London: Hutchinson; also New York: Harper & Row (1962). E, F, G, K, L, N.

——, 1962. The simulation of learning and decision-making behavior, in [AG], N$_5$.

Paycha, F., 1959. Medical diagnosis and cybernetics, in [N], pp. 635–659. M$_1$, M$_2$.

Peirce, C. S., 1887. Logical machines, *American Journal of Psychology*, 1:165–170. G$_8$.

Pendergraft, E., 1961. *Machine Language Translation Project, 9th Quarterly Progress Report*, 1 May 1961–31 July 1961, U.S. Army Signal Corps Contract DA 36-039 SC 78911, File No. 19678-PM 59-91-91 (6909). H$_1$.

Penfield, W., and Rasmussen, T., 1950. *The Cerebral Cortex of Man*, New York: Macmillan. K$_3$; 23, 34.

Penrose, L. S., 1959a. Automatic mechanical self-reproduction, in *New Biology*, Baltimore: Penguin, no. 28, pp. 92–117. P$_4$.

——, 1959b. Self-reproducing machines, *Scientific American*, 200(6):105–112, 114, 202. P$_4$.

Pervin, I. A., 1959. On algorithms and programming for playing at dominoes, *Doklady Akademii Nauk. SSSR*, 124(1):31–33; translated in *Automation Express*, 1(8):26–28 (1959). C$_1$, P$_5$; 12, 34.

Petrick, S. R., 1961a. Talking to a computer, *New Scientist*, May 18, 10(235):370–372. D$_7$, D$_2$.

——, 1961b. Use of a list processing language in programming simplification procedures, *Proceedings of the 2d Annual AIEE Symposium on Switching Circuit Theory and Logical Design*, **AIEE S-134**:18–24. H$_1$, H$_3$.

Pfeiffer, J., 1952. This mouse is smarter than you are, *Popular Science*, March, 160:99–100. P$_7$; 13, 34 (Shannon, 1952).

——, 1955. *The Human Brain*, New York: Harper & Row. K$_3$, K$_4$; 35.

Piaget, J., 1926. *The Language and Thought of the Child*, New York: Harcourt, Brace & World; New York: Meridian Books, Inc. (1955), M10. G$_4$, G$_5$; 22.

——, 1950. *The Psychology of Intelligence*, New York: Harcourt, Brace & World. G$_4$; 22.

——, 1954. *The Construction of Reality in the Child*, New York: Basic Books, Inc., Publishers (with list of author's books available in English). G$_4$; 22.

Pierce, J. R., 1950. See J. J. Coupling.

——— and David, E. E., 1958. *Man's World of Sound,* Garden City, N.Y.: Doubleday. D₇, H₁, K₃; 12, 13, 15, 34, 35, 31.

———, 1961. *Symbols, Signals and Noise,* New York: Harper & Row. H₅, H₇, I₃, D.

Pitts, W., 1943. A general theory of learning and conditioning, *Psychometrika,* **8**(1):131. E₈.

——— and McCulloch, W. S., 1947. How we know universals, *Bulletin of Mathematical Biophysics,* **9**:127–147. D₁₂, D₆, K₃, N₁; 23, 21, 36.

———, 1955. Extended remarks in [E], pp. 108–111, and in [J]. L, D₁, K₄.

Poincaré, H., 1954. Science and hypothesis, excerpt in [H]. G₇, G₄, J₂; 22, 21.

Polanyi, M., 1957. Problem-solving, *British Journal of Philosophy of Science,* **8**:89; reproduced in Polanyi, M., *Personal Knowledge,* London, 1958, pp. 120–135. C, G, G₆, J₂; 24.

Poletayev, I. A., 1958. *Signal,* Soviet Radio; cited in Joint Publications Research Service Report 2211-N, 1960.

Polya, G., 1954. *How to Solve It,* Princeton, N.J.: Princeton (rev. ed., Anchor A-93). G₄, G₅, J₂, I₁, I₅, F₆; 35, 36.

———, 1954*a.* Induction and analogy in mathematics, *Mathematics and Plausible Reasoning,* vol. 1, Princeton, N.J.: Princeton; also New York: Dover. G₇, G₄, J₂, G₅, I₁, I₅, F₆.

Popper, K. R., 1950. Indeterminism in quantum physics and in classical physics, *British Journal of Philosophy of Science,* **1**:117–133, 173–195.

———, 1960. The logic of scientific discovery, review by Good, *Mathematical Review,* **21**:1171–1173. I₅, I₄, I₆, I₁, L; 24, 36, 21.

Post, E., 1943. Formal reductions of the general combinatorial decision problem, *American Journal of Mathematics,* **65**(2):197–215. H₂ A₇ (Minsky, 1961*d*).

Prawitz, D., Prawitz, H., and Vogera, N., 960. A mechanical proof procedure and its realization in an electronic computer, *Journal of the Association for Computing Machinery* (ACM), **7**(2):102–128. C₁ G₇; 12, 21, 34, 32, 31.

Precker, J. A., 1954. Toward a theoretical brain-model, *Journal of Personality,* March, **22**:310–325. K₃.

Pribram, K., 1959. On the neurology of thinking, *Behavioral Science,* October, **4**:265–287. K₃.

Pringle, J. W. S., 1951. On the parallel between learning and evolution, *Behaviour,* **3**:174. C₁₀.

Prinz, D. G., 1952. Robot chess, *Research,* **5**:261. P₅.

Prywes, N., 1961. Data processing aspects of some psychological experiments, *Perceptual and Motor Skills,* **12**:155–160.

——— and Gray, H. J., 1962. The organization of a multilist type associative memory, *Gigacycle Computing Systems,* AIEE Publication 5-136, Jan. 29–Feb. 2, 87–101. B₁, C₆, C₃, E₅, H₂, M₁.

Quastler, H., 1957. The complexity of biological computers, *IRE Transactions on Electronic Computers,* **EC-6**(3):192–194. K₄.

Quine, W. V. O., 1955. A proof procedure for quantification theory, *Journal of Symbolic Logic,* **20**:141–149. C_1, G_7.

Rabin, M. O., and Scott, D., 1959. Finite automata and their decision problems, *IBM Journal of Research and Development,* April, **3**:114–125. A_1, A_4, A_7; 21.

Rapoport, A., 1948. Cycle distribution in random nets, *Bulletin of Mathematical Biophysics,* **10**. B_6, B_4; 21.

—— and Shimbel, A., 1949. Mathematical biophysics, cybernetics, and general semantics, *Review of General Semantics,* **6**:145. N, B_6.

——, 1956. On the application of the information concept to learning theory, *Bulletin of Mathematical Biophysics,* **18**:317. E_9, H_7.

Rappaport, D. (ed.), 1951. *The Organization and Pathology of Thought,* New York: Columbia. G_4; 22.

Rashevsky, N., 1940. *Advances and Applications of Mathematical Biology,* Chicago: University of Chicago Press. B_6, B_5, D_1, E_8, K_3, N; 21, 31, 32.

——, 1945*a*. The mathematical biophysics of some mental phenomena, *Bulletin of Mathematical Biophysics,* **7**:115. K_3; 21.

——, 1945*b*. Mathematical biophysics of abstraction and logical thinking, *Bulletin of Mathematical Biophysics,* **7**:133–148. G_6, D, G_8.

——, 1946. The neural mechanism of logical thinking, *Bulletin of Mathematical Biophysics,* **8**:29–40. K_3, G_6, G_8.

——, 1960. *Mathematical Biophysics,* Chicago: University of Chicago Press, 1938 (rev. ed., New York: Dover, 2 vols.). B_6, B_5, D_1, E_8, K_3, N; 21, 31, 32, 36.

Ray, L. C., and Kirsch, R. A., 1957. Finding chemical records by digital computers, *Science,* **126**(3278):814. M_1; 12, 34, 36.

Razran, G., 1958. Soviet psychology and psychophysiology, *Science,* Nov. 14, **128**:1187–1194.

Reich, D. L., and Ernst, H. A., 1960. *A Mechanical Hand,* Quarterly Progress Report 56, pp. 156–157, Research Laboratory of Electronics, Massachusetts Institute of Technology, Cambridge, Mass. N_1; 13, 12, 33, 34.

Reitman, W. R., 1959. Heuristic programs, computer simulation and higher mental processes, *Behavioral Science,* **4**:330–335. G_1, K_3, J_2, J_1; 31. (Ernst, 1962).

——, 1961. Programming intelligent problem-solvers, in [AF], pp. 26–33. G_1, H_3, J_2, J_1, P_6; 31.

——, 1962. Book review, *Science,* Mar. 2. L_5 (Taube, 1961), L_2.

Richards, P. I., 1951. Machines which can learn, *American Scientist,* **39**:711. P_5, E.

——, 1952. On game-learning machines, *Scientific Monthly,* **74**(4):201–205. P_5, E.

Roberts, L. G., 1960. Pattern recognition with an adaptive network, *IRE International Convention Record,* pt. 2, pp. 66–70. D_{13}, D_{12}, E_3, D_{10} (Rosenblatt, 1958).

——, 1962. Picture coding using pseudo-random noise, in [AA], pp. 145–154. D_6.

Robinson, A., 1957. Proving a theorem (as done by man, logician, or machine), *Proceedings of the Cornell Summer Institute of Logic, Transcription*, Ithaca, N.Y.: Cornell. G₆, G₇, G₄; 36.

——, 1960. On the mechanization of the theory of equations, *Bulletin of the Research Council of Israel*, **9F**(2):47–70.

Rochester, N., 1953. Symbolic programming, *IRE Transactions on Electronic Computers*, **EC-2**(1):10–15. H₃.

——, Holland, J. H., Haibt, L. H., and Duda, W. L., 1956. Test on a cell assembly theory of the action of the brain, using a large digital computer, *IRE Transaction on Information Theory*, **IT-2**(3):80–93. K₂, B₄, B₆; 12, 34 (Hebb, 1949).

——, Goldberg, S. H., and Edwards, D. J., 1959. *Machine Manipulation of Algebraic Expressions*, Quarterly Progress Report 55, pp. 132–134, Research Laboratory of Electronics, Massachusetts Institute of Technology, Cambridge, Mass. H₄, H₃; 14 (LISP), 34.

Rogers, H., Jr., 1959. The present theory of Turing machine computability, *Journal of the Society of Industrial and Applied Mathematics* (SIAM), **7**(1):114–130. A₄, A₇; 35.

——, 1960. Review of Gödel's proof by Newman and Nagel, *American Mathematics Monthly*, January, **67**:98. A₇ L₂; 31.

Rome, B. K., and Rome, S. C., 1959. "Leviathan: A Simulation of Behavioral Systems, to Operate Dynamically on a Digital Computer," International Conference for Standards on a Common Language for Machine Searching and Translation, Cleveland. N₇.

Rosenblatt, F., 1958a. *The Perceptron, a Theory of Statistical Separability in Cognitive Systems*, Report VG-1196-G-1, Cornell Aeronautical Laboratory, Buffalo, N.Y. B₄, B₅, D₁₃, D₁₀, E₃, K₁, D₉; 13, 33, 39 (Roberts, 1960; Bledsoe, 1959; Hawkins, 1961; Papert, 1961; Keller, 1961; Minsky, 1960, 1961a).

——, 1958b. The perceptron: A probabilistic model for information storage and organization in the brain, *Psychological Review*, November, **65**:386–407. B₄, B₅, D₁₃, E₃, K₁, M, D₉; 13, 33.

——, 1959a. *On the Convergence of Reinforcement Procedures in Simple Perceptrons*, Report VG-1196-G-3, Cornell Aeronautical Laboratory, Cornell University, Buffalo, N.Y. D₁₃, D₉, E₃, E₄; 21.

——, 1959b. Two theorems of statistical separability in the perceptron, in [N], vol. I, pp. 421–456. B₄, B₅, D₉, D₁₃; 21.

——, 1960a. Perceptual generalization over transformation groups, in [U]. B₄, B₅, D₁₃, D₉, D₁₂, F, I₃; 11, 33, 36.

——, 1960b. Perceptron experiments, *Proceedings of the IRE*, March, **48**:301–309.

——, 1962. *Principles of Neurodynamics*, Cornell Aeronautical Laboratory Report 1196-G-8; Washington, D.C.: Spartan. B₅, D₁₃, D₉, D₁₄, E, K₁, K₃; 12, 13, 21, 23, 34, 36.

Rosenblith, W. A., 1959. Some quantifiable aspects of the electrical activity of the nervous system (with emphasis upon responses to sensory stimuli), *Review of Modern Physics*, **31**(2):532–545. 12, 23, 34, 32, 31.

Rosenbloom, P. C., 1950. *The Elements of Mathematical Logic,* New York: Dover. H₂, L₂; 31, 35.

Rosenblueth, A., Wiener, N., and Bigelow, J., 1943. Behavior, purpose and teleology, *Philosophy of Science,* **10**:18–24. N₂, L.

——— and ———, 1950. Purposeful and non-purposeful behavior, *Philosophy of Science,* **17**:318, N₂, L.

Ross, T., 1933. Machines that think, *Scientific American,* April, **148**:206–208. L₂.

Rothstein, J., 1954. Information, organization and systems, *IRE Transactions on Information Theory,* **IT-4**:64–66. H₇, H₅, N.

Russell, B., 1940. *History of Western Philosophy,* New York: Simon and Schuster. L₃.

Russell, D. H., 1956. *Children's Thinking,* Boston: Ginn. G₅; 22.

Russell, G., 1957. *Learning Machines and Adaptive Control Mechanisms,* Radar Research Establishment Memorandum 1369, British Ministry of Supply, Malvern, England. E, N, N₁, B₅, C, D₁₄, I; 13, 34 (Ashby 1952a, Uttley, 1954–1957).

Ryle, G., 1949. *The Concept of Mind,* London, Hutchinson. L, L₄, H₅, I₅; 24.

Salveson, M. E., 1955. The assembly-line balancing problem, *Transactions of the American Society of Mechanical Engineers,* **77**:(16). (Tonge, 1959). G₁₁.

Samuel, A. L., 1959a. Some studies in machine learning using the game of checkers, *IBM Journal of Research and Development,* **3**(3):210–229. P₅ (Checkers), G₂, M₁, E₄, E₃, D₄, C₃, E₁₀, M₁; 12, 34, 36.

———, 1959b. Machine learning, *Technology Review,* November, **62**:42–45.

———, 1960a. Programming a computer to play games, in *Advances in Computers* (F. Alt, ed.), New York: Academic. P₅; 31, 32, 35.

———, 1960b. Letter to the editor, *Science, 132,* (no. 3429, September 16). L₂, L₃ (Incorrectly labelled volume 131 on cover).

———, 1962. Artificial intelligence—a frontier of automation, *Annals of the American Academy of Political and Social Science,* March, **340**:10–20.

Samuelson, P. A., 1947. *Foundations of Economic Analysis,* Cambridge, Mass.: Harvard.

Sapir, E., 1939. *Language,* New York: Harcourt, Brace and World. H₁, H₅.

Schultz, H., 1938. *The Theory and Measurement of Demand,* Chicago: University of Chicago Press.

Schutzenberger, M. P., 1954. A tentative classification of goal-seeking behavior, *Journal of Mental Science,* **100**(1):97–102. N₂.

Scott, P., and Williams, K. G., 1959. A note on temporal coding as a mechanism in sensory perception, *Information and Control,* **2**(4):380–385. D₆, H₇.

Scriven, M., 1953. The mechanical concept of mind, *Mind,* April, **62**:230–240. L.

Sebestyen, G. S., 1960. *Classification Decisions in Pattern Recogntion,* Report 381, Research Laboratory of Electronics, Massachusetts Institute of Technology, Cambridge, Mass. D₉, D₁₁.

————, 1961. Recognition of membership in classes, *IRE Proceedings on Information Theory,* **IT-7**(1):40. D₉, D₁₁.

Selfridge, O. G., 1948. Some notes on the theory of flutter, *Archives of the Institute of Cardiology, Mexico,* **18**(2):177–187. B₆; 22.

————, 1955. Pattern recognition and modern computers, in [E], pp. 91–93. D₁, D₄, D₁₁, D₃, D₈, E₉, I₂, I₁; 12, 34, 33, 36 ([X], Dinneen, 1955).

————, 1956. Pattern recognition and learning, in [I], p. 345; also in *Methodos,* **8**:31. D₁₁, D₁, D₈, D₄, D₃, E₉, I₂, I₁, J₁, C₆, C₈, P₅, H₅, G₃, I₃.

———— and Minsky, M. L., 1956*b*. "Digital Computers and Pattern Recognition," Annual Meeting of the AAAS. Paper does not seem to exist.

————, 1959. Pandemonium: a paradigm for learning, in [N], pp. 511–529. D₁₄, D₁₃, C₈, E₃, B₂, D₁₁, K₂; 12, 34, 33, 36.

———— and Neisser, U., 1960. Pattern recognition by machine, *Scientific American,* **203**(3):60–68. D₁, D₂, D₃, D₆, D₁₀, D₁₂, D₁₄; 31, 35 (Byrnes, 1959; Gold, 1960; Doyle, 1960, [X]).

Shaginyan, M., 1959. *In the World of Cybernetics,* Joint Publications Research Service Report 718-D, U.S. Department of Commerce, Washington, D.C. N.

Shannon, C. E., and Weaver, W., 1949*a*. *The Mathematical Theory of Communication,* Urbana, Ill.: University of Illinois Press. H₇, H₁, I₃.

————, 1949*b*. Synthesis of two-terminal switching networks, *Bell System Technical Journal,* January, **28**(1):59–98. A₂, A₃ I₆.

————, 1949*c*. Communication theory of secrecy systems, *Bell System Technical Journal,* October, **28**(4):656–715. H₇.

————, 1950*a*. Automatic chess player, *Scientific American,* February, **182**: 48. P₅, G₂, G₃, F₆; 33.

————, 1950*b*. Programming a digital computer for playing chess, *Philosophy Magazine,* March, **41**:356–375. P₅, G₂, G₃, F₆; 33; also in [H].

————, 1952. Presentation of a maze-solving machine, in [B], 8th conference, pp. 173–180. E₁₀, P₇; 13, 34.

————, 1954. Computers and automata, *Proceedings of the IRE,* **41**(10): 1234–1241; also *Methods,* **6**:115. A₁, B₁.

————, 1955. Game-playing machines, *Journal of the Franklin Institute,* **260**(6):447–453. P₅, F₄, I₁, E₁₀; 13, 34 (Hagelbarger, 1955, [X]).

————, 1956. A universal Turing machine with two internal states, in [G]. A₄.

————, 1959. Von Neumann's contributions to automata theory, *Bulletin of the American Mathematical Society,* **64**(3, pt. 2):123–129. 31.

Shaw, J. C., Newell, A., Simon, H. A., and Ellis, T. O., 1958. A command structure for complex information processing, *Proceedings of the Western Joint Computer Conference* (WJLL), May 6–8. H₃, H₄; 15, 35, 38 (Newell, 1957*b*).

Shepard, R. N., and Chang, J. J., 1961*a*. *Stimulus Generalization in the Learning of Classifications,* mimeographed report, Bell Telephone Laboratory. E₂, D.

————, Hovland, C. I., and Jenkins, H. M., 1961*b*. Learning and memorization of classifications, *Psychological Mongraphs,* **517**(75). E₂, D.

Sherman, H., 1959. A quasi-topological method for machine recognition of line patterns, in [R], D_{10}, D_5, D_8; 21, 34.

Shimbel, A., 1950. Contributions to the mathematical biophysics of the central nervous system, with special reference to learning, *Bulletin of Mathematical Biophysics,* **12**:24. E, K_3.

Sholl, D. A., and Uttley, A. M., 1953. Pattern discrimination and the visual cortex, *Nature,* **171**:387–388. B_6, D, K_3.

––––––, 1956. *The Organization of the Cerebral Cortex,* London: Methuen. K_3.

Shoulders, K. R., 1960. On microelectronic components, interconnections, and system fabrication, in [V]. B_1, B_2.

Shubik, M., 1960a. Games, decisions and industrial organizations, *Management Science,* **6**:455–474. P_8, P_1, P_2.

––––––, 1960b. Bibliography on simulation, gaming, artificial intelligence, and allied topics, *Journal of American Statistical Association,* **55**(292):736–751. P_8, P_1, P_2, N_3; 32.

Shultz, G. L., 1957. Use of IBM 704 in. simulation of speech-recognition systems, *Proceedings of the Eastern Joint Computer Conference,* (EJCC), pp. 214–218. D_7; 12, 34.

Simmons, R. F., 1960. *Anticipated Developments in Machine Literature Processing in the Next Decade,* SP-129, System Development Corporation, Santa Monica, Calif. M_1.

Simon, H. A., 1955. A behavioral model of rational choice, *Quarterly Journal of Economics,* February, **69**:99. P_2.

–––––– and Newell, A., 1956a. Models: Their uses and limitations, in *The State of the Social Sciences* (White, ed.), Chicago: University of Chicago Press. G_4.

––––––, 1956b. Rational choice and the difficulty of the environment, *Psychological Review,* March, **63**:129. P_2, G_5.

––––––, 1957. *Models of Man,* New York: Wiley. F_6, G_4; 22, 21.

–––––– and Newell, A., 1958. Heuristic problem-solving, *Operations Research,* **6**(1):1–10. J_1, J_2, G; 35.

––––––, 1960. *The New Science of Management Decision,* New York: Harper & Row.

––––––, 1961a. Modelling human mental processes, in [Z], pp. 111–120. G, G_4, J_1, J_2.

––––––, 1961b. The control of the mind by reality: Human cognition and problem solving, in *Control of the Mind* (Farber and Wilson, ed.), pp. 219–232, New York: McGraw-Hill. E_2, G_3, G_4, J_2, L_2.

––––––, 1961c. Experiments with a heuristic complier, RAND Corporation Paper P-2349, Santa Monica, Calif.

Singer, J. R., 1961. Electronic analog of the human recognition system, *Journal of the Optical Society of America,* January, **51**:61–69. D, E, B.

Skinner, B. F., 1953. *Science and Human Behavior,* New York: Macmillan. G_5, E_2; 22, 35.

––––––, 1957. *Verbal Behavior,* New York: Appleton-Century-Crofts. H_5, H_1, E_2, E_3.

––––––, 1961. *Cumulative Record: Enlarged Edition,* New York: Appleton-

Century-Crofts; contains a number of earlier papers. E_1, E_2, E_3, H_1, L_1, L_3, L_4, G_5.

Slagle, J., 1961. *A Computer Program for Solving Problems in Freshman Calculus* (*SAINT*), doctoral dissertation, Massachusetts Institute of Technology, Cambridge, Mass. G_1, G_{10}, G_7, J_1, J_2, D_4, H_4; 12, 14, 21, 34.

Sluckin, W., 1954. *Minds and Machines*, London: Pelican; Baltimore: Penguin. E, N; 35.

———, 1958. Information theory, probability models and psychology, *Penguin Scientific News*, **47**:65. H_7, I_1.

Sobolev, S. L., Kitor, A. I., and Lyapunov, A. A., 1958. *The Basic Features of Cybernetics*, JPRS/DC-L-15, Library of Congress Photoduplication Service, Washington, D.C. N.

Solomonoff, R. J., 1957. An inductive inference machine, *IRE National Convention Record*, pt. 2, pp. 56–62. I_4, I_6, J_1, G_5, E_6, D_{11}; 33, 36.

———, 1958b. The mechanization of linguistic learning, in [AB]; also in *Zator Technical Bulletin* ZTB-125, ASTIA Document AD 212226. I_2, I_3, I_4, H_2.

———, 1959. A new method for discovering the grammars of phrase structure languages, in [R], ASTIA Document AD 210390. I_2, I_4, I_3, I_6, H_2, E_6.

———, 1959b. On machines to learn to translate languages and retrieve information, *Zator Technical Bulletin*, AFOSR-TN-59646. I_2, H_2, M_1.

———, 1960. A preliminary report on a general theory of inductive inference, *Zator Technical Bulletin* ZTB-138, Contract AF 49(638)-376, Zator Company, Cambridge, Mass. I_2, I_1, I_5, I_6, A_4, A_6; 21, 24.

Somenzi, V., 1956. Can induction be mechanized? in [I], p. 226. L_2, I_5.

Sperry, R. W., 1951. Mechanisms of neural maturation, in *Handbook of Experimental Psychology* (S. S. Stevens, ed.), pp. 236–280, New York: Wiley. K_3.

———, 1952. Neurology and the mind-brain problem, *American Scientist*, **40**:291. D_1, L_4, K_4.

Spiegelthal, E. S., 1960. Redundancy exploitation in the computer solution of double-crostics, *Proceedings of the Eastern Joint Computer Conference* (EJCC), pp. 39–56. G_3, C_5.

Spilsbury, R. J., 1952. Mentality in machines, *Proceedings of the Aristotelian Society*, **26**: suppl., 61–86. K_4, M_4.

Sprick, W. and Ganzhorn, K., 1959. An analogous method for pattern recognition by following the boundary, in [R], pp. 238–244. D_{11}, D_{10}, D_3; 13.

Stein, P., and Ulam, S., 1957. Experiments in chess on electronic computing machines, *Computers and Automation*, September, **6**:14. P_5, G_2, J_1 (Kister, 1957; Bernstein, 1958a).

Steinbuch, K., 1958a. Automatic symbol recognition. *Nachrichtentechnische Zeitschrift*, **11**(4):210, (5):237; *Electrical Engineering Abstract*, nos. 3722, 4872. D_{10}, D_3, D_4; 13, 31, 32, 36.

———, 1958b. Automatic speech recognition, *Nachrichtentechnische Zeitschrift*, September, **11**:446. D_7.

———, 1961. Die Lernmatrix, *Kybernetik*, **1**(1), 36–45. (Kudielka, 1961). E_4.

516   BIBLIOGRAPHY

Stevens, M. E., 1957. *A Survey of Automatic Reading Techniques,* Report 5643, National Bureau of Standards, Washington, D.C. D$_{10}$, D$_3$, D$_1$; 31, 32 (Stevens, 1961a).

————, 1959. A machine model of recall, in [R], pp. 309–315. M$_1$, M$_2$, E$_5$; 12, 34.

————, 1961a. *Automatic Character Recognition—a State-of-the-art Report,* NBS Technical Note 112, PB No. 161613, Washington, D.C. D$_{10}$, D$_1$, D$_2$, D$_4$, D$_5$, D$_8$, D$_9$, D$_{12}$, E$_7$; 31, 36, 35, 32 (549 references).

————, 1961b. Abstract shape recognition by machine, *Proceedings of the 1961 Eastern Joint Computer Conference* (EJCC) (Computers—key to total systems control), **21**:332–351. D$_8$, D$_{11}$, D$_{12}$ (Deutsch, 1955).

Stevens, S. S. (ed.), 1951. *Handbook of Experimental Psychology,* New York: Wiley. D$_6$, D$_7$, E, G, H, M.

Strachey, C. S., 1952. Logical or non-mathematical programmes, *Proceedings of the Association for Computing Machinery* (ACM), September, Ontario, Canada. P$_5$, H$_4$.

Sutherland, N. S., 1959. Stimulus analysing mechanisms, in [N], pp. 575–609. D$_1$, D$_6$, E$_1$, K$_3$; 22, 23, 31, 32, 36.

Sutherland, W. R., Mugglin, M. G., and Sutherland, I., 1958. An electromechanical model of simple animals, *Computers and Automation,* **7**:6–8, 23–25, 32. N; 13.

Sutro, L., 1959. Emergency simulation of the duties of the president of the United States, in [P], pp. 314–323. N$_4$; 12, 33, 36.

Swallow, R., and Weston, P., 1959. On the design of artificial nerve nets, in [O], pp. 34–46. B$_6$.

Tarjan, R., 1958. Neuronal automata. *Cybernetica,* **1**(3):189. A$_2$, B$_6$.

Taube, M., 1959. Man-machine relationships, January–February, *Datamation.* P$_3$.

————, 1960. Letter to the editor, Aug. 26, *Science.* L$_2$.

————, 1961. *Computers and Common Sense, The Myth of Thinking Machines,* New York: Columbia. K$_4$, L$_1$.

Taylor, W. K., 1956. Electrical simulation of some nervous system functional activities, in [I]. K$_3$.

————, 1959a. Pattern recognition by means of automatic analog apparatus, *Proceedings of the Institute of Electrical Engineers,* pt. B, no. 106, pp. 198–209. D; 13.

————, 1959b. Automatic control by visual signals, in [N], pp. 843–861. D$_3$, D$_{10}$, D$_{13}$; 13.

Thomson, R., and Sluckin, W., 1954a. Cybernetics and mental functioning, *British Journal of Philosophy of Science,* **4**:130; *Psych. Abstract* 3532. N$_4$.

———— and ————, 1954b. Machines, robots, and minds, *Durham University Journal,* **15.** L$_4$.

Thorpe, W. H., 1956. *Learning and Instinct in Animals,* Cambridge, Mass.: Harvard. E$_1$; 35 (Tinbergen, 1951).

Tinbergen, N., 1951. *The Study of Instinct,* New York: Oxford. E$_1$, E$_{10}$, D$_{14}$.

Tonge, F. M., 1960. An assembly line balancing procedure, *Management Science,* **7**(1):21–42. F$_4$, J$_1$, J$_2$, G$_1$, H$_4$, C$_4$, C$_5$, C$_6$; 14, 34, 36, 31.

————, 1961a. *A Heuristic Program for Assembly Line-balancing*, Englewood Cliffs, N.J.: Prentice-Hall.

————, 1961b. The use of heuristic programming in management science, *Management Science*, April, 7(3).

Troll, J. H., 1954. The thinking of men and machines, *Atlantic Monthly*, July, pp. 62–65. L₂.

Tsien, H. S., 1954. *Engineering Cybernetics*, New York: McGraw-Hill. N.

Turing, A. M., 1936. On computable numbers, with an application to the *Entscheidungsproblem*, *Proceedings of the London Mathematics Society*, (ser. 2) **42**:230–265, **43**:544 (1937). A₄, A₇, L₁.

————, 1950. Computing machinery and intelligence, *Mind*, October, **59** (n.s. 236):433–460; also reprinted in [H], pp. 2099ff., and in *Methodos*, **6**:195 (1954). L, L₂, L₃, L₄, E; 24, 36 (Kleene, 1952, chap. 30).

————, 1953. Author of part of chap. 25, pp. 288–295, of *Faster than Thought* (B. V. Bowden, ed.), London: Pitman. P₅, G₂ (Chess), D₁₃, J₁; 12 (Hand-simulated), 34 (Newell, 1958b).

Uhr, L., 1959a. Machine perception of printed and hand-written forms by means of procedures for assessing and recognizing gestalts, in *Preprints of the 14th National Meeting of the Association for Computing Machinery, Boston*, Preprint 34. Ann Arbor, Mich.: Mental Health Research Institute. D₁₁, D₅, D₁₀.

————, 1959b. Latest methods for the conception and education of intelligent machines, *Behavioral Science*, **4**:248–251 (review of reference [P]).

————, 1960. Intelligence in computing machines: The psychology of perception in people and in machines, *Behavioral Science*, **5**:177–182. D₆, D₁₁.

———— and Vossler, C., 1961a. Suggestions for self-adapting computer models of brain functions, *Behavioral Science*, **5**:91–97. D, K, E₇.

————, 1961b. A possibly misleading conclusion as to the inferiority of one method for pattern recognition to a second method to which it is guaranteed to be superior, *IRE Transactions on Electronic Computers*, **EC-10**: 96–97. D₉, D.

———— and Vossler, C., 1961c. A pattern recognition program that generates, evaluates, and adjusts its own operators, in [A], pp. 555–569. D₁₁, I₂, I₄.

———— and ————, 1961d. Recognition of speech by a computer program that was written to simulate a model for human visual pattern recognition, *Journal of the Acoustical Society*, **33**:1426.

————, ————, and Uleman, J., 1962a. Pattern recognition over distortions, by human subjects and by a computer simulation of a model for human perception, *Journal of Experimental Psychology*, **63**:227–234.

————, 1962b. Pattern recognition computers as models for form perception, *Psychological Bulletin*, in press.

Unger, S. H., 1958. A computer oriented toward spatial problems, *Proceedings of the IRE*, **46**(10):1744–1750. B₂ H₃, A₁, D₉, D₈.

————, 1959. Pattern detection and recognition, *Proceedings of the IRE*, **47**(10):1737–1752. B₂, H₃, D₈, D₁, D₁₀, D₅; 36.

Uttley, A. M., 1954. The classification of signals in the nervous system, *E. E. G. Clinical Neurophysiology*, **6**:479. D₁, K₃, D₁₄, D₉, D₁₃, B₄, B₅, B₆.

————, 1955. The probability of neural connections, *Proceedings of the Royal Society*, (B)144:229. B₄, K₃; 23.

————, 1956a. Conditional probability machines, in [G], pp. 253–275. I₁, E₅, E₉, D₉, B₂, B₆.

————, 1956b. Temporal and spatial patterns in a conditional probability machine, in [G], pp. 277–285. I₁, E₅, E₉, D₉, D₁, D₁₄.

————, 1956c. Conditional probability as a principle of learning, in [F], pp. 830–856. D₁₄, D₁₃, D₉, E₅, I₁.

————, 1959a. The design of conditional probability computers, *Information and Control*, April, 2:1–24. I₁, E₅, E₉, D₉; 13, 34 (Kudielke, 1961).

————, 1959b. Conditional probability computing in a nervous system, in [N], pp. 121–146. I₁, B₂, B₄, B₆, B₅, K₃, E₅, D₁₃, D₁₄, D₉.

————, 1961. The engineering approach to the problem of neural organization, *Progress in Biophysics*, 2:25–52.

————, 1962. Properties of plastic networks, *Biophysical Journal Supplement*, Rockefeller Institute Press, in press.

Verbeek, L. A. M., 1960a. On error-minimizing neuronal nets, in [W]. B₃, A₆, N₆, B₂.

————, 1960b. Reliable computation with unreliable circuitry, in [S]. B₃, A₆, B₂.

Vinacke, W. E., 1962. *The Psychology of Thinking*, New York: McGraw-Hill. J₂, G₄; 22.

Von Foerster, H., 1949. Quantum mechanical theory of memory, in [B], 6th conference. M₃, K₃.

————, 1957. Basic concepts of homeostasis, in *Homeostatic Mechanisms*, Brookhaven Symposia in Biology, no. 10, Upton, N.Y., pp. 216–242. N₆, N₅; 21.

————, 1959. Some aspects in the design of biological computers, in [O], pp. 47–64. A₂, B₂, B₄, B₆, D₁ N₅; 13.

————, 1960. On self-organizing systems and their environments, in [U], pp. 31–50. N₅.

———— and Zopf, G. W., Jr. (eds.), *Principles of Self-organization*, New York: Pergamon. B₆, C, D₁₁, E.

Wada, H. et al., 1959. An electronic reading machine. in [R], pp. 227–232. D₃, D₁₀, D₁₃.

Wald, A., 1950. *Statistical Decision Functions*, New York: Wiley, P₂.

Wall, P. D., and Melzak, R., 1962. Neural mechanisms which discriminate events on the skin, in [AA], pp. 120–125. D₇, K₃, N₆.

Wallace, R. A., 1952. The maze-solving computer, *Proceedings of the Association for Computing Machinery* (ACM), May, Toronto, Pittsburgh, Pa.: Rimbach, pp. 119–125. P₇, E₁₀.

Walter, W. G., 1950. An imitation of life, *Scientific American*, 182(5):42. E₈, K₄; 13.

————, 1951. A machine that learns, *Scientific American*, 185(2):60. E₈, K₄; 13, 34.

————, 1953. *The Living Brain*, New York: Norton. K₃; 23, 31, 35, 36.

————, 1954. Networks of neurons, Brooklyn Information Networks Symposium, Brooklyn Polytechnic Institute, Brooklyn, N.Y., p. 185. B_6.

Wang, H., 1957. A variant to Turing's theory of computing machines, *Journal of the Association for Computing Machinery* (ACM), 2:63. A_4, A_6 L_2; 21 (Minsky, 1961*d*).

————, 1960*a*. Toward mechanical mathematics, *IBM Journal of Research and Development*, 4(1):2–22. G_7, H_2, J_1, J_2, C_1, L_2, C_2, C_5; 21, 12, 34, 36 (Minsky, 1961*a*).

————, 1960*b*. Proving theorems by pattern recognition, I, in [T], p. 220. G_7.

————, 1961. *Proving Theorems by Pattern Recognition*, II, Bell Telephone Laboratories, Inc., Murray Hill, N.J., unpublished. G_7.

Ware, (ed.), 1960. Soviet computer technology—1959, *IRE Transactions on Eectronic Computers*, March, pp. 72–120. B_1.

Watanabe, S., 1960. Information-theoretic aspects of inductive and deductive inference, *IBM Journal of Research and Development*, 2(4):208–231. I_5, I_1, I_4, M_2; 21, 12, 34.

Watson, A. J., 1959. Some questions concerning the explanation of learning in animals, in [N], pp. 693–728. E_1, D_{11}, E_4; 22, 36.

Weber, C. O., 1949. Homeostasis and servo-mechanisms for what? *Psychological Review*, 56:234–236. N_6, N.

Wechsler, D., 1958. The nature of intelligence, in *The Measurement and Appraisal of Adult Intelligence*, Baltimore: Williams & Wilkins. L_2.

————, 1960. Intelligence, quantum resonance and machine thinking, *Transactions of the New York Academy of Sciences*, 22(4):259–266. L_2, K_3, M.

Weinberg, M., 1951. Mechanism in neurosis, *American Scientist*, January, 39:74–98. N_4.

Weir, J. M., 1958. "A Learning Process Suitable for Mechanization," presented at the 11th national meeting of the Association for Computing Machinery, Los Angeles, Calif., August, 1956, "A Physical Model of an Abstract Learning Process," presented at the 13th national meeting of the Association for Computing Machinery, June, 1958. E, I_4.

Wertheimer, M., 1945. *Productive Thinking*, New York: Harper & Row. G_4, J_2.

White, G. M., 1959. Penny matching machines, *Information and Control*, December, 2:349–363. I_1, E_9, P_1, P_5; 21.

Wickelgren, W., 1962*a*. A simulation program for conservative focusing, *Behavioral Science*, April, 7:245–247.

———— and Cohen, D. H., 1962*b*. *An Artificial Language and Memory Approach to Concept Attainment*, Psychological Reports, 10:815–827.

Widrow, B., 1959. Adaptive sampled-data systems—a statistical theory of adaptation, IRE WESCON Convention, San Francisco. N_1, E_9, C_8.

Wiener, N., and Rosenblueth, A., 1946. Conduction of impulses in cardiac muscle, *Archives of the Institute of Cardiology, Mexico*, 16:205–265. B_6.

————, 1948. *Cybernetics*, New York: Wiley. H_7, N_1, N_6, N_2, N_3, N_4, D_{12}, E_3, K, L, G_2, P_5 (Chess) (New material concerning learning and game playing.)

————, 1949a. *Extrapolation, Interpolation, and Smoothing of Stationary Time Series,* Cambridge, Mass.: Technology Press, Massachusetts Institute of Technology. I₁, D₉.

————, 1949b. Sensory prostheses, in [B]. D.

————, 1950a. *The Human Use of Human Beings,* Boston, Mass.: Houghton Mifflin. N₂.

————, 1950b. Speech, language and learning, *Journal of the Acoustical Society of America,* **22**:696–697. H₁, D₇.

————, 1958. My connection with cybernetics: Its origin and its future, *Cybernetics,* **1**(1):1–14. N.

————, 1960. Some moral and technical consequences of automation, *Science,* May 6. N₃.

Wilkes, M. V., 1953. Can machines think? *Discovery,* **14**:151; also in *Proceedings of the IRE,* October, **41**:1230. L₂.

————, 1956a. Appendix on Can machines think?, in *Automatic Digital Computers,* London: Methuen; New York: Wiley. L₂.

Williams, J. D., 1960. *Toward Intelligent Machines,* RAND Corporation Paper P-2170, Santa Monica, Calif. L₂.

Williams, T., 1956. *Translating from Ordinary Discourse into Formal Logic,* ASTIA Document AD98813, Research Department, Avion Division, ACF Industries. H₁, H₂, H₄.

Willis, D. G., 1959. Plastic neurons as memory elements, in [R]. M₁, B₆ (K₁, D₁₃), E₃; 12, 34 (Not *made* of plastic!) (Kudielka, 1961).

————, 1960. The functional domain of complex systems, in [W]. C₃, C₅.

Wisdom, J. O., 1951. The hypothesis of cybernetics, *General Systems Yearbook,* **1**:111; also in *British Journal of Philosophy of Science,* **2**:1, 248, 312. N; 24.

————, 1952. Mentality in machines, *Proceedings of the Aristotelian Society,* **26**; suppl. 1–26. L.

Wozencraft, J., and Horstein, M., 1961. Coding for two-way channels, in [X]. H₇, J₁.

Wright, M. A., 1959. Can machines be intelligent? *Process Control and Automation,* January, **6**:2–6. L₂.

Wulfeck, J. W., and Taylor, J. H., (eds.), 1957. *Form Discrimination as Related to Military Problems,* Publication 561, National Academy of Sciences, National Research Council, Washington, D.C. D₁.

Wyckoff, L. B., 1954. A mathematical model and an electronic model for learning, *Psychological Review,* **61**:89–97. E.

Yngve, V. H., 1956. A programming language for mechanical translation, *Mechanical Translation,* July, **5**(1). H₄, H₁.

————, 1961. A model and an hypothesis for language structure, *Proceedings of the American Philosophical Society,* **104**:444–466. H₁, H₂.

————, 1962. Computer programs for translation. *Scientific American,* June, **206**(6): 68–76.

Yntema, D. B., and Torgerson, W. S., 1961. Man-computer cooperation in decisions requiring common sense, in [AF], pp. 20–26. P₃.

Young, J. Z., 1956. The organization within nerve cells, *Endeavor,* January, **15**:5–19. K₃.

————, 1957. *Doubt and Certainty in Science,* New York: Oxford. K, L, M; 23, 34.

Zemanek, H., Kretz, H., and Angyan, A. J., 1960. A model for neurophysiological functions, in [X], pp. 270–284. E_1, E_8, I_1, K_3.

Some Symposia, Proceedings, and Other Special Collections Concerning Artificial Intelligence

[A] Teleological mechanisms, *Annals of the New York Academy of Science,* **50:**189. (L. K. Frank, G. E. Hutchinson, W. K. Livingston, W. S. McCulloch, and N. Wiener.)

[B] Von Foerster, H. (ed.), *Cybernetics: Circular Causal and Feedback Mechanisms in Biological and Social Systems,* transactions of the 6th (1949), 7th (1950), 8th (1951), 9th (1953), and 10th (1955) conferences, sponsored and published by the Josiah Macy, Jr., Foundation, New York.

[C] Jeffress, L. A. (ed.), 1951. *Cerebral Mechanisms in Behavior: The Hixon Symposium,* New York: Wiley; also London: Chapman & Hall, 1951, (von Neumann, McCulloch, Lashley, Kluver, Kohler, Halstead, and discussants.)

[D] Couffignal, L. (ed.), 1952. *Les Machines à Penser,* Paris: Editions de Minuit.

[E] *Proceedings of the 1955 Western Joint Computer Conference,* Session on Learning Machines, W. H. Ware, Chairman, pp. 85–111, Mar. 1–3, 1955. (Clark and Farley, Selfridge, Dinneen, Newell; discussion by W. Pitts and G. A. Miller.)

[F] *Proceedings of the 1st International Congress on Cybernetics,* Namur, Belgium, June, 26–29, 1956, Paris; Gauthier-Villars; 2d conference, reference [AB].

[G] Shannon, C. E., and McCarthy, J. (eds.), 1956. Automata studies, *Annals of Mathematics Studies,* vol. 34, Princeton, N.J.: Princeton.

[H] Newman (ed.), 1954. *The World of Mathematics,* vol. 4, New York: Simon and Schuster. (von Neumann, 1951; Poincaré, 1954; Shannon, 1950*b*; Turing, 1950.)

[I] Cherry, C. (ed.), 1956. Information theory, *Proceedings of the 3d London Symposium on Information Theory,* London: Butterworth; also New York: Academic, 1956.

[J] Tompkins, H. E. et al., 1956. Symposium on the design of machines to simulate the behavior of the human brain, *IRE Transactions on Electronic Computers,* **EC-5:**240–255. (H. E. Tompkins, moderator; McCulloch, Oettinger, Schmitt, Rochester, Pitts, Rothstein, others.)

[K] Jackson, W. (ed.), 1953. Communication theory, *Proceedings of the 2d London Symposium on Applications of Communications Theory,* London: Butterworth.

[L] Carr, J. W., III, 1958. *Computer Programming and Artificial Intelligence:* An Intensive Course for Practicing Scientists and Engineers, University of Michigan, Ann Arbor: Summer Conference, College of Engineering.

[M] Liapunov, A. A. (ed.), 1959. *Problems of Cybernetics,* JPRS 876-D, Joint Publications Research Service, Washington, D.C. This is a serial; translations available from Pergamon Institute, New York and Oxford.

[N] Blake, D. V., and Uttley, A. M. (eds.), 1959. *Proceedings of the Symposium on Mechanisation of Thought Processes,* National Physical Laboratory, Teddington, England, London: H. M. Stationary Office, 2 vols.

[O] von Foerster, H. (ed.), 1959. *The Realization of Biological Computers,* Report 5, Electrical Engineering Research Laboratory, University of Illinois, Urbana, Ill.

[P] *Proceedings of the Western Joint Computer Conference,* Mar. 3–5, 1959.

[Q] *Proceedings of the Eastern Joint Computer Conference,* Dec. 9–13, 1959.

[R] *Proceedings of the International Conference on Information Processing* (ICIP), 1959, Paris: UNESCO House.

[S] Steele, E. J. (ed.), 1960. (USAF Air Research and Development Command) Symposium on BIONICS. (P. Armer, H. E. Savely, M. Blum, L. Verbeek, J. Cowan, L. Stark, W. S. McCulloch, B. A. Schreiver, P. M. Kelly, A. Novikoff, W. P. Tanner, W. C. Dersch, E. E. Loebner, L. A. de Ross, L. Vallese, K. K. Maitra, W. A. van Bergeijk, L. D. Harmon, W. Reitman, P. Metzelaar, R. J. Lee, R. Ryle, T. Scott, L. Steinman, H. V. Noble, M. Taube, O. H. Schmitt, and E. J. Steele.)

[T] *Communications of the Association for Computing Machinery,* 3(1960); preprints of the Conference on Symbol Manipulation Programs.

[U] Yovitts, M., and Cameron, S. (eds.), 1960. *Self-organizing Systems,* New York: Pergamon. (Farley, von Foerster, Estes, Rosenblatt, Newell et al., Milner, Campbell, Pask, McCulloch, Burks, and others.)

[V] *Proceedings of the Western Joint Computer Conference,* May 3–5, 1960.

[W] von Foerster, H. (ed.), 1960. *Illinois Symposium on Principles of Self-Organization,* University of Illinois, Urbana, Ill., to be published. (G. Pask, W. R. Ashby, A. Rapaport, S. Beer, L. Verbeek, M. Blum, J. Cowan, L. Lofgren, R. W. Sperry, R. L. Beurle, G. W. Zopf, F. A. Hayek, J. K. Hawkins, J. R. Platt, A. Novikoff, C. A. Rosen, D. G. Willis, F. Rosenblatt, and P. H. Greene.)

[X] Cherry, C. (ed.), 1961. *Proceedings of the 4th London Symposium on Information Theory,* London: Butterworth; also New York: Academic.

[Y] *Proceedings of the IRE,* 1961. Special computer issue; review articles about artificial intelligence, automatic programming, adaptive servomechanisms, adaptive networks, etc.

[Z] *Proceedings of the Western Joint Computer Conference,* May 9–11, 1961.

[AA] David, E. E. (ed.), 1962. Special issue on sensory information processing, *IRE Transactions on Information Theory,* **IT-8**:2, 74–191.

[AB] 2d International Congress on Cybernetics, Sept. 3–10, 1958, Namur, Belgium, Association de Cybernétique.

[AC₁] Delafresnaye, J. F. (ed.), 1954. *Brain Mechanisms and Consciousness,* Council for International Organizations of Medical Sciences, Oxford: Blackwell Scientific Publications.

[AC₂] Delafresnaye, J. F. (ed.), 1961. *Brain Mechanisms and Learning,* Oxford: Blackwell Scientific Publications.

[AD] Greenberger, M. (ed.), 1962. *Management and the Computer of the Future,* New York: Wiley.

[AE] *Proceedings of a Conference on Learning Automata* (Lernende Automaten), 1961, Technische Hochschule, Karlsruhe, Germany, Apr. 11–14, 1961, Oldenbourg, Munich, 1961.

[AF] Marill, T. (ed.), 1961. Special issue on artificial intelligence, *IRE Transactions on Human Factors in Electronics,* **HFE-2:**1.

[AG] Symposium on Biosimulation Organized by the Barth Foundation at Locarno, Switzerland, June–July, 1960.

[AH] Liapunov, A. A. (ed.), *Problems of Cybernetics,* no. 1 (1958), no. 2 (1959), no. 3 (1960), no. 4 (1960), no. 5 (1961).
Seminar on Cybernetics in Moscow University, 1959–1960; *All Union Conference on Computer Mathematics and Technology,* 1960. These all contain papers in the Artificial Intelligence area, and I have not attempted to characterize their content. For a listing of titles for these and other Soviet literature, with numbers and prices of the Office of Technical Services and other available translations, see Morris D. Friedman, *8th Reference Bibliography (Artificial Intelligence—Soviet Bloc),* MIT Lincoln Laboratory Library, Dec. 27, 1961, ASTIA MIT Hayden Library and see Feigenbaum, 1961c, for an interpretation of this literature.

Index